The Longman Companion to

Imperial Russia, 1689–1917

David Longley

Longman

An imprint of **Pearson Education**

Harlow, England · London · New York · Reading, Massachusetts · San Francisco · Toronto · Don Mills, Ontario · Sydney
Tokyo · Singapore · Hong Kong · Seoul · Taipei · Cape Town · Madrid · Mexico City · Amsterdam · Munich · Paris · Milan

Pearson Education Limited
Edinburgh Gate
Harlow
Essex CM20 2JE
England

and Associated Companies throughout the world

Visit us on the World Wide Web at:
www.pearsoneduc.com

First published 2000
© David Longley 2000

ISBN 0–582–31989–7 CSD
ISBN 0–582–31990–0 PPR

British Library Cataloguing-in-Publication Data

A catalogue record for this book is available from the British Library

Library of Congress Cataloging-in-Publication Data

Longley, David, 1938–
    The Longman companion to Imperial Russia / David Longley.
        p. cm. — (Longman companions to history)
    Includes bibliographical references and index.
    ISBN 0–582–31990–0 — ISBN 0–582–31989–7
    1. Russia—History—1613–1917. I. Title: Imperial Russia. II. Title.
    III. Series.
  DK113.L66 2000
  947—dc21   99–057966

Set by 35 in 9.5/12pt New Baskerville
Produced by Pearson Education Asia (Pte.) Ltd.
Printed in Singapore

Contents

Preface

Throughout I have assumed that the typical reader will be non-Russian-speaking, and so have not given the Russian title for books, plays, poems, etc. I have however given it for journals and newspapers, as these often appear in English-language texts. I do, however, give translations of these titles either immediately after the Russian, or in the list of abbreviations, or in the Glossary. In all transliterations, I have omitted the hard and soft signs, as the pronunciation differences these make are inaccessible to non-Russian-speakers (as they are to many non-Russian Russian-speakers). In my List of Placenames, however, I have included soft signs in the modern names as appropriate, to conform with the way in which they normally appear in modern atlases.

I have assumed that the reader, even if non-Russian-speaking, will want to pronounce Russian names correctly. Unlike French, which has a constant stress on the last syllable of the word, in Russian the stress can come anywhere. Stress is important, as it is very pronounced and its position can alter the entire sound of the word, as the sound of unstressed vowels is different from stressed ones (see pp. 407–9). I have, therefore, placed an accent over the stressed syllable. Where this is missing, it is probably simply because I do not know where it should be. Some surnames (e.g. Basakov) just do not appear in any of the standard works of reference. In some cases (Nóvikov, Novikóv), the stress differs from family to family or even person to person (as does Fórbes, Forbés in Scotland). I can only apologize for any hurt susceptibilities I may have inadvertently caused if I have got this wrong.

Purists may object to my transliteration of Russian names. Why Alexander and Alexei, when other names are transliterated rather than translated? And if Alexander, why not Peter, rather than Pëtr? My answer is that I have aimed to make things as easy as possible for non-Russian-speakers. Alexander is a lot easier to absorb than Aleksandr, and the difference in pronunciation is not significant. In any case, as far as the x or *ks* are concerned, our system of transliteration is illogical. Yes, Russians use two letters to convey the sound of our letter x, but does this mean that we must do so? After all, we use four letters *shch* to convey the single Russian Щ, so if this can work one way, why not in the other? On the other hand, there are significant phonic differences between Pëtr and Peter and Mikhaíl and Michael, and so I have kept the Russian forms to convey the flavour of the Russian names. For this reason, although I write Alexándrovich with an *x*, I have stressed the *a* to help the reader pronounce it properly.

Surnames of people who became well-known in the West before the currently accepted transliteration systems were devised, do present some difficulties, as the accepted spelling is often very different from a strict transliteration. In these cases, I usually give the commonly known spelling for the well-known figure, but the normal transliteration for those not so well-known. Thus Tchaikovsky the composer, but Chaikóvskii the revolutionary, although these are the same name to Russians.

Clearly in a book of this kind, the author's main problem lies in what to put in and what to leave out. Some readers will disagree with my decisions. For example, in the Culture section, I know that some will feel that Chekhov is underrepresented as, although I have put in all of his plays, I have almost none of his stories. The problem here is that he wrote so many that their titles alone would almost fill my word quota for the entire book, so I have merely included his first stories to show when he began. The same is true of Pushkin. Ostróvskii and Saltýkov-Schedrín, on the other hand, in terms of their long-term literary merit may seem overrepresented. But they were immensely popular in their day, with hardly a year going past without something new by them, and thus were a major part of the contemporary literary scene, whatever we may think about them now.

As this is a book about pre-Revolutionary Russia, I have used the Julian (Old Style) calendar as the basis for dating. Where events have an international dimension, I have added the Gregorian date (e.g. 3/15 September). This can become somewhat cumbersome at times (e.g. when the two calendars span different months or even years), but my experience is that people, even distinguished scholars, can be misled by taking one calendar for the other and so a little encumbrance seemed a small price to pay.

All locations are St Petersburg, unless otherwise indicated.

I should like to thank Eino and Ritva Ketola for their help with the Finnish section, Jo and Jim Forsyth for their guidance through the subtleties of the Russian language, Michael Moss for correcting me on the two calendars, and my wife and children for their patience, encouragement and understanding for a project that has seriously disturbed their lives. Finally, I should like to thank Hilary Shaw, Verina Pettigrew and Emma Mitchell at Pearson Education, who are everything an author could hope for as editors: encouraging, kind, yet critical. Their good-natured but penetrating criticism has helped me avoid many *folies d'auteur* and has made this book easier to use. I have not always followed their advice, and any errors that remain are mine.

List of Abbreviations

ATS	Alexandrinskii Theatre St Petersburg
BdC	*Bibliotéka dlia chténiia/The Reading Library*
BTM	Bolshoi Theatre Moscow
BTS	Bolshoi Theatre St Petersburg
E	*Epókha/The Epoch*
L	*Listók/The News-sheet*
M	*Moskvitiánin/The Muscovite*
MGL	*Moskóvskii gorodskói listók/Moscow City News-sheet*
MKhaT	Moskóvskii Khudózhestvennyi Teátr/Moscow Arts Theatre
Mo	*Molvá/Rumour*
MTB	*Moskóvskaia teatrálnaia bibliotéka E. N. Rassokhinoi/E. N. Rassokhina's Moscow Theatrical Library*
MTM	Mályi Theatre Moscow
MTS	Maríinskii Theatre St Petersburg
MV	*Moskóvskii véstnik/Moscow Herald*
n.s.	new style (i.e. date according to the western, Gregorian, calendar)
NV	*Nóvoe vrémia/New Times*
o.s.	old style (i.e. date according to the Julian calendar)
OZ	*Otéchestvennye zapíski/Notes of the Fatherland*
PK	Petersburg Committee of the Bolshevik Party
PPS	Polish Socialist Party
PSR	*Pártiia sotsialístov revoliutsionérov/*Party of Socialist Revolutionaries
PZ	*Poliárnaia zvezdá/Pole Star*
RA	*Rússkii arkhív/Russian Archive*
RB	*Rússkaia beséda/Russia Conversation*
RM	*Rússkii mír/The Russian World*
RMS	Russian Musical Society, Moscow
RMusS	Russian Museum, Saint Petersburg
RMy	*Rússkaia mysl/Russian Thought*
RS	*Rússkaia stariná/Russian Antiquity*
RSL	*Rússkoe slóvo/Russian Word*
RSDRP (b)	*Rossíiskaia sotsiál-demokratícheskaia rabóchaia pártiia (bolshevikóv)/*Russian Social-Democratic Workers' Party (Bolsheviks)

RSDRP (m)	*Rossíiskaia sotsiál-demokratícheskaia rabóchaia pártiia (menshevikóv)*/Russian Social-Democratic Workers' Party (Mensheviks)
RSl	*Rússkoe slóvo/The Russian Word*
RV	*Rússkii véstnik/The Russian Herald*
Rved.	*Rússkie védomosti/The Russian Gazette*
S	*Sovreménnik/Contemporary*
SDKPiL	Social-Democracy of the Kingdom of Poland and Lithuania
SO	*Syn otéchestva/Son of the Fatherland*
Sor	*Sorevnovátel/The Emulator*
SPV	*Sankt Peterbúrgskii véstnik/Saint Petersburg Herald*
SR	Socialist Revolutionary
ST	*Sévernye tsvetý/Northern Flowers*
STM	Soldóvnikov Theatre, Moscow
Str	*Strekozá/The Dragon-Fly*
SV	*Sévernyi véstnik/Northern Herald*
TGM	Tretiakóv Gallery, Moscow
V	*Vrémia/Time*
VE	*Véstnik Evrópy/Messenger of Europe*
WPT	Winter Palace Theatre

List of Maps

Map 1   European Russia showing the Provinces, the Jewish Pale of Settlement, and Russian Poland

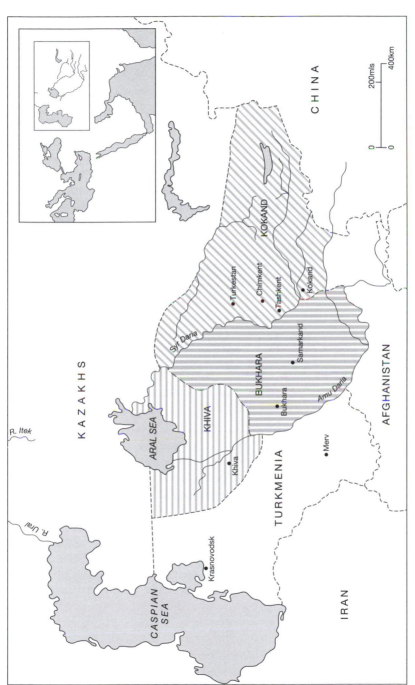

Map 3   The Russian Conquest of Central Asia

Map 4   The Russian Fronts in the First World War

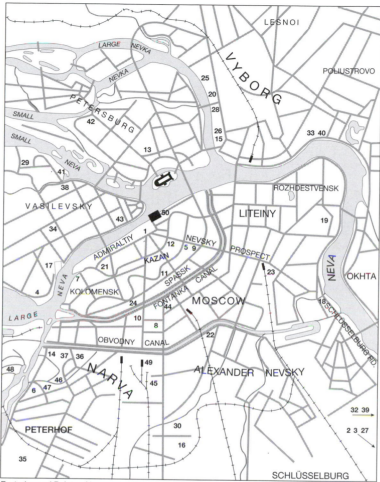

Factories and Points of Interest

1 Aleksandrovsk Garden
2 Aleksandrovsk Machine Works
3 Atlas Iron & Copper Foundry & Machine Plant
4 Baltic Shipyards
5 City Duma
6 Ekaterinhof Spinnery
7 Franco-Russian Machine Building Works
8 Free Economic Society
9 Gostinyi Dvor
10 Government Stationers
11 Haymarket (*Sennoi rynok*)
12 Kazan Cathedral and Square
13 Kirchner Bindery
14 L. L. König Spinnery
15 Lessner Machine Works
16 Mechanized Shoe Factory
17 Nail Plant
18 Nevsky Shipbuilding and Machine Works
19 Nevsky Spinnery
20 Nevsky Thread Factory ("Nevka")
21 New Admiralty Shipyards
22 New Spinnery
23 Nikolaev Railroad Station
24 Nikol'skii Market
25 Nikol'sk Weaving Factory
26 Nobel' Plant
27 Obukhov Steel Mill
28 Old Sampson Spinning and Weaving Factory
29 Osipov Leather Works
30 Ozoling Machine Plant
31 Palace Square
32 Paul Factory
33 Phoenix Machine Construction Works
34 Possel' Horseshoe Works
35 Putilov Plant or Works
36 Russian-American Rubber Factory
37 Russian Spinnery
38 Siemens & Halske Electric Works
39 Spassk & Petrovsk Cotton Mills
40 St. Petersburg Metal Works
41 St. Petersburg Pipe Plant
42 St. Petersburg Rolling & Wire Mill
43 St. Petersburg University
44 Technological Institute
45 Train Car Construction Plant
46 Triumphal Arch (Narva Gates)
47 Triumphal Spinnery
48 Voronin, Liutsh & Cheshire Weaving Factory
49 Warsaw Railroad Station
50 Winter Palace

Map 5   Pre-Revolutionary St Petersburg

I dedicate this book to my mother
Patricia Elisabeth Longley, 1914–1998
who always intended to write a book of
this kind

SECTION ONE

Internal Politics

1.1 Central Government and General Politics

Peter I, 1689–1725

1689
Peter deposes Sophia and assumes sole power (12 Sept.).

1690
Birth of Tsarévich Alexei Petróvich (Feb.).

mid 1690s
Creation of the *Preobrazhénskii Prikáz* under F. Iu. Romodánovskii.

1696

Feb.
Death of Ivan V.

Nov.–Dec.
Landowners ordered to finance shipbuilding.

1697–98
The 'Great Embassy' to the West.

Preobrazhénskii Prikáz entrusted with internal security while Peter is abroad.

1698

8–16 June
Revolt of the *Stréltsy*.

17–19 June
Revolt suppressed by Gordon and Shéin.

25 Aug.
Peter returns to Moscow.

26 Aug.
Peter publicly shears the beards off Shéin and Romodánovskii.

7 Sept.
'Investigation' (i.e. torture and punishment) of *Stréltsy* begins.

1699

12 Feb.
Peter shears short the caftans worn by guests at a dinner held by Lefort.

Private Chancellery established to control the expend-iture of the *Prikázy*.

Tax on beards introduced.

19 Dec.
Julian calendar adopted. New year to begin on 1 Janu-ary (previously 1 September) and dating to be from birth of Christ not beginning of the world.

1700

Jan.
Boyars, nobles and all urban-dwellers instructed to wear 'Hungarian' dress.

19 Jan.
The *Gold*, *Silver* and *Special Barrel Prikázy* joined to form the *Armoury*.

Feb.	*Foreign Countries* and the *Cavalry Prikázy* joined to form the *Commissar's Prikáz*, named after its chief, Ober-Komissar Ia. F. Dolgorúkii, later renamed the *War Prikáz*.
	Stone Prikáz replaced by the Department of the Quartermaster General S. I. Iazýkov, responsible for army food supply. (1717, named *Proviántskii Prikáz*.)
19 May	Tsarévich Alexander Archílovich of Imereti placed in charge of the *Canon Prikáz*, renamed Artillery *Prikáz*.
1701	All men and women except the clergy and peasants to wear 'German, Saxon or French' clothes (Jan.).
1702	Marriage without the consent of both bride and bridegroom prohibited.
1708–10	Russia divided into eight *gubérnii*: Moscow, Ingermanland, Kiev, Smolénsk, Kazán, Azóv, Archangel, Siberia, each with a governor controlling military, civil, judicial and financial affairs.
1709	Last award of the title of *boyár* (P. M. Apráksin).
1710	Peter's niece, Anna Ivánovna, marries Frederick William, Duke of Kurland.
1711	Last award of the title of *Okólnichi* (A. Iushkóv).
	Creation of ninth *gubérniia* of Vorónezh. *Uézdy* combine into *províntsii*.
28 Feb.	Establishment of the Senate of nine officials with judicial, administrative and some legislative powers.
5 Mar.	Creation of the *fiskáls*: 500 officials, under the *oberfiskál*, to root out offences that weakened government: embezzlement, tax evasion, etc.
Oct.	Grand Duke Alexéi Petróvich marries Charlotte of Brunswick-Wolfenbüttel.
1712	St Petersburg becomes the capital.
	Peter's second marriage to Catherine Alexéevna (the future Catherine I).
1713	Peter pilots into port the first Dutch ship to visit St Petersburg.
24 Apr.	Creation of boards of *landráty*, of eight to twelve men, depending on the size of the *gubérniia*, to take decisions by majority vote and with whom the governor has to consult. *Landráty* to be appointed by the Senate from two lists of candidates drawn up by governors.
1714	Fusion of *vótchina* with *poméste*, both now regarded as private property.
17 Mar.	More precise definition given to the duties and responsibilities of the *fiskály*.

| 23 Mar. | Inheritance Law forbids the sale, mortgage or division among heirs of urban and landed property, which must now pass undivided to one son (not necessarily the oldest). (Repealed 1730.) |

1715

28 Jan.	*Uézdy* and *províntsii* abolished. *Gubérnii* divided into *dóli* (units of 5,536 households) governed by *landráty*. The board of *landráty* as advisers to the governor was abolished, but two *landráty* were to serve with the governor in two-monthly tours of duty. Extra layers of *gubérniia* officials created: a vice-governor, who either assisted the governor or governed part of the *gubérniia* himself. A *landrichter*, to administer justice. An *oberproviánt* and a *proviantméister*, in charge of grain collection.
Oct.	Charlotte of Wolfenbüttel dies giving birth to a son (the future Peter II).
Nov.	Creation of an Inspector General, V. N. Zótov, over the Senate.

1716

Aug.	Peter's ultimatum to Alexei to join the army or enter a monastery.
Autumn	Alexei flees to Austria.
1717	Peter's second visit to Western Europe.
Aug.	P. A. Tolstoy visits Alexei in Naples.
Dec.	Announcement of the formation of nine 'Colleges' to replace the *Prikázy*, and their presidents. (Comes into operation, February 1720.)
1718	I. F. Romodánovskii succeeds his father as head of the *Preobrazhénskii Prikáz*.
31 Jan.	Alexei returns to Moscow, is tortured and renounces his right to the throne.
End Mar.	Creation of the Secret Chancellery under P. A. Tolstoy to investigate Alexei, whose denunciations lead to widespread arrests and executions. Romodánovskii ultimately controls this as well as the *Preobrazhénskii Prikáz*.
24 June	Alexei condemned to death.
26 June	Alexei 'dies in prison', probably tortured to death.
26 Nov.	*Gubérnii* increased to eleven, subdivided into *províntsii* (50 in all), each of which was administered by a *voevóda*. *Províntsii* subdivided into *distríkty* (replacing the *dóli*), administered by *zémskii komissár*. *Gubérniia* retains only military and judicial powers. *Voevódy* answerable only to the Senate in financial, police and commercial

	affairs, and the governor was *voevóda* for the chief town of the *gubérniia*. *Zémskie komissáry* responsible for finding run-away serfs, collecting taxes, supplying and quartering of troops.
1719	Landowners possessing more than 40 serf households commanded to build a house and live on Vasílevskii Island, St Petersburg.
1720	
Feb.	First model *magistrát* established in St Petersburg.
28 Feb.	Government organized in nine 'Colleges': Foreign Affairs (Chancellor: G. I. Golóvkin, Vice-Chancellor: P. P. Shafírov); War (A. D. Ménshikov, A. Wegde); Admiralty (F. M. Apráksin, C. Cruys); *Kámer-kollégiia* (D. Golítsyn); Justice (A. A. Matvéev); *Revizión-kollégiia* (Ia. F. Dolgorúkii); *Kommérts-kollégiia* (P. A. Tolstoy); *Shtats-kontór-kollégiia* (I. A. Músin-Púshkin); *Berg-Manufacktúr-kollégiia* (James Bruce).
1721	Establishment of the College of the Holy Synod (Procurator: S. Iavórskii; Vice-Procurator: F. Prokopóvich); the College of the *Glávnyi Magistrát*, to administer towns; and the Vótchina College, to administer noble estates.
July	Colleges subordinated to the Senate.
Sept.?	At the end of the war with Sweden, Peter assumes the title of Emperor/*Imperator*. Austria opposes this as dividing Christianity. Britain and Austria recognize the title, 1742; France and Spain, 1745.
1722	Mining and Manufactures separated into two Colleges.
24 Jan.	Promulgation of the Table of Ranks, (see pp. 29–30). *Herald Master* to supervise registration of young nobles for service. *Senior Secretary for Petitions* to investigate complaints against Colleges and Senate.
5 Feb.	New law on succession stipulates that the monarch may choose whomsoever he wishes as his successor.
27 Apr.	*Generalprokurór* (P. I. Iaguzhínskii) to control the Senate, procurators and *fiskáls*. Officers of the guards to watch over Senate proceedings.
1724	Charter of municipal institutions confirms the division of the urban population into two guilds and *tsékhy*, below which come the *pódlye liúdi* or common people (50–90% of the people). Urban government conducted by the *magistrát*, consisting of a president and several members. Officials, elected for an indefinite period, must come from the first guild, but were

	elected by the first and second guilds. The *magistrát* had administrative, judicial and police duties, and collection of the poll tax. The common people were unrepresented, but they and the guilds elected elders to voice their interests.
7 May	Coronation of Catherine, Peter's second wife, as Empress of Russia.
1725	Death of Peter. Under pressure from the Preobrazhénskii and Semënovskii Guards, a manifesto is issued by the *Generalitét*, the Senate and the Holy Synod proclaiming Peter's second wife as the Empress Catherine I (28 Jan.).

Catherine I, 1725–27

1725	*Preobrazhénskii Prikáz* merged with the Secret Chancellery to form the *Preobrazhénskaia Kantseliáriia*.
5 Mar.	Military personnel checking census returns are recalled to their units.
1726	
8 Feb.	Creation of Supreme Privy Council of six members: A. I. Osterman (Vice-Chancellor), A. D. Ménshikov (War), P. A. Tolstoy, G. I. Golóvkin (Foreign Affairs), F. M. Apráksin (Navy), D. M. Golítsyn.
17 Feb.	Duke of Holstein appointed to Supreme Privy Council.
11 Mar.	Senate downgraded to the status of a College, losing the title 'Governing' to become the 'High' Senate. Procurator-General P. I. Iaguzhínskii transferred to the court post of Senior Stablemaster and not replaced.
1727	
24 Feb.	Reform of local government: 14 *gubérnii*, subdivided in provinces, further subdivided into *uézdy*. Governor of a *gubérniia* had administrative, judicial, financial and military functions and was appointed by and was responsible to the Senate. The *uézd voevóda* was responsible to the provincial *voevóda*, who was responsible to the Governor. *Voevóda* made responsible for collection of the poll tax, through the landowners. The *magistráty* were now subject to the control of the *voevóda*.
Mar.	Catherine consents to the marriage of Grand Duke Peter Alexéevich to Maria Ménshikova.
6 May	Death of Catherine. Conference of Supreme Privy Council, Senate, Holy Synod, *Generalitét* and Guards officers choose Peter's grandson, Peter Alexéevich to be emperor. In the event of Peter dying childless, the

succession is to pass to Catherine's daughter Anna Petróvna and her descendants, then to Elizabeth Petróvna and her descendants. (No mention is made of descendants of Peter the Great's half-brother, Ivan V.)

Peter II, 1727–30
1727

25 May	Engagement of Peter II to Maria Ménshikova.
End July	Duke and Duchess (Anna Petróvna) of Holstein return to Kiel.
Aug.	Abolition of the *Glávnyi Magistrát*.
8 Sept.	Arrest of Ménshikov, deprived of his offices and decorations and deported first to his estate in Oranienburg, then to Berëzov in Siberia. (Dies 1729.) Rule of the Supreme Privy Council dominated by Dolgorúkii family.

1728

Jan.	Capital returns to Moscow.
Feb.	A. G. and V. L. Dolgorúkii appointed to Supreme Privy Council.
May	Death of Duchess of Holstein (Anna Petróvna) soon after giving birth to a son (the future Peter III).
12 Sept.	Provincial governors and *voevódy* given full judicial and administrative powers.

1729

4 Apr.	Abolition of the *Preobrazhénskaia Kantseliáriia*.
13 Nov.	Peter II engaged to Catherine Dolgorúkaia

1730

19 Jan.	Peter II dies of smallpox at 1 a.m. on the day he should have married Catherine Dolgorúkaia.
19 Jan.	On the death of Peter, the Supreme Privy Council (D. M. and M. M. Golítsyn, G. I. Golóvkin, A. G., M. V., V. L. and V. V. Dolgorúkii, A. I. Osterman) choose Anna Ivánovna, daughter of Ivan V and duchess of Kurland, as empress on condition that she should not remarry nor designate an heir; she should retain the present Supreme Privy Council of eight members, without whose permission she would not make war or peace, raise taxes, promote beyond the 6th *chin*, grant titles or estates, or make use of state revenues. The armed forces were to be placed under the Supreme Privy Council. Nobles were not to be deprived of life, honour or property without trial.

	In the morning, the choice of successor is approved by the Senate, Synod and *Generalitét*, who are not, however, informed of the 'conditions'. In the evening, a delegation led by V. L. Dolgorúkii takes the proposals to Anna Ivánovna in Mitau. Another delegation, inspired by F. Prokopóvich, R. G. Löwenwolde and Iaguzhínskii arrives in Mitau to persuade Anna not to sign.
28 Jan.	Anna accepts the 'Conditions' of the Supreme Privy Council.
2 Feb.	'Conditions' announced officially in Moscow.

Anna Ivánovna, 1730–40

1730

15 Feb.	Anna enters Moscow.
25 Feb.	Anna publicly tears up the 'Conditions' of the Supreme Privy Council.
	New entourage: R. G. Löwenwolde (Grand Marshal of the Court); B. C. Münnich (army commander); A. I. Osterman (Foreign Affairs); E. J. Bühren (Birón). Dolgorúkiis sent into exile.
4 Mar.	Supreme Privy Council abolished. Senate re-established as 'Ruling Senate' with a membership of 21.
Oct.	Iaguzhínskii restored as Procurator-General of the Senate.
Dec.	Repeal of inheritance law of 1714.
1731	
Mar.	Revival of the *Preobrazhénskaia Kantseliáriia* in charge of internal security.
Apr.	*Preobrazhénskaia Kantseliáriia* renamed the Chancellery for Secret Investigatory Affairs under A. I. Ushakóv.
10 Nov.	Creation of the 'Cabinet of Her Imperial Majesty', composed of three ministers: Osterman, Cherkáskii, Golóvkin.
End	Iaguzhínskii appointed Ambassador in Berlin.
1732	Capital returns to St Petersburg.
1734	On death of Golóvkin, Iaguzhínskii enters the cabinet. Osterman assumes title of 'First Minister'.
1736	Compulsory military and civil service for the nobility limited to 25 years. Families with two or more males are allowed to retain one son at home to manage their estates (31 Dec.). (Implemented in 1739 at the end of the Turkish War, and soon unofficially modified because of huge demand for retirement.)

1737	Re-establishment of the office of *Glávnyi Magistrát*.
Jan.?	Revision of Table of Ranks. Noble boys were to be presented to local governors at the ages of seven and 12. If they failed a literacy test at 16, they were to be ordinary soldiers or sailors. Those who passed were to be allotted service at 20.
1738	A. P. Volýnskii enters the cabinet (Apr.).
1740	A. M. Cherkásskii made Chancellor.
27 June	Torture and execution of A. P. Volýnskii, accused of plotting to bring Elizabeth to the throne.
June	A. P. Bestúzhev-Riúmin enters the cabinet.
Aug.	Birth of Ivan Antónovich (Ivan VI), son of Anna's niece Anna Leopóldovna and of Anthony of Brunswick.
17 Oct.	Death of Anna. Bühren (Birón) made regent of infant heir, Ivan VI.

Ivan VI, 1740–41

1740	Münnich and Preobrazhénskii Regiment arrest Bühren (Birón). Anne of Brunswick proclaimed regent (9 Nov.).
1741	
Mar.	Osterman ousts Münnich as 'First Minister'.
24 Nov.	Guards Regiments told to prepare for departure to the Swedish front.

Elizabeth, 1741–61

1741	
25 Nov.	Elizabeth, second daughter of Peter I and Catherine, seizes power with the help of the Preobrazhénskii Regiment. Brunswick family exiled to Kholmogóry near Archangel. Osterman and Münnich sentenced to death, commuted to exile in Siberia.
	Creation of 'Supreme Council' or 'Council of Eleven': A. P. Bestúzhev-Riúmin (Foreign Affairs until 1758), A. M. Cherkásskii, G. P. Chernyshëv, N. F. Golovín, A. B. Kurákin, V. Ia. Levashëv, A. Messino, A. P. Narýshkin, Iu. Iu. Trubetskói, N. Iu. Trubetskói, A. I. Ushakóv. Abandoned after a few weeks.
12 Dec.	Powers of the Senate increased. Cabinet replaced by Her Majesty's Special Chancellery (headed by I. A. Cherkásov).
1742	
5 Feb.	Karl Peter Ulrich of Holstein-Gottorp arrives in Russia.

7 Nov.	Karl Peter Ulrich proclaimed heir to the throne (future Peter III).
1743	Re-establishment of *magistráty*.
1744	
Jan.	Sophia von Anhalt Zerbst (Catherine II) arrives in Russia.
28 June	Sophia converts to Orthodoxy as Catherine Alexéevna.
June	Bestúzhev-Riúmin made Chancellor and Mikhaíl Vorontsóv Vice-Chancellor.
1745	Marriage of Catherine and Grand Duke Peter (21 Aug.).
1746	A. I. Ushakóv replaced by A. I. Shuválov as head of the Secret Chancellery.
1754	
13 May	Beginning of land survey to delimit privately owned from state land and to verify all land titles. Non-nobles forced to sell land.
20 Sept.	Birth of Paul Petróvich.
1756–62	Seven Years' War
1756	Creation of the Conference at the Imperial Court (War Cabinet): Grand Duke Peter Fĕdorovich, S. F. Apráksin, A. P. and M. P. Bestúzhev-Riúmin, A. B. Buturlín, M. M. Golítsyn, A. I. and P. I. Shuválov, N. Iu. Trubetskói, M. I. Vorontsóv. Meets twice weekly. By the end of the war it is deciding general policy (14 Mar.). (Abolished 1762.)
1757	Elizabeth's first stroke (8 Sept.).
1758	A. P. Bestúzhev-Riúmin disgraced, Vorontsóv appointed Chancellor (14 Feb.).
1761	Death of Elizabeth (25 Dec.).

Peter III, 1761–62
1762

29 Jan.	Abolition of the Conference at the Imperial Court (created 1756).
18 Feb.	Emancipation of the nobility. Serving nobles may retire in peacetime subject to Imperial consent. Those not of officer rank must serve 12 years before applying. Nobles may travel freely abroad, but must return if summoned. Wealthy nobles may educate children at home, the state would supervise the education of the children of poor nobles.
21 Feb.	Abolition of Secret Chancery. St Petersburg Police Chief placed in charge of police throughout Russia.
28 June	Peter deposed by Catherine and Guards.

Catherine II, 1762–96

1762

28 June	Catherine proclaimed empress.
29 June	Peter abdicates.
5 July	Assassination of Peter III at Ropsha, by Guards under Alexei Orlóv.
6 July	Catherine's manifesto denouncing Peter.
22 Sept.	Coronation of Catherine.
Oct.	Catherine reaffirms the abolition of the Secret Chancellery (although this probably continues to function unofficially under S. I. Sheshkóvskii).
28 Dec.	Manifesto creating the 'Imperial Council'. (Never implemented.)

1763

	Grigórii Orlóv made grand master of the Ordnance.
11 Feb.–18 Mar.	Commission to examine the freedom of the nobility.
4 June	'Manifesto of Silence' forbids 'improper discussion and gossip on matters concerning the Government'.
22 July	Freedom of entry to Russia given to all foreigners, who could choose their place of domicile and practise their own religion.
End Oct.	Nikíta Pánin made senior member of College of Foreign Affairs (until 1781).
15 Dec.	Reform of the Senate, whose legislative powers were reduced and duties confined to administrative and judicial. It was divided into six Departments which could issue an *ukáz* by unanimous vote if it was consistent with existing law: 1. State and Political Affairs; 2. Justice; 3. Territories with their own laws (Livonia, Ukraine, etc.) and Education; 4. Armed forces and New Serbia; 5 & 6 as 1 & 2, but in Moscow. The presidents of the Colleges of War, Navy and Foreign Affairs were given direct access to the empress. Reform of Local Government: imposes greater uniformity of establishment. Salaries and pensions introduced. Offensive against corruption.

1764

26 Feb.	Secularization of Church lands.
Feb.	A. A. Viázemskii made Procurator-General.
21 Apr.	Powers of provincial governors increased. They regain police powers.
June–July	Catherine tours Estonia and Livonia.
4 July	Murder of Ivan VI.
11 Oct.	*Gubérniia* governors to redraw *uézdy* to contain approximately 30,000 inhabitants, and centrally situated

uézd towns and to provide maps and lists of towns in their *gubérniia.*

1765 New land survey decreed (19 Sept.).

1766

12 June Land survey begins (continues into 1840s by which time most of European Russia has been covered).

14 Dec. All free estates and central government offices invited to send deputies to the Legislative Commission.

1767

30 July Catherine's *Instruction* to the Legislative Commission.

31 July Legislative Commission opens in Moscow (Marshal: A. I. Bíbikov).

14 Dec. Legislative Commission prorogued.

1768

18 Feb. Legislative Commission reopens in St Petersburg.

28 Feb. Supplement to the *Instruction* dealing with the Police.

8 Apr. Supplement to the *Instruction* dealing with expenditure, revenue and state administration.

4 Nov. First meeting of the 'Council': Z. G. Chernyshëv, A. M. Golítsyn, G. G. Orlóv, N. I. Pánin, P. I. Pánin, K. G. Razumóvskii, A. A. Viázemskii, M. N. Volkónskii.

1769

12 Jan. Last session of full Legislative Commission.

22 Jan. 'Council attached to the Court' to coordinate policy during the war. (Composition as on 4 November minus Golítsyn and Volkónskii.)

1772

Aug. A. S. Vasílchikov becomes Catherine's favourite while Orlóv is in Fokshani.

Early Sept. G. Orlóv dismissed.

1773

June G. Orlóv readmitted to the Council.

29 Sept. Wedding of Paul Petróvich to Natália Alekséevna (Wilhelmina of Hesse Darmstadt).

1774

End Feb. G. A. Potëmkin replaces Vasílchikov as favourite.

19 Dec. Instruction to Hundredsmen (*sótskie*), provides for the election in each village every December of hundredsmen, fiftiethmen and tenthmen, to carry out police duties.

1775

5 Nov. Fundamental Law for the Administration of the *gubérnii* establishes structure of local government which lasted until 1864, and the territorial division until 1917.

Gubérnii were to be redrawn as units of 300–400,000 and subdivided into *uézdy* of 20–30,000. The intermediary unit, the province, was abolished. Two *gubérnii* formed a *naméstnichestvo*, and the senior of the two governors became the *naméstnik*. By 1785, the 25 *gubérnii* had been redivided into 41. By 1796, there were 50 *gubérnii* and 493 *uézdy*.

Administrative, judicial and financial functions were separated. Administration was the governor's responsibility, with the right to correspond directly with the Empress, and with a seat in the Senate. Orders to be issued by a collegial board composed of the governor, deputy-governor and two appointed councillors. Finance was the responsibility of the Treasury Chamber, under the deputy-governor, assisted by a finance director and collegial board. It was responsible for the census, local income and expenditure, tax collection, maintenance of state buildings, the salt monopoly and liquor taxes. It had no judicial powers.

Judicial bodies were responsible to the collegial board. The highest judicial bodies in each *gubérniia* were a civil and a criminal court, whose members were appointed, which dealt with cases from all estates with appeal to the Senate. Below them, each estate had its own courts. The nobility had a higher land court, with an appointed judge and assessors elected from the nobility, and an *uézd* court with elected judge and assessors. Towns had a *gubérniia magistrát*, with two appointed judges and four assessors elected by the *kuptsý* and *meshcháne*, and a town *magistrát* with elected judges and assessors. At village level, administrative and judicial functions were united in the *zémskii isprávnik*, who chaired the lower land court and executed the orders of the collegial board. Where villages were owned by nobles, the *isprávnik* should be chosen by them, where there were few or no nobles, he should be appointed from among those with *chin*. The town equivalent of the *isprávnik* was the *gorodníchi*, who was also in command of small detachments of armed guards.

Procurators were appointed to the *gubérniia* board, to the *gubérniia magistrát*, the higher land court and the higher summary court. Their function was to ensure that legality was observed and that the different institutions did not encroach on each other. They were responsible both to the governor and to the Procurator-General in St Petersburg.

The Board of Social Welfare was responsible for schools, hospitals, almshouses and houses of correction. Primary schools, voluntary in attendance and free to the poor, were to be established in villages with a higher summary court. Corporal punishment was forbidden. The establishment of hospitals, workhouses and houses of correction were also provided for.

The marshal of the nobility and the town head, first encountered in the elections to the Legislative Commission, were given permanent status. Elected every three years, they were responsible for the welfare of widows and orphans. The marshal of nobility also organized the election of noble assessors and officials of the various courts.

1776

Jan.–Feb.	P. Zavadóvskii replaces Potëmkin as favourite.
15 Apr.	Death of Grand Duchess Natália Alekséevna.
End June–Aug.	Grand-Duke Paul Petróvich visits Berlin.
26 Sept.	Paul Petróvich marries Maríia Fëdorovna (Sophia Dorothea of Württemberg).

1777	Birth of Alexander Pávlovich (Alexander I) (12 Dec.).
1778	Ivan Rímskii-Kórsakov replaces Zavadóvskii as favourite (May).
1780	Alexander Lanskói replaces Rímskii-Kórsakov as favourite (Easter).
1781	Nikíta Pánin replaced by I. A. Osterman at College of Foreign Affairs. A. A. Bezboródko becomes Catherine's principal adviser on Foreign Affairs (Sept.).

1782

8 Apr.	Police Ordinance: organization and powers of police in towns; codification of civil and criminal law, laying down penalties.
	Glávnyi Magistrát abolished.
1783	Abolition of *Shtats-kontór-kollégiia* (College of State Revenue). On the death of Grigorii Orlóv, Catherine gives the palace of Gátchina to Paul Petróvich.
1784	Death of Lanskói from diptheria (25 June).
1785	Alexander Ermólov becomes favourite.
21 Apr.	Charter to the nobility. Nobility defined as hereditary. Rank, estate, honour or life could not be lost

without trial by peers. Noble rank could be forfeit for breach of oath, treason, robbery, etc. Noblewomen marrying commoners did not lose rank, but their children did. Nobles immune from corporal punishment. Nobles serving in non-commissioned ranks in the armed forces to be punished as officers. Nobles were free from service, had exclusive right to buy serf villages, to establish manufactures etc. on their estates, were free from personal taxation and from billeting obligations. The *gubérniia* Noble Assembly to meet every three years, when summoned by the governor, who could not attend sessions or the election of local officials. The marshal of nobility to administer oath of allegiance to elected noble officials and to preside over election of his successor. The Noble Assembly was to discuss local needs and elect representatives to present these to Empress, to levy voluntary taxes, and to keep a register of nobles in the *gubérniia*, composed of: 1. Those ennobled by crowned heads, or whose nobility was 100 years old; 2. Those who had risen to noble rank in the armed forces (14th *chin*); 3. Those who had risen to noble rank in the bureaucracy (8th *chin*); 4. Foreign nobles; 5. Those with titles of prince, count or baron; 6. Those whose undisputed nobility was lost in the mists of antiquity.

The Charter also laid down 15 proofs of nobility to be produced by those who wished to be recognized as noble.

1786	Abolition of the College of Justice and of the *Vótchina* College.
July	Alexander Dmítriev-Mamónov replaces Ermólov as favourite.
1789	Platón Zúbov replaces Dmítriev-Mamónov as favourite (June).
1791	Death of Potëmkin (5 Oct.).
1793	Alexander Pávlovich marries Elizavéta Alexéevna (Louise of Baden) (28 Sept.).
1794	A. S. Makárov succeeds Sheshkóvskii as head of the Secret Chancellery.
End	La Harpe dismissed (returns to Switzerland in early 1795).
1796	
25 June	Birth of Nicholas Pávlovich (Nicholas I).
6 Nov.	Death of Catherine.

Paul I, 1796–1801

1796	Alexander Kurákin made Vice-Chancellor, and Alexei Kurákin Procurator-General.
26 Nov.	Wearing of round hats forbidden. Radíshchev pardoned.
Nov.–Dec.	Reform of the Senate.
Dec.	Vice-Chancellor to control the Secret Chancellery, now renamed Secret Expedition (Makárov probably continues to run it).
12 Dec.	Reform of local government structure, replacing the *naméstnichestvo* with the *gubérniia.*
1797	
3 Jan.	Nobles convicted of crimes involving loss of legal status lose immunity from flogging.
5 Apr.	Coronation of Paul. Crown made hereditary in house of Romanov. Order of succession defined. Creation of the Ministry of the Property of the Imperial Family (*Minísterstvo udélov*). First usage of the term Ministry.
29 Nov.	Paul accepts the title of 'Protector' of the Maltese Order of the Knights of St John.
1798	
13 Jan.	Publication of Paul's comprehensive dress code.
27 Oct.	Paul elected Grand Master of the Maltese Order of the Knights of St John.
1799	*Gubérniia* Noble Assemblies discontinued (14 Oct.).
1800	
18 Apr.	The importation of books or music forbidden.
14 May	Election of local government officials abolished (except for nobility). Local officials to be appointed by the Senate.
24 Oct.	Provincial marshals of the nobility to be elected by the county marshals by correspondence.
1801	Murder of Paul I by L. Bennigsen, P. A. Pahlen, P., V. and N. Zúbov (11 Mar.).

Alexander I, 1801–25

1801	
15 Mar.	Alexander pardons those imprisoned and exiled by Paul.
19 Mar.	Police powers limited.
26 Mar.	Council Attached to the Court (established 1769) abolished.
30 Mar.	Establishment of Permanent Council of 12 elder statesmen.

31 Mar.	The ban on the importation of books and music lifted. The use of private printing presses is permitted.
2 Apr.	Catherine's Charter to the Nobility (1785) and regulations for the towns restored. Secret Expedition abolished.
5 June	Alexander announces his intention to restore the ancient authority of the Senate.
6 June	Platón and Nicholas Zúbov exiled to their estates.
12 June	First meeting of the 'Unofficial Committee': A. Czartorýski, N. N. Novosíltsev, P. A. Stróganov, V. P. Kochubéi.
18 June	Dismissal of P. A. Pahlen.
July	Senate discusses P. V. Zavadóvskii's report on its future.
5 Aug.	Unofficial Committee opposes legislative powers for the Senate, proposing instead purely judicial powers.
6 Aug.	Creation of the Commission to codify the laws (Zavadóvskii, Radíshchev).
15 Sept.	Coronation of Alexander I. Creation of the Commission for the Review of Formerly Criminal Cases (A. B. Kurákin, Novosíltsev, O. P. Kozodávlev, A. S. Makárov). (Abolished 5 Feb. 1816.)
27 Sept.	Torture abolished.
Oct.	Dismissal of N. P. Pánin.
1802	
6 Jan.	Unofficial Committee opposes election of Senators.
2 Feb.	Preliminary censorship abolished.
8 Sept.	Senate's prerogatives and duties affirmed. Eight Ministries replace the Colleges. Ministers to be appointed by and responsible to the Emperor, but also subject to the supervision of the Senate, to whom they must submit accounts of their actions. Ministers must confer with each other in a Committee of Ministers before reporting to the Emperor. Interior: V. Kochubéi; Justice: G. R. Derzhávin; Trade: N. P. Rumiántsev; Navy: N. S. Mordvínov (then P. V. Chichagóv); War: S. K. Viazmitínov; Foreign Affairs: V. P. Kochubéi; Finance: A. I. Vasílev; Education: P. V. Zavadóvskii.
1803	Senate's rights under the decree of 8 September 1802 do not extend to new or recently confirmed legislation (21 Mar.).
1804	First committee on censorship.
13 Nov.	Senate reprimanded for failing to prevent the continued use of torture.

1805	Paul's decree forbidding the formation of masonic lodges repealed.
5 Sept.	Creation of the Committee of Higher Police (Viazmitínov, Lopukhín, Kochubéi). Functions and procedures of the Committee of Ministers regulated.
1806	Precautionary measures to be taken against French citizens resident in Russia (28 Nov.).
1807	
12 Jan.	Creation of Committee for Public Safety (Lopukhín, Makárov, Novosíltsev). (Abolished 17.i.1829.)
27 June	Arakchéev granted the power to issue decrees in the name of the Emperor.
1808	
31 Aug.	Reform of the Committee of Ministers.
Dec.	Speránskii appointed assistant Minister of Justice.
1809	
3 Apr.	Court appointments no longer entitle their holders to *chin* (i.e. became merely honorary).
6 Aug.	Promotion above a certain *chin* open only to those passing an examination or holding a university degree.
Oct.	Speránskii completes his plan for constitutional reform.
15 Oct.	Creation of the Address Office for the registration of foreigners.
1810	
1 Jan.	Creation of the State Council according to a plan drawn up by Speránskii. Arakchéev resigns as War Minister over Speránskii's plan for the State Council.
July	Alexander visits Arakchéev at Gruzinó.
25 July	Ministries reorganized according to Speránskii's principles. Police removed from Ministry of Interior and placed under new Minister of Police (A. D. Balashëv).
1811	
25 June	Further reorganization of Ministries according to Speránskii's principles.
7 Aug.	I. de St Glin made head of the Police Ministry's Special Chancellery.
1812	
18 Mar.	Speránskii exiled to his estates in Nízhnii Nóvgorod. M. L. Magnítskii exiled to Vólogda.
20 Mar.	Decree regulating the Committee of Ministers.
Summer	Alexander I reads the Bible for the first time.
1814	Nicholas Pávlovich engaged to Princess Charlotte of Prussia (23 Oct.).

1815	Alexander's first meeting with Baroness Krüdener (4 June).
1816	
5 Feb.	Commission for the Review of Formerly Criminal Cases abolished.
30 Mar.	Formation of the Independent Corps of Internal Security Troops (E. F. Komaróvskii).
16 Aug.	Alexander tells Moscow nobility that the victory over Napoleon was God's work.
18 Aug.	Alexander visits Arakchéev's mother in her apartment in Moscow.
30 Aug.	Speránskii and Magnítskii pardoned.
1817	Nicholas Pávlovich marries Princess Charlotte of Prussia (Alexandra Fëdorovna) (1 July).
1818	Birth of Alexander Nikolaevich (Alexander II) (17 Apr.).
1819	
13/25 July	Nicholas Pávlovich is told of Konstantín Pávlovich's renunciation of the throne.
Oct.	Alexander approves Novosíltsev's *Charter for the Russian People* proposing a federal structure for a constitutional Russia.
1822	
Aug.	Capodistria resigns from Russian service over their failure to intervene in Greece.
1 Aug.	Decree forbidding secret societies (including Masonic lodges).
1825	
19 Nov.	Death of Alexander I in Taganróg.
27 Nov.	Nicholas Pávlovich (the future Nicholas I) swears allegiance to Konstantín Pávlovich as Konstantín I.
Dec.	For the Decembrist Revolt see pp. 57–9.

Nicholas I, 1825–55

1825	
14 Dec.	Nicholas Pávlovich ascends the throne as Nicholas I.
Dec.	Arakchéev dismissed.
1826	
Early	Establishment of the First Department of His Majesty's Own Chancery to receive reports from all Government Agencies, and of the Second Department to codify the Laws (Balugiánskii and Speránskii).
3 July	Establishment of the Third Department of His Majesty's Own Chancery to organize police matters and of the Ministry of the Imperial Court and Properties.

30 Sept.	Ministerial reports for 1826 to be presented to the Committee of Ministers on 1 January 1827, for discussion before presentation to the Tsar.
6 Dec.	Committee of the Sixth of December established to work through the papers of Alexander I and advise Nicholas on reform (abolished 1834). V. P. Kochubéi (chair), D. N. Blúdov, D. V. Dáshkov, I. I. Díbich, A. N. Golítsyn, M. M. Speránskii, P. A. Tolstoy, I. V. Vasílchikov.
1828	Establishment of the Fourth Department of His Majesty's Own Chancery to oversee charitable institutions.
26 May	Publication of the first volume of Balugiánskii and Speránskii's *Fundamental Laws of the Russian Empire* (45 vols in all by 1.iv.1830).
1829	Committee for Public Safety closed (17 Jan.).
1831	Authority of the Assemblies and Marshals of the Nobility enhanced (6 Dec.).
1832	Speránskii and Balugiánksii's *Digest of the Laws of the Russian Empire* (15 vols) published. Introduction of the social category of 'Honorary Citizen' (*pochëtnyi grazhdanín*).
4 Dec.	S. S. Uvárov's report to the Tsar advocating 'Orthodoxy, autocracy and nationality'.
1833	State Council approves Speránskii and Balugiánskii's revision of the laws (Jan.)
1834	As a result of Admiral Chichagóv's refusal to return to Russia (see p. 343), residence abroad limited to five years for nobles and three for non-nobles (17 Apr.).
1835	Speránskii and Balugiánskii's law code comes into effect (1 Jan.).
1836	Fifth Department of His Majesty's Own Chancery is established in the spring to deal with state peasants (P. D. Kiselëv).
1837	Establishment of the Ministry of State Domains to supervise state lands and peasants (Kiselëv until 1857). The post of Governor-General abolished except for St Petersburg, Moscow and the borderlands. *Gubérniia* boards are subordinated to the governors, who become the sole persons in charge in their *gubérniia*.
3 June	Introduction of new *uézd* police network subordinate to the governor.
1841	Alexander Nikoláevich marries Mariia Alexándrovna (Wilhelmina Maria of Hesse) (16 Apr.).

1842	Law standardizes the format of reports from *gubérniia* governors and requires *gubérniia* offices to maintain records according to standard procedures.
1845	
26 Feb.	Birth of Alexander Alexándrovich (Alexander III).
June	Personal Nobility acquired only by reaching 9th *chin* (rather than 14th).
1846	Establishment of the Sixth Department of His Majesty's Own Chancery to draw up an administrative plan for Transcaucasia.
1847	Uvárov's circular condemns Slavophilism which 'may be used by ill-intentioned persons for the excitement of minds and the spreading of dangerous propaganda, criminal and obnoxious' (30 May).
1848	
23 Feb.	A. F. Orlóv, head of the Third Section, summoned to report on the periodical press.
27 Feb.	Ménshikov Committee on censorship established (A. S. Ménshikov, P. I. Degai, D. P. Buturlín, L. V. Dubbelt, M. A. Korf, A. S. Stróganov).
2 Apr.	Ménshikov Committee replaced by the Buturlín Committee, inaugurating an 'era of censorship terror' (Buturlín, Degai, Korf). (Dissolved 6.xii.1855.)
1855	Death of Nicholas I (18 Feb.).

Alexander II, 1855–81

1855	Alexander's first decree thanks the Guards for saving Russia in December 1825 (19 Feb.).
1856	D. A. Miliútin's memorandum advising the Tsar not to prolong the War in the Crimea (1 Jan.).
1857	Committee of Ministers set up, after a plan prepared by D. N. Blúdov. Its existence remains secret for four years.
1858	Ministers to submit their reports to special commissions of the State Council and others nominated by the Tsar, who would return them to the ministers with comments, before presentation to the Tsar (11 Apr.).
1861	Official establishment of the Committee of Ministers.
19 Feb.	Emancipation of the serfs.
8 Nov.	Establishment of the Commission for the reform of the legal system: Blúdov (chairman), V. P. Butkóv, N. A. Butskovskii, P. N. Danevskii, P. P. Gagárin, A. M. Plávskii, K. P. Pobedonóstsev, D. A. Rovínskii, S. P. Shúbin, N. I. Stoianovskii, A. P. Vilinbakhov.

1862	Sukhozanét, Putiátin, Muravëv, and Kniazhévich replaced as ministers by D. A. Miliútin, A. V. Golovnín, A. A. Zelënyi, and M. Kh. Reitern (Jan.).
1864	
1 Jan.	*Zémstvo* statute.
20 Nov.	Procedural code for law courts.
1866	Creation of a Ministry of Posts and Telegraph (I. M. Tolstoy). Reports of the State Controller made available to the public.
28 Oct.	Alexander Alexándrovich marries Princess Sophie Frederica Dagmar of Denmark (Maria Fëdorovna).
21 Nov.	Limitation of *zémstvos'* right to tax.
1867	Presiding officers of *zémstvo* assemblies empowered to determine the scope of the debate. The publication of the proceedings of *zémstvo* assemblies is prohibited without the authorization of administrative officials (13 June).
1868	Ministry of Posts and Telegraph incorporated into the Ministry of the Interior.
6 May	Birth of Nicholas Alexándrovich (Nicholas II).
1869	Revision of standard *gubérniia* report form (13 Apr. also 19 June 1870).
1872	Press law. Offences committed by the press removed from the jurisdiction of the courts and now to be dealt with by the Council of Ministers.
7 July	Offences against the state, punishable by loss of rank, become the jurisdiction of a special session of the Senate, but may be placed in the jurisdiction of the Supreme Criminal Court by Imperial order.
1873	Authorities empowered to prohibit press discussion of measures contemplated by the government (16 June).
1877	Regulations on the conduct of troops during public disorders introduced (29 Oct.).
1878	
9 May	Cases involving disobedience to civil authorities removed from the jurisdiction of the normal criminal courts.
24 May	Imperial decree on administrative exile.
20 Aug.	Alexander II appeals to all estates to rally to the defence of public safety against the revolutionaries.
1879	
5 Apr.	Alexander appoints the governors-general of Moscow, Kiev, Warsaw, Khárkov (Lóris-Mélikov), St Petersburg

	(Gúrko) and Odessa (Totleben) as 'regional military dictators' authorized to use any measure necessary, including exile, to maintain peace in educational establishments.
9 Apr.	Security Law institutes rotas for doormen, forbids the sale of arms without permission from the city governor, and empowers the Senate to refuse confirmation as justices to people of unacceptable political views.
2 May	Police to be armed with revolvers.
19 Aug.	Governors empowered to intervene in *zémstvo* affairs.

1880

12 Feb.	Creation of the Supreme Executive Commission with comprehensive police powers, chaired by M. T. Lóris-Mélikov (the 'dictatorship of the heart' of M. T. Lóris-Mélikov).
23 Aug.	Law of 19.viii.1879 giving governors power over *zémstvos* repealed.
22 Dec.	Lóris-Mélikov asks *zémstvos* for proposals for reform of local administration.

1881

| 1 Mar. | Alexander II approves Loris-Melikov's 'constitution', i.e. the establishment of a commission to which the *zémstvos* and towns were to send representatives to examine, in a purely consultative capacity, legislative bills before submission to the State Council. (Shelved by Alexander III.)
Assassination of Alexander II. |

Alexander III, 1881–94

1881

29 Apr.	Imperial Manifesto asserting the new Tsar's complete faith in autocracy.
30 Apr.	Resignation of Lóris-Mélikov and Abazá.
5 May	Resignation of D. Miliútin.
13 June	Grand Duke Konstantín Nikoláevich dismissed from all his posts.
14 Aug.	Government empowered to declare a state of emergency anywhere in the country, giving officials extra-legal executive powers of closure, arrest and imprisonment, etc. (enacted 'provisionally' for three years, but in force until 1917).

1882

| 12 Apr. | Establishment of the Commission on *zémstvo* reform: M. S. Kakhánov (chair), M. E. Kovalévskii, S. A. |

	Mordvínov, A. A. Pólovtsev, I. I. Shamshín (abolished 1.v.1885).
4 May	N. P. Ignátev dismissed as Minister of the Interior after the rejection of his plan to summon a *Zémskii sobór*.
27 Aug.	'Provisional' censorship rules: all newspapers and journals that had received three previous warnings must submit to preliminary censorship. A committee of the Procurator of the Holy Synod, the Ministers of the Interior, Education and Justice, could suspend any publication indefinitely and debar its editors and publishers from editing or publishing anything else.

1885

20 May	Disciplinary powers of the Minister of Justice over the judiciary increased.
5 Nov.	All acts of the Tsar to have equal force no matter how they were enacted.

1886

Limits set on the number of the Tsar's relatives who may be officially designated as members of the Imperial Family (2 July).

1887

12 Feb.	Minister of Justice can order a trial to be held in camera to protect 'the dignity of State power'.
28 Apr.	Term of service on *vólost* courts increased to three years.

1889

7 July	Crimes against state officials to be heard in special courts without a jury.
12 July	The peasant *vólost* made subject to the Land Captain (*zémskii nachálnik*), a member of the local nobility appointed by the Ministry of the Interior. The *vólost* justices abolished, and cases previously heard by them become the jurisdiction of the Land Captain. In the towns, justices give way to 'town judges' appointed by the Minister of Justice.

1890

Zémstvo reform. *Zémstvo* assemblies to be elected by three separate electoral colleges: nobles, all others except peasants, and peasants. Membership of the first two colleges was determined by land ownership and they voted directly. Membership of the peasant college was irrespective of landholding, but they voted indirectly. 57.1% of the seats were assigned to the nobility; 13.3% to the others; 29.6% to the peasants. This ensured that the nobility dominated the *zémstvos*. All were subject to disciplinary measures by the Ministry of the Interior (13 June).

1892	Municipal Government Act. The right to vote restricted to owners of immovable property over a certain value (11 June).
1893	Abolition of flogging of women prisoners (29 Mar.).
1894	Death of Alexander III (20 Oct.).

Nicholas II, 1894–1917

1894	Marriage of Nicholas II to Alice of Hesse-Darmstadt (Alexandra Fëdorovna) (14 Nov.).
1899	Goremýkin's proposal to introduce *zémstvo* institutions into the Western Provinces is vetoed by the Tsar on Witte's advice.
Oct.	Dismissal of Goremýkin.
1900	
12 June	Limits set on *zémstvos'* taxation powers. Their statutory powers to provision the population removed.
Aug.	Communication between *zémstvos* and towns to make joint representation to the government on matters outside their jurisdiction is forbidden.
1901	Famine forces the government to return to the *zémstvos* their powers to provision the population.
7 May	State Council stripped of most of its judicial responsibilities, and its decision-making process is streamlined.
1903	Police reform (5 May).
1904	
30 July	Birth of Alexei Nikoláevich.
Aug.	Appointment of Sviatopólk-Mírskii as Minister of the Interior: 'the Political Spring of Sviatopólk-Mírskii'.
11 Aug.	Corporal punishment no longer administrable by *vólost* courts.
12 Dec.	Decree 'On Plans for the Improvement of the Social Order' promises to ease press censorship, provide state insurance for factory workers, define the scope of local government, reduce discrimination against national minorities, limit the application of exceptional laws and improve the lot of the peasants.
1905	For the events of the 1905 Revolution, see pp. 70–2.
6 Aug.	Committee of Ministers relieved of the responsibility of drafting legislation for constitutional reform.
17 Oct.	October Manifesto.

19 Oct.	Creation of the Council of Ministers, whose chairman might recommend ministerial appointments to the Tsar.
Oct.	Witte's cabinet: A. F. Rédiger (War), A. A. Birilëv (Navy), V. B. Fredericks (Imperial Court), V. N. Lamsdorff (Foreign Affairs), S. S. Manúkhin (Justice), P. N. Durnovó (Interior), A. D. Obolénskii (Holy Synod), I. P. Shípov (Finance), D. A. Filosófov (State Controller), N. N. Kutler (Agriculture), K. S. Nemesháev (Transport), V. I. Timiriázev (Trade & Industry), I. I. Tolstoy (Education).

1906

25 Apr.	Goremýkin's cabinet: A. F. Rédiger (War), A. A. Birilëv (Navy), V. B. Fredericks (Imperial Court), A. P. Izvólskii (Foreign Affairs), V. N. Kokóvtsov (Finance), P. K. Shvanebakh (State Controller), P. A. Stolýpin (Interior), A. A. Shirínskii-Shikhmátov (Holy Synod), P. Kaufman (Education), A. S. Stishinskii (Agriculture), I. G. Shcheglovítov (Justice), N. K. Schaffhausen-Schoenberg-Ek-Schaufuss (Transport).
26 Apr.	First Duma convened.
18 July	First Duma dissolved.

1907

20 Feb.	Second Duma convened.
3 June	Stolýpin's *coup d'état*: Second Duma dissolved. New electoral law introduced.
1 Nov.	Third Duma convened.

1910

12 Mar.	Guchkóv elected Duma President.
May	Duma passes bill extending *zémstvos* to the Western Provinces.

1911

Mar.	Guchkóv replaced by Rodziánko as Duma President. The Western *zemstvo* crisis: State Council rejects the Duma bill. Stolýpin passes it under Article 87.
1 Sept.	Assassination of Stolýpin.

1912

25 Jan.	Questions raised in the Duma about Raspútin's influence.
24 Mar.	Raspútin banished to his village in Siberia.
11 Apr.	Makárov defends the Lena massacre in the Duma: 'So it has been, so it will be.'
15 Nov.	Fourth Duma convened.

1914

16 July	Law on the Administration of the Army in the Field in Wartime divides Russia into two: a military zone governed by the military, and a rear zone governed by the government.
26 July	Duma one-day session to vote support for the war. Only the *Trudoviki* and Social-Democrats (Bolshevik and Menshevik) vote against.

1915

Jan.	Three-day session of the State Duma.
19 July	State Duma reconvened.
3 Sept.	State Duma prorogued

1916

6 Feb.	Nicholas II addresses the State Duma at its first session of the year.
20 June	State Duma prorogued.
1 Nov.	State Duma reconvened. Purishkévich attacks Raspútin in the Duma.
18 Dec.	Murder of Raspútin.
1917	Duma reconvened (14 Feb.).

1.1.1   The Romanov Dynasty, 1613–1917

Michael Romanov	1613–45	Elizabeth (Petróvna)	1741–61
Alexei (Mikháilovich)	1645–76	Peter III (Kárlovich)	1761–62
Fëdor III (Alexéevich)	1676–82	Catherine II	1762–96
Ivan V (Alexéevich) (Regent: Sophia)	1682–89	Paul I (Petróvich)	1796–1801
Peter I (Alexéevich)	1689–1725	Alexander I (Pávlovich)	1801–25
Catherine I	1725–27	Nicholas I (Pávlovich)	1825–55
Peter II (Alexéevich)	1727–30	Alexander II (Nikoláevich)	1855–81
Anna (Ivánovna)	1730–40	Alexander III (Aleksandrovich)	1881–94
Ivan VI (Antónovich)	1740–41	Nicholas II (Aleksandrovich)	1894–1917

1.1.2   The Table of Ranks

Chin[1]	Land Forces[2]	Navy	Civil	Court
1	General-Field Marshal	General-Admiral	Chancellor Actual Privy Counsellor First Class	
2	1716–96: Général-en-chef After 1796: General of infantry, cavalry, artillery or engineers	Admiral	Actual Privy Counsellor	Senior Marshal
3	Lieutenant-General	Vice Admiral	Procurator-General	Senior Stablemaster
4	Major-General	Rear Admiral	Until 1724: College President Privy Counsellor	Senior Chamberlain
5	1722–99: Brigadier	1722–99: Captain-Commander	Herald Master	Chamberlain
6	Colonel	First Captain	College Procurator	Stablemaster
7	Lieutenant-Colonel After 1884: Cossack Major	Second Captain	Senior Secretary of Colleges of War, Admiralty and Foreign Affairs	Chamberlain of HIH the Empress
8	1731–97: First and Second Major Before 1884: Major, Cossack Major After 1884: Captain	18th Century: Third Captain Before 1884 & 1907–11: Lieutenant-Captain From 1912: Senior Lieutenant	Senior Secretary of other Colleges	Titular Chamberlain

Chin[1]	Land Forces[2]	Navy	Civil	Court
9	Before 1884: Captain After 1884: Staff Captain	18th century: Lieutenant-Captain After 1884: Lieutenant 1907–11: Senior Lieutenant	Titular Counsellor	Court Master of Ceremonies
10	1705–98: Lieutenant-Captain Before 1884: Staff Captain After 1884: Lieutenant	Before 1884: Lieutenant After 1885: Midshipman	College Secretary	
11	Before 1884: Lieutenant		Ship's Secretary	
12	18th century: Under-Lieutenant After 1884: Cornet	Before 1885: Midshipman	Provincial Secretary	
13	Ensign Before 1884: Cornet		Provincial Secretary, Senate Secretary, Synodal Registrar, Cabinet Registrar	
14	18th Century: *Fendrik*	18th century: Midshipman	College Registrar	Court Butler

[1] All 14 military and naval ranks and the first eight civil and court ranks carried with them exemption from the poll tax and the right to own serfs.

[2] Ranks in the Guards were two higher than those in the army generally (i.e. a Guards captain was 7th *chin*).

1.1.3   Chairmen of the Committee of Ministers

1827–?	V. P. Kochubéi
1832–?	N. N. Novosíltsev
1838–?	I. V. Vasílchikov
?–April 1856	A. I. Chernyshëv
April 1856–September 1858	A. F. Orlóv
January 1862–19.ii.1864	D. N. Blúdov
1864–74	P. P. Gagárin
1874–20.xii.1879	P. N. Ignátev
1879–81	P. A. Valúev
1881–86	M. Kh. Reitern
1887–95	N. K. Bunge
1895–1903	I. N. Durnovó
17.viii.1903–19.x.1905	S. Iu. Witte

1.1.4   Chairmen of the Council of Ministers

20.x.1905–14.iv.1906	S. Iu. Witte
22.iv–9.vii.1906	I. L. Goremýkin
9.vii.1906–1.ix.1911	P. A. Stolýpin
12.ix.1911–29.i.1914	V. N. Kokóvtsov
30.i.1914–20.i.1916	I. L. Goremýkin
20.i–10.xi.1916	B. V. Stürmer
10.xi–27.xii.1916	A. F. Trépov
27.xii.1916–1.iii.1917	N. D. Golítsyn

1.1.5   Ministers of the Interior (MVD)

8.ix.1802–7	V. P. Kochubéi
1807–11	A. B. Kurákin
1811–19	O. P. Kozodávlev
1819–23	V. P. Kochubéi
1823–28	V. S. Lanskói
1828–31	A. A. Zakrévskii
1832–38	D. N. Blúdov
1839–41	A. G. Stróganov
1841–52	L. A. Peróvskii
August 1852–August 1855	D. G. Bíbikov
August 1855–February 1861	S. S. Lanskói
February 1861–9.iii.1868	P. A. Valúev
9.iii.1868–27.ix.1878	A. I. Timáshev
27.ix.1878–1880	L. S. Mákov
August 1880–4.v.1881	M. T. Lóris-Mélikov
4.v.1881–4.v.1882	N. P. Ignátev

4.v.1882–April 1889	D. A. Tolstoy
April 1889–1895	I. N. Durnovó
1895–20.x.1899	I. L. Goremýkin
20.x.1899–2.iv.1902	D. S. Sipiágin
4.iv.1902–15.vii.1904	V. K. Plehve
25.viii.1904–18.i.1905	P. D. Sviatopólk-Mirskii
22.i–22.x.1905	A. G. Bulýgin
October 1905–22.iv.1906	P. N. Durnovó
25.iv.1906–1911	P. A. Stolýpin
1911–12	A. A. Makárov
1912–14.vi.1915	N. A. Maklakóv
14.vi-26.ix.1915	N. B. Shcherbátov
26.ix.1915–3.iii.1916	A. N. Khvostóv
3.iii–7.vii.1916	B. V. Stürmer
7.vii–16.ix.1916	A. A. Khvostóv
16.ix.1916–1.iii.1917	A. D. Protopópov

1.1.6 Ministers of Justice

8.ix.1802–8.x.1803	G. R. Derzhávin
October 1803–10	P. V. Lopukhín
1810–14	I. I. Dmítriev
1814–17	D. P. Troshchinskii
1817–27	D. I. Lobánov-Rostóvskii
1829–39	D. V. Dáshkov
1839	D. N. Blúdov
1839–October 1862	V. N. Pánin
October 1862–67	D. N. Zamiátnin
1867	S. N. Urúsov
1867–30.v.1878	K. I. Pahlen
30.v.1878–85	D. N. Nabókov
1885–93	N. A. Manaséin
1894–January 1905	N. V. Muravëv
January–November 1905	S. S. Manúkhin
November 1905–April 1906	M. G. Akímov
April 1906–6.vii.1915	I. G. Shcheglovítov
6.vii.1915–7.vii.1916	A. A. Khvostóv
7.vii–20.xii.1916	A. A. Makárov
20.xii.1916–1.iii.1917	N. A. Dobrovólskii

1.1.7 Ministers of Posts and Telegraph

1866–67	I. M. Tolstoy
1867–9.iii.1868	A. I. Timáshev
9.iii.1868	subsumed into Ministry of the Interior

1.1.8   Ministers of Police

25.vii.1810–4.xi.1819	A. D. Balashëv (nominally only 1812–15.10.1819)
1812–15.x.1819	S. K. Viazmitínov (acting minister)
4.xi.1819	Ministry reabsorbed into Ministry of Interior

1.1.9   Directors of the Third Department

3.vii.1826–44	A. Kh. Benkendoff
1844–27.vi.1856	A. F. Orlóv
27.vi.1856–66	V. A. Dolgorúkov
1866–74	P. A. Shuválov
1874–76	A. L. Potápov
1876–4.viii.1878	N. V. Mezentsóv
August 1878–26.ii.1880	A. R. Drenteln
26.ii.1880	subsumed into Ministry of the Interior

1.2 The Armed Forces

1682	*Stréltsy* massacre the supporters of Natália Naríshkina (Peter the Great's mother) and appoint Sophia (Peter's half-sister) as regent.
Late 1680s	Peter creates the Preobrazhénskii and Semënovskii Regiments on his estate at Preobrazhénskoe.

Peter I

1693	Warship-building begins in Archangel.
1694	First Archangel ships assembled as the White Sea Fleet, commanded by Vice-Admiral Buturlín.
1695	Warship-building begins at Vorónezh.
1696	Warship-building begins in Taganróg.
1697	Fifty-eight young men sent abroad to train as naval officers.
1698	Patrick Gordon crushes the revolt of the *Stréltsy* whose regiments are disbanded. Officer training school established in the Preobrazhénskii Regiment. School of Navigation opened in Azóv. Establishment of the *Voénnyi Morskói Prikáz* (Department of the Navy).
1699	Volunteers and conscripts enlisted to form new regiments (Nov.).
1700	Moscow landlords with more than 40 peasant households to provide recruits for officer training (May).
Nov.?	After Narva, 47 new infantry and five grenadier regiments are formed.
1701	Establishment of the *Prikáz Voénnykh Del* (Department of Military Affairs) (until 1706), of the *Prikáz Artilleríi* (Artillery Department) (until 1714), of the *Admiraltéiskii Prikáz* (Admiralty Department), and of the First Artillery School. Seizure of church bells for recasting as canon. 25,000 former members of cavalry units summoned to Moscow.
1702	Formation of nine new cavalry units.
1703	Fortification of Kronstadt.
1705	First recruit levies (early in the year, and December) produce 45,000 men (between 1705 and 1715 there

are 12 levies, normally at one man per 20 peasant households). Special cavalry levy: one man per 80 peasant households. Ship-building begins in St Petersburg Admiralty Yard.

| 1706 | War *Prikáz* replaced by the War Chancellery (until 1719). Foreign officers entering Russian service are no longer automatically promoted to rank higher than that held at home. Two infantry levies. Three cavalry levies. Levy of 1,000 men for the Navy. |

1708–11 Army reorganized on a territorial basis, not for recruiting, but for drawing of revenue.

1709 School of Military Engineering established in Moscow.

1711 Military establishment:

Field infantry	42 regiments	62,000 men
Garrison troops	two dragoon, 30 infantry	58,000 men
Cavalry	33 regiments	44,000 men
Artillery	one regiment	
Cossacks		approx. 100,000 men

First of a series of edicts (1719, 1724) to prevent the promotion to officer rank of anyone who had not served in the ranks of a guards regiment. After the Pruth five foreign generals, six colonels and 45 staff officers are dismissed.

1712 War with Turkey leads to the formation of militia forces recruited from former soldiers in Ukraine and the Baltic. Thirty sons of noblemen sent to France to train as officers.

1714 Artillery *Prikáz* replaced by Artillery Chancellery. Only guardsmen eligible for commissions in the army.

1716 Military statute: systematic regulations replace a series of *ad hoc* rules. Twenty young men sent to France to train as naval officers; 20 to Amsterdam, 30 to Venice.

1718 Establishment of the poll tax, payable by all adult males entered on the census registers, except nobles, soldiers, priests. The tax was allocated to the army, to be collected by the War College.

1718–19 Establishment of the War College.

1719 Establishment of the Leib-Regiment of Dragoons and of the School of Military Engineering.

1720 Naval Statute systematizes the organization of the Navy.

1721 Every army officer, irrespective of origin, is elevated to the hereditary nobility (16 Jan.) (confirmed in the

| | Table of Ranks, 1722 (see pp. 29–30)). Only Russians to be promoted to officer rank in the Artillery. |
| **1722** | Ménshikov informs the Senate that many regiments have not received their pay and had deserted *en masse* (Oct.). |

Catherine I
| **1727** | Two thirds of army officers sent home to save money (Feb.). |
| **1727–28** | Collection of poll tax transferred from the army to local landowners. |

Anna Ivánovna
| **1730** | Creation of Izmáilovskii Guards Regiment (Colonel: Karl Gustav Löwenwolde, Lieut.-Col.: James Keith), officered mainly by members of the Baltic nobility. Commander-in-chief of the army: B. C. Münnich. |
| **1730–34** | Construction of the 'Ukrainian Line' of fortresses from the Donéts to the Dniépr. |

Ivan VI
| **1740** | Bühren (Birón)'s intention to change the composition of the guards regiments, posting the noble-rankers to army regiments as officers and replacing them with commoners, leads to his arrest and downfall. |

Elizabeth
1741	Grenadier company of the Preobrazhénskii Regiment renamed 'Her Majesty's Own Company' (*Leibkompániia*) in recognition of its role in placing Elizabeth on the throne. Its officers and men are raised to noble status and granted estates and serfs from confiscated estates (after 25 Nov.).
1742	V. V. Dolgorúkii pardoned, restored to his rank of Field Marshal and made President of the War College. Vice-President: S. F. Apráksin.
1756	Apráksin recalled to St Petersburg and charged with treason (Oct.).
1757	V. V. Fermór made Commander-in-chief.
1760s	Average price paid for a substitute recruit = 150 rubles.

Peter III
| **1762** | Peter orders reorganization of the army along Prussian lines. The guards to wear Prussian-style uniforms |

(Jan.), and Peter threatens to introduce new units of Holstein Guards to replace the existing guards regiments.

Catherine II

1762

In October, 15 officers arrested for conspiring to replace Catherine by Ivan VI.

Military Commission to review establishment of armed forces (Nov.).

1764

4 July

V. Ia. Miróvich attempts to take control of Schlüsselburg, to free Ivan Antónovich and proclaim him Tsar. Ivan is killed by his guards who are later rewarded by Catherine.

17 Aug.

Special court set up to try Miróvich and some 50 officers for treason.

9 Sept.

Miróvich condemned to death.

1768

I. G. Chernyshëv appointed Vice-President of the Admiralty (until 1796). Unrest among officers believing Catherine intends to emancipate the serfs.

8 Oct.

Recruit levy of one in 300 raises 19,500.

6 Nov.

Golítsyn to command the First Army, to concentrate around Kiev, march into Polish Podolia, take Kameniec Podolski, advance and take the Turkish fort of Khotín. Rumiántsev to command the Second Army, to concentrate in New Russia for an offensive against the Crimea and to defend the First Army's communications.

14 Nov.

Second levy raises the total recruited to 50,747.

1769

Golítsyn replaced by Rumiántsev (13/24 Aug.).

1770s

Average price paid for a substitute recruit = 300 rubles.

1772

Conspiracy in the Preobrazhénskii Regiment to depose Catherine and place Paul on the throne (June).

1773

In August, a recruit levy of one in 100, the 6th since 1767, raises 74,739, a total of 323,360 in five years.

1774

22 July

P. Pánin to command the forces engaged in putting down Pugachëv Revolt.

19 Aug.

Suvórov is sent to assist him.

1775

Potëmkin bans powder, ribbons and curls in the cavalry and pike regiments under his command.

1776

Military settlements first mooted by Potëmkin and Rumiántsev.

1780s

Average price paid for a substitute recruit = 400 rubles.

1782	Recruit levy raised to one in 200 and one in 100 for *odnodvórtsy*.
1783	Recruit levy set at two in 500.
1784	Recruit levy set at one in 500.
1785	Recruit levy set at two in 500.
1786	Recruit levy set at one in 500.
1787	
Aug.	Recruit levy of two in 500.
Sept.	Recruit levy of three in 500.
1789	Rumiántsev replaced by N. V. Repnín as commander of Ukrainian army (8/19 Mar.).

Paul I

1796	
7 Nov.	Paul declares himself chief of all guards regiments. Alexander Pávlovich to command the Semënovskii Regiment, Konstantín the Izmáilovskii and Nicholas to be Colonel of the Horse Guards. Arakchéev made commandant of St Petersburg. S. I. Pleshchéev, I. I. Shuválov, F. Rostopchín, G. G. Kushelëv, N. O. Kotliubitskii and A. I. Nelídov become Paul's adjutants.
7 Nov.?	Paul cancels the current recruitment levy.
8 Nov.	N. I. Saltykóv promoted to Field Marshal. Rostopchín, Kushelëv, Arakchéev and Oboliáninov all promoted to Lieutenant-General.
9 Nov.	N. V. Repnín promoted to Field Marshal.
10 Nov.	Gátchina army arrives in St Petersburg and is merged with the existing guards regiments.
11 Nov.	P. I. Melissino promoted to Général-*en-chef*.
12 Nov.	I. G. Chernyshëv promoted to Field Marshal and made President of the Naval College.
29 Nov.	New Regulations for the infantry and cavalry based on Frederick the Great's Regulations of 1726 and 1757.
1797	
6 Feb.	Suvórov dismissed from service and deprived of the right to wear a uniform.
Autumn	Recruitment levy, cancelled in 1796, now implemented.
1798	Establishment of a military orphanage, with places for 800 soldiers' sons (23 Dec.).
1799	Suvórov returns to the army as a Lieutenant-General, commanding the Russo-Austrian troops in Italy (9 Feb.).
By 1801	One-quarter of all officers resign during Paul I's reign (i.e. 3,500 officers in addition to the 340 generals and 2,261 staff officers dismissed by Paul).

Alexander I
1801

12 Mar.	Karázin advocates military settlements.
Mar.	Alexander reinstates some 12,000 officers dismissed by Paul.
9 Apr.	Uniform reform abolishes curls, but retains the pigtail. Wide, long Prussian greatcoats replaced by short narrow ones.
24 June	Military Commission reviews regulations but changes very little.

1802

8 Sept.	War and Naval Ministries established.
5 Dec.	Military service of 12 years for nobles not attaining officer rank.

1803

26 Apr.	Alexander recalls Arakchéev to service.
26 May	Arakchéev appointed Inspector-General of Artillery.

1806

	Divisional system introduced.
30 Nov.	*Ukáz* on the formation of a militia (*milítsiia*). Most of those called up were not used as militiamen, who should have been released as soon as hostilities ended, but were drafted into the army and thus subject to service for life.
2 Dec.	Pigtails abolished.
24 Dec.	Bénigsen replaces Kámenskii as Commander-in-chief.

1807

	Publication of the first volume of Khátov's translation of Guibert's *Essai général de tactique* (vol. 2, 1810).
10 Oct.	Swedish ambassador reports rumours of a possible army coup against Alexander.

1809

	M. A. Fonvízin's military history *circle*.
9 Nov.	First military settlement established in Mogilёv *gubérniia*.

1810

	P. A. Rakhmánov's *Voénnyi zhurnál*, Russia's first theoretical military journal (closed 1811). N. S. Mordvínov advocates a system in which some troops are set aside to produce food for the remainder.
28 June	Alexander entrusts Arakchéev with the formation of military settlements.

1811

	New Army Regulations encompass fighting in column as well as in line; establish special sharpshooter units, and for the first time include the training of troops in target practice. Light infantry regiments increased from 20 to 54.

1812

June	Arakchéev appointed Chairman of the State Council Department of War.
17 July	Alexander appeals to the Moscow nobility for men for a new militia, renamed *opolchénie* to disassociate it from the bad experience of the *milítsiia* of 1805. He promises that at the end of hostilities all militiamen shall return home.
29 July	First men enrolled into the Moscow militia.
10 Aug.	Russian generals, dissatisfied with strategy of withdrawal, demand the replacement of Barclay de Tolly.
17 Aug.	Kutúzov appointed Commander-in-chief.
Sept.	Barclay de Tolly retires from the War Ministry.
Dec.	Alexander criticizes his generals, is distressed by the shabby appearance of the troops and their 'loss of discipline' and ensures that rigorous drilling resumes. Rioting breaks out among the militiamen of Pénza *Gubérniia*

1813

	Death of Kutúzov in Bunzlau, Prussian Silesia (16 Apr.). Wittgenstein's appointment as his successor is resented by Tormásov and Milorádovich, both senior to Wittgenstein and both Russian. Alexander is forced to take command of their corps, thus dividing the Russian army.

1815

Summer	Partisans disarmed and the militia dissolved immediately the war is over.
5 Aug.	Work to begin again on military settlements, the first settlement to be near Novgorod on the river Vólkhov.
27 Aug.	Creation of the 'Army Gendarme Regiment', from the former Borisoglébskii Dragoons, to act as a Military Police Force. Its men received double pay.
29–30 Aug./ 10–11 Sept.	The Parade at Vertus (France): 150,000 Russian soldiers march past the Duke of Wellington, the Austrian and Russian Emperors and the King of Prussia.
3 Sept.	Second Battalion of the Count Arakchéev Grenadier Regiment, commanded by Major von Finken, establishes the first military settlement on the river Vólkhov.
Autumn	Clear-out of fighting generals in favour of Arakchéevites begins. New drill regulations cause great dissatisfaction
12 Dec.	Establishment of the Main Staff in charge of central army administration, to which the War Minister is formally subject (abolished 1832).

1816	In November A. N. and M. N. Muravëv found the Society of Military Men who Love Science and Literature, and restart *Voénnyi zhurnál* (F. N. Glínka, editor).
1817	Regulations for the military settlements state that they are being created to do away with all the burden associated with the present recruiting system, and to satisfy the needs of the state economy by reducing expenditure on the maintenance of the armed forces (11 May). Disorders among the Bug Cossacks, protesting against their transfer to the status of military settler; 64 condemned to death.
1818	New Regulations for light troops stress accuracy of fire and dispersed formations. New Regulations for heavy infantry make columns the formation for the attack.
1819	
18 Aug.	Disorders in Chugúev military settlements in the Chugúev Lancers and Taganróg Lancers: over 2,000 arrests; 273 men condemned to death, commuted to 3,000–12,000 blows running the gauntlet; the remainder are exiled; 29 women to be birched; 50 officers demoted and dismissed.
24 Nov.	Nicholas Pávlovich opens the Army Engineering School.
1820	Further trouble among the Bug Cossacks: thirty men condemned to between 500 and 3,000 strokes of the rod and exile to the Siberian Corps. Infantry regulations updated.
16–17 Oct.	Mutiny in the Semënovskii Guards Regiment caused by the appointment of a martinet, Colonel Schwartz, as commander. Arakchéev and Alexander attribute it to 'outside influences'.
2 Nov.	Semënovskii Guards Regiment disbanded.
1821	
Mar.	Unrest among Russian officers over the dispatch of Russian troops to Piedmont.
Apr.	Guards regiments moved from St Petersburg to the north-western *gubérniias.*
	Trial of officers of Semënovskii Guards Regiment. Colonel Schwartz dismissed.
1822	New Infantry regulations re-establish the line as the attack formation, with 20 paces between each line.
6 Feb.	Major V. F. Raévskii arrested in Odessa for distributing revolutionary propaganda among his soldiers.

Mar.	Captain Nórov released after a sentence of six months imprisonment for offering his resignation after a dressing down by Grand Duke Nikolai Pávlovich.
1825	Arakchéev informs the Education Minister of an Imperial decree that only material supplied by himself may be published about the military settlements.

Nicholas I

1827	Raévskii condemned to exile in Siberia (see 1822) (15 Oct.).
1828	Creation of Naval Staff. Secret Committee to decide on the campaign of 1829: A. I. Chernyshëv, V. P. Kochubéi, K. F. Toll, I. V. Vasílchikov.
1829	Admiral P. V. Chichagóv refuses Nicholas's summons to return to Russia.
1830	Sailors take part in cholera riots in Sebastopol (30 June).
1831	Naval Staff renamed Main Naval Staff, and headed by A. S. Ménshikov (until 1856). New recruiting system introduced. Mutiny in the military settlements in Novgorod *Gubérniia*: 2,672 men put on trial; 83 knouted, 1,581 condemned to run the gauntlet, during which 11 died. General Danílov refused to carry out the punishments.
1832	Main Staff (created 1815) dissolved, retaining nominal existence inside War Ministry.
1834	Military service reduced from 25 to 15 years.
1838	A project to translate well-known foreign books on military history and theory put forward by the publisher Glazunóv. Editors-in-chief were Médem and Senkóvskii, those taking part were Miliútin, Stuermer, Bogdanóvich, Goremýkin, Vúich, Kuzmínskii.
1839	Codification of the military laws.
1854	Senate *ukáz* announces naval conscription (3 Apr.).

Alexander II
1855

19 Feb.	F. V. Ridiger appointed commander of the guards.
24 Feb.	M. D. Gorchakóv appointed commander in the Crimea.
4 June	F. V. Ridiger's memorandum to Alexander II attributes the army's failure to centralization and ignorance of the principles of warfare.

23 June	Ridiger's second memorandum suggests the abolition of excessive centralization; that training methods be changed to train soldiers as individuals; that the educational level of officers be increased and higher command improved; that a referee system be put in place for promotion to higher posts; and that a special commission to examine these questions be established.
20 July	Establishment of the Ridiger Commission: Ridiger (chair), Baránov, Barántsev, Bariátinskii, P. A. Dannenberg, Gechevich, Glínka, Kártsov, Kurdiúmov, Loshkarëv, Maksímovich, Merkhelevich. From February 1856, Miliútin. Terms of Reference: 1. Battle regulations; 2. Weaponry; 3. Physical development of officers and men; 4. Peacetime training; 5. Referee system for officers; 6. Officer promotion.
1856	Grand Duke Konstantín Nikoláevich replaces Ménshikov as Chief of Naval Staff.
29 Mar.	In the Ridiger Committee, Miliútin recommends three-year military service.
1857	Abolition of the Department of Military Settlements (15 Dec.).
1860	
Aug.	D. A. Miliútin appointed Assistant War Minister.
Oct.	115 officers of the Nicholas General Staff Academy protest against its director.
1861	Troops placed on alert in case of post-Emancipation disturbances.
May	Sukhozanét appointed acting viceroy for Poland.
9 Nov.	Miliútin appointed War Minister.
1862	Miliútin begins restructuring of War Ministry (completed 1869).
15 Jan.	Miliútin's memorandum advocating universal conscription.
1863	
17 Apr.	Running the gauntlet abolished.
14 May	The *kadétskie korpusá* replaced by military *gimnázii*, to provide a general non-Classical six-year secondary education and higher military schools to provide specialized military training.
1870	Heiden Commission examines plans for reorganization of the army (17 Nov.).
1872	Inquiry into the distribution of revolutionary propaganda in the naval colleges (Apr.).

1874	Conscription Law (the 'Miliútin Reform'): all men, regardless of social status, become liable for military service at the age of 20. Those actually to serve, to be chosen by ballot. Exemptions only for medical reasons. Length of service reduced according to educational qualifications (1 Jan.).
	Disturbances among the Urals Cossacks over Conscription Law.
1877	Regulations on the conduct of troops during public disorders (29 Oct.).
1879	Military History Commission established on 29 March (abolished 6.xii.1911).

Alexander III

| 1882 | Military *gimnázii* revert to military academies. |
| 5 Apr. | After Skóbelev's speeches, military personnel are forbidden to make political statements or to publish any political work without permission. |

Nicholas II

1904	Kuropátkin appointed commander of Manchurian Army (7 Feb.).
1905	
8 June	Establishment of the Council of National Defence.
Oct.	Sveaborg, Kronstadt and Vladivostók mutinies.
22 Nov.	War Minister V. V. Sákharov killed in Sarátov.
1906	
1 Jan.	*Military Voice* (*Voénnyi gólos*) published by V. K. Shneur (closed 5 Sept.).
7 Mar.	Military service reduced to three years in the infantry and artillery, four years in other services.
16 May	General Zabélin's secret memorandum arguing that the War Ministry will benefit from good relations with the State Duma.
1907	Commission for National Defence in the State Duma is established towards the end of the year. A. Guchkóv (chair).
1908	'Young Turks' (Iurii Danílov, N. N. Golovín, V. I. Gúrko, von Korf, A. S. Lukómskii) meet Duma members in Gúrko's flat to discuss cooperation (disbanded 1910).
1909	Decree on disbanding of Council of National Defence (12 Aug. but *de facto* disbanded 1908).

1914

16 July	Russian mobilization begins.
2 Aug.	Grand Duke Nikolái Nikoláevich appointed Commander-in-chief with N. N. Ianushkévich as Chief of Staff.
7 Aug.	Militia mobilized.

1915

July	North-western Front divided into Western (Alekséev) and Northern (Rúzskii) Fronts.
Aug.	Nicholas II replaces Grand Duke Nikolái Nikoláevich as Commander-in-chief.
23 Aug.	Alekséev replaces Ianushkévich as Chief of Staff and Evert replaces Alekséev as commander of the Western Front.

1.2.1 Presidents of the War College

September 1728–1730	M. M. Golítsyn
1742–	V. V. Dolgorúkii
1763–July 1774	Z. G. Chernyshëv (technically Vice-President until July 1773)
July 1774–5.x.1791	G. A. Potëmkin
October 1791–1802?	N. I. Saltykóv

1.2.2 Ministers of War

1802–7	S. K. Viazmitínov
31.xii.1807–1.i.1810	A. A. Arakchéev
8.i.1810–September 1812	M. D. Barclay de Tolly
1812–15	A. I. Gorchakóv
1815–19	P. P. Konovnítsyn
1819–23	P. I. Meller-Zakomélskii
April 1824–27	A. I. Tatíshchev
1828–52	A. I. Chernyshëv
April 1852–April 1856	V. A. Dolgorúkov
April 1856–16.v.1861	N. O. Sukhozanét
16.v.1861–21.v.1881	D. A. Miliútin
21.v.1881–1.i.1898	P. S. Vannóvskii
1.i.1898–1904	A. N. Kuropátkin
1904–22.xi.1905	V. V. Sákharov
1905–9	A. F. Rédiger
1909–13.vi.1915	V. A. Sukhomlínov
13.vi.1915–13.iii.1916	A. A. Polivánov
13.iii.1916–3.i.1917	D. S. Shuváev
3.i.–1.iii.1917	M. A. Beliáev

1.2.3   Naval Ministers

September–December 1802	N. S. Mordvínov
December 1802–11	P. V. Chichagóv
1811–27	I. I. de Traversé
1827–36	A. V. von Müller
1836–55	A. S. Ménshikov
1855–57	F. P. Vrángel
1858	N. F. Metlín
1860–76	N. K. Krabbe
1876–80	S. S. Lesóvskii
1880–82	A. A. Peshchurov
1882–88	I. A. Shestakóv
1888–96	N. M. Chikhachëv
1896–1903	P. P. Týrtov
1903–May 1905	F. K. Avelán
June 1905–11.i.1907	A. A. Birilëv
11.i.1907–8.i.1909	I. M. Díkov
8.i.1909–18.iii.1911	S. A. Voevódskii
18.iii.1911–1.iii.1917	I. K. Grigoróvich

1.3 Social Unrest and Revolution

Peter I

1694–96	Kizhí uprising by Karelian assigned peasants in the Butenant metallurgy works.
1697	Conspiracy led by *Strélets* colonel Ivan Zickler (Feb.).
1698	Revolt of the *Stréltsy*.
1703	Kungur uprising by assigned peasants in the Kaménskii works.
1705–6	Revolt in Ástrakhan.
1707–9	Don, Zaporózhian and Ukrainian Cossack revolts (see p. 163).
1709–10	Peasant revolt in the Volga Basin.
1718	Unrest in Moscow as torture and executions follow arrest of Alexei Petróvich (Feb.–July).
1719–27	About 200,000 peasants run away (mainly to Poland) to avoid the poll tax.
1723	Army man special barriers on the frontiers to catch fleeing peasants (from 8 Mar.).
1723–27	Moscow *Sukónnyi dvor* workers protest over transfer to private ownership.

Anna Ivánovna

1732–36	Peasant disturbances as harvest failure spreads from Smolensk *Gubérniia* to the whole of Russia.
1738	Near Kiev, clergy and townspeople recognize a pretender as Alexei Petróvich.

Elizabeth

1757–63	Widespread peasant unrest and flight into Poland.
1760	All social groups given the right to send unruly members to Siberia (Dec.).

Peter III

1762	Peasants warned not to believe rumours of their impending freedom (19 June).

Catherine II

1762	Repetition of Peter's warning of 19 June (4 July).
1763	P. Pánin's investigation blames peasant flights on the religious oppression of Old Believers, landowners' abuse of the recruitment levy, the ill treatment of recruits, the power of landowners over their serfs, and the cost of salt and spirits. A. A. Viázemskii tours the Urals, punishing the leaders of the disorders, and investigating the causes of unrest among assigned peasants.
13 May	Amnesty for pre-1762 fugitives, with permission to settle on state land and six years' immunity from taxes and labour dues.
11 July	Peasants to bear costs of military expeditions to restore order.
Aug.	Troops cross into Poland and recover 2,000 serfs.
1767	Twenty-seven serf risings.
1769	Iaík Cossack mutiny crushed by General Traubenberg.
1770	The Danubian Army infects Moscow with the plague.
1771	
Aug.	400–500 plague deaths per day in Moscow.
16/27 Sept.	Moscow plague riots, after Archbishop Ambrosius removes a miracle-working icon from a city gate to prevent cross-infection among crowds gathering there. G. G. Orlóv burns houses, disinfects, etc., to control the plague. Plague ends in December. Total dead around 200,000.
1772	
Mar.	Cossacks support F. I. Bogomólov's claim to be Peter III.
Nov.	Don Cossacks riot when authorities try to arrest ataman Efrémov.
Dec.	Bogomólov arrested, dies on way to Siberia.
1773–75	**Pugachëv Revolt**
1773	
Jan.	Fresh Iaík Cossack disturbances. Traubenberg killed.
June	General Freymann restores order, and imposes harsh punishments.
July	In Iaítsk, Emelián Pugachëv claims to be Peter III, and promises to restore the old free Cossack way of life.
17 Sept.	Pugachëv's first Manifesto.
19 Sept.	Pugachëv fails to take Yaítsk.
5 Oct.	Pugachëv begins siege of Orenbúrg (defended by I. A. Reinsdorp) and offers to restore to the Bashkirs their traditional way of life.

Early Nov.	Pugachëv defeats punitive force sent from Kazán, commanded by V. A. Kar.
6 Nov.	Pugachëv's College of War at his headquarters in Berda, outside Orenbúrg: I. & B. Baimekóv, I. Pochitálin, M. A. Shvanovich, A. Vitoshnov.
Mid Nov.	Pugachëv defeats punitive force from Simbírsk. Revolt spreads to Bashkiria.
End Nov.	Zarúbin Chíka begins the siege of Ufá.
29 Nov.	A. I. Bíbikov appointed to put down rebellion.
26 Dec.	Bíbikov arrives in Kazán and sets up the Kazán Commission to investigate the causes of the rebellion and to punish the guilty.
End Dec.	Ília Arápov occupies Samára.

1774

Jan.	Pugachëv begins forcible recruitment. An attack on Urals copper foundries, led by Salavát Iuliáev and I. Kuznetsóv, takes Cheliabinsk but fails to take Kungúr and Ekaterinbúrg. Siege of the Great Dalmátov Monastery.
24 Jan.	Chíka attack on Ufá repulsed.
14 Mar.	Government troops relieve Great Dalmátov.
22 Mar.	P. M. Golítsyn defeats Pugachëv at Tatíshchevo.
23 Mar.	Pugachëv abandons Berda as Golítsyn's vanguard enters it.
23–24 Mar.	Government troops under I. I. Mikhelson defeat Chika and relieve Ufá.
7 Apr.	Death of Bíbikov.
16 Apr.	Yaítsk relieved. F. F. Shcherbátov takes over from Bíbikov.
18 June	Osa surrenders to Pugachëv.
5 July?	Shcherbátov replaced by P. S. Potëmkin as head of the Kazán Commission.
12 July	Pugachëv takes and burns Kazán. Mikhelson disperses the rebels at Kazán.
13 July	Mikhelson enters Kazán, and defeats Pugachëv, who moves south.
23 July	Pugachëv in Alatyr.
26 July	Pugachëv in Saránsk.
1 Aug.	Pugachëv in Pénza.
6 Aug.	Pugachëv takes Samára.
13 Aug.	Pugachëv's Manifesto to the Don Cossacks.
21 Aug.	Outside Tsarítsyn, Don Cossacks recognize that Pugachëv is not Peter III.
25 Aug.	Mikhelson's last battle with Pugachëv south of Tsarítsyn.

15 Sept.	Iaík Cossacks deliver Pugachëv to the authorities. Pánin conducts savage reprisals against Pugachëv's supporters.
End Sept.	Establishment of a Special Commission of the Secret Department of the Senate to try the rebel leaders in Moscow (M. N. Volkónskii, S. I. Sheshkóvskii, P. S. Potëmkin). The Kazán Commission is wound up.
4 Nov.	Pugachëv drawn through the streets of Moscow in an iron cage.
24 Nov.	Salavát Iuliáev captured in Bashkiria.
30 Dec.	Trial of Pugachëv.

1775

10 Jan.	Execution of Pugachëv leaders.
15 Mar.	Amnesty for all offences committed during Revolt. Estimated casualties: killed by rebels: 1,572 nobles, 237 clerics, 1,037 officers and officials, 600 government troops (and 1,000 wounded). 20,000 rebels killed (excluding Bashkirs and those killed in Pánin's reprisals).
1777	Great flood of St Petersburg.

Paul I

| **1796** | Marked increase in peasant uprisings in November extending into 1797. |

Alexander I

1812	Rebellion of militiamen in Penza *Gubérniia*, in the belief that their contribution against Napoleon should have led to their emancipation (Dec.).
1816	Disorders in Dorpat University lead to students being expelled from the city.
1819	August von Kotzebue, dramatist and agent of the Russian government, is assassinated in Mannheim on 10 March by Jena University student, Karl Sand. After this, Russian students are forbidden to attend certain German universities.
1824	Great flood of St Petersburg.

1825

| Sept. | Serfs murder Arakchéev's mistress, Anastasia Mínkina, on his estate at Gruzinó. |
| 14 Dec. | Decembrist Revolt (see pp. 57–9). |

Nicholas I

| **1826** | Peasant unrest in Kiev *Gubérniia*. Ringleaders knouted. |

1828	Suicide of I. I. Sukhónin after the failure of his revolt among the workers of the Blagodátnyi and Kliníchnyi factories in Zabaikália (1 Dec.).
1829	Twenty Urals workers condemned to death after a factory riot (20 Sept.).
1830	Cholera riots in Sebastopol (30 June) and in Kursk and Tambóv *Gubérniias.*
1831	Cholera riot in St Petersburg (22 June).
1832	Moscow University student unrest.
1838	Kiev University closed until May 1839. A Military-Medical Academy student dies during his punishment for striking the Academy's director: to run a 500-blow gauntlet three times.
1840	Twenty-one peasants killed and 24 wounded, in a riot in Vítebsk *Gubérniia* over an 'erroneous understanding of their right to freedom'.
1841	Peasant riots around Riga.
1842	Peasant riots in Perm *Gubérniia*, extending into 1843, lead to 69 deaths.
1847	Peasant clashes with troops in Vítebsk *Gubérniia* (Spring).
1848	
20 Feb.	News of the French Revolution reaches St Petersburg.
22 Feb.	News of the Second French Republic reaches St Petersburg.
14 Mar.	Imperial Manifesto on Revolution: 'Take heed, O nations, and submit, for God is with us!' Strict limitations imposed on the publication of news about foreign disturbances.
27 Mar.	Ménshikov Committee established to recommend ways of limiting the circulation of unwelcome ideas.

Alexander II

1855	Peasant riots and clashes with the military in Kiev, Zvenígorod, Chigírin, Umansk and Cherkássia (Mar.–Aug.).
1856–63	**The beginning of student and industrial unrest**
1856	Students clash with officers of the local garrison in Kazán (Autumn).
1857	Kazán University student protest when Ivan Úmov is sent to the army for three years for having 'insulted' the university authorities.
13 July	Disturbances in the Izhóra Admiralty Works, St Petersburg.

Sept.	Police injure Moscow students who had refused them entry to the university.
Oct.	Alexander frees Kiev students imprisoned for kicking an army officer's dog.
End	First student friendly society in St Petersburg. First student newspapers appear.

1858

Jan.	Dobroliúbov in *Sovreménnik* takes up Kazán students' request for the resignation of Professor V. F. Bervi, on the grounds that he is ignorant of his subject. Bervi is forced to resign.
Apr.	Strike at the Wright Cotton Mill, St Petersburg.
Autumn	Student disturbances in Khárkov, 13 expelled. Moscow student disturbances in sympathy with Kazán students force two lecturers to resign. Ten students expelled, 100 suspended for a year.

1859

Jan.	Eighteen Kazán students dismissed for supporting a liberal lecturer. Followed by a mass protest exodus of students from the university. Unrest among workers of the Maxwell Cotton Mill, St Petersburg *Gubérniia*.
Dec.	Disturbances at the Goleníshchevskaia Works, St Petersburg.

1860   Workers at the Alexandróvsk Machine Works, St Petersburg, petition the management for higher wages (Jan.).

1861

17 Feb.	Russian and Polish students attend a requiem mass in St Petersburg to commemorate the fallen in the Warsaw disturbances.
28 Feb.	Demonstrations at Shévchenko's funeral in St Petersburg.
12 Apr.	The Bézdna Affair: troops fire on peasant demonstrators who were claiming that the true terms of the Emancipation had been concealed from them. Their leader, Anton Petróv, is executed on 18 Apr.
Apr.	Kazán student demonstration at a church service in memory of the victims of the peasant revolt in Bézdna, followed by the dismissal of one staff member (A. P. Shchápov) and nine students, and the exile of two priests who took the service.
May	Metropolitan Filarét writes to the Tsar about 'anti-religious and political works' circulating in Moscow University. Peasant unrest in Pénza, Kalúga, and Vorónezh *Gubérnii*.

22 Sept.	Lecture rooms closed in St Petersburg University to prevent student meetings.
23 Sept.	Beginning of a series of student demonstrations culminating in a clash with the military on St Isaac's Square (Nov.), followed by arrests, imprisonments and trials in St Petersburg. Troubles spread to Moscow, Kíev, Khárkov and Kazán.
Oct.	Kazán University handed over to the military and temporarily closed.
20 Dec.	St Petersburg University closed (until August 1863 for most faculties).

1862

Feb.	Students and intellectuals organize the Free University of St Petersburg.
5 Mar.	Arrest of history professor P. V. Pávlov marks the end of the Free University.
May	Fires in St Petersburg attributed to 'radical groups active in the Sunday Schools', lead to the closure of the latter.

1866–68   **The White Terror**

1866

4 Apr.	Dmitrii Karakózov's attempt on the Tsar.
24 June	Uprising of Polish and Russian forced labour convicts constructing the Baikál railway. Leaders shot.
1867	Police and academic authorities ordered to share information on students' political views (26 May).
	Famine in Archangel, Vólogda, Olónets, Nóvgorod, Orël, Kostromá, Túla and Riazán *Gubérniias*, extending into 1868.
1869	New wave of student unrest.
15 Mar.	Military-Medical Academy closed until 24 March after student disorders.

1870

22 May	Névskii Works Strike.
13 June	Trial of 62 Névskii strikers (sentenced to 3–7 days confinement).
1872	Three-day riot in Khárkov (17–19 Apr.).
1873	N. A. Liubímov's article in *Russkii véstnik* attacking university autonomy (Feb.).
	Famine in Samára extending into 1874.

1874

| 15 Feb. | Strike in the Semiánnikov factory. |
| Summer | The Movement to the People ('The Mad Summer of '74'). |

17 Oct.	Disorders in the Medical-Surgical Academy and in the Mining Institute.
18 Oct.	Disorders in the Technological Institute.
1875	The Chigírin affair: peasants from the Chigirin District of Kiev *Gubérniia* are arrested for refusing to accept the system of land distribution implemented after the Emancipation (May).
1876	
30 Mar.	Demonstrations during the funeral of the student P. F. Chernyshëv.
Nov.	S. M. Solovëv resigns his university post over government support for N. A. Liubímov, who had been censured by Moscow University Council after 50 of his 65 students had walked out in protest at his views on university autonomy.
6 Dec.	Kazán Square student demonstration.
1877	
21 Feb.–14 Mar.	Trial of the 50 (for the Movement to the People). Closure of the Artists Club after a speech at a students' ball in honour of Nekrásov and a collection taken for the Kazán Square demonstrators on trial.
17 June	Trial of the Chigirin peasants. At about the same time, police uncover a secret society of about 1,000 peasants in Chigirin led by Iakov Stefánovich. Arrested in September 1877, he escaped in May 1878.
Oct.	The Trial of the 193 (continues until January 1878).
1878	
24 Jan.	Vera Zasúlich's attempt on the life of St Petersburg governor F. F. Trépov.
31 Mar.	Demonstrations after Vera Zasúlich's acquittal.
5 Apr.	An attack on the rector of Kiev University leads to the expulsion of 140 students.
4 Aug.	S. Kravchínskii kills gendarme chief N. V. Mezentsóv.
Autumn	Student unrest in St Petersburg leads to 142 arrests.
15–18 Dec.	Student disturbances at the Khárkov Veterinary Institute.
1879	
9 Feb.	D. N. Kropótkin, governor of Khárkov, shot by G. D. Goldenberg.
13 Mar.	Unsuccessful attempt on the life of gendarme chief A. R. Drenteln.
2 Apr.	A. K. Solovëv's attempt on the life of Alexander II.
31 July	Cabinet gives Tolstoy power to tighten control over students.

5 Nov.	Tolstoy's university regulations transfer disciplinary powers from the academics to the administration and inspectorate.

1880

6 Feb.	Tolstoy presents his proposals for a new university charter to the cabinet.
20 Feb.	I. Mlodétskii's attempt on the life of Lóris-Mélikov.
14 Apr.	Dismissal of Tolstoy as Minister of Education after student unrest in Moscow University leads to 400 arrests. A. A. Sabúrov shelves the new charter (implemented in 1884).
1881	Assassination of Alexander II (1 Mar.).

Alexander III

1882

19 May	Trial of 100 students in Odessa.
30 Oct.	Student disorders in Kazán lead to the closure of the university.
13 Dec.	Hunger strike in Odessa prison.

1883

22 Feb.–6 Mar.	Disorders at the New Admiralty Agricultural College. Nearly 200 students expelled.
7 Mar.	New Admiralty Agricultural College closed.
1885	Strike at the Morózov Works, Orékhovo-Zúevo (7–17 Jan.).
1886	Press forbidden to mention the nationwide celebrations of the 25th anniversary of peasant emancipation (19 Feb.).
1887	Student disorders and clashes with police in Moscow, Odessa and Kazán (Dec.).
1888	Street disorders in Samára, Tiflis.
17 Oct.	Twenty-one killed when the Imperial train crashes in Borki station.
1889	Six killed and many wounded when troops clash with political deportees in Yakútia (21 Mar.).
1890	St Petersburg, Moscow, Kiev, Khárkov, Odessa, Warsaw, Dorpat student demonstrators demand the restoration of the 1863 University statute and the admission of Jews.
1891	'The Great Famine', extending into 1892, affects 30 million people.
Aug.	Peasant rioting begins. St Petersburg flooded.
1892	Iuzóvka factory entirely demolished in rioting involving 30,000 people.
1893	Don Cossack riots.

Nicholas II

1895	United council of student *zemliáchestvos* arrested in Moscow.
1896	
18 May	1,300 crushed to death in Khodynka Field, Moscow, during Nicholas II's coronation celebrations.
24 May–17 June	Some 30,000 textile workers strike in St Petersburg.
Nov.	700 arrests at a demonstration to commemorate the victims of Khodynka Field, organized by the reconstituted Moscow student council of *zemliáchestvos*.
1897	Student disturbances after a female student commits suicide in the Peter-Paul Fortress (Mar.).
1899	
8 Feb.	Student strikes close St Petersburg University after police use whips on student rioters. The strike spreads to Riga and Warsaw.
5 May	Army fires on strikers at the Feniks Factory and at the Jute Mills, killing 93.
6–17 May	Serious disturbances in Riga after the killing of the Jute workers.
1901	
Feb.	P. Karpóvich, a twice-expelled former student, kills the Minister of Education, N. P. Bogolépov.
25 Feb.	Moscow student demonstration.
4 Mar.	Kazán Square student demonstration dispersed by police.
11 Mar.	Kiev student demonstration.
Mar.	Lagóvskii's attempt on the life of Podbedonóstsev.
7–17 May	During the strike known as 'The Obúkhov Defence', workers are killed and wounded; 37 workers put on trial.
8 May–7 June	Strikes in St Petersburg in sympathy with the 'Obúkhov Defence'.
28 Nov.–2 Dec.	Student disorders in Khárkov.
1905–7	See pp. 70–2.
1908	Purishkévich founds the Union of Michael the Archangel (11 Mar.).
1912	Lena Gold Fields massacre: police fire on workers killing 200 (4 Apr.).
1914	
7–10 July	Street disturbances and strikes coincide with Poincaré's visit to St Petersburg.
4 Aug.	German Embassy sacked.
1915	
27–30 May	Moscow anti-German riots.

5 June	Kostromá strikers shot down.
Early Aug.	Putílov factory workers' meetings to discuss proposed 'mobilization of industry'. Numerous Putílov workers arrested.
10 Aug.	Ivánovo-Voznesénsk strikers protesting against the war are shot down.
17–19 Aug.	Widespread protest strikes in Petrograd at Ivánovo-Voznesénsk shootings.
2–5 Sept.	Three-day strike in the Putílov factory over the arrest of workers who spoke to Duma deputies when these visited the factory and, from 3 September, over the prorogation of the State Duma.

1916

4 Feb.	Putílov factory strike. General Tumánov threatens Putílov and Lessner workers with mobilization.
6 Feb.	Putílov factory closed down.
10 Feb.	Putílov factory takes on workers again.
16 Feb.	Renewed strikes at Putílov.
22 Feb.	Duma deputies Skóbelev, Tuliakóv and Kháustov visit Putílov. Sit-in strike begins.
23 Feb.	Putílov factory closed down. Sacked workers called up into the army.
29 Feb.	Government takes over Putílov factory and shipyard.
1–3 Mar.	Widespread strikes in support of Putílov workers.
14 Mar.	General Polivánov sacked as War Minister because of his inability to solve the Putílov troubles, and replaced by Shuváev, thought to be able to talk to the workers.
Oct.	Soldiers from 181 Regiment, stationed on the Vyborg Side, help workers from the Russkii Renault factory fight the police. The regiment is transferred from the capital in December.

For the February Revolution, see pp. 73–9.

1.3.1   The Revolutionary and Labour Movements

Alexander I

1814

30 July	Semënovskii Guards return to St Petersburg from France. (For dissatisfaction in the army, see pp. 40–2).
After 30 July	Creation of the Semënovskii officers' *Artél*. General Staff officers create the 'Holy *Artél*'.
1816	Formation of the 'Union of Salvation' (The Society of True and Loyal Sons of the Fatherland), A. N.

	Muravëv, N. M. Muravëv, M. I. and S. I. Muravëv-Apóstol, S. P. Trubetskói and I. D. Iakúshkin, inspired by the Prussian *Tugenbund*.
1821	
1–21 Jan.	Moscow meeting of the Union of Welfare: I. G. Búrtsev, I. A. and M. A. Fonvízin, F. N. Glínka, P. Kh. Grabbe, I. D. Iakúshkin, N. I. Komaróv, M. N. Muravëv, K. A. Okhótnikov, M. F. Orlóv, N. I. Turgénev.
25 May	Benckendorff warns Alexander of the existence of secret societies in the army.
1824	In the Spring, Russian and Polish revolutionaries meet in Kiev (Bestúzhev, A. Jabłonowski, S. Krzyżanowski, S. Muravëv-Apóstol).
1825	Secret Congress of the United Slavs, near Zhitomir (Mar.).

Nicholas I

1825	
13 Dec.	Arrest of Pavel Pestél.
14 Dec.	Revolt of the Moscow Guards Regiment, Senate Square, St Petersburg.
17 Dec.	Establishment of the Committee of Investigation into the Decembrist Revolt: A. I. Tatíshchev, V. F. Adlerberg, A. Kh. Benkendorff, A. I. Chernyshëv, D. N. Blúdov, A. N. Golítsyn, P. V. Goleníshchev-Kutúzov, V. V. Levashëv, Grand Duke Mikhaíl Pávlovich.
30 Dec.	S. Muravëv-Apostol marches the Chernígov Regiment to Vasilkov near Kiev.
31 Dec.	Chernígov Regiment reaches Motovilovka.
1826	
3 Jan.	General Geismar defeats the Chernígov Regiment outside Trilesy.
30 May	Committee of Investigation presents its report to Nicholas I.
3 June	Supreme Criminal Court opens.
9 July	Supreme Criminal Court passes sentence on 579 Decembrists: 290 acquitted; 289 guilty: five to be quartered; 31 to be decapitated; 85 to be exiled to Siberia; 134 to suffer loss of military rank and to be posted to other units; four to be deported (20 died before the trial; the fate of 10 is unknown). Admiral N. S. Mordvínov is the only judge to refuse to vote for the death penalty. Nicholas commutes the five

	quarterings to hangings and the 31 decapitations to exile to Siberia for life.
13 July	Five Decembrists hanged in the Peter-Paul Fortress, St Petersburg (M. P. Bestúzhev-Riúmin, P. G. Kakhóvskii, S. I. Muravëv-Apóstol, P. I. Pestél, K. F. Ryléev).
1834	Herzen, Ogarëv and members of the Moscow Saint-Simonist Group arrested (July).
1840	Bakúnin leaves Russia.
1845	Publication of Petrashévskii's *Pocket Dictionary of Foreign Words Which Have Entered the Vocabulary of the Russian Language*, vol. 1.
1846	Petrashévskii's *Pocket Dictionary of Foreign Words Which Have Entered the Vocabulary of the Russian Language*, vol. 2, is banned a month after publication.
Jan.	Foundation of the Kiev Brotherhood of Cyril and Methodius, with a programme of the emancipation of the serfs and Ukrainian nationalism through the creation of a federated Slav republic with broad local autonomy.
1847	Herzen leaves Russia.
1849	
23 Apr.	Petrashévskii circle (F. and M. Dostoevskii, Iastrzhémbskii, Káshkin, Toll, Golovínskii, Dúrov, Pleshchéev, A. A. Kuzmín) arrested.
22 Dec.	Mock-execution of members of the Petrashévskii circle.
1850	Herzen, *From the Other Shore*, is published in the *Deutsche Monatsschrift*.
1851	Herzen, *Du développement des idées révolutionnaires en Russie* and *Le people russe et le socialisme* are both published in Nice and seized by the French government.
1853	Herzen founds the Free Russia Press in London (21 Feb.).

Alexander II

1855	First number of Herzen's *Pole Star* (1 Aug., 8 issues in all).
1857	Herzen and Ogarëv's *Kólokol* published fortnightly in London from 1 July until 1867.
1859	Iu. M. Molosov and N. Satilov found *The Library of Kazán Students in Moscow University*.
1861	
1 July	An article in *Kólokol* answers 'Land and Freedom' to the question 'What do the People Need?'
July	Publication of the first clandestine leaflet, *Velikorús* (*The Great Russian*).

Sept.	M. I. Mikháilov sentenced to penal servitude in Siberia for his leaflet *To the Young Generation*. Publication of the second and third issues of *Velikorús* (no more published).
Nov.	In *Kólokol*, Herzen urges expelled university students to 'go to the people'.
1862	The first Land and Freedom is founded by N. A. Serno-Solovévich.
Jan.	Chernyshévskii writes his *Unaddressed Letters* (published in London in 1874).
May	P. G. Zaichnévskii issues *Young Russia*.
7 July	Arrest of Chernyshévskii and N. A. Serno-Solovévich.
1863	Formation of the Ishútin Group in Moscow.
Apr.–May	The Kazán Conspiracy, (see p. 178).
1864	Demise of the first Land and Freedom.
1865	Arrest of N. M. Iádrintsev and G. N. Potánin for 'plotting the separation of Siberia from Russia' (Spring).
1866	
4 Apr.	Attempt on the Tsar's life by Dmitrii Karakózov, a member of the Ishútin Group.
7 Dec.	Petrashévskii dies in Siberia.
1867	G. A. Lopátin and F. Volkhóvskii found The Society of the Ruble. Bakúnin founds his League of Peace and Freedom in Geneva.
1868	Peter Lavróv's *Historical Letters* published in *Nedélia* (*The Week*) (1869). Publication of Bakúnin and Necháev's *Revolutionary Catechism*.
Sept.	First issue of Bakúnin's *The People's Cause*.
1869	Mark Natansón and N. V. Chaikóvskii establish the Chaikóvskii Circle in the Military-Medical Academy.
26 Mar.	Tkachëv arrested.
Aug.–Nov.	Necháev founds The People's Reckoning.
21 Nov.	Necháev organizes the murder of Iván Ivanóv and flees to Switzerland.
1870	Formation of the Russian section of the First International.
1871	Trial of Necháev's associates, (July–Aug.).
1872	Formation of the Odessa terrorist group with Zheliábov as a member, and of the Dolgúshin group. Publication of Bakúnin's translation of vol. 1 of *Das Kapital*. The Moscow Socialist-Revolutionary group (S. Kliachkó, V. Bátiushkova, Armfeld, Tsákin and Tikhomírov) carries out propaganda among the workers.

Aug.	Necháev extradited from Switzerland.
9/21–14/26 Aug.	The Hague Congress of the Socialist International expels Bakúnin.

1873

Jan.	Necháev sentenced to 20 years' hard labour followed by exile to Siberia.
1 Aug.	First number of Lavróv's *Forward!* (48 issues published in Zürich and London until 1876).
Sep.	Dolgúshin arrested near Moscow.
Dec.	Tkachëv escapes abroad.

1874

Summer	The Movement to the People ('The Mad Summer of '74').
9–15 July	Trial of Dolgúshin.

1875

Jan.	Z. K. Ralli's *The Worker* published in Geneva monthly until 1876.
Spring	E. O. Zaslávskii sets up the South Russian Workers' Union in Odessa.
1 Dec.	Tkachëv's *The Tocsin* published in Geneva until 1877.

1876   The second Land and Freedom founded in October (name adopted only in 1878).

1877

21 Feb.–14 Mar.	Trial of the 50.
23–29 May	Trial of the members of the South Russian Workers' Union.
18 Oct.	The Trial of the 193 (lasts until 23.i.1879).

1878

31 Mar.	Trial of Vera Zasúlich.
4 Aug.	S. M. Kravchínskii, of Land and Freedom, kills gendarme chief N. V. Mezentsóv.
23 Dec.	S. N. Khaltúrin and V. P. Obnórskii set up the Northern Union of Russian Workers.

1879

9 Feb.	G. D. Goldenberg shoots D. N. Kropótkin, governor of Khárkov.
13 Mar.	Leon Mírskii's unsuccessful attempt on gendarme chief A. R. Drenteln.
2 Apr.	A. K. Solovëv, of Land and Freedom, fires five shots at Alexander II.
17–21 June	The Lipetsk preliminary conference of Land and Freedom endorses the assassination of Alexander II as one of the organization's main objectives.

24 June	The Vorónezh Congress of Land and Freedom accepts the recommendations of the Lipetsk pre-conference (G. V. Plekhánov votes against).
26 Aug.	Executive Committee of Land and Freedom votes to assassinate Alexander II.
Oct.	Land and Freedom splits into The People's Will and Plekhánov's Black Repartition.
18 Nov.	Zheliábov's attempt to blow up Alexander II's train at Alexandrovsk.
19 Nov.	Alexander Mikháilov's attempt to blow up Alexander II's train near Moscow.
1880	Publication of *The Programme of Worker-Members of the Party of the People's Will* early in the year.
Jan.	First issue of *Black Repartition*.
17 Jan.	Police uncover The People's Will's printing press (in existence since 22.viii.1879).
22 Jan.	Police seize Black Repartition's printing press.
5 Feb.	Stepan Khaltúrin's bomb in the Winter Palace kills 11 and wounds 56.
15 Feb.	Northern Union of Russian Workers' *Workers' Dawn* (one issue only published).
20 Feb.	I. Mlodétskii of The People's Will's attempt on the life of M. T. Lóris-Mélikov.
22 Feb.	Molodétskii hanged.
Dec.	Publication of the first issue of the Workers' Sections of Black Repartition's *Grain* (nos 2–6 published in Russia).
1881	Assassination of Alexander II (1 Mar.).

Alexander III
1881

26–29 Mar.	Trial of Gésia Gelfman, Nikolái Kibálchich, Timoféi Mikháilov, Sofia Peróvskaia, Nikolái Rysakóv, and Andréi Zheliábov for the assassination of Alexander II. All are condemned to death.
3 Apr.	Assassins of Alexander II hanged, except for Gelfman, who was pregnant.
	Demise of Black Repartition.
1882	
14 Feb.	Police seize The People's Will's press in Odessa.
May	Plekhánov's translation of *The Communist Manifesto* published in Geneva.
18 Dec.	Police seize the People's Will's press in Odessa.
1883	Stepniák's *Underground Russia* published in London.

10 Feb.	Vera Figner arrested.
13/25 Sept.	Formation of the Group for the Emancipation of Labour in Geneva.
Early winter	Formation of D. Blagóev's Party of Russian Social Democrats.
1884	The *Programme of the Social-Democratic Group for the Emancipation of Labour* published in Geneva in the summer.
1885	Publication of Plekhánov, 'Our Differences,' (Geneva), and of Stepniák, *Russia under the Tzars*, 2 vols (London).
Jan.	Blagóev's *Worker*, no. 1, published.
July	*Worker*, no. 2, published.
Autumn	Formation of P. V. Tochísskii's social-democratic organization (named The Association of Saint Petersburg Workers in late 1886).
1887	
1 Mar.	Alexander Uliánov's group's attempt on the life of Alexander III.
8 May	Alexander Uliánov (Lenin's brother) hanged.
1888	The second Proletariat formed in Warsaw (Feb.).
1890	
Feb.	The Group for the Emancipation of Labour publish *Sotsiál-demokrát*.
19 Apr./1 May	May Day celebrated in Warsaw (first time in Russian Empire).
1891	
15 Apr.	Workers participate in the funeral of N. V. Shelgunóv.
5 May	M. I. Brúsnev's group organize May Day celebrations.
4/16–10/ 22 Aug.	Second Congress of the Second International, Brussels.
1892	Lenin's Marxist group formed in Samára.
2 Feb.	Julius Mártov's first arrest.
Dec.	Mártov's St Petersburg Group for the Emancipation of Labour formed.
1893	Third Congress of the Second International, Zürich (25–31 July/6–12 Aug.).
1894	Formation of the Central Group of the Union of Socialist Revolutionaries in Sarátov and of the Kiev Organization of Socialist Revolutionaries. Publication of J. Mártov's 'On Agitation'.
Apr.	Formation of the Central Workers' Circle, Moscow.
June	Publication of V. I. Lenin, 'Who the "Friends of the People" Are' (hectograph).

Nicholas II

1895	Formation of Socialist Revolutionary groups in Vorónezh, Poltáva and Khárkov and of Social-Democratic groups in Nízhnii Nóvgorod, Kozlóv, Kostromá, Pénza, Odessa, Shúia. Publication of N. Béltov (G. V. Plekhánov), *On the Development of the Monist View of History*.
18–19 Feb.	Meeting of representatives of Social-Democratic groups from St Petersburg, Moscow, Kiev and Vílna.
Feb.	Formation of a Social-Democratic Circle in Odessa.
Nov.	Formation of the Union of Struggle for the Emancipation of the Working Class (J. Mártov, I. M. Liakhóvskii, G. M. Krzhizhánovskii, V. I. Lenin, V. V. Starkóv).
9 Dec.	The leaders of the Union of Struggle for the Emancipation of the Working Class are arrested (Krzhizhánovskii, Lenin, Starkóv, A. A. Vanéev).
1896	The Sarátov Union of Socialist Revolutionaries publish their *Basic Program*.
Mar.	Geneva Union of Russian Social-Democrats' *The Worker*, no. 1–2.
May	Formation of the Workers' Cause, Kiev.
15/27 July	Fourth Congress of the Second International opens, London (ends 20 July/1 Aug.).
8 Dec.	Publication of the Workers' Cause's *Forwards*, no. 1, Kiev.
1897	Formation of the St Petersburg Group of Socialist Revolutionaries. The Sarátov Central Union of Socialist Revolutionaries moves to Moscow.
Mar.	Kiev Social-Democratic groups form the Kiev League of Struggle for the Emancipation of the Working Class.
Apr.	Formation of the Union of Nikoláev Workers, part of the South Russian Workers' Union (members include Trotsky).
Aug.	Publication of the Kiev League of Struggle for the Emancipation of the Working Class's *Workers' Paper*, no. 1. Socialist Revolutionaries from Vorónezh, Kiev, St Petersburg, Poltáva and Khárkov set up the PSR in Vorónezh.
Sept.	First Congress of the Bund, Vilnius.
20 Oct.	Union of Nikoláev Workers' *Our Cause*, no. 1.
Oct.	Publication of *Workers' Thought*, no. 1.
Nov.	Second Congress of the PSR.
1898	
1–3 Mar.	First Congress of the RSDRP, Minsk.

12 Mar.	Leaders of the St Petersburg Group of Socialist Revolutionaries arrested.
Nov.	First Congress of the League of Russian Social-Democrats Abroad, Geneva.
Autumn	Lenin, *The Tasks of the Russian Social-Democrats*, published in Geneva.

1899

Jan.	*Workers' Thought*, no. 5, becomes the official organ of the St Petersburg Union of Struggle.
24 Mar.	Lenin, *The Development of Capitalism in Russia*, published in St Petersburg.
Apr.	Publication of the League of Russian Social-Democrats' *Workers' Cause*, no. 1.
Autumn	The Minsk group of Socialist Revolutionaries form the Workers' Party for the Political Emancipation of Russia (branches established in Ekaterinosláv, Vítebsk, Dvinsk, Grodno, Zhitomir, Vilkovishki).

1900

	Vademecum for the editors of 'Rabochee delo' published, with a preface by G. V. Plekhánov in Geneva.
Jan.	Publication of the Ekaterinosláv Committee RDSRP's *Southern Worker*, no. 1.
May	The League of Struggle and its supporters set up the Social-Democrat Organization in Geneva.
16 Jul.	Lenin leaves Russia.
10/23–14/ 27 Sept.	Fifth Congress of the Second International, Paris: 12 delegates from the Bund, 9 from the RSDRP, 3 from the PSR, and 5 others.
24 Dec.	Publication of *The Spark* (*Iskra*), no. 1, in Leipzig.
End	Formation of the Northern Workers' Union with branches in Vladímir, Ivánovo-Voznesénsk, Kostromá and Iároslavl.

1901

Jan.	Publication of *Revolutionary Russia*, organ of the PSR (76 issues until 1905).
Apr.	Publication of *The Dawn*, no. 1 (editors: Lenin, Plekhánov) in Stuttgart.
Mar.	PSR member Lagóvskii's attempt on the life of Podbedonóstsev.
June	Representatives of *Iskra*, *Sotsiál-demokrát*, the League of Russian Social-Democrats, Struggle (*Borbá*), and the Bund meet in Geneva.
Oct.	Formation of the League of Russian Revolutionary Social-Democracy Abroad in Geneva.

Dec.	Formal foundation of the PSR by Evno Ázev and George Gershuni.
1902	
Jan.	Samára Conference of *Iskra* organizations in Russia.
2 Apr.	Minister of the Interior, D. S. Sipiágin, assassinated by PSR member S. V. Balmashëv.
26 Apr.	Trial of Balmashëv.
July	Attempt on the life of the governor of Khárkov, Obolénskii, by PSR member F. Kachúr.
1903	
May	PSR member E. Dulébov shoots and kills the governor of Ufá, Bogdanóvich. Arrest of PSR leader Gershuni, who is succeeded by E. Ázev.
17/30 July	Second Congress of the RSDRP opens in Brussels (until 24 July/6 Aug.) then moves to London (29 July/ 11 Aug.–10/23 Aug.).
1904	
15 July	Egor Sazónov of the PSR assassinates the Minister of the Interior, V. K. Plehve.
10 Nov.	Trial of Sazónov.
1905	
12/25 Apr.– 27 Apr./10 May	Third (Bolshevik) Congress of the RSDRP, London.
Apr./May	(Menshevik) Congress of the RSDRP, Geneva.
Nov.	PSR suspends terror activities.
12–17 Dec.	First (Bolshevik) Conference of the RSDRP, Tammerfors.
Dec.–Jan. 1906	First Congress of the PSR, Imatra, decides to renew the terror.
1906	
10/23 Apr.– 25 Apr./8 May	Fourth (Unification) Congress of the RSDRP, Stockholm.
12 Aug.	PSR blow up Stolýpin's summer residence on Aptékarsky Island, St Petersburg.
Oct.	Successful raid on a bullion transport in St Petersburg enables the extreme advocates of terror in the PSR to establish the Union of Socialist-Revolutionary-Maximalists.
3–7 Nov.	Second (First All-Russian) Conference of the RSDRP, Tammerfors.
1907	Second Congress of the PSR (early in the year).
Apr.	Arrests decimate the SR-Maximalists.
30 Apr./13 May–19 May/1 June	Fifth Congress of the RSDRP, London.
21–23 July	Third (Second All-Russian) Conference of the RSDRP, Kotka.

5–12 Nov.	Fourth (Third All-Russian) Conference of the RSDRP, Helsingfors.
End	Central Committee of the PSR flee abroad.
1908	Ázev uncovered as a government agent.
21–27 Dec./3–9 Jan. 1909	Fifth Conference of the RSDRP, Paris.
1912	
5/18–17/30 Jan.	Sixth (Bolshevik) Conference of the RSDRP, Prague.
Aug.	(Menshevik) Conference of the RSDRP, Vienna.
1914	Bolshevik Duma leader R. Malinóvskii (later exposed as a police spy) suddenly resigns his seat and goes abroad (May).
1916	
31 Jan./13 Feb.	Bolshevik victory in elections to *Strakhovói sovét*. Two delegates and nine alternates elected.
Early Feb.	Bolshevik campaign against the proposed measures for the militarization of labour.

1.3.2   The Democratic Movement

1859	The Tver nobility protest to Alexander II against the decree of November 1858, forbidding them to discuss the peasant question. Their marshal, A. M. Únkovskii, is deported to Viátka (23 Feb. 1860).
1860	The Vladímir nobility petition for devolution of government, the rule of law and the abolition of special privileges (Jan.).
1862	Tver nobility's address to the Crown argues that the Emancipation Act violates the principles of justice and of economics, and calls for a representative assembly (Feb.).
1865	Moscow nobility request the Crown to call the representatives of the people (Jan.).
1867	A. P. Shuválov exiled after a speech to the St Petersburg *Zémstvo* assembly attacking the law of November 1866, limiting their right to tax. The *zémstvo* is closed until summer (Jan.).
1870	Moscow Duma statement on press freedom (written by I. Aksákov). Moscow mayor Cherkásskii dismissed (17 Nov.).
1872	The Moscow nobility petitions the Tsar to abolish administrative exile (Feb.).
1878	I. P. Petrunkévich, leader of the Chernigov *Zémstvo*, exiled after its address to the Tsar calling for free

	press, schools, learning and public opinion to offer effective opposition to the revolutionaries (Aug.).
1881	Formation of the *Zémstvo* Union.
1888	*Zémstvo* organization in Cherepovetsk closed. Its president, N. F. Rumiántsev, and other members of the board exiled for constitutional agitation.
1895	Nicholas II dismisses the idea of *zémstvo* participation in government as 'senseless dreams' and reaffirms his belief in autocracy (17 Jan.).
1896	First *zémstvo* conference, Nízhnii Nóvgorod (Aug.).
1901	'Private' *zémstvo* conference, Moscow (Feb.).
1902	*Liberation*, no. 1, published in Stuttgart (editors: P. N. Miliukóv, P. B. Struve) (June).

1903

20–22 July	Union of Liberation founded as an illegal organization in Schaffhausen, Switzerland.
Sept.	The Union of Liberation founded by a *zémstvo* conference in Khárkov.

1904

3–5 Jan.	Formal foundation of the Union of Liberation.
Sept.	Conference of radical and revolutionary groups in Paris, organized by the Finnish Party of Active Resistance, attended by the Union of Liberation (Struve, Miliukóv), the PSR (Chernóv, Ázev), and six national minority parties (Finland, Poland, Georgia, Armenia, Latvia).
Oct.	Union of Liberation plan of action: 1. *Zémstvos* to demand constitutional government; 2. Political agitation at banquets organized to celebrate the 40th anniversary of the legal reforms; 3. *Zémstvos* to promote professional unions.
6–9 Nov.	First *zémstvo* conference in St Petersburg calls for civil liberties, equality before the law, democratization and expansion of local government, political amnesty, repeal of state of emergency legislation, and the summoning of a legislative assembly.

1905

May	The Union of Unions (chair: P. Miliukóv) is formed by the Union of Liberation and the professional unions of university teachers, doctors, veterinarians, railway employees, journalists and authors, *zémstvo* assembly members, engineers, bookkeepers and accountants, teachers, pharmacists, and the unions of female and Jewish emancipation.

6 June	Nicholas II receives a delegation from the Union of Unions.
July	Conference of *zémstvo* leaders in Moscow approves a new draft constitution. *Zémstvo* constitutionalists and the Union of Unions launch the Constitutional Democratic Party (Kadets). Formation of the Peasants' Union.
12–18 Oct.	First congress of the Kadet Party, Moscow. Miliukóv elected leader.
6–13 Nov.	Sixth Congress of *Zémstvos* and Towns, Moscow, demands that the Duma function as a Constituent Assembly.
Dec.	Foundation of the Union of the 17th October, the 'Octobrist Party,' led by A. I. Guchkóv.

1906

5–11 Jan.	Second congress of the Kadet Party.
Feb.	First issue of the Kadet newspaper *Rech* (daily until 1918).
21–25 Apr.	Third congress of Kadet Party.
18 June	Union of Russian People murders the Kadet Duma Deputy, M. I. Hertsenstein.
10 July	200 Kadet, Social-Democratic and Trudovik Duma deputies sign the Výborg Manifesto.
23–28 Sept.	Fourth congress of the Kadet Party, Helsingfors.
12–18 Dec.	Trial and imprisonment of the signatories of the Výborg Appeal.

1907

14 Mar.	Union of Russian People murders the Kadet Duma Deputy, G. B. Iollos.
28 June	*Rech* prints the names of Iollos's killers.
23–25 Oct.	Fifth congress of the Kadet Party, Helsingfors.

1914

Jan.	Government suspends the Tver *Zémstvo*.
30 July	Formation of the All-Russian *Zémstvo* Union for the Relief of Sick and Wounded Soldiers (president G. E. Lvov).
Aug.	Formation of the All-Russian Union of Towns.
1915	Formation of the Progressive Block (Nationalist, Octobrist, *Zémstvo* Octobrist, Progressist and Kadet parties in the Duma, and the Centre and Academic groups in the State Council) (19 July).

1916

18–22 Feb.	Sixth congress of the Kadet Party.
1 Nov.	Miliukov's 'Is this stupidity or is it treason?' speech to the State Duma.
10 Dec.	Police close the *zémstvo* conference in Moscow.

1.3.3   The Revolution of 1905–7

1905

9 Jan.	Bloody Sunday.
19 Jan.	Tsar receives a delegation of workers selected by the governor-general of St Petersburg, D. F. Trépov, and 'forgives them'.
4 Feb.	PSR member I. P. Kaliáev kills Grand Duke Sergéi Alexandrovich, Moscow.
Feb.	Russian army defeated at Mukden.
6 Feb.	Agrarian disorders begin in Kholzovki, Kursk *Gubérniia*.
18 Feb.	Nicholas II announces his intention to convoke a consultative assembly and orders the Committee of Ministers to draft legislation for constitutional reform.
17 Apr.	Decree on religious tolerance repeals discriminatory laws against dissenters.
May	Baltic Fleet sunk in the Straits of Tsushimá.
June	Troops used against strikers in Łódż.
13 June	General strike in Odessa.
14–24 June	Mutiny on board the battleship *Potëmkin*.
6 Aug.	First Manifesto on the creation of the State Duma, 'the Bulýgin Duma'.
Aug.	First conference of the Peasants' Union, Moscow.
27 Aug.	Universities granted autonomy.
23 Sept.	Moscow printers' strike.
6 Oct.	Moscow–Kazán railway strike.
9 Oct.	Telegraph workers join strike. Witte tells the Tsar he has two alternatives: to crush the revolution and impose a dictatorship, or to grant a constitution.
12 Oct.	General Strike. Nicholas II orders St Petersburg governor, D. F. Trépov, to adopt more aggressive measures.
13 Oct.	First meeting of the St Petersburg Soviet of Workers' Deputies.
17 Oct.	'The October Manifesto': 1. Grants freedom from arrest, freedom of opinion, of the press, of assembly and of association; 2. Promises to extend the law of 6 Aug. to enfranchise all classes of the population; 3. Grants that no law shall be promulgated without the approval of the State Duma. *Izvestia of the St Petersburg Soviet*, no. 1, published.
18 Oct.	N. E. Bauman killed in clash between radical and monarchist groups, Moscow.
20 Oct.	Major demonstrations at Bauman's funeral, Moscow.

21 Oct.	St Petersburg Soviet calls off the General Strike. Partial amnesty allows revolutionaries to return to Russia.
26–27 Oct.	Kronstadt mutiny.
1 Nov.	St Petersburg Soviet's renewed call for a strike meets with little response.
5 Nov.	St Petersburg Soviet calls off its strike.
6–12 Nov.	Peasants' Union conference, Moscow, calls for the transfer of all land to the toilers of the soil, a constituent assembly, and a political alliance between the peasantry and the proletariat.
8 Nov.	A. I. Dubróvin forms the Union of Russian People.
14 Nov.	Moscow Bureau of the Peasants' Union arrested.
16 Nov.	Telephone and telegraph strike.
19 Oct.	Council of Ministers established.
30–31 Oct.	Vladivostók mutiny.
24 Nov.	'Provisional rules' abolish preliminary censorship for items published in cities. Severe penalties decreed for those 'commenting favourably on criminal acts'.
26 Nov.	G. S. Khrustalëv-Nosar, president of the St Petersburg Soviet, arrested.
27 Nov.	Soviet elects a presiding committee of three (including Trotsky) to replace Nosar and appeals to the armed forces.
3 Dec.	All members of the St Petersburg Soviet arrested.
10 Dec.	Moscow uprising.
11 Dec.	Electoral law amended to give representation to the urban population and industrial workers.
Dec.	Nicholas II accepts honorary membership of the Union of Russian People for himself and his son (as do Pobedonóstsev, Plehve, Goremýkin).

1906

9–10 Jan.	Armed uprising in Vladivostók, leading (11.i.1906) to 'Vladivostók Republic', crushed on 19.i.1906.
18 Feb.	Severe penalties for those spreading false information about state agencies and officials.
20 Feb.	Decree on the structure of the new legislature: two chambers: the State Duma and the State Council. Members of the State Duma to be chosen according to the law of 6 August 1905 (as amended 11 Dec.). Half the members of the State Council to be nominated by the Tsar; of the other half six were to be elected by the clergy, 56 by the zémstvos, 18 by the nobility, six by the Academy of Sciences and the

	universities, 12 by commerce and industry and two by the Finnish Diet.
4 Mar.	'Provisional rules' guaranteeing the right of assembly and of association.
8 Mar.	Budgetary rules exclude about one-third of national expenditure from the Duma's jurisdiction.
23 Apr.	Publication of the *Fundamental Laws of the Russian Empire.*
26 Apr.	'Provisional rules' abolish preliminary censorship.
27 Apr.	Opening of the First State Duma.
13 May	Goremýkin replies to the Duma's 'address to the throne'.
18 June	Union of Russian People murders the Kadet Duma Deputy, M. I. Hertsenstein.
9 July	Dissolution of the First Duma.
17–20 July	Sveaborg mutiny.
19–20 July	Mutinies in Kronstadt and on the *Pámiat' Azóva.*
20 July	Suppression of the Sveaborg mutiny.
12 Aug.	PSR 'Maximalists' blow up Stolýpin's summer residence on Aptékarsky Island, St Petersburg, killing 32 and wounding 22.
19 Aug.	Most political cases entrusted to specially constituted courts martial, with summary powers.
15 Sept.	Provincial governors directed to maintain public order at any cost, including the use of 'patriotic and monarchical organizations'. Political parties may be banned if their aims 'though formally within the law, are not sufficiently clear'.
Sept.–Nov.	Trial of the members of the St Petersburg Soviet.
1907	
30 Jan.	Union of Russian People's attempt on the life of S. Iu. Witte.
Jan.–Feb.	Elections to Second State Duma.
20 Feb.	Opening of the Second State Duma.
14 Mar.	Union of Russian People murders the Kadet Duma Deputy, G. B. Iollos.
4 May	Police, after a raid on the rooms of Social-Democratic Duma member I. P. Ozols, claim to have found plans for fomenting mutiny in the armed forces.
27 May	Attempt on the life of S. Iu. Witte by the Union of Russian People.
1 June	Stolýpin requests the Duma to waive the immunity of the Social-Democratic deputies.
3 June	Dissolution of the Second State Duma. Publication of a revised electoral law: Stolýpin's *'coup d'état'* of 3 June 1907.

1.3.4   The Revolution of February 1917

1916

13 June	General S. S. Khabálov appointed commander of Petrograd Military District.
Dec.	Police seize the PK's printing works.
30 Dec.	During his last audience with the Tsar, British ambassador Sir George Buchanan warns that the army will not support him in a revolution.

1917

2 Jan.	Ten members of the PK arrested.
3 Jan.	Khabálov complains to A. I. Guchkóv that 'outsiders' are attending meetings of the Workers' Group of the War Industries Committee and are discussing 'demands of a revolutionary nature'. The authorities must receive advance notice of any future meetings, to which they will send a representative. The Council of Ministers postpones the reconvening of the State Duma, from 12 January to 14 February.
5 Jan.	The Okhrána warns that rumours of the impending dissolution of the State Duma may give rise to disorders.
6 Jan.	Newspapers announce that the Duma will reconvene on 14 February.
9 Jan.	Strikes and demonstrations to commemorate 'Bloody Sunday' (1905) in Petrograd (about 140,000), Moscow, Khárkov, Bakú and Nízhnii Nóvgorod. *Rech* publishes an appeal from members of the Progressive Block for the Tsar to appoint a government 'enjoying the confidence of the country'.
11 Jan.	The chairman of the Workers' Group of the War Industries Committee, K. A. Gvozdëv, refuses to allow a representative of the authorities to attend its meetings. The Ministry of Transport calls on railwaymen not to participate in the Workers' Group of the War Industries Committees.
12 Jan.	Police disperse demonstrators demanding 'Bread' in Moscow.
13 Jan.	A. I. Guchkóv informs Khabálov that the War Industries Committee supports the Workers' Group's refusal to have a representative of the authorities at its meetings or to notify the authorities of any future meetings.
16 Jan.	Khabálov repeats his complaint to Guchkóv about the Workers' Group and warns that, should his requests not be complied with, he will prevent any future meetings.

17 Jan.	Police raid the Workers' Group premises in the belief that a meeting is taking place there, but leave once they are satisfied that it is not.
20 Jan.	Police raid the Workers' Group premises, interrupting a meeting of 11 members chaired by Gvozdëv, on the grounds that the city governor had not been notified. The vice-chairman of the War Industries Committee, M. I. Teréshchenko, rejects the police demand that they should have been notified of the meeting. The police take statements and withdraw.
21 Jan.	At a meeting of the Special Council for Defence, Rodziánko and Kárpov confront the War Minister, Beliáev, with the claim that the army is supplying the Petrograd police with machine guns to fire on the people. Beliáev denies all knowledge of this.
24 Jan.	Leaflets appear in the factories, issued by the Workers' Group of the War Industries Committee, calling for a strike and demonstration to coincide with the reconvening of the Duma on 14 February, to demand the overthrow of the autocracy and the creation of a provisional government.
26 Jan.	Police raid the premises of the Workers' Group of the War Industries Committee during the night, and arrest the following group members in their homes: Bogdánov, Breido, Emeliánov, Gudkóv, Gvozdëv, Iákovlev, Kachálov, Kuzmín, Shílin and four members of the Group's propaganda committee. During the night, Guchkóv and Konoválov, members of the Central War Industries Committee, plead the case of the Workers' Group with the Chairman of the Council of Ministers, Prince Golítsyn.
27 Jan.	The Central War Industries Committee pledges support for the Workers' Group.
30 Jan.	Newspapers publish the government announcement that the Workers' Group had been arrested for plotting to overthrow the regime and establish a Social-Democratic republic.
31 Jan.	The Bureau of the Central War Industries Committee's reply to the government statement of the day before states that, although it has political differences with the Workers' Group, it agrees with its assessment of the regime and its view that the government is incapable of winning the war.

1 Feb.	Anonymous leaflets calling on workers to demonstrate on 14 February appear in the factories.
5 Feb.	Petrograd Military District is removed from the Northern Front. General Khabálov is made its commander, with wide powers. The Okhrána warns that food shortages and high prices may lead to rioting.
6 Feb.	PK calls for a strike on 10 February, the anniversary of the trial of the Bolshevik Duma deputies.
8 Feb. (Wed.)	Strike begins in the Izhóra Works, Kolpinó.
9 Feb. (Thurs.)	Late at night a message from Khabálov is posted around Petrograd, warning that demonstrators and strikers on 14 February will be met with armed force.
10–12 Feb (Fri.–Sun.)	Shrovetide holiday. Many factories closed.
10 Feb. (Fri.)	Morning newspapers carry Khabálov's warning to strikers on 14 February. A letter from Miliukóv in *Rech* appeals to workers not to strike or demonstrate on that day. Izhóra workers are locked out until 15 February. A demonstration called by the PK to commemorate the trial of the Bolshevik Duma deputies (10–20 Feb. 1915) is unsuccessful. Rodziánko tells the Tsar that the Duma finds it difficult to work with the government, and asks him to prolong its mandate for the duration of the war.
13 Feb. (Mon.)	A one-day strike called by the Bolshevik Russian Bureau of the Central Committee is unsuccessful. Bakers' shop windows in the Narva District are broken.
14 Feb. (Tues.)	About 60 factories on strike. There is a poor response to the Workers' Group call for a demonstration. All demonstrations are dispersed by police. In the State Duma, reconvened on this day, the government is much attacked in a stormy debate on the Minister of Agriculture, Rittikh's report on the food situation. 1,400 Kronstadt sailors stage a hunger strike in support of the Progressive Block.
15 Feb. (Wed.)	About 25 factories (25,000 workers) strike in Petrograd. A student demonstration is dispersed by police.
16 Feb. (Thurs.)	Khabálov announces the impending introduction of bread rationing.
17 Feb. (Fri.)	Putílov strike begins. The State Duma condemns the arrest of the Workers' Group.
18 Feb. (Sat.)	Demonstrations for bread begin on the Petrograd Side. Further debate on the food crisis in the Duma. The Duma presidium rules that the Bolshevik deputies

in exile in Siberia must continue to receive their Duma salaries, as they remain elected members.

20 Feb. (Mon.) Strike begins at the Lébedev Jute Mills. Some bakers' shops on the Petrograd Side are pillaged.

21 Feb. (Tues.) Meetings are held in all shops in the Putílov factory to discuss the threatened lockout.

22 Feb. (Wed.) Nicholas II leaves Tsárskoe seló for Stávka. The Putílov workers are locked out. In the evening, a workers' delegation from the Putílov factory asks Kerensky to intervene on their behalf in the Duma. Putílov and Lébedev workers agitate on the Výborg Side for support, but the Bolshevik agitator Kaiúrov calls on women workers not to strike or demonstrate on International Women's Day.

23 Feb. (Thurs.) **International Women's Day**
Around 100,000 on strike (fewer than on 9 Jan. or 14 Feb.). The first red banners with revolutionary slogans are seen in the south-west of Petrograd. An Inter-District Group leaflet calls on workers and soldiers to struggle against the tsarist regime. A Bolshevik leaflet for International Women's Day contains no call for a strike.

Early morning The Bolshevik agitator Kaiúrov makes a last attempt to prevent women workers coming out on strike, but joins them when they persist.

9 a.m. Strike begins on Výborg Side.

Midday? Cossacks allow Výborg Side workers to cross the river.

p.m. The police unsuccessfully attempt to prevent workers entering the centre of the city. Bread demonstrations take place outside the City Duma on the Névskii Prospékt.

4–5 p.m. Výborg Side workers call factories in the Litéiny district out on strike.

5.20–6.20 p.m. The State Duma discusses an emergency resolution on the events in the Putílov and Izhóra factories, and passes Miliukóv's resolution to involve the voluntary organizations in food distribution.

Late evening The Bolshevik leadership decide to support a continuation of the strike.
Khabálov holds a meeting to discuss the food crisis: P. I. Leliánov (mayor of Petrograd), D. I. Dëmkin (deputy mayor), V. K. Weiss (food commissioner), A. P. Balk (city governor), Colonel V. I. Pavlénkov (troop commander), K. I. Globachev (Okhrana commander), M. Ia. Klýkov (gendarme commander).

24 Feb. (Fri.)	Closure of the Izhóra Works begins. The Council of Ministers decides to hand over food administration to the Petrograd City government. Deputations of manufacturers and of bakers petition Khabálov about the food crisis.
Midday	Strike virtually universal. Pavlénkov informs Balk that Petrograd is now under military government. Great crowds on the Névskii Prospékt. Orators address the crowds outside the Kazán Cathedral and on Známenskii Square. A bomb is thrown at mounted police on Karavánnaia.
p.m.	Orators address the crowds outside Kazán Cathedral and on Známenskii Square. Elections to the soviets begin in working-class districts.
25 Feb. (Sat.)	Strike now general. Stones are thrown at mounted police and a police superintendent is beaten up on Výborg Side. A striker from the Pipe Works, Vasílevskii Island, is shot dead by an officer.
4–5 p.m.	A Cossack kills a policeman on Známenskii Square. Khabálov issues an order that, unless they have returned to work by 28 Feb., workers benefiting from exemption from the draft will be mobilized into the army.
Evening	Petrograd City Duma meeting discusses the food problem.
Night	Arrest of remaining members of the Workers' Group of the War Industries Committee and other militants (including members of the PK). A ministerial meeting in the apartment of Prince Golítsyn decides to prorogue the State Duma.
26 Feb. (Sun.)	The Tsar, at Stávka, learns for the first time of 'minor disturbances' in Petrograd.
p.m.	Troops fire on the crowd on Známenskii Square. One company of the Pávlovskii Guards mutinies.
About 4 p.m.	Pávlovskii guardsmen fire on the police across the Ekateríninskii canal.
Evening	Golítsyn, using a blank form over the Tsar's signature, prorogues the State Duma.
27 Feb. (Mon.)	
Early morning	Mutiny of the garrison.
Morning	Colonel Kutépov is given command of a body of troops and told to drive the workers out of the city centre (by afternoon, his force has melted away). The prisons are opened and the prisoners freed.

12.40 p.m.	Rodziánko sends a telegramme to the Tsar asking him to appoint a prime minister 'enjoying the nation's confidence' to form a cabinet, warning him that 'tomorrow may be too late'.
2–3 p.m.	Duma elects a 'Provisional Committee to Restore Order and to Deal with Institutions and Individuals': Rodziánko (chair), N. S. Chkheídze, I. I. Dmtriúkov, M. A. Karaúlov, A. F. Kérenskii, A. I. Konoválov, V. N. Lvov, P. N. Miliukóv, N. V. Nekrásov, V. A. Rzhévskii, S. I. Shidlóvskii, V. V. Shulgín. On their release from prison, Gvozděv and Chkheídze form a Provisional Executive Committee of the Petrograd Soviet (Gvozděv, B. O. Bogdánov, N. Iu. Kapelinskii, K. S. Grinévich, Chkheídze, M. I. Skóbelev, Frankorússkii) and call for elections to the Soviet, to meet that evening.
6 p.m.	Ministers ask the Tsar to replace them with a government acceptable to the Duma.
9 p.m.	The Petrograd Soviet of Workers' Deputies meets in the Tauride Palace and elects an Executive Committee: Chkheídze (chairman), M. I. Skóbelev (vice-chairman), A. F. Kérensky (vice-chairman), Iu. Steklóv, N. N. Sukhánov, A. Shliápnikov, P. A. Alexandróvich, Kapelinskii. The Provisional Committee of the State Duma decides to take power.
Midnight	The Provisional Committee of the State Duma changes its name to the Executive Committee of the State Duma and adds Colonel Engelhardt to its number.
28 Feb. (Tues.)	
1 a.m.	Nicholas II leaves Stávka for Petrograd.
10 a.m.	*Izvestia of the Petrograd Soviet*, no. 1, is published. Tsarist ministers are arrested. A strike begins in the Kronstadt dockyard. Troops march to the Duma, where they are addressed by prominent Duma members.
	The Executive Committee of the Duma nominates commissars to oversee the work of the ministries: M. I. Aréfev, I. N. Efrémov, D. P. Kapníst, A. M. Máslennikov (Interior); A. A. Barýshnikov, K. K. Chernosvítov (Post Office); P. P. Grónskii, Kalúgin (Telegraph); A. P. Savvatéev, N. V. Sávich (Naval and War); I. P. Demídov, Kapníst, Vasílchikov, N. K. Vólkov (Agriculture); M. S. Adzhémov, V. P. Basakov, V. A. Maklakóv (Justice); S. N. Rodziánko, N. A. Rostóvtsev (Trade and Industry); V. A. Vinográdov and I. V. Titóv

| | (Finance); I. V. Gódnev (Senate); V. Pepeliáev (Governor of Petrograd). A. A. Búblikov is placed in charge of the railways. |

First plenary session of the Petrograd Soviet.

Nominated party members added to the Executive Committee of the Petrograd Soviet: B. S. Batúrskii, B. O. Bogdánov (Mensheviks); V. M. Mólotov (Bolshevik); N. S. Rusánov, V. M. Zenzínov (SRs); G. M. Erlich, M. Rafes (Bund); Bramson, N. V. Chaikóvskii (Trudoviks); A. V. Peshekhónov, Chernolússkii (Popular Socialists); K. Iurénev (Inter-District); P. Stuchka and Kozlóvskii (Latvian Socialists).

Night Kronstadt mutiny. Admiral Víren and other officers are killed. Nicholas II's train turns back towards Pskov, as Liuban and Tosno are in the hands of the revolutionaries.

1 Mar. (Wed.) The Executive Committee of the Petrograd Soviet decides (by 13 votes to 8) not to participate in the Provisional Government.

Evening Nicholas II arrives in Pskov.

Night Soviet representatives negotiate with the Duma Committee over the conditions on which the Soviet would support a Provisional Government. The first meeting of the united Petrograd Soviet of Workers and Soldiers Deputies approves Order No. 1.

2 Mar. (Thurs.) The Petrograd Soviet becomes the Petrograd Soviet of Workers' and Soldiers' Deputies. The Provisional Government is formed: G. E. Lvov (Prime Minister and Interior); A. I. Guchkóv (War); P. N. Miliukóv (Foreign Affairs); N. V. Nekrásov (Transport); A. I. Konoválov (Trade and Industry); A. A. Manúilov (Education); M. V. Teréshchenko (Finance); V. Lvov (Holy Synod); A. I. Shingarëv (Agriculture); A. F. Kérensky (Justice).

By 2.30 p.m. The front commanders advise Nicholas II to abdicate.

p.m. Nicholas II in Pskov signs an abdication manifesto on behalf of himself and of his son, Alexei, drafted in Stávka.

Evening Guchkóv and Shulgín arrive in Pskov to discover that Nicholas has already abdicated.

3 Mar. (Fri.) Mikhaíl Alexandrovich abdicates. Mutiny begins in the fleet at Helsingfors.

SECTION TWO

Social, Economic and Cultural Developments

2.1 Religion and the Church

Peter I

1689	Jesuits expelled from Russia. Huguenots invited to settle in Russia.
1690	Death of Patriarch Joachím in March, and appointment of Adrián.
1691	Jesuits return to Russia.
1692	Creation of Peter's 'Most Drunken Synod'.
1696	The monk Avráam presents Peter with a written protest against his innovations. He is exiled to a remote monastery.
1700	The book copyist G. Talitskii proclaims that Peter is the antichrist. After the death of Patriarch Adrián the Patriarchy falls into abeyance.
1701	The Church loses its estates, which are transferred to the Monastery Prikáz under I. A. Músin-Púshkin.
1702	Decree on religious toleration for non-Orthodox Christians, but forbidding proselytism.
1703	Government to abstain from persecuting the Old Believer Vyg Community, in return for it supplying the new Onéga arms factories with iron ore. Stefán Iavórskii's *Signs of the Coming of Antichrist and the End of Time* published as a refutation of Talitskii.
1706	Establishment of an independent Anglican congregation in Moscow.
1708	The Orthodox Church anathematizes Mazépa (Nov.).
1709	Old Believer group allowed to return to Pskov district from the Baltic.
1711	New bishops to be chosen only from a list approved by the Senate.
1713	Foundation of the Monastery of Saint Alexander Névskii in St Petersburg.
1715	Persecution of Vetka and Starodúb Old Believers ceases, and they are granted land, in reward for their guerrilla actions against the Swedes.
1716	Institution of a new bishops' oath: they cannot increase the number of clergy in their diocese or build

'unnecessary' churches; must ensure that monks do not travel without written permission; they are not to interfere in secular affairs. The persecution of Old Believers is relaxed, but they must register with the authorities and be taxed at double the rate for others. Confession is made compulsory.

1718   Church attendance on Sundays and holidays made compulsory. Old Believers, who have refused to register, to be sentenced to hard labour for life.

1719   Government decrees to be read out in churches. Absentees to be punished.

17 Apr.   Jesuits expelled from Russia.

1721   *Spiritual Regulation* of the Church replaces the Patriarchy by a 'Spiritual College' (later: Holy Synod): President, Stefán Iavórskii (25 Jan.). Priests must reveal to the civil authorities any intent to commit crime admitted during confession. Priests must keep registers of births, marriages and deaths. The number of priests is to be regulated by the state. Mixed marriages with other Christian denominations are allowed on condition that there is no conversion from Orthodoxy and that the children are raised as Orthodox.

1722   No new churches may be built without approval from the Senate. Clerics are classified with vagrants and beggars as persons prohibited from entering St Petersburg. Publication of Feofán Prokopóvich, *The Legality of the Monarch's Will.*

11 Mar.   I. V. Boltín, an army officer, appointed first Over-Procurator of the Holy Synod.

1723   Taking of holy orders forbidden. Vacancies in monasteries must be filled by former soldiers. The Anglican congregation moves to St Petersburg.

Sept.   Holy Synod recognized by the patriarchs of Antioch and Jerusalem.

1724   The job of monasteries is defined as the relief of the sick, aged, destitute and orphans as well as the training of the Church hierarchy (Jan.).
Old Believers, other than peasants, retaining their beards, must wear a copper medallion.

Anna Ivánovna

1731   The 'Commission for the Conversion of those of other faiths in Kazán, Nízhnii Nóvgorod and Elsewhere' is given overall responsibility for Moslem communities.

| 1740 | The Commission for the Conversion ... etc. renamed Office of the Converted. Emergence of the Dukhobór sect around Khárkov. |

Elisabeth
| 1754 | Anglican Chapel opened in St Petersburg. |
| 1760 | Monasteries and ecclesiastical dignitaries may not sell their peasants, or remove them from their land. They may only deport them to Siberia with the consent of the village assembly and peasant officials (13 Dec.). |

Peter III
1762
| 29 Jan. | Edict of tolerance for Old Believers, allowing those abroad to return to Russia. |
| 21 Mar. | Secularization of Church land. |

Catherine II
1762
12 Aug.	All Church land returned to the Church.
29 Nov.	Commission on Church lands: Metropolitan Dmítrii Séchenov (Nóvgorod), Archbishop Gavríil Kremenétskii (St Petersburg), Bishop Silvester Starogódskii (Pereiaslávl'-Zaléskii), and S. Gagárin, A. S. Kozlóvskii, B. A. Kurákin, G. N. Teplóv, I. I. Vorontsóv.
13 Dec.	Amnesty to Old Believers renewed.
1763	G. A. Potëmkin appointed assistant procurator of the Holy Synod.
1 Apr.	Metropolitan Arsényi of Rostóv, who had denounced Catherine and the secularization of Church lands, is found guilty of *lèse majesté*, stripped of ecclesiastical rank and sentenced to hard labour in a distant monastery, without access to writing materials.
May	A College is established to administer Church lands before the Commission of 29 Nov. 1762 submits its report.
1764	
26 Feb.	Decree on Secularization of Church lands also lays down establishment of Church.
2 Apr.	Office of the Converted abolished.
1767	Arsényi, who had continued to denounce Catherine's right to the throne and her policy of secularization of Church lands, is condemned to solitary confinement in Réval, with non-Russian-speaking guards who do not even know his name.

7 June	Bishops' courts are forbidden to sentence priests to corporal punishment.
30 July	Catherine's *Instruction* speaks of 'prudent toleration of other Religions' and that 'The human Mind is irritated by Persecution'.
1769	Old Believers allowed to testify in court.
12 Feb.	Regulations for the St Petersburg Catholic Community stipulate that there should be six priests, who must be Franciscans; the community should elect a superior and eight syndics to manage its financial affairs; there should be a school exclusively for Catholic children; Church and school building to be exempt from town taxes; priests not to proselytize; disputes to be referred to the Justice College for Livonian, Estonian and Finnish Affairs, which would not intervene in matters of dogma.
1771	Old Believer communities established in Moscow at Preobrazhénskoe and Rogózhsk. The ban on corporal punishment is extended to deacons.
1772	
2 July	*Ukáz* against the *khlystý*.
14 Dec.	No papal bull or brief, no ecclesiastical ordinance of foreign provenance, to be published in Belorussia without the authority of the Russian government.
1773	
13 June	Holy Synod instructed to leave matters pertaining to other faiths to the secular authorities.
Sept.	Catherine undertakes to respect the religious *status quo* in Belorussia.
22 Nov.	Creation of Catholic bishopric of Mogilëv, to be in charge of all Catholics in Russia. First bishop: S. Siestrencewicz-Bohusz.
Nov.	Catherine ignores the bull dissolving Jesuit order and removes them from the jurisdiction of Bishop Siestrencewicz.
1777	Authorization given for a Jesuit novitiate in Pólotsk (16 Feb.).
1782	Old Believers no longer to be called schismatics, to pay double taxes or to wear distinctive clothing.
Feb.	Creation of Uniat bishopric of Pólotsk, with jurisdiction over all Uniats in Russian Empire. The see is temporarily left vacant.
20 Feb.	Catherine unilaterally raises the Catholic see of Mogilëv to an archbishopric and installs Siestrencewicz.

1784	Catherine appoints Iráklii Lisóvskii Uniat bishop of Mogilëv.
10 Jan.	Siestrencewicz consecrated archbishop of Mogilëv with papal approval, but Catherine forces a change in oath, removing promise to attack heretics and schismatics.
1785	Potëmkin establishes an *edinovérie* monastery and a number of Old Believer churches in the Crimea. Old Believers become eligible for public office.
1786	Catholic Church forbidden to acquire estates.
1785	Catherine accepts recommendation of Orenbúrg governor, O. A. Ingelstrom, to build mosques, caravanserais and schools for Muslims (4 Sept.).
1786	Moslem schools placed under the authority of the Commission on National Schools.
1788–89	Moslem Spiritual Assembly, with authority throughout the Empire, established in Orenbúrg (later moved to Ufá).
1795	Abolition of Uniat bishoprics of Pinsk, Luck and Brest as 'unnecessary'.

Alexander I

1803	Appointment of members to the Holy Synod limited to short terms only.
1804	Dukhobórs allowed to move as a community to designated land in the Crimea (16 Dec.).
1807	Establishment of a Commission to reorganize education in the seminaries headed by Speránskii. The governor-general of Siberia, I Pestél, orders the Dukhobórs, as a 'threat to public order', to be drafted into the army.
1808	New structure of ecclesiastical schools set up, according to the recommendations of the Speránskii commission.
1812	The Russian Bible Society is founded in St Petersburg by A. N. Golítsyn, A. Turgénev, and V. M. Popóv (Dec.).
1813	Alexander I joins the Bible Society (15 Feb.).
1814	Alexander I meets the Quakers Allen and Grellet in London (June).
1816	Jesuits expelled from St Petersburg and Moscow (2 Jan.).
1817	Creation of Ministry of Education and Spiritual Affairs, headed by Golítsyn.
	Dukhobórs in the armed forces are excused from taking the oath of allegiance after one of their number refuses to do so.

1818	The Quakers Allen and Grellet visit Russia at Alexander's invitation.
1819	Lindl and Gossner, former Catholic priests from Bavaria, begin preaching a reformed Catholicism in St Petersburg.
1820	
13 Mar.	Jesuits expelled from Russia.
11 Apr.	Old Believers no longer subject to criminal prosecution but are banned from holding state office.
1821	Madame Krüdener opens her salon in St Petersburg.
1822	Lindl is expelled from Russia.
1824	V. M. Popóv, the secretary of the Bible Society, is prosecuted for publishing Gassner's *L'Évangile selon Saint Mathieu*. Gassner is exiled and his book burnt.
15 May	On Golítsyn's resignation, the Holy Synod regains a separate identity.
1825	Members of the *Subótnik* heresy are condemned to serve in the army and be exiled to Siberia (20 Jan.).

Nicholas I

1825	Publication of the Bible in Russian is postponed (7 Nov.).
1826	The Bible Society is liquidated. Old Believer prayer houses built since 1816 are to be closed and new ones not to be permitted. Old Believers are again designated as 'schismatics'.
1828	The clergy are obliged 'to warn parishioners against false and dangerous rumours, to strengthen them in good morals and in submission to their masters, and to try by all means to prevent disturbances among the peasantry'.
1835	
14 Mar.	Old Believer schools in Moscow closed down.
2 Apr.	Old Believers banned from state employment.
1837	Old Believers and sectarians are divided into 'less harmful', 'more harmful' and 'especially harmful'. 'Especially harmful' groups (*Molokáne*, *Dukhobórs*, *Khlystý* and *Skoptsý*) are forbidden to hold prayer meetings. The *Khlystý* and *Skoptsý* are designated criminal, and liable to automatic transportation to Siberia.
1838	Children of the *bespopóvtsy* are declared illegitimate and subject to forcible conversion to Orthodoxy.
1839	The Uniat Church has its connection with Rome severed and is absorbed into the Orthodox Church.

1841	Restrictive laws against sects 'to safeguard the Orthodox Faith of our forefathers' (21 May). The Dukhobórs are banished to Transcaucasia.
1844	Archpriest Pávskii dismissed from his teaching post as a result of his translations of the *Book of Job* and *Song of Songs* (12 Mar.). The translations are destroyed.
1847	Concordat between Russia and Rome.
1849	Golovín, *Mémoires d'un prêtre russe*, published in Leipzig.
1850	Sectarians forbidden to attend secondary schools and universities.

Alexander II
1856

Jan.	Old Believer services permitted at Rogózhsk, Moscow.
9 Feb.	Old Believers who had refused to serve in the militia during the Crimean War tried by court martial.
July	At the insistence of Metropolitan Filarét, Old Believer services banned at Rogózhsk.
1858	Establishment of a Special Commission under Pavel Mélnikov to look into the Old Belief. An unofficial instruction is given not to persecute Old Believers.
1864	Establishment of the Pánin Committee on Old Belief.
1874	State recognizes Old Believer marriages as legal, but the law has little practical effect (19 Apr.).

Alexander III

1883	Dissenters (except *skoptsý*) may receive passports, engage in commercial and industrial enterprise, hold minor office, and conduct religious meetings in their homes and churches. However, they may not build new places of worship, wear religious vestments outside their churches, or conduct religious propaganda. Proselytism is made an Orthodox monopoly. The conversion of an Orthodox to any dissenting faith to be punished by imprisonment or exile to Siberia (3 May).
1893	State begins paying salaries to priests.
1894	Stundism declared an 'especially dangerous sect' and its prayer meetings forbidden (4 June).

Nicholas II

| 1895 | Dukhobórs refuse to serve in the army and burn their weapons. The Church begins publication of *Missionary Survey* as part of offensive against sects. |
| 1897 | In the census, more than one Russian in ten admits to being a dissenter. |

1899	Mass exodus of the Dukhobórs to Cyprus and Canada.
1900	Grand Duke Sergei Alexandrovich proposes that Old Believers be considered an 'especially dangerous' group.
1901	Lev Tolstoy is excommunicated by the Orthodox Church. Old Believers petition the Tsar to relieve them of police persecution.
Sept.	M. A. Stakhóvich calls for religious toleration at the Orël Missionary Congress.
Nov.	Organization of the Religious-Philosophical Society.
1903	*New Way*, journal of the Religious-Philosophical Society, begins publication.
26 Feb.	Nicholas promises 'consistent observance of the decrees on tolerance, enacted in the fundamental laws'.
1904	Nicholas promises a number of religious reforms, including religious toleration for Old Believers (12 Dec.).
1905	
17 Apr.	Temporary enactment on religious liberty. Anyone may leave the Orthodox Church for any other Christian faith, with no loss of rights or other penalties. 'Old Ritualists' to replace 'schismatics' as the official designation of Old Believers. Non-Orthodox Christian congregations are allowed to own property, their clergy exempted from military service and prayer houses previously sealed to be opened.
18 Aug.	Those wishing to leave the Orthodox Church for other Christian faiths must notify the local police, who will inform the provincial governor and the Orthodox clergy. The provincial governor must approve the change within one month.
1906	Bill on Freedom of Religious Belief introduced into the First Duma (12 May). It falls when the Duma is dissolved.
1907	Commission on Freedom of Religious Belief set up by Second Duma (20 Mar.). It comes to nothing as Duma is dissolved.
1908	Fourth All-Russian Missionary Congress, Kiev, calls for reforms to Orthodox monasteries to end drunkenness and fornication.
1909	*Vékhi* (*Landmarks*) (essays by N. A. Berdiáev, S. N. Bulgákov, M. O. Gershenzón, A. S. Izgóev, B. A. Kistiakóvskii, P. B. Struve, S. L. Frank) published in Moscow.

1910	Synod condemns the practices deplored by the 1908 Missionary Congress.
1912	Synod rejects A. I. Morózov's request that the state fund Old Believer schools.
1914	Old Believers disqualified from teaching in state schools (13 Jan.).
1915	N. B. Shcherbátov, Minister of the Interior, tells the Duma that some Baptists are 'undoubted tools of the German government' (3 Aug.).

2.1.1 Procurators of the Holy Synod

11.v.1722–25	Colonel I. V. Boltín
1725–26	Captain A. P. Baskákov
1726	Captain R. Raévskii
1726–41	vacant
1741–53	Ia. P. Shakhovskói
1753–58	A. I. Lvov
1758–63	Major-General A. S. Kozlóvskii
1763–68	I. I. Melissino
1768–74	Brigadier P. P. Chébishev
1774–86	S. V. Akchúrin
1791	A I. Naúmov
1791–97	A. I. Músin-Púshkin
1797–99	V. A. Khovánskii
1799–1803	D. I. Khvostóv
1803	A. A. Iákovlev
1803–17	A. N. Golítsyn
1817–33	P. S. Meshchérskii
1833–36	S. D. Necháev
1836–55	General N. A. Protásov
1855–56	A. I. Karasévskii
1856–62	A. P. Tolstoy
1862–65	General A. P. Akhmátov
1865–80	D. A. Tolstoy
1880–October 1905	K. P. Pobedonóstsev
October 1905–April 1906	A. D. Obolénskii
April–July 1906	A. A. Shirínskii-Shikhmátov
July 1906–February 1909	P. P. Izvólskii
February 1909–2.v.1911	S. M. Lukiánov
2.v.1911–5.vii.1915	V. K. Sabler (Desiatovskii)
5 July–26.ix.1915	A. D. Samárin
1.x.1915–7.viii.1916	A. N. Vólzhin
7.viii.1916–1.iii.1917	N. P. Ráev

2.2 Education

Peter I

1700	Arabic numerals come into general usage.
1701	Foundation of a School of Artillery and of Farqharson's school of mathematics and navigation in Moscow. The Moscow Academy is revived by Stefán Iavórskii. The First Russian Reader is published.
1703	A mathematics textbook is published. Ernst Glück founds his *gimnáziia* in Moscow (which closes in 1715 through lack of demand).
1706	A Russian Grammar is published.
1707	A School of Medicine is founded in Moscow.
1712	A School of Engineering is founded in Moscow.
1714	Two graduates of the Moscow Navigation School to be sent to each province as teachers in the new Mathematical or Navigational Schools for the sons of landlords and officials, without a certificate from which young noblemen could not get married. These schools close in 1744.
1715	Farqharson's school moves to St Petersburg to become the Naval Academy.
1716	A School of Mining is founded in Moscow. Peter has the Königsberg manuscript of the Nestorian Chronicle copied and the copy brought to Russia.
16 Jan.	Nobles excluded from the Mathematical schools, henceforth reserved for children of the lower estates.
1717	Publication of V. N. Tatíshchev's *Mirror of Honour for Youth.*
1720	Peter approaches Christian Wolff, Professor of Philosophy and Physics at Halle, for help in setting up a Russian Academy of Sciences.
1721	The *Spiritual Regulation* establishes parochial schools.
1721–22	J. D. Schumacher tours Europe to contact scholars for the Academy of Sciences.
1722	First Russian work on dynamics published. Russian chronicle texts to be copied and collected in the Synodal Library.

1724	Senate decides to found an Academy of Sciences (29 Jan.).
1725	Academy of Sciences opens in St Petersburg, with a *gimnáziia* attached (Aug.).

Anna Ivánovna

1731	Foundation of the *Kadétskii kórpus* (29 June).
1732	Garrison schools for the children of soldiers of all ranks. G. F. Müller publishes the journal *Russian History Collection.*
1733	V. E. Adadúrov, mathematician, is elected the first Russian associate member of the Academy of Sciences.

Elizabeth

1742	M. V. Lomonósov becomes the first Russian Academician.
1747	Provision of 20 scholarships for the Academy *gimnáziia*, open to all except poll-tax payers.
1750	Foundation of the Naval Cadet Corps.
1755	
12 Jan.	The Senate approves Ivan Shuválov's proposal for the foundation in Moscow of a University and of two *gimnázii*, one for nobles, one for non-nobles.
Apr.	Moscow University opens, with Shuválov as its curator.
1756	Moscow University graduates are granted privileges in the civil and military services (17 May).
1758	Foundation of the Academy of Arts. A *gimnáziia* is established in Kazán. All potential private tutors must be examined by the Academy of Sciences or Moscow University.
1759	The *Kadétskii kórpus* publishes its own journal, *Time off.* John Locke's *On Education* is translated into Russian.

Catherine II

1763	I. I. Bétskoi appointed as principal adviser in education, director of the *Kadétskii kórpus* and president of the Academy of Arts. A Commission on Education is set up: P. H. Dilthey, Rev. D. Dumaresq (from 1764), T. von Klingstedt, G. F. Müller, G. N. Teplóv.
1 Sept.	Moscow Orphanage founded.
1764	
12 Mar.	Bétskoi's *General Plan for the Education of Young People of both Sexes* is published.
Apr.	Foundation of a Foundlings Hospital in Moscow.

May	Foundation of the Smólny Institute for Noble Girls, Russia's first girls school, and of the first school for boys from non-privileged families (except serfs) under the auspices of the Academy of Arts and the Military Academy.
1765	Foundation of a school for girls from non-privileged families (except serfs).
Nov.	First Russian students attend British universities.
1766	The *Kadétskii kórpus* curriculum is broadened and corporal punishment forbidden (11 Sept.).
1768	Legislative Commission sub-committee on education established in May (abolished 1771).
1770	Legislative Commission sub-committee produces a plan for compulsory male education, based on the Prussian model of one village school per 100–250 households. (Never implemented.)
1772	Prokófii Demídov endows the Moscow orphanage with a school of commerce. An orphanage is founded in St Petersburg.
1773	Foundation of the Mining Academy.
1775	
Mar.	Catherine appeals to 'Messieurs les philosophes' to produce an educational plan for Russia.
Aug.	Diderot hands F. M. Grimm his *Plan d'une université ou d'une éducation publique dans toutes les sciences* to be taken to Russia. Catherine receives this in Jan. 1776.
5 Nov.	Creation and funding of Boards of Social Welfare responsible for *gubérniia* and *uézd* schools.
1777	N. I. Nóvikov founds his St Catherine's day school for pupils of both genders (Nov.).
1778	Nóvikov founds his second school, St Alexander's (Aug.).
1779	Demídov's school of commerce moves from Moscow to St Petersburg.
1781	Catherine founds and funds a school attached to St Isaac's Cathedral (16 Feb.). Six further schools are founded attached to churches in St Petersburg.
1782	Advisory Commission on Education (F. Aepinus, A. M. Golítsyn, I. I. Melissino, S. Pallás) advises Catherine to follow the Austrian Felbiger system.
4 Sept.	Arrival of T. I. Jankovich de Mirjevo, sent by Joseph II to advise Catherine on the Austrian education system.
7 Sept.	Commission on National Schools composed of Aepinus, Jankovich, P. I. Pastukhóv, P. V. Zavadóvskii (chair), is established to oversee the founding of

schools, training of teachers, and provision of text-books. New teaching methods are introduced into St Petersburg schools.

1783 Publication of *A Guide to Teachers* and *The Duties of Man and Citizen*, based on Felbiger's works.

1784 Commission on National Schools inspects all St Petersburg private schools and teachers. One foreign school and all Russian schools, except for Nóvikov's, are closed. All foreign schools remaining open placed under the Commission. Nóvikov's two schools transferred to the state system. Pupils from the schools that have been closed are to transfer to the new national schools.

1785 Commission inspects Moscow schools to ensure only authorized books in use (Oct.).

1786 Foundation of a High School in St Petersburg with a teachers' training school attached (closed in 1801). Three new universities planned, in Pénza, Chernígov and Pskov (never implemented).

5 Aug. Statute of National Education creates a two-tier network of high schools and primary schools (known as people's schools) in *uézd* towns, free, co-educational, and open to all free classes. Curriculum and teaching methods are closely regulated at every level. Corporal punishment abolished. Governors in 25 *gubérnii* are ordered to set up new schools immediately. Russia now has 40 lay schools, including village and private schools, with 136 teachers and 4,398 pupils.

1788 New schools ordered in a further 16 *gubérnii* (3 Nov.).

1790 Total school enrolment = 16,525, i.e. one pupil per 1,573 inhabitants.

Paul I

1796 Russian students abroad recalled home. Russia has 316 schools, 744 teachers, 17,341 pupils (about 7% of whom are girls).

1797 Decree on foundation of a school for training men for government service (14 Jan.).

1798 Decrees founding the University of Dorpat (19 Apr. and 9 May).

Alexander I

1802 Ministry of Education created on 8 Sept.

1803 Provisional Statute for Schools (26 Jan.) divides Russia into six school regions under a curator and a member of the Central School Board. Four types of school: universities, *gimnázii*, county schools and parish schools. Three universities, 42 *gimnázii*, 405 county schools to be established. The government is to finance universities and *gimnázii*, local authorities to fund county and parish schools.

St Petersburg Teachers' Training College reopens (1819, becomes St Petersburg University). Publication of the *Journal of the Ministry of Education*, no. 1.

1804	Foundation of the universities of Khárkov and Kazán (5 Nov.).
1811	S. S. Uvárov introduces intensive Latin courses into St Petersburg *gimnázii*.
1816	A. N. Golítsyn begins a campaign to sweep away 'ungodly, liberal and revolutionary' tendencies in the schools. A Khárkov professor is dismissed for teaching that Napoleon's crime was violating the natural rights of the people rather than the traditional rights of monarchs.
1817	Golítsyn's post changed to Minister of Education and of Spiritual Affairs. Introduction of *gimnáziia* tuition fees.
1819	Foundation of the Imperial University, St Petersburg. Curator: D. P. Rúnich.
Early	After inspecting Kazán University, M. L. Magnítskii recommends it 'should be publicly destroyed'.
June	Magnítskii appointed head of Kazán University, where he purges non-Russian professors and introduces a curriculum based on the Bible and 'piety, in accordance with the principles of the Holy Alliance'.
8 Nov.	First Lancastrian school established.
1820	Magnítskii becomes curator of the Kazán Educational District. Seweryn Potocki is replaced as curator of Khárkov Educational District by E. V. Karnéev, a supporter of the Bible Society. A. P. Obolénskii, of the Bible Society, replaces P. I. Kutúzov as curator of Moscow Educational District.
1821	History, ancient languages and geography replace 'harmful' subjects (philosophy, political economy, commerce and technology) in *gimnáziia* syllabuses. D. P. Rúnich replaces S. S. Uvárov as curator of St Petersburg Educational District, where he dismisses four university professors, 'for teaching in a spirit contrary to Christianity and subversive to the social order'. Their books are withdrawn from circulation.

Nicholas I

1828	Central government takes charge of county schools whose curriculum now corresponds to the junior years of the *gimnázii* and increases from two to three years. *Gimnáziia* curriculum increases to seven years. In year four, the courses divide between those offering classical languages to pupils aspiring to university entrance and those emphasizing natural history, mathematics and law to pupils not proceeding to higher education. Broad humanitarian subjects are dropped (8 Dec.).
1830	Trial of four teachers at Nezhin Lyceum 'for a harmful influence on the young people'. Those who are foreign are deported, while their Russian colleagues are placed under police supervision (27 Oct.).
1832	Uvárov's report to the Tsar advocating 'Orthodoxy, autocracy and nationality' (4 Dec.).
1833	Uvárov's first circular as Minister, proclaims 'Orthodoxy, autocracy and nationality' (2 Apr.).
1834	Foundation of Kiev University. Creation of the Archaeographical Commission. The *Journal of the Ministry of Education*, no. 1 (1834) publishes Uvárov's ideas on Orthodoxy, autocracy and nationality.
14 Mar. **1835**	Moscow Old Believer schools closed.
22 June	Schools brought under tighter state control. Education curators to reside in their regional university town and supervise provincial, country, and parish schools.
26 June	Universities Charter. Universities no longer the Ministry of Education's principal organ in the school region, and are brought under the Educational District curator's control. University courts abolished. Students to wear uniform, and their behaviour, manners and appearance subject to an inspectorate, under the orders of the curator. Theology, Church History and Church Law compulsory for all students. New chairs of Russian and Slavic History established. Pogódin is appointed the first professor of Russian History at Moscow University, and Ustriálov first professor of Russian History at St Petersburg University.
1839	F. G. W. Struve founds the Púlkovo observatory.
1845	*Gimnáziia* and university tuition fees are increased, to limit 'the excessive influx into higher and secondary schools of young men born in the lower strata of society for whom higher education is useless'.

1846	Publication of the Archaeographical Commission's *Complete Collection of Russian Chronicles*, vol. 1: *The Tale of Bygone Years* (Laurentian text).
1847–48	Khárkov and Kiev school districts are removed from the jurisdiction of the curators and subordinated to the provincial governors-general.
1849	*Gimnázii* redefined as *realschulen* (*Realgimnázii*).
30 Apr.	Student enrolment reduced to 300 per university.
Sept.	Uvárov forced to resign as Minister of Education after the Buturlín Committee objects to an article he had commissioned from I. I. Davadov, 'On the Significance of Russian Universities'.
11 Oct.	University charter amended. Rectors appointed, not elected, and not to hold a chair. Minister of Education empowered to replace elected deans with nominees. University and *gimnáziia* student body declines as a result of restrictive legislation.
1850	University deans to exercise the strictest supervision over the content of lectures. University teaching of philosophy and of European constitutional law is discontinued. Teaching of logic and psychology is entrusted to theologians, to ensure its conformity with Orthodox Church doctrine.
1851	Publication of S. M. Solovëv's *History of Russia from Ancient Times*, vol. 1 (then one per year until 1879; 29 vols in all).

Alexander II

1856	A. S. Nórov recommends a secondary curriculum based on the Classics and on the Orthodox faith. N. I. Pirogóv, 'Questions of Life,' is published in *Morskoi sbornik*, 85, no. 2.
1858	Disciplinary powers of educational curators confined to the university campuses, outside which students are subject to the same laws as ordinary citizens. Authorization is given for the creation of locally financed girls' day schools with six and three-year courses. *Maríinskoe Védomstvo* begins the establishment of state-financed girls' day schools.
14 Oct.	Pirogóv's first Sunday School in Kiev.
1859	Sunday School Movement begins in St Petersburg.
1861	
June	Putiátin's new university regulations forbid 'absolutely any meetings without permission of superiors', and

impose a 50 ruble tax on university enrolment while curtailing state stipendiaries and exemptions from fees, thereby restricting entrance to the wealthy.

Dec. A draft charter for Russian universities is translated into English, French and German and circulated to Russian and foreign places of learning. K. D. Kavélin is sent abroad to study French, German and Swiss higher schools.

1862 Fires in St Petersburg, attributed to 'radical groups active in the Sunday Schools', leads to their closure until 1864 (May).

1863
18 June University charter repeals most of the 1835 restrictions. Wide powers given to university councils consisting of faculty members and elected officers, subject to the general supervision of the curators of the school regions. Government-appointed inspectors are deprived of their powers. Elective university courts given jurisdiction over student disciplinary offences. Women are excluded from the universities.

Sept. Debate begins between M. N. Katkóv and *Sovreménnik* over the Classics and the *Realschulen*.

1864
14 July Primary schools to be established by the 'free cooperation of the government, the clergy, village communes and private persons', to promote 'true religious and moral principles' and to impart 'useful elementary knowledge'.

19 Nov. Constitutions for seven-year *gimnázii* and four-year *progimnázii*, incorporating Nórov's 1856 recommendations, assert that education is for all regardless of gender or social class. Power is devolved from St Petersburg to the regions. Schools to be governed by a council. Teaching week to be 12 hours, with extra payment for extra hours. Both classical and *realschule* traditions are maintained, but only graduates of classical schools are eligible for university entrance.

1865 Foundation of Odessa University. The Ministry of Education takes over schools previously under the Ministry of the Imperial Court and Properties.

1866
13 May Alexander II decrees that education 'must be conducted in the spirit of true religion, respect for the

	right of property and preservation of the foundations of public order'.
12 Nov.	Provincial education authorities are required to provide St Petersburg with all timetables currently in use.
1867	Police and academic authorities ordered to pool information on the political views of students (26 May). Annual examinations are restored in secondary schools. The St Petersburg Historico-Philological Institute is set up to train classical language-teachers. The Ministry of Education takes over schools previously under the Ministry of State Domains. The first Russian female doctor graduates from Bern University.
1868	State supervision is extended to private schools and tutors.
1869	Introduction of Higher Courses for Women, Moscow. State censorship is introduced for school textbooks. Establishment of the office of inspector of primary schools. Warsaw University is reopened as a Russian University.
1870	Establishment of girls' *gimnázii* and *progimnázii* (24 May).
1871	The *gimnáziia* curriculum is made exclusively classical (i.e. the *Realgimnázii* are abolished), and the powers of the inspectorate are increased (30 June).
1872	Introduction of a four-year course for midwives, affiliated to the Military Medical Academy, 'on an experimental basis' (abandoned 1882).
15 May	Creation of *Realschulen* to offer 'a general education, though directed towards practical needs and the acquisition of technical knowledge'.
31 May	County schools reorganized as City Schools.
Aug.	Tolstoy requests university councils to propose amendments to the 1863 charter.
Nov.	Samára Seminary graduates denied university entrance.
8 Dec.	Publication of uniform rules for examinations.
1873	
Feb.	N. A. Liubímov's article in *Rússkii véstnik* attacking university autonomy begins a public debate.
June	The Ministry of the Interior forbids Russian women to enroll as students in Zürich University.
1874	Provincial and county marshals of the nobility become *ex officio* chairmen of schools boards, whose powers are restricted to financial and administrative matters. Academic questions now become the prerogative

of the directors and inspectors of primary schools, appointed by the Ministry of Education (24 May). A Committee on student disturbances, chaired by P. A. Valúev, recommends drastic curtailment of university autonomy, stricter government control over teaching and the limitation of student numbers. Latin and Greek are introduced as optional subjects in girls' *gimnázii*. The Ministry of Education takes over schools operating among the nomadic tribes (Kirghiz, Bashkir, Tartar).

1875	I. D. Deliánov's committee to examine the working of the universities (21 Apr.).
1876	Rules for the establishment of Higher Courses for Women published (9 Apr.).
1877	Higher Courses for Women introduced in St Petersburg.
1878	Tomsk University founded (opens 1888).
1879	Tolstoy disbands St Petersburg Pedagogical Society.
Jul.	Tolstoy's regulations to tighten control over students.
1880	
6 Feb.	Tolstoy presents his proposals for a new university charter to the cabinet.
14 Apr.	Dismissal of Tolstoy as Minister of Education. A. A. Sabúrov shelves the new charter (implemented in 1884).

Alexander III

1882	Higher Courses for Women to be gradually closed (6 Aug.). St Petersburg Medical School for Women closed.
1884	Universities are deprived of autonomy. Rectors, deans and lecturers to be appointed by the Ministry of Education. The powers of regional curators of education are to be extended. Student body denied all corporate rights. The cost of higher education is raised (13 Aug.).
1886	Final closure of the Higher Women's Courses.
1887	
21 Jan.	Students are forbidden to form *zemliáchestva*.
Spring	University fees raised to limit access to the wealthy.
11 Apr.	State Council cuts off funds to *gimnázii* preparatory classes.
18 June	Deliánov's 'Cook's Circular' directs educational authorities to 'free the *gimnázii* and *progimnázii* from children of coachmen, menials, cooks, washerwomen, small shopkeepers and the like. For, excepting occasionally

	gifted children, it is completely unwarranted for the children of such people to leave their position in life.'
26 June	University tuition fees increased from 10 to 50 rubles per year.
1888	Vocational schools established under the Ministry of Education (7 Mar.).
1890	New *gimnáziia* curriculum reduces hours assigned to Latin and Greek (20 July). *The Russian School* and *The Education Herald* begin publication.
1892	*Technical Education* begins publication.
1893	Princess Ténisheva establishes her factory school in Briánsk. *Zémstvos* are 'invited' to finance church schools.
1894	Princess Ténisheva sets up her School of Art (1895–98) directed by Répin; teachers included Bilíbin, Chekhónin, Serebriakóva (closed 1904).

Nicholas II

1896	Princess Ténisheva founds a second Art School in Smolénsk (closed 1904).
1898	Foundation of the Moscow University Pedagogical Society.
1899	
8 July	Bogolépov's circular recognizes the dissatisfaction of teachers and pupils with the academic sterility of Russian schools.
29 July	'Temporary Rules' for the readmission of students expelled for participating in disorders. Expelled students to be drafted into the army for the period of their expulsion, even if not otherwise liable for military service.
Aug.	New loyalty oath introduced for teaching staff.
1902	Hours assigned to teaching classical languages reduced.
1905	'Provisional rules' restore the right of academic bodies to choose their officers and to make appointments, but do not repeal the Act of 1884 (27 Aug.).
1906	*Zémstvos* may establish six-year primary schools.
1907	Education Minister presents bill on universal primary education to the Duma (1 Nov.).
1908	Compulsory education for eight to eleven year olds to be enforced gradually (3 May).
1910	
12 June	Duma passes new University statutes.
24 Nov.	L. A. Kasso withdraws the new University statutes without consulting Duma.

1911

12 Jan.	Kasso's University statutes effectively deprive them of autonomy.
Feb.	Resignation of prominent Moscow University academics (Kliuchévskii, Paul Vinográdov, Kizevetter) over government attacks on university freedom.
12 Feb.	Duma passes law on universal primary education. The State Council rejects a bill passed by the Duma, making primary schools the responsibility of the *zémstvos* and towns.

1912

5 June	State Council rejects Duma bill on universal primary education.
28 June	Six-year primary schools reorganized.

2.2.1 Ministers of Education

8.ix.1802–1810	P. V. Zavadóvskii
1810–16	A. K. Razumóvskii
1817–15.v.1824	A. N. Golítsyn (Minister of Spiritual Affairs)
15.v.1824–28	A. S. Shishkóv
1828–33	K. A. Lieven
1833–20.x.1849	S. S. Uvárov
27.i.1850–54	P. A. Shirínskii-Shikhmátov
1854–58	A. S. Nórov
March 1858–June 1861	E. P. Kovalévskii
June 1861–December 1861	E. V. Putiátin
January 1862–14.iv.1866	A. V. Golovnín
14.iv.1866–22.iv.1880	D. A. Tolstoy (and Procurator of the Holy Synod)
22.iv.1880–24.iii.1881	A. A. Sabúrov
24.iii.1881–22.iii.1882	A. P. Nikolái
22.iii.1882–December 1897	I. D. Deliánov
1898–February 1901	N. P. Bogolépov
February 1901–April 1902	P. S. Vannóvskii
April 1902–4	G. E. Saenger/Zenger
1904–October 1905	V. G. Glázov
31.x.1905–April 1906	I. I. Tolstoy
April 1906–8	P. M. Kaufman
1908–10	A. N. Schwartz
1910–14	L. A. Kasso
8.i.1915–26.xii.1916	P. N. Ignátev
28.xii.1916–1.iii.1917	N. K. Kulchítskii

2.3 Finance, Industry, Trade and the Bourgeoisie

Peter I

1698   Establishment of the Sérikov and Dubróvskii woollen mills, Moscow. Currency devaluation.

1699   Town tax and excise duty collection transferred from the *voevódy* to *burmístry* (elected by the *kuptsý* to the *Burmístrskaia paláta* or *Rátusha* in Moscow and *zémskaia izbá* in other towns) (30 Jan.). The building of the Nevianskii works inaugurates heavy industry in the Urals.

1700   Establishment of the *Mining Prikáz* to take charge of finding and excavating 'silver, gold and other' ores (24 Aug.).

1700–20   State and private factories built in the Urals.

1703–5   Lípetsk metallurgy works built.

1703–7   Olónets metallurgy works built.

1705   Salt and tobacco made a state monopoly. *Sukónnyi dvor* woollen mills opened in Moscow.

1707   Cotton factory built on the river Iaúza, Moscow.

1709–11   Artillery and Admiralty works built in St Petersburg.

1710   Domestic distilling forbidden. Spirits to be bought in state Kabakí (9 Feb.).

1711   Decree allowing 'People of all ranks to trade in any commodity anywhere.'

1712   Creation of the *Kommértz-kollégiia* (College of Trade) (Feb.).

1712–18   Túla 'Armaments Yard' built.

1716   Nobles allowed to distil spirits. State monopoly on foreign trade relaxed. Trade in all commodities except potash and tar may be carried out by merchants after the payment of duty.

1718   The household tax is replaced by the poll tax, to be paid by all adult males on the census registers, except nobles, soldiers and priests (26 Nov.). The first census is carried out to establish those liable for the poll tax.

1719	All the Tsar's subjects may 'seek, smelt, melt and refine all metals'. Creation of the *Berg-Manufaktúr-kollégiia* (College of Mining and Manufactures).
1719–23	Landowners concealing peasants from the poll tax census to be punished with fines, the galleys and confiscation of their serfs. Bailiffs so doing to be sentenced to death or corporal punishment. Those denouncing offenders to be rewarded with their serfs.
1721	Factory owners allowed to buy serfs for industry (18 Jan.). These must be removed from the land and attached permanently to the factory itself, not to the person of the factory owner.
1722	Factories are temporarily allowed not to return runaway serfs to their owners. Admiralty regulations, subsequently adopted by all state-owned factories, fix the length of the working day for workers in Admiralty factories.
11 Jan.	Poll tax set at 80 kopeks per head.
27 Apr.	Townspeople to be designated by category. The merchants' guilds to be defined by capital not occupation – 1st guild: those with a capital of 100–500 rubles, 2nd guild: 50–100 rubles, 3rd guild: 10–50 rubles. Below the merchants came the craftsmen, registered in craft unions (which were tax-gathering bodies not organizations to foster craft).
1723	The *Berg-Manufaktúr-kollégiia* (College of Mining and Manufactures) is split into the *Berg-kollégiia* (College of Mining) and the *Manufacktúr-kollégiia*, this latter is to regulate the hiring of labour in manufacturing industry and to transfer state-owned factories to private ownership. State tobacco monopoly ends. British Factory forced to move from Moscow to St Petersburg. The Ekaterinbúrg metallurgy works is built. *Zémskie kommissáry* to be elected by landowners to collect the poll tax.
1724	Sestrorétsk arms factory built. *Ukáz* establishes the rates of pay for hired labour and assigned workers. Levy of the poll tax begins: 74 kopeks per peasant; 80 kopeks per merchant and townsperson.
1725	Nízhne-Tazhílsk iron, steel and copper foundry built.
26 Jan.	Landowners no longer to be sent to the galleys for concealing peasants liable for the poll tax.

Catherine I

1725	'Harsh punishments' for landowners guilty of concealing peasants liable for the poll tax remitted and their lands returned. Instead they are fined 12 kopeks per soul. Death penalty for bailiffs guilty of the same offence reduced to confiscation of property (14 Feb.).
25 Feb.	Poll tax reduced to 70 kopeks per peasant and arrears up to 1723 waived.
14 June	Assigned workers in Urals factories exempted from military levy. Instead the factory is to arm and train to defend the factory the number that they would otherwise have sent to the army.
1727	College of Manufactures abolished.
9 Jan.	Unpublished report 'On the improvement of the country's internal affairs' describes the ravages imposed by the poll tax.
9 Feb.	Supreme Privy Council sets up Commission under Golítsyn to review the level and collection of the poll tax.
24 Feb.	Creation of the *Doímochnaia kantseliáriia* (Arrears Office) under A. L. Pleshchéev to collect poll tax arrears.

Peter II

1729	A. Demídov builds a metallurgy works at Kolyvano-Voskresénsk in the Altái (1747, taken over by Imperial cabinet). Introduction of bills of exchange whose use is restricted to *kuptsý*.

Anna Ivánovna

1731	*Kámer-kollégiia* (College of State Revenues) is restored specifically to deal with the poll tax. Landowners are made responsible for poll-tax collection. Military units to collect arrears.
1732	A. S. Máslov, over-procurator of the Senate, given overall responsibility for the collection of poll tax arrears (10 Oct.).
1733	Máslov's office renamed the *Doímochnyi Prikáz* (Arrears Ministry).
1735	Landowners become responsible for poll tax arrears as well as collection (23 Jan.). Willim Elmzel's Glass Works established in St Petersburg. (After 1777, owned by G. A. Potëmkin, who moved it to Ózerki, outside St Petersburg. 1792, becomes state property and renamed the Imperial Glass Manufactury).

| 1736 | *Ukáz* defines category of serfs 'eternally bound' to factories and forbids the sale of serfs from the land to manufactures owned by merchants (7 Jan.). |
| 1740–60 | Many metallurgy works built in the Urals. |

Elizabeth

1741	Regulations define conditions of work in woollen industry.
1744	Merchants again permitted to buy serfs for industry.
1745	Névskii porcelain factory built near St Petersburg.
1752	Number of serfs that can be purchased for each loom, blast furnace, etc. regulated.
1753	Internal customs duties and charges on the movement of merchandise abolished.
1754	Foundation of the Bank of the Nobility and of the Commercial Bank. The building of new metallurgical works within 200 versts of Moscow banned. Usury prohibited.
1757	Heavy import and export duties introduced.
1760	Ban on metallurgy around Moscow rescinded.

Peter III
1762

17 Jan.	Price of salt reduced.
23 Mar.	*Ukáz* condemns monopolies.
29 Mar.	Non-noble merchants forbidden to purchase serf villages for industry.

Catherine II
1762

31 July	Anti-monopoly policy strengthened.
8 Aug.	Prohibition on non-noble purchase of serf-villages reiterated.
1763	Tax imposed on blast furnaces and copper foundries.
9 Apr.	A. A. Viázemskii introduces regulations for industry and mining. Peasants to be assigned to one establishment and allowed to return to their village in the summer. Managers forbidden to demand more work than necessary to pay off the poll tax. Teams to elect their own elders to supervise pay and disputes with management.
May	College of Economy re-established.

Dec.	Commerce Commission, directly responsible to Catherine, established to study trade and devise ways of developing it.
1764	Local government becomes responsible for poll tax collection (23 Apr.).
1765	Commission set up to investigate mining and foundries, and to consider whether industry should be publicly or privately owned (July).
1766	
18 Jan.	Francis Gardner obtains permission to open a porcelain factory at Verblikí, near Moscow.
1 Sept.	Tariff laws to take effect from 1.iii.1767.
1770–71	Tomsk iron works built.
1773–75	Great damage done to Urals industry during Pugachëv Revolt.
1773	A. R. Vorontsóv becomes president of the *Kommértz-kollégiia* (College of Trade) (until 1793).
1775	
15 Mar.	State permission no longer needed to set up a workshop or practise a craft (i.e. all classes can now participate in manufacture).
17 Mar.	Status of *kupéts* confined to those with capital of over 500 rubles. All others to be *meshcháne* (common towns people). *Kuptsý* continue to be divided into three guilds, and to pay a tax of 1% of declared capital per annum instead of the poll tax. They also have to pay for exemption from the recruit levy.
1779	Iron foundries no longer need to sell part of their production to the state.
21 May	*Ukáz* specifies what work may be demanded of assigned workers, and increases their pay.
22 Nov.	Abolition of the *Manufaktúr kollegiia* (College of Manufacture). Freedom for all to establish manufactories is reaffirmed.
1781	P. V. Zavadóvskii made director of newly created State Bank.
1782	Bank of the Nobility wound up and its assets transferred to the Commercial Bank. Tariffs increased.
28 June	Nobles granted free exploitation of their lands above and below the soil.
1783	Abolition of the *Shtats-kontór-Kollégiia* (College of State Expenditure).
1784	Abolition of the *Kámer-kollégiia* (College of State Revenue) and of the *Berg-kollégiia* (Mining College).

| 1785 | Charter to the towns (21 Apr.): no taxes to be imposed on towns without the confirmation of the sovereign; nobles living in towns to be subject to all town taxes; towns entitled to set up schools, mills, inns, etc. 'Towns societies', composed of all registered citizens, could elect officials (for which there was a property qualification) to listen and reply to proposals from the governor, and present collective petitions to the governor. Towns are divided into districts (*chásti*), subdivided into *kvartály*. The *gorodníchi*, appointed by the Senate, is to preside over a board (*upráva*) assisted by two appointed commissioners, and two councillors selected by the local *magistrát*. Six categories of registered citizens are established: 1. Owners of immovable property; 2. Three guilds of merchants; 3. Registered craftsmen; 4. Foreigners and citizens of other towns; 5. 'Distinguished citizens' (those who had been elected to official posts more than once, university graduates, artists, those with capital over a certain amount, etc.); 6. Those who were born or lived in the town but did not belong to the other groups. Three urban institutions are established: 1. Urban society as a whole; 2. The town duma (*óbshchaia dúma*), composed of representatives of the six categories of town dwellers, separately elected every three years by the whole urban society. 3. A six-man executive board (*shestiglásnaia dúma*), of which the president was the *gorodskáia golová* elected by the town duma. Regulations drawn up for the *tsékhi* (craft guilds). Each branch of production to elect its own officials, who would be part of the town duma, they in turn elected a member to the six-man duma. Hours and days of work were also regulated. |

1786	Commercial Bank absorbed into the State Loan Bank.
1787	First State Budget.
1788	*Revizión-kollégiia* (Audit College) abolished.
1793	Protectionist policies adopted (8 Apr.).
1794	G. R. Derzhávin becomes president of the *Kommértz-kollégiia* (College of Trade).

Paul I
1796

| 19 Nov. | Colleges of Mining (*Berg-kollégiia*) and Manufactures (*Manufaktúr-kollégiia*) restored. |
| 4 Dec. | Creation of the office of State Treasurer. |

31 Dec.	Townspeople to contribute to the maintenance of local administration.
1797	
10 Feb.	*Kámer Kollégiia* (College of State Revenues) restored.
Autumn	Bank of Assistance for the Nobility established.
18 Dec.	Noble estates to be taxed. Revenue to go to maintenance of local officials. Townspeople to contribute to maintenance of the police.
1798	Non-nobles may purchase serfs for factories on conditions established in 1752 (16 Mar.).
1800	Creation of the Ministry of Commerce.

Alexander I

1810	Issuing of paper money prohibited; specific weight and fineness of silver ruble defined (2 Feb.).
1811	Ministry of Commerce abolished (25 June).
1812	Speránskii introduces progressive taxation from 1% to 10% on the revenue from landed estates.
9 Apr.	Paper ruble becomes the only legal tender.
1816	Rights of non-nobles to buy serfs for factories abolished.
1820	Sávva Morózov buys his freedom from serfdom for 17,000 rubles.

Nicholas I

1827	Silver made legal tender for all payments to the government.
1830	Gold made legal tender for all payments to the government.
1832	Creation of the estate of *Honorary Citizen* (10 Feb.).
1833	P. L. Schilling demonstrates his electric telegraph in St Petersburg.
1836	Introduction of auditing of *gubérniia* accounts (30 Dec.).
1839	The Kankrín monetary reforms (1843): the silver ruble made the basic monetary unit. Promissory notes remain legal tender but at the set rate of exchange of 3.50 rubles to the silver ruble (1 June).
1841	Issue of a new paper currency, treasury notes (*kredítnye biléty*).
1843	Compulsory exchange of promissory notes for treasury notes, now renamed state notes (*gosudárstvennye* biléty) (1 June).
1843–51	Construction of the Moscow–St Petersburg railway.

| 1845 | Penal Code (Section 1791) states that 'wilful disobedience to factory owners and managers', if expressed in collective action, is deemed to be 'rebellion against lawful authorities' and punishable by penal servitude. Section 1792 makes strikes punishable by up to three months imprisonment. |

Alexander II

1855	Establishment of a Committee on foreign railway legislation (Oct.).
1856	Foundation of the Russian Steamship Company.
Mar.	Baron Stieglitz in Paris to discuss railway finance with French banking interests. V. A. Tatárinov sent to Western Europe to study the budgetary provisions of the major powers.
Aug.	Stieglitz given permission to build a railway from St Petersburg to Peterhof.
1857	First postage stamps issued for internal mail. Rates of duty on imported machinery, semi-manufactured goods and raw materials, and import prohibitions, considerably reduced.
26 Jan.	Formation of the General Company of Russian Railways, headed by Stieglitz, and controlled by a Dutch, British and French banking syndicate.
9 Apr.	Finance Committee set up to examine state expenditure (N. N. Ánnenkov, M. D. Gorchakóv, A. S. Ménshikov).
1858	Depression (until the mid-1860s)
5 Nov.	Committee of Ministers considers Tatárinov's budgetary proposals and sets up a committee under A. D. Gúrev to draw up reforms for Departments of State.
1859	
13 Feb.	Gúrev Committee report recommends wide-ranging reform.
22 May	New regulations for Departmental budgets.
1860	
31 May	State Bank established.
26 Oct.	Tax farming in spirits abolished.
1861	General Company of Russian Railways given considerable government subsidies and relieved of its obligations to build some lines. However the Russian government now appoints four of the 14 board members and its headquarters is moved from Paris to St Petersburg.

1862

1 May	State Bank exchanges notes for gold rubles at a pre-determined rate.
22 May	Establishment of formal procedure for compiling and publishing annual budgets for state bodies (implemented 1.i.1863).

1863

1 Jan.	State Budget to be published annually. Excise duty imposed on alcohol.
Aug.	Run on gold forces State Bank to cease exchanging notes for gold.
1864	Postage stamp system extended to foreign mail. Boards of Inspection in all *gubérnii* to oversee state financial transactions. Virtual abolition of export prohibitions.
1865	Policy of granting railway concessions only to foreign companies relaxed to allow Russian finance to participate. Russia's first loan and savings association founded in Kostromá *Gubérniia*.
1868	Substantial reduction in tariffs. Responsible officials forbidden to participate in private railway companies. Concession given to Great Northern Telegraph Company to erect a line between Russia and Denmark.
1869	Great Northern Telegraph Company constructs a line connecting Russia with Sweden. Both the Swedish and Danish lines give Russia direct telegraph connection with Britain.
1873	Direct telegraph link with France. Depression (until 1876).
1874	Black Sea Telegraph Company establishes a line between Odessa and Constantinople.
1877	Customs duties to be paid in gold instead of paper rubles.
1879	Foundation of the Nobel Oil Company.
1880	State becomes active in railway building and administration. Salt Tax abolished.
June	Iron and pig iron subject to customs duties.
Dec.	10% increase in all customs duties.

Alexander III

1882	Depression (until 1887).
1 June	Employment of children under the age of 12 prohibited. Employment of children between 12 and 15 limited to eight hours per day. Children not to work on holidays or Sundays and their hours to be arranged to permit them to attend school. (Effective from 1.v.1884.)

15 June	Inheritance and gift tax introduced.
1883	Goujon Works built in Moscow.
1884	Factory Inspectorate established in 10 Districts (12 June).
1885	Foundation of the State Bank of the Nobility.
20 May	Tax on income from capital introduced.
3 June	Night work of women and young people in textile mills forbidden.
1886	Labour laws forbid fines, except for workers' welfare, prohibit the lowering of contractual wages, require the regular payment of wages in cash, introduce pay-books, but also make participation in strikes punishable by imprisonment (3 June).
1890	Factory inspectors empowered to lift the prohibition on night work for women and juveniles, and to allow the employment of children as young as 10 (24 Apr.).
1891	Depression (until mid-1890s).
17 Mar.	Building of the Trans-Siberian Railway begins.
11 June	Tariff Act marks the height of a policy of protectionism.
1893	Siberia Railway Committee formed.
1 June	Russo-German tariff war. Witte introduces punitive tariffs for goods from countries denying Russia most favoured nation status.
8 June	State monopoly in the manufacture of spirits introduced in four *gubérnii* (gradually extended to the entire Empire).
1894	Russo-German commercial treaty ends the tariff war (7 Mar.).

Nicholas II
1897

3 Jan.	Currency reform devalues the ruble.
2 June	Working day limited to $11\frac{1}{2}$ hours on normal working days and 10 hours on Saturdays and the days before a holiday.
12 Aug.	Minister of the Interior directs provincial governors to use extra-judicial procedures for dealing with striking workers.
26 Aug.	Introduction of the Gold Standard.
14 Nov.	Currency reform devalues the ruble.
1899	Recession until 1903.
1900	Tariffs increased (July).
1903	Tariff Act confirms the increases of 1900.
2 June	Employers are financially responsible for industrial accidents leading to disability or death.

10 June	Creation of 'factory elders'.
1904	Russo-German commercial treaty renewed.
1906	'Provisional rules' legalize trades unions and employers' organizations (4 Mar.).
1912	Establishment of sickness benefit funds and employer-funded insurance against accidents at work (23 June).
1914	Shops selling alcohol closed 'temporarily' (July).
22 Aug.	Sale of alcoholic drink prohibited.
1915	Building of Murmansk Railway begins (Oct.) (completed November 1916).

2.3.1 Ministers of Finance

1802–6	A. I. Vasílev
1807–10	F. A. Golubtsóv
1810–23	D. A. Gúrev
1823–44	E. F. Kankrín
May 1844–51	F. P. Vrónchenko
April 1852–23.iv.1858	P. F. Brok
23.iv.1858–January 1862	A. M. Kniazhévich
23.i.1862–8.vii.1878	M. Kh. Reitern
8.vii.1878–25.x.1880	S. A. Greig
25.x.1880–7.v.1881	A. A. Abazá
7.v.1881–December 1886	N. Kh. Bunge
January 1887–30.viii.1892	I. A. Vyshnegrádskii
30.viii.1892–August 1903	S. Iu. Witte
August 1903–4	E. D. Pleske
5.ii.1904–October 1905	V. N. Kokóvtsov
28.x.1905–April 1906	I. P. Shípov
22.iv.1906–29.i.1914	V. N. Kokóvtsov
30.i.1914–1.iii.1917	P. L. Bark

2.3.2 Minister of Commerce

8.ix.1802–25.vi.1811	N. P. Rumiántsev

2.3.3 Ministers of Trade and Industry

27.x.1905–February 1906	V. I. Timiriázev
18 February–April 1906	M. M. Fëdorov
1906–7?	D. A. Filosófov
1907?–8.i.1908	I. P. Shípov
8.i.1908–9?	V. I. Timiriázev
18.ii.1915–1.iii.1917	V. N. Shakhovskói

2.3.4   Managers-in-Chief of Transport and Public Buildings

1811–12	Prince George of Oldenburg
1812–18	F. P. Devolant
1819–22	A. Bétancourt (Betankúr)
1822–33	A. Duke of Württemberg
1834–42	K. F. Tol
1843–55	P. A. Kleinmíkhel
Autumn 1855–October 1862	N. V. Chévkin

2.3.5   Ministers of Transport

October 1862–April 1869	P. P. Mélnikov
April 1869–September 1871	V. A. Bóbrinskii
September 1871–74	A. P. Bóbrinskii
1874–4.xi.1888	K. N. Posét
4.xi.1888–89	G. E. Pauker
1889–91	A. Ia. von Giubbenet
17.ix.1891–30.viii.1892	S. Iu. Witte
30.viii.1892–17.xii.1894	A. K. Krivoshéin
17.xii.1894–October 1905	M. I. Khilkóv
28.x.1905–April 1906	K. S. Nemesháev
25.iv.1906–9	N. K. Schaffhausen-Schoenberg-Ek-Schaufuss
1909–27.x.1915	S. V. Rúkhlov
30.x.1915–10.xi.1916	A. F. Trépov
10.xi.1916–1.iii.1917	E. B. Kríger-Voinóvskii

2.3.6   State Controllers

1811–23	B. B. Kamenhausen
1827–54	A. Z. Khitrovó
1854–55	A. G. Kushelёv-Bezboródko
1855–62	N. N. Ánnenkov
1863–71	V. A. Tatárinov
1871–74	A. A. Abazá
1874–78	S. V. Greig
1878–89	D. M. Sólskii
1889–99	T. I. Filíppov
1899–1905	P. L. Lobko
October 1905–April 1906	D. A. Filosófov
April 1906–12 September 1907	P. A. Shvanebakh
12.ix.1907–21.i.1916	P. A. Kharitónov
21.i.1916–30.xi.1916	N. N. Pokróvskii
1.xii.1916–1.iii.1917	S. G. Feodósev

2.4 Serfdom, the Peasantry and Agriculture

Peter I

1698   20,000 peasants work on Volga–Don Canal.

1699–1714   Peasant levies for forced labour building canals, draining marshes, building cities, at an average of 17,000 per annum (1699–1701, 20,000 per annum for work in Vorónezh shipyards).

1701   Almost 9,000 peasants working to build Taganróg (Summer).

1705   First forced settlement in St Petersburg.

1709   Over 10,000 peasants conscripted to build St Petersburg.

1713   12,000 conscripted peasants build fortresses in South Russia for the Turkish war (Mar.).

1717   Sale and purchase of young men as army recruits legalized (17 Dec.).

1719   Poll tax makes various groups of peasant (black peasants, *odnodvórtsy*, Tartars and other non-Slavic peoples of the Volga basin), who had hitherto avoided enserfment, liable for taxes, quit-rent and conscription. Senate empowered to remove an owner who mistreats his serfs and to appoint his wife or children administrators of his estate.

1720   Legality of selling and buying recruits for the army confirmed (29 Oct.).

1721   Sale of serfs apart from the land condemned but not forbidden.

1723   Entire servile population liable to the poll tax. All distinctions between serfs and other bondsmen eliminated (9 Jan.). *Obrók* set at 40 kopeks per male state peasant per year.

1724   Serfs need their master's written permission to engage in trade away from his estate. First use of 'State Peasant', to describe those made taxable in 1719.

Catherine I

1725	Early in the year, Iaguzhínskii reports that the peasantry are facing starvation.
1726	Catherine decrees the establishment of the *Kollégiia ekonómii* (College of Economy), to administer Church lands and peasants. A. Matvéev reports extreme impoverishment among the peasantry (Aug.).
1727	Serfs prohibited from joining the army without their masters' consent. *Kollégiia ekonómii*, although administered by clerics, is made subordinate to the Senate.
7 Jan.	Iaguzhínskii reports that most Polish estates harbour runaway Russian serfs.

Peter II

1728	Barriers along Western borders strengthened to catch runaway peasants (5 Mar.).

Anna Ivánovna

1730	Serfs forbidden to own urban property.
1734	Landlords obliged to provide seeds for their serfs (measure provoked by the famine of 1733–34 and repeated in 1750 and 1761 to little effect) (Apr.).
1735	Population of parts of Russia officially estimated to have declined by one half because of runaways, and that the condition of the remaining peasants was worsened by liability for the fugitives' poll tax.
1736	Landlords allowed to decide on the punishment for runaway serfs (6 May).
1737	Serfs only permitted to purchase agricultural land with their master's permission, and in his name (1 Aug.).
1738	*Kollégiia ekonómii* (College of Economy) taken over entirely by the Senate, and run by Lieutenant-General A. Ia. Vólkov.

Elizabeth

1744	Serfs may only move away from their master's estates with their master's written permission and a passport from the local governor.
1746	Purchase of serfs by non-nobles prohibited.
1747	Legality of selling and buying recruits for the army confirmed.
1753	State Bank of the Nobility created to provide the nobility with credit at below market rates (7 May).

1754

13 May   Female serfs may not marry anyone not owned by their master without his written permission. Masters may not base a claim to ownership of a serf on any record predating the 1719 census.

15 June   Czartoryski estates reported to contain 'several thousand' fugitive Russian serfs.

1758   Estates containing bonded labour not owned by nobles, to be taken over by the Crown.

1760   *Obrók* for state peasants raised to one ruble per head (12 Oct.). Average *obrók* for serfs between one and two rubles.

13 Dec.   Landlords (except ecclesiastical ones) allowed to deport delinquent serfs to Siberia and credit male deportees to their liability to provide army recruits. The deported peasant ceased to be a serf.

Peter III
1762
31 Jan.   Civil administration and landlords to assume full control over poll tax collection.

19 June   Landowners assured that the state would maintain them in peaceful ownership of their estates. Peasants ordered to render complete obedience to their masters.

Catherine II
1762   Average price of a male serf = 30 rubles.

1763   Peter Pánin proposes legislation defining the rights of landlords over their serfs.

1764   Secularization of Church lands (26 Feb.). Former Church peasants become known as 'economic peasants' after the *Kollégiia ekonómii* (College of Economy). Their *obrók* is set at 1.50 rubles a year and poll tax at 70 kopeks.

1765   Owners given the power to sentence serfs to penal servitude in Siberia and to claim them back whenever they pleased (17 Jan.).
                   College of the Navy empowered to receive and employ serfs sentenced by their masters to hard labour for unruliness. Sievers proposes legislation to limit landlord power over their serfs. Pastor Eisen asked to prepare a plan to introduce peasant ownership of land in Ropsha.

1766   Pastor Eisen dismissed. Sale of adult male serfs forbidden three months before a recruit levy. Land sold by state peasants to other social groups to be restituted without compensation. No further transfers of such land to be allowed, even between state peasants themselves.

1767	Reassertion of the 1649 law prohibiting serfs from complaining about their masters. Punishment increased to knout or penal servitude for life (22 Aug.).
1768	Acceptance of 'free' or 'voluntary' peasant recruits for the army forbidden. Dária Saltykóva deprived of title of nobility, publicly exhibited in Moscow as a 'torturer and murderer' and imprisoned for torturing to death some 75 serfs.
1769	*Obrók* from all tax payers except serfs raised to two rubles. Average serf *obrók* in the 1670s = two to four rubles (July).
1771	Sale of serfs apart from the land forbidden at public auctions.
1775	Freed serfs may not be re-enserfed, even voluntarily (17 Mar. and 6 Apr.).
1780s	Average price of a male serf = 80 rubles.
1783	*Obrók* for state peasants raised to three rubles. Average serf *obrók* = four rubles.
1790s	Average price of a male serf = 200 rubles.
1794	Poll tax increased to one ruble. Average serf *obrók* = five rubles.

Paul I

1796	Peasants' attachment to their allotments extended to all Southeastern regions including the Caucasus and Don (12 Dec.). Right of individual (but not collective) petitions by serfs to the Crown restored (12 Dec.).
1797	
29 Jan.	Serfs to show complete obedience to their masters, under threat of severe punishment.
5 Apr.	Landowners prohibited from making their serfs work on Sundays. For the remaining six days serf labour to be divided equally between the landowner's land and that of the serfs themselves. (Reassertion of the much violated provision of the code of 1649.) Ministry of Property of the Imperial Family introduced. First usage of the term 'Ministry'.
6 Apr.	Senate promulgation of the Manifesto of 5 April omits the limitation of serf labour to three days a week.
18 Dec.	*Obrók* for state peasants increased to 3.5–5.5 rubles.

Alexander I

1801

28 May	Advertising for the sale of serfs without land forbidden.
12 Dec.	The right to own agricultural land extended to merchants, burghers and state peasants.
1803	Law creates a new class of 'free agriculturalists' intended primarily for serfs who have obtained their freedom by voluntary agreement with their owners (20 Feb.).
1807	The emancipation of whole villages of serfs without land prohibited (14 Dec.).
1808	The sale of serfs 'like cattle' at markets and fairs prohibited (14 July).
1809	Decree of 1765, allowing owners to sentence serfs to penal servitude, repealed.
1810	Wealthy merchants permitted to own populated agricultural estates, provided these were bought from the Crown and not from individuals.
1812	Free Economic Society Essay Competition on the respective merits of servile and free labour.
1814	Personal nobles prohibited from acquiring serfs, although they may keep those they already have.
1816	Kiselëv memorandum advocates serf emancipation (27 Aug.).
1818	Arakchéev, Novosíltsev and Mordvínov's proposals for serf emancipation.
1819	Average *obrók* is eight rubles per male serf (but could be as high as 40 rubles).
1822	The right of owners to deport serfs to Siberia is confirmed, but they are no longer credited against the recruit quota for the army.
1825	The hiring of serfs to manufacturers prohibited (law not enforced).

Nicholas I

1826

12 May	Nicholas condemns rumours of impending emancipation and orders serfs to obey their masters.
6 Dec.	First Committee on the Peasant Question: Kochubéi (chair), Blúdov, Dáshkov, Díbich, Speránskii, Vasílchikov.
1827	Serfs forbidden entry to *gymnázii* and universities. Gentry's rights to send serfs to Siberia restricted.
1829	Committee established to examine the sale of serfs without land.

1832	Serf labour on landlords' land restricted to a maximum of three days per week (see 5–6.iv.1797).
1834	Military service reduced from 25 to 15 years.
1835	Committee set up to examine the condition of state peasants.
1837	Supervision of state lands and peasants transferred from the Ministry of Finance to the new Ministry of State Domains.
1839	Second Secret Committee on the Peasant Question: Blúdov, Kiselëv, Ménshikov, Orlóv, Pánin, Stróganov, Tuchkóv.
1841	Nobles without populated estates may not buy peasants separately from the land to which they are attached.
1842	Gentry who are former serfs forbidden to acquire populated estates.
Mar.	Nicholas I describes serfdom 'in its present form' as 'an evil for all concerned'.
2 Apr.	Landlords may free their peasants from personal bondage if they are given use of a portion of land in return for payment of a fixed annual rent in cash or kind.
1844	Household serfs permitted to buy their freedom.
1845	Limits set on landowners' rights to inflict physical punishment.
1846	Committee on the Eradication of Serfdom in Russia established, chaired by Alexander Nikoláevich (Mar.).
1847	Serfs permitted to buy their freedom when the estate on which they live is being sold by auction (8 Nov.).
1848	
Mar.	Serfs acquire the right to immovable property.
21 Mar.	Nicholas tells St Petersburg nobility of his intention to preserve 'the unshakable power and right of the serf-owners over their serfs'.
1853	Leasehold ownership of populated estates forbidden.
12 Feb.	Absentee landowners made criminally responsible for the actions of their overseers.
1854	Decree raising a militia (widely interpreted among the peasantry as signalling emancipation) (3 Apr.).
1855	Manifesto on the Militia (29 Jan.).

Alexander II

1856	Kiselëv dismissed from the Ministry of State Properties.
30 Mar.	Alexander II's speech to the Moscow Gentry: 'It is better to abolish serfdom from above . . .'

1857

1 Jan.	Secret Committee on the Peasant Question: V. P. Butkóv (secretary), V. F. Ádlerberg, D. N. Blúdov, N. V. Chévkin, V. A. Dolgorúkov, P. P. Gagárin, A. M. Korf, S. S. Lanskói, A. F. Orlóv (chair), Ia. I. Rostóvtsev.
Apr.	M. N. Muravëv appointed to the Secret Committee.
20 Nov.	Nazímov Rescript: Alexander rejects a request from the Lithuanian gentry to free their serfs without land. Instead, they were to arrange for their peasants to retain their homesteads, and purchase them from their former lords within a stipulated time. They were to be able to rent enough farmland to meet their needs, and be organized in communes. This document laid down the basic principles of the Emancipation of 1861.

1858

8 Jan.	'Secret Committee' renamed 'Main Committee' and joined by V. N. Pánin.
20 June	Kiselëv's system to be retained on state lands and extended to Crown lands.

1859

4 Mar.	Editorial Commission of 38 members established under Ia. A. Rostóvtsev: V. V. Apráksin, I. P. Arapétov, A. P. Bulgákov, V. I. Bulýgin, N. Kh. Bunge, V. A. Cherkásskii, K. I. Domontóvich, P. P. Gagárin, Iu. A. Gagemeister, G. P. Galagán, K. I. Getsevich, A. K. Giers, B. D. Golítsyn, S. P. Golítsyn, A. A. Grabianka, O. F. Iaroshínskii, N. V. Kalachóv, N. A. Kristofari, E. I. Lamánskii, M. N. Liuboshchinksii, N. A. Miliútin, F. I. Paskévich-Erivánskii, N. N. Pávlov, A. V. Popóv, M. P. Pozen, M. Kh. Reitern, Iu. F. Samárin, N. P. Semënov, P. P. Semënov(-Tian-Shánskii), N. P. Shíshkin, P. P. Shuválov, Ia. A. Solovëv, V. V. Tarnóvskii, A. N. Tatárinov, A. P. Zablótskii-Desiátovskii, B. F. Zalésskii, N. I. Zheleznóv, A. D. Zheltúkhin, S. M. Zhukóvskii.
1860	Death of Rostóvtsev (6 Feb.). V. N. Pánin becomes chairman of the Editorial Commission.
1861	Emancipation of the proprietal serfs (19 Feb.).
1863	Emancipation of the serfs of the Imperial Family, on terms more favourable than those granted the proprietal serfs.
1866	Statute on land reform for State Peasants, who receive as permanent allotments all the lands, except forests,

which were at the time in their continuous usage (24 Nov.).

1872   Establishment of the Valúev Commission on agriculture.

Alexander III
1881

22 May   The leasing of state land by peasant communes made easier.

28 Dec.   The period of 'temporary obligation' terminated. The redemption of allotments made compulsory for all former serfs. Redemption payments reduced.

1882   Foundation of the State Peasant Bank (18 May).

1883   Poll tax partially abolished (and 1884).

1886

18 Mar.   The breaking up of a peasant household not recognized unless approved by two-thirds majority of the commune.

12 June   Breach of contract by an agricultural labourer becomes a criminal offence.

1887   Poll tax (law of 18.v.1885) and *obrók* completely abolished and replaced by redemption payments (to extend until 1931!) (1 Jan.).

1889   Abolition of justices appointed by the *zémstvos* and the Ministry of Justice. Establishment of Land Captains (12 July).

1893

8 June   Communal repartition of land subject to the approval of the Land Captain.

14 Dec.   Sale of communal land by village communes prohibited. Withdrawals from the commune become subject to approval by the village assembly.

1894

7 Feb.   Repayment of redemption payments arrears extended over a longer period.

3 June   Passport Law introduced. Peasants cannot obtain a passport to move from their village without the consent of the village assembly. Junior family members also need the consent of the family elder, which can be overruled by the Land Captain.

Nicholas II
1896   Redemption payments period extended into the 1950s (13 May).

1902	Witte convenes the Special Conference on the Needs of Agriculture (Jan.) (dissolved 1905).
1903	Collective responsibility for taxes abolished (12 Mar.).
1904	All redemption payments arrears written off (11 Aug.).
1905	
30 Mar.	Special Conference on the Needs of Agriculture dissolved.
3 Nov.	Imperial Manifesto pledges to relieve the distress of the peasantry 'without doing injury to the other land-owners'. Redemption debt halved for 1906 and cancelled as of 1.i.1907. Regulations governing the Peasant Land Bank liberalized to allow 100% mortgages on land.
1906	
5 Oct.	Peasants allowed to circulate freely throughout the Empire without seeking permission from the commune.
9 Nov.	The 'Stolýpin Land Reform' passed as a temporary measure under Article 87. Every householder in a repartitional commune allowed to claim a share of the land as private property. In those with hereditary tenure, the land was deemed to have already passed into private ownership. The household elder became sole owner of what had previously been considered family property.
1910	Land Law introduced (14 June): 1. Confirms the provisions of the decree of 9.xi.1906; 2. Individual ownership has replaced communal ownership in all communes where no redistribution of land has taken place since the allocation under the Emancipation decree.

2.4.1   Ministers of the Imperial Court and Properties

1826–52	P. M. Volkónskii
1852–56	L. A. Peróvskii
1857–70	V. F. Adlerberg
1870–81	A. V. Adlerberg
1881–6.v.1897	I. I. Vorontsóv-Dáshkov
6.v.1897–1.iii.1917	V. B. Fredericks

2.4.2   Head of the Fifth Section of His Majesty's Own Chancery

April 1836–December 1837	P. D. Kiselëv

2.4.3   Ministers of State Domains

December 1837–April 1856	P. D. Kiselëv
April 1856–57	V. A. Sheremétev
17.iv.1857–December 1861	M. N. Muravëv
January 1862–72	A. A. Zelënyi
1872–79	P. A. Valúev
1879–24.iii.1881	A. A. Lieven
24 March-4.v.1881	N. P. Ignátev
4 May 1881–93	M. N. Ostróvskii

2.4.4   Minister of Agriculture and State Domains

1893–October 1905	A. S. Ermólov

2.4.5   Ministers of Agriculture

October 1905–29.i.1906	N. N. Kutler
February–April 1906	A. P. Nikólskii (acting)
April–July 1906	A. S. Stishínskii
July 1906–8	B. A. Vasílchikov
1908–27.x.1915	A. V. Krivoshéin
10.xi.1915–21.vii.1916	A. N. Naúmov
21 July–14.xi.1916	A. A. Bóbrinskii
29.xi.1916–1.iii.1917	A. A. Rittikh

2.5 Culture

Peter I

1698	Russian translations of foreign works published by Jan Tessing, Amsterdam.
1699	Tessing publishes first reasonably accurate map of Ukraine and the Black Sea area.
Mar.	Women appear publicly in Moscow for the first time at a dinner given by Peter for the representative of the Elector of Brandenburg.
1700	Introduction of the simplified 'civic alphabet'.
1702	Kopievskii's Russian calendar is published in Amsterdam.
1702–3	Building constructed on Red Square for the presentation of plays in Russian and German.
1703	Publication begins of *Védomosti* (*Gazette*), the first official government newspaper.
16 May	A. D. Ménshikov and the military engineer Kirchenstein break the ground with a sword on an island in the Nevá delta to mark the spot for the construction of a fortress called Sankt-Piter-Burkh (the site of the present Peter-Paul Fortress).
1706	Domenico Tressini builds the Fortress of St Peter and St Paul (completed 1744).
1710	Work begins on Tressini's Summer Palace on the Nevá for Peter the Great (completed 1714), and Gottfried Schädel's Summer Palace on Vasilevskii Island for Ménshikov (completed 1714).
c. **1712**	I. N. Nikítin paints his *Portrait of the Empress Elizabeth as a child*.
1712	Work begins on Tressini's Cathedral of St Peter and St Paul (completed 1733).
1713	Work begins on Schädel's Palace at Oranienbaum for prince Ménshikov (completed 1725).
1715	Naval Academy pupils begin mapping the Russian Empire.
Before 1716	Nikítin paints the portrait of Natália Alexéevna (Peter the Great's sister).

1716	Peter starts buying pictures in Italy through an agent and asks Cosimo III of Tuscany to allow young Russians to study painting at the Florence Academy. Le Blond's Château for Peter I is built at Strélna.
1717	
8 Jan.	Le Blond's *Ideal Plan for St Petersburg.*
Early	Jean-Marc Nattier paints *The Battle of Poltava* and his *Portrait of the Empress Catherine.*
May	Nattier paints his portrait of Peter the Great and Caravaque paints the portrait of Peter the Great's daughters, Anne and Elizabeth.
Dec.	Peter I becomes a member *'hors de tout rang'* of the French Academy of Sciences.
1718	Decree orders establishment of 'assemblies' in St Petersburg, where men and women (whose presence was compulsory) could meet for chess, dancing, etc. (Dec.).
	Work begins on Mattarnovy's Kunstkamera (later the Library of the Academy of Sciences) (completed 1825).
1719	Building of the Museum of Natural History.
1720	Daniel Messerschmidt goes on his First Siberian journey. Le Blond builds the Palace of Peterhof.
1722	Work begins on Tressini's Twelve Colleges on Vasílii Óstrov (completed 1733).
1724	I. T. Pososhkóv completes his *Book on Poverty and Wealth.* Titus Bering is ordered to discover if Siberia is joined to North America.
Before 1725?	Nikítin paints his portrait of Peter the Great.

Catherine I

1725	Publication of Kantemír's *Russian and French Dictionary* (1725–26).
1726	Nikítin paints his portrait of S. G. Stróganov.

Peter II

1728	Library of the Academy of Sciences opened to the public.

Anna Ivánovna

1730	Kantemír translates Fontenelle's *Entretiens sur la pluralité des mondes* (only published in 1740 as the Church objected to its rejection of Ptolemaic astronomy). Captain John Philips, as Grand Master of Russia, creates the first Masonic Lodge. Nikítin paints his *Portrait of a Hetman.*

1733   Luigi Madonis's instrumentalists and singers arrive in St Petersburg (until 1762).
1735   Domenico dall'Oglio, composer and violinist, arrives in Russia (until 1764).
1736   First Italian opera performed in Russia, Araja's *La Forza dell'amore e dell'odio*, Theatre of the Imperial Court (Jan.).
1738   Luigi Madonis composes *Twelve diverse symphonies for violin and bass*.
1740   Mikhaíl Golítsyn is condemned to 'marriage' to Anna Buzheninova and spends a 'honeymoon night' in a house built of ice on the frozen Nevá (Jan.). Kantemír's translation of Fontenelle's *Entretiens sur la pluralité des mondes* is published.

Elizabeth
1741   Lomonósov elected to the Academy of Sciences. Work begins on Rastrelli's Summer Palace on the Fontánka (completed 1744).
1742   Charles de Sérigny's French Theatre visits Russia. Work begins on M. G. Zemtsóv's Aníchkov Palace for Alexei Razumóvskii (completed by Rastrelli, 1744).
1744   Première of A. P. Sumarókov's *The Piety of Marcus Aurelius* in Kiev, and of Araja's *Seleuco*, WPT.
1745   Première of Araja's *Scipione*, WPT. Voltaire requests admission to the Academy of Sciences and to write the history of Peter the Great.
1746   Voltaire elected honorary member of the Academy of Sciences. A Russian translation of Voltaire's *Histoire de Charles XII*, part 1, is published.
1747   Première of Araja's opera *Mitridate*, WPT. Rastrelli begins the reconstruction of Peterhof (completed 1752), and building the Church of St Andrew, Kiev (completed 1767).
1748   Première of the first opera to have a Russian subject, Araja's *L'Asilio della pace*, WPT. Sumarókov translates *Hamlet*. Work begins on Rastrelli's Cathedral for the Smólny Convent (completed 1757).
1749   French translation of Kantemír's *Satires* published in London. Vishniakóv paints his *Portrait of Sarah Fermor*. Work begins on Rastrelli's Great Palace of Tsárskoe seló (completed 1752).
1750   Première of Araja's *Bellerofonte*, WPT and of Sumarókov's *Khórev* and *Artistona*. Work begins on Rastrelli's

Stróganov Palace on the Névsky Prospékt (completed 1754). F. G. Vólkov opens a public theatre at Iároslavl.

1751 Première of Araja's *Eudossa incoronata*, WPT. Sumarókov's *Sinave et Trouvore* is published simultaneously in French and Russian. Lomonósov's *Demofont* is published.

1752 Baron Spicker translates Kantemír's *Satires* into German.

1753 Argunóv paints his portrait of P. B. Sheremétev.

1754 Work begins on Rastrelli's Winter Palace (completed 1762). First French-language journal in Russia *le Chaméléon littéraire* is published by Théodore-Henri de Tschudy (closed 1755).

1755 Première of the first opera with a libretto written by a Russian (Sumarókov's adaptation of a story from Ovid's *Metamorphoses*), Araja's *Céphale et Procris*, WPT (27 Feb.). Lomonósov founds the journal *Monthly Writings*, intended to be a Russian *Encyclopédie* (1758, edited by G. F. Müller and renamed *Writings and Translations for the Use and Entertainment of Officials*) (closed 1764).

1756 First issue of *Moskóvskie védomosti/Moscow Gazette* published daily until 1917. First public Russian theatre opens with Sumarókov as director until 1761.

1756–61 Vishniakóv paints the portraits of M. S. Iákovlev and S. S. Iákovleva.

1757 Ivan Shuválov founds the Imperial Academy of Fine Arts.

1758 The French painter Jean-Baptiste Le Prince arrives in Russia (until 1763). Publication of Sumarókov's *Hermit*.

Jan. Tocqué's portrait of the Empress Elizabeth.

31 Jan. Publication of P. Svistunóv's translation of Molière's *Bourgeois gentilhomme*.

29 Oct. Première of Dancourt's *Le Tuteur trompé, battu et content* (trans: A. A. Vólkov), Russian Theatre.

1759 Publication of Sumarókov's journal *Trudoliubivaia pchela* (*The Busy Bee*) (Jan.–Dec.) and of P. Pastukhóv's journal *Prazdnoe vremia* (*Time off*). Voltaire's *Histoire de Pierre le Grand* published in Geneva (1759–63).

1760 A. P. Lósenko paints his portraits of Sumarókov and of I. I. Shuválov. Publication of Svistunóv's translation of Voltaire's *L'Indiscret* and of M. M. Kheráskov's weekly paper *Poléznoe Uveselénie* (*Useful Entertainment*) (closed 28.vi.1762).

1761	Publication of Svistunóv's translation of Molière's *Amphitrion*.
6 June	Chappe D'Auteroche in Tobólsk to observe the passage of Venus.

Peter III
1762	Antrópov paints his *Portrait of Peter III*.

Catherine II
1762	Establishment of the Commission on the building of St Petersburg and Moscow: I. I. Betskói, Z. Chernyshëv, M.-K. Dáshkov. First Russian publication of Kantemír's satires (18 years after his death). Publication of Fonvízin's translation of Voltaire's *Alzire*. D'Alembert declines the post of tutor to Grand Duke Paul Petróvich. Bernardin de St Pierre arrives in Russia (until 1764).
9/20 Aug.	Diderot declines Shuválov's invitation to continue publication of the *Encyclopédie* (suspended in France by royal command since 1759) in Riga.
1762–65	Rókotov paints his *Portrait of Count I. G. Orlov*.
1763	B. Galuppi appointed Imperial Court *kapellmeister*. Lósenko paints his portrait of F. G. Vólkov.
Jan.–June	I. F. Bogdanóvich's monthly journal *Nevínnoe uprazhnénie* (*Innocent Exercise*).
Jan.–Dec.	Kheráskov's monthly journal *Svobódnye chasý* (*Leisure Time*).
6 Sept.	Rousseau's *Emile* banned in Russia.
1764	Foundation of the Hermitage Art Gallery by the purchase of E. I. Gostovskii's collection in Berlin. Le Prince paints the first of his many Russian pictures *Le joueur de balalaïka* and *Scène de la vie quotidienne en Russie*. D. I. Fonvízin writes *Korion*.
Jan.–Dec.	V. D. Sankóvskii's monthly journal *Dóbroe namerénie* (*Good Intentions*).
26 Sept.	Première of F.-A. D. Philidor's *Le maréchal ferrant* at the Court Theatre.
1765	Publication of S. Glébov's translation of Diderot's *Le père de famille* (first performed in the early 1770s).
May	Catherine buys Diderot's library, while leaving him the lifetime enjoyment of it, and giving him an annual pension.
28 June	Official inauguration of the Academy of Fine Arts.
22 Aug.	Foundation of the Free Economic Society, the first Russian secular cultural institution (closed Oct. 1917).

17 Oct.	Première of I. P. Elágin's *A Russian Frenchman.*
1766	Publication of Trediakóvskii's translation of Fénelon's *Télémaque.* G. Müller appointed director of the archives of the College of Foreign affairs. Work begins on Rinaldi's Palace of Gátchina (completed 1781).
Jan.	Elágin made director of Court Spectacles and Music.
9 Apr.	Free Economic Society's Essay Competition on 'What is more useful to society, that a peasant should own the land or only moveable property, and how far should his rights over the one or the other extend?' won by Beardé de l'Abbaye (against competition which included Voltaire and Marmontel), who argued for emancipation. Second prize to the French physiocrat Graslin.
1767	Three volumes of translations of articles from the *Encyclopédie* published in Moscow. G. Orlóv invites Rousseau to Russia.
Spring	Catherine and her entourage translate Marmontel's *Bélisaire.*
Aug.	Pierre-Paul Lemercier de la Rivière arrives in Russia (until Mar. 1768).
1768	Russian translation of Marmontel's *Bélisaire* published in Moscow. M. M. Shcherbátov appointed official historiographer. Beardé de l'Abbaye's essay published in Russian. Ia. P. Kozélskii's *Philosophical Propositions* denounces the Russian political system. Publication of Charpentier's *Les Elémens de la langue russe* in St Petersburg and of Chappe d'Auteroche's *Voyage en Sibérie* in Paris. Müller begins publishing the first three volumes of Tatíshchev's *Russian History* 18 years after the latter's death (vol. 3: 1774).
Aug.	Thomas Dimsdale inoculates Catherine and Paul Petróvich against smallpox.
4 Nov.	Catherine founds and endows the Society for the Translation of Foreign Books.
1769	Catherine sponsors and contributes to the journal *Vsiákaia vsiáchina/Anything and Everything*, edited by G. V. Kozítskii, which gives rise to a host of short-lived satirical journals over the next five years: *To i së/This and that* etc., some of which are extremely critical of serfdom and society. Fonvízin's *The Brigadier* performed at Court. Bashílov's translation of Voltaire's *Candide* is published. Levítskii paints his *Portrait of the Architect A. F. Kokórinov.*

1 May	N. I. Nóvikov's[1] weekly journal *Trúten* (*The Drone*) (closed 27 April 1770).
1770	Catherine II's *L'antidote*, a reply to Chappe d'Auteroche's hostile picture of Russia in his *Voyage en Sibérie*, is published in Amsterdam. Lósenko paints *Vladímir and Rogneda*. Publication of a Russian *samizadat* version of Voltaire's *Histoire de Pierre le grand* (bound manuscript 'translated by a student of Moscow University' probably Nikolái Nikoláevich Bántysh-Kámenskii, sometime between 1770 and 1780). Velten builds the Chesme Palace.
June–July	Nóvikov's monthly journal *Boltún* (*The Babbler*) (two issues only).
1771	Work begins on I. E. Staróv's country house at Bogoróditsa (Túla) for A. G. Bóbrinskii (completed 1776). Authorization given for first private printing press. Publication of Fonvízin's translation of *The Elegy of Marcus Aurelius* and of Kheraskóv's epic poem *The Battle of Chesme*.
1 Feb.	Sumarókov's *Dimitri the Pretender*, Imperial Theatre.
1772	Publication of Nóvikov's *Historical Dictionary of Russian Writers* and of his translation of Le Jeune's *La philosophie française contemporaine*. Fonvízin reads *The Brigadier* to Grand Duke Paul Petróvich. Première of M. I. Popóv's comic opera *Aniuta*.
12 Apr.	Nóvikov's weekly journal *Zhivopísets* (*The Painter*) (closed June 1773).
1773	Work begins on Staróv's house and Church for S. V. Gagárin at Nikólskoe (completed 1776). Lósenko paints *Hector's Farewell to Andromaque*.
Oct.	Diderot arrives in St Petersburg (until 4.iii.1774).
1774	Levítskii paints his portrait of Diderot. Sumarókov's *Satires and Elegies* published, and Catherine II's play *The Lady Writer and her Family* is published anonymously.
1775	Work begins on Rinaldi's Bolshoi Theatre, St Petersburg (completed 1783 at the place where the Conservatoire now stands).
Oct.	Kniazhnín's translation of Corneille's *Le Cid, La Mort de Pompée* and *Cinna* is published (put on sale by Nóvikov, 1779).

---

[1] There is a dispute about how he pronounced his name. It may have been Novikóv. I am here following B. O. Unbegaum, *Russian Surnames* (Oxford, 1972), p. 321.

1776	Work begins on Felten's Kamenoóstrovskii Palace for Grand Duke Paul Petróvich (completed 1780), and on V. I. Bazhénov's Palace at Tsarítsyno (left uncompleted 1785).
8 July	Nóvikov's weekly journal *Koshelëk* (*The Purse*) (closed Oct.).
1777	Publication of Kniazhnín's translation of Voltaire's *Henriade*.
10 Jan.	Condorcet and Buffon elected to the Russian Academy.
Spring	A. B. Kurákin imports the Masonic Order of Templars into Russia.
Sept.	Nóvikov's journal *Útrennyi svet* (*Morning Light*) (closed Aug. 1780).
1778	Work begins on Staróv's Cathedral for Alexander Nevskii Lávra (completed 1790).
End	Catherine buys Voltaire's library of 6,814 books after his death, which she proposes to house in a reproduction of the *chateau* of Ferney at Tsárskoe seló.
1779	Première of A. O. Ablésimov's comic opera *The Miller, the Wizard, the Quack and the Matchmaker*. D. S. Bortniánskii appointed principal of the Imperial Chapel. Publication of Kheráskov's *Rossiada* in Moscow.
Jan.	Nóvikov's journal *Módnoe ezhemésiachnoe izdánie* (*Monthly Fashion Journal*) (closed Dec.).
31 July	Voltaire's library arrives in St Petersburg.
7 Nov.	Première of V. Pashkévich's comic opera *Misfortune from a Carriage* (libretto by Kniazhnín).
1780	Publication of Catherine II's anti-Masonic satire *Le secret de la société anti-absurde dévoilé par quelqu'un qui n'en est pas*.
27 Dec.	Première of Fonvízin's *Brigadier*, Knipper-Dmitriévskii's Russian Theatre.
1781	Work begins on Quarenghi's English Palace at Tsárskoe seló (completed 1789).
1782	Work begins on Charles Cameron's Palace of Pávlovsk (completed 1786). Derzhávin writes his *Ode à Félice*.
7 Aug.	Unveiling of Falconet's Bronze Horseman.
24 Sept.	Première of Fonvízin's *The Callow Youth*, Knipper-Dmitriévskii's Russian Theatre.
Dec.	Princess E. Dáshkova is appointed director of the Academy of Sciences.
1783	Dáshkova is appointed president of the Russian Academy of Letters. Derzhávin's *Ode à Félice* published in Dáshkova's *Sobesédnik*. Première of D. I. Khvostóv's

	The Russian Parisian. Levítskii paints his *Portrait of Catherine II as Legislator.* Work begins on Quarenghi's Hermitage Theatre (completed 1787) and on Staróv's Tauride Palace for Potëmkin (completed 1789; in 1906 it became the State Duma).
15 Jan.	Anyone may establish a printing press as long as the police are notified, and manuscripts submitted to them for approval.
22 Feb.	Première of Grétry's comic opera *Les deux avares,* Moscow.
1783–84	Dáshkova and O. P. Kozodávlev edit *Companion for Lovers of the Russian Language.*
1784	Argunóv paints his *Portrait of an unknown peasant woman in Russian costume.* Publication of Tatíshchev's *Russian History,* vol. 4. Work begins on Quarenghi's Academy of Sciences Building (completed 1787).
23 Sept.	Nóvikov's *History of the Jesuit Order* is banned.
1785	Publication of Kheráskov's epic poem *Vladímir.*
1785–89	Iván Rakhmáninov's translation of Voltaire's works (three volumes).
1786	Première of E. I. Fomín's *Gallant Boeslavich of Novgorod* (libretto by Catherine II). Shchúkin paints his *Portrait of the Architect I. M. Felten.* Shcherbátov writes *On the Corruption of Morals in Russia* (published 1896).
15 Jan.	Première of Giuseppe Sarti's opera *Armida e Rinaldo,* at the opening of the Hermitage Theatre.
11 Oct.	Première of Bortniánskii's comic opera *Le Faucon,* Palace of Gátchina.
1787	Publication of Bogdanóvich's play *Slavs.*
2 Jan.	Première of Fomín's comic opera *Coachmen at the Stage,* BTS.
15 Jan.	Première of Russian translation of Beaumarchais's *Le Mariage de Figaro,* Petróvskii Theatre, Moscow.
1788	Police prevent publication of Fonvízin's journal *Starodúm.*
1789	I. A. Krylóv's monthly *Póchta dukhóv* (*Courier of the Spirits*) (closed August). Work begins on Kazakóv's Palace of Ostánkino for prince Sheremétev (completed 1796).
23 Nov.	Première of N.-M. Dalayrac's comic opera *Nina, ou la Folle par amour,* Stróganov Palace.
1790	Russian translation of Charles Compan's *Dictionnaire de danse* published in Moscow.
May	Radíshchev, *Journey from St Petersburg to Moscow,* published by himself.

May–Sept.	Karamzín's journey to France.
24 July	Radíshchev condemned to death for *lèse majesté*. (4 Sept., commuted to ten years in Siberia with loss of noble status; 1796, released by Paul I.)
22 Oct.	Première of V. A. Pashkévich and Carlo Canobbio's *The Early Rule of Olég* (libretto by Catherine II), Hermitage Theatre.
1791	Karamzín's *Moskóvskii zhurnál* (*Moscow Journal*) (closes after one year), in which he publishes his *Letters of a Russian Traveller*. Suppression of Kniazhnín's *Vadím of Nóvgorod*. First Russian fashion magazine: *Magazín anglíiskoi, frantsúzskoi i nemétskoi nóvykh mod* (*Magazine of New English, French and German Fashions*).
1792	Publication of Karamzín's *To forgiveness* (*Moskóvskii zhurnál*).
Feb.–Dec.	Krylóv's journal *Zrítel* (*The Spectator*). Krylóv's printing-house searched, and Krylóv placed under police surveillance.
June	Karamzín's *Poor Lisa* (*Moskóvskii zhurnál*, vol. VI, part 3).
Aug.	Nóvikov sentenced to 15 years' imprisonment in Schlüsselburg (released Nov. 1796).
1793	Krylóv's journal *Sankt-Petersbúrgskii Merkúrii* (*The St Petersburg Mercury*).
1793–94	Burning of Voltaire's works.
1794	G. R. Derzhávin's *Monument to a Hero* published in Riga. Publication of A. I. Músin-Púshkin's *Historical Research on the Site of the Old Russian Principality of Tmutarakán* and of Karamzín's journal *Agláia* (2 issues only, closed 1795). Borovikóvskii paints *Catherine II walking in the park at Tsárskoe seló*. Quarenghi builds a country house at Lialichyi (Chernígov) for P. Zavadóvskii.
1795	Derzhávin accused of Jacobinism for his versification of Psalm 81 (written 1780, published 1787). Músin-Púshkin buys the manuscript of *The Tale of Igor's Raid* from the archimandrite of the Spáso-Iaroslávskii monastery. Borovikóvskii paints his *Portrait of Gavríil Románovich Derzhávin* and *Portrait of Khristinia, a peasant woman from Torzhók*.
End June	Elisabeth Vigée-Lebrun arrives in Russia (until 1801).
1796	Vigée-Lebrun paints her portrait of Grand-Duchesses Alexandra Pávlova and Eléna Pávlovna. Quarenghi builds the Alexander Palace at Tsárskoe seló.

June	Vigée-Lebrun becomes a member of the St Petersburg Academy.
Sept.	Russia's borders sealed: all imported literature admitted only through Riga, Odessa or the Polish border.

Paul I

1797	Levítskii paints *Portrait of N. I. Nóvikov*. Claude-Carloman de Rulhière's *Histoire ou Anecdotes sur la révolution de Russie en l'année 1762* published in Paris.
1798	In April, Auguste Poirot, dancer, Pierre Chevalier, ballet-master, and Madame Chevalier, née Poirot, singer, arrive in St Petersburg.
1799	Première of Derzhávin's *Chicane*. Vigée-Lebrun paints her *Portrait of the Empress Maria Fëdorovna* and Shchúkin paints *Portrait of Paul I*.
5 Nov.	Première of Sarti and Fonbrune's *L'Arivée de Thétis et Pélée en Thessalie*, Imperial Theatre, Gátchina.
1800	Vigée-Lebrun's *Self Portrait* is donated to the Academy of Fine Arts. Músin-Púshkin's edition of *The Tale of Igor's Raid* published. Borovikóvskii paints portraits of Paul I as Grand Master of the Order of Malta and of A. B. Kurákin.
12 July	Première of Chevalier's ballet, *Une héroïne du village*.
Sept.	Première of Sarti's ballet, *Les Amours de Flore et de Zéphire*, Imperial Theatre, Gátchina.

Alexander I

1801	Work begins on Voroníkhin's Kazán Cathedral (completed 1811), and on Quarenghi's additional wings to the palace of Ostánkino. Première of Didelot's ballet, *Apollo et Daphné*.
1802	Publication of Karamzín's journal *Véstnik Evrópy* (*Messenger of Europe*), in which he publishes parts of his *Letters of a Russian Traveller* too controversial to have been published in 1791–92, and of Zhukóvskii's translation of Gray's *Elegy* (*VE*).
1803	Publication of Shishkóv's *An Enquiry into Old and New Styles in the Russian Language*, and of Karamzín's *Martha the Mayoress* (*VE*). Alexander allocates 120,000 rubles for the translation of works by Adam Smith, Bentham, Beccaria, Montesquieu, Tacitus, etc.
30 Nov.	Appointed 'Official Historiographer', Karamzín resigns the editorship of *VE*.

1804	Work begins on Thomas de Thomon's Stock Exchange (completed 1811). Première of V. Ózerov's *Oedipus in Athens*.
1805	Première of Ózerov's *Fingal* and of Didelot's ballet, *Zéphire et Flore*, Hermitage Theatre.
1806	Première of Ózerov's *Dmitri Donskoi*. Foundation of the Moscow State Theatre. Work begins on A. Zakhárov's Admiralty (completed 1823).
9 July	All manuscripts submitted for publication to be examined by officials of the Ministry of Education.
1807	Publication of the journal *Rússkii véstnik* (*The Russian Herald*) (edited by S. Glínka).
1808	Première of Ózerov's *Polyxena*.
1809	Publication of Russian translation of Voltaire's *Histoire de Pierre le grand*.
3 Jan.	Première of Didelot's ballet, *Psyché et l'Amour*, Hermitage Theatre.
1810	Première of Didelot's ballet, *Laure et Henri*.
1811	Ministry of Police given broad powers over publications.
Mar.	First monthly meeting of the *Beséda* group (Shishkóv, Derzhávin, Krylóv, Gnédich, Katénin) (dissolved 1816).
15 Mar.	Karamzín gives his *Memoir on Ancient and Modern Russia* to Alexander I.
1812	Publication of Zhukóvskii's *A Bard in the Russian Warriors' Camp* and of Bátiushkov's *My Penates*.
1813	Bátiushkov's *On the Ruins of a Castle in Sweden* and *To Dáshkov* published.
1814	Alexander Pushkin's first poems and Bátiushkov's *The Ghost of a Friend* published.
1815	Formation of the *Arzamás* literary circle (Bátiushkov, Dáshkov, Davýdov, Karamzín, Vasílii Púshkin, A. Turgénev, Uvárov, Vígel, Alexander Voéikov, Zhukóvskii; 1816–17: Nikíta Muravëv, Mikhaíl Orlóv, N. Turgénev) (dissolved April 1818).
1817	Minister of Education, Golítsyn, prohibits the discussion in print of government activities without preliminary authorization by the minister concerned (10 Feb.).
1818	*Sorevnovátel* (*The Emulator*), journal of the Free Society of Lovers of Russian Letters, published monthly until 1825. Work begins on Montferrand's St Isaac's Cathedral (completed 1858).
Early	Publication of Karamzín's *History of the Russian State*, vols 1–8.

14 May	*Ukáz* states: 'All questions pertaining to government policies may be discussed only in accordance with the wishes of the authorities, who know better what information should be given to the public; private persons must not write on political topics, either for or against.'
1819	
Mar.	Formation of the *Green Lamp* literary circle.
1 May	Première of Didelot's ballet, *Raoul de Créqui*, BTS.
1820	Publication of Pushkin's *Ruslán and Liudmílla*, of Ryléev's *To the Favourite* and of Viázemskii's *Indignation*.
5 May	Pushkin banished to South Russia until July 1824 because of his 'freedom poems'.
1821	Publication of Bestúzhev's 'Journey to Réval' (*Sor*).
1822	Publication of Pushkin's *Captive of the Caucasus*. Masonic lodges closed (1 Aug.).
1823	Première of Didelot's *The Captive of the Caucasus* (after Pushkin), BTS (15 Jan.). Moscow State Theatre changes its name to the Mályi Theatre. Formation of the *Liubomúdrye*/Lovers of Wisdom (president: Odóevskii; secretary: Venevítinov; Khomiakóv, Koshelëv, I. V. and P. V. Kiréevskii, Pogódin, N. Rozhálin, Shevyrëv) (dissolved Dec. 1825). Publication of Ryléev and Bestúzhev's journal *Poliárnaia zvezdá* (*Pole Star*) (closed 1825), of Bestúzhev's 'Roman and Olga' (*PZ*), and 'Wenden Castle', and of Orést Sómov's essay 'Romantic Poetry' (*Sor*).
1824	Viázemskii's *Sankt-Peterburg* and Bestúzhev's 'Neuhausen Castle' published.
9 Aug.	Pushkin in enforced residence on his estates at Mikháilovskoe, near Pskov.
1825	Pushkin completes *Borís Godunóv* (published 1831). Publication of Pushkin's *Evgénii Onégin*, chapter 1 (Feb.), Bestúzhev's 'The Réval Tournament', and of A. S. Griboédov's *Woe from Wit* (with cuts imposed by the censor. Complete text published 1913; first partial performance 1827, first complete performance 1831). Also published: Délvig's literary miscellanies *Sévernye tsvetý* (*Northern Flowers*) (until 1831), N. A. Polevói's monthly journal *Moskóvskii telegráf* (*Moscow Telegraph*) (closed April 1834) and F. V. Bulgárin's monthly journal *Sévernaia pchëla* (*Northern Bee*) (after 1831, jointly edited by N. I. Grech, and from 1860 with P. S. Úsov; closed 1864).

Nicholas I

1826	Bestúzhev's 'Eisen Castle' published as 'Blood for Blood'.
10 June	Law on censorship gives censors almost unlimited powers.
Summer	Iazýkov's 'Pushkin cycle' of poems published.
Sept.	Pushkin freed from banishment after meeting Nicholas I.
Oct.	Pushkin, *Evgénii Onégin*, chapter 2, published.
1827	Publication of Pushkin's *Gypsies* (written 1824) and of his *Evgénii Onégin*, chapter 3 (Oct.). Also published: Sómov's first 'Survey of Russian Literature' (*ST*) (then annually until 1831), and Mikhail Pogódin's monthly journal *Moskóvskii véstnik* (*Moscow Herald*) (closed 1830). Officers of the Caucasus Corps in Ereván perform extracts from Griboédov's *Woe from Wit* (first complete performance, 1831).
1828	Publication of Viázemskii's *The Russian God*.
Jan.	Pushkin, *Evgénii Onégin*, chapters 4 and 5 published.
Mar.	Pushkin, *Evgénii Onégin*, chapter 6 published.
22 Apr.	Censorship liberalized.
1829	Publication of Gnédich's translation of *The Iliad*, of Pushkin's *Poltáva*, of Zagóskin's *Iúrii Milosóvskii, or the Russians in 1612*, of F. Bulgárin's *Iván Výzhigin* (Russia's first best-seller: 6,000 copies sold) and of Délvig's literary almanachs *Podsnézhnik* (*Snowdrop*) (until 1830).
1 Dec.	Chaadáev finishes the first of his eight *Lettres philosophiques*.
2 Dec.	Performance of part of Act 1 of Griboédov's *Woe from Wit*, benefit performance for the actress M. I. Valberkhova (complete performance, 1831).
1830	Pushkin completes *Tales of Bélkin*. Publication of Bestúzhev's 'The Test' (*SO*).
1 Jan.	Délvig's *Literary Gazette* (published every five days for 18 months).
Feb.–Mar.	Publication of N. V. Gógol's 'A Midsummer's Night's Eve' (*OZ*).
Mar.	Pushkin, *Evgénii Onégin*, chapter 7 published.
19 Oct.	Pushkin burns chapter 10 of *Evgénii Onégin*.
Dec.?	Publication of Vladímir Odóevskii's *Beethoven's Last Quartet* (*ST*).
1831	Publication of Pushkin's *Borís Godunóv* and *Mozart and Salieri*, of Bestúzhev's 'Lieutenant Belozór', and of N. I. Nadézhdin's monthly *Teleskóp* (closed 1836).

26 Jan.	First complete performance of Griboédov's *Woe from Wit*, BTS.
Sept.	Publication of Gógol's *Evenings on a Farm near Dikanka*, part 1.
1832	Bestúzhev's 'The Frigate *Hope*' and 'Ammalat Bek' published.
Jan.	Pushkin, *Evgénii Onégin*, chapter 8 published.
1833	Publication of Odóevskii's *Motley Fairy Tales*.
6 Dec.	Pushkin's *Bronze Horseman* is turned down by the censor.
1834	Archaeographical Commission established. Extracts from Pushkin's *Bronze Horseman* published as *Petersburg: an Extract from a Poem*. Pushkin's *Queen of Spades* (*BdC* vol. 2, book 3) and his *Tales of Bélkin* are published, as are Bestúzhev's 'Nikítin the Sailor' and Osip Senkóvskii's monthly journal *Biblióteka dlia chténiia* (*Reading Library*) (closed 1865). Montferrand's Alexander Column is erected on Palace Square.
5 Apr.	Closure of Polevói's *Moskóvskii Telegráf* because of a hostile review of Kúkolnik's patriotic play, *The Hand of the Almighty Saved the Fatherland*.
Sept.	Publication of Belínskii's 'Literary reveries' (*Mo* no. 38).
1835	Manuscript copies of Karamzín's *Memoir on Ancient and Modern Russia* circulate. Pushkin and Gógol's monthly journal *Moskóvskii nabliudátel* (*Moscow Observer*) published (closed 1837).
Jan.	Gógol's *Arabesques* is published.
Mar.	Gógol's *Mírgorod* is published.
Dec.	Belínskii begins to publish regularly in *Teleskóp*.
1836	
June	Pushkin's monthly journal *Sovreménnik* (*Contemporary*) published (closed 1866).
July	Extracts published from Nadézhda Dúrova's *The Cavalry Maiden* (*S* no. 2).
19 Apr.	Première of Gógol's *The Inspector General*, ATS.
Sept.	Publication of Gógol's 'The Nose' (*S* no. 3) and of F. I. Tiútchev's *Poems sent from Germany* (*S* nos 3–4).
End Sept.	Russian translation of Chaadáev's first *Lettre philosophique* published (*Teleskóp* no. 15).
28 Oct.	Chaadáev declared insane and placed under police and medical supervision. The censor, Bóldyrev, dismissed, Nadézhdin banished to Ust-Sysolsk (1841). *Teleskóp* closed down.
27 Nov.	Publication of Pushkin's *The Captain's Daughter* (*S* no. 4.).

9 Dec.	Première of M. I. Glínka's *A Life for the Tsar*, BTS.
1837	Publication of Pushkin's *Rusálka* (written 1832) (*S* no. 6), of his *Bronze Horseman* (written 1833) (*S* with alterations by Zhukóvskii as demanded by the censors) and of his *Arab of Peter the Great* (*S* vol. 6, no. 2), also of a truncated version of Karamzín's *Memoir on Ancient and Modern Russia*, introduction by Pushkin (*S* no. 5), and of Chaadáev's *Apologie d'un fou*.
27 Jan.	Pushkin is fatally wounded in a duel with the baron d'Anthès.
29 Jan.	Death of Pushkin. Pletněv takes over the editorship of *Sovreménnik*.
1838	
Jan.	Turgénev's first publication: 'Evening' (*S* no. 1).
Mar.	Belínskii *de facto* editor of *Moskóvskii nabliudátel* (nominal editor: V. Andrósov).
4 Dec.	Lérmontov finishes *Demon*.
1839	A. A. Kraévskii's monthly journal *Otéchestvennye zapíski* (*Notes of the Fatherland*) published (closed 1884). The publication of extracts from Lérmontov's *Demon* in *OZ* is postponed because of Lérmontov's exile.
Aug.	Belínskii becomes literary critic for *OZ* and *Literatúrnoe pribavlénie k Rússkomy invalídu* (*Literary Supplement to the Russian ex-Serviceman*).
1840	Publication of Lérmontov's *A Hero of Our Time* (May).
1841	Russian Academy of Letters becomes the second department of the Academy of Sciences (humane sciences). Pogódin's monthly journal *Moskvitiánin* (*The Muscovite*) (closed 1856) and Shevyrëv's 'A Russian looks at the present state of Europe' (*M* no. 1) published.
1842	Censors forbid the publication of Lérmontov's *Demon* (Kraévskii does manage to publish some extracts). (Complete poem published in Karlsrühe, 1856).
21 May	Publication of Gógol's *Dead Souls*, vol. 1.
9 Dec.	Première of Gógol's *The Wedding*, ATS and of Glínka's *Ruslán and Liudmíla*, BTS.
Dec.	Publication of Gógol's 'The Overcoat'.
1843	
5 Feb.	Première of Gógol's *The Gamblers*, BTM.
Apr.	Publication of Turgénev's *Parasha*.
Autumn	Granóvskii delivers his public lectures on Russia and Europe.
1844	First complete publication of Odóevskii's *Russian Nights*.

1845	Publication of Nekrásov's *Physiology of St Petersburg.*
1846	Belínskii leaves *OZ* (1 Apr.). Panáev and Nekrásov take over the editorship of *S.* Publication of Dostoevskii's *The Double* (*OZ* no. 2), an extract from S. T. Aksákov's *A Family Chronicle*, and Nekrásov's *Petersburg Miscellany*, containing writings by Herzen, Panáev, Odóevskii, Sollogúb, Belínskii and Dostoevskii (*Poor Folk*).
1847	
Jan.	Herzen leaves Russia. Belínskii joins *S.* Publication of Dostoevskii's *A Novel in Nine Letters* (*S* no. 1) and Turgénev's 'Khor and Kalínich' (*S* no. 1). (Other stories from *A Huntsman's Sketches: S* 1847, nos 2, 5, 10; 1848, no. 2; 1849, no. 2.)
12 Jan.	Gógol's *Selected Passages from Correspondence with Friends* is severely cut by the censors.
Feb.	Publication of I. A. Goncharóv's *A Common Story* (*S* no. 2) and of Turgénev's 'Pëtr Petróvich Karatáev' (*S* no. 2).
14–15 Mar.	A. N. Ostróvskii's *Picture of a Family* published (*MGL*). (Censor forbids theatrical production; première 1855.)
May	Publication of Turgénev's 'Ermolái and the Miller's Wife', 'My Neighbour Radílov', 'Ovsiánikov the Freeholder', 'Lgov' (*S* no. 5).
3–5 June	Ostróvskii's *Notes of an Inhabitant of Zamoskvoréchie* published (*MGL*).
2/15 July	Belínskii's writes his famous letter to Gogol from Salzburg.
Oct.	Publication of Turgénev's 'The Bailiff', 'The Estate Office' (*S* no. 10).
1848	Tatíshchev, *Russian History*, vol. 5 published 98 years after the author's death.
Feb.	Publication of Turgénev's 'Raspberry Water', 'The Country Doctor', 'The Lone Wolf', 'Lebedian', 'Tatiána Borísovna and her Nephew', 'Death' (*S* no. 2).
Sept.	*Chténia* (*Reading*), journal of Moscow University's Society of Russian History and Antiquities, publishes D. I. Gippius's Russian translation of Giles Fletcher's *Of the Rus Commonwealth* (1591). The Buturlín Committee closes the journal and the secretary of the Society, O. M. Bodniánskii, is transferred to Kazán University. (Banned again in 1864, finally published in 1905).
Dec.	Publication of Dostoevskii's *White Nights* (*OZ* no. 12).

1849

Feb. Publication of Turgénev's 'The Hamlet of Shchigrovo Province', 'Chertopkhanov and Nedopiuskin', 'Forest and Steppe' (*S* no. 2).

22 Apr. Arrest of Dostoevskii and other members of the Petrashévskii Circle.

30 Sept. Trial of Dostoevskii (sentenced to death on 16 November).

14 Oct. Première of Turgénev's *The Bachelor*, ATS (published *OZ* no. 9).

23 Nov. Moscow première of Turgénev's *Lunch at the Marshal of Nobility's* (published 1856).

22 Dec. Mock execution of Dostoevskii and the other members of the Petrashévskii Circle.

24 Dec. Dostoevskii leaves for hard labour in prison at Omsk (until 23 Jan. 1854), then service as a soldier in 7th Siberian Infantry Battalion (until July 1859), then exile in Tver (until 16 Dec. 1859).

1850

Jan. Publication of Turgénev's 'The Rendezvous' (*S* no. 1).

Apr. Publication of Turgénev's 'Diary of a Superfluous Man' (*OZ* no. 4).

Nov. Publication of Turgénev's 'The Singers' (*S* no. 11).

1851

18 Jan. Première of Turgénev's *A Girl from the Provinces*, MTM (published *OZ* no. 1).

Feb. Publication of Turgénev's 'Bezhin Meadow' (*S* no. 2).

Mar. Publication of Turgénev's 'Kasian from Fair Springs' (*S* no. 3).

10 Dec. Première of Turgénev's *It breaks where it's thinnest* (flops after three performances) (published *S* 1848 no. 11).

1852

7 Jan. Première of Turgénev's *Impecuniosity*, ATS (published 1846 *OZ* no. 10).

11 Feb. Gógol burns the manuscript of vol. 2 of *Dead Souls*.

21 Feb. Death of Gógol.

18 July Publication of Turgénev's *Huntsman's Sketches*.

Nov. Publication of Tolstoy's *Childhood* (*S* no. 9).

1853

14 Jan. Première of Ostróvskii's *Don't Sit on Another Man's Sledge*, BTM.

12 Feb. Première of Ostróvskii's *A Young Man's Morning*, Teatr-Tsirk (published *M* 22.xi.1850).

Mar. Publication of Tolstoy's 'The Raid' (*S* no. 3).

Apr.	Tiútchev's poems published by I. S. Turgénev.
July	Chernyshévskii joins the staff of *OZ*.
20 Aug.	Première of Ostróvskii's *The Poor Bride*, MTM.

1854

25 Jan.	Première of Ostróvskii's *Poverty is no Crime*, MTM.
Sept.	Publication of Tolstoy's *Boyhood* (*S* no. 9).
3 Dec.	Première of Ostróvskii's *You Can't Live as You Please*, MTM (published *M* 17–18 Sept. 1855).

1855

Jan.	Publication of Turgénev's *A Month in the Country* (*S* no. 1, with cuts by the censor) (première 1872), and of Tolstoy's 'Notes of a Marker' (*S* no. 1).

Alexander II
1855

Apr.	Publication of Tolstoy's 'Felling the Forest' (*S* no. 4).
June	Publication of Tolstoy's 'Sebastopol in December' (*S* no. 6).
Sept.	Publication of Tolstoy's 'Sebastopol in May' (*S* no. 9).
1856	Formation of the Moscow Actors' Circle. Aksákov's *A Family Chronicle* is published in Moscow and a complete version of Lérmontov's *Demon* is published by A. I. Filosófov in Karlsrühe.
Jan.	Publication of Tolstoy's 'Sebastopol in August 1855' (*S* no. 1).
9 Jan.	Première of Ostróvskii's *Your Drink, My Hangover*, MTM.
Jan.–Feb.	Publication of Turgénev's *Rúdin* (*S* nos 1–2).
Apr.	Publication of Tolstoy's 'The Blizzard' (*S* no. 4).
May	Publication of Tolstoy's 'Two Hussars' (*S* no. 5).
Aug.	Publication of Turgénev's 'Lunch at the Marshal of Nobility's' (*S* no. 8) and of the first of M. E. Saltykóv-Shchedrín's *Provincial Sketches* (*RV* vol. 4 book 2–1857, vol. 10 book 1).
Dec.	Publication of Tolstoy's 'The Caucasus Memoirs of an Officer Reduced to the Ranks' sometimes entitled 'Meeting a Moscow Acquaintance in the Detachment' (*BdC* no. 12).

1857

Jan.	Publication of Tolstoy's *Youth* (*S* no. 1).
Mar.	Publication of Tolstoy's 'Song of the Battle on the River Chernyi on 4 August 1855' (*PZ* no. 3).
Sept.	Publication of Tolstoy's 'From the notes of Prince D. Nekliúdov' (*S* no. 9).

Oct.	Publication of Saltykóv-Shchedrín's 'The Bridegroom' (*S* no. 10) and of his 'Pazúkhin's Death' (*RV* vol. 11, book 1).
28 Oct.	Première of Ostróvskii's *A Festive Dream before Dinner*, ATS (published *S* no. 2).
Nov.	Première of Ostróvskii's *Keep it in the Family!* in Irkutsk (St Petersburg première, 1861) (published *M* 1850 no. 6).
Dec.	Publication of Saltykóv-Shchedrín's 'The Arrival of the Inspector' (*RV* book 2).
16 Dec.	Third Department bans performance of Ostróvskii's *A Profitable Post*, scheduled for 20 December.
1858	Herzen publishes Shcherbátov's *On the Corruption of Morals in Russia* in London. Publication of Aksákov's *Years of Childhood* in Moscow and of Goncharóv's *Frigate Pallas*.
Jan.	Publication of Saltykóv-Shchedrín's 'A Christmas Story' (*Atenei* pt. 1, no. 5).
Feb.	Publication of Saltykóv-Shchedrín's 'Provincial Ambition' (*BdC* no. 2).
Aug.	Publication of Tolstoy's 'Albert' (*S* no. 8).
1 Sept.	Première of Ostróvskii's *They Could not Get on*, ATS (published *S* no. 1).
1859	Publication of the monthly journal *Rússkoe slóvo* (*The Russian Word*) (closed 1866).
Jan.	Turgénev's *A Nest of Gentlefolk* and Tolstoy's 'Three Deaths' both published in *S* no. 1.
Jan.–Apr.	Publication of I. A. Goncharóv's *Oblómov* (*OZ* nos 1–4).
Feb.	Publication of Saltykóv-Shchedrín's 'A Happy Life' (*S* no. 2).
Mar.	Publication of Saltykóv-Shchedrín's 'General Zubátov' (*MV* no. 3).
Apr.	Publication of Tolstoy's *Family Happiness* (*RV* nos 7–8).
May	Publication of Saltykóv-Shchedrín's 'Gegemóniev' (*MV* no. 15).
July	Publication of Saltykóv-Shchedrín's 'Mrs. Padeikova' (*RB* no. 16).
23 Oct.	Censors ban production of Ostróvskii's *The School Girl* (première 1862).
Nov.	First concert of the Russian Musical Society, set up by Grand Duchess Eléna Pávlovna and Anton Rubinstein.
Nov.	Publication of Saltykóv-Shchedrín's 'Buried Alive' (*MV* no. 46).

16 Nov.	Première of Ostróvskii's *The Storm*, MTM (published *BdC* 1860 no. 158).
Winter	Tolstoy organizes a school on his estate at Iásnaia Poliána.
16 Dec.	Dostoevskii returns to St Petersburg.
1860	Chaadáev's first *Lettre philosophique* (complete), published by I. S. Gagárin in the French journal *Correspondant*.
Jan.	Publication of Turgénev's *On the Eve* (*RV* no. 1) and of Saltykóv-Shchedrín's 'The Gnashing of Teeth' (*S* no. 1).
Feb.	Publication of Chernyshévskii's translation of J. S. Mill, *Principles of Political Economy* (*S* nos 2–10).
1 Sept.	Publication of Dostoevskii's *Notes from the House of the Dead* (*RM* no. 67; 1861: nos 1, 3, 7; *V* 1861 nos 4, 9–11; 1862, nos 2, 3, 5, 12).
10 Oct.	Première of Ostróvskii's *One Old Friend is Worth Two New Ones*, ATS (published *S* no. 9).
1861	
16 Jan.	Première of Ostróvskii's *Keep it in the Family!*, ATS (published 1850 *M* no. 6).
Jan.–July	Publication of Dostoevskii's *The Insulted and the Injured* (*V* nos 1–7).
Feb.	Publication of Saltykóv-Shchedrín's 'Our Friendly Rubbish' (*S* no. 2).
Oct.	Publication of Saltykóv-Shchedrín's 'Slander' (*S* no. 10).
27 Oct.	Première of Ostróvskii's *Our Own Dogs are Fighting, Don't Bring in any One Else's*, MTM (published *BdC* no. 3).
Nov.	Publication of Saltykóv-Shchedrin's 'Our Silly Business' (*S* no. 11).
1862	First publication of three of Chaadáev's *Lettres philosophiques* (*Oeuvres choisies de Pierre Tchadaïev, publiées pour la première fois par le p. Gagarin, de la Compagnie de Jésus*). The other five were first published in 1935, in Russian translation (*Lituratúrnoe naslédstvo*, nos 22–24), and in the original French only in 1966 (*Forschungen zur osteuropäischen Geschichte*, vol. 2).
27 Jan.	Première of Ostróvskii's *The School Girl*, amateur production, Teátr Peterbúrgskogo Passázha (professional production, 1863).
30 Jan.	Première of Turgénev's *The Lodger*, BTM (published as *Other People's Food*, *S* 1857 no. 3).
Feb.	Publication of Turgénev's *Fathers and Children* (*RV* no. 2).

Apr.	Publication of Saltykóv-Shchedrín's 'Recent Comedies' (*V* no. 4).
27 Apr.	Saltykóv-Shchedrín's 'Silly Dissipation', due for publication in *S* no. 5, banned by the censor. (Published 1910.)
June	Police raid Iásnaia Poliána.
Sept.	Publication of Saltykóv-Shchedrín's 'Our Provincial Day' (*V* no. 9).
20 Sept.	Foundation of the St Petersburg Conservatoire under Anton Rubinstein.
Nov.	Publication of Dostoevskii's 'A Nasty Tale' (*V* no. 11).
14 Dec.	Chernyshévskii begins writing *What is to be Done?* while a prisoner in the Peter-Paul Fortress (completed 4.iv.1863).
1863	Publication of V. I. Dahl's *Explanatory Dictionary of the Living Russian Language* (1863–66) and of Nekrásov's *Frost the Red Nosed*.
1 Jan.	Première of Ostróvskii's *Seek and You shall Find*, ATS (published *V* 1861 no. 9).
Jan.	Publication of Tolstoy's 'The Cossacks' (*RV* no. 1) and of Saltykóv-Shchedrín's *Our Life in Society* (*S* nos 1–5, 9, 11–12; 1864, nos 1–3).
Jan.–Feb.	Publication of Saltykóv-Shchedrín's 'Innocent Stories' (*S* nos 1–2).
Feb.	Publication of Tolstoy's 'Polikúshka' (*RV* no. 2).
Feb.–Mar.	Publication of Dostoevskii's 'Winter Remarks on Summer Impressions' (*V* nos 2–3).
Mar.	Publication of Saltykóv-Shchedrín's 'After the Dinner Party' (*S* no. 3) and of Ostróvskii's *Troubled Times* (*S* no. 3).
Mar.–May	Publication of Chernyshévskii's *What is to be Done?* (*S* nos 3–5).
Sept.	Publication of Saltykóv-Shchedrín's *Pompadours and Pompadourettes* (*S* no. 9; 1864 nos 1, 3, 8; *OZ* 1868 nos 2, 11; 1871 nos 1, 5; 1873 nos 3, 9, 11; 1874 no. 4).
27 Sept.	Première of Ostróvskii's *A Profitable Post*, ATS (published *RB* 1857 no. 1).
2 Oct.	Première of Ostróvskii's *Hard Times*, MTM.
21 Oct.	Première of Ostróvskii's *The School Girl*, MTM (published *BdC* 1859 no. 1).
1864	
Mar.	Publication of Dostoevskii's *Notes from the Underground* (*E* nos 1–2, 4).
9 Oct.	Première of Ostróvskii's *The Jokers*, ATS (published *S* no. 9).

1865

Jan.–Feb.	Publication of Tolstoy's *War and Peace*, part 1 (*RV* nos 1–2).
28 Apr.	Première of Ostróvskii's *The Governor*, MTS (published *S* no. 1).
30 Aug.	The first public performance of Tchaikovsky's music: Johann Strauss the younger conducts Tchaikovsky's *Dances of the Hay Maidens* in Pávlovsk Park.
29 Sept.	Première of Ostróvskii's *In a Lively Place*, MTM (published *S* no. 9).
1866	Publication of Dostoevskii's *The Gambler.*
Jan.	Publication of Dostoevskii's *Crime and Punishment* (*RV* nos 1, 2, 4, 6–8, 11, 12).
Apr.	Première of Ostróvskii's *The Abyss*, MTM (published *SPV* nos 1, 4, 5, 6, 8, Jan.).
3 June	*Sovreménnik* and *Rússkoe slóvo* suppressed.
9 Dec.	Première of Ostróvskii's *Kuzmá Zakhárich Mínin: the Man with a Withered Arm*, ATS (published *S* 1862 no. 1).
1867	
30 Jan.	Première of Ostróvskii's *Dimtri the Pretender and Vasilii Shuiskii*, MTM (published *VE* no. 1).
23 Nov.	Première of Ostróvskii's *Túshino*, ATS (published *Vsemírnyi trud* no. 1).
1868	Publication of Tolstoy's *War and Peace*, 6 vols (Moscow, 1868–69). Vasílii Peróv paints *The Last Inn by the Town Gate* (TGM).
3 Jan.	Première of Ostróvskii's *Vasilísa Melénteva*, MTM (published *VE* no. 2).
Jan.	Saltykóv-Shchedrín becomes editor of *OZ*. Publication of Dostoevskii's *Idiot* (*RV* nos 1, 2, 4–12 and supplement to no. 12 dated 17 Jan. 1869) and of Saltykóv-Shchedrín's 'A New Narcissus' (*OZ* no. 1).
3 Feb.	Nikolai Rubinstein conducts the first performance of Tchaikovsky's Symphony no. 1, *Winter Daydreams*, RMS.
Feb.	Publication of Saltykóv-Shchedrín's *Letters from the Provinces* (*OZ* nos 2, 4, 5, 9, 10; 1869 nos 3, 8, 11; 1870 nos 3, 4, 9).
Mar.	Publication of Tolstoy's 'A Few Words about *War and Peace*' (*RA* no. 3).
1 Nov.	Première of Ostróvskii's *There's enough Stupidity in Every Wise Man*, ATS (published *OZ* no. 11).
1869	Publication of Goncharóv's *The Precipice.*

Jan.	Publication of Saltykóv-Shchedrín's *The Story of a Town* (*OZ* nos 1–4, 9).
15 Jan.	Première of Ostróvskii's *The Passionate Heart*, MTM (published *OZ* no. 1).
30 Jan.	First performance of Tchaikovsky's *Voevóda*, BTM.
Feb.	Publication of Saltykóv-Shchedrín's 'The Tale of How One Peasant Fed Two Generals', the first of his *Fairy Tales* (*OZ* no. 2. Others: *OZ* no. 3; 1880 no. 1; 1884 no. 1; *Sbornik 25 let*, 1884; *Rved* 25 Dec. 1884; 15 Jan., 12 Feb., 13 Mar., 23 Apr., 19 May, 2 June, 23 June 1885; 14 Feb., 7 Sept., 14 Sept., 19 Sept. 1886).
Oct.	Publication of Saltykóv-Shchedrín's *The Gentlemen from Tashkent* (*OZ* nos 10–11; 1870 no. 11; 1871 nos 9, 11; 1872 nos 1, 9).
1870	St Petersburg première of Pushkin's *Borís Godunóv*, with cuts by the censor. M. I. Semévskii publishes an expurgated edition of Shcherbátov, *On the Corruption of Morals in Russia* (written 1786–87) (*RS* 1870–71). Karamzín's *Memoir on Ancient and Modern Russia* (written 1810–11) is published without cuts as a supplement to *RA*. The *Peredvízhniki* (Wanderers) (Miasoédov, Kramskói, Peróv, Ge, Shíshkin, Vasílev, Savrásov, Klodt, Kámenev) form the Society for Travelling Art Exhibitions.
4 Mar.	First performance of Tchaikovsky's *Romeo and Juliet* (first version), Moscow.
22 Mar.	The Mámontovs arrive in Abrámtsevo.
16 Sept.	Première of Ostróvskii's *Easy Money*, ATS (published *OZ* no. 2).
1871	Vasílii Peróv paints his *Portrait of Alexander Ostróvskii* (TGM), and Alexei Savrásov paints *The Rooks have Returned* (TGM). Semévskii publishes a complete edition of A. T. Bólotov's *The Life and Adventures of Andrei Bólotov written by himself for his Descendants* (written 1789–1816) (4 supplements to *RS*, 1871–73).
Jan.	Publication of Dostoevskii's *The Devils* (*RV* nos 1, 2, 4, 7, 9–11; 1872 nos 11–12) and of Saltykóv-Shchedrín's *Summing up* (*OZ* nos 1–4, 8).
7 Oct.	Première of Ostróvskii's *Comes the Reckoning*, MTM (published *OZ* no. 9).
1 Nov.	Première of Ostróvskii's *The Forest*, ATS (published *OZ* no. 1).
28 Nov.	First Exhibition of the *Peredvízhniki*, Academy of Arts.

1872	Peróv paints his *Portrait of Dostoievskii* (TGM). Kramskói paints *Christ in the Wilderness* (TGM). Illarión Priáshnikov paints *Peasants Driving Home* (TGM). Vasilii Vereshchágin paints *The Apotheosis of War* (TGM).
Jan.	Publication of Tolstoy's *Prisoner in the Caucasus*, and of Saltykóv-Shchedrín's *The Petersburg Diary of a Provincial* (*OZ* nos 1–8, 10–12).
13 Jan.	Première of Turgénev's *A Month in the Country*, MTM (flops after five nights) (published 1855 *S* no. 1).
5 Feb.	First performance of Tchaikovsky's *Romeo and Juliet* (second version).
26 Oct.	Première of Ostróvskii's *A Comedian of the Seventeenth Century*, MTM (published *OZ* 1873 no. 2).
Nov.	Publication of Turgénev's *The End of Chertopkhanov* (*VE* no. 11).
1873	Ilia Répin finishes *The Volga Boatmen* (begun 1870) (RMusS) and Vereshchágin paints *Mortally Wounded* (TGM).
1 Jan.	First performance of Rimskii-Korsakov's *The Maid of Pskov*, MTS.
26 Jan.	First performance of Tchaikovsky's Symphony no. 2 (*Little Russian*), Moscow.
11 May	Première of Ostróvskii's *The Snow Maiden*, MTM (published *VE* no. 9).
17 Aug.	Tolstoy's appeal for the Samára famine.
22 Nov.	Première of Ostróvskii's *Late Love*, MTM (published *OZ* 1874 no. 1).
1874	Work begins on Vladímir Sherwood's Historical Museum, Moscow (completed 1883). Mámontov founds the colony of artists in Abrámtsevo.
27 Jan.	First performance of Músorgskii's *Borís Godunóv* (libretto after Pushkin and Karamzín), MTS.
Mar.	Turgénev's *The Living Relics* published in *Clubbing Together. A Literary Miscellany of Works by Russian Writers in Aid of those Suffering from Hunger in Samara Province.*
12 Apr.	First performance of Tchaikovsky's *Oprichnik*, MTS.
28 Nov.	Première of Ostróvskii's *Hard-Earned Bread*, MTM (published *OZ* no. 11).
1875	
Jan.	Publication begins of Tolstoy's *Anna Karénina* (completed Apr. 1877).
Summer	Valentín Seróv's first visit to Abrámtsevo.
Oct.	Publication of Saltykóv-Shchedrín's *The Golovëv Family* (*OZ* nos 10, 12; 1876 nos 3, 5, 8, 12; 1880 no. 5).

13 Oct.	First performance of Tchaikovsky's First Piano Concerto, Boston MA.
7 Nov.	First performance of Tchaikovsky's Symphony no. 3, (*Polish*), RMS.
28 Nov.	Première of Ostróvskii's *The Wealthy Brides*, ATS (published *OZ* 1876 no. 2).
8 Dec.	Première of Ostróvskii's *Wolves and Sheep*, ATS (published *OZ* no. 11).

1876

18 Nov.	Première of Ostróvskii's *Truth is Good, but Happiness is Better*, MTM (published *OZ* 1877 no. 1).
24 Nov.	First performance of Tchaikovsky's *Vakúla the Smith*, MTS.

1877

Kramskói paints his *Portrait of the Poet Nikolái Nekrásov* (TGM).

Feb.	Publication of Saltykóv-Shchedrín's *A Contemporary Idyll* (*OZ* nos 2–4; 1878 nos 2–4; 1882 nos 9–12; 1883 nos 1, 5).
20 Feb.	First performance of Tchaikovsky's *Swan Lake*, BTM.
25 Feb.	First performance of Tchaikovsky's *Francesca da Rimini*, Moscow.
28 Oct.	Première of Ostróvskii and N. Ia. Solovëv's *A Happy Day*, MTM (published *OZ* no. 7).
8 Nov.	Première of Ostróvskii's *The Last Sacrifice*, MTM (published *OZ* 1878 no. 1).
17 Nov.	First performance of Tchaikovsky's *Variations on a Rococo Theme*, Moscow.
26 Dec.	Première of Ostróvskii and Solovëv's *Bulýgin's Wedding*, MTM (published *OZ* 1878 no. 5).

1878

Vasilii Polénov paints *A Moscow Courtyard* (TGM). Shíshkin paints *Rye* (TGM). Victor Vasnetsóv paints *News from the Front* (TGM).

10 Feb.	First performance of Tchaikovsky's Symphony no. 4, Moscow.
Aug.	Publication of Saltykóv-Shchedrín's *The Sanctuary of Mon Repos* (*OZ* no. 8; 1879 nos 2, 8, 9, 11).

1879

Vereshchágin paints *Shipka-Sheinovo: General Skóbelev at Shipka* (TGM).

Late Jan.	Maria Sávina revives Turgénev's *A Month in the Country*, ATS, with great success.
Jan.	Publication of Dostoevskii's *Brothers Karamázov* (*RV* nos 1–2, 4–6, 8–11; 1880 nos 1, 4, 7–11).
29 Mar.	First performance of Tchaikovsky's *Eugene Onégin*, MTM.
2 Nov.	Première of Ostróvskii and Solovëv's *The Savage Woman*, MTM (published *VE* 1880 no. 1).

10 Nov.	Première of Ostróvskii's *The Girl Without a Dowry*, MTM (published *OZ* no. 1).
21 Nov.	Première of Ostróvskii's *A Heart is not a Stone*, ATS (published *OZ* 1880 no. 1).
1880	Vasnetsóv paints *After Prince Igor's Battle with the Polóvtsy* (TGM).
9 Mar.	Chekhov's first short story 'Letter to a Learned Neighbour' published (*Str* no. 10).
6 June	Unveiling of Alexander Opekúshin's Pushkin monument, Moscow (speech by Turgénev).
8 June	Dostoevskii's speech on Pushkin to the Society of Lovers of Russian Literature.
Sept.	Publication of Saltykóv-Shchedrín's *Abroad* (*OZ* nos 9–11; 1881 nos 1, 2, 5, 6).
6 Nov.	Première of Ostróvskii and Solovёv's *It Shines but Gives out No Heat*, MTM (published *Ogonёk* 1881, vol. 5, nos 6–10).
14 Nov.	Première of Ostróvskii's *The Slave Women*, MTM (published *OZ* 1881 no. 1).
26 Dec.	Première of Ostróvskii and P. M. Nevézhin's *Caprice*, MTM (published *OZ* 1881 no. 3).
1881	Répin paints his *Portrait of Músorgskii* (TGM). Vasilii Súrikov paints *The Morning of the Execution of the Stréltsy* (TGM).
31 Jan.	First performance of Tchaikovsky's Symphony no. 2 (*Little Russian*) (second version).

Alexander III
1881

July	Saltykóv-Shchedrín's *Letters to Auntie* published (*OZ* nos 7–9, 11–12; 1882 nos 1–5).
31 Oct./12 Nov.	First performance of Tchaikovsky's Second Piano Concerto in G, op. 44, New York.
22 Nov.	First performance of Tchaikovsky's Violin Concerto in D, op. 35, Vienna.
20 Dec.	Première of Ostróvskii's *Talent and its Admirers*, MTM (published *OZ* 1882 no. 1).
1882	Vasnetsóv paints *The Knight at the Crossroads* (RMusS).
29 Jan.	First performance of Rimskii-Korsakov's *The Snow Maiden*, MTS.
17 Mar.	First performance of Glazunóv's Symphony no. 1, conducted by Balákirev, Free Music School.
8 Aug.	First performance of Tchaikovsky's *1812*, Moscow.
21 Nov.	Première of Ostróvskii and Nevézhin's *Plus ça change . . .*, MTM (published 1951).

26 Dec.	Première of Ostróvskii's *The Handsome Man*, MTM (published *OZ* 1883 no. 1).
1883	Nikolai Iaroshénko paints *The Girl Student* (Kiev Museum of Russian Art). Répin finishes his *Easter Procession in Kursk* (begun 1880) (TGM), and paints his portraits of Pavel Tretiakóv (TGM) and of Vladimir Stásov (RMusS). Work begins on A. Parland's Church of the Resurrection of the Saviour on the Blood, on the spot where Alexander II was assassinated (completed 1907).
23 Nov.	First performance of Tchaikovsky's Symphony no. 1 (third version), Moscow.
1884	Iaroshénko paints his *Portrait of the Actress Strépetova* (TGM). Work begins on M. Chichagóv's Korsh Theatre, Moscow (completed 1885).
15 Jan.	Première of Ostróvskii's *Guilty but Innocent*, MTM (published *OZ* 1888 no. 1).
3 Feb.	First performance of Tchaikovsky's *Mazépa*, BTM.
20 Apr.	*Otéchestvennye zapíski* closed down.
Summer	Seróv paints *The Amazon* (private collection, Moscow).
5 July	125 works by various authors removed from public libraries.
1885	Répin paints *Ivan the Terrible and His Son Ivan, 16 Nov. 1581* (TGM). M. P. Beliáev founds the Russian Symphony Concerts.
9 Jan.	Première of Ostróvskii's *Not of This World*, ATS (published *RMy* 1885 no. 2). Mámontov's Krotkóv Private Opera Company opens at the Lianozov Theatre, Moscow, with a performance of Dargomýzhkii's *Rusálka*.
20 Sept.	Censor bans Chekhov's *On the High Road* (published and premièred, 1914).
1886	Vasnetsóv paints *My Native Land*, (TGM). Publication of the first collection of Chekhov's writings, *Speckled Stories*.
21 Feb.	First performance of Músorgskii's *Khovánshchina*.
11 Mar.	First performance of Tchaikovsky's Manfred Symphony, Moscow.
19 Apr.	First performance of Tchaikovsky's *Romeo and Juliet* (third version), Tiflis.
Early summer	Seróv paints *At the Window* (TGM).
15 Oct.	First Russian Symphony Concerts, Konónov Hall. (Also 22, 29 Oct. and 5 Nov. 1 and 3 conducted by Rimskii-Korsakov, 2 and 4 conducted by G. O. Dütsh.)
Autumn/winter	Seróv's paintings of Abrámtsevo (TGM).
22 Dec.	Concert organized by Beliáev to honour Rimskii-Korsakov's 25 years as a musician.

1887	Súrikov paints *The Boyarina Morózova* (TGM). Répin paints his *Portait of the composer Mikhaíl Glínka.* Publication of the second collection of Chekhov's stories, *In the Twilight.* Closure of Mámontov's Krotkóv Private Opera Troupe.
Jan.	Publication of Tolstoy's *Power of Darkness.* Censor forbids performances.
Sept.	Seróv paints his *Young Girl with Apricots* (TGM).
Oct.	Publication of Saltykóv-Shchedrín's *Old Times at Poshekhonie* (*VE* nos 10–12; 1888 nos 3, 4, 9–12; 1889 nos 1–3).
19 Nov.	Première of Chekhov's *Ivánov* (first version), Korsh Theatre, Moscow (published *MTB*, 24 Jan. 1888).
1888	Iaroshénko paints *Life is Everywhere* (TGM). Répin completes *They did not expect him* (begun 1884) (TGM).
19 Feb.	Première of Chekhov's *Swan Song*, Korsh Theatre, Moscow (published *Sezón*, Jan. 1887).
22 Feb.	Première of Tolstoy's *Power of Darkness*, Théatre Libre Antoine, Paris (Russian première 1896).
28 Oct.	Première of Chekhov's *The Bear*, Korsh Theatre, Moscow, (published *NV* no. 4491, 30 Aug. 1888).
5 Nov.	First performance of Tchaikovsky's Symphony no. 5.
1889	Sergéi Ivánov paints *On the Road: Death of a Migrant Peasant* (TGM). Mikhail Nésterov paints *The Boy Bartholomew's Vision* (TGM) and completes *The Hermit* (begun 1888) (TGM). Work begins on Alexander Pomerántsev's Upper Trading Rows (known as GUM in Soviet times), Moscow (completed 1893).
31 Jan.	Première of Chekhov's *Ivánov* (revised version), ATS (published *SV* no. 3).
12 Apr.	Première of Chekhov's *The Proposal*, Stolíchnyi artistícheskii kruzhók (published *MTB*, Dec. 1888).
1 Oct.	Première of Chekhov's *A Tragic Role*, German Club.
30 Dec.	Première of Tolstoy's *The Fruits of Enlightenment*, in a private house (published Moscow, 1891).
1890	Nikolai Ge paints *What is Truth?* (TGM). Vrúbel paints *Seated Demon* (TGM). Work begins on D. Chichagóv's Moscow City Duma (completed 1892). Censor bans Tolstoy's *Kreutzer Sonata.*
3 Jan.	First performance of Tchaikovsky's *Sleeping Beauty*, MTS.
24 June	Publication of Chekhov's 'From Siberia' (*NV* 55142–47 (24–29 June), 5168 (20 July), 5172 (24 July), 5202 (23 Aug.)).

23 Oct.	First performance of A. Borodín's *Prince Igor*, MTS.
28 Nov.	First performance of Tchaikovsky's string sextet in D, op. 70, *Souvenir de Florence*.
7 Dec.	First performance of Tchaikovsky's *The Queen of Spades*, MTS.
18 Dec.	Chaliápin's first operatic role: 'stolnik' in Moniuszko's *Halka*, Entreprise Semënova-Samárskogo, Ufá.
27 Dec.	Première of Chekhov's *The Wood Demon*, Abrámova's Theatre, Moscow.
1891	Répin completes *The Zaporózhian Cossacks Write to the Turkish Sultan* (begun 1880) (RMusS).
13 Apr.	S. A. Tolstáia's audience with Alexander III to ask for a relaxation of censorship over her husband's 'Kreutzer Sonata' (published 1890 in his *Collected Works*, vol. 13, but refused separate publication).
Autumn	Seróv paints his *Portrait of Konstantín Alexéevich Koróvin* (TGM).
6 Nov.	First performance of Tchaikovsky's *Voevóda*, symphonic ballad, Moscow.
1892	Ge paints *The Crucifixion* (Musée d'Orsay, Paris). Isaak Levitán paints *Evening Bells* (TGM). Publication of Dmítri Merezhkóvskii's *Symbols* and of Maxim Gorky's *Makar Chudra*, the first of Gorky's works to be published, Tiflis.
20 Oct.	First performance of Rimskii-Korsakov's *Mlada*, MTS.
6 Dec.	First performance of Tchaikovsky's *Nutcracker*, MTS.
1893	Nikolai Kuznetsóv paints his *Portrait of Tchaikovsky* (TGM). Work begins on F. Shékhtel's house for Z. G. Morózova (completed 1896).
17 Apr.	First performance of Rachmaninov's *Aleko*, Moscow.
Oct.	Publication of Chekhov's *Sakhalín Island* (*RMy* nos 10–12; 1894 nos 2, 3, 5–7. 19 chapters. Chapters 20–24 added on publication as a book, Moscow, 1895. Chapter 22 published separately in *Help to the Hungry*, Moscow, 1892).
16 Oct.	First performance of Tchaikovsky's Symphony no. 6 (*Pathétique*).
25 Oct.	Death of Tchaikovsky.
1894	Levitán paints *Above Eternal Peace* (TGM). Seróv completes *Alexander III and his family* (begun 1892) (lost).
Early	Seróv paints *At the Battle of Kulikóvo* (RMusS).
20 Mar.	First performance of Rachmaninov's *The Rock*, Moscow.
Mar.–June	Seróv paints his *Portrait of N. S. Leskóv* (TGM).

Nicholas II

1895	Nikolai Bogdánov-Bélskii paints *Mental Arithmetic* (TGM). Censor allows performances of Tolstoy's *Power of Darkness*, except in 'popular' theatres.
7 Jan.	First performance of Tchaikovsky's *Third Piano Concerto.*
15 Mar.	First performance of Rachmaninov's *First Symphony*, St Petersburg.
Summer	Seróv paints *In Summer* (TGM), and *Portrait of Maríia Iákovlevna Lvóva* (private collection, Paris).
Oct.	Seróv paints *October, Domotkanovo* (TGM).
1896	Nízhnii Nóvgorod Exhibition. Vrúbel paints *The Fortune Teller* (TGM). Publication of Shcherbátov, *On the Corruption of Morals in Russia* (complete text). Shékhtel builds his house for A. V. Morózov, Moscow. Reopening of Mámontov's Private Opera Company.
Autumn	Seróv paints *Peasant Woman in a Cart* (RMusS).
17 Oct.	Première of Chekhov's *The Seagull*, ATS (published *RMy* 1896 no. 12).
1897	Bogdánov-Bélskii paints *At the School Door* (RMusS). Nésterov paints *The Youth of St Sergius of Radónezh* (Samára Art Museum). Vrúbel paints his *Portrait of S. I. Mámontov* (TGM).
Jan.	Diághilev's exhibition of German and British watercolours, Stieglitz Museum (Hermann, Bartels, Liebermann, Lavery, Austen-Brown, Guthrie, Paterson).
Early	Seróv's portraits of Maríia Fĕdorovna Morózova (RMusS), and of Grand Duke Pável Alexandrovich (TGM).
22 June	At a meeting in the *Slaviánskii Bazár* Restaurant, Moscow, Stanislávskii and Nemiróvich-Dánchenko decide to found the Moscow Arts Theatre (MKhaT).
Oct.	Diághilev's exhibition of Scandinavian painters (Thaulow, Werenskiold, Zorn), Society for the Encouragement of the Arts.
30 Dec.	First performance of Rimskii-Korsakov's *Sadko*, Mámontov's Private Opera, Soldóvnikov Theatre, Moscow.
1898	Vasnetsóv paints *Bogatýrs* (TGM).
15 Jan.	Diághilev's exhibition of Russian and Finnish artists (Koróvin, Levitán, Seróv, Sómov, Benois, Blomstedt, Gallen-Kallela, Edelfeldt), Stieglitz Museum.
Early	Seróv paints *In the Village: Peasant Woman with a Horse* (TGM).
Feb.–Mar.	Seróv paints his portrait of Rimskii-Korsakov (TGM).

5 Apr.	Publication of Leonid Andréev's 'Bargamot and Garaska' (*Kurér*).
14 Oct.	Première of Tolstoy's *Tsar Fëdor* marks the opening of MKhaT.
10 Nov.	Publication of the first two issues of Diághilev's *Mir iskússtva* (dated Jan. 1899) (closed autumn 1904).
1899	Levitán paints *Twilight: Haystacks* (TGM). Seróv paints *Children. Sásha and Iúra Seróv* (RMusS). Súrikov paints *Suvórov's Army Crossing the Alps in 1799* (RMusS). Work begins on William Walcot's Hotel Metropol, Moscow (ceramic panel by Vrúbel) (completed 1904). Tolstoy's *Resurrection* published with illustrations by Leonid Pasternak (*Niva*).
22 Jan.	Diághilev's International Exhibition of Paintings (The First *Mir iskússtva* Exhibition), Stieglitz Museum.
11 Sept.	Arrest of Sávva Mámontov on charges of misappropriation of funds.
26 Oct.	Première of Chekhov's *Uncle Ványa*, MKhaT (published 1897).
1900	Vrúbel paints *The Swan Princess* (TGM). Work begins on Shékhtel's house for S. P. Riabushínskii, Moscow (completed 1902). Permission is given for the separate publication of Tolstoy's 'Kreutzer Sonata'.
Jan.	Second *Mir iskússtva* exhibition, Stieglitz Museum.
Apr.	Successful Russian participation in the *Exposition Universelle*, Paris.
June	Seróv paints his portrait of Nicholas II. Nicholas II agrees to subsidize *Mir iskússtva* (15,000 rubles per year).
28 Nov.	Première of Chekhov's *The Wedding* and *The Jubilee*, Society for Art and Literature at the Moscow Sporting Club (published Moscow, Oct. 1890 and May 1892).
1901	Shékhtel builds the Russian Pavilion at the Glasgow Exhibition. Publication of *Art Treasures of Russia*, ed. A. Benois.
Jan.	Third *Mir iskússtva* exhibition, Academy of Arts.
31 Jan.	Première of Chekhov's *Three Sisters*, MKhaT (published *RMy* 1901 no. 2).
27 Oct.	First performance of Rachmaninov's *Second Piano Concerto*, Moscow.
1902	Léon Bakst paints *The Supper* (RMusS). Work begins on G. Baranóvskii's Eliséev building, Névskii Prospékt (completed 1904) and on P. Siuzor's Singer building, Névskii Prospékt (completed 1904). Shékhtel builds the Moscow Arts Theatre and the Iaroslavl Railway

	Station, Moscow. Vasnetsóv builds the Tretiakóv Gallery, Moscow.
Mar.–Apr.	Fourth *Mir iskússtva* exhibition.
Spring	Seróv paints his portrait of Mikhaíl Abrámovich Morózov (TGM).
18 Dec.	Première of Maxim Gorky's *Lower Depths*, MKhaT.
1903	Répin paints his portrait of Pobedonóstsev (RMusS). Moscow Historical Museum publishes a facsimile of Griboedov's manuscript of *Woe from Wit*.
Feb.–Apr.	Fifth *Mir iskússtva* exhibition.
Sept.	Seróv paints his portraits of F. F. Sumarókov-Élston, F. F. Iusúpov and of Z. N. Iusúpova (RMusS).
Dec.–Jan.	First exhibition of the *Union of Russian Artists*, Moscow.
1904	Mikhail Lariónov paints *Rain* (Musée Pompidou). Seróv paints his *Portrait of Sergei Diághilev* (RMusS). Work begins on Alexander Gogen's Kshesínskaia house (completed 1906). S. Rachmaninov appointed conductor of BTM (until 1906).
17 Jan.	Première of Chekhov's *The Cherry Orchard*, MKhaT.
Jan.	Publication of *Vésy* (*The Scales*), symbolist magazine (closed 1909).
May.	*Crimson Rose* exhibition in Sarátov (Borísov-Musátov, Vrúbel, Kuznetsóv).
1 Oct.	Rimskii Korsakov's *May Night* opens S. I. Zimín's private opera, Moscow (closed 1917) STM.
13 Dec.	Isadora Duncan dances at the Hall of the Nobility. (Second performance, 16 Dec.)
1905	Work begins on S. Maliútin and N. Zhúkov's Pértsov apartment house, Moscow (completed 1907).
Jan.	Second exhibition of the *Union of Russian Artists*.
7 Jan.	Russian artists publish a letter in support of *zémstvos* (*Rved.*).
9 Jan.	Seróv and Polénov witness the slaughter from the windows of the Academy of Arts.
10 Jan.	Stravínskii arrested during student demonstration.
18 Feb.	Seróv and Polénov demand the resignation of Grand Duke Vladimir Alexandrovich from the presidency of Academy of Arts.
6 Mar.	Diághilev's historical exhibition of Russian portraits, Tauride Palace.
10 Mar.	Seróv resigns from Academy of Arts.
16 Mar.	Rimskii-Korsakov's open letter to the director of the Conservatoire.
19 Mar.	Rimskii-Korsakov dismissed from the Conservatoire.

27 Mar.	First performance of Rimskii-Korsakov's *Kashchei the Immortal*, Kommissarzhévskaia Theatre.
Apr.	Z. Grzhébin's magazine *Zhúpel* (banned after three issues).
20 Apr.	Fokine's first ballet productions: *Acis and Galatea* and *Polka with a Little Ball*, MTS.
July	Seróv's bitter paintings on the January massacres reproduced in *Zhúpel*.
Sept.	Seróv paints his *Portrait of Maxim Gorky* (Gorky Museum, Moscow).
Nov.	Dobuzhínskii's painting *October Idyll* reproduced in *Zhupel*.
Dec.	Seróv's painting *Well done, my Brave Boys! Where is your Glory Now?* reproduced in *Zhúpel* (RMusS).
1906	Leon Bakst paints his *Portrait of Zinaída Gíppius* (TGM). Dobuzhínskii completes painting *Man in Glasses* (begun 1905). Anna Akhmátova's first published poem, *On his hand are many shining rings*, appears in *Sirius*, ed. Gumilëv, Paris.
Jan.	First issue of Nikolái Riabushínskii's art journal *The Golden Fleece* (closed 1910).
6 Oct.–15 Nov.	Diághilev's exhibition of Russian painting, Salon d'Automne, Grand Palais, Paris.
30 Dec.	Première of Alexander Blok's *The Showman*, Kommissarzhévskaia's Theatre, (published *Fakél* (*The Torch*), April).
1907	Alexandre Benois paints *Parade in the Reign of Paul I* (RMusS). Sómov paints his *Portrait of Alexander Blok* (TGM). Publication of Sologúb's *The Petty Demon*.
10 Feb.	Première of the ballet *Chopiniana*, MTS.
Mar.	First exhibition by the Symbolist *Blue Rose* group.
Apr.	Publication of Blok's *The King on the Square* (*Zolotóe runó*, no. 4).
27 Apr.	First performance of Stravínskii's Symphony no. 1 in E Flat.
3/16 May	Diághilev's *Concerts historiques russes* (16, 19, 23, 26, 30 May), Théâtre National de l'Opéra, Paris.
25 Nov.	First performance of Cherepnín's *Le Pavillon d'Armide*, MTS.
12 Dec.	Première of Leonid Andréev's *The Life of Man*, MKhaT.
27 Dec.–15 Jan.	*Stefanos/Wreath* Exhibition, Stróganov School, Moscow.
1908	Russia's first feature film: Alexander Drankov, *Sténka Rázin* (score by M. Ippolítov-Ivánov). First showing of Alexander Khanzhónkov's film, *Drama in a Gypsy Camp*. Publication of Leoníd Adréev's 'The Seven who were hanged'.

26 Jan.	First performance of Rachmaninov's *Second Symphony*, St Petersburg.
24 Mar.	*Venók/Wreath* Exhibition.
Apr.	Publication of the satirical weekly *Satirikon* (closed 1913).
5 Apr.–11 May	*Golden Fleece* Exhibition, Moscow.
6/19 May	Diághilev produces Músorgskii's *Borís Godunóv* (with Chaliapin singing the lead), Théâtre National de l'Opéra, Paris.
5 June	Censor bans Rimskii-Korsakov's *Le Coq d'Or.*
30 Sept.	Première of Maurice Maeterlinck's *L'oiseau bleu*, MKhaT (Stanislávskii and Nemiróvich-Dánchenko's last joint production).
20 Dec.	Ida Rubinstein's performance of Oscar Wilde's *Salome*, St Petersburg Conservatoire.
1909	Vasilii Kandínskii paints *Cupolas* (*Destiny: the Red Wall*) (Kustódiev Museum, Ástrakhan). Zinaida Serebriakóva paints *Self-Portrait at Toilette* (TGM). A. Erikhson builds the *Iar* restaurant, Moscow. A. Bélyi's *The Silver Dove* is published (*Vésy*).
Spring	Seróv paints *Anna Pávlova in Les Sylphides* (reproduced on the poster for the *Ballets russes* season in Paris) (RMusS).
13/19 May– 20 May/2 June	First of Diághilev's *saisons russes*, Théatre du Châtelet, Paris:
6/19 May	Cherepnín, *Le pavillon d'Armide*, Borodín, *The Polovtsian Dances*, Glínka, *Ruslán and Liudmílla*, Tchaikovsky and others, *Le Festin*, Théâtre du Châtelet, Paris.
12/25 May	Rimskii-Korsakov, *Ivan the Terrible* (*Pskovitianka*), Théâtre du Châtelet, Paris.
20 May/2 June	Chopin, *Les Sylphides*, Árenskii, *Cleopatra*, Glínka, *Ruslán and Liudmílla* (Act 1), Théâtre du Châtelet, Paris.
25 May/7 June	Alexander Seróv, *Judith*, Théâtre du Châtelet, Paris.
7 Oct.	Première of Rimskii-Korsakov's *Le Coq d'Or*, Soldóvnikov Theatre, Moscow.
Oct.	*Apollón*, ed. by Sergei Makóvskii, journal of the Acmeists (monthly until 1918).
15/28 Nov.	First performance of Rachmaninov's *Third Piano Concerto*, New York.
1910	Kandínskii paints *The Lake* (TGM). Teffi's *First Book of Humorous Stories* is published.
21 Feb.	First performance of Prokófiev's *First Piano Sonata*, Moscow.
7 Mar.–11 Apr.	First exhibition of the *Union of Youth* (David Burliúk, Chagall, Exter, Filónov, Kliun, Malévich, Rózanova, Matvejs, Tátlin, Udaltsóva) (twice yearly until 1913).

7/20 May	Diághilev produces *Carnaval* (Schumann, Glazunóv, Liádov, Rimskii-Korsakov, Cherepnín), Theater des Westens, Berlin.
22 May/4 June	Diághilev produces Rimskii-Korsakov's *Sheherazade*, Théâtre National de l'Opéra, Paris.
June	Seróv paints his *Portrait of Ida Rubinstein* (RMusS).
5/18 June	Diághilev produces Adam's *Giselle*, Académie Nationale de Musique, Paris.
12/25 June	Diághilev produces Strávinskii's *Firebird* and *Les Orientales* (Árensky, Borodín, Glazunóv, Grieg, orchestrated by Strávinskii), Théâtre National de l'Opéra, Paris.
Sept.	Publication of Saltykóv-Shchedrín's 'Silly Dissipation' (censored 1862) (*Niva* no. 9).
22 Nov.	First performance of Prokófiev's *Dreams*, St Petersburg.
10 Dec.–11 Jan.	First *Bubnóvyi valét* exhibition, Moscow (Kandínskii, Jawlensky, Lariónov, Goncharóva, the Burliúk brothers, Malévich) (yearly until 1917).
1911	First showing of Iákov Protozánov's film, *The Prisoner's Song*. Lariónov paints his *Portrait of Vladimir Tátlin* (Centre Pompidou, Paris), and his *Soldier in a Wood* (Scottish Gallery of Modern Art, Edinburgh). Tátlin paints *Self-Portrait as a Sailor* (RMusS). Natalia Goncharóva paints *The Washerwomen* (RMusS). Malévich paints *Portrait of Ivan Kliun* (RMusS). Serebriakóva paints *Girl with a Candle* (RMusS).
6 Jan.	Scandal of Chaliápin and Maríinskii chorus 'kneeling to the Tsar' after a performance of *Borís Godunóv*.
25 Jan.	Nijinsky dismissed from the Imperial Theatres after a member of the Imperial family complained that he was 'insufficiently dressed' in *Giselle* (Mariinksii Theatre, 24 Jan.).
Mar.	First performance of Skriábin's *Prometheus*, Moscow.
Apr.	Goncharóva and Lariónov form the *Donkey's Tail* Group.
6/19 Apr.	Diághilev produces Weber's *Le Spectre de la Rose* (orchestrated by Berlioz), Casino de Monte-Carlo.
13/26 Apr.	Diághilev produces Cherepnín's *Narcisse*, Théâtre de Monte-Carlo.
24 May/6 June	Diághilev produces Rimskii-Korsakov's *Sadko*, Théâtre du Châtelet, Paris.
31 May/13 June	Diághilev produces Stravinsky's *Petrúshka*, Théâtre du Châtelet, Paris.
Sept.	Publication of N. G. Chernyshévskii's *Memoirs* (written 1883–86) (*Sovreménnyi mir* (*The Contemporary World*) nos 9–11).

23 Sept.	Première of Tolstoy's *The Living Corpse*, MKhaT (published *RSl*).
Oct.–Nov.	Matisse visits Moscow and St Petersburg at the invitation of Sergei Shchúkin.
17/30 Nov.	Diághilev produces Tchaikovsky's *Swan Lake*, Royal Opera House, Covent Garden.
Dec.	*Donkey's Tail* breaks with *Jack of Diamonds*.
1912	Alexandra Exter paints *A Bank of the Seine* (Iároslavl Art Museum). Boris Kustódiev paints *Merchant Women* (Kiev Museum of Russian Art). Lariónov paints *Blue Rayonism* (Private collection, Paris). Malévich paints *The Knife Grinder* (Yale University). Kuzmá Petróv-Vódkin paints *The Red Horse takes a Bath* (TGM). Olga Rózanova paints *The Oil Stove* (TGM). Serebriakóva paints *Village of Neskuchnoe* (RMusS). Akhmátova's *Evening* is published.
11 Mar.–8 Apr.	*Donkey's Tail* exhibition, Moscow (Lariónov, Goncharóva, Malévich and Tátlin).
Apr.	First issue of *Soiúz molodézhi/Union of Youth*.
30 Apr./13 May	Diághilev produces Reynaldo Hahn's *Le Dieu Bleu*, Théâtre du Châtelet, Paris.
7/20 May	Diághilev produces Balákirev's *Thamar*, Théâtre du Châtelet, Paris.
16/29 May	Diághilev produces Debussy's *L'Après-Midi d'un Faune*, Théâtre du Châtelet, Paris.
26 May/8 June	Diághilev produces Ravel's *Daphnis and Chloë*, Théâtre du Châtelet, Paris.
25 July	First performance of Prokófiev's *First Piano Concerto*, Moscow.
Nov.	M. I. Teréshchenko sets up *Sírin* publishing house.
Dec.	Futurist manifesto, *A Slap in the Face for Public Taste*, marks the formation of the *Hylea* Group.
1913	Goncharóva paints *Aeroplane above a Train* (Kazan Art Museum). Kandínskii paints *Composition No. 6* (Hermitage) and *Composition No. 7* (TGM). Malévich paints *An Englishman in Moscow* (Stedelijk Museum, Amsterdam). Serebriakóva paints *The Bathhouse* (RMusS). Osip Mandelshtám's *Stone* is published, as is, for the first time, the complete text of Griboédov's *Woe from Wit* (written 1825).
Jan.	Diághilev produces Tchaikovsky's *L'Oiseau d'or*, Vienna Opera.
Feb.	Première of Blok's *The Unknown Woman*, The Young Actors' Studio, Moscow Literary Circle (published *Vesy* 1907 nos 5–7).

24 Mar.–7 Apr.	Lariónov's exhibition *Mishén/Target* (children's drawings, Chagall, Pirosmanashvili) and launches his Rayonist manifesto.
Apr.	Boris Pasternak's first published poems in *Lirika* miscellany.
2/15 May	Diághilev produces Debussy's *Jeux*, Théâtre des Champs-Elysées, Paris.
16/29 May	Diághilev produces Stravínskii's *The Rite of Spring*, Théâtre des Champs-Elysées, Paris.
23 May/5 June	Diághilev produces Músorgskii's *Khovánshchina*, Théâtre des Champs-Elysées, Paris.
30 May/12 June	Diághilev produces Florent Schmitt's *La Tragédie de Salomé*, Théâtre des Champs-Elysées, Paris.
Aug.	Publication of Blok's *Róza i krest* (*Sirin* no. 1), and of Andrei Bélyi's *Peterbúrg* (*Sirin* nos 1–3).
23 Aug.	First performance of Prokófiev's *Second Piano Concerto*, Pávlovsk.
30 Nov.	First performance of Rachmaninov's *The Bells*, St Petersburg.
2 Dec.	Première of Maiakóvskii's *Vladimir Maiakovskii*, Luna-Park Theatre.
3 Dec.	Première of Matiúshin's opera *Victory over the Sun* (text by Khlebnikov and Kruchënykh), Luna-Park Theatre.
Dec.	Publication of Pasternak's *Twin in the Storm Clouds*.
Dec.?	Victor Shklovskii delivers his lecture 'Resurrection of the Word' at the *Stray Dog* nightclub (published in 1914 as a pamphlet).
1914	Nathan Altman paints his *Portrait of Anna Akhmátova* (RMusS). Pavel Filónov paints *Shrovetide Carnival* (RMusS). Serebriakóva paints *At Breakfast* (TGM). Roman Klein builds the Coliseum Cinema, Moscow. Kruchënykh and Khlébnikov's *Te li le*, illustrated by Rózanova, and Akhmátova's *Rosary* are published.
3/16 Apr.	Diághilev produces Schumann's *Papillons* (orchestrated by Cherepnín), Casino de Monte-Carlo.
1/14 May	Diághilev produces Richard Strauss's *The Legend of Joseph*, Théâtre National de l'Opéra, Paris.
11/24 May	Diághilev produces Rimskii-Korsakov's *Le Coq d'Or*, Théâtre National de l'Opéra, Paris.
13/26 May	Diághilev produces Stravínskii's *Le Rossignol*, Théatre National de l'Opéra, Paris.
19 May/2 June	Diághilev produces Steinberg's *Midas*, Théâtre National de l'Opéra, Paris.
25 May/6 June	Diághilev produces Borodín's *Prince Igor*, Theatre Royal, Drury Lane, London.

13/26 June	Diághilev produces Rímskii-Kórsakov's *May Night*, Theatre Royal, Drury Lane, London.
July	Première of Chekhov's *On the High Road*, Malákhovskii Theatre, near Moscow (written 1884; banned 1885; published Moscow 1914).
1915	Marc Chagall paints *The Poet Reclining* (Tate Gallery, London). Exter paints *Town at Night* (RMusS). Filónov paints *Three at Table* (RMusS). Ivan Kliun paints *Suprematism* (TGM). Liubóv Popóva paints *Violin* (TGM) and *The Philosopher* (RMusS). Serebriakóva paints *Harvesting* (Odessa Picture Gallery). Ivan Búnin's *The Gentleman from San Francisco* is published.
10 Jan.	Première of Fokine's ballet, *The Dream* (music by Glínka), MTS.
Feb.	*Tramway V: First Futurist Exhibition*, organized by Ivan Puni.
10 Mar.	First performance of Rachmaninov's *Vespers*, Moscow.
Sept.	Publication of Maiakóvskii's *A Cloud in Trousers*.
24 Oct.	First performance of Prokófiev's *Simfonietta in A major*, Petrograd.
28 Nov.	Fokine's charity ballet performance for war orphans.
Dec.	*0.10. The Last Futurist Painting Exhibition* featuring Malévich's Suprematist paintings. Publication of the second enlarged edition of Mandelshtám's *Stone*.
7/20 Dec.	Diághilev produces Rimskii-Korsakov's *Soleil de Nuit*, Grand Théâtre, Geneva.
1916	Dobuzhínskii paints *The Kiss* (Ókunev Collection). Kustódiev paints *Shrove Tuesday* (TGM). Malévich paints *Supremus No. 56* (RMusS). Nésterov completes *The Land of Russia* (*The People's Soul*) (begun 1914) (TGM). Kruchënykh's *War*, illustrated by Rózanova, is published.
16 Jan.	First performance of Prokófiev's *Scythian Suite*, Petrograd.
Feb.	Publication of Maiakóvskii's *The Spinal Flute*.
Mar.	Tátlin's exhibition *Magazín/The Shop* (featuring Ródchenko's paintings).
12/25 Aug.	Diághilev produces Fauré's *Las Meniñas* and Liádov's *Kikimora*, Teatro Eugenia-Victoria, San Sebastián.
10/23 Oct.	Diághilev produces Richard Strauss's *Till Eulenspiegel*, Manhattan Opera House, New York.
1917	First performance of Prokófiev's 'Akhmátova songs' (5 Feb.).

SECTION THREE

Nationalities

3.1 The Baltic States

Peter I

1710   Livonia and Estonia incorporated into Russian Empire, retaining charters and privileges.

1721   Treaty of Nystad confirms acquisition of Livonia and Estonia (30 Aug.).

Elizabeth

1750   Baltic nobility forbidden to serve in foreign (i.e. Prussian) armies.

Catherine II

1762   George Browne becomes governor of Livonia. Catherine confirms Livonian privileges.

1765   Patent defining status of peasantry (12 Apr.). Peasants guaranteed ownership of movable property. Money dues not to be levied, labour dues to be levied at the discretion of landowners, who must publish norms by 1.viii.1765, according to the amount of cultivated land. Peasants granted access to lower courts (*Ordnungsgericht*), and could complain against landowners.

1775   George Browne becomes governor of Livonia and Estonia.

1776–77   Prosecution of Major von Klodt and his wife for torturing a ten-year-old serf-girl to death.

1777   The sale, gift or mortgaging of Livonian feudal land is forbidden (14 Feb.).

1779   Livonian nobles petition Catherine to recognize all Livonian land as allodial.

Aug.   Governor George Browne presents selected Baltic nobles with plan to introduce 1775 statutes into Baltic.

7 Nov.   C. H. von Rosenkampf for Livonia and G. R. von Ulrich for Estonia petition Catherine against the introduction of the statutes of 1775.

1781   In the autumn, the Senate decrees that a census must take place in the Baltic every 20 years, as in the rest of Russia. Towards the end of the year, C. H. von Rosenkampf is arrested for embezzlement.

1782	Browne is ordered to divide Livonia and Estonia into *uézdy* (3 Dec.).
1783	
3 May	Distinction between feudal tenure and allodial land abolished. Poll tax introduced.
29 Oct.	New Institutions based on 1775 statutes inaugurated in Riga.
10 Dec.	New institutions inaugurated in Réval.
1784	Catherine orders that assessors to higher and lower summary courts should not be nobles but 'village dwellers', and confirms the right of peasants to complain about their masters (4 Sept.).
1785	Charter to the Nobility alters legal foundation of government and nobility in Livonia. Followed by much noble protest.
1786	
7 Aug.	Catherine orders the immediate implementation of the Charter of Nobility.
14 Aug.	*Landräte, Landtag* and *Landrat* College abolished.
1792	Governor George Browne dies in office.

Alexander I

1804	Serfs in Livonia no longer personally dependent on their owners, are permanently attached to their allotments, have their property rights recognized and their obligations towards the estate owners defined (as are the latter's powers over them) (20 Feb.).
1807	Livonian pattern of emancipation is extended to Estonia, except Kurland, in a form more unfavourable to the peasantry (27 Aug.).
1807–16	Agrarian depression in the Baltic provinces.
1816	Personal freedom is conferred on the peasants of Estonia, but they are deprived of their allotments, have their freedom of movement, property rights and rights of self-government curtailed. Landlords granted considerable police powers (23 May).
1817	Estonian pattern of emancipation extended to Kurland (25 Aug.).

Nicholas I

1836	Orthodox Cathedral built in Riga.
1848	'Long Live the Livonian Republic' is pasted on the Cathedral doors in Riga (3/15 Mar.).

| 1849 | Circulation of Iurii Samárin's strongly anti-Baltic-German *Letters from Riga*. |

Alexander II

1857	F. R. Kreutzwald's epic poem *Kalevipeg* establishes the literary Estonian language. J. W. Jannsen's Estonian newspaper for peasant readers appears.
1864	Bishop Walter's sermon urges Estonians and Latvians, as 'fragments of tribes disappearing from history', to become Germanized in their own interest (9 Mar.).
1867	Use of Russian as the official language made compulsory. Publication of 2 vols of Samárin's *Borderlands of Russia*.
1868	Formation of the Latvian Association/*Latveishu Biedriba*, Riga.
Nov.	Samárin rebuked by the Tsar for the anti-German tone of *Borderlands of Russia*.
1870	Estonian students' association formed.
1871–76	Samárin publishes four more volumes of *Borderlands of Russia*, abroad.
1876	Latvian daily newspaper *The Voice* (*Balss*) begins publication.
1878	Publication of K. R. Jacobson's Estonian newspaper *Sakala* (until 1882).

Alexander III

1886	Trial of Greifenhagen, mayor of Réval, and of Büngert for opposing the use of Russian in official business.
1887	Teaching in primary schools to be in Russian. Primary school administration to be on the Russian model.
1893	Dorpat renamed Iúrev, Dinaburg renamed Dvinsk, Dinamünde renamed Ust-Dvinsk (17 Jan.). Orthodox cathedral built in the middle of the walled city of Réval.

Nicholas II

| 1895 | Congress of New Course/*Iauna-strava*, Riga (28 Jan.). |
| 1897 | First leaflet in Latvian, calling for bread and freedom, issued by *Iauna-strava* and students of the Riga Polytechnic (19 Apr.). |

3.2 Poland

Catherine II
1795–96   Ninety-six estates and over 121,000 serfs taken from Polish landlords to reward Russian conquerors.

Paul I
1796

12 Dec.   Autonomous elective judiciary and *dietines* (local noble assemblies) restored throughout the Polish provinces under Russian rule.

Dec.   Stanisław Poniatowski invited to St Petersburg. Poland's external debts are charged to the Russian Treasury. 12,000 Polish prisoners, taken in 1795 and now doing forced labour, are released. Kościuszko and Ignacy Potocki are freed.

1797   Stanisław Poniatowski attends Paul's coronation (5 Apr.).

Alexander I
1802

          Dietines brought increasingly under supervision of Crown officers.

1806

Nov.   French invasion of Poland.

16/28 Nov.   Murat takes Warsaw.

5 Dec.   Czartoryski presents Alexander with his *Memorandum on the Need to re-establish Poland in order to pre-empt Bonaparte.*

1807

2/14 Jan.   Napoleon appoints a Governing Commission of five 'directors' in French-occupied Poland. Joseph Poniatowski is in charge of creating a Polish army.

[1] For Russian relations with Poland before 1795 see section 4.2 Russia and the Baltic, pp. 215–27.

25 June/7 July	Treaty of Tilsit creates the Grand Duchy of Warsaw from former Prussian Poland.
9/21 Dec.	Duchy of Warsaw abolishes serfdom.
1808	Poniatowski introduces French-style conscription in the Grand Duchy of Warsaw.
1809	Judiciary in Russian Poland begins to function mainly on Russian rather than Polish Law.
6/18 Apr.	Secret convention between Alexander and Prince Schwarzenberg of Austria. The Russians, while appearing to respect the Treaty of Erfurt (30 Sept./ 12 Oct. 1808, see section 4.5 Russia and Western Europe, p. 287), would not oppose Austrian action in Poland.
7/19 Apr.	Austrian invasion of the Grand Duchy of Warsaw leads to an insurrection. Austrians withdraw.
2/14 Oct.	Treaty of Schönbrunn joins New Galicia to the Duchy of Warsaw.
1811	Alexander informs Czartoryski of his firm decision to restore Poland (6 Jan.).
1812	Nesselrode memorandum argues that Alexander's 'deep emotional commitment to the restoration of Poland' is 'entirely opposed to the interests of Russia'.
June–Dec.	Some 96,000 men from the Duchy of Warsaw fight in the *Grande armée* against Russia.
Oct.	Alexander resumes negotiations with Czartoryski over restoration of Poland under Russian protection.
1813	
Feb.	Russian army enters Warsaw.
2/14 Mar.	Provisional Supreme Council to rule the Grand Duchy of Warsaw set up: General V. Lanskói (president), N. Novosíltsev, Lubecki, Wawrzecki.
1815	
13/25 May	Principles of the Constitution of the Kingdom of Poland, drawn up by Adam Czartoryski, are issued in Vienna.
28 May/9 June	Treaty of Vienna gives most of former Duchy of Warsaw to Russia, to become a kingdom with the Russian Tsar as king.
8/20 June	Kingdom of Poland proclaimed in Warsaw. Formation of the Society of True Poles.
15 Nov.	Constitution for the Kingdom of Poland. Hereditary monarchy, whose king was the Emperor of Russia, represented in Poland by the Viceroy and an appointed state council. Poland to have broad and comprehensive

autonomy, except for foreign relations, which were the preserve of the Imperial government. Poland to have its own army. Only Polish citizens were eligible for public office. Polish to be the language of administration and the courts, and the Napoleonic Code the basis for the judicial system. Bicameral Diet to meet every two years: Senate, whose members were appointed for life by the Crown; Lower House, elected by the landed gentry and burghers. Property qualifications to restrict franchise and eligibility for membership of the Diet. Diet may not initiate legislation, but could petition the Crown. Freedom of worship and of the press, civil rights and the peasantry's right to own land were guaranteed. Konstantín Pávlovich (Alexander's brother) is appointed Commander-in-chief of the Polish Army. Poles who had fought with Poniatowski are released from Siberian exile. N. Novosíltsev is appointed high commissioner of the Imperial government in Poland (a post not in the constitution).

19 Nov./1 Dec.	Stanisław Potocki becomes Minister of the Board of Religious Denominations and Public Instruction (until 9.xii.1820).
1816	Opening of Warsaw University, Warsaw Institute of Agronomy, Warsaw Polytechnic (17/29 Nov.).
1817	Adam Mickiewicz and Tomasz Zan found the Philomatic Society.
6/18 Mar.	Decree on the Church proclaimed.
1818	
16/28 Jan.	Concordat with the Catholic Church.
15 Mar.	Alexander I opens the first Diet with a speech lauding 'free institutions' and announces his intention to extend these to the entire Russian Empire.
17/29 Apr.	General Józef Zajączek becomes the first Viceroy (until July 1826).
1 Oct.	Publication of the *Daily Home and Foreign Gazette*, no. 1 (suppressed).
1819	Formation of the 'Universal Union', of the 'Union of Free Poles' and of K. Machnicki and W. Łukasziński's 'National Freemasons'.
16/28 May	Censorship imposed on newspapers and periodicals.
4/16 July	Censorship extended to all publications.
Nov.	Prefects introduced into the Warsaw lyceum as the beginning of religious and moral supervision over all schools.

1820	In the Diet, government bills increasing the powers of the Governor-General are blocked by the Kalisz Group, led by the Niemojowski brothers. (Diet not reconvened until May 1825.) Stanisław Potocki's *Journey to Darktown* is published.
May	Marriage of Konstantín Pávlovich to Joanna Grudzińska.
27 Nov./9 Dec.	Potocki dismissed.
1821	
2/14 Aug.	Russian Commissioner given power over the Board of Religion and Instruction.
13/25 Sept.	Freemasonry banned. Masons join W. Łukasziński's National Patriotic Society. Formation of the Philodelphist Society and the Green League.
1822	Members of the Patriotic Society arrested (Apr.).
1823	
May	Student disturbances in Wilno.
July	Novosíltsev commission investigates secret societies.
2 Sept.	J. N. Janowski and E. A. Odynets arrested.
23 Oct.	A. Mickiewicz and T. Zan arrested.
1824	
5/17 Apr.	Czartoryski dismissed.
14 Aug.	Trial of Patriotic Society members. Mickiewicz and Zan are exiled. J. Lelewel is dismissed from Warsaw University.
1825	
Feb.	Alexander amends the constitution to have Diet sessions held *in camera.*
May	Diet is reconvened, but leaders of the opposition are excluded.
21 Aug.	Alexander forbids publication of the proceedings of the Diet because of oppositionist speeches.

Nicholas I

1826	Formation of the Committee of enquiry (Hauke, Novosíltsev, S. Zamoyski) into the 'Polish Conspiracy' (i.e. the Patriotic Society) (7 Feb.). Reports to Konstantín Pávlovich on 22 December.
1828	
10/22 May	Polish Senate, by 40 votes to two (Krasinski and Novosíltsev), find those accused in 1826 not guilty of treason and send the ringleader, Seweryn Krzyżanowski, to prison for only three years.
25 May/6 June	Konstantín Pávlovich has the senators arrested and the verdict suspended.

17/29 Aug.	Nicholas instructs the Administrative Council to discover whether the verdict of the Senate was the result of incompetence or treason.
Dec.	Formation of P. Wysocki's secret association in the School of Infantry Cadets.

1829

Mar.	Nicholas has the prisoners from the Patriotic Society sent to Siberia in chains.
24 Apr.	Nicholas is crowned King of Poland in Warsaw.
17/29 May	Attempt on Nicholas's life in Warsaw.

1830

17/29 Nov.	Polish uprising begins with an attempt to assassinate Konstantín Pávlovich.
18/30 Nov.	Administrative Council condemns the uprising, and co-opts Czartoryski, Radziwiłł, Kochanowski, Pac, Niemcewicz and Chłopicki.
20 Nov./2 Dec.	Konstantín Pávlovich meets the Administrative Council at Wierzbno. He promises not to attack Warsaw, and to intercede with Nicholas.
21 Nov./3 Dec.	Re-formation of the 'Patriotic Society'. The Administrative Council changes its name to 'Provisional Government of the Kingdom of Poland' and appoints Chłopicki Commander-in-chief of the Polish Army.
23 Nov./5 Dec.	Chłopicki declares himself dictator.
28 Nov./10 Dec.	Lubecki and Jezierski go to St Petersburg to negotiate with Nicholas.
5/17 Dec.	Nicholas rejects any negotiations and orders the Administrative Council to resume its duties in its original composition; military commanders to assemble their troops at Płock; and all irregular formations to be disbanded.
6/18 Dec.	Diet reassembles.
8/20 Dec.	Diet confirms Chłopicki as dictator and declares the insurrection national.
26 Dec./7 Jan.	Nicholas demands Chłopicki's unconditional surrender.

1831

1 Jan.	Independent Polish Judiciary abolished.
6/18 Jan.	Chłopicki resigns.
8/20 Jan.	Diet appoints Michał Radziwiłł as Commander-in-chief.
11/23 Jan.	Díbich, in command of First Russian Army on the Polish frontier, demands unconditional Polish surrender.
13/25 Jan.	Diet deposes Nicholas as King of Poland.

18/30 Jan.	Formation of the national government under Czartoryski (S. Barzykowski, W. Niemojowski, T. Morawski, Lelewel).
24 Jan./5 Feb.	Díbich leads the Russian Army into Poland.
13/25 Feb.	Indecisive battle of Grochów.
19/31 Mar.	Battle of Dembe Wielkie. Polish victory.
14/26 May	Battle of Ostrolenko. Russian victory.
29 May/10 June	Dibích dies of cholera.
3/15 June	Konstantín Pávlovich dies of cholera.
27 Aug./8 Sept.	Paskévich takes Warsaw.
23 Sept./5 Oct.	Remains of Polish Army cross the Prussian frontier and surrender, most emigrate to France and Britain. M. N. Muravëv, 'the hangman', becomes military governor of Grodno.
6/18 Oct.	Czartoryski stripped of the title of Senator.
Nov.	Polish Committee set up in Paris with B. Niemojowski as president.
Dec.	Polish Permanent National Committee established in the same building as Lafayette's Committee, with Lelewel as president.
1832	
2/14 Feb.	Polish Constitution of 1815 replaced by an 'Organic Statute', making Poland an organic part of the Russian Empire. Polish Diet and Army abolished.
May	University of Wilno closed. All schools in the Wilno area closed for two years. 200 Roman Catholic monasteries closed.
28 June	2,338 Polish estates sequestered.
1833	Closure of the Lyceum of Krzemieniec.
8 Nov.	St Vladimir University of Kiev opens as the centre for the Russification of the Western Provinces.
1834	Schools in the Wilno area reopened with Russian as the language of instruction.
	Czartoryski's Polish 'government' set up in the Hôtel Lambert, Paris.
1836	First appearance of David Urquart's *Portfolio*, containing papers taken in Warsaw from Novosíltsev (until 1844). The teaching of Polish ceases.
1837	Polish *wojewodztwa*/provinces reorganized as ten Russian *gubérnii*.
1838	Creation of the Orthodox diocese of Warsaw. Uvárov reports to Nicholas that 'the establishment of Russian education in the Lithuanian provinces may be considered definitely completed'.

1839	Education Commission abolished. 'School Region of Warsaw' subordinated to the Russian Ministry of Education.
1840	The words 'Belorussia' and 'Lithuanian *gubérnii*' forbidden. The Russian legal code supplants the Polish code in the Western Provinces.
1841	Polish State Council abolished. The Russian Senate becomes Poland's Supreme Court. Catholic Church lands are secularized.
1843	Attempt on the life of Nicholas I in Poznania (7 Sept.).
1844	Landlords in 'Western Russia' are ordered to submit lists (inventories) of their 'immovable properties' to the *gubérniia* authorities, identifying the lands cultivated by serfs and the duties they had to perform (15 Apr.).
1846	Kamieński trial in Warsaw (students accused of an attempt on the life of Paskévich).
5 Mar.	Three Polish nobles hanged for an attempted uprising in Siedlce.
1847	Russian Criminal Code replaces Napoleonic Code in Poland. Concordat is signed with the pope (remains a dead letter until 1856).
26 May	Decree on the preparation of inventories, applying only to the South-Western Provinces. Serf plots to be inviolable. Rules limiting serf obligations to be read aloud to the serfs by the marshal of the nobility in the presence of the *uézd* police commander and the local priest. (Revised 29.xii.1848.)
10 Sept.	Any serf-owner in the South-West violating the decree of 26 May to be subject to military court martial.
1849	Russian weights and measures replace Polish ones.
1851	Customs barriers abolished between Russia and Poland.
1852	D. G. Bíbikov extends the regulations on inventories to all the Western Provinces (22 Dec.). This is followed by protests of the north-western and White Russian gentry, supported by Alexander Nikoláevich (the future Alexander II).
1854	Nicholas puts aside the decree of 22.xii.1852. Instead, landlords in Western Provinces to form committees to establish their own rules for the drawing up of inventories (5 Apr.).
1855	
Feb.	Only Russians to be appointed to official posts in Poland (rescinded 1857).
May	New regulations for inventories for White Russia.

Alexander II

1855	Bíbikov dismissed because his inventories policy is too harsh on landowners (Aug.).
1856	Implementation of the Concordat of 1847.
31 Mar.	Military rule in Poland ends. Polish émigrés and exiles amnestied.
11 & 15 May	Alexander II speaks in Warsaw on the future of Poland.
1857	Agricultural Society legalized. President: A. Zamoyski.
Autumn	Establishment of a medical academy in Warsaw.
1859	Polish press established in Zhitomir.
1860	Demonstrations at the funeral of the widow of General Sowiński (11 June).
1861	
15/27 Feb.	Five killed when troops disperse a Warsaw demonstration of 200,000 people to greet the annual general meeting of the Agricultural Society.
16/28 Feb.	Archbishop Fijałkowski, Zamoyski and Małochowski present Gorchakóv with a set of demands for constitutional reform in Poland to be sent to the Tsar.
20 Feb.	Further demonstrations at the funerals of the five killed on 15 February.
Mar.	Petition with 60,000 signatures asking Alexander for reforms in Poland.
13/25 Mar.	Alexander grants a Council of State, a Commission of Public Instruction and Religion, and the election of local assemblies.
15/27 Mar.	Alexander Wielopolski appointed head of the Commission of Public Instruction and Religion, a member of the Council of Administration, Organizer of the Council of State, director of agrarian reform and of Jewish emancipation, head of the departments of Justice and the Interior and adviser to the viceroy.
18 May	Death of M. D. Gorchakóv.
12 Aug.	Demonstrations all over Lithuania to commemorate the union of Poland and Lithuania of 1413 (Union of Lublin).
2/14 Oct.	State of emergency declared.
3/15 Oct.	Occupation of the churches on the anniversary of the death of Kościuszko, followed by mass arrests.
10 Oct.	Mogilëv nobility petition the Tsar to reopen Wilno University. Their chairman is sentenced to 18 months imprisonment.
11/23 Oct.	Resignation of Wielopolski.
28 Oct./9 Nov.	Liders takes over and imposes harsh military rule.

1862

Feb.	Feliński is made archbishop of Warsaw and pursues a policy of reconciliation with Russia.
19 Feb./3 Mar.	Those arrested during the state of emergency are amnestied. Local assemblies, elected in 1861, are allowed to meet.
15/27 May	Elections to Warsaw city assembly.
15/27 June	Viceroy A. N. Liders wounded by a Polish revolutionary. Wielopolski is reinstated.
21 June/3 July	Konstantín Nikoláevich wounded by a Polish revolutionary (Jaroszyński).
1/13 Sept.	A. Zamoyski presents a petition on behalf of 300 Polish nobles demanding full independence for Poland reunited with Lithuania and Ruthenia. Alexander refuses to accept the petition and exiles Zamoyski.
	Wielopolski implements his programme of re-Polonizing Poland. Warsaw High School is opened as a Polish university. Poles replace Russians in administrative posts. A Polish lyceum is founded in Lublin as well as numerous Polish *gymnázii*. Polish becomes the official state language.
Dec.	*Kólokol* publishes a letter from the Society of Russian Officers in Poland, appealing for political action to prevent bloodshed and avert armed intervention.

1863

2/14 Jan.	Forced conscription into the Russian army of young men believed to have been active in street demonstrations.
4/16 Jan.	Central National Committee calls the nation to arms.
10/22 Jan.	Polish soldiers in the Russian army mutiny.
28 Feb./12 Mar.	Marian Langiewicz becomes 'dictator of Poland'.
9/21 Mar.	Langiewicz flees to Austria. Central National Committee declares itself the National Government.
20 Mar./1 Apr.	Imperial Manifesto grants partial amnesty to Polish insurgents laying down their arms by 1 May.
Apr.–May	The Kazán Conspiracy. H. Kienewicz of the Polish National Committee and a group of Kazán University students publish a false manifesto from the Tsar, promising 'full liberty to all Our subjects', eternal ownership of the land to peasants, and ordering 'the soldiers of Our army to return to their homes'.
1 May	Muravëv 'the hangman' is appointed governor-general of Wilno.
4 July	Wielopolski dismissed.

19 Sept.	Attempt on the life of F. F. Berg.
Oct.	Romuald Traugutt assumes the leadership of the insurrection (arrested August 1864).

1864

2/14 Mar.	Nikolai Miliutin's land reform, covering the *gubérnii* of Wilno, Kovno, Grodno, Minsk and part of Vitebsk, emancipates the peasantry on much more favourable terms than the Russian reform of 1861.
1/13 May	'Pacification' of Poland declared to be complete.
6 June	Execution of the 'Kazán Conspirators': Iwanicki, Kienewicz, Mroczek and Stankevich.
24 July/5 Aug.	Execution of Traugutt, Krajewski, Toczyski, Żuliński and Jeziorański.

1865	Kaufman replaces Muravëv as governor-general of Wilno.

1866

Jan.	Breach with the papacy over Poland.
5 Feb.	End of military rule.
7 Dec.	All of Poland's privileges as a separate kingdom removed.

1867

16 May	Statute on land reform for State peasants in the nine Western Provinces.
25 May	Polish émigré Berezowski's attempt on Alexander II's life in Paris.

1868

17 Feb.	Internal self-government in Poland abolished.
July	The use of the Polish language in public is forbidden.
1869	University of Warsaw reopened as a Russian University.
1870	Widespread disorder over the banning of the Polish language.
1872	Russian judicial reforms of 1864 extended to cover Poland.
1874	Congress Kingdom abolished.

Alexander III

1882	Ludwig Waryński's *Proletariat* group is formed in Warsaw (Aug.) (dissolved 1885).
1883	A. Apúkhtin, Warsaw Educational District curator until 1897, pursues a policy of Russification.
16 Apr.	Disorders in Warsaw University.
3 Sept.	Publication of *Proletariat*, no. 1 (no. 2: 19 Sept.; no. 3: 8 Oct.; no. 4: 8 Dec.; no. 5: 1884).
1885	Teaching in primary schools to be in Russian, except for classes in religion and in 'the native tongue of the

	pupils'. Poles forbidden to buy land in Kiev, Podólsk, Volynia, Kovno, Grodno, Vítebsk, Mogilëv or Minsk *gubernii*. Police arrest the *Proletariat* group. Waryński dies in prison.
1886	The Polish League is formed in Rapperswil, Switzerland. The Polish Bank becomes a branch of the Russian State Bank.
1887	Khárkov University student, Józef Piłsudski, exiled to Siberia.
1891	Demonstrations to commemorate the 1791 Constitution (3 May).
1892	Formation of the Polish Socialist Party (PPS) in Paris.
23 Aug.	M. Zieliński's attempt on the life of governor-general Gúrko.
1893	
Summer	First Congress of the PPS, Wilno.
Aug.	Rosa Luxemburg and Julian Marchlewski found the Social-Democracy of the Kingdom of Poland (dissolved 1900). Feliks Dzierżyński founds the Social-Democracy of Lithuania (dissolved 1900).
1894	
7–15 Feb.	Second Congress of the PPS.
26–27 Feb.	First Congress of the Social-Democracy of the Kingdom of Poland, Warsaw.
	Demonstrations to commemorate Kościuszko's uprising.

Nicholas II

1895	Third Congress of the PPS, Wilno (16 June).
1896	First Congress of the Social-Democracy of Lithuania, Wilno (Apr.).
1897	
6 Feb.	Second Congress of the Social-Democracy of Lithuania, Wilno.
7–21 Nov.	Fourth Congress of the PPS, Warsaw.
1900	
20 Feb.	Demonstrations in Warsaw at the funeral of the worker Studziński.
25 July	Demonstrations in Warsaw at the funeral of the worker E. Vengrzhinovich.
6/19–8/21 Aug.	First Congress of the SDKPiL, Otvotsk, near Warsaw.
1–5 Sep.	Fifth Congress of the PPS, Skierniewice.
1901	Second (Third) Congress of the SDKPiL (15/28–17/30 Sept.).

1904	Piłsudski attempts to recruit a Polish legion to fight with Japan against Russia.
28 Sept.	Twenty killed when police fire on a crowd in Białystok.
13 Nov.	Gun battle in Warsaw between PPS supporters and the police.
1905	
28 Jan.	PPS and SDPKiL call a general strike (400,000 workers for four weeks).
Apr.	Polish language reinstated in private, but not state, schools. Polish School Board given official approval.
24 May	Praga workers sack the red-light district of Warsaw.
22–24 June	Barricades go up in Łódź.
21 July	Execution of Stefan Okrzei, member of the PPS Battle Organization, in Warsaw. Poles allowed to buy land in the Western Provinces.
1906	All factories in Łódź closed. Thousands deported to the villages (16/29 Dec.). Eighth Congress of PPS, Lwów.
1907	Project for Polish Constitution presented to Second Duma is instrumental in its dissolution.
1908	PPS splits into PPS (*Lewica*) and PPS (*Rewolucja*).
1911	PPS (*Rewolucja*) splits into the New PPS and Feliks Perl and Tomasz Arciszewski's PPS (*Opozucja*) (1916).
1914	
19 July/3 Aug.	Piłsudski forms the Polish legions.
24 July/6 Aug.	Piłsudski's abortive invasion of Russian Poland.
26 July/8 Aug.	Polish Duma deputies pledge loyalty to the Tsar during the war.
1/14 Aug.	Grand Duke Nikolái Nikoláevich issues a proclamation containing vague promises to Poland.
28 Aug./10 Sept.	Central Citizens' Committee (W. Grabski) formed in Warsaw and a Warsaw Committee is established (Zdzisław Lubomirski).
Nov.	Dmowski and Wielopolski's National Committee is formed.
Dec.	Governors of Russia's Polish *gubérnii* told that Nikolái Nikoláevich's proclamation would apply only to German and Austrian Poland.
1915	
Jan.	Paderewski's fund-raising campaign in the USA.
Mar.	Tsar grants municipal autonomy to Warsaw (denied since 1863).

June	Goremýkin Commission on Poland promises 'self government' if the Polish lands were reunited.
23 July/5 Aug.	Germans enter Warsaw.
12/25 Aug.	Germans at Brest.
5/18 Sept.	Germans in Wilno.
	Polish University re-established in Warsaw.

1916

June	Sazónov's plan for an autonomous Poland, with two chambers and a viceroy appointed by the Tsar.
23 Oct./5 Nov.	Austrians and Germans promise an Independent Poland after the war and create a Provisional Council of State (TRS) in Warsaw.
Nov.	Woodrow Wilson supports an independent Poland after meeting Paderewski.

1917

8/21 Jan.	Woodrow Wilson's first State of the Union Address speaks of a 'united Poland' with access to the sea.
26 Feb./8 Mar.	France recognizes Russia's right to determine her own Western frontier in return for Russian recognition of French claims on Alsace-Lorraine.
2/15 Mar.	Abdication of Nicholas II.
16/29 Mar.	Russian Provisional Government promises independence to the Poles, deferring details to the Constituent Assembly.

3.2.1   Viceroys of Poland

17/29.iv.1818–July 1826	General Joseph Zajączek
July 1826–June 1831	vacant
June 1831–April 1856	I. F. Paskévich
April 1856–18.v.1861	M. D. Gorchakóv
23 May–6.viii.1861	N. O. Sukhozánet (acting)
12 August–5.x.1861	K. K. Lambert
10–28.x.1861	N. O. Sukhozanét (acting)
28.x.1861–15.vi.1862	A. N. Liders
20.vi.1862–19.x.1863	Grand Duke Konstantin Nikolaevich[2]
19.x.1863–1874	F. F. Berg

[2] His appointment was made on 15 May, but he did not arrive in Warsaw until 20 June.

3.3 New Russia, South Russia and Ukraine

1687	Suspecting the Cossacks of having set fire to the steppe, V. V. Golítsyn arrests *hétman* Samoilóvich and replaces him with I. S. Mazépa (June).

Peter I

1696	Boyar Duma decides to send 3,000 families to settle the Volga region and to establish a permanent garrison in Azóv (4/14 Nov.). Ivan Tolstoy becomes governor of Azóv.
1701	Peter orders construction of Taganróg.
1703	Tolstoy ordered to settle soldiers, townspeople, workers and Swedish prisoners in Taganróg.
1708	Don Cossack revolt led by *atamán* Bulávin.
7 June	Bulávin calls on Turks to take Azóv.
Autumn	Bulávin's henchman Nekrásov goes to Constantinople for help. He fails, but his horde roams the steppe until the war of 1733–35.
Oct.	Mazépa allies his Cossacks to the Swedes.
Nov.	Ménshikov destroys Mazépa's capital Baturin. I. I. Staropádskii elected *hétman*.
1709	
Early	Zaporózhian *hétman* Hordienko demands that Russian forts in his territory be destroyed and all Russian and Ukrainian landlords banished.
May	Iákovlev destroys Zaporózhian *Sech*. Zaporózhians move to Lower Dniépr.
1710–14	Zaporózhian Cossack rump under Philip Orlyk wage guerrilla warfare on the steppe.
1715	Ottoman Serbs led by Mikhail Milorádovich, who had organized Montenegrin revolt in 1711, are resettled in Little Russia.

Catherine I

1726	First Austrian Serbs settled in *Slobodskáia Ukraína*.

Anna Ivánovna

1734	Zaporózhians swear fealty to Anna, and are allowed to return to the *Sech*. Office of *hétman* lapses.

Elizabeth

1743	Russian government ignores the Code of Rights of the Little Russian People compiled by Ukrainian lawyers.
1749	The fortress of St Dmitrii of Rostóv is built on the Lower Don.
1750	Zaporózhian *hétman* re-established (K. Razumóvskii).
1751	Razumóvskii invested as *hétman*. Elizabeth confirms privileges and franchises of Little Russia (13 Mar.). Little Russian affairs moved from Senate to College of Foreign Affairs.
1752	Establishment of autonomous 'New Serbia' (Governor: Horvat) (11 Jan.).
1753	S. Efrémov becomes Don Cossack *atamán*.
1754	Creation of 'Slavianoserbia' (Governors: Shévich, Prerádovich). Russian government begins granting military rank to favoured members of Don Cossack *starshiná*, and treating their officials as paid government servants.
1756	General census of Little Russia (completed 1769).
1760	Razumóvskii forbids peasants to leave the land without landlord's consent.
1761	Children of Little Russian nobility refused admission to the Russian *Kadétskii kórpus*.

Catherine II

1762	Manifesto permits the settlement of foreigners except Jews (4 Dec.).
1763	Ukrainian peasants need landlord's written permission to give up their tenancy and move from one landlord to another. Reform of the Little Russian legal system.
11 June	Privileged status of New Serbia ended. Russian governor (A. P. Melgunóv) replaces Horvat.
22 July	Manifesto grants all foreigners freedom of entry to Russia, and creates the Office of Foreign Settlers.
1764	
22 Mar.	New Serbian settlements become 'Government of New Russia'.
June	Slavianoserbia joined to New Russia.
22 July	Creation of the Chancery for the Protection of Foreigners, with College status, to foster settlement.

	Foreigners wishing to settle in the Russian Empire may choose their place of residence and occupation, and freely exercise their religion.
10 Nov.	Hetmanate replaced by Little Russian College (president: P. A. Rumiántsev) with four Russian and four Little Russian members. Rumiántsev remains governor of Little Russia until 1796.
1764–74	Active recruitment of foreigners to settle in Russia leads to the establishment of German colonies on the Volga, and to large settlements on the southern borders of New Russia.
1765	Freedom of peasant movement abolished in some Ukrainian provinces.
1767	Children of Little Russian nobility admitted to the *Kadétskii kórpus* and Smólnyi Institute.
1768	Zaporózhian *hétman* P. Kalnyshévskii calls on Russian troops to defend the *starshiná* during a mutiny.
1771	Imperial Council allows Nogáis, who have switched allegiance from the Porte to Russia, to settle in Kubán (3/14 Mar.).
1774	Potëmkin becomes governor-general of New Russia (31 Mar.).
1775	Potëmkin becomes governor-general of Azóv and New Russia.
15 Jan.	Iaík Cossacks reorganized. Iaítsk renamed Uralsk, river Iaík renamed Urál.
15 Feb.	Don Cossack statute divides the administration into military (remaining under Cossack hierarchy) and civil (justice and taxation) branch which is taken over by Russia. Don Cossack lands incorporated into Azóv *Gubérniia*. Cossack regimental commanders are considered as having attained officer rank, and therefore hereditary nobility, but are placed below Russian army majors.
6 June	Zaporózhian Cossacks surrender to Russian regular army under P. A. Tekelli at the *Sech*. The last *hétman* P. Kalnyshévskii and the *starshiná* are interned.
3 Aug.	End of Zaporózhian Host proclaimed.
1776	Volga Cossack Host broken up and most transferred to the Térek and the Caucasus (5 May).
1778	Foundation of Khérson.
1781	Cossack lands to be taken over by new Treasury Boards and Cossacks to be given status equivalent to state peasants (26 Oct.).

1782	1775 Local Administration Statute is introduced into Little Russia. Hetmanate disappears. Three *gubérnii* are created: Kiev, Chernígov and Nóvgorod Sevérsk. Old titles and ranks of office based on the Lithuanian Statute, Magdeburg Law or Little Russian custom are replaced by those in the 1775 Statute (Jan.).
1783	Poll tax is extended to Little Russia and *Slobodskáia Ukraína*. Freedom of movement for all Ukrainian peasants is abolished (3 May).
1784	Ekaterinosláv is founded on the banks of the Dniépr.
2 Feb.	Entire Tartar Khanate, except the Kubán, to be the new *óblast* of Tauris, until increased population qualified it as *gubérniia*. All Kazán Tartar *mirzas* (heads of landowning families) are given the status of Russian nobles.
30 May	Crimean Tartar *mirzas* are given Russian noble status.
1785	Potëmkin becomes governor-general of Ekaterinosláv and Tauris and actively encourages settlement of Orthodox immigrants. Ukrainian bishoprics are redrawn to coincide with *gubérnii*.
Apr.	Charter to the Towns is extended to Ukraine.
1786	Secularization of Ukrainian Church lands (10 Apr.). Cossacks transferred to ordinary dragoon regiments.
1787	
7 Jan.	Catherine begins her journey to the South.
29 Jan.	Catherine arrives in Kiev.
25 Apr.	Catherine meets Stanislas Augustus of Poland in Kánev.
12 May	Catherine meets Joseph II in Khérson.
22 May	Catherine and Joseph in Inkerman.
11 July	Catherine returns to Tsárskoe seló.
Sept.	M. N. Krechétnikov replaces Rumiantsev as Governor of Ukraine.
1789	Recruit levy extended to Ukraine. For 25 years, Little Russian Cossacks were recruited into the army just like other peasants and posted to ordinary units.
Paul I	
1798	Sale of serfs without land prohibited in Ukraine (16 Oct.).
Alexander I	
1812	Annexation of Bessarabia, granted the use of the Romanian language in the courts and administration, the continued use of local law and a large role for the local gentry in administration.

1818	New statute for Bessarabia, superseding all others, grants wide autonomy.
1819	Disorders in the Don Cossack Lands. Ring-leaders exiled to Siberia.
1823	Mikhaíl Vorontsóv becomes governor of New Russia.
1824	Curtailment of Bessarabian privileges begins.

Nicholas I

1826	Peasant unrest in Kiev *Gubérniia* over rumours of impending emancipation. Unpopular landlords are beaten. Ring-leaders are arrested, knouted and sent to Siberia.
1828	Bessarabian autonomy abolished.
1831	Russian Legal Code replaces the Lithuanian Code in Belorussia.
1837	D. G. Bíbikov is made governor-general of Kiev, Volýnia and Podólia.
1840	Russian Legal Code replaces the Lithuanian Code in Kiev, Volýnia and Podólia.
1846	
Jan.	Creation of the Kiev Brotherhood of Cyril and Methodius, which calls for emancipation of the serfs and Ukrainian nationalism through the creation of a federated Slav republic, with broad local autonomy.
19 June	Shevchénko's Ukrainian poems banned.
1847	Arrest of the Brotherhood of Cyril and Methodius (27 Mar.) (N. I. Kostomárov exiled to Sarátov until 1857, and Taras Shevchénko sent to Siberia as a private soldier).

Alexander II

| 1855 | A. G. Stróganov becomes governor of New Russia (until 1864). |
| 1876 | Commission on separatist activities in Ukraine recommends the closure of the south-western section of the Geographical Society and the prohibition of all publications, theatrical performances and song recitals in Ukrainian (5 June). Publication of M. Dragománov/ Drahomaniv's *The Problem of Little Russian Literature* (Vienna). |

Alexander III

| 1881 | Ignátev slightly eases restrictions on the publication of literature in Ukrainian. |

1883   Tolstoy re-imposes the restrictions on publication in Ukrainian.

Nicholas II

1901   Formation of the Revolutionary Ukrainian Party.

1904   Publication of the *Ten Commandments* of the Ukrainian People's Party.

1905   People's Party and Radical Democratic Party congress demands a legislative assembly in Kiev and for Ukrainian to become the official language (June).

1906   40 Ukrainian nationalists (*Ukrainska hromada*) sit in the First Duma (Apr.).

1908   Formation of the Society of Ukrainian Progressives (TUP).

3.4 Finland

Alexander I
1808

6/18 Feb.	Imperial proclamation promises the Finns 'the preservation of their privileges, religious freedom, liberties, rights and other advantages', and invites them to send deputies to a Diet in Åbo.
8/20 Feb.	Russian invasion of Finland.
20 Mar./1 Apr.	Imperial manifesto declares Finland to be part of Russian Empire.
Summer	Finnish guerrilla warfare against the Russians.
5/17 June	Imperial Manifesto to the Finns.
1809	Speránskii draws up a new constitution for Finland.
20 Jan./1 Feb.	Alexander summons the Finnish Diet to meet in Borgå on 10 Mar.
15/27 Mar.	Declaration of Borgå: Alexander promises to respect Finnish traditions and rights.
7/19 July	Diet dispersed (not reconvened until 1863).
6/18 Aug.	Creation of a Government Council, consisting of two departments, administration of the law, and direction of the economy, but with no rights to initiate legislation or to levy new taxes. Fourteen members chaired by the governor-general.
5/17 Sept.	Treaty of Fridrikshamn: Sweden cedes Finland and the Åland Islands to Russia. The new Russo-Swedish frontier to be the river Torneå.
1810	Speránskii is made Chancellor of the Finnish University in Åbo.
1811	Alexander confirms the privileges of the Finnish University and grants funds. Foundation of the Bank of Finland.
11/23 Dec.	'Old Finland' joined to the Grand Duchy.
1812	As from 1817, no one to be appointed to public office in Finland without a knowledge of Russian, to be tested by examination.
1816	Government Council is renamed the Finnish Senate, the members of which are to be chosen

only from Finnish citizens resident in Finland (9/
21 Feb.).

Nicholas I

1826	Creation of the office of Secretary of State for Finland.
1828	After the Fire of Åbo, the Finnish University moved to Helsingfors and renamed the Imperial Alexander University.
1847	Finnish Language Association is set up at Helsingfors University (16/28 Mar.).
1850	Publication of books in Finnish forbidden, except for books on agriculture and religion.

Alexander II

1856	Alexander II presides over the reforming Senate.
1862	Establishment of the 'January' Commission (Jan.).
1863	
6/18 June	Diet summoned for early September.
End June	Alexander II visits Finland.
20 July/1 Aug.	Finnish to be officially recognized as an official language with the same status as Swedish by the end of 1883.
6/18 Sept.	Diet reopened by Alexander II (first meeting since 1809).
1863	Finnish to become the official language 'within twenty years'.
1865	The Survey and Forests Office, Post Office, State Bank and Customs must serve the public in Finnish if requested.
1866	Schools Reform ends church control of elementary education and introduces Finnish as the language of instruction.
1869	Diet reorganized as a legislative assembly.
1873	Establishment of elected town councils. First Finnish-speaking secondary school opens at Helsingfors.
1878	Creation of a Finnish Army.

Alexander III

1886	Finnish now given equal status with Swedish 'in all official business and correspondence' (6/18 Mar.). Diet can initiate legislation in all matters except the Fundamental Laws, armed forces and the press.
1890	Finnish Post Office subordinated to Russian Post Office.

1891	Imperial Manifesto aims to circumscribe the Finnish Constitution (28 Feb.).

Nicholas II

1899	Creation of the Finnish Workers Party.
Jan.	Diet rejects legislation incorporating the Finnish Army into the Russian Army.
3/15 Feb.	Legislation affecting both Finland and Russia removed from the jurisdiction of the Finnish Diet.
Aug.	Finnish postal services absorbed into the Russian Post Office.
1900	Beginning of Passive Resistance.
June	Russian becomes the compulsory language for the Finnish Senate records.
1901	Finnish Army disbanded (June). Finns to be conscripted into the Russian Army.
1902	Conscription riots (Apr.).
1904	
June	Eugen Shauman kills governor-general Bóbrikov and then commits suicide.
Sept.	Finnish Party of Active Resistance's conference of radical and revolutionary groups is held in Paris.
1905	
Oct.	Finnish general strike.
22 Oct.	Finnish rights restored. Law of 3.ii.1899 repealed.
1906	Creation of a single-chamber Diet elected by universal suffrage (July).
1907	Formation of the National trades union movement *Suomen Ammattijärjestö*.
1908	Finnish administration subordinated to Russian Council of Ministers (20 May). Finnish conscription abandoned. Instead, Finland is to make a contribution to defence costs.
1909	Establishment of the Kharitónov Committee on Russo-Finnish relations prior to Duma legislation.
1910	Russian State Duma decides that it will enact legislation affecting Finland 'if its effects are not limited to the internal affairs of that region' (17 June).

3.4.1   Governors-General of Finland

1808–9	G. Sprengtporten
1809–10	M. D. Barclay de Tolly
1810–24	F. F. Steinheil

1824–31	A. A. Zakrévskii
1831–55	A. S. Ménshikov
1855–61	F. F. Berg
1861–66	P. I. Rokassóvskii
1866–81	N. V. Adlerberg
1881–97	F. L. Heiden (Geiden)
1898–1904	N. I. Bóbrikov
1904–5	I. M. Obolénskii
1905–8	N. N. Gerard
1908–9	V. A. Bekman
1909–17	F. A. Sein

3.5 The Jews

Catherine I

1727   *Ukáz* expelling all Jews from Russia and Little Russia (never implemented).

1738   A Jew and the naval officer he was accused of having converted to Judaism are burned alive in St Petersburg (15 July).

Elizabeth

1742   Jews prohibited from residing in Russia, and to be deported unless they adopt Orthodox Christianity (2 Dec.).

Catherine II

1762   Jewish settlement in New Russia tolerated, but not explicitly allowed (Dec.).

1764   Catherine orders Prince Dáshkov, with the Russian Army in Poland, to protect Jews wishing to emigrate to Russia.

Apr.   Settlement of Jews unofficially allowed in New Russia and the Baltic.

1769   Specific permission for Jews to settle in New Russia for the first time (17 Nov.).

1780   Jews in Mogilëv and Pólotsk *Gubérnii* permitted to register as *kuptsý* or *meshcháne* (Jan.).

1783   Jews participate in local elections in Mogilëv and Pólotsk, and are elected as local officials. Catherine orders the governor, P. B. Passek, to see that elected Jews can carry out their duties.

1786   Jews given equal civil rights in former Polish provinces (7 May).

1794   Jews to pay double the tax paid by Christians of equivalent status (23 June).

Alexander I

1802   Establishment of the Committee for the Organization of Jewish Life (Nov.) (Derzhávin, Valerián Zúbov,

	Speránskii, Kochubéi, Czartorýski and Potocki. P. V. Lopukhín replaces Derzhávin).
1804	1802 Committee's Statute of Jewish Life (9 Dec.): The Jewish Pale of Settlement to be extended to include the Caucasus and the Province of Ástrakhan. Jews within the Pale to enjoy 'the protection of the law on the same basis as the other subjects of the Crown'. Jewish children to be admitted to Russian schools without restriction and be eligible for university degrees. Jews debarred from leasing agricultural land, keeping inns and distilling spirits. Jews divided into four categories: farmers, manufacturers and artisans, merchants, and burghers.
1806	Project for the establishment of Jewish agricultural colonies in south Russia initiated.
1825	Jews residing outside the cities within 50 *versts* of the frontier to be removed.

Nicholas I

1826	Jews forcibly removed from St Petersburg, Kiev and Sebastopol.
1827	Jews to be liable for 25 years military service (26 Aug.). Enlistment to be at the age of 12. Nicholas 'reduces' the death sentence, imposed on two Jews for illegally attempting to cross the frontier, to running a gauntlet of 12,000 strokes.
1835	The Pale of Settlement redefined and the disabilities to which Jews were subject codified (e.g. a prohibition on employing gentiles). Digest of Imperial Legislation classifies Jews as 'aliens'.
1842	Jewish schools brought under the Minister of Education (22 June).
1844	
13 Nov.	Establishment of Jewish parish and district schools on the Russian model, with a mixed body of Jewish and gentile teachers. A secret Rescript declares Nicholas's intention to do away with Jewish confessional schools.
19 Dec.	*Kahals* (Jewish autonomous communities) dissolved.
1850	The wearing of Jewish dress is prohibited.
1851	Jewish women are forbidden to shave their heads on marriage.

Alexander II

1856	Conscription of Jews to be on same basis as other subjects (26 Aug.).

1859	Jewish merchants of the first guild allowed to live outside the Pale (16 Mar.).
1861	Jews with higher university degrees allowed to live outside the Pale (27 Nov.).
1865	Skilled Jewish artisans and craftsmen allowed to live outside the Pale (28 June).
1866	Settlement of Jews in agricultural areas of Southern Russia stopped.
1870	Municipal Government Act limits the number of Jews on municipal councils to one-third. Jews may not be elected mayor.
1871	Odessa *pogróm.*
1878	Kutais 'ritual murder' trial (all acquitted).
1879	Jewish graduates allowed to live outside the Pale.

Alexander III

1881

15–17 Apr.	Elisavetgrád *pogróm.*
26–27 Apr.	Kiev *pogróm* spreads to surrounding townships.
1 May	Aleksándrovsk *pogróm.*
3–4 May	Odessa, Remny, Smela and Volochisk *pogróms.*
12 July	Borispol *pogróm.*
20 July	Nezhin and Lubny *pogróms.*
6 Aug.	Borzna *pogróm.*
25 Dec.	Warsaw *pogróm.*
1882	'Provisional Rules' forbid Jews to settle in rural areas, even inside the Pale (3 May).

1883

Feb.	Pahlen Commission reviews existing legislation on the Jews.
May	Rostov-on-Don *pogróm.*
Aug.	Many killed in Ekaterinosláv *pogróm.* Nízhnii Nóvgorod *pogróm.*
Nov.	Krivói Rog *pogróm.*
1887	*Numerus clausus* established for Jews in universities and *gimnázii*: 10% of the student body within the Pale; 5% outside it; 3% in St Petersburg and Moscow (July). Secret order states that all Jews sentenced to exile be sent exclusively to Yakútia. Rostov-on-Don and Taganróg removed from the Pale.
1889	Persons of 'non-Christian persuasion' are only allowed to practise law with the permission of the Minister of Justice (Nov.).
1890	Further administrative action against Jews reduces percentage admitted to educational establishments.

	Deportations take place of foreign Jews from Russia, and of Russian Jews from towns outside the Pale.
12 July	*Zémstvo* reform explicitly disenfranchises Jews.
Nov.	Tolstoy leads a writers' protest to the government against the persecution of Jews.
Dec.	London Guildhall protest meeting against the persecution of Russian Jews.
1891	1865 Law permitting Jewish artisans to practise their trade outside the Pale partially repealed. 2,000 Jewish artisans deported from Moscow.
1892	Municipal reform disenfranchises Jews (11 June). In towns within the Pale, Jewish municipal councillors to be appointed by the provincial office of *zémstvo* and municipal affairs, and must not exceed 10% of the membership.
1893	The use of Christian names by Jews is made a criminal offence.

Nicholas II

1903

6–7 Apr.	Kishinëv *pogróm*, provoked by P. A. Krusheván, editor of *The Bessarabian*. Over 700 houses and 600 businesses ransacked. Hundreds killed and wounded.
Aug.	Gomel *pogróm*.

1905

Apr.	Zhitomír *pogróm*.
10 July	Kiev *pogróm*.
1 Aug.	Białystók *pogróm*.
18 Oct.	Simferópol *pogróm*.
18–20 Oct.	Iároslavl *pogróm*.
18–21 Oct.	Over 500 killed in the Odessa *pogróm*.
8 Nov.	A. I. Dubróvin forms the *Union of Russian People*.
24 Nov.	One hundred towns added to the list of places where Jews may live.
Dec.	Nicholas II accepts honorary membership of the Union of Russian People for himself and his son (as do Pobedonóstsev, Plehve, Goremýkin).

1906

Jan.	Publication of G. V. Butmi de Kautsman's *The Protocols of the Elders of Zion* (St Petersburg and Kazán).
13–14 Jan.	Gomel *pogróm*.
13 Mar.	Yalta *pogróm*.
1 May	Vólogda, Muróm and Simbírsk *pogróms*.
1 June	Białystok *pogróm*.

10 July	Odessa *pogróm*.
24 Aug.	Stolýpin announces his intention of removing restrictions on Jews 'that had outlived their usefulness'.
26 Aug.	Siedlce *pogróm*.
10 Dec.	The Tsar rejects Stolýpin's proposals for liberalizing legislation relating to the Jews.
1907	
28 Feb.	Elizavetgrád *pogróm*.
8–12 May	Odessa *pogróm*.
19 June	Odessa *pogróm*.
1912	Jews declared ineligible to be justices of the peace (15 June).
1913	Beilis trial held in Kiev (25 Sept.–28 Oct.).
1914–17	Jews subject to countless persecutions as 'spies' in the zone behind the front line. Some two million Jewish evacuees seek refuge in the rear.

3.6 The Caucasus

Catherine II

1782	New road built to Georgia.
1783	Treaty of Geórgievskoe guarantees existing dynasty and territorial integrity of Georgia (24 July). Georgian rulers to receive investiture in Russia and Georgian nobles given Russian noble status.
1784	Proclamation of Russian suzerainty read aloud in Tiflis by P. S. Potëmkin (24 Jan.).
1795	
Sept.	Persians overrun Georgia, sack Tiflis and withdraw.
Early Oct.	I. V. Gudóvich ordered to dispatch a force to Georgia.
Early Dec.	Two battalions from Gudóvich's force cross the Dariel Pass into Georgia.
1796	Valerián Zúbov's expedition (Apr.) (see p. 206).

Paul I

1797	
Sept.	Last Russian units leave Georgia.
Dec.	Chavchavádze, Georgian minister in St Petersburg, requests assurance that Russia will defend Georgia according to the Treaty of 1783.
1798	Imperial declaration of renewed Russian protection over Georgia (8 Aug.).
1799	
16 Apr.	P. I. Kovalénskii appointed Imperial Envoy to Georgia with orders to see that 'nothing is ever done contrary to the interests of the Imperial Court'.
7 Sept.	King Giorgi requests the incorporation of Georgia into the Russian Empire.
8 Nov.	Kovalénskii arrives in Tiflis.
26 Nov.	Russian Jäger regiment under I. P. Lázarev arrives in Tiflis.
Nov.?	Paul promises Armenians an autonomous national home in Georgia.

1800

10 July	Paul orders General Knorring to send fresh troops from the Caucasian Line to Georgia.
Summer	Georgian delegation arrives in St Petersburg with *Petitionary Articles*, i.e. conditions for the voluntary incorporation into Russia.
3 Aug.	Kovalénskii recalled. Relations with Georgian Court entrusted to Lázarev.
Sept.	General Guliakóv arrives in Georgia with Kabardian Musketeer Regiment.
7 Nov.	Russians and Georgians repel Omar Khan's invasion.
15 Nov.	Paul orders Knorring to reinforce Georgian garrison and, on King Giorgi's death, to prevent any nomination of a new king without Russian consent.
19 Nov.	Paul informs Georgian delegation of his consent to the *Petitionary Articles*, including that guaranteeing the Georgian Crown to Giorgi's heirs.
Early Dec.	Paul decides that Georgia must be annexed.
17 Dec.	Imperial Council of State discusses Músin–Púshkin's memorandum on Georgia. The majority is against outright and unilateral annexation, but in the light of the Emperor's views the decision and the minutes are altered.
18 Dec.	Paul decrees the unilateral annexation of Kartlo-Kakhetia (Georgia).
28 Dec.	Death of King Giorgi. Establishment of a temporary administration of Lázarev, Ioane Batonishvíli, Egnate Tumanishvíli.

1801

8 Jan.	Delegation returns to Tiflis and, unaware of Paul I's change of mind, present the rescripts from Paul I to Georgi's son David Batonishvíli.
15 Jan.	David Batonishvíli and Lázarev draw up new conditions for Georgia's incorporation into Russia.
18 Jan.	Imperial decree on the annexation of Georgia published in St Petersburg. Georgian delegation leaves again for St Petersburg.
16–17 Feb.	Decree on annexation of Georgia published in Tiflis.

Alexander I
1801

11 and 15 Apr.	Council of State discusses the Georgian question. Although Alexander expresses his 'extreme loathing' for annexation, the Council decides to proceed, as

the retention of Georgia 'is essential to the prestige of the Russian monarchy'. It recommends that General Knorring be sent to Tiflis to set up a temporary administration and to discover if the population wants annexation.

22 May	Knorring removes David Batonishvíli from power and sets up a Provisional Government of four Georgian noblemen under General Lázarev.
24 July	A. R. Vorontsóv and V. Kochubéi's memorandum to the Tsar arguing against unilateral annexation.
28 July	Knorring presents his report to the Tsar.
8 Aug.	Council of State considers Knorring's report and the Vorontsóv–Kochubéi memorandum. Council accepts Knorring's arguments for annexation, but Alexander refers the matter to the 'Unofficial Committee'.
13 Aug.	Unofficial Committee discusses Georgia and decides against unilateral annexation, arguing for a protectorate.
12 Sept.	Imperial Manifesto announces the unilateral annexation of Georgia and the removal of the Bagratid dynasty. New system of administration drawn up by Platón Zúbov and P. G. Butkóv: Georgia is divided into five *uézdy*, with administrative centres in Tiflis, Gori, Dusheti, Telavi and Sighnaghi. The commander-in-chief of the Caucasian Line becomes supreme head of the government in Tiflis. Executive authority to be a council of Russian and Georgian officials under the commander-in-chief's deputy, the administrator of Georgia. Administration divided into executive, financial, criminal and civil *expeditions*, each to be headed by a Russian official over four Georgian councillors. Knorring becomes first head of government, with P. I. Kovalénskii as administrator.

1802

12 Apr.	Knorring publishes the annexation decree in Tiflis.
8 Sept.	P. D. Tsitsiánov replaces Knorring and Kovélenskii, accused of corruption.

1803

18 Feb.	Tsitsiánov arrives in Tiflis. He rounds up the remaining Bagratids and sends them into exile in Russia.
Dec.	Mingrelia taken into Russian protection. Administration left to the princely house (until 1857).

1804

3 Jan.	Tsitsiánov takes Ganjeh, one of the key fortresses in Azerbaijan, and renames it Elizavetpól.

20 June	Tsitsiánov begins siege of Eriván (abandoned early September).
Summer–autumn	Popular uprising against Russian rule along the Georgian Military Highway. Tsitsiánov confirms privileges of Georgian nobility, with same rights over serfs as the Russian nobles. Estates confiscated by Georgian monarchy returned. School opened in Tiflis for the sons of the aristocracy.
1805	War with Persia. Tsitsiánov holds out against heavy odds.
1806	Tsitsiánov killed outside the walls of Bakú, in an unsuccessful attempt to take it (8 Feb.). Bakú and Derbent taken by the Russians.
1807	Treaty of Finkenstein between French and Persians (4 May). Napoleon undertakes to help Persians recover Georgia. (French military mission in Persia until Tilsit, when they are replaced by the British, until 1812). Russia goes to war with Turkey.
1808	Unsuccessful attempt to take Eriván.
1809	Gudóvich replaced by General A. Tormásov, who takes Poti. Abkházia is taken under Russian protection. A rebellion takes place in Imereti, led by King Solomon.
1810	Solomon's rebellion defeated by Colonel Simonóvich (Jan.). Russians take Sukhum-Kaleh (Sukhumi). Solomon escapes from Russian prison. A second Imereti rebellion is crushed and the country divided into four districts, under martial law.
1810–12	Plague and famine in Georgia.
1811	Solomon turns to the Turks for aid (Jan.). The Russians take Akhalkalaki. Guria is incorporated into the Russian Empire. The Catolicos Antoni II is sent into enforced retirement in St Petersburg and replaced by a representative of the Russian Synod, Metropolitan Varlaám, with the title of Exarch of Georgia.
1812	
Spring	Peasant revolt in Kakhetia (crushed by Paulucci in the summer).
May	Treaty of Bucharest between Russia and Turkey restores Poti and Akhalkalaki to Turkey but makes no provision in favour of Solomon.
Summer	Rtíshchev's regime gives greater involvement to the Georgian nobility.
1813	Treaty of Gulistan between Russia and Persia recognizes Russia's acquisition of Eastern and Western Georgia.

1815	Death of Solomon in Trebizond (19 Feb.).
1815?	Exarch Varlaám, considered too pro-Georgian, replaced by Exarch Theophilact Rusánov, who tries to replace the Georgian liturgy with the Slavonic one.
1816	Ermólov conducts numerous expeditions into the Caucasus mountains, pursuing a policy of great savagery towards the native population (until 1827).
1818	Russians build the fort of Grozny ('Threatening').
1819	Russian annexation of Shekki. Georgian nobles, accused of treason, exiled to Siberia.
1820	The arrest of the archbishops of Gelati and Kutais for opposing Theophilact is followed by an uprising in Imereti.
Aug.	Russian annexation of Shirvan.
1821	Russian and foreign concerns in business in Georgia granted special customs concessions and other privileges for ten years. Civil War breaks out in Abkházia (crushed in 1822).
1822	Russian annexation of Karabágh.

Nicholas I

1826	Persian surprise attack on Georgia and the Karabágh. The Russo-Georgian Army under Madátov wins the Battle of Shamkhor.
14/26 Sept.	Arrival of Paskévich results in the collapse of the Persian Army at Ganjeh.
1827	Kazi Mulla preaches holy war against the Russians in Daghestan.
13 Oct.	Russians take Eriván.
1828	Treaty of Turkmanchai establishes Russia's frontier on the Araxes. War breaks out with Turkey. Paskévich takes Akhaltsikhe, Kars and Erzerum.
1829	Treaty of Adrianople provides for Russian retention of Poti, Akhalkalaki and Akhaltsikhe. Guria placed under direct Russian rule.
1830	Formation of a Secret Society for the re-establishment of an independent Georgia under Bagratid rule (composed of Elizbar Eristavi, Alexander Orbeliani and other members of their clans).
1832	General Veliamínov invades Kazi Mulla's territory, capturing Dargo and Gimri. Kazi Mulla killed.
9 Dec.	Orbeliani–Eristavi conspiracy betrayed to the authorities. Ten of the accused condemned to death by quartering, commuted to exile in Russia.

1833	Formation of a Ministerial Committee for the Organization of the Trans-Caucasian Territory.
1836	Kazi Mulla's successor, Shamíl, begins raiding Russian positions.
1837	Commission under P. V. Hahn recommends standardization of Caucasian administration along Russian lines. Nicholas I tours the Caucasus and is persuaded by Hahn to dismiss Rozen, who preferred a more devolved system. Shamíl rejects an invitation to meet Nicholas. 3,000 Russian troops land at Adler, at the mouth of the river Mzymta.
1838	Russians land at Sochi and Tuapse and build forts. General von Grabbe leads an expedition into Chechniá, capturing Shamíl's stronghold of Ahulgo, but Shamíl escapes.
1840	Adoption of Hahn's proposals for Caucasian administration (10 Apr.). Widespread Circassian raids on Russian forts.
1841	Peasant revolt in Guria, blamed on Hahn's over-centralization, leads to his dismissal (spring).
1842	Chernyshëv and Pozen tour the Caucasus to examine the administration.
Oct.	Sixth Section of His Majesty's Own Chancery set up to ensure the Emperor's close supervision of Caucasian affairs (director: Pozen).
1843	Widespread raids by Shamíl.
1845	Vorontsóv's raid into Chéchnia and Ichkéria incurs heavy Russian losses but brings no results (May).
1846	Shamíl's raid on Kabarda threatens the Georgian Military Highway.
1854	Vorontsóv granted leave to go abroad for medical treatment (Mar.). Nikolái Andréevich Read made temporary commander of the Caucasus Corps.

Alexander II

1857	General Evdokímov pursues a policy of systematic deforestation of the Caucasus to flush out Shamíl.
1858	Evdokímov takes Shatoy and penetrates into Daghestan.
1859	Shamíl captured (25 Aug.).
1862	Evdokímov moves into Circassia and begins to transport the population into the Russian steppe (Feb.).
1864	Defeat of the Circassians (May). 400,000 Circassians, about half the population, emigrate to Turkey. The

	remainder are transported into the Russian steppe. Circassia is repopulated with Russians. Discontent grows in Georgia over the harsh conditions of the peasant emancipation there.
1865	New taxes give rise to strikes and disorders in Tiflis. Troops fire on the crowds killing about 40. Members of 'Young Georgia' and 'Young Armenia' arrested.

Alexander III

1885	Dondukóv-Kórsakov closes about 500 Armenian Church schools.
1886	Dondukóv-Kórsakov reverses his decision on Armenian schools.

Nicholas II

1896	Armenian Church schools replaced by Russian schools under the Education Ministry (Jan.). The cost to be met by the confiscation of Church funds previously dedicated to education.
1903	Armenian Church funds confiscated (12 June). Armenian passive resistance begins. Russians encourage ethnic strife between Azeris and Armenians.
1905	
Feb.	Bakú *pogróm* of Armenians. Fighting between Armenians and Muslims. Peasant revolt in Guria: peasants withhold taxes, boycott Russian institutions, and establish a republic ruled by the RSDRP. Georgian clergy demand an autocephalous Church.
29 Aug.	Numerous casualties when Cossacks attack a socialist demonstration outside Tiflis town hall.
1907	I. Chavchavádze murdered (28 Aug.). A Bishop and an archimandrite, demanding an autocephalous church, are dismissed.
1908	Georgian nationalist murders Russian Exarch Nikon in Tiflis (28 May).
1912	Georgian peasants removed from the state of 'temporary obligation' and begin redemption payments.

3.6.1 Commanders-in-chief and Viceroys in the Caucasus

1801–2	K. von Knorring
1802–6	P. D. Tsitsiánov
1806–9	I. V. Gudóvich

February 1809–11	A. P. Tormásov
1811–12	F. O. Paulucci
1812–16	N. F. Rtíshchev
1816–28.iii.1827	A. P. Ermólov
1827–31	I. F. Paskévich
1831–37	G. V. Rozen
1837–42	E. A. Golovín
1842–44	A. I. Neidgart

Viceroys in the Caucasus

17.xi.1844–29.xi.1854	M. S. Vorontsóv
January–June 1854	N. A. Read (acting)
29.xi.1854–17.vi.1856	N. N. Muravëv
22.vii.1856–1862	A. I. Bariátinskii
1862–1881	Grand Duke Mikhaíl Nikoláevich

Commanders-in-chief in the Caucasus

1882–90	A. M. Dondukóv-Kórsakov
1890–6.xii.1896	S. A. Sheremétev
12.xii.1896–1905	G. S. Golítsyn

Viceroys in the Caucasus

1905–15	I. I. Vorontsóv-Dáshkov
1915–1.iii.1917	Grand Duke Nikolái Nikoláevich

3.7 Russia in Asia

Peter I
1705–11   Bashkír uprising against Russian rule.

Anna Ivánovna
1731   Kazákh Little Horde accepts Russian suzerainty.
1734   Kazákh Middle Horde accepts Russian suzerainty.

Catherine II
1795   Shah of Persia invades Caucasus (see p. 198).
1796
Apr.   Expeditionary force under Valerián Zúbov leaves Kirliar.
Summer   Zúbov occupies Bakú, Shamakhi and Ganjeh.
Autumn   Zúbov crosses the Araxes and takes up winter quarters on the Maghan Steppe.

Paul I
1796   Zúbov expedition recalled (Nov.).

Nicholas I
1836   Kazákh revolt led by Isatay Taimánov (until 1838).
1837   Kazákh revolt led by Kenesary Kazymov (until 1847).
1845   Military bases established at Turgai and Irgiz.
1847   Military base established at Raimsk on the Aral Sea. N. Muravĕv becomes governor-general of Eastern Siberia (until 1861).

Alexander II
1866   Territories seized since 1847 annexed as the governorship-general of Turkestan. Governor-general: K. P. von Kaufmann (until 1883).
1876   Abolition of the Khanate of Kokand, annexed to Russia as the Fergana Region (19 Feb.). Military governor: M. D. Skóbelev (until 1877).

Nicholas II

1903
Admiral E. I. Alekséev appointed viceroy of Kwantung (with Port Arthur) and Amúr (20 July).

1904
Alekséev appointed commander-in-chief in the Far East (recalled Oct.).

3.8 Russian America

Ivan VI
1741   Following Titus Bering, Russian fur traders penetrate
                Alaska.

Catherine II
1770s   Siberian merchant Shélikov equips expeditions to the
                Kuriles.
1783   Further expeditions to the Kuriles and mainland
                Alaska (until 1789).

Paul I
1797   Creation of the United American Company.
1799   United American Company renamed the Russian-
                American Company and made responsible for Russian
                settlements in America north of 55th parallel. Its
                administrative centre was Novo-Arkhangélsk, Sitka
                Island, Alaska.

Alexander I
1812   Building of a Russian colony at Fort Ross (California).
1821   Alexander tries to prevent foreign powers from whal-
                ing between the Sea of Okhótsk and Russian Alaska.

Nicholas I
1841   Sale of Fort Ross to Captain John Sutter.
1854   To avoid British attack, the affairs of the Russian-
                American Company transferred fictitiously to an
                American company (1 May until 1.v.1857).

Alexander II
1862   Russian-American Company's Charter expires (1 Jan.).
                Gold found in Alaska.
1863   Inter-Departmental Committee reports that Russian
                colonies in America 'present a picture of complete
                stagnation' (May).

1866   Secret negotiations between William Henry Seward
                           and Edward Stoeckl, Russian Minister to Washington,
                           over the sale of Alaska to the USA (Dec.).
1867
17/29 Mar.   USA buys the Russian-American Company (i.e. Alaska)
                           for US$7,200,000.
28 Mar./9 Apr.   US Senate ratifies the purchase of the Russian-
                           American Company.
6/18 Oct.   USA officially takes possession of Alaska.

SECTION FOUR

Foreign Policy and War

4.1 Foreign Policy Outline

1695–1700	Azóv Campaigns
1700–21	Great Northern War
1710–11	Loss of Azóv
1733–38	War of the Polish Succession
1735–39	Turkish War: withdrawal from the Southern Steppe
1741–43	Swedish War (War of the Hats)
1756–62	The Seven Years' War
1768–74	The Conquest of the Southern Steppe to the Black Sea
1772	First Partition of Poland
1776–83	Conquest of the Crimea
1787–91	Turkish War
1788–90	Swedish War
1792–1800	Wars of the French Revolution
1793	Second Partition of Poland
1795	Third Partition of Poland
1806–12	Turkish War
1808–9	Invasion and Annexation of Finland
1821–41	The Greek Revolt and the Mohammed Ali Crises
1841–53	The Dispute over the Holy Places
1853–54	Turkish War
1854–56	The Crimean War
1869–85	Anglo-Russian Rivalry in Afghanistan
1875–78	The Bosnian Crisis and the Russo-Turkish War
1881–87	The Bulgarian Crisis
1890–1907	Rapprochement with France and Rivalry with Britain in the Far East
1911–13	The Balkan Wars
1914–17	The First World War

4.1.1 Ministers of Foreign Affairs

8.ix.1802–January 1804	A. R. Vorontsóv
January 1804–8.vi.1806	A. J. Czartoryski
8.vi.1806–September 1807	A. E. Budberg
September 1807–August 1814	N. P. Rumiántsev

August 1814–April 1856	K. V. Nesselrode (1816–22 jointly with Capodistria)
1816–Summer 1822	J. Capodistria (jointly with Nesselrode)
April 1856–82	A. M. Gorchakóv
April 1882–January 1895	N. K. Giers
6.i.1895–18.viii.1896	A. B. Lobánov-Rostóvskii
1896–1.i.1897	N. P. Shíshkin
1.i.1897–8.vi.1900	M. N. Muravëv
June 1900–April 1906	V. N. Lamsdorff
April 1906–10	A. P. Izvólskii
1910–7.vii.1916	S. D. Sazónov
7 July–10.xi.1916	B. V. Stürmer
30.xi.1916–1.iii.1917	N. N. Pokróvskii

4.2 Russia and the Baltic

Peter I

1699	Russo-Polish anti-Swedish Alliance (Nov.).
1700–21	**Great Northern War**
1700	
8/19 Aug.	Russia declares war.
Aug.	Russia invades Ingria. Russian siege of Narva begins.
7/18 Nov.	Charles XII scatters Russians outside Narva. Peter the Great flees.
9/20 Nov.	Battle of Narva: Swedes annihilate the Russian army under de Croy although outnumbered five to one.
1701	
Feb.	Peter meets Augustus at Birsen and promises to make no claims on Livonia or Estonia and to supply the Poles with men and money.
17 June	Swedes defeat a Russian-Polish-Saxon army and relieve Riga.
1702	
Jan.–Dec.	Russian invasion of Ingria.
7 Jan.	Battle of Erestfer. Russian victory.
18 July	Battle of Hummelshof. Russian victory.
Oct.	Russians take Nöteborg which they rename Schlüsselburg.
1703	Foundation of St Petersburg in Swedish Ingria (16 May).
1704	
4 July	Russians take Dorpat.
9 Aug.	Russians take Narva.
1705	Russian army under Ogilvie occupies Kurland.
1706	
July	Russians driven out of Kurland back to Pinsk.
Aug.	Charles XII invades Saxony.
Sept.	Charles rejects Peter's peace overtures and imposes Treaty of Altranstädt on Augustus, replacing him with Stanisław Leszczyński on the throne of Poland.
1707	Negotiations between Peter and Francis Rakoczi, whom Peter wants as Polish king. Retreating Russian army lays waste to Swedish Baltic provinces.

1708

21 Dec./1 Jan.	Charles XII invades Russia.
17/28 June	Charles crosses the Berezína at Borísov.
23 June/4 July	Battle of Golovchino. Swedish victory.
27 June/8 July	Swedes advance to Mogilëv.
July–Oct.	Russian retreat using scorched earth tactic. Swedes suffer from hunger. Charles marches south into Ukraine to join forces with Mazépa.
Sept.–Oct.	Swedish army under Lybecker driven back from St Petersburg into Finland.
28–29 Sept./ Oct. 9–10	Battle of Lesnáia. Swedish relief army under Lewenhaupt is defeated and burns a vital supply train.
21 Oct.	Lewenhaupt and 6,000 survivors join Charles.

1709

Spring	Russians under Goltz invade Poland.
30 Apr.–27 June	Swedes besiege Poltáva.
27 June	Battle of Poltava. Russian victory.
28 June	Swedish army capitulates at Perevolochna. Charles and Mazépa flee to Ottoman territory.
July	Saxony invades Poland.
Aug.–Dec.	Russian invasion of Poland.
26 Sept.	Peter meets Augustus in Torún and replaces him on Polish throne.
Oct.	Peter raises the partition of Poland with Frederick I of Prussia at Marienwerder.

1710	Russians under Apráksin take Výborg. Russians take Elbling, Riga and Réval. Livonia and Estonia incorporated into Russia, retaining charters and privileges. Peter's niece, Anna Ivánovna, marries Frederick William, Duke of Kurland.
1711	Russians take Borgå and Åbo.
1713–14	Russians occupy the whole of Finland to Åland Islands.
1714	Battle of Gangut (26–27 July). Russian naval victory ends Swedish domination of Baltic.
Autumn	Russian troops occupy Umeå in Sweden for one month.
1715–17	Uprising of the Polish nobles against Augustus II.
1715	Prussia declares war on Sweden (1 May).
1716	
Apr.	Peter's niece Catherine Ivánovna marries Charles-Leopold, Duke of Mecklenburg-Schwerin. Russian alliance with Mecklenburg.

3 June	Convention with Denmark to invade Sweden.
Mid Sept.	Planned invasion of southern Sweden cancelled. Danes demand Russian troops evacuate to Mecklenburg.
Nov.	Russian intervention against Polish nobility. Russian treaty with Augustus confines the Polish Army to a maximum of 24,000 men.
1717	Russian troops withdrawn from Mecklenburg (Summer).
1718	
May	Russo-Swedish peace talks open at Lövö.
Dec.	Charles XII killed.
1718–19	Anti-Russian unrest in Poland.
1719	
Jan.	Treaty of Vienna.
July–Aug.	Unsuccessful Osterman mission to Stockholm. Lövö talks abandoned. Russian troops land in Southern Sweden.
1719–20	Under pressure of Treaty of Vienna, Russian troops withdrawn from Poland.
1720	
Jan.	Secret alliance with Prussia.
Feb.	Anglo-Swedish alliance. Russian troops land in Northern Sweden.
Nov.	George I urges Swedes to make peace with Russia.
1721	
Feb.	Peace talks begin in Nystad.
11/22 May	Peace conference officially opens.
May–June	Russian troops continue to devastate Northern Sweden.
30 Aug./10 Sept.	Peace of Nystad ends Great Northern War.
1724	Peter's daughter, Anna Petróvna, marries Charles-Frederick, Duke of Holstein-Gottorp (Nov.). The marriage contract includes a promise that Russia would intervene 'if necessary' to uphold his claim to the Swedish throne.

Catherine I

| **1726** | Abortive Russian attempt to impose Ménshikov as Duke of Kurland. |

Peter II

| **1727** | Russian troops occupy Kurland and expel Maurice de Saxe, who had been elected to the throne by the local Diet (Aug.). |

Anna Ivánovna

1732	Treaty with Denmark and Austria (Mar.) (see p. 261).
1733–38	**War of the Polish Succession**
	The death of Augustus II left two claimants to the Polish throne: Augustus III of Saxony (supported by Austria and Russia) and Stanisław Leszczyński (supported by France, Spain and Sardinia).
1733	
Feb.	Death of Augustus II.
12 Sept.	Lacy leads a Russian invasion of Poland following the re-election of Stanisław Leszczyński to the Polish throne. Stanisław flees to Danzig.
24 Sept.	Frederick Augustus of Saxony elected Augustus III of Poland.
1734	
Jan.–June	Siege of Danzig (Lacy until March, then Münnich).
2 June	Fall of Danzig. Stanisław flees to Prussia.
1734–35	Civil war in Poland.
1736	Abdication of Stanisław (Jan.).
1737	Russians impose Bühren/Birón as Duke of Kurland by force of arms.
1741–43	**Russo-Swedish War (War of the Hats)**

Ivan VI

1741	Sweden declares war (27 July).
23 Aug.	Battle of Wilmanstrand. Russian victory.

Elizabeth

1741	Elizabeth's negotiations with the Swedish commander Lewenhaupt (Nov.) are broken off when the latter demands that Russia cede all its Baltic territories.
1742	Russian invasion of Finland.
1743	Treaty of Åbo (7 Aug.) ends the war with Sweden.

Peter III

1762	
1 Mar.	Peter III's note to Denmark demanding the return of Schleswig.
16 Apr.	Bühren/Birón abdicates as Duke of Kurland in favour of George of Holstein.
21 May	Peter orders Rumiántsev to occupy Mecklenberg.
24 May	Russian ultimatum to Denmark.

Catherine II

1762　Bühren/Birón agrees to protect Orthodoxy in Mitau, to favour Russian merchants, to have no dealings with Russia's enemies and to allow free passage for Russian troops (4/15 Aug.).

1763

Apr.	Russia achieves restoration of Bühren/Birón in Kurland.
24 Sept./5 Oct.	Death of Augustus III of Poland.
6/17 Oct.	The Chernyshёv plan defines Russian policy to Poland. Russia to support a candidate for the Polish throne. Troops to be stationed along the Russo-Polish border, which is to be 'modified' in Russian strategic interests.
6/17 Dec.	Death of the Elector of Saxony (French and Austrian candidate for the Polish throne).

1764

Mar.	Russian troops enter Poland at request of the Czartorýskis.
31 Mar./11 Apr.	Russo-Prussian Treaty. A separate convention binds Frederick to support Stanisław Poniatowski to the Polish throne.
12/23 Apr.	Russia and Prussia pledge support for Polish 'dissidents' (Orthodox and Protestants).
May	Russians, under M. K. Dáshkov, pursue and defeat Branicki and Radziwiłł.
July	Russia and Prussia call for the restoration of dissidents' rights in Poland.
26 Aug./6 Sept.	Stanisław Poniatowski elected king.

1765　Russo-Danish Defensive Alliance formed (28 Feb./11 Mar.).

1766

Sept.–Oct.	Russian envoy to Poland (N. V. Repnín) presses the case for dissidents' rights.
24 Sept./4 Oct.	Repnín orders Russian troops to occupy Cracow and Wilno to support his case.
13/24 Nov.	Polish Diet reaffirms discrimination against the dissidents.

1767

26 Feb./9 Mar.	Proclamation of Confederation of Słuck for Orthodox dissidents in Lithuania, and of Torún for Protestant dissidents, under the protection of Russian troops.
11/22 Apr.	Russo-Danish Treaty to exchange Holstein for Oldenburg.
June	General Confederation of Radom summons a Diet in Poland.

3/14 Aug.	Pánin informs Repnín that Russian support for Polish dissidents was to obtain 'once and forever, through our co-religionists and the Protestants, a firm and reliable party legally entitled to participate in the affairs of Poland'.
Mid Sept.	Russian troops moved to the outskirts of Warsaw and Repnín is joined by von Saldern.
24 Sept./5 Oct.	Extraordinary Polish Diet opposes Russian demands. Repnín and von Saldern have numerous opponents of Russian policy arrested and deported to Russia.

1768

13/24 Feb.	Extraordinary Polish Diet adopts Warsaw Treaty.
Mar.	The rejection of the Russo-Polish Treaty by the Confederation of Bar leads to civil war in Poland with strong Russian intervention.

1769   Austria starts moving troops into Zips (Feb.).

31 Mar./11 Apr.	Repnín replaced by M. N. Volkónskii.
2/13 Sept.	Battle of Orékhovo. Russian (A. V. Suvórov) victory.

1770   French send Dumouriez to Poland to unite confederates.

7/18 Oct.	Suvórov commands Russian troops around Lublin.

1771

10/21 May	Battle of Tyniec. Suvórov defeats Walewski.
12/23 May	Battle of Landskron. Suvórov defeats Dumouriez.
22 May/2 June	Battle of Zamosc. Suvórov defeats Pulawski.
May	Catherine's Council decides to lay claim to Polish Livonia, in return for which Poland would be compensated with Moldavia and Wallachia.
Dec.	Pánin invites Austria to join Prussia and Russia and 'compensate herself in Poland'.

1772

6/17 Feb.	Russo-Prussian Convention on Poland.
7/18 Mar.	Preliminary Austro-Prusso-Russian agreement on Poland.
5 Aug.	**First Partition of Poland**
8/19 Aug.	Royal *coup d'état* in Sweden destroys Russian policy there.

1773

1/12 June	Holstein ceded to Denmark.
14/25 July	Paul Petróvich cedes Oldenburg and Delmenhorst to Frederick Augustus of Lübeck.
12/23 Aug.	Treaty of Alliance with Denmark.
30 Sept.	Polish Diet accepts partition, and Catherine's terms: maintenance of *liberum veto*; the Crown to remain elective, but open to native Poles only; relatives of the

king and queen to be excluded from high office; king not to command troops; death penalty for apostasy against Catholicism to be abolished.

1777	Gustavus III of Sweden visits St Petersburg as the 'Count of Gothland'.
1780	
9/20 July	'Armed Neutrality': convention with Denmark over rights of neutral shipping.
1/12 Aug.	Sweden joins 'Armed Neutrality'.
1787	At their meeting in Kánev, Stanisław Poniatowski tries to persuade Catherine to accept constitutional reform in Poland in return for Polish support against the Porte (May).
1788–90	**Russo-Swedish War**
1788	
20 June/1 July	Diplomatic relations broken off.
22 June/3 July	Swedes bombard Nyslott.
6/17 July	Naval battle of Hogland (Admiral Grieg). Indecisive.
12/23 July	Gustavus III besieges Fridrikshamn but withdraws in August.
1/12 Aug.	Over 100 Swedish and Finnish nobles sign the Pact of Anjala, denouncing Gustavus for engaging in war unconstitutionally and proposing that Catherine negotiates peace on the basis of the 1721 frontier.
End Aug.	Denmark declares war on Sweden.
28 Sept./9 Oct.	Danish armistice with Sweden.
Oct.	Polish 'Four Years' Diet' dismantles the 1773 system of government.
9/20 Nov.	Prussia 'guarantees' Polish borders.
1789	
May	Russia agrees to remove troops from Poland.
30 June/11 July	Porte undertakes to pay Sweden a subsidy as long as war lasts.
26 July	Naval battle of Åland (Chichagóv). Inconclusive.
13/24 Aug.	First naval battle of Svensksund. Russian victory (Kruse and Nassau-Siegen).
1790	
Feb.	Prussia demands Danzig and Torún in return for alliance and commercial treaty with Poland.
18/29 Mar.	Prusso-Polish Defence Treaty. 1. Prussia to regard as *causus foederis* any attempt by Russia or Austria to intervene in Polish affairs. '2. The two high contracting parties will do all that they can to guarantee and conserve for each other reciprocally the tranquil

possession of states, provinces and towns that they possess at the time of the present treaty.' 3. Prussia undertakes to send 14,000 skirmishers and 4,000 cavalry immediately should Poland be attacked.

2/13 May	Chichagóv defeats the Swedes at the battle of Réval.
4/15 May	The Swedes win the battle of Fridrikshamn.
2–9 July	The Russians under Nassau-Siegen lose the second naval battle of Svensksund, losing 53 ships sunk or captured.
3/14 Aug.	Peace of Verelä signed on the basis of the *status quo ante*.

1791

22 Apr./3 May	Polish Diet accepts new constitution: 1. Elections to the throne abolished, monarchy made hereditary (Elector of Saxony and his heirs to succeed Poniatowski). 2. Executive power conferred on king and council of state. 3. Legislative power to reside in a Diet of two chambers. 4. *Liberum veto* and confederations abolished.
7/18 Oct.	Secret Treaty with Sweden.

1792

27 Jan./7 Feb.	Austro-Prussian Alliance.
29 Mar./9 Apr.	Catherine's Council discusses policy towards Poland and decides to invade only with the consent of Austria and Prussia.
10/21 Apr.	Russia informs Berlin and Vienna of its intention to form a Confederation and to invade Poland.
28 Apr./8 May	F. Potocki, S. Rzewuski and K. Branicki in St Petersburg sign an Act of Confederation, with Catherine's participation, to restore the ancient constitution of Poland.
7/18 May	Russian troops invade Poland. Poles accompanying Russian forces proclaim the Confederation, dating it from Targowice on 3/14 May, i.e. before the Russian invasion.
11/22 May	Polish Diet appoints Stanisław dictator and dissolves.
14/25 May	Russians in Wilno announce the General Confederation of Lithuania.
13/24 July	Stanisław accedes to the Confederation of Targowice.

1793

12/23 Jan.	**Second Partition of Poland**
27 May/7 June	Chichagóv ordered to act against the shipping of Denmark and Sweden, which had refused to join the trade ban on France.
11/22 July	Polish Diet accepts Russian partition.

13/24 Sept.	Polish Diet accepts Prussian partition.
5/16 Oct.	Russo-Polish Alliance makes the rump of Poland a Russian protectorate.

1794

Apr.	Danish-Swedish convention to protect their shipping against Russia.
Mar.	Polish uprising under Tadeusz Kościuszko, sparked off by the reduction of the Polish Army by Russian envoy Ingelstrom.
24 Mar./4 Apr.	Kosciuszko defeats Russians at Raclawice.
3/14 Apr.	Warsaw uprising against Russians.
11/22 Apr.	Revolt spreads to Russian-occupied Lithuania and Kurland.
20 Apr./1 May	Catherine's Council decides to coordinate with the Prussians and Austrians.
25 Apr./6 May	Rumiántsev commands repression of Polish revolt. Repnín commands repression in Lithuania.
7/18 May	Kosciuszko proclaims the emancipation of Polish peasantry (never implemented).
26 May/6 June	Battle of Rawka: Russo-Prussian victory over the Poles.
4/15 June	Prussians occupy Cracow.
28 Sept./9 Oct.	Kosciuszko defeated and taken prisoner by Fermór at Maciejowice.
24 Oct./4 Nov.	Suvórov's troops sack Praga (suburb of Warsaw) killing 20,000 civilians.
28 Oct./8 Nov.	Suvórov occupies Warsaw.
23 Dec./3 Jan. 1795	Treaty with Austria partitioning Poland.

1795

Aug.	Austro-Russian partition treaty presented to Prussia as an ultimatum.
13/24 Oct.	**Third Partition of Poland** with Austria and Prussia.

Paul I

1796

	Russian Emperors become rulers of Kurland (15/26 Nov.).

1800

	Second Armed Neutrality (5/16 Dec.).

Alexander I

1805

	Russo-Swedish Alliance (Jan.).

1808

8/20 Feb.	Invasion of Finland.
16/28 Mar.	Note circulated to foreign courts announcing the annexation of Finland.
Summer	Finns wage guerrilla warfare.

1809

Mar.   Barclay de Tolly crosses the ice of the Gulf of Bothnia and occupies the Åland Islands.

5/17 Sept.   Peace of Fridrikshamn.

1812   Treaty with Sweden (Apr.).

4.2.1 Treaties

1699

21 Apr.   **Vorónezh**: Between Russia and Denmark to end Swedish domination of the Baltic.

11 Nov.   **Preobrazhénskoe**: Anti-Swedish alliance between Russia and Poland-Saxony. Russia to take Ingria, Augustus to take Kurland. After this the Danes ratify the Vorónezh agreement.

1700

18 Aug.   **Travendal**: Denmark withdraws from the war, returning Schleswig to Sweden.

1706

24 Sept.   **Altranstädt**: Augustus of Saxony abdicates the Polish throne, recognizes Stanisław Lesczynski as king, and breaks his alliance with Russia.

1709

9 Oct.   **Thorn**: Russo-Saxon alliance.

1714

June   **Russo-Prussian Treaty**: Russia to take Estonia, Ingria, Karelia and Výborg; Prussia to take Stettin.

1715

Oct.   **Greifswald**: Russia to retain Ingria, Karelia and Estonia. Hanover to give Russia support for the retention of Livonia. Hanover to take Bremen and Verden.

1716

Apr.   **Treaty with Mecklenburg-Schwerin**: Signed on the occasion of the marriage of Peter's niece Catherine with Charles-Leopold of Mecklenburg-Schwerin. Russia to give armed support to M-S against all internal and external enemies. M-S to acquire Swedish port of Wismar. Russia to use M-S as base of operations against the Swedes. Russians to have the right to trade in M-S on the same basis as the Mecklenburgers.

1719

Jan.   **Vienna**: Between Augustus II, Austria and Britain, providing for the forced evacuation of Russian troops from Poland.

1720

Feb.   **Secret Treaty of Potsdam**: Russia and Prussia agree to preserve intact the free elective constitution of the Polish monarchy and the 'liberties' of Poland, including the *liberum veto*.

1721

30 Aug./10 Sept.   **Nystad**: Between Russia and Sweden. Russia acquires Livonia, Estonia, Ingria and part of Karelia, but returns the rest of Finland to Sweden. Russia pays an indemnity to Sweden. Russia is not to intervene in internal Swedish struggles or in the succession to the Swedish throne.

1738

Nov.   **Vienna**: Stanisław abdicates the throne of Poland to become Duke of Lorraine; Lorraine to become French on the death of Stanisław; Augustus recognized as King of Poland.

1743

7 Aug.   **Åbo**: Russia extends its frontier in Finland to the river Kymi, including Nyslott Wilmanstrand and Fridrikshamn.

1764

31 Mar./11 Apr.   **Russo-Prussian Alliance**

1765

28 Feb./11 Mar.   **Russo-Danish Defensive Alliance**: Russia and Denmark each guarantees the other's possessions and binds themselves to assist the other in the event of attack, except if Russia were attacked by the Porte, when this assistance could take the form of a subsidy.

1767

11/22 Apr.   **Russo-Danish Treaty**: On the majority of Grand Duke Paul, Russia to give up Holstein, Denmark to cede Oldenburg and Delmenhorst to a junior branch of the house of Holstein-Gottorp.

1768

24 Feb./6 Mar.   **Warsaw**: Russia guarantees for all time the constitution, form of government, freedoms and laws of Poland. All nobles, whether Catholic or dissident, to have equal rights, but the king must be Catholic, and Catholicism to be the religion of the Polish state. Various military and civil offices open to non-Catholics. Both parties guarantee the territorial integrity of the other. A separate agreement specifies which matters of state are subject to the *liberum veto*.

1769

2/13 Dec.   **Russo-Danish Treaty**: Any alteration in the Swedish constitution to be *casus foederis*. In which event, Denmark is to invade Sweden across the Norwegian border, and Russia to invade Sweden across the Finnish border.

1772

5 Aug.   **First Partition of Poland:** Poland loses about one-third of its territory. Russia acquires White Russia and all territory to the Dvina and Dniépr (about 1,800,000 people, mostly Orthodox). Austria takes Red Russia, Western Podolia, Lwów and part of Cracow (about 2,700,000 people). Prussia takes Polish Prussia except Gdánsk and Torún (416,000 people).

1790

3/14 Aug.   **Verälä/Wereloe**: Ends Russo-Swedish War and restores the *status quo ante*.

1791   **Secret Treaty with Sweden**: Russia to supply Gustavus with 8,000 troops, warships, or 300,000 rubles per annum for an invasion of France planned for 1792.

1793

12/23 Jan.   **Convention of St Petersburg – Second Partition of Poland**: Russia takes most of Lithuania and Western Ukraine, including Podolia (over 250,000 square kilometres and over 3,000,000 people). Prussia takes Gdánsk, Torún and South-west Poland (1,000,000 people).

5/16 Oct.   **Polish Alliance**: For mutual defence, with the army command going to Russia. Russia may introduce forces into Poland after consultation with the Polish government. In time of war, Russia may recruit Polish troops or increase the size of the Polish Army. Poland to refrain from alliances with other powers without Russian consent. Polish foreign envoys to act in concert with Russians. The Polish constitution is not to be altered without Russian consent. Orthodox Poles to be subordinate to the metropolitan of Kiev.

1794

23 Dec./3   **Treaty with Austria**: 1. Austria accedes to the parti-
Jan. 1795   tion treaty between Russia and Prussia of 12/23 January 1793, thereby gaining Russian recognition of her right to exchange the Netherlands for Bavaria. 2. Poland is distributed between Russia, Austria and Prussia. 3. Secret alliance against Prussia and a renewal

of the alliance against Turkey, with an agreement over its partition (a restatement of the agreement of 10/21 September 1782, see p. 252). Russia agrees to future Austrian acquisitions in France and Venice in compensation for the advantages obtained by Russia and Prussia in 1793.

1795

13/24 Oct   **Third Partition of Poland**: Russia obtains the remainder of Lithuania, Belorussia and Ukraine (120,000 square kilometres). Kurland is incorporated into Russia (1796). Austria receives remainder of Galicia (October 1796: including Cracow). Prussia received Mazovia with Warsaw.

1799

Oct.   **Alliance with Sweden**

1800

5/16 Dec.   **Second Armed Neutrality**: Based on the Armed Neutrality of 1780, Russia, Sweden, and Denmark unite to defend the freedom of the seas. Prussia signs on 7/18 December.

1809

5/17 Sept.   **Fridrikshamn**: Sweden cedes Finland and the Åland Islands to Russia. The new Russo-Swedish frontier to be the river Torneo.

1812

Apr.   **Treaty with Sweden**: Removes the danger of Swedish attack on Finland in the event of war with France, in return for Alexander's promise to support Swedish claims on Norway.

4.3 Russia and the Ottoman Empire

1687 V. V. Golítsyn and P. Gordon's advance south is defeated when Khan Selim Girey sets fire to the Steppe (May–June).

Peter I
1689
Mar. Golítsyn and Gordon's second advance into the southern Steppe.
Mid Apr. Golítsyn joins I. S. Mazépa.
15/26 May Victory over Tartars in the Steppe.
20/31 May Russians arrive at Perekóp, to find Tartars entrenched. They withdraw North.
1692 Crimean Tartars burn Nemirov (Ukraine).
1695–1700 **Azóv Campaign**
27 June Gordon and A. S. Shéin camp outside Azóv.
5 Aug. First unsuccessful attack on Azóv.
Aug. B. P. Sheremétev and Mazépa sweep down the Dniepr to take the Turkish fortresses of Gazy-Kerman, Taman, Nustretkermen and Saginkermen.
25 Sept. Second unsuccessful attack on Azóv.
1696
Spring Warship construction begins at Vorónezh.
27 May Russian fleet arrives off Azóv.
19 July Russians take Azóv.
1698 Congress of Carlowitz (Nov.). P. Voznítsyn demands that Russia retain its conquests and that Turkey surrender Kerch. Turks demand surrender of Azóv and four forts on the lower Dniépr taken by Sheremétev.
1699
14/24 Jan. Russo-Turkish stalemate at Carlowitz. No peace treaty, only two-year armistice.
July E. I. Ukráintsev sent to Constantinople to negotiate peace.
1700 Peace of Constantinople (13/24 June).
1704 Tolstoy agreement (Dec.).

1705	Ukráintsev agreement (22 Oct./2 Nov.).
1710–11	Loss of Azóv.
1710	Ottomans declare war (Nov.).
1711	
Jan.	Unsuccessful Tartar raid on Vorónezh. Peter tries to avoid war by writing to the Sultan.
28 Feb./11 Mar.	Russia declares war on the Ottomans.
Mar.	Russia calls on the Montenegrins and on the Christian Peoples under Turkish Rule 'to fight for faith and fatherland . . . [to drive out] the descendants of the heathen Mohammed . . . into their old fatherland, the Arabian sands and steppes'.
8–9/19–20 July	Battle of the Pruth. Ottoman (Baltadji) victory. Peter obliged to seek peace.
10/21 July	Treaty of the Pruth.
1717	Tartar raid up the Volga penetrates to the outskirts of Sarátov, Pénza and Vorónezh.
1723	Alarmed at Peter's successes against the Persians in the Caucasus, the Turks invade Georgia.
1724	Treaty of Constantinople (July).

Catherine I

| 1725 | Russian support for the Ottoman attempt to secure Western Caucasus leads to the Turkish-Persian War. |

Anna Ivánovna

1733	Russia protests when Crimean Tartars pass through Russian-held Northern Caucasus on their way to help the Porte in its war with Persia. Tartars recalled to the Crimea.
1735–39	**Russo-Turkish War**
1735	
June	Renewed attempt by Crimean Tartars to pass through North Caucasus leads to Russian attacks on Azóv and the Crimea.
Aug.	Russians under B. C. Münnich cross the Don.
Sept.	Ambassador in Constantinople (Veshniakóv) recalled.
1736	
May	Münnich's first raid into the Crimea.
June	Leóntev takes Kinbúrn and Lacy retakes Azóv, but then withdraws.
Aug.	Münnich withdraws from Crimea.
1737	
June–July	Münnich captures (2 July) and then abandons Ochákov.

Aug.–Oct.	Russo-Austro-Turkish peace conference at Nemirov fails to reach any agreement over Russian demands for Eastern frontier at river Kubán and Western at Dniestr, (later revised to Berda).

1738

May	Ostermann requests the French (Villeneuve) to begin negotiations with the Turks (May). Sticking point: Azóv, which the Turks wished to have demolished. Turkish formula to demolish Azóv and build two equidistant fortresses, one Russian, one Turkish – prevails.
Summer	Lacy's invasion of the Crimea is unsuccessful. Russians evacuate Ochákov and Kinbúrn.

1739

July–Sept.	Münnich takes Khotín and advances to Jassy.
7/18 Sept.	Treaty of Nissa.

Catherine II
1768–74   **The Conquest of the Southern Steppe to the Black Sea**
1768

25 Sept./6 Oct.	Turkey declares war when the Russians refuse to withdraw from Poland after Russian irregulars pursue Poles into Turkish territory and destroy the town of Balta.
Autumn	Iu. V. Dolgorúkii sent to Montenegro to foment anti-Turkish revolt.
6/17 Nov.	Imperial Council defines war aims: freedom of navigation in the Black Sea, a fortress/port on the Black Sea, new frontiers with Poland.
1769	Crimean Tartars (Kirim Girey) invade Ukraine (15/ 26 Jan.), lay waste Elizavetgrád Province and join the Confederates in Poland.
Apr.–May	A. M. Golítsyn's unsuccessful attempt to take Khotín.
May	Russians under de Vernes take Azóv.
June	Golítsyn's second unsuccessful attempt to take Khotín.
22 July/2 Aug.	Kirim Girey attacks Golítsyn, but is beaten back.
26 July/6 Aug.	A Baltic Fleet Squadron under G. A. Spirídov sets sails for the Mediterranean to support the Greek revolt with landings in Morea. He is followed later in the year by two further squadrons under J. Elphinston and S. Grieg.
2/12 Aug.	Golítsyn withdraws across the Dniestr.
29 Aug./9 Sept.	Battle of Kameniec. Ali Pasha attacks Golítsyn, but is defeated.
6/17 Sept.	Golítsyn's victory on the Dniestr.
10/21 Sept.	Golítsyn takes Khotín.
16/27 Sept.	Golítsyn replaced by Rumiántsev.

26 Sept./7 Aug.	Russians (I. K. Elmpt) occupy Jassy.
16/27 Oct.	Catherine formulates the policy of encouraging the independence of the Crimean Tartars.
Nov.	N. A. Karázin occupies Bucharest.

1770

Mar.	Baltic squadrons arrive off Morea.
10/21 Apr.	Russians capture Navarino.
26 May/6 June	Russians abandon Navarino.
17/28 June	Battle of Riabaia Mogíla on the Pruth. Rumiántsev puts Turkish-Tartar Army to flight.
24–27 June/ 5–8 July	Battle of Chesme (Elphinston, S. Greig, A. G. Orlóv, Spirídov). Turkish fleet anihilated.
7/18 July	Rumiántsev defeats the Turks at the junction of the rivers Larga and Pruth.
17/28 July	P. Pánin begins the siege of Bender.
21 July/1 Aug.	Battle of the River Kagúl. Rumiántsev forces the Turks back behind the Danube. Russians then take the Turkish fortresses along the Danube and Pruth.
26 July/6 Aug.	Rumiántsev takes Izmail.
10/21 Aug.	Rumiántsev takes Kilia.
28 Aug./8 Sept.	Rumiántsev takes Akkerman.
Sept.	Porte requests joint Austrian-Prussian mediation.
16/27 Sept.	Pánin takes Bender.
16/27 Sept.	Catherine's Council defines war aims: Azóv, Taganróg, independence of the Crimea, the opening of the Black Sea and a new status for the Principalities (Moldavia and Wallachia).
10/21 Nov.	Rumiántsev takes Brailov, and goes into winter quarters near Jassy.

1771

Jan.	Spirídov accepts the surrender of 18 Aegean islands, which are incorporated into the Russian Empire as the Duchy of the Archipelago Islands.
3/14 June	V. M. Dolgorúkov[-Krýmskii] invades the Crimea.
29 June/10 July	Dolgorúkov takes Kaffa (Feodósiia). Selim Girey flees to Turkey.
24 Oct./5 Nov.	Catherine's Council redefines war aims: return the Principalities to Turkey in exchange for Ochákov and Kinbúrn.

1772

19/30 May	Armistice signed in Giurgevo.
27 July/ 8 Aug.	G. G. Orlóv and A. M. Obréskov begin peace negotiations with Turks (Osman Efendi) in Fokshani.
17/28 Aug.	Orlóv ultimatum breaks off negotiations.

1/12 Sept.	Catherine's Council decides policy in case of Swedish attack: lay waste to the Principalities and evacuate their inhabitants to Russia; the army to withdraw beyond the Dniépr and concentrate on holding the Crimea.
20 Nov./1 Dec.	Obréskov conducts new negotiations in Bucharest.
1773	
21 Mar./1 Apr.	Bucharest negotiations broken off.
Spring	Rumiántsev renews hostilities with a cautious campaign beyond the Danube.
10/21 May	A. V. Suvórov raids Turtukai.
17/28 June	Suvórov's second raid on Turtukai. Peace negotiations follow as the Pugachëv Revolt breaks out.
1774	
9/20 June	Rumiántsev crosses the Danube.
10/21 June	Battle of Kozludzha. Suvórov victory.
20 June/1 July	Turks ask for an armistice.
10/21 July	Peace of Kuchuk Kainardji.
1776–1783	**Conquest of the Crimea**
1776	A. A. Prozoróvskii seizes Perekóp (Nov.).
1777	Revolt in the Crimea against the pro-Russian Khan, Shagin Girey (Oct.).
1778	
Feb.	Revolt against Shagin Girey put down with the help of Russian troops.
July	Exodus of Christians from the Crimea, supported by Russian troops, shatters the Crimean economy.
1779	Treaty of Ainalikawak (10/21 Mar.).
1780	Civil war in the Crimea (Winter).
1782	
May	Shagin Girey flees to Kerch. The Porte is inclined to support the new khan, Bahadir Girey, despite Treaty of Ainalikawak.
3/14 Aug.	Potëmkin ordered to restore Shagin Girey.
Oct.	With the help of Austrian mediation in Constantinople, Shagin Girey is restored as Khan of the Crimea.
14/25 Dec.	Catherine authorizes Potëmkin to annex the Crimea in certain circumstances.
1783	
8/19 Apr.	Catherine orders Russian annexation of the Crimea.
20/31 July	Annexation completed.
1787–91	**Turkish War**
1787	
15/26 July	Turkish ultimatum.
13/24 Aug.	Turks declare war.
20/31 Aug.	Turkish ships fire on Russian ships near Ochákov.

1/12 Oct.	Battle of Kinbúrn. Suvórov repels Turkish landing.
1788	
June	Suvórov repels Turkish landing on Dniépr/Bug estuary.
27 July/7 Aug.	Battle of Ochákov. Suvórov, wounded in the throat, repels Turkish sortie.
16/27 Dec.	Potĕmkin takes Ochákov.
1789	
21 June/2 July	Battle of Fokshani. Russo (Suvórov)–Austrian (Coburg) victory.
11/22 Sept.	Battle of Rymnik. Suvórov–Coburg victory.
28 Sept./9 Oct.	Turks surrender Akkerman.
13/24 Oct.	New Sultan, Selim III, declares the war a Holy War.
3/14 Nov.	Potĕmkin takes Bender.
1790	
May	Ushakóv raids north Anatolian shore at Sinope, Samsun and Anapa.
June–Aug.	Joint Suvórov–Coburg campaign around Bucharest.
8/19 July	Naval battle of Kerch (Ushakóv). Inconclusive but frustrates Turkish landing.
11/22 Dec.	Suvórov takes Izmail.
1791	
End Mar.	Repnín crosses the Danube.
3/14 June	Turks defeated at Babadag.
22 June/3 July	Russians take Anapa.
29 June/10 July	Turks defeated at Machin.
31 July/11 Aug.	Preliminary Russo-Turkish peace agreement at Galatz. Russian victory over the Turkish fleet at Cape Kaliakra.
29 Dec./ 9 Jan. 1792	Peace of Jassy.

Alexander I

1806–12	**Turkish War**
1806	
26 Apr.	Porte announces its intention to close the Straits to Russian warships and troopships.
23 Nov.	Russian troops enter Moldavia.
27 Dec.	Porte declares war on Russia.
1807	Seniávin's victory over the Turkish Fleet at Athos (18/30 June).
1812	Treaty of Bucharest (16/28 May).

The Eastern Question

1821–41	**The Greek Revolt and the Mohammed Ali Crises**
1814	Greek merchants found *Philike Hetairia/The Friendly Society* in Odessa.

1816	G. A. Stróganov, ambassador to the Porte, instructed to ensure the full implementation of the Treaty of Bucharest.
1817	John Capodistria refuses presidency of *Philike Hetairia*.
1820	Alexander Ypsilantis becomes president of *Philike Hetairia*.
1821	
Mar.	Ypsilantis leads an army across the Pruth into Moldavia and Wallachia from Bessarabia, and appeals to Alexander for help. Alexander rejects this, in the conviction that the Greek revolt is fermented by revolutionary clubs in Paris. Revolt against the Turks breaks out in Morea.
Apr.	Revolt spreads to the Greek islands.
23 Apr.	Sultan Mahmud has the Greek Patriarch and three priests hanged in front of the Orthodox cathedral in Istanbul.
May	Turks stop Greek ships with wheat from Odessa passing through the Straits.
7 June	Ypsilantis defeated by the Turks at Dragatsani.
July	French do not respond to Alexander's proposal for a Franco-Russian alliance to intervene in Greece.
1822	Greek revolt increasingly successful in Morea and the islands. The Sultan appeals for help to Mohammed Ali of Egypt.
Apr.	Turkish massacre 20,000 Greeks in Chios.
Aug.	Diplomatic relations broken off with the Porte. British present the Porte with Russian demands: 1. Reduction of Turkish forces in the Principalities. 2. Re-establishment of freedom of shipping in the Black Sea. 3. Guarantees of future good government for Greece.
1823	Mahmud II forbids Greek ships to sail under the Russian flag (Apr.).
1824	
Jan.	Alexander calls for a conference on the Greek question: 1. Moslem yoke should not be imposed on Christian subjects; 2. Full independence should not be conceded. 3. Creation of three autonomous principalities (Eastern, Western and Southern Greece), with similar status to Moldavia and Wallachia.
June	St Petersburg conference of the ambassadors of the Powers lasts for only two meetings, as neither Greeks nor Turks are prepared to accept the proposed principalities.

July	Invasion of Crete by Egyptian soldiers under Ibrahim Pasha.

1825

End Feb.	Ibrahim Pasha invades Morea.
End Mar.	Ibrahim Pasha besieges Navarino.
7 Apr.	The four Powers agree to propose mediation with the Porte.
Aug.	Nesselrode writes that in future 'Russia will follow her own views exclusively and will be governed by her own interests', with regard to Greece.
Sept.	Russian armies concentrate on the borders of Moldavia and Wallachia.

Nicholas I
1826

5/17 Mar.	Russian note to the Porte demands: 1. The restoration of the privileges of the Principalities. 2. That the treaty of Bucharest be respected with regard to Serbia. 3. The dispatch of a Turkish plenipotentiary to the Russian frontier to negotiate outstanding issues. If this were not done within six weeks, war would ensue.
31 Apr./12 May	Sultan accepts the Russian ultimatum, withdraws Turkish troops from the Principalities and sends plenipotentiaries to Akkerman.
May	Sultan Mahmud issues an edict to create a regular army.
2/15 June	Massacre of Janissaries in Istanbul.
25 Sept./7 Oct.	Convention of Akkerman.

1827

Mar.	Capodistria elected president of Greece for seven years.
May	New Greek government draws up a Republican constitution.
June	Turks recapture Athens.
24 June/6 July	Treaty of London (see p. 288).
4/16 Aug.	Porte rejects the armistice.
8/20 Oct.	Anglo-Franco-Russian fleet annihilates Turco-Egyptian fleet at Navarino Bay.
18/30 Nov.	Porte repudiates the Convention of Akkerman and proclaims war against the infidels.
8/20 Dec.	Mahmud II, as Caliph, calls on all Muslims to aid him in a Holy War against Russia.

1828

Jan.	Russia proposes that the allies penetrate the Straits and dictate peace to the Sultan.

End Feb.	Straits virtually closed to foreign ships.
Mar.	Nesselrode instructs Admiral Heiden (Russian commander in the Mediterranean) to support the Greeks with arms and equipment.
Before 12/ 24 Apr.	Nicholas tells the Austrian ambassador that the Greeks 'do not deserve' liberation.
14/26 Apr.	Russia declares war on Turkey.
27 May	Russian troops cross the Danube.
Early June	Russian troops occupy the Principalities, but fail to take Shumla and Silistria, and retreat across the Danube for the winter.
23 June	Paskévich takes Kars.
20 Sept./2 Oct.	Egyptian troops begin to embark.
1829	Díbich appointed commander of Danubian Army.
30 May	Turks defeated at Kulevcha.
18 June	Silistria capitulates.
30 July/11 Aug.	The Porte accepts the Treaty of London.
8 Aug.	Adrianople surrenders.
Aug.	Committee convened to consider Russia's future attitude to Turkey: V. P. Kochubéi (chairman), Nesselrode, D. Dáshkov and three others).
2/14 Sept.	Treaty of Adrianople.
4 Sept.	Kochubéi Committee declares that 'the advantages of preserving the Ottoman Empire exceed its disadvantages', but should it collapse, Russia must take 'the most energetic measures to ensure that the exit from the Black Sea is not seized by any other power'.
Sept.	P. D. Kiselëv appointed Russian plenipotentiary in Moldavia and Wallachia (9.v.1834). He endows the Principalities with a Constitution.
1830	Convention of St Petersburg (26 Apr.).
1831	Egyptian Army under Ibrahim Pasha marches into Syria (Autumn).
1832	
25 Apr./7 May	Convention on Greek Independence.
15/27 May	Ibrahim takes Acre.
3/15 June	Ibrahim takes Damascus.
4/16 July	Ibrahim takes Aleppo.
9/21 July	Sultan signs protocol recognizing Greek independence.
Summer	Sultan sounds out A. P. Buténev, Russian ambassador to the Porte, on the possibility of Russian help against the Egyptians.
14 Oct./6 Nov.	Nesselrode promises a Russian squadron to help the Sultan against Mohammed Ali if required.

9/21 Dec.	N. N. Muraviëv arrives in Istanbul to prepare for Russian military aid to Turkey. Ibrahim routs the Turks at Koniah and advances to Brusa.
1833	
1/13 Jan.	Muraviëv in Cairo, with Austrian support, persuades Mohammed Ali to make peace with the Sultan.
8/20 Jan.	Ibrahim Pasha ignores the peace agreement and advances on Istanbul.
21 Jan./2 Feb.	Sultan asks Russia to send a fleet and an army to help him against the Egyptians.
4/16 Feb.	Mohammed Ali demands the cession to Egypt of Syria and Adana.
8/20 Feb.	Russian fleet anchors off the Golden Horn.
18/30 Mar.	Turks accept Mohammed Ali's terms, and ask for Russian troops to defend Istanbul.
23 Mar./4 Apr.	Russian troops land at Buyukdéré, in the Bosphorus (14,000 by 10/22 Apr.).
23 Apr./5 May	A. F. Orlóv's diplomatic mission to Istanbul.
26 June/8 July	Treaty of Unkiar-Skelessi.
28 June/10 July	Russians withdraw from the Bosphorus.
1834	Russo-Turkish Convention settles the frontier in the Caucasus, provides for a Russian troop withdrawal from the Principalities, and the cancellation of the Turkish war debt to Russia (7/29 Jan.).
1839	
15/27 July	Ambassadors of the Five Powers present the Porte with a joint note, stating that they have reached 'agreement on the eastern question', and urging Turkey 'to suspend all definite decisions without their concurrence'.
Aug.	Nesselrode memorandum to Nicholas that, as the Porte was unlikely to renew Unkiar Skelessi in 1841, a comprehensive international agreement for the closure of the Straits to warships was desirable.
22 Oct./3 Nov.	Hatt-i Sherif of Gülhané, by which the Sultan declares his intention to create a legislative council and institute the rule of law.
1840	London Convention (3/15 July) (see section 4.5 Russia and Western Europe, pp. 288–9).
1841	Straits Convention (1/13 June) (see section 4.5 Russia and Western Europe, p. 289).
1841–53	**The Dispute over the Holy Places** (see section 4.7 Russia and the Crimean War, pp. 299–302).
1854–56	**The Crimean War** (see section 4.7 Russian and the Crimean War, pp. 301–7).

Alexander II

1858

May | French and Russian support for the Montenegrins after their defeat of Turkey at Grahovo prevent Turkish retaliation.

7/19 Aug. | Convention of Paris (see p. 289).

Dec. | France and Russia support the overthrow of the pro-Austrian prince Alexander Karageórgevich in Serbia and his replacement by the pro-Russian Milosh Obrénovich.

1859 | The assemblies of both Principalities elect Alexander Cuza thereby accomplishing the creation of Romania.

1866 | On the election of Charles of Hohenzollern-Sigmaringen as King Carol I (Feb.), Russia withholds recognition and demands that severe measures be taken against the new Kingdom of Romania (the former Principalities) as the August 1858 Convention had confined the succession to Romanian citizens.

1867

Apr. | On the outbreak of a revolt in Crete, Russia urges the Porte to transfer Crete to Greece (see pp. 256, 287).

1868 | Russia recognizes the Kingdom of Romania.

1869 | Conference of the Great Powers (including Russia) in Paris advises George I of Greece to comply with the Turkish ultimatum to cease giving aid to the Cretan rebels (Jan.).

1870 | The Gorchakóv note of 19/31 October to the Powers repudiates the Black Sea provisions of the Treaty of Paris (1856), arguing that this was justified *de jure* because the Treaty had already been breached over Romania (1866) and by Palmerston's dispatch of warships to the Black Sea (1857, see p. 279), and *de facto* because it was inadmissible that 'the security of Russia should depend on a fiction that had not stood the test of time'.

1871

Jan. | London Conference (Austria-Hungary, Britain, France, Germany, Italy, Turkey, Russia) convenes to discuss the Gorchakóv note.

1/13 Mar. | Powers abrogate the Black Sea clauses of the Treaty of Paris. The principle of closing the Straits is maintained, but the Sultan is given authority to open them to friendly powers in time of peace 'in order to secure the execution of the stipulations of the Treaty of Paris'.

	Both Russia and Turkey are empowered to maintain navies, fortifications and arsenals in the Black Sea.
1875–78	**The Bosnian Crisis and the Russo-Turkish War**
1875	
June	Anti-Turkish revolt breaks out in Herzegovina.
Aug.	Russia rejects Prince Milan of Serbia's request for military aid.
Oct.	Milan informed that Russia would not oppose Turkish opposition to Serbia unless Serbia refrains from aggressive measures against the Turks.
1876	
May	Cherniáev arrives in Belgrade to command the Serbian army. Anti-Turkish revolt breaks out in Bulgaria.
June	Serbia and Montenegro conclude military alliance. A. N. Kartsóv, Russian consul-general in Belgrade, told to stop Serbia declaring war on Turkey.
July	Serbia and Montenegro declare war on Turkey.
20 Aug./1 Sept.	Cherniáev defeated by the Turks.
End Aug.	Serbia and Montenegro sue for peace.
18/30 Oct.	Russia imposes armistice on the Turks by threatening to break off diplomatic relations.
1/13 Nov.	Partial Russian mobilization.
End Nov.	Alexander II appoints V. A. Cherkásskii 'civil governor of Bulgaria'.
1877	
16/28 Feb.	Peace restored between Turkey and Serbia on the basis of the *status quo ante bellum*.
19/31 Mar.	London Protocol (see p. 289).
28 Mar./9 Apr.	The Porte rejects the London Protocol.
4/16 Apr.	Russo-Romanian military and political conventions.
12/24 Apr.	Russia declares war on Turkey. Turkey declares war on Romania.
9/21 May	Romania declares independence from the Ottoman Empire.
15/27 June	Russians cross the Danube.
4/16 July	Russians take Nicopolis.
7/19 July	I. V. Gúrko seizes the Shipka Pass and proceeds towards Adrianople.
8/20 July	First unsuccessful attempt to take Plevna.
18/30 July	Second unsuccessful attempt to take Plevna.
18/30 July	Suleiman Pasha forces Gúrko to withdraw to the Shipka.
30–31 Aug./ 11–12 Sept.	Third unsuccessful attempt on Plevna.

4/16 Nov.	Russians take Kars.
28 Nov./10 Dec.	Russians take Plevna.
1878	
8/20 Jan.	Russians take Adrianople.
19/31 Jan.	Armistice ends hostilities.
12/24 Feb.	Russians occupy San Stefano.
19 Feb./3 Mar.	Treaty of San Stefano.
16/28 Mar.	Romania rejects the Treaty of San Stefano.
Mid Apr.	Grand Duke Nikolái Nikoláevich replaced as commander by Totleben after he refuses to occupy the shores of the Bosphorus.
27 Apr./9 May	Totleben also rejects the occupation of the shores of the Bosphorus, and recommends the withdrawal of the Russian army to Adrianople.
Late May	P. Shuválov replaces Ignátev as ambassador to the Porte.
1/13 June	Congress of Berlin opens.
1/13 July	Treaty of Berlin.
1879	
27 Jan./8 Feb.	Russo-Turkish Peace Treaty, followed by Russian withdrawal.
Apr.	Constitution for the new Bulgaria (the Trnovo Constitution) drafted in Russia, grants universal suffrage, limitations on the powers of the throne, and freedom of the press, assembly and association.
End Apr.	Prince Alexander of Battenberg elected Prince of Bulgaria.
May	Russian evacuation of Bulgaria begins (completed by September).

Alexander III

1881–87	**The Bulgarian Crisis**
1881	Prince Alexander of Bulgaria's *coup d'état* of 27 Apr./ 9 May. The liberal government is forced to resign and is replaced by a provisional government under General Ehrnroth, the Russian representative. The constitution is set aside and Alexander assumes dictatorial powers for seven years.
1882	Prince Alexander appoints a new Bulgarian government, headed by the Russian general Sóbolev, and with the Russian general Kaulbars as minister of war (July).
1883	
Mar.	All Bulgarian ministers resign in protest against Sóbolev and Kaulbars.

Sept.	Alexander of Bulgaria restores the Trnovo Constitution. Sóbolev and Kaulbars recalled to Russia.
1885	
6/18 Sept.	Bulgarian nationalists, led by Stambulov, kidnap the Turkish governor of Eastern Rumelia and force Prince Alexander to accept the union of the two Bulgarias.
Late Sept.	Russia protests against the union as a violation of the Treaty of Berlin and withdraws Russian officers serving with the Bulgarian army.
2/14 Nov.	Serbia declares war on Bulgaria, but is defeated within two weeks.
10/22 Dec.	Armistice between Bulgaria and Serbia.
1886	
8/20 Aug.	Pro-Russian Bulgarian officers, led by Radko-Dmitriev, force Prince Alexander to abdicate and establish a pro-Russian government.
11/23 Aug.	Pro-Russian government in Bulgaria overthrown by Stambulov who invites Alexander to return.
26 Aug./7 Sept.	Alexander abdicates for the second time after failing to win the approval of Alexander III of Russia, and nominates three regents to choose the next prince.
Nov.	Waldemar of Denmark, unanimously elected prince by the Bulgarian national assembly, declines under Russian pressure.
Dec.	The regents offer the throne of Bulgaria to Ferdinand of Saxe-Coburg-Gotha.
1887	
Early	Unsuccessful Russian attempts to persuade the Sultan to block the election of Ferdinand.
2/14 Aug.	Ferdinand crowned King of Bulgaria in Trnovo. (Russia protests and withholds recognition until 1896.)

Nicholas II

1896	Government accepts Nelídov's proposal to occupy the upper Bosphorus (Nov.).
1908	
22 Sept./5 Oct.	Ferdinand proclaims himself king of an independent Bulgaria.
23 Sept./6 Oct.	Austria annexes Bosnia and Herzegovina.
1911–13	The Balkan Wars
1911	
Sept.	Italo-Turkish War leads to the Italian annexation of Tripoli and Cyrenaica (Treaty of Lausanne, Oct. 1912).

Nov.	Charýkov's proposals to the Porte for the removal of restrictions to Russian warships passing through the Straits.

1912

19 Feb./13 Mar.	Serbo-Bulgarian anti-Ottoman Alliance.
Mar.	Charýkov disavowed by St Petersburg and replaced as ambassador in Constantinople.
16/29 May	Greco-Bulgarian anti-Ottoman Alliance.
24 Sept./7 Oct.	Austro-Russian note admonishing Balkan States.
25 Sept./8 Oct.	Montenegro declares war on Turkey (followed by Serbia, Bulgaria and Greece): **The First Balkan War**. Turkey is rapidly defeated.

1913

17/30 May	Peace of London.
June	**Second Balkan War**: Bulgaria, unable to accept the division of territories imposed by the peace of London, goes to war against Serbia, Greece and Romania.
28 July/10 Aug.	Treaty of Bucharest.
1914–17	**The First World War** (see section 4.8 Russia and the First World War pp. 308–10).

4.3.1   Treaties

1700

13/26 June	**Constantinople**: Thirty year peace. Turkey recognizes Russia's refusal to acknowledge tribute obligation to the Crimean Khan. Russia to have permanent embassy in Constantinople on an equal footing with other Powers. Russian pilgrims to have unhindered right of access to the Holy Land. Russia to retain Azóv. Region between Perekóp and Taganróg to remain uninhabited (sovereignty over this territory was not spelled out). Region south of Azóv, in Kubán, to be joined to Azóv. Turkey to regain Gazy-Kerman. The surrounding fortresses of Taman, Nustretkermen and Saginkermen to be destroyed. No new town to be built on the Lower Dniépr between Ochákov and the Sech of the Zaporózhian Cossacks. Turks may build a town between Kizy-Kerman and Ochákov to serve as a crossing place for merchants and travellers.

1704

Dec.	**Tolstoi Agreement**: I. Tolstoy, Governor of Azóv, agrees with Ottomans that Southern frontier of

Azóv territories will be the river Eia (Yeya). Ottomans also accept the Russian right to build new towns, Taganróg and Kámennyi Zaton, on the Lower Dniépr.

1705
22 Oct./2 Nov.   **Ukraíntsev Agreement**: E. I. Ukraíntsev, signatory of the Treaty of Constantinople, obtains from Porte recognition of Russian sovereignty over territories between the Bug and the Dniépr.

1711
10/21 July   **The Pruth**: Russia surrenders Azóv. Taganróg, Kamenka (Kámennyi Zaton) and the new Russian fortress on the Samára to be destroyed. No new towns to be built in these regions. Russia to cease protecting Cossacks. Russians lose right of representation at Constantinople. Terms very vague and open to various interpretations.

1712
5/16 Apr.   **Constantinople**: Replaces Treaty of the Pruth and is much more precise. Russia retains Left Bank Ukraine, but gives up its claims to Right Bank (Polish) Ukraine except for Kiev. Russo-Turkish frontier fixed at a line midway between the Orël and the Samára (i.e. roughly where Ekaterinosláv would later be). All in all, Russia was thrown back to its position in the seventeenth century.

1713
5/16 June   **Adrianople**: Renewed the terms of Treaty of Constantinople, but Russia loses the right for unhindered access to the Holy Land for its pilgrims.

1720
5/16 Nov.   **Constantinople**: Makes Treaty of 1712 a Perpetual Peace. Russia regains the right of representation at Constantinople and Russian pilgrims regain the right of unhindered access to the Holy Land.

1721   Russia is obliged to evacuate troops from Polish territory. If any outside power enter Poland to make the monarchy hereditary, to change the constitution or to dismember the country, the Porte, 'whose interest is that the ancient liberty of the country should survive', would not prevent Russian intervention.

1724   **Constantinople**: Russians recognize Turkish conquest of Georgia in return for Turkish recognition of Russian conquests on the Caspian.

1739

7/18 Sept.

Nissa: (Signed by de Villeneuve, French ambassador to the Porte, on Russia's behalf.) Russia surrenders all conquests. Azóv to be destroyed and replaced by two equidistant fortresses, one Turkish, one Russian (Cherkássk). Azóv's territory, as defined in the treaty of 1700, to remain unpopulated and to serve as a barrier between Russia and Turkey. Taganróg not to be rebuilt. Russia not to build any ships in the Black Sea or Sea of Azóv. In a supplementary treaty (3/14 October), Villeneuve accepts frontiers very unfavourable to Russia, except that the Western frontier remains as per Ukraíntsev Agreement. Nonetheless, Russia ratifies the treaty.

1772

1/12 Nov.

Karasubazar: Russians (Shcherbínin) recognize and promise to defend the independence of the Crimea from the Ottoman Empire. Russians annex the fortresses of Kerch and Enikale.

1774

10/21 July

Kuchuk-Kainarji: Negotiated directly between Rumiántsev and the Grand Vizir, without any diplomats present, ends war with the Ottomans. Russia acquires Kinbúrn, Enikale, Kerch, and the coast between the Bug and the Dniépr. They secure the right of free navigation for commercial shipping in Turkish waters. The Crimean Tartars are recognised as 'independent', on condition that they accept the Sultan as Caliph; Wallachia and Moldavia are returned to Turkey in return for an indemnity of 4.5 million rubles, and on condition that they are leniently governed, and Russia retains the right to intervene on behalf of the Christians in the Ottoman Empire. Russia is given the right to build an Orthodox Church in Galata (Istanbul), and the Turks promise protection for Christian churches.

1779

10/21 Mar.

Ainalikawak: The Porte accepts the independence of the Crimea, and Shagin Girey as Khan of the Crimea. Russians agree to religious investiture of Crimean khans and that *kadis* (judges) belong to the spiritual (i.e. Turkish) authority. Russia agrees to evacuate the Crimea.

1791

29 Dec./
  9 Jan. 1792

Jassy: Ends war with Ottomans. Russia obtains Ochákov and a boundary along the Dniestr, but returns Moldavia and Bessarabia.

1794

23 Dec./
  3 Jan. 1795

Russo-Austrian Agreement: Includes secret provisions for the dismemberment of the Ottoman Empire.

1812

16/28 May

Bucharest: Ends war with the Porte. Bessarabia ceded to Russia, whose frontier is now the Pruth and the northern-most branch of the Danube. The Principalities to be retained as Turkish vassals, but with autonomous status. Those parts of Serbia which rebelled in 1804 to be made autonomous, but Turks still to man the Serbian fortresses. *Status quo ante bellum* restored on the Caucasian frontier of Turkey. Russians withdraw from Anapa.

1826

23 Mar./4 Apr.

Anglo-Russian Protocol: Britain to offer to mediate between Turks and Greeks, with the object of making Greece an independent vassal state of the Ottoman Empire. The Sultan to have 'a certain share' in the nomination of its rulers. The agreement should not be dissolved even should Russia go to war with the Turks. The protocol provided for intervention by the Powers 'jointly or separately' between the Porte and Greece.

25 Sept./7 Oct.

Akkerman: The Porte agrees to re-establish all the privileges of the Principalities and to grant similar ones to Serbia, and recognizes Russia's right to retain her existing possessions in the Caucasus. Sukhúmi and other points on the coast of Abkházia recognized as Russian territory. Merchantmen flying the Russian flag to have freedom of navigation on all domestic waterways of the Ottoman Empire.

1828

7/19 July

London Protocol: authorizes a French expeditionary force to Greece.

1829

10/22 Mar.

London Protocol: Provides for the establishment and frontiers of an autonomous Greek state, a tributary of the Sultan, under a prince chosen by the signatory Powers.

2/14 Sept.   **Adrianople**: (Signatories: Sadik Efendi, Abdul Kadir Bey, Alexei Orlóv, F. Pahlen.) There are 16 articles: 1. Ends the war. 2. Russia restores Moldavia, Wallachia, Banat, Rumelia, etc. to the Ottoman Empire. 3. Russia annexes the mouth of the Danube. Turkey to demilitarize the right bank of the Danube, to dismantle military establishments in the Principalities, and to withdraw her troops from there. 4. The Porte recognizes the Russian annexation of former Turkish and Persian territories in the Caucasus, including the Black Sea coast with Anapa and Poti. 5. 'Privileges and immunities' to be restored to Moldavia and Wallachia. 6. Serbia to be granted the benefits conferred by the convention of Akkerman. 7. Freedom of Russian trade in Turkey, and freedom of trade and navigation in the Black Sea. 8. The Porte to indemnify losses incurred by Russian citizens. 9. The Porte to pay an indemnity to Russia. 10. The Greek question to be settled in accordance with the Treaty of London of 24 June/6 July 1827 and the London Protocol of 10/22 Mar. 1829. 11. Russia will withdraw from the Principalities only when these conditions have been met. 12. Peace and restoration to take place immediately. 13. Amnesty to all those taking part in military operations. 14. All prisoners of war to be returned. 15. All previous agreements between Russia and Turkey, except those modified by the present one are confirmed. 16. Treaty to be ratified within six weeks.

1830
9/21 July   **London Protocol**: Independence for Greece, with frontiers including Attica, Boeotia and Euboea, with only a strip north of the Gulf of Corinth. Greece would include the Cyclades, but not Crete or Samos. The new state to be guaranteed by Russia, France and Britain. The form of government to be an hereditary monarchy whose prince might not be chosen from the reigning families of the guaranteeing Powers.

1833
26 June/8 July   **Unkiar-Skelessi**: (Russian signatories: Alexei Orlóv, Buténev.) Defensive alliance between Russia and Turkey including six articles and one separate clause. 1. Eternal peace between the two countries. 2. Confirms the Treaty of Adrianople, the Convention of St Petersburg (26.iv.1830) and the Constantinople

Protocol of 9/21.vii.1832. 3. Russia undertakes to place land and sea forces at the disposal of the Sublime Porte, whenever the two parties consider necessary. 4. The cost to be borne by the country requesting aid. 5. The treaty to last for eight years in the first instance. 6. The treaty to be ratified within two months. Separate clause: Ottoman aid to Russia can take the form of closing the Straits to foreign ships.

1877

4/16 Apr.   **Russo-Romanian Military Convention**: Regulates the passage of Russian troops through Romanian territory.

4/16 Apr.   **Russo-Romanian Political Convention**: Binds Russia 'to maintain and respect the political rights of the Romanian state . . . as well as to maintain and defend the actual integrity of Romania'.

1878

19 Feb./3 Mar.   **San Stefano**: (Signatories: Ignátev, Nelídov, Saffet, Sadullah.) Comprises 29 articles. 1. Bulgaria: (a) to become autonomous, under the suzerainty of the Sultan, to whom it would pay a tribute; (b) to have an elected prince, elective assembly and national militia; (c) frontiers to comprise all the territory between the Danube, the Black Sea and the Aegean, including Rumelia and Macedonia, but excluding Adrianople and Salonika; (d) Turkish troops to be withdrawn and all Turkish fortresses on the Danube to be razed; (e) the new regime to be supervised for two years by a Russian commissary supported by a Russian army of occupation. 2. The Porte recognizes the independence of Montenegro, Serbia and Romania. 3. Montenegro to acquire parts of Herzegovina, the Sanjak of Novibazar and of Albania, including the Adriatic ports of Spizza, Antivari and Dulcigno. 4. Serbia to acquire part of the Sanjak of Novibazar and Old Serbia (Kosovo). 5. Russia to acquire Dobrudja and the Danube Delta, which it might transfer to Romania in return for the parts of Bessarabia lost in 1856. 6. The Porte to introduce reforms into Bosnia and Herzegovina as proposed by the Constantinople conference, subject to modification by Russia, Austria and the Porte. 7. Political institutions introduced to Crete in 1868 to be extended to Epirus, Thessaly, and 'other parts of European Turkey for which no special organization is provided in this treaty'. 8. Turkey to

pay an indemnity to Russia, which is to withdraw its troops within three months, except from Bulgaria. 9. The Straits to remain open in peace and war to merchantmen bound for Russian ports.

1/13 July   **Berlin**: 1. Russia gains Bessarabia, Kars, Ardahan and Batum, but renounces Bayazid and Alashkert acquired at San Stefano. 2. Bulgaria loses over half the territory assigned at San Stefano, including access to the Aegean, and is split into two parts: (i) the autonomous province of Bulgaria north of the Balkan range, with its own representative institutions and an elected prince 'confirmed by the Sublime Porte with the consent of the Powers'; (ii) the autonomous province of Eastern Rumelia south of the Balkans 'under the direct political and military authority of the Sultan'. Turkish troops to be removed and fortresses razed in Bulgaria. They may remain on the frontier between Eastern Rumelia and Bulgaria, but may only be brought into other parts of the province at the request of the Christian governor and with the consent of the Powers. Police functions in Eastern Rumelia to be carried out by a native gendarmerie and militia. The use of *bashi-bazouks* and Circassians is prohibited. 3. Austria-Hungary gains the right to occupy and administer Bosnia and Herzegovina and to maintain garrisons and 'military and commercial routes' in the Sanjak of Novibazar. 4. Montenegro's independence recognized, but it loses substantial territory allocated at San Stefano, in Novibazar, Herzegovina and Dalmatia. 5. Serbia's independence recognized. 6. Romania has its independence recognized and is given the Danube Delta and Dobrudja in return for Bessarabia, lost to the Russians. 7. The Internationalization of the Danube, and the closure of the Straits is reaffirmed, (but see p. 248). 8. Russia to withdraw from Bulgaria within nine months, and from Romania three months after the evacuation of Bulgaria.

1913

17/30 May   **London**: Turkey relinquishes all European territories west of the Enos-Midia line, and the island of Crete.

28 July/10 Aug.   **Bucharest**: Bulgaria loses most of her gains under the Treaty of London, as well as Southern Dobrudja to Romania, Serbia and Greece.

4.4 Russia and the Central Powers

1686	Russia joins anti-Turkish Alliance with Austria, Venice and Poland (Mar.).

Peter I

1695–1700	**Azóv campaigns**
1697	
Feb.	Russo-Austro-Venetian anti-Ottoman offensive alliance.
July	Treaty of Friendship with Prussia.
1698	Congress of Carlowitz (Nov.). Austrians, Poles and Venetians make peace.
1700–21	**Great Northern War**
1714	Russo-Prussian Treaty (June).
1717	Peter in Potsdam on his way back from his visit to France (19–23 Sept.).

Catherine I

1726	
Feb.	Osterman becomes Vice-Chancellor with a policy of close alliance with Austria, friendly relations with Prussia and Denmark, and hostility to France.
6 Aug.	Russo-Austrian Treaty.

Anna Ivánovna

1732	Treaty with Austria and Denmark (Mar.).
1733–38	**War of the Polish Succession** (see p. 218)
1735	Lacy marches to Saxony with 20,000 troops and joins the Austrians near Heidelberg, but further advance stopped by Austro-French armistice (June).
1735–39	**Russo-Turkish War**
1735	Lacy and his troops recalled to Russia. Austria backs Russia half-heartedly (Nov.).
1737	Austria enters the Russo-Turkish war (June).
1739	Treaty of Belgrade between Austria and the Porte (1/12 Sept.).

Elizabeth

1743	The 'Botta conspiracy', allegedly involving the Austrian Ambassador Botta, in a plot to restore Ivan VI (Summer).
1746	Defensive alliance with Austria (22 May).
1756–63	**The Seven Years' War**
1756	Russia adheres to Treaty of Versailles (31 Dec./ 11 Jan.).
1757	
22 Jan./2 Feb.	Russo-Austrian Treaty.
15/26 Mar.	Russia enters Seven Years' War against Prussia.
May	S. F. Apráksin's indecisive advance into East Prussia. Great losses through disease.
June	V. V. Fermór takes Mémel.
19/30 Aug.	Battle of Gross-Jägersdorf. Apráksin and P. A. Rumiántsev defeat the Prussians (H. von Lehwaldt).
27 Aug./7 Sept.	Instead of pursuing Lehwaldt, Apráksin withdraws.
16/27 Oct.	Apráksin replaced by Fermór.
1758	
Jan.	Fermór occupies East Prussia.
4/15 Aug.	Fermór begins siege of Küstrin.
14/25 Aug.	Battle of Zorndorf. Frederick II defeats Fermór.
15/26 Aug.	Fermór withdraws to Königsberg.
Nov.	Russians withdraw from East Prussia.
1759	New tactics: to join with Austrians and destroy Prussians in Silesia.
Apr.–May	Slow advance of Fermór leads to his dismissal (8 May).
19/30 June	P. S. Saltykóv replaces Fermór.
12/23 June	Saltykóv defeats the Prussians under Wedell at the battle of Paltzig.
23 July/3 Aug.	Saltykóv reaches Frankfurt-on-Oder.
1/12 Aug.	Saltykóv and the Austrians under London defeat Frederick II at the battle of Kunersdorf.
1760	
18 Sept.	Saltykóv replaced by A. B. Buturlín.
28 Sept./9 Oct.	Z. G. Chernyshëv takes Berlin, withdrawing after two days.
1761	
1–4/12–15 Aug.	Buturlín crosses Oder to join Loudon.
9/20 Aug.	Outmanoeuvred, Frederick withdraws to Bunzelwitz, but disagreements between allies mean that no effective action is taken against him.
29 Aug./9 Sept.	Buturlín withdraws to winter quarters.

Sept.	Rumiántsev besieges Kolberg.
5/16 Dec.	Kolberg falls, giving Russia control of Eastern Pomerania.

Peter III
1762

12/23 Feb.	Russia informs its allies that it intends to negotiate peace with Prussia.
5/16 Mar.	Treaty of Stargrad.
24 Apr./5 May	Treaty of St Petersburg.
5/16 June	Military Alliance with Prussia.

Catherine II

28 June/9 July	Manifesto denouncing Peter for making peace with Frederick, although Saltykóv ordered to continue withdrawing troops from Prussia.
29 June/10 July	Catherine informs all courts of her intention to maintain peace with all powers.
1/12 July	Catherine informs Frederick II that she will abide by Peter's peace treaty, but refuses to ratify treaty of alliance.
Oct.	Austria issues ban on Hungarian emigration to Russia.
1763	Second Austrian ban on emigration to Russia. Prussia and most major European countries follow suit.
1764	Russo-Prussian Treaty (31 Mar./11 Apr.).
1767	Russo-Prussian military Alliance (Apr.).
1768–74	**The Conquest of the Southern Steppe to the Black Sea**
1769	Russo-Prussian Treaty (12/23 Oct.).
1770	Prince Henry of Prussia's protracted visit to Russia, (from September to February 1771), during which 'adjustments' to Polish frontiers are discussed.
1771	
Mid Feb.	Pánin informs Prussian envoy (V. F. Solms) that Russia might give up demands on the Porte in return for compensation in Poland.
Feb.	Austrian negotiations with the Porte on entry into the war on the Turkish side.
25 June/6 July	Austro-Turkish Treaty: The Porte to pay 20,000 purses of 500 piastres to Austria and to cede part of Wallachia to Austria if, by mediation or by force, Austria secures the return of all Russian conquests in Turkey and a guarantee of the political independence and territorial integrity of Poland.

1772

Feb.	Russo-Prussian agreement.
5 Mar.	**First Partition of Poland**
27 July/8 Aug.	Austrian (F. M. Thugut) and Prussian (J. C. von Zegelin) ministers attend Russian peace negotiations with the Turks in Fokshani.
20 Nov./1 Dec.	Prussians and Austrians do not attend the peace negotiations with the Turks in Bucharest.

1776–83   **Conquest of the Crimea**

1776

Apr.	Prince Henry of Prussia's second visit to St Petersburg.
22 Aug./2 Sept.	Border convention signed between the Powers partitioning Poland.

1777	Renewal of the Russo-Prussian Treaty (20/31 Mar.).
1778	Russo-Prussian Treaty lapses (20/31 Mar.). Russian mediation between Prussia and Austria in the War of Bavarian Succession leads to the Treaty of Teschen (2/13 May 1779).
1780	Eclipse of Pánin and the ascendancy of Potëmkin leads to a pro-Austrian policy.
End May	Joseph II meets Catherine at Mogilëv where they discuss her 'Greek Project' (to drive the Turks out of Europe and restore the Byzantine Empire, ruled by Catherine's second grandson, Konstantín. In return, Austria is to receive the whole of the Western Balkans).
18/29 Nov.	Maria Theresa's death makes a Russo-Austrian treaty possible.
1781	Secret Russo-Austrian Treaty.

1782

10/21 Sept.	Catherine's letter to Joseph II on possible future acquisitions: Russia to take Ochákov, the coast between the Bug and the Dniestr and an island or two in the Greek archipelago. A kingdom to be formed from Moldavia, Wallachia and Bessarabia to remain independent of Russia and Austria. Catherine raises the 'Greek Project' again, hoping that Austria would assist Konstantín to the throne in Constantinople.
Oct.	Austrian mediation in Constantinople helps the Russians restore Shagin Girey as Khan of Crimea.

1787	Joseph II and Catherine tour the Crimea (Apr.–May).
1787–91	**Turkish War**

1788

Feb.	Austria declares war on the Porte.
4/15 Sept.	Austrians take Khotín.

1789

21 June/2 July	Battle of Fokshani. Russo (Suvórov)-Austrian (Coburg) victory.
11/22 Sept.	Battle of Rymnik. Suvórov–Coburg victory.
3/14 Nov.	Austrians take Belgrade.
4/15 Nov.	Coburg takes Bucharest.

1790

20/31 Jan.	Prusso-Turkish alliance commits Prussia to declaring war on Russia and Austria in the spring and not to lay down arms until occupied territories are restored to the Sultan.
June–Aug.	Joint Suvórov–Coburg campaign around Bucharest.
16/27 July	Reichenbach: Austrian armistice with the Turks on the basis of the *status quo ante bellum*.

1791

24 July/4 Aug.	Austro-Turkish Peace signed at Sistovo. Austria returns almost all conquests.
16/27 Aug.	'Declaration of Pillnitz', by which Austria and Prussia proclaim their intention of restoring the French monarchy.

1792–95   Partitions of Poland

1792

3/14 July	Renewal of Austro-Russian Treaty of 1781, reaffirming support for the unreformed constitution and boundaries of Poland.
27 July/7 Aug.	Russo-Prussian Treaty: re-establishment of the old Polish constitution.

1793	**Second Partition of Poland** (12/23 Jan.) (see pp. 222–3).
1794	Treaty with Austria (23 Dec./3 Jan. 1795) (see pp. 223, 263).

1795

Aug.	Austro-Russian partition treaty presented to Prussia as an ultimatum.
13/24 Oct.	**Third Partition of Poland** (see p. 223).
1796	Catherine orders a force of 60,000 to join the Austrians against the French.

Paul I

1796	Paul recalls the expeditionary force from Austria (25 Nov.).

Alexander I

1802	Alexander visits Frederick William III and Queen Louise of Prussia in Memel (June).

1804

4/16 July	Russo-Austrian military convention.
25 Oct./6 Nov.	Russo-Austrian Alliance against France.

1805

28 July/9 Aug.	Austria joins Russo-British Alliance.
End Oct.	Alexander visits Frederick William of Prussia at Potsdam, where the two pledge eternal friendship.
22 Oct./3 Nov.	Russo-Prussian Convention.
14/26 Dec.	Treaty of Pressburg: Austria makes peace with France.

1806   Russo-Prussian secret military convention (July).

1807

Apr.	Alexander meets Frederick William at Memel.
14/26 Apr.	Convention of Bartenstein.

1808   King of Prussia visits St Petersburg, (26 Dec./ 7 Jan. 1809–9/21 Jan. 1809).

1809

6/18 Apr.	Secret convention with Austria.
June	Golítsyn leads an army of 32,000 into Galicia, but does not engage with the Austrians.

1811   Scharnhorst in St Petersburg to negotiate the forming of a German Legion under Gneisenau to operate behind the French lines (5 Oct.).

1812

Summer	Alexander I appoints a 'German Committee', with Stein as a member, to encourage Prussian resistance to Napoleon.
Before 12/ 24 Dec.	Russian command urges the 'German people' to rise up against the French.
18/30 Dec.	Convention of Tauroggen.

1813

Jan.	Alexander sends Boyen to the King of Prussia to offer an offensive and defensive alliance.
15/27 Feb.	Treaty of Kalisch.
7/19 Mar.	Convention of Breslau.
17/29 Mar.	Treaty of Kalisch.
4/16 May	Austrian Chancellor Stadion supports Russo-Prussian ultimatum to Napoleon (see p. 274).
15/27 June	Secret Treaty of Reichenbach.

1815   Formation of the Holy Alliance (14/26 Sept.).

1821–41   **The Greek Revolt and the Mohammed Ali Crises**

1825   Metternich proposes the recognition of the independence of Morea and the Greek islands (rejected by Alexander and Nesselrode) (3/15 Jan.).

Nicholas I

1829	Metternich declares the Holy Alliance to be 'dead' (27 Sept./9 Oct.).
1830	Metternich and Nesselrode sign the *Chiffon de Carlsbad*, in which both governments declare their intention to protect the existing order against French subversion (25 July/6 Aug.).
1833	
1/13 Jan.	Austrian support helps Muravëv persuade Mohammed Ali to make peace with the Sultan.
6/18 Sept.	Münchengrätz Agreement.
3/15 Oct.	Convention of Berlin.
1837	Prussian officers, including Hellmuth von Moltke, begin training the Turkish army (Nov.).
1840	London Convention (3/15 July) (see pp. 288–9).
1841	(For events relating to the Ottoman Empire 1841–56, see section 4.7 Russia and the Crimean War, pp. 299–307.)
1848	
21 Apr./2 May	Prussian army invades Schleswig-Holstein on the order of the Frankfurt Parliament, but withdraws after a Russian ultimatum.
20 June/2 July	Prussian-Danish Treaty restores *status quo ante* to Schleswig and Holstein.
21 Sept./3 Oct.	Austrian government declares war on Kossuth and his supporters.
1849	
Early	Russian troops enter Transylvania at the request of the local military commander but are defeated by Hungarians led by Polish émigré General József Bem.
Mar.	Schwarzenberg appeals to Russia for military help.
2/14 Apr.	Kossuth declares the Independence of Hungary.
8/20 May	Nicholas orders the army into Hungary.
9/21 May	Francis-Joseph and Nicholas meet in Warsaw.
29 May/10 June	Austro-Russian Convention.
6/18 June	Paskévich crosses the Carpathians into Hungary.
30 July/11 Aug.	Kossuth abdicates and flees to Turkey.
1/13 Aug.	Hungarian army surrenders to the Russians.
1852	Treaty of London (26 Apr./8 May).
1853–56	(For events relating to the Crimean War, see section 4.7 Russia and the Crimean War, pp. 299–307.)

Alexander II

1857	Alexander meets Francis-Joseph in Weimar (Sept.).
1858	Alexander meets the Prussian Regent, Prince William, in Warsaw (11 Sept.).
1859	Bismarck appointed Prussian ambassador in St Petersburg (until 1862).
1860	Alexander, Francis-Joseph and the Prince Regent of Prussia meet in Warsaw.
1862	Bismarck offers Prussian assistance in Poland (Sept.).
1863	
27 Jan./8 Feb.	Russo-Prussian Convention.
5/17 Apr.	Austrian note on the Polish question presented simultaneously with British and French notes (see p. 280), stresses the probable effect of the uprising on Austrian Galicia.
1864	
Jan.	Gorchakóv informs Austria and Prussia of his intention to mass troops in Finland should Sweden come to Denmark's help over Schleswig-Holstein.
Apr.–June	At the London Conference, Brunnóv first presses for the implementation of the 1852 agreements on Schleswig-Holstein, then presses the claims of the Duke of Oldenburg to the provinces.
1866	Alexander assures William of Prussia that, despite Russian reservations on Prussian policy, under no condition 'would Russia join the enemies of Germany' (31 July).
1867	German Confederation supports Russian demand that Crete be transferred to Greece (Apr.).
1870	
June	Ems Conference between, Alexander, Gorchakóv, William of Prussia and Bismarck.
July	On the outbreak of the Franco-Prussian War, Russia informs the French ambassador that, should Austria attack Prussia, Russia would attack Austria.
19/31 Oct.	Four days after the Bazaine's capitulation at Metz, Russia repudiates the Black Sea provisions of the Treaty of Paris (1856) (see section 4.7 Russia and the Crimean War, p. 306).
1871	William telegraphs Alexander that 'Prussia will never forget that she owes it to you that the war has not assumed extreme dimensions'. Alexander replies 'I am happy that I was in a position to prove to you my sympathy as a devoted friend' (Jan.).

1872

June	Archduke William and a group of Austro-Hungarian officers attend Russian manoeuvres.
Sept.	Alexander, William and Francis-Joseph meet in Vienna.

1873   **League of the Three Emperors (Dreikaiserbund)**

Apr.–May	William I visits St Petersburg as the guest of Alexander II.
24 Apr./6 May	Secret Russo-German Convention.
May/June	Alexander's state visit to Vienna.
25 May/6 June	Secret Convention of Schönbrunn.
10/22 Oct.	Germany accedes to the Secret Convention of Schönbrunn.

1874   Francis-Joseph pays a state visit to St Petersburg (Feb.).

1875–78   **The Bosnian Crisis and the Russo-Turkish War**

1875

Aug.	Austria-Hungary, Germany and Russia propose the appointment of a consular commission of the Powers to examine affairs in Herzegovina.
18/30 Dec.	Andrássy Note (sponsored by Austria-Hungary, Germany and Russia) proposes a mixed commission of Muslims and Christians to supervise reform in Bosnia and Herzegovina.

1876

Mar.	Austria and Russia warn Milan and Nicholas of Montenegro not to enter into an anti-Turkish alliance.
1/13 May	Berlin Memorandum restates the proposals of the Andrássy Note, reinforced by 'effective measures that may appear necessary in the interest of general peace.'
26 June/8 July	Alexander II and Francis-Joseph meet at Reichstadt (see p. 265).
Mid Dec.	Constantinople Conference: (see p. 281).

1877

3/15 Jan.	Russo-Austrian military and political conventions.
Late Jan.	Delegates and ambassadors of the six Powers leave Constantinople in protest at the failure of the conference.
19/31 Mar.	London Protocol.
10/22 Apr.	Gorchakóv protests at the reappointment of ambassadors to the Porte by Austria-Hungary and Germany.
27 Nov./9 Dec.	Alexander sends Francis-Joseph and William an outline of the proposed settlement with the Porte.
27 Dec./ 8 Jan. 1878	Francis-Joseph criticizes the Russian proposals on the grounds that they violate the Reichstadt Agreement and the Convention of January 1877, denies the Russians the right to conclude peace without prior consultation

with Vienna, claims the right to occupy Bosnia and Herzegovina, opposes the creation of a Big Bulgaria and its occupation by Russian troops, and refuses to recognize the validity of any changes in the Treaty of Paris unless they are confirmed by all the signatories.

1878

4/16 Jan.   Alexander accepts Austria's right to occupy Bosnia-Herzegovina, agrees in principle to the convocation of a European conference, but rejects Francis-Joseph's other points.

Early Feb.   Andrássy proposes the convocation of the signatories of the Treaty of Paris. Gorchakóv accepts on condition that it be a congress attended by leading European statesmen.

Late Feb.   Bismarck agrees to chair a congress to be held in Berlin.

1/13 June   Opening of the Congress of Berlin: Gorchakóv and Shuválov, Beaconsfield, Salisbury, Andrássy, W. H. Waddington (France), Luigi Conti (Italy). Serbia, Montenegro, Greece and Romania send delegations but do not take part in the Congress.

1/13 July   Treaty of Berlin (see p. 248).

1879

3/15 Aug.   Alexander complains to William I of German 'anti-Russian' activities.

22–23 Aug./   Alexander and William meet at Alexándrovo and
3–4 Sept.   make up.

25 Sept./7 Oct.   Austro-Hungarian-German Alliance.

Alexander III

1881–87   **Renewed League of the Three Emperors**

1881

6/18 June   Secret Alliance between Austria-Hungary, Germany and Russia.

28 Aug./9 Sept.   Alexander III and William I meet in Danzig.

1882

12 Jan.   General Skóbelev's anti-German pan-Slav speech in St Petersburg on the anniversary of the taking of Gheok Teppe.

5/17 Feb.   General Skóbelev's anti-German pan-Slav speech to Serbian students in Paris.

25 June   Sudden death of General Skóbelev.

1884

15/27 Mar.   Renewal of the Russo-Austro-German Alliance.

5/17–10/22 May   Prince William of Prussia (future William II) visits St Petersburg.

3/15–5/17 Sept.	Alexander, William and Francis-Joseph meet at Skierniewice in Russian Poland.
1885	
28 Mar./9 Apr.	Bismarck instructs the German ambassador in Constantinople to insist that the Porte keep the Straits closed in the event of a Russo-British War over Afghanistan.
Aug.	Alexander and Francis-Joseph meet at Kremsier.
13/25 Nov.	Austrian ultimatum to Bulgaria brings peace between Bulgaria and Serbia.
1886	Katkóv begins a campaign against Germany and Austria's role in the Bulgarian crisis in *The Moscow Gazette/Moskóvskie védomosti.*
1887	
8 Mar.	Katkóv reveals the existence of the Dreikaiserbund in an article in *Moskóvskie védomosti.*
6/18 June	After the Bulgarian incident, Russia refuses to renew the Dreikaiserbund, but signs a Treaty of Reinsurance with Germany.
1888	
June	William II becomes Kaiser.
July	William II's state visit to Russia.
1889	Alexander's state visit to Germany (Oct.).
1890–1907	**Russo-British Rivalry in the Far East**
1890	
5/17 Mar.	Bismarck forced to resign as German Chancellor.
9/21 Mar.	William II assures Alexander that Bismarck's resignation will not affect the Russo-German Alliance.
15/27 Mar.	Germany refuses to renew the Reinsurance Treaty.
Aug.	During William II's state visit to Russia, Giers unsuccessfully tries to renew the Alliance.

Nicholas II

1897	Agreement with Austria (May).
1902	The Russians, French and British protest when Germany obtains from the Porte the concession to build the Berlin–Baghdad Railway.
1903	Nicholas and Francis-Joseph meet at Mürzsteg and reaffirm the terms of the May 1897 Treaty (Oct.).
1904	
Oct.	Nicholas and William II each appoint a military attaché to be attached to the other's personal suite.
14/27 Oct.	After the Dogger Bank incident, William II proposes a defensive Russo-German alliance against Britain.

15/28 Oct.	Nicholas requests William to draw up such an alliance to include France (project ultimately abandoned).
Dec.	Russia agrees to provide military support for Germany, should the coaling of the Russian Baltic Fleet lead to war between Germany and Britain.
1905	Nicholas and William II sign the Björkö Treaty, promising 'mutual aid' in case of war with a third European power. The treaty was immediately disavowed by the respective Foreign Ministers (11/24 July).
1907–9	**The Bosnian Crisis**
1907	
Sept.	Izvólskii talks with Aehrenthal in Vienna on the possible reopening of the Straits and Austrian annexation of Bosnia and Herzegovina.
16/29 Oct.	Secret Agreement with Germany on the Åland Islands.
1908	
Jan.	Aehrenthal announces the Austrian intention to build a railway through the Sanjak of Novibazar from Sarajevo to Mitrovica.
2/15–3/16 Sept.	Buchlau conversations between Izvólskii and Aehrenthal. Each agrees not to oppose the other's demands over the opening of the Straits and the annexation of Bosnia and Herzegovina. Aehrenthal also agrees to withdraw Austrian troops from Novibazar and to abandon the railway project.
23 Sept./6 Oct.	Austria annexes Bosnia and Herzegovina.
1909	
4/17 Mar.	Russian cabinet decides that war over Bosnia is not within its means.
9/22 Mar.	Under German pressure, Russia approves the Austrian annexation of Bosnia and Herzegovina.
1910	Nicholas and Sazónov visit Potsdam (Nov.).
1911–13	**The Balkan Wars**
1911	Russo-German Agreement (6/19 Aug.).
1912	
21–22 June	Nicholas II and Wilhelm II meet at Baltíiskii Port.
Dec.	Conference of the ambassadors of the Powers, chaired by Sir Edward Grey, meets in London to sort out the Balkan crisis.
1913	Powers support Austria's demand for an independent Albania.
Oct.	Russia supports Austrian demands for a Serbian withdrawal from Albania.

Nov.	Russia protests at Liman von Sanders's mission to Turkey.
1914–17	**The First World War** (see section 4.8 Russia and the First World War, pp. 308–10).

4.4.1 Treaties

1714

June	**Russo-Prussian Treaty**: Divides Swedish Empire. Prussia to have Stettin, Russia to have Estonia, Ingria, Karelia and Výborg.

1726

6 Aug.	**Russo-Austrian Treaty**: Military treaty making Russia part of the Austro-Spanish League. Contracting parties guarantee each other's possessions, undertake to render military assistance in time of war, and to conclude no separate peace. Secret clause: Austria to assist in returning Schleswig to the Duke of Holstein and to assist Russia in war against Ottomans.

1732

Mar.	**Treaty with Austria and Denmark**: Denmark to pay monetary compensation to the Duke of Holstein for the loss of Schleswig and to recognize the Pragmatic Sanction. Russia and Austria to guarantee Danish frontiers.

1746

22 May	**Austrian Alliance**: Provides an Austrian guarantee for the Duke of Holstein's German possessions.

1756

31 Dec./11 Jan.	**Russia adheres to Treaty of Versailles**: Defensive alliance signed 20 Apr./1 May between Austria and France, providing for the restoration of Silesia to Austria. In a secret clause, Russia agrees to assist France in the event of the latter being attacked by Britain in Europe.

1757

22 Jan./2 Feb.	**Austrian Alliance**: Each party to provide at least 80,000 troops against Prussia. Neither party to conclude a separate peace until Silesia is returned to Austria and Saxony liberated and indemnified. Austria to pay Russia an annual subsidy of one million rubles. Russia to acquire Kurland if East Prussia is given to the Poles.

1762

5/16 Mar.   **Stargrad**: Armistice with Prussia.

24 Apr./5 May   **St Petersburg**: Russia to return all conquests to Prussia. A twenty-year friendship established between Russia and Prussia. Each to have most favoured nation status for trade. Each to aid the other with troops in case of attack, except if Prussia were attacked by Britain or France, or if Russia were attacked by Persia or the Tartars, when aid was to be financial only. Prussian ownership of Silesia and Glatz is guaranteed. Prussia to support the Russian conquest of Schleswig by force of arms if necessary. Prussia and Russia to determine the Polish succession. Russia to gain Kurland.

1764

31 Mar./11 Apr.   **Prussian Alliance**: Each guarantees the other's European possessions, including Russia's possession of Holstein. In the event of attack by a third power, each to provide the other with 10,000 infantry and 2,000 cavalry. Secret clauses: 1. If Russia is attacked by the Porte or Prussia by a power beyond the Weser, military assistance could be replaced by a subsidy of 400,000 rubles per year. But if Austria joined the Porte, Prussia would enter the war on Russia's side. 2. Each agrees to observe the existing balance of political parties in Sweden, and to concert their efforts in the event of any threat to the Swedish government. 3. King of Prussia guarantees Holstein to Grand Duke Paul. 4. Any changes to the Polish constitution to be opposed by force of arms if necessary. Treaty to last for eight years.

1769

12/23 Oct.   Renewal of Prussian Alliance: Agreement reached on what changes would be considered an overthrow of Sweden's fundamental laws. Swedish attack on Russia or the restoration of absolutism in Sweden to be seen as *casus foederis*, in which case, Frederick to invade Swedish Pomerania.

1772

5 Aug.   **First Partition of Poland**: (see p. 226).

1781

May–June   **Secret Treaty with Austria**: Mutual defence of territory, including Polish acquisitions but excluding Russia's Asiatic and Austria's Italian possessions. Russia was only liable to pay a subsidy in the event of an attack on the Austrian Netherlands. Existing treaties between both parties and the Porte to be guaranteed. Should the Porte fail to honour these, or to declare war on either party, the other would come to its assistance within three months.

1793

12/23 Jan.   **Convention of St Petersburg**: The second Partition of Poland signed with Prussia.

1795

23 Dec. 1794/ 3 Jan.   **Russo-Austrian Agreement**: Catherine supplies an expeditionary force of 60,000 men against the French.

1805

22 Oct./3 Nov.   **Russo-Prussian Convention**: Frederick William to present to Napoleon peace terms substantially the same as those of the Anglo-Russian Treaty of 30 Mar./ 11 Apr. (see p. 286). Should Napoleon refuse, Prussia would enter the war on the side of the Allies.

1807

14/26 Apr.   **Convention of Bartenstein**: Confirms the Russo-Prussian Alliance, invites the adherence of Austria, Britain, Sweden and Denmark, and lays out plans for Europe in the event of victory over the French. Guarantees Turkey's independence and territorial integrity.

1809

6/18 Apr.   **Secret Convention**: Signed by Alexander and Prince Schwarzenberg of Austria, the Russians, while appearing to respect the Treaty of Tilsit, would not oppose Austrian action in Poland.

1812

18/30 Dec.   **Convention of Tauroggen**: Prussian General Yorck signs an agreement with the Russian commander that he will withdraw his Prussian corps from the *Grande armée* and announce their neutrality.

1813

15/27 Feb.   **Kalisch**: Close military alliance between Russia and Prussia, which stipulates the size of their respective contingents and promises to compensate Prussia for Polish territory lost to Russia at Tilsit.

7/19 Mar.   **Convention of Breslau**: (Signatories: Stein and Nesselrode for Russia, Hardenberg and Scharnhorst for Prussia.) Comprises ten articles, including: 1. Limits the war against France to the liberation of German soil. 2. Creates a central Council, representing both powers, to create provisional administrations in liberated territories. 5. Divides liberated Germany into five parts. 4. Legalizes the raising of the Prussian *landwehr* and *landsturm*.

17/29 Mar.   **Kalisch**: Austria (still officially France's ally) agrees to evacuate Poland without fighting the Russians.

15/27 June   **Secret Treaty of Reichenbach**: Austrian military alliance with Russia and Prussia. Austria undertakes to declare war on France should Russo-Prussian terms be rejected by Napoleon, and not to conclude any separate peace with France.

1815

14/26 Sept.   **Holy Alliance**: Signed by Alexander, Francis I of Austria and Frederick William III of Prussia, a declaration of vague Christian principles to guide rulers in their relations with their subjects and each other.

8/20 Nov.   **Renewal of the Quadruple Alliance**: Each signatory to supply 60,000 men in the event of any attempt to violate the Treaty of Paris. Future meetings to be held to ensure the implementation of the Treaty (the Congress System).

1833

6/18 Sept.   **Münchengrätz**: Agreement between Russia and Austria to maintain the Ottoman Empire under its present dynasty, and to oppose any change in its form of government. Includes two secret articles: 1. Mohammed Ali to be prevented from acquiring any direct or indirect influence over any part of European Turkey. 2. Should the partition of the Ottoman Empire become inevitable, Austria and Russia will act only in agreement with each other.

3/15 Oct.   **Convention of Berlin**: Russia, Prussia and Austria renew the Holy Alliance to preserve the European order. In a letter from Nicholas to Frederick William III (23 Sept./5 Oct.), Prussia is specifically exempted from any obligation to intervene in the Levant.

1852   **London**: Austria, Britain, France, Prussia and Russia settle the succession to the Danish Crown (including Schleswig-Holstein) on Prince Christian of Glücksburg, his consort and their male issue.

1863

27 Jan./8 Feb.   **Russo-Prussian Convention**: Russian troops authorized to enter Prussian territory in pursuit of Polish rebels.

1873

24 Apr./6 May   **Secret Russo-German Convention**: Guarantees mutual military assistance if either is attacked by another European Power. (Bismark refused to ratify.)

25 May/6 June   **Secret Convention of Schönbrunn**: Ensures the unity of action of the Emperors of Austria-Hungary and Russia, irrespective of changes that might occur in the composition of their governments. Specific reference made to 'the protection of the peace of Europe from any subversive attempts (*bouleversements*)'. In case of aggression by a third Power, both parties to seek a common understanding not to conclude outside alliances, and, if necessary, to make arrangements for joint military action.

1876

26 June/8 Aug.   **Reichstadt Agreement**: Signed by Alexander II and Francis Joseph II and their Foreign Ministers. 1. If Turkey wins the war with Serbia and Montenegro, Austria and Russia will act together to protect the Christian populations and enforce a minimum of reform. 2. If Turkey loses the war, Austria and Russia will work together to establish a new order in the Balkans: (a) there is to be no large Slav state; (b) Russia to acquire the parts of Bessarabia lost in 1856; (c) Austria to annex Bosnia and (according to Andrássy but not Gorchakóv) Herzegovina; (d) other Turkish territories in Europe to be partitioned between Bulgaria, Serbia, Romania, Montenegro, Greece and Albania; (e) Constantinople to become a free city.

1877

3/15 Jan.   **Russo-Austrian Military Convention**: Should Russia go to war with Turkey: 1. Austria to remain benevolently neutral and not to take part in any action under its treaty of 3/15 April 1856 with France and Britain to maintain the Treaty of Paris. 2. Russia to be allowed to occupy Bulgaria. 3. Austria to occupy Bosnia and Herzegovina, when it deems this to be desirable. 4. Serbia, Montenegro and the Sanjak of Novibazar to be a neutral zone prohibited to both Austrian and Russian troops.

3/15 Jan.   **Russo-Austrian Political Convention**: Restates the agreements of Reichstadt and sanctions the annexation of Bosnia and Herzegovina by Austria and of Bessarabia by Russia. Each power promises to support the other should any of these territorial changes come before a conference of the Powers.

1881
18 June

Secret Russo-Austro-German Alliance: If any one of the parties should become involved in war with a fourth Great Power, the other two will retain a benevolent neutrality and work for a peaceful settlement of the dispute. This would apply to a war with Turkey should the three courts have agreed in advance on the results of such a war. The three Powers agree to coordinate their policies in the Balkans, where no modifications of the *status quo* would be tolerated except by agreement of all three Powers. All three agree to respect and defend the closure of the Straits. Austria's right to annex Bosnia, Herzegovina and the Sanjak of Novibazar is recognized. The three Powers agree not to oppose the union of Bulgaria and Eastern Rumelia.

1887
6/18 June

Secret Russo-German Reinsurance Treaty: 1. Should either go to war against a third party, the other to remain benevolently neutral and to work for the localization of the conflict. This does not apply to war against France or Turkey resulting from a German or Russian attack. 2. Germany recognizes Russia's 'historically acquired' rights in the Balkans, 'especially the legitimacy of her preponderant and decisive influence in Bulgaria and Eastern Rumelia'. No change in the *status quo* in the Balkans to take place without the consent of both Russia and Germany. 3. Reaffirms the provision of the 1884 Treaty on the closure of the Straits. In an additional and highly secret protocol, Germany undertakes (a) to assist Russia in 're-establishing in Bulgaria a regular and legal government'; (b) not to allow the restoration of Alexander of Battenberg; (c) to remain benevolently neutral should the Emperor of Russia 'find himself under the necessity of assuming the task of defending the entrance to the Black Sea', the key to his Empire.

1897
May

Agreement with Austria: maintains the *status quo* in the Balkans or, should this not be possible, signatories agree to consult each other on future change.

1907

16/29 Oct.   **Secret Agreement with Germany**: Germany approves Sazónov's attempts to obtain the reversal of the clause in the Treaty of Paris (1856) demilitarizing the Åland Islands.

1911

6/19 Aug.   **Russo-German Agreement**: Germany undertakes to seek no economic concessions in northern Persia. Russia agrees to withdraw all obstacles to the construction of the Berlin–Baghdad Railway.

4.5 Russia and Western Europe

Peter I

1697–98   **The 'Great Embassy' to the West.** Peter visits Kurland, Brandenburg, Holland, England and Austria, working in shipyards in Amsterdam and Deptford.

1715   First French consul appointed to St Petersburg (Lavie).

Oct.   Treaty of Greifswald with Hanover.

1716–17   Peter's second visit to Western Europe (May–June 1717 in France, then in Holland).

1717   Treaty of Amsterdam (Aug.).

Catherine I

1726   British Fleet appears off Réval (May).

Anna Ivánovna

1731   Diplomatic relations resumed with Britain towards the end of the year.

1734   Commercial Treaty with Britain.

Elizabeth

1741   French Ambassador La Chétardie helps Elizabeth carry out her *coup d'état* (25 Nov.).

1742   Anglo-Russian Treaty of Alliance.

1744   La Chétardie expelled (6 June).

1746   Diplomatic relations with France broken off.

1747   Alliances with Britain (June and Dec.).

1748   Russian troops under Repnín sent to the Rhine under the terms of the 1747 British alliance, but arrive after the war has ended (Jan.).

1755

June   Sir Charles Hanbury-Williams appointed British ambassador.

19 Sept.   Russo-British Treaty.

1756   Convention of Westminster between Britain and Prussia destroys Bestúzhev-Riúmin's pro-British, anti-Prussian, anti-French system (Jan.). Resumption of diplomatic relations with France.

31 Dec./ 11 Jan. 1757	Russia accedes to the Treaty of Versailles (Franco-Austrian Alliance).

Catherine II
1762

29 June/10 July	Catherine declares her intention to maintain peace with all Powers.
Aug.	Earl of Buckinghamshire appointed British ambassador (until Jan. 1765).
1763	Unsuccessful attempt to negotiate new Russo-British Alliance (Sept.). D. A. Golítsyn becomes ambassador in Paris (until 1767).
1764	G. Macartney arrives to negotiate commercial treaty (Oct. until June 1767).
1766	Russo-British Commercial Treaty (20 June/1 July).
1775	Catherine rejects a British request for 20,000 troops for use in the American colonies (Summer).
1778	Russia rejects an alliance with Britain (Dec.).
1779–80	Disputes with Britain over British detention of neutral shipping and seizure of cargoes.
1780–83	Formation of the 'Armed Neutrality' with Denmark (1780), Sweden (1780), the United Provinces (briefly, January 1781), Prussia (May 1781), Austria (October 1781), Portugal (1783) and the Two Sicilies (1783). France and Spain supported the principles (April 1780).
1781	
4/15 Jan.	Dutch plenipotentiaries sign 'Armed Neutrality' in St Petersburg, unaware that their country is at war with Britain.
Jan.	Catherine agrees to mediate jointly with Austria in the Anglo-French conflict.
Mid-Feb.	Catherine offers to mediate in the Anglo-Dutch conflict.
1 Oct.	Paul Petróvich and Maríia Fëdorovna ('le comte et la comtesse du Nord'), begin a tour of Europe (until 1782).
1785	Comte de Ségur appointed French Ambassador (until 1789).
1786	Russo-British Commercial Treaty lapses (11/22 Jan.).
1787	Commercial agreement with France.
1789	Charles-Édouard Genêt becomes the French *chargé d'affaires*.
1791	
Jan.	Pitt's anti-Russian policy.

16/27 Mar.	British ultimatum to Russia to make peace with the Porte on the basis of the *status quo ante bellum* or British Fleets would be dispatched to the Baltic and Black Seas, and Prussian troops would advance into Livonia.
31 Mar./11 Apr.	British Cabinet drops ultimatum for strict *status quo*.
9/20 June	The Flight to Varennes. French envoy ceases to be received by Catherine.
24 Sept.	Catherine calls on European Powers not to recognize any act of the French National Assembly.
1792–1800	**Wars of the French Revolution**
1792	French envoy, Genêt, expelled (8 July).
1793	
8/19 Feb.	Diplomatic relations with France broken off. Franco-Russian Commercial Treaty of 1787 annulled and trade between the two countries prohibited. Russian ports closed to French shipping. All Russian subjects in France recalled, and all French subjects in Russia expelled unless they swore allegiance to the Bourbons. Importation of French books and papers banned.
14/25 Mar.	Preliminary agreement with Britain to renew the treaty of 1766.
1795	Treaty with Britain (7/18 Feb.). Russian ships under Admiral Khanýkov sail in the North Sea with Admiral Duncan.
Paul I	
1797	Anglo-Russian Commercial Treaty.
Nov.	Russia gives refuge and money to Condé's French émigré corps.
1798	
Feb.	Pension of 200,000 rubles per annum paid to Louis XVIII in Mitau.
July	Russian Baltic squadron sails with the British Fleet in the Channel.
Nov.	Russo-Turkish Fleet takes the Ionian Islands from the French.
13/24 Dec.	Russo-British Alliance.
1799	
20 Feb./1 Mar.	Admiral Ushakóv takes Corfu.
Apr.	Suvórov marches from Vienna.
10/21 Apr.	Suvórov's victory at Brescia.
16/27–17/ 28 Apr.	Suvórov's victory over Moreau on the Adda, and entry into Milan.
7/18 June	Suvórov's victory on the Trebbia.

11/22 June	Anglo-Russian Convention for a joint invasion of Holland.
4/15 Aug.	Suvórov's victory at Novi.
7/18 Sept.	17,000 Russian troops land at the Texel.
13/24–14/25 Sept.	Suvórov's crossing of the St Gotthard Pass.
14/25 Sept.	A. M. Kórsakov defeated by Masséna at Zurich.
Sept.	Nelson prevents Ushakóv from taking Malta.
Oct.	Russian army in Switzerland capitulates.
6/18 Oct.	Russian forces at the Texel capitulate.
1/13 Nov.	Russians and Austrians clash over the taking of Ancona.
27 Dec./8 Jan. 1800	Suvórov recalled to Russia.

1800

Mar.	Condé's corps dismissed from Russian service.
24 Aug./5 Sept.	British occupy Malta and refuse to surrender it to Paul. Bonaparte promises to return it to Russia.
Aug.–Oct.	Embargo on, then burning of, British shipping and arrest of British seamen.
5/16 Dec.	Second Armed Neutrality (see p. 227). British ambassador recalled. British impose an embargo on merchantmen of neutral Powers.
1801	Louis XVIII expelled from Mitau (Jan.). Vasilii Orlóv and 23,000 Cossacks leave for conquest of India (12 Jan.).

Alexander I

1801

Mar.	Orlóv's Cossacks recalled. S. Vorontsóv becomes ambassador in London.
5/17 June	Convention of St Petersburg.
26 Sept./8 Oct.	Franco-Russian Treaty.
1803	French request the recall of Count Morkóv as ambassador to France (Nov.).

1804

Apr.	Alexander protests at the execution of the duc d'Enghein. Napoleon's reply compares Russian interest in the duc d'Enghein with the failure to prosecute the murderers of Paul I.
30 Apr./12 May	France withdraws its ambassador, comte d'Hédouville.
Aug.	Russia recalls its *chargé d'affaires* in Paris, Pëtr Oubril.
11 Sept.	Novosíltsev receives instructions for negotiating an alliance with Britain: the creation of federations of Italian and German states; Russia to have sovereignty over all Poland and, if possible, Moldavia, Cattaro, Corfu, Malta, Constantinople, and the Dardanelles;

in the case of the partition of the Ottoman Empire, the Emperor to become 'Protector of the Eastern Slavs'.

Nov.   Novosíltsev's secret mission to London to propose the formation of an Anglo-Russian anti-French league.

1805

30 Mar./11 Apr.   Anglo-Russian Treaty.

20 Nov./2 Dec.   Battle of Austerlitz. Russian defeat.

1806

8/20 July   Oubril signs a peace treaty with France in Paris. The Russian government refuses to ratify this, arguing that Oubril had exceeded his instructions.

13/25 Nov.   Bennigsen's first encounter with the French west of Warsaw.

16/28 Nov.   Murat occupies Warsaw. The Holy Synod's Appeal, read out in churches throughout Russia, denounces Napoleon as an enemy of peace and a usurper of the French Crown.

14/26 Dec.   Battle of Pułtusk. Russian (Bennigsen) victory. Battle of Golymino. Russian (Golítsyn) defeat.

15/27 Dec.   Bennigsen withdraws to Ostrolenko.

1807

Jan.   Bennigsen forces Ney to withdraw south of Königsberg.

27 Jan./8 Feb.   Battle of Eylau. Inconclusive. Enormous losses on both sides. Bennigsen withdraws to Königsberg. Napoleon later commented 'ce n'était pas une bataille, mais un carnage'.

29 May/ 10 June   Battle of Heilsberg. Russian victory.

2/14 June   Battle of Friedland. Russian defeat.

9/21 June   Franco-Russian Armistice signed.

13/25 June–27 June/9 July   Napoleon and Alexander meet at Tilsit.

15/27 June   Britain adheres to the Convention of Bartenstein (see p. 263).

25 June/7 July   Peace of Tilsit (ratified 27 June/9 July). General R. Savary becomes French ambassador in St Petersburg.

26 Aug./7 Sept.   Seniávin's fleet leaves Tenedos to escape from the British.

25 Oct./6 Nov.   Seniávin's storm-damaged fleet puts in to Lisbon, where the British blockade it.

26 Oct./7 Nov.   Relations with Britain broken off.

Dec.   Savary replaced by the marquis de Caulaincourt as French ambassador.

1808

21 Jan./2 Feb.   Napoleon writes to Alexander encouraging his ambitions on Finland, Turkey and Asia.

Sept.	Seniávin surrenders his fleet to the British.
15/27 Sept.–2/ 14 Oct.	Erfurt Conference between Alexander and Napoleon.
30 Sept./12 Oct.	Treaty of Erfurt.

1809

Apr.–Oct.	Russia gives France only token assistance in the war against Austria.
10/22 Nov.	Russian convention abolishing Poland received in Paris. Napoleon orders Caulaincourt to accept this and proposes marriage to Alexander's sister, Anna Pávlovna.
23 Dec./ 4 Jan. 1810	Caulaincourt and Rumiántsev sign the Convention abolishing Poland.

1810

25 Jan./6 Feb.	Napoleon announces his engagement to Marie Louise of Austria (his letter announcing this crosses Alexander's refusal of his proposal to Anna Pávlovna on the grounds that, at the age of 15, she was too young).
29 Jan./10 Feb.	Napoleon repudiates the agreement on Poland.
Sept. and Oct.	Napoleon requests Alexander to adopt the Trianon Tariff and to close Russian ports to neutral shipping.
19/31 Dec.	Alexander imposes a heavy tariff on goods imported over the land frontier (chiefly affecting France), while easing tariffs imported by sea, providing the importer was not at war with Russia.

1812

11/23 June	*Grande armée* crosses the Niemen.
12/14 June	Barclay's army withdraws.
17/29 June	Barclay rejects idea of a stand at Drissa and continues to retreat into Russia.
27 June/9 July	Alexander announces the end of the retreat and forecasts a 'new Poltáva'.
5/17 July	Alexander leaves the army under pressure from his advisers, but fails to nominate a commander-in-chief.
11/23 July	Davout prevents Bagratión's army from joining Barclay at Mogilëv.
22 July/3 Aug.	Bagratión's and Barclay's armies join outside Smolénsk.
26 July/7 Aug.– 7/19 Aug.	At Smolénsk, Barclay appears to offer battle but continues the withdrawal.
17 Aug.	Kutúzov appointed commander-in-chief.
26 Aug./ 7 Sept.	Battle of Borodinó. Inconclusive. Kutúzov withdraws past Moscow.
2/14 Sept.	French enter Moscow, which is set on fire.
12/24 Oct.	Battle of Maloiaroslávets. Napoleon fails to destroy Kutúzov's army. French retreat begins.

4/16–5/17 Nov.	Battle of Krásnoe, the French foil an attempt to cut them off.
14/26–16/28 Nov.	Crossing of the Berezína.
13 Dec.	Last French troops leave Russia.

1813

1/13 Jan.	Russian troops cross the Nieman.
20 April/2 May	Battle of Lützen. French victory. Wittgenstein withdraws East.
25–26 Apr./7–8 May	French take Dresden.
8/20–9/21 May	Battle of Bautzen, French victory.
23 May/4 June–4/16 Aug.	Armistice.
2–3/14–15 June	Treaties of Reichenbach.
4/16 May	Russo-Prussian ultimatum. War will be resumed on 1 June unless: 1. Austria is returned to its 1805 frontiers, extending to the Po and Mincio in Italy. 2. Prussia is restored according to the Treaty of Kalisch. 3. The Confederation of the Rhine is dissolved. 4. The Grand Duchy of Warsaw is dissolved. 5. Holland is separated from France. 6. The Bourbons are restored in Spain. 7. France withdraws entirely from Italy.
14–15/26–27 Aug.	Battle of Dresden. French victory.
4–6/16–18 Oct.	Battle of Leipzig. French defeat.
27 Oct./8 Nov.	Napoleon rejects a peace offer giving France frontiers at the Alps and Rhine.

1814

17/29 Jan.	Conference of Châtillon: Stadion (Austria); Razumóvskii (Russia); Castlereagh, Aberdeen and Sir Charles Stewart (Britain); Humboldt (Prussia); Caulaincourt (France). France offered 'its natural frontiers'.
25 Feb./9 Mar.	Treaty of Chaumont.
19/31 Mar.	Alexander I enters Paris.
31 Mar./11 Apr.	Treaty of Fontainebleau.
May	Alexander insists that Louis XVIII sign a 'Charter' with the French people, and is active in its drafting.
18/30 May	First Treaty of Paris.
21–23 May/2–4 June	Allied troops withdraw from Paris.
23 May/4 June– 14/26 June	Alexander and Ekaterína Pávlovna visit Britain.
June 1814– June 1815	Congress of Vienna: Metternich (Austria); Hardenberg and Humboldt (Prussia); Castlereagh and Wellington (Britain); Alexander I, Czartorýski, Stein, Razumóvskii, Capodistria, Nesselrode (Russia); Talleyrand (France); Cardinal Consalvi (Papacy).

1815

18 Feb./2 Mar.	Napoleon returns to France – 'The Hundred Days.'
29 May/9 June	Treaty of Vienna.
6/18 June	Battle of Waterloo. French defeat.
June–Nov.	Establishment of a provisional government of France, known as the Conference, composed of Castlereagh and Wellington (Britain); Razumóvskii and Capodistria (Russia); Metternich and Wessenberg (Austria); Hardenberg and Humboldt (Prussia).
28 June/10 July	Alexander I returns to the Elysée Palace, Paris.
8/20 Nov.	Second Treaty of Paris.

1818

Sept.–Nov.	Congress of Aix-la-Chapelle. Settles the question of French indemnities and the withdrawal of the armies of occupation. France admitted to the Quintuple Alliance. Also discusses the Slave Trade, the status of the Jews, etc.

1820

Oct.–Dec.	Congress of Troppau. Russia, Prussia and Austria accede to the Troppau Protocol, directed against revolution. Britain refuses to interfere in the internal policies of other states.

1821–41   **The Greek Revolt and the Mohammed Ali Crises**

1821	Congress of Laibach (31 Dec.1820/12 Jan.–30 Apr./12 May).

1822

Aug.	Viscount Strangford presents Russian demands to the Porte when the Russians break off relations.
8/20 Oct.–2/14 Dec.	Congress of Verona.

1824

June	Canning recalls his ambassador, Sir Charles Bagot, as a means of evading participation in the St Petersburg Conference. Ottoman affairs entrusted to Stratford Canning.
Nov.	Stratford Canning arrives in St Petersburg.

1825

7/19 Mar.	Stratford Canning's audience with the Tsar.
Mar.	Pro-Greek *Société Philanthropique* formed in France (Chateaubriand, Benjamin Constant, Sebastiani).
Oct.	Stratford Canning becomes British ambassador in Istanbul (until 1829).

Nicholas I

1826

18 Feb.	Duke of Wellington arrives in St Petersburg.

23 Mar./4 Apr.	Anglo-Russian Protocol.
1827	
24 June/6 July	Treaty of London.
Aug.	Allies instruct their navies to cut off supplies from Egypt.
22 Aug./3 Sept.	Capodistria accepts Allied armistice.
Sept.	Allied blockade of Morea and other Greek islands.
8/20 Oct.	Battle of Navarino. Anglo-Franco-Russian fleet annihilates Turco-Egyptian fleet.
5/17 Dec.	British, Russian and French ambassadors leave Istanbul.
1828	
17/29 Jan.	At the opening of Parliament, George IV 'deeply laments' Navarino as an 'untoward event'.
18/30 Jan.	Wellington refers to Turkey as an 'ancient ally' whose 'existence as an independent and powerful state' is 'necessary to the well-being' of Britain.
8/20 Apr.	France declines Wellington's offer to enforce the Treaty of London without the Russians.
14/26 Apr.	Britain is hostile to the Russo-Turkish War, but continues to cooperate with Russia for a diplomatic solution to the Greek question.
7/19 July	Allies agree that a French expedition under General Maison should be sent to Morea to expel Ibrahim.
28 July/9 Aug.	Admiral Codrington signs a convention with Mohammed Ali for the evacuation of Egyptian troops from Greece.
Early Sept.	Russian, French and British representatives (Ribeaupierre, Guilleminot, Stratford Canning) meet on the island of Poros.
30 Nov./12 Dec.	Poros Conference recommends an autonomous Greek state, including Attica, Thessaly and Euboea, ruled by an hereditary prince. The Greeks to pay an annual tribute, but Turkish landowners to be completely expropriated.
1829	Poros Conference recommends terms more favourable to Greece: a land frontier from the Gulf of Arta on the West to the Gulf of Volo in the Aegean, including most of the small islands and some of the large ones (10/22 Mar.).
1830–31	**Polish Crisis**
1831	Lafayette founds the Franco-Polish Committee in Paris.
1832	French parliament votes 224–19 to grant a subsidy to the Polish emigration.

15/27 Nov.	Lord Ponsonby becomes British ambassador to the Porte (until 1841).
20 Dec./1 Jan. 1833	Britain refuses military aid to the Sultan.

1833

9/21 Feb.	Admiral Roussin, the French ambassador, promises to force Mohammed Ali to drop his claim for Adana, if Russian troops withdraw from Turkey.
Feb.	Nicholas approaches the Austrian ambassador, Ficquelmont, on the course to be taken should the Ottoman Empire collapse.
25 Feb./9 Mar.	Mohammed Ali rejects the French terms.
May	Nicholas rejects Stratford Canning as British ambassador and recalls Kh. A. Lieven from the London Embassy.
May	British Fleet sent to the eastern Mediterranean.
Aug.	Britain and France protest against Unkiar-Skelessi and urge the Turks not to ratify it.

1834

Jan.	Ponsonby empowered to summon the British Mediterranean squadron to the Straits should the Russians threaten to seize Constantinople. He proposes that British ships be sent to the Black Sea to support the Circassian struggle against Russia.
Apr.	Quadruple Alliance of Britain, France, Portugal and Spain.
Sept.	David Urquart, secretary to the British Embassy in Istanbul, after a visit to Circassia, suggests that the Circassians declare independence from Russia and request help from Britain. Palmerston has him removed from the Embassy as a 'danger to the peace of Europe'.
1835	Urquart's *Portfolio* publishes secret Russian documents on Poland. British officers sent to help improve the Turkish Army.
Mar.	Wellington government deprives Ponsonby of the right to summon the Fleet.
June	Palmerston restores Ponsonby's right to summon the Fleet.
Nov.	Palmerston proposes a Franco-British anti-Russian treaty with Turkey.
11/23 Sept.	Urquart re-appointed secretary to the Embassy in Istanbul.
Oct.	Lord Durham arrives in St Petersburg as British ambassador (until summer 1837).

1836	The Russians seize the *Vixen*, a British ship allegedly carrying arms to the Circassians, in the port of Sudjuk-Kalé (Nov.).
1837	Urquart is recalled for his part in the *Vixen* affair (26 Feb./10 Mar.).
1838	
13/25 May	Mohammed Ali declares his intention to proclaim himself an independent ruler. Russia prepares to seize the Straits in the event of a Turco-Egyptian war.
4/16 July	In an audience with the British and Russian consuls, Mohammed Ali withdraws his declaration of 13/25 May.
Aug.–Sept.	Palmerston fails to replace Unkiar-Skelessi with a Five-Power protectorate over Turkey.
Sept.	Turkish squadron joins the British Mediterranean Fleet for a training cruise.
1839	
Mar.	British officers arrive in Istanbul to train the Ottoman Navy.
15/27 July	Five-Power note to the Porte (see p. 237).
Sept.	London Mission of F. I. Brunnóv, offering to allow Unkiar-Skelessi to lapse if a satisfactory agreement can be reached. Franco-British differences delay an agreement.
Dec.	Brunnóv's second offer: Nicholas consents to French and British ships entering the Straits should British troops be sent through the Bosphorus to defend Constantinople, and gives definite assurances on Russian aims in Central Asia.
1840	
3/15 July	London Convention.
5/17 July	French learn the terms of the London Convention.
30 Aug./11 Sept.	British Fleet bombards Beirut.
Aug.	Walewski persuades Mohammed Ali to renounce Crete and Adana in return for hereditary title to Egypt, and lifelong title to Syria.
2/14 Sept.	Sultan rejects Walewski's terms and declares Mohammed Ali deposed as viceroy of Egypt.
Sept.	British aid guerrilla war against the Egyptians in the Lebanon.
23 Oct./4 Nov.	British, Austrian and Turkish Fleets bombard Acre.
15/27 Nov.	Napier and Mohammed Ali sign a convention leaving the latter in control of Egypt in return for his surrender of the Turkish Fleet.

1841

1/13 Feb.	Sultan declares Mohammed Ali hereditary ruler of Egypt.
4/18 Feb.	Ibrahim Pasha's army returns to Egypt.
	Lord Ponsonby replaced as ambassador to the Porte by Stratford Canning.
1/13 June	Straits Convention.
1854–56	(See section 4.7 Russia and the Crimean War, pp. 299–307.)

Alexander II

1857	Palmerston sends a fleet to the Black Sea when he believes Russia has interpreted the Bessarabian frontier too much to its advantage.
13/25 Sept.	Alexander II and Napoleon III meet in Stuttgart (until 16/28 Sept.) and discuss a Franco-Russian alliance.
1858	
7/19 Aug.	Convention of Paris.
Sept.	Alexander II meets Prince Napoleon in Warsaw.
1859	
Mar.	Secret Treaty of St Petersburg.
25 Mar.	Napoleon III tells Kiselëv that the time has come for France and Russia to press for the revision of the Vienna Treaty of 1815 and the Paris Treaty of 1856.
Apr.	Massing of Russian troops on the Austrian border helps French to win the war in Italy.
Oct.	Conference of Alexander II and the Russian ambassadors to London, Paris, Berlin and Vienna. Kiselëv unsuccessfully pleads for a formal French alliance.
1860	
Spring	French support Russian proposal for concerted action to force the Porte to fulfil its Treaty of Paris obligations towards its Christian subjects.
Summer	French fail to support Russian proposal for collective action on behalf of the Porte's Christian subjects.
Sept.	Russia withdraws its mission to Turin in protest at the Sardinian occupation of the Papal States.
1862	Kiselëv replaced in the Paris embassy by Andrei Budberg. De Ségur, the French consul-general in Warsaw, expelled for alleged secret dealings with Polish subversives.
Aug.	Russia recognizes the unified Kingdom of Italy.
1863	**Polish Crisis**

1/13 Feb.	French note calls attention to the fact that the Polish question was arousing unprecedented sympathy in France.
18 Feb./2 Mar.	British note states that Russian action in Poland is a violation of the 1815 Vienna Treaty and urges that the rebels be amnestied and Alexander I's constitution restored. (Denmark, Italy, Holland, the Pope, Portugal, Spain, Sweden, and Turkey also send notes to Russia on Poland.)
5/17 Apr.	Britain, France and Austria present simultaneous, but not identical, notes to Russia on the Polish question. British note expands on its note of 18 Feb./2 Mar. French note makes no reference to the 1815 Treaty, but laments the effect of the uprising on the peace of Europe. (For the Austrian note see p. 256.)
15/27 May	Britain, France and Russia officially accept the deposition of King Otto of Greece.
5/17 June	Britain, France and Austria present a six-point programme for the solution of the Polish question: 1. A general amnesty. 2. A national government in accordance with the constitution of 1815. 3. Access for Poles to public office. 4. Freedom of conscience, and removal of restrictions on the Catholic Church. 5. Polish to be the exclusive official language of government and education. 6. Army recruitment to be regulated by law. Russia rejects any foreign intervention in Russo-Polish relations.
1/13 July	Treaty of London.
1864	Russia recalls its ambassador to Rome (Spring).
1866	Britain, France and Prussia reject Russian demands for severe measures against the new Kingdom of Romania (Feb.) (see p. 238).
27 Nov.	Russia breaks off diplomatic relations with the Holy See.
1867	France and Italy support the Russian demand that Crete be transferred to Greece. With British support, the Porte rejects this demand, and crushes the Cretan revolt (Apr.).
1869–85	**Anglo-Russian rivalry in Afghanistan**
1869	Clarendon proposes that Afghanistan be accepted as a neutral zone between British and Russian possessions. Gorchakóv accepts but negotiations become bogged down over the definition of Afghanistan.

1870	Gorchakóv note to the Powers repudiating the Black Sea provisions of the Treaty of Paris (19/31 Oct.) (see p. 306).
1873	Anglo-Russian agreement over Afghanistan is immediately invalidated by the Russian occupation of Khiva (Jan.).
1875–78	**The Bosnian Crisis and the Russo-Turkish War**
1876	
Jan.	France, Italy and (reluctantly) Britain accept the Andrássy Note.
May	France and Italy accept the Berlin Memorandum. Britain rejects it and sends a fleet to Besika Bay.
Mid Dec.	Constantinople Conference: Austria-Hungary, Britain (Lord Salisbury and Sir Henry Elliott), France, Germany, Italy, Russia (Ignátev). Agree to create the autonomous states of Eastern and Western Bulgaria. Turks then admitted, but reject the proposals. Conference ends in a deadlock (8/20 Jan. 1877).
1877	
Late Jan.	Delegates and ambassadors of the six Powers leave Constantinople in protest at the failure of the conference.
19/31 Mar.	London Protocol.
Apr.	Sir Henry Layard becomes British ambassador to the Porte.
24 Apr./6 May	Britain warns Russia that it will not remain neutral if the war threatens its vital interests (Suez Canal, Egypt, Constantinople, the Straits, the Persian Gulf).
18/30 May	Russia gives assurances to Britain on Suez, Egypt, the Persian Gulf and India. Should the question of Constantinople and the Straits arise, this would be decided by general agreement. Constantinople should not belong to any of the Powers, although a temporary occupation could not be ruled out.
18/30 June	British Fleet ordered to Besika Bay.
16/28 July	British warn that a fleet might be sent to the Straits to prevent a Russian occupation of Constantinople.
1878	
3/15 Jan.	British declaration that no changes in the 1856 settlement can be made without the agreement of all signatories.
11/23 Jan.	British Fleet ordered to Constantinople.
12/24 Jan.	Orders to British Fleet countermanded.

14/26 Jan.	Gorchakóv announces that the question of the Straits is one of 'general concern'.
27 Jan./8 Feb.	British Fleet ordered to Constantinople.
1/13 Feb.	British Fleet enters the Dardanelles.
4/16 Mar.	Beaconsfield refuses to participate in the Congress proposed by Andrássy unless every item of the Russo-Turkish settlement is brought within its purview. Russia rejects this.
15/27 Mar.	British Cabinet decides to call up reserves, to move troops from India to Malta and Asia Minor, and to occupy portions of Turkish territory in order to restore the balance of power in the Mediterranean. This last point leads to the resignation of Lord Derby (Foreign Secretary).
20 Mar./1 Apr.	New Foreign Secretary, Lord Salisbury, issues a circular note indicting the Treaty of San Stefano, accusing Russia of wishing to install itself as the leading power in the Balkans.
28 Mar./9 Apr.	Gorchakóv challenges Britain to say what it wants.
15/27 Apr.	German efforts to mediate between Britain and Russia fail.
17/29 Apr.	Shuválov offers Salisbury direct negotiations.
12/24 May	Britain demands that Turkey conclude an anti-Russian alliance and allow Britain to occupy Cyprus so that it can 'make necessary provision for the execution of her engagement'. (Convention signed 23 May/4 June.)
18/30 May	Salisbury–Shuválov conversations lead to three memoranda that form the basis of the Congress of Berlin.
25 May/6 June	Salisbury and Andrássy agree to cooperate at the Congress of Berlin.
1/13 June	Congress of Berlin opens.
24 June/6 July	Salisbury announces that 'the obligations of Her Britannic Majesty relating to the closure of the Straits do not go further than the engagement with the Sultan to respect in this matter His Majesty's independent determination in conformity with the spirit of the existing treaties'.
26 June/ 8 July	British occupy Cyprus.
30 June/12 July	Russians reply to Salisbury that the closure of the Straits is a European principle binding on all Powers, not only as regards the Sultan but also the other signatories of the treaties of 1841, 1856 and 1871.
1/13 July	Treaty of Berlin (see p. 248).

Alexander III

1881–87	**The Bulgarian Crisis**
1884	Anglo-Russian commission for the Afghan border (July).
1885	
Feb.	Russian occupation of Penjdeh.
20 Feb./4 Mar.	Queen Victoria appeals to Alexander not to allow Russian and Afghan troops to clash.
5/17 Mar.	Russians agree not to advance pending settlement of the Afghan border.
18/30 Mar.	Russian defeat of the Afghans at Ak-Teppe almost leads to war with Britain.
10/22 May	Preliminary Russo-British agreement on the Afghan border in Penjdeh.
29 Aug./10 Sept.	Final Russo-British agreement on the Afghan border.
Autumn	Britain supports (while Russia opposes) the recognition of unification of the two Bulgarias.
1886	Russia protests after Lord Salisbury describes Radko-Dmitriev and his followers as 'traitors debauched with foreign gold' (Aug.).
1890–1907	***Rapprochement* with France and rivalry with Britain in the Far East.**
1891	
July	French Fleet visits Kronstadt.
15/27 Aug.	French and Russian governments agree to come to an understanding on measures to adopt 'immediately and simultaneously' in case of a threat to peace.
1892	
5/17 Aug.	Franco-Russian military agreement.
6 Nov.	Witte memorandum predicts the Trans-Siberian Railway will supersede the Suez Canal as the principal trade route to China.
1893	
15/27 Dec.	Russia ratifies the military agreement with France.
23 Dec./4 Jan. 1894	France ratifies the military agreement with Russia.

Nicholas II

1894–96	The Armenian massacres in Asia Minor and Constantinople arouse European opinion against Turkey and contribute to an estrangement between Britain and the Porte.
1895	
10/23 Apr.	Britain refuses to join the Russo-Franco-German protest against the terms of the Sino-Japanese Treaty of Shimonoseki (see p. 294).

1896	Nicholas II visits Paris.
1897	Franco-Russian Alliance officially announced during President Félix Faure's state visit to St Petersburg (Aug.).
1898	Russian circular note proposing a disarmament congress (12 Aug. and 30 Dec.).
1899	Peace conference in The Hague in response to Russian notes (May–June). Attended by 20 European Powers, the USA, Mexico, Japan, China, Siam and Persia, the conference agrees on the rules of warfare and establishes the International Court at The Hague.
1902	
17/30 Jan.	Anglo-Japanese Agreement: each to remain neutral in a war involving the other, but would come to the other's aid should a third party join in against the other.
3/16 & 7/ 20 Mar.	Franco-Russian declarations supporting the independence of China and Korea and the open-door policy in the Far East.
1904	
8/21 Oct.	Dogger Bank incident.
Oct.	Anti-Russian press campaign in Britain.
1906	
Apr.	British bankers participate in the floating of a loan for Russia for the first time since the Crimean War.
June	Nicolson–Izvólskii conversations on a Russo-British *rapprochement.*
1907	Second Hague conference meets on the initiative of the Russian government.
Mar.	Russian Fleet visits Portsmouth.
18/31 Aug.	Anglo-Russian Convention.
1908	
21 Jan./3 Feb.	Izvólskii fails to convince the Council of Ministers that, given the projected Austrian railway in Novibazar, a military alliance with Britain would now be in Russia's interest.
June	Edward VII visits Nicholas II in Réval.
26 Sept./9 Oct.	Sir Edward Grey approves Izvólskii's plan to open the Straits, as long as it applies to the warships of all nations.
1909	Nicholas II visits Victor Emmanuel in Racconigi (Oct.).
1910	Sir George Buchanan becomes British Ambassador (Summer).
1911–13	**The Balkan Wars**

1912

27 July–5 Aug.   Poincaré visits St Petersburg.

Dec.   Conference of the Ambassadors of the Powers, chaired by Sir Edward Grey, meets in London to try to sort out the Balkan crisis.

1913   French Ambassador, Georges Louis, recalled at Sazónov's request (Feb.).

1914   Buchanan warns the Tsar that differences in North Persia 'might prove fatal to the Anglo-Russian understanding' (June).

1914–17   (See section 4.8 Russia and the First World War, pp. 308–10.)

4.5.1   Treaties

1715

Oct.   **Greifswald**: Treaty with Hanover. Russia to retain Ingria, Karelia and Estonia (and originally Livonia, but the text was later altered to remove this). In return, Hanover was to take Bremen and Verden.

1717

Aug.   **Amsterdam**: Treaty of friendship with France and Holland. Of little practical significance.

1747

June and Dec.   **Anglo-Russian Treaties**: Provide for an annual British subsidy for Russia in return for 30,000 Russian troops at British disposal in Kurland, and another army of 30,000 on the Rhine, in return for further subsidy.

1755

Sept.   **Anglo-Russian Treaty**: Britain to pay Russia an annual subsidy of £100,000. Russia to maintain on the frontiers of Livonia and Lithuania an army of 55,000 men, to be available for service abroad (for an additional subsidy of £500,000) in the event of an attack on Hanover. (Ratified 1.ii.1756.)

1780–82   **Armed Neutrality**: The signatories demanded free passage for neutral ships from port to port and along the coasts to combatants and freedom for neutral ships to carry enemy goods, except for contraband. Only an effective blockade would be recognized as legal.

1793

14/25 Mar.   **Treaties with Britain**: Renews Commercial Treaty of 1766. A second treaty bound each party also to help the other in the war with France, not to conclude a separate peace, to close their ports to all French ships, to prohibit French trade with neutral countries.

1795
7/18 Feb.   **Treaty with Britain**: Mutual assistance against France. Russia to provide an expeditionary corps, Britain a naval squadron or an annual subsidy of 500,000 rubles. Russia to provide a squadron of 12 warships and six frigates to assist the British Fleet in the Channel and the Atlantic. A British squadron was to act in the Baltic if Russia was attacked. British ports to be open to Russian ships if war were to break out with the Porte.

1801
5/17 Mar.   **Convention of St Petersburg**: Signed by Lord St Helens and Peter Pánin. Effectively ends the Armed Neutrality, with some concessions to Russia. (Denmark signs, October 1801; Sweden in March 1802.)

1805
30 Mar./11 Apr.   **Anglo-Russian Treaty**: The two governments agree to form a European league for the liberation of North Germany, Holland, Switzerland and Italy from French domination. Britain to pay an annual subsidy of £1,250,000 for every 100,000 men contributed against France, provided the number was not less than 400,000.

1806
8/20 July   **Peace Treaty with France**: The integrity and independence of the Ottoman Empire is guaranteed. Both parties to bring about peace between Prussia and Sweden. French and Russian claims in Italy and the Adriatic are settled. France to withdraw her troops from Germany.

1807
25 June/7 July   **Tilsit**: (Signatories: Ch.-M. Talleyrand, A. Kurákin, D. Lobánov-Rostóvskii.) Comprises 29 Articles, seven secret clauses and a Russo-French Alliance of nine articles.
Main Treaty: Peace between France and Russia. Part of Prussia to be retained by the King of Prussia 'out of regard for' the Emperor of Russia. The Duchy of Warsaw, under the King of Saxony, to comprise all Polish provinces formerly held by Prussia, except for Białystok. Danzig to be a free city. Russia's Polish possessions to be recognized as Russian in perpetuity. Russia to withdraw its troops from the Danubian Principalities. Russia recognizes Joseph Bonaparte as King

of Naples, Jerome Bonaparte as King of Westphalia and Louis Bonaparte as King of Holland, and recognizes the Confederation of the Rhine. Alexander to mediate between France and Britain, and Napoleon to mediate between Russia and Turkey. Commercial relations to be restored, and ambassadors exchanged. *Secret Treaty*: Russia to hand Cattaro over to the French, to recognize French sovereignty over the Ionian Islands and the King of Naples's claim on Sicily. France not to pursue any Turkish subject, especially Montenegrins, who may have opposed them.

Treaty of Alliance: France and Russia to make common cause on land and sea in all European wars. All differences between them to be settled diplomatically. Britain would be offered Hanover in return for mediation, the recognition of all flags on the seas, and the restoration of all French, Spanish and Dutch colonies seized since 1805. If peace with Britain was not achieved by 1 November, or if Britain had not fulfilled its terms by 1 December, Russia would declare war on Britain, and Austria, Sweden, Denmark and Portugal would be compelled to join an anti-British coalition. If the Sultan refused to accept French mediation, or if this failed to produce satisfactory results within three months, France would make common cause with Russia against Turkey, and they would reach an agreement on the liberation of European Turkey except Constantinople and Rumelia.

1808

30 Sept./12 Oct.   **Erfurt**: Confirms the anti-British Alliance. Napoleon recognizes Russia's right to Finland, Wallachia and Moldavia and the Danube as the frontier between Russia and Turkey. France will support Russia should Austria ally with Turkey. Russia will support France should Austria declare war on France. The convention to remain secret for ten years.

1813

2–3/14–15 June   **Reichenbach**: Britain insists on Prussian support for the aggrandizement of Hanover (2/14 June) before joining Prussia and Russia against France. Britain agrees to pay £1,000,000, plus £250,000 towards the upkeep of Russian vessels in British ports. Prussia renounces all claims on territories Britain claims for Hanover, and Russia undertakes to support the enlargement of Hanover. Prussia, Russia and Britain agree to coordinate their military activities and not to sign a separate peace with France.

1814

25 Feb./9 Mar.	**Chaumont**: Establishes the Quadruple Alliance – Russia, Prussia, Austria, Britain.
31 Mar./11 Apr.	**Fontainebleau**: Napoleon abdicates but retains the title of emperor and rule over the island of Elba.
18/30 May	**First Treaty of Paris**: France is reduced to its 1792 frontiers.

1815

28 May/9 June   **Vienna** ends the Napoleonic Wars. France reduced to its pre-1789 frontiers. Russia acquires the Grand Duchy of Warsaw. Austria acquires Lombardy, Venice, Dalmatia, Tyrol, Vorarlberg, Salzburg and East Galicia. Prussia acquires Saxony, Posen, Swedish Pomerania, Westphalia and the Rhineland. Britain acquires Malta, Heligoland, Cape Colony, Mauritius and the protectorate of the Ionian Islands. The German Confederation replaces the Holy Roman Empire. Belgium and Holland unite as the Kingdom of the Netherlands. Sweden acquires Norway. The Republic of Cracow is established. Swiss neutrality is confirmed, and Neuchâtel and Geneva join the Confederation. The former ruling houses are restored in Naples, Sardinia, Tuscany, and Modena. The Papal States are reconstituted.

8/20 Nov.   **Second Treaty of Paris**: France reduced to its 1790 frontiers (i.e. loses Belgium, Germany West of the Rhine and parts of Savoy), has to pay an indemnity of 700 million francs, and to pay for an army of occupation of 150,000 men.

1827

24 June/6 July   **London**: Britain, France and Russia agree to set a term to the struggle between Turkey and Greece. They offer the Porte their mediation and insist on an immediate armistice. They propose that the Greeks shall be governed by authorities of their own choice, subject to the approval of the Porte and that they shall pay a fixed annual tribute to the Sultan as their suzerain. Turkish proprietors on Greek soil shall be bought out with fair compensation. The frontiers of the new state to be determined by negotiation between the Powers and the two belligerents. The Powers renounce

any territorial or commercial advantages to themselves and agree to guarantee the new settlement. In an additional secret clause they undertake to inform the Porte of their decision to enter on consular relations with the Greeks and that, if either belligerent refuses to agree to an armistice, the three Powers will 'by means which circumstances may suggest to their prudence', but 'without . . . taking part in the hostilities . . . jointly exert all their efforts to accomplish the object of such an armistice'.

1840
3/15 July
  London Convention: (Signatories: Palmerston, Brunnóv, Neumann (Austria), Bülow (Prussia).) Lays down the terms of settlement between Mohammed Ali and the Porte, that is Mohammed Ali to be offered Egypt as an hereditary possession and Southern Syria, including Acre, for life, on condition that he surrender Northern Syria, Adana, Crete and Arabia. The Convention also provides for military and naval measures to support them. Article IV confirms the 'ancient rule' of closing the Straits to warships.

1841
1/13 June
  Straits Convention: Britain, Russia, France, Austria and Prussia pledge to observe the rule that the Sultan, 'so long as he is at peace', will not admit foreign warships in the Straits, except light vessels in the service of legations of friendly Powers. Russia retains the rights secured by the treaties of Kuchuk Kainardji, Akkerman and Adrianople, but relinquishes the special position acquired by Unkiar-Skelessi (which is allowed to lapse).

1858
7/19 Aug.
  Convention of Paris: Signed by Russia, Britain, France, Austria and Turkey, the Principalities to remain separate, but their institutions to be similar. Turkish suzerainty to be nominal. The new regime to be guaranteed by the Powers.

1859
Mar.
  Secret Treaty of St Petersburg: Russian government undertakes to maintain friendly neutrality towards France in the event of a Franco-Austrian War.

1863
1/13 July
  London: The Protecting Powers and Denmark recognize the succession of Prince William of Denmark as

George I of Greece, and the union of Greece and the Ionian Islands.

1864

17/29 Mar.   **London**: Britain, France and Russia guarantee the Hellenic Kingdom as a constitutional monarchy.

1877

19/31 Mar.   **London Protocol**: A watered down version of the Constantinople Conference agreements.

1885

10 Sept.   **Russo-British Agreement on the Afghan Border**: Russia to retain Penjdeh, but the Afghans retain the Zulfikar pass.

1892

5/17 Aug.   **Franco-Russian Military Agreement**: Signed by the French and Russian chiefs of staff. 1. If France were attacked by Germany, or by Italy supported by Germany, Russia would employ all her available forces to fight Germany. 2. If Russia were attacked by Germany, or Austria supported by Germany, France would employ all her available forces to fight Germany. 3. A mobilization of the armies of the Triple Alliance (Germany, Austria, Italy) would be countered by immediate mobilization of France and Russia. 4. France to use 1.3 million troops against Germany; Russia to employ 7–800,000. 5. The general staffs of the two countries to coordinate plans. 6. Neither Russia nor France to conclude a separate peace.

1907

18/31 Aug.   **Anglo-Russian Convention**: (Signatories Izvólskii and Sir Arthur Nicolson.) Defines and delimits the spheres of influence in Persia, Tibet and Afghanistan.

1909

Oct.   **Racconigi**: Russia promises to view with benevolence Italian interests in Tripoli and Cyrenaica; Italy agrees to take a similar view of Russian interests in the Straits.

4.6 Russia and Asia

Peter I

1692	Unsuccessful embassy to China to establish diplomatic and commercial relations.
1715	A. P. Volýnskii sent as the Tsar's permanent representative to the Shah of Persia.
1716–17	Military expedition to Khiva and Bokhara annihilated in an ambush near Khiva.
1722	
May	War with Persia.
23 Aug.	Russians take Derbent.
1723	
Summer	Russians take Bakú.
12 Sept.	Treaty of St Petersburg.

Anna Ivánovna

1732	Treaty of Rasht.
1735	Treaty of Gandjeh.

Alexander I

1804	
Jan.	Russians under Tsitsiánov invade Persia.
Sept.	Siege of Eriván. Russians forced to retire.
1812	Battle of Aslanduz. The Russians surprise and rout Abbas Mirza on the river Aras (19/31 Oct.).
1813	Treaty of Gulistan (30 Sept./12 Oct.).
1819	N. N. Muravëv's mission to Khiva. Ministry of Foreign Affairs establishes a permanent Asia Desk. Alexander I establishes the Asiatic Committee to consider ways of improving trade with Asia.

Nicholas I

1826	
June	The Persian government denounces the Treaty of Gulistan. Persian troops under Abbas Mirza cross the Russian border and occupy Lenkoran, Elizavetpól and Karabágh, reaching Tiflis.

Sept.	Madátov retakes Elizavetpól.
10 Sept.	Paskévich arrives in Elizavetpól.
14/26 Sept.	Battle of Ganjeh. Abbas Mirza defeated by Paskévich.
1827	Paskévich takes Eriván and advances towards Teheran (1 Oct.).
1828	Treaty of Turkmanchai (10/22 Feb.).
1836	At Russian instigation, Persia declares war on Afghanistan.
1837	Palmerston complains to the Russian ambassador in London after the Russian Minister in Teheran, Colonel A. S. Simónich, participates in the Persian siege of Herat. Nesselrode persuades Nicholas to recall Simónich.
1839	V. A. Peróvskii's unsuccessful military expedition to Khiva (Nov.).
1846	Russians reach the Aral Sea and the mouth of the river Syrdaria.
1849	
Feb.	Special committee established to investigate the Amúr.
July	G. I. Nevelskói's ship enters the Amúr.
3 Aug.	Nevelskói sails between Sakhalín and the mainland, proving Sakhalín to be an island.
1850	Nevelskói establishes Nikoláevsk on the Amúr (13 Aug.). Penetration of the Ili basin (until 1854).
1853	Russian-American Company empowered to administer Sakhalín and appoint a governor. V. Peróvskii goes up the Syrdaria and establishes the fort of Peróvsk, 350 miles south-east of the Aral Sea.
Aug.	Admiral Putiátin's naval squadron visits Nagasaki.
Oct.	Russian forces land in Sakhalín (until 1854).
1854	Muravëv sails up the Amúr and founds the city of Khabárovsk. Foundation of the fortress of Vérnyi ('Loyal').
22 Dec.	Putiátin begins formal negotiations with the Japanese.
1855	Russo-Japanese Treaty (7 Feb.).

Alexander II
1858	
May	Treaty of Aigun.
June	Treaty of Tientsin.
12 Aug.	Treaty of Yedo.
1858	N. P. Ignátev's mission to Peking. Chinese refuse to accept the territory between the Ussuri and the Pacific as Russian. Muravëv sails down the Amúr and

	finds the spot for the future Vladivostók ('Ruler of the East').
Sept.	Ignátev's mission to Khiva and Bokhara.
1860	
July	Foundation of Vladivostók.
2/14 Nov.	Treaty of Peking.
1862	Japanese mission to St Petersburg to discuss Sakhalín. Japanese seek frontier on 50th parallel, Russians claim the entire island. No agreement reached.
1864	
July	M. G. Cherniáev, sent to Siberia to establish a line of forts from Peróvsk to Vérnyi, captures Chimkent and envelopes the Kazakh steppe.
Oct.	Cherniáev's unsuccessful attempt to take Tashkent.
21 Nov.	Gorchakóv's circular justifying Russian expansion into Central Asia by reference to the expansionary policies of Britain, France, Holland and the USA.
1865	Cherniáev captures Tashkent (17 June). The Amir of Bokhara declares a Holy War. Russians occupy part of the Khanate of Bokhara.
1866	Cherniáev's unsuccessful campaign in Bokhara leads to his dismissal. Russians take Khodjent. The Khan of Kokand accepts Russian peace terms. Territories seized since 1847 annexed as the governorship-general of Turkestan (governor-general: K. P. von Kaufmann until 1883).
1867	Further Japanese mission on Sakhalín fails to reach agreement.
1868	
Jan.	Treaty of Kudair.
2 May	Kaufmann captures Samarkand.
June	Kaufmann defeats the Bokharans on the Zerbulak Heights near Katta-Kurgan.
18 June	Khan of Bokhara makes peace with Russia, accepting the loss of territory and Russian trade rights.
1869	Establishment of Krasnovódsk on the eastern littoral of the Caspian.
1870	Unsuccessful Japanese attempt to obtain American mediation over Sakhalín.
1871	Occupation of Kuldja (returned to China 1883).
1873	
12 Aug.	Kaufmann takes over Khiva, which becomes a protectorate.
16 Sept.	Bokhara becomes a protectorate.

1875	Treaty of St. Petersburg (25 Apr./7 May). The revolt against Kudair, Khan of Kokand, becomes a Holy War against Russia and is met by punitive expeditions by Kaufmann and M. D. Skóbelev.
1876	
Jan.	Skóbelev captures Andizhan.
19 Feb.	Annexation of Kokand.
1879	N. P. Lomákin's disastrous campaign against the Turkoman tribesmen. Treaty of Livádia.
1881	Skóbelev's victory at Gheok Teppe and the massacre of the male population leads to the annexation of Turkoman country (12/24 Jan.).

Alexander III

1881	Treaty of St Petersburg (Aug.).
1883	Korean government offers Russia an ice-free port and invites Russian officers to train the Korean Army. Offer withdrawn under British pressure.
1884	Annexation of Merv (6/18 Feb.).
1885	Occupation of Penjdeh (Feb.).

Nicholas II

1895	
Apr.	Nicholas writes of the need for an ice-free port in the Pacific, south of Korea.
10/23 Apr.	Russia, France and Germany protest against the terms of the Sino-Japanese Treaty of Shimonoseki which cedes to Japan the Liaodong peninsula, Formosa/Taiwan and the Pescadores. Japan restores the Liaodong peninsula to China.
July	Witte arranges a Franco-Russian loan to China to pay off its indemnity to Japan, under the terms of the Treaty of Shimonoseki.
Dec.	Establishment of the Russo-Chinese Bank.
1896	
21 May/3 June	Secret Russo-Chinese Treaty.
27 May/9 June	Russo-Japanese Protocol on Korea.
1897	
Nov.	Russian protest at the German seizure of Kiaochow.
Dec.	Russian fleet anchors in Port Arthur and presents demands to the Chinese government to compensate for the German occupation of Kiaochow.
1898	
14/27 Mar.	Russia obtains a 25-year lease on the Liaodong peninsula, including Port Arthur and Dálnyi, and

	the right to build a railway between Port Arthur and Harbin.
15/28 Apr.	Reaffirmation of the Russo-Japanese Protocol of 1896 with Russian recognition of Japanese special economic interests in Korea.
1899	Muravëv endorses the Open Door policy for China (Dec.).
1900	
May	Boxer Rebellion.
July	Witte memorandum argues that control of the Manchurian Railway will give Russia control of China. Lamsdorff proclaims Russia's determination to prevent the partition of China. The Russians occupy Manchuria.
Nov.	Russia obtains a concession in Tientsin.
1902	
17/30 Jan.	Anglo-Japanese Alliance.
3/16 & 7/ 20 Mar.	Franco-Russian declarations supporting the independence of China and Korea and the open-door policy in the Far East.
26 Mar./8 Apr.	Russo-Chinese Convention.
1903	Final attempt by the Japanese to reach an agreement with Russia (end July).
1904–5	**The Russo-Japanese War**
1904	
22 Jan./5 Feb.	Japanese break off diplomatic relations with Russia.
25 Jan./8 Feb.	Japanese attack on Port Arthur.
Apr.	Japanese victory over Zasúlich on the Yalu.
31 Mar./13 Apr.	Japanese sink the *Petropavlovsk*, with admiral S. O. Makárov on board.
May	Japanese capture Nanshan and Dálnyi.
28 July/10 Aug.	Japanese (Togo) destroy the Port Arthur Fleet.
Aug.	Battle of Liaoyang. Russian (Kuropátkin) defeat.
15 Sept.	Kuropátkin's Sha-ho offensive peters out after great losses.
Oct.	Baltic Fleet leaves for the Far East.
6/19 Dec.	Russians (A. M. Stoessel) surrender Port Arthur after an 148-day siege.
End Dec.	A. V. Míshchenko's Cossack raid on Japanese communications.
1905	
Jan.	Battle of Sandepu: Russian victory (O. K. Grippenberg).
25 Feb.	Battle of Mukden. Japanese victory. Linévich replaces Kuropátkin as commander.
14/27 May	Battle of Tsushimá. Japanese (Togo) destroy the Russian Baltic Fleet.

18/31 May	Japanese request that Roosevelt invite them and the Russians to a peace conference.
28 July/10 Aug.	Opening of the peace conference at Portsmouth, New Hampshire.
23 Aug./5 Sept.	Treaty of Portsmouth.
1907	
15/28 June	Russo-Japanese agreement on fisheries and trade.
17/30 June	Russo-Japanese Convention.
1910	
21 June/4 July	Russo-Japanese Treaty.
16/29 Aug.	Japanese annexation of Korea.
1911	Outer Mongolia proclaims its independence from China and becomes *de facto* a Russian dependency (Dec.).
1912	Secret Russo-Japanese Treaty (25 June/8 July).

4.6.1   Treaties

1723
12 Sept.   **Treaty of St Petersburg**: Ends war with Persia. Russia obtains Bakú, Derbent, Rasht and the Persian provinces on the west and south shores of the Caspian. The Shah to have the use of Russian troops to maintain internal order.

1727   **Kiakhta**: Defines the boundary with Mongolia from the river Argun to the Eniséi.

1732   **Rasht**: Ends the war with Persia. Russia waives its right to territory south of the river Kura.

1735   **Gandjeh**: Restores to Persia provinces ceded to Russia in 1723. No Russian presence allowed south of the Térek.

1813
12 Oct.   **Gulistan**: Russia granted the right to maintain a fleet in the Caspian and obtains recognition of its sovereignty over much of the Caucasus, including Georgia.

1828
10/22 Feb.   **Turkmanchai**: Ends war with Persia. Russia acquires Nakhicheván and Eriván, and the right to maintain a navy in the Caspian.

1855
7 Feb.   **Treaty with Japan**: Sakhalín recognized as a joint possession. Japanese sovereignty over the Kurile Islands

recognized from Etoforu south; Russian from Urup north. Shimoda, Hakodate and Nagasaki to be open to Russian ships.

1857	**Russo-Japanese Trade Treaty**
1858	
May	**Aigun**: Negotiated by Muravëv and a local Chinese commander. 1. The Chinese recognize Russian sovereignty over the left bank of the Amúr from the river Aigun to the Sea. 2. The Ussuri region, from the junction of the river Ussuri to the shore, placed under joint Russo-Chinese administration. 3. Russian and Chinese citizens granted exclusive rights of navigation on the Amúr, Ussuri and Sungari. (Not ratified by Peking until 1860.)
June	**Tientsin**: Putiátin obtains for Russia all privileges in China previously secured by Britain, France and the USA.
12 Aug.	**Yedo**: Putiátin negotiates an exchange of permanent resident diplomatic missions with Japan and for the development of trade without government interference.
1860	
2/14 Nov.	**Peking**: Establishes new Chinese-Russian border: 1. Recognizes Russian sovereignty over the territories stipulated in the Treaty of Aigun. 2. Grants Russian sovereignty over the area between the Ussuri and the Gulf of Tartary. 3. Grants Russia trading privileges in Mongolia and Chinese Turkestan.
1868	
Jan.	**Kudair**: Khanate of Kokand becomes a Russian protectorate.
1875	
25 Apr./7 May	**St Petersburg**: Russia acquires Sakhalín from Japan in return for recognizing Japanese rule over all the Kurile islands. Freedom of trade and fishing rights given to the Japanese in the Okhótsk ports and Kamchatka.
1879	**Livadia**: China cedes to Russia large sections of Kuldja, including the Tian Shan mountain pass. (Chinese government disavowed its envoy and refused to ratify.)
1881	
Aug.	**St Petersburg**: Russia retains a smaller section of Kuldja than granted by Treaty of Livadia, but receives an indemnity of 9,000,000 rubles and trading concessions in China, Mongolia and Chinese Turkestan.
1884	**Russo-Korean Treaty**: Russia receives the right to trade with Korea and establish a diplomatic mission in Seoul.

| May/3 June | **Secret Russo-Chinese Treaty**: Defensive alliance against Japan. The Russo-Chinese Bank granted a concession to build the Chinese Eastern Railway across Manchuria. |
| 27 May/9 June | **Russo-Japanese Protocol**: Both countries to respect the independence of Korea and to cooperate in the administrative and financial rehabilitation of Korea. |

1902

| 26 Mar./8 Apr. | **Russo-Chinese Convention**: Russia to withdraw from Manchuria within 18 months, at six month intervals, ending in October 1903. |

1905

| 23 Aug./5 Sept. | **Treaty of Portsmouth**: (Signatories: S. Iu. Witte, Baron Komura.) Ends the Russo-Japanese War. Russia acknowledges Japan's paramount interests in Korea. Russia cedes Southern Sakhalín to Japan, as well as its lease of the Liaodong peninsula (including ceding all public works and properties there), and the Southern Manchurian Railway from Port Arthur to Changchun. Russia renounces any concessions in Manchuria. |

1907

| 17/30 June | **Russo-Japanese Convention**: Each promises to respect the other's territorial integrity and to uphold the open-door policy in Manchuria. Secret articles give Japan a free hand in Korea and recognize Southern Manchuria and Inner Mongolia as being in the Japanese sphere of influence, and Northern Manchuria and Outer Mongolia as being in the Russian sphere of influence. |

1910

| 21 June/4 July | **Russo-Japanese Treaty**: Confirms the spheres of influence outlined in the 1907 Convention but omits any reference to Chinese territorial integrity or the open-door policy. Secret articles provide for common action to safeguard 'special interests' in their respective spheres of influence. |

1912

| 25 June/8 July | **Secret Russo-Japanese Treaty**: Amplifies and redefines the provisions of the 1907 and 1910 treaties with respect to the partition of Mongolia and Manchuria. |

4.7 Russia and the Crimean War

Nicholas I

1841–53	**The Dispute over the Holy Places**
1841	Nicholas approves the renovation of two Orthodox monasteries in Jerusalem for use as hostels for Russian pilgrims (Apr.).
1842	Stratford Canning arrives in Istanbul (Jan. until June 1852). Britain vetoes the appointment of P. D. Kiselëv as *hospodar* of Wallachia. France demands to be allowed to help in the repair of the Church of the Holy Sepulchre.
1843	French consulate established in Jerusalem. Nesselrode sends Uspénskii to study the religious situation in the Holy Land.
Sept.	Nicholas has two interviews with Fiquelmont in Warsaw to discuss a possible partition of the Ottoman Empire.
1844	
Mar.	Orlóv's discussions with Metternich on the partition of the Ottoman Empire.
19/31 May	Nicholas I visits London (28 May/9 June).
23 May/4 June	Nicholas's conversations with Peel and Aberdeen (and 24 May/5 June).
7/19 Sept.	Nesselrode's memorandum to Aberdeen, summarizing the June talks with Nicholas I: Russia and Britain vitally interested in the independence and territorial integrity of Turkey. The fate of the Christian subjects of the Ottomans depends largely on the concerted action of the Great Powers, whose duty is 'to use all their influence to maintain the Christian subjects of the Porte in a state of submission to their sovereign authority'. Should the Empire collapse, Britain and Russia to agree on a common course.
1845	Aberdeen confirms Nesselrode's view of the London talks, but adds that they only bind the Peel/Aberdeen government (9/21 Jan.).

1846	On the fall of the Peel government in June, neither Palmerston nor Sir John Russell feel bound by the Nesselrode memorandum.
1847	Establishment of the Latin (i.e.Catholic) Patriarchate of Jerusalem.
1848	
Feb.	Uspénskii heads a Russian ecclesiastical mission to Jerusalem.
2/14 Apr.	The Russians inform the Porte that their troops will enter the Principalities should there be revolutionary outbreaks there.
June	Bucharest uprising, followed by a Russian occupation of Moldavia.
Sept.	Omer Pasha sent to Wallachia to crush the insurgents. Russian troops enter Wallachia to assist the Turks.
1849	(For Russian help to the Habsburgs in suppressing the Hungarian Revolution, see p. 255.)
19 Apr./1 May	Convention of Balta Liman.
5/17 Sept.	Austrian and Russian governments break off relations with the Porte to protest against its refusal to extradite Polish and Hungarian revolutionaries.
4/16 Oct.	Fuad Pasha, special emissary of the Porte, received by Nicholas.
7/19 Oct.	Nicholas drops the demand for the extradition of Polish revolutionaries.
15/27 Oct.	British and French Mediterranean squadrons sent to the neighbourhood of the Dardanelles.
19 Oct./1 Nov.	British squadron under Admiral Parker, encouraged by Stratford Canning, enters the Straits (until 1/13 Nov.).
1/13 Nov.	Palmerston admits that Parker's act had violated the Straits Convention.
1850	Louis Napoleon, supported by Austria, demands the reassertion and enforcement of the 1740 religious concessions to the Latins in Jerusalem.
1851	Nicholas vetoes a proposal that all churches and shrines in the Holy Places be under joint Catholic and Orthodox possession (Autumn).
1852	Treaty between Greece and the Protecting Powers provides that successors to the Greek throne must be Orthodox.
28 Jan./9 Feb.	Porte makes concessions to the Latins, conflicting with promises made to the Orthodox.
Apr.	Nicholas assures the British of Russian support in the event of a French attack on Belgium.

26 Apr./8 May	Treaty of London (see p. 264).
May	The Sultan allows the French warship, *Charlemagne*, to pass through the Dardanelles to Constantinople.
June	Stratford Canning leaves Istanbul after failing to persuade the Turks to carry out reforms (Apr. 1853).
10/22 Nov.	Ózerov promises the Sultan Russian help in case of a French attack.
Dec.	Turks settle the dispute over the Holy Places in France's favour by granting the Latins the key of the Church of the Nativity in Bethlehem.
End	Basili, the Russian consul in Jerusalem, resigns. Omer Pasha, governor of Bosnia, declares war on Montenegro.
28 Dec./ 9 Jan. 1853	Nicholas I's conversations with Sir George Hamilton Seymour, British Ambassador (second conversation: 2/14 Jan.) on measures to be taken on the collapse of the Ottoman Empire.

1853

2/14 Jan.	Nesselrode writes to Sir John Russell, urging him to 'bring the French cabinet back to counsels of prudence' in the Near East.
16/28 Feb.	Ménshikov arrives in Istanbul to bring about the dismissal of Fuad Pasha, the Turkish Foreign Minister, and an agreement on the Holy Places.
22 Feb./6 Mar.	Fuad Pasha replaced by Rifaat Pasha.
24 Feb./8 Mar.	Colonel Rose, British *chargé d'affaires* in Istanbul, summons the British Mediterranean squadron to Vourla in response to a Turkish request for help.
6/18 Mar.	French squadron ordered to Salamis.
24 Mar./5 Apr.	Stratford de Redcliffe (Canning) returns to Istanbul (until 1858).
22 Apr./4 May	Ménshikov and the French ambassador sign Stratford de Redcliffe's protocol on the Holy Places.
23 Apr./5 May	Ménshikov demands an agreement from the Porte guaranteeing the position of the Orthodox subjects of the Empire within five days.
28 Apr./10 May	The Porte promises to respect the rights of its Orthodox subjects and the immunities of the Greek Church, but refuses to sign an agreement with Russia.
1/13 May	Ménshikov secures the replacement of Rifaat Pasha by Reshid Pasha.
5/17 May	Turkish Grand Council rejects the Russian demand for agreement over the Orthodox Christians.
6/18 May	Reshid offers Ménshikov a compromise (and again on 8/20 May).

9/21 May	Ménshikov's note to Reshid states that any declaration safeguarding merely the religious rights of the Orthodox would be regarded as a hostile act by the Russians.

1853–54   The Russo-Turkish War

1853

15/27 May	Ménshikov leaves Istanbul. Diplomatic relations broken off.
19/31 May	Nesselrode tells Reshid that unless Ménshikov's terms are accepted within eight days, the Russian army will enter the Principalities. The British government empowers Stratford de Redcliffe to summon the Mediterranean squadron to Constantinople.
1/13 June	British Fleet arrives in Besika Bay.
2/14 June	French Fleet arrives in Besika Bay.
2/16 June	Reshid rejects the Russian demands.
21 June/3 July	Russian troops begin to cross the river Pruth.
24 June/6 July	Gorchakóv enters Bucharest.
12/24 July	'The Vienna Note' produced by a meeting between Buol and the ambassadors of Britain, France and Prussia to settle the Russo-Turkish dispute. The Sultan is asked to promise to observe the spirit and letter of the treaties of 1774 and 1829 as regards the rights of the Orthodox Church, to extend to the Orthodox all privileges enjoyed by other Christian sects and to make no change in the existing position of his Christian subjects without the agreement of the French and Russian governments.
24 July/5 Aug.	Russia accepts the Vienna Note.
8/20 Aug.	Turkish Grand Council rejects the Vienna Note but indicates that it will be acceptable if changed to make it clear that the privileges of the Orthodox derive entirely from concessions by the Sultans, not from agreements with Russia.
26 Aug./7 Sept.	Russia rejects the amendments and issues a memorandum interpreting the Vienna Note as giving Russia the right of intervention on behalf of the Orthodox.
30–31 Aug./ 11–12 Sept.	Anti-Russian riots in Istanbul. Two British and two French warships sail through the Dardanelles to protect foreigners.
5/17 Sept.	France and Britain abandon the Vienna Note.
12/24 Sept.	Nicholas I meets Francis-Joseph at Olmütz. Nesselrode and Buol agree that the Vienna Note be re-submitted after the Turkish rejection with a written denial of

	any Russian intention to interfere in the internal affairs of the Ottoman Empire. This is rejected by the British government.
13/25 Sept.	Turkish Grand Council decides to declare war on Russia.
17/29 Sept.	Sultan ratifies the decision to declare war on Russia.
28 Sept./10 Oct.	Gorchakóv presented with Turkish ultimatum to evacuate the Principalities within a fortnight, or war would begin.
9/21 Oct.	Redcliffe summons the British Fleet to Istanbul.
11/23 Oct.	Turkish batteries fire on a Russian flotilla on the Danube.
15/27 Oct.	Omer Pasha crosses the Danube with a Turkish Army.
3/15 Nov.	French and British squadrons anchor in the Bosphorus.
17/29 Nov.	Nesselrode tells Castelbajac that Russia will accept the good offices of Britain, France, Austria and Prussia.
18/30 Nov.	Battle of Sinope: Russian naval victory.
25 Nov./7 Dec.	Britain warns that if Russian troops cross the Danube, British ships will intercept Russian supply ships.
29 Nov./11 Dec.	Meyendorff, Russian ambassador in Vienna, urges a quick peace, as Russia could not hope for victory in a long war with Turkey supported by the Powers.
1/13 Dec.	The Porte agrees to open negotiations under Four-Power mediation.
23 Dec./4 Jan. 1854	British and French squadrons enter the Black Sea.

1854

Jan.	Orlóv's mission to Vienna to bind Austria to neutrality in any future conflict with Britain and France. Francis-Joseph unwilling to promise this if Russians cross the Danube. Russia must also undertake to evacuate the Principalities and to make no change in the territorial situation of the Ottoman Empire, whatever the outcome of the war.
8/20 Jan.	Buol and the French, British and Prussian ambassadors in Vienna propose a peace conference in a neutral city, and a Russian evacuation of the Principalities. Russia rejects this.
20 Jan./1 Feb.	Russia told that French and British ships will prevent any movement of men or supplies from one Russian port to another.
25 Jan./6 Feb.	Russian ambassadors leave London and Paris.
28 Feb./12 Mar.	Britain and France sign a treaty with the Porte to defend Turkish territory against Russia.
16/28 Mar.	Britain and France declare war on Russia.

1854–56	The Crimean War
1854	
8/20 Apr.	Austro-Prussian Treaty.
22 May/3 June	Austria demands Russian evacuation of the Principalities.
2/14 June	Austro-Turkish Treaty.
17/29 June	Nicholas agrees to evacuate the Principalities, if Austria will prevent the British or French armies from entering them.
July	Austro-French negotiations in Paris produce the Four Points: 1. Russian renunciation of any special rights in Serbia and the Principalities and agreement to their replacement by a general guarantee of the Powers. 2. Free navigation on the Danube. 3. Revision of the Straits Convention of 1841 'in the interests of the Balance of Power in Europe'. 4. Russian renunciation of any claim to protect the Orthodox Christians of the Ottoman Empire.
17/29 July	The British government accepts the Four Points.
End July	Russian troops begin evacuating the Principalities.
27 July/8 Aug.	The Four Points adopted as Allied war aims.
Aug.	Russia rejects the Four Points.
8/20 Aug.	Austrian troops begin occupying the Principalities.
1/13 Sept.	British and French troops land in the Crimea.
8/20 Sept.	Battle of the Alma. Allied victory.
10/22 Oct.	General mobilization of Habsburg forces.
26 Sept./8 Oct.	Siege of Sebastopol begins.
13/25 Oct.	Battle of Balaklava (charge of the Light Brigade). Indecisive.
24 Oct./5 Nov.	Battle of Inkerman. Allied victory.
10/22 Nov.	Austrian general mobilization cancelled.
16/28 Nov.	Russia accepts the Four Points.
20 Nov./2 Dec.	Formation of an Austro-Franco-British Alliance for the defence of the Principalities.
Early Dec.	Britain expands the Third Point to mean the end of Russian domination of the Black Sea, including the destruction of Sebastopol as a *sine qua non*.
5/17 Dec.	Secret agreement between Britain and France for the destruction of Sebastopol and the reduction of the Russian Black Sea Fleet to four warships (also note of 7/19 Dec.).
22 Dec./ 3 Jan. 1855	Austria assures the Russians that the Allies will not demand the destruction of Sebastopol or the limitation of Russian sea power in the Black Sea.

Alexander II
1855

3/15 Mar.	Vienna Peace Conference (23 May/4 June). Russian representatives: A. M. Gorchakóv, V. P. Titóv. Breaks down over differences over the Third Point.
June	Austrian army reduced to peacetime strength.
4 Aug.	Battle of the Chernyi. Russian defeat.
27 Aug.	Evacuation of Sebastopol.
5/17 Oct.	French encourage Austria to present Allied peace terms in St Petersburg. Napoleon III establishes direct contact with the Russian government.
9/21 Nov.	Swedish agreement with the Western Powers not to cede any territory to Russia, nor to allow any to be occupied by Russian troops.
16/28 Nov.	N. N. Muravëv takes Kars.
16/28 Dec.	Austrian ultimatum presented in St Petersburg.
24 Dec./ 5 Jan. 1856	Russia accepts the Austrian demands but refuses to cede any territory and rejects the idea of further concessions 'in the European interest'.
31 Dec./ 12 Jan. 1856	Buol informs the Russians that unless the Austrian conditions are accepted unconditionally by 6/18 Jan. 1856, diplomatic relations will be broken off.

1856

2/14 Jan.	Prussians adhere to Austrian ultimatum.
3/15 Jan.	Imperial Council urges Alexander to accept the Austrian ultimatum.
4/16 Jan.	Alexander accepts the Austrian ultimatum.
20 Jan./1 Feb.	Preliminary peace terms signed.
13/25 Feb.	Paris Peace Conference.
18/30 Mar.	Peace of Paris.
18/30 Mar.	Renewed Straits Convention.
18/30 Mar	Russo-Turkish Convention limiting their forces in the Black Sea.
3/15 Apr.	Tripartite Treaty.
1857	Austrians withdraw from the Principalities (Mar.).

4.7.1   Treaties

1849

19 Apr./1 May	**Convention of Balta Liman**: Russia and Turkey agree to deprive the assemblies of Moldavia and Wallachia of some of their powers, that the *hospodars* are to be appointed for seven years only, that the Turks will

oversee administrative reforms, and that both powers can send in troops in case of disorders.

1854

8/20 Apr.   **Austro-Prussian Treaty**: Both promise to cooperate if either is attacked and to force Russia out of the Principalities, but will only go to war if Russia crosses the Balkan mountains and threatens Constantinople.

2/14 June   **Austro-Turkish Treaty**: Ottoman Empire transfers its sovereign rights in the Principalities to Austria until the end of the war.

1856

18/30 Mar.   **Peace of Paris**: (Signatories Clarendon, Cowley, Buol-Schauenstein, Hübner, Walewski, Bourqueney, Manteuffel, von Hatzfeldt, Orlóv, Brunnóv, Cavour, di Villamarina, Aali, Mehemmed Djemil.) Comprises 34 Articles. Russia to restore Kars and other Ottoman territories. The Allies to restore Sebastopol and other territories to Russia, in return for which Russia will evacuate the mouth of the Danube. The Ottoman Empire to be admitted to the Concert of Europe; any differences with other states to be settled henceforth by the mediation of the Powers. The Sultan informs the other Powers of a *firman* ameliorating the conditions of his Christian subjects, and the Powers take note, while not being able to interfere. Revision of the Straits Convention of 1841, neutralizing the Black Sea, now open to merchant ships of all nations and closed to warships of all nations, except the coastal defence vessels of Russia and Turkey. Russia and Turkey are not to have any military–maritime arsenals on their coasts. The Danube to be open to free navigation. The Principalities and Serbia to remain under the suzerainty of the Porte, without any Power having any protection over them, but are to retain their privileges and immunities, including independent, national administrations, freedom of worship, legislation and commerce. The Principalities to have a national frontier defence force, but Serbia to be garrisoned with Ottoman troops. No military intervention, by the Porte or anyone else, may take place in the Principalities or Serbia without the consent of the Powers. The Russo-Turkish frontier in Asia to be examined by a mixed commission.

18/30 Mar.   **Renewed Straits Convention**: (Signatories as for the Peace of Paris.) Renews the Convention of 1/15 July

1841 with 'some modifications of detail which do not affect the principle on which it rests'. The Straits to remain closed to warships in time of peace, except for light vessels in the service of the missions of foreign Powers and no more than two light vessels which the contracting parties are entitled to station at the mouths of the Danube.

18/30 Mar.   **Russo-Turkish Convention limiting their forces in the Black Sea**: (Signatories: Orlóv, Brunnóv, Aali, Mehemmed Djemil.) Comprises Three articles. Both parties agree to maintain no more than six steam warships of 800 tons maximum and four steam or sailing warships of 200 tons maximum.

3/15 Apr.   **Tripartite Treaty**: Austria, Britain and France guarantee the independence and territorial integrity of the Ottoman Empire.

4.8 Russia and the First World War

1914

8/21 Feb.	Special Conference in St Petersburg to discuss the 'problem' of the Straits and Constantinople.
June	British naval squadron visits Kronstadt.
15/28 June	Assassination of Archduke Francis-Ferdinand in Sarajevo by Gavrilo Princip.
7/20–10/23 July	State visit of President Poincaré to St Petersburg.
10/23 July	Austrian ultimatum to Serbia.
15/28 July	Austria declares war on Serbia.
16/29 July	Russian mobilization begins.
18/31 July	German Ambassador Pourtales demands that Russia cease to mobilize within 12 hours or war will be declared.
19 July/1 Aug.	Germany declares war on Russia.
24 July/6 Aug.	Austria declares war on Russia.
28 July/10 Aug.	The cruisers *Göben* and *Breslau* enter the Dardanelles and are 'sold' to Turkey.
4/17 Aug.	Russian advance into East Prussia.
4/17 Aug.	Battle of Stallupönen. German (von François) victory over Russians (von Rennenkampf).
7/20 Aug.	Battle of Gumbinnen (Prittwitz against Rennenkampf). Inconclusive.
	Prittwitz replaced by Hindenburg and Ludendorff.
12/25–17/ 30 Aug.	Battle of Tannenberg/Soldau. German (von François) victory over Samsónov. Samsónov's army surrenders to the Germans. Samsónov commits suicide.
21 Aug./3 Sept.	Russians take Lemberg and push Austrians behind the Carpathians (29 Aug./11 Sept.).
27 Aug./9 Sept.– 1/14 Sept.	Battle of the Masurian Lakes. François defeats Rennenkampf.
23 Aug./5 Sept.	Treaty with France and Britain.
15/28 Sept.–18/ 31 Oct.	German offensive in the South-west in support of the Austrians pushes the Russians back to pre-war lines.
16/29–17/ 30 Oct.	Turks bombard Sebastopol, Odessa, Feodósia and Novorossíisk.
20 Oct./2 Nov.	Russia declares war on Turkey.
23 Oct./5 Nov.	Britain declares war on Turkey.

24 Oct./6 Nov.	France declares war on Turkey.
29 Oct./11 Nov.	Battle of Łódź. Technically a Russian victory, but signals the end of the Russian advance into Poland.
1/14 Nov.	Grey informs the Russians that the British government accepts that the fate of the Straits and Constantinople should be decided in conformity with Russian interests at the end of the war.
16/29 Dec.	Battle of Sarikamish. Iudénich halts Turkish advance into the Caucasus.

1915

18/31 Jan.	Battle of Bolimov. German feint towards Warsaw. First use of poison gas by the Germans.
25 Jan./7 Feb.	Second battle of the Masurian Lakes. German victory.
19 Feb./4 Mar.	Russian programme for the Straits presented to Britain. Meeting of the Finance Ministers of Russia, Britain and France.
27 Feb./12 Mar.	Britain accepts the Russian programme for the Straits.
9/22 Mar.	Russians take Przemyśl and advance into the Carpathians.
28 Mar./10 Apr.	France accepts the Russian programme for the Straits.
12/25 Apr.	Austro-Germans halt the Russian advance in the Carpathians.
18 Apr./1 May	German counter-offensive begins.
21 May/3 June	Austro-Germans retake Przemyśl.
9/22 June	Austro-Germans retake Lemberg.
10/23 June	Austro-Germans begin crossing the Dniestr.
22 July/4 Aug.	Germans take Warsaw.
5/18 Aug.	Germans reach the Bug.
6/19 Aug.	Nicholas II dismisses Nikolai Nikoláevich and takes command of the army himself, with M. V. Alekseev as his Chief of Staff.
12/25 Aug.	Germans take Brest-Litovsk.
20 Aug./2 Sept.	Germans take Grodno.
5/18 Sept.	Germans take Vilno. End of German advance (500 kilometres).
1/14 Oct.	Bulgaria declares war on Russia.
Dec.	Allied Conference at Chantilly.
29 Dec./11 Jan. 1916	Iudénich's advance into Turkey begins (until Apr.).

1916

20 Jan./2 Feb.	France and Britain 'incensed' over appointment of the 'pro-German' B. V. Stürmer as chairman of the Council of Ministers.
3/16 Feb.	Iudénich takes Erzerum.
25 Feb./9 Mar.	Sykes–Picot Agreement on the dismembering of Asiatic Turkey.

5/18 Mar.	Unsuccessful Russian offensive around Vilno.
13/26 Apr.	Franco-Russian convention ratifies the Sykes–Picot Agreement. Russia's share to include Trebizond, Erzerum, Bayazid, Van, Bitlis, part of Kurdistan and a strip of Black Sea coast west of Trebizond.
Apr.	Russians take Trebizond.
22 May/4 June	Brusílov offensive begins (until 7/20 Sept.).
12/25 July	Battle of Erzincan. Iudénich's victory over Vehip Pasha.
14/27 Aug.	Romania declares war on Austria and Germany.
Late Oct.	Buchanan's speech warning of 'Inner Germans'.
19 Nov./2 Dec.	Agreements with France and Britain on the Straits and Constantinople made public in the State Duma.
23 Nov./6 Dec.	Germans take Bucharest.
1917	
16/29 Jan.	Allied representatives arrive in Petrograd.
19 Jan./1 Feb.	Allied Conference opens in Petrograd. **Britain**: Buchanan, Lord Milner, Lord Revelstoke, General Sir Henry Wilson. **France**: Gaston Doumergue, Maurice Paléologue, General de Castelnau. **Italy**: Carlotti di Riparbella, General di Ruggieri-Laderchi, Vittorio Scialoja. **Romania**: Ion Bratianu (attended one session only). **Russia**: P. L. Bark, General M. A. Beliáev, Admiral I. K. Grigoróvich, General V. Gúrko, A. A. Nerátov, N. N. Pokróvskii, Admiral A. I. Rúsin, S. D. Sazónov, Grand Duke Sergéi Mikhailovich, V. N. Shakhovskói, E. Voinóvskii-Kríger. **Chairman**: Foreign Minister, N. N. Pokróvskii.
4/17 Feb.	Lord Milner's memorandum to Nicholas II.
7/20 Feb.	Allied Conference ends.
8/21 Feb.	Allied representatives leave Petrograd.
21 Feb.	N. N. Pokróvskii urges the Tsar to land troops in the Bosphorus in order to ensure Russian possession of the Straits.

4.8.1   Treaties

1914	
23 Aug./5 Sept.	**Treaty with France and Britain**: Britain, France and Russia undertake not to sign a separate peace and to reach a preliminary agreement on what peace terms will be acceptable.

SECTION FIVE

Glossary

Abrámtsevo   A country house outside Moscow which was first, when owned by the Aksákovs (q.v.), a centre of Slavophilism and panslavism and then, when owned by Mámontov (q.v.), a centre of the arts.

Ádskaia póchta   *Hell's Postbox*, a satirical journal (1905–7).

apanage peasants   A term used in English to describe court peasants after Paul I's Act of 5 April 1797, placing them under the *Udél*, translated as 'Department of the Apanage'. Strictly speaking, this is a mistranslation, for 'Apanage' refers to property set aside to provide for the *younger* children of kings and princes, whereas *Udél* refers to *all* inalienable property belonging to the Imperial Family.

arshín   A measure of length (71 centimetres or 28 inches), one-third of a *sázhen* (q.v.).

artél   Generally, a mutual aid society, or a society organizing lodging and food in common for its members. With regards to the Decembrist Movement, it has the specific meaning of an officers' dining club.

Article 87   Article 87 of the Constitution of the State Duma allowed the government to pass emergency legislation while the State Duma was in recess, although this legislation had subsequently to be confirmed by the State Duma. Stolýpin made great use of this provision to pass legislation that he believed the Duma would reject by the simple expedient of proroguing it for a few days while he passed 'emergency decrees'. The most notable example was his land reform, passed under Article 87 in November 1906, but only confirmed by the Duma in June 1910.

Arzamás   A literary circle of 1815–18, whose members included Bátiushkov, Dáshkov, Karamzín, Turgénev, Uvárov, Zhukóvskii, etc.

assigned peasants   *See* factory serfs.

atamán   A Cossack leader. Among the Don Cossacks the leader of the entire Host. Among the Zaporózhians, a lesser leader, under the *hétman*.

bárshchina   Labour service carried out by serfs for their masters.

bashi-bazouks   Turkish irregular troops with a reputation for lawlessness and brutality.

Berg-kollégiia   College of Mining (1723–84).

Berg-Manufaktúr-kollégiia   College of Mining and Manufactures (1719–23).

Beséda   *Beséda liubítelei rossíiskoi slóvesnosti/Gathering of Lovers of Russian Literature*, a literary group of 1811–16 primarily designed to combat modernism in literature.

Bespopóvtsy   Old Believers who had no priests, as they believed that apostolic succession had been broken during the reign of the antichrist.

Biblióteka dlia chténiia   *The Readers' Library*, the first 'thick' journal, edited by Osip Senkóvskii (1834–65), and much disliked by the liberal intelligentsia.

Birzhevýe védomosti   *Stock Exchange Gazette*. A liberal St Petersburg newspaper (1880–1917).

Black hundreds   Right-wing thugs, forerunners of the fascists and Nazis, who conducted *pogróms* against Jews and left-wing parties. The main Black Hundred organizations were the Union of Russian People, founded in 1905, and The Union of St Michael the Archangel, founded in 1908. Nicholas II was an honorary member of the Union of Russian People, whose members murdered two Kadet Duma deputies, 1906–7, and attempted to murder Sergei Witte in 1907.

black peasants   Peasants, not bonded serfs, who farmed land that was not owned by private landlords but was considered by the princes to be their own patrimony. They bought and sold their land but paid money dues to the prince.

black repartition   A term used among the peasantry to mean the complete redistribution of land from private and state owners to the peasantry.

Black Repartition   In 1879 *Land and Freedom* split into G. V. Plekhánov's Black Repartition (*Chërnyi peredél*), which advocated mass agitation, and The People's Will (*Naródnaia vólia*), which advocated terror as a means of achieving social revolution.

Bolshevik   A 'member of the majority', originally a faction of the Russian Social-Democratic Workers' Party which supported Lenin from the party's Second Congress in 1903. From 1912 it became a separate party.

Boyar   The highest Russian nobility before the reign of Ivan the Terrible. Whereas they owned their land outright and could choose whom to serve, Ivan more or less wiped them out, substituting for them the *Poméshchiki* ('placed men') who were placed on their estates in return for state service.

Bubnóvyi valét   *Jack of Diamonds*, an art group formed by the Burliúks and Kandinsky in 1910.

Bund   The General Jewish Workers' Union in Lithuania, Poland, and Russia.

Burmístr (pl. burmistry)   A Russian attempt to say burgomeister, the elected head of a municipality.

Burmístrskaia paláta   A Town Hall. *See also Rátusha.*

Castrates   See Skoptsý.

chast' (pl. chásti)   A subdivision of a town.

Chërnyi peredél   See 'Black Repartition'.

chin   A position on the Table of Ranks.

Chinóvnik   A person who serves the state and is given *chin*. Consequently the term was most commonly used to mean 'bureaucrat'.

Church peasants   Peasants in bondage to monasteries, cathedrals, city churches or (rarely) village churches. They were especially numerous in the *gubérnii* of Nóvgorod, Archangel, Nízhnii Nóvgorod and Moscow. The Monastery of Saint Sergius and the Trinity near Moscow owned over 106,000 serfs and was the largest serf-owner in the country before the reign of Catherine the Great.

Circassians   People of the north-western Caucasus who emigrated *en masse* to Turkey in the 1860s rather than submit to transportation into the Russian steppe.

College   (*Kollégiia*) Department of State, 1720–97. A forerunner of the Ministries.

commune *(mir, óbshchina)*   An institution of peasant self-government. Normally composed of elected representatives it worked with the assembly of all males from the village (*skhod*) to organize agricultural work, redistribute land, collect taxes, decide who was liable for drafting to the army, negotiate with the serf-owner, etc.

Cossack   A member of a free and (originally) democratic military brotherhood (Host), mostly made up of runaway serfs, who lived in the borderlands of the Russian Empire and lived mainly from pillage. Some of these, like the Zaporózhian, were originally exclusively male and celibate. They enjoyed special status in the Russian armed forces. As the borderlands became more peaceful in the eighteenth century, so the Cossacks progressively turned to agriculture.

Court peasants   Peasants who were privately owned by the Imperial court.

distríkt   From 1718 to 1727, a 'district' or subdivision of a province, administered by a *zémskii komissár*.

Doímochnaia kantseliariia   Arrears Office created in 1727 for the collection of poll tax arrears.

Dukhobórs   'Spirit fighters': a religious sect that arose among the peasantry around Khárkov *c.* 1740 and spread rapidly. After much persecution, most of them emigrated to Canada at the end of the nineteenth century.

Duma   The State Duma was the Russian Parliament, 1906–17. The city and town dumas were city or town councils, 1785–1917.

economic peasants   The name given to former Church peasants in the immediate aftermath of the secularization of Church lands, 26 Feb. 1764.

economists   Lenin's term for those Social-Democrats who believed that the economic struggle (for wages, better conditions, etc.) would automatically lead workers into political conflict.

edinovérie   An agreement between Old Believers and the Orthodox Church whereby the former would be allowed to preserve their own ritual, as long as they recognized the authority of the latter.

factory serfs   There were three categories of these: 1. (*posessiónnye*) Serfs who belonged to the factory itself, not to the owner; 2. (*pripísnye*) State peasants who had been temporary assigned to a factory, normally to earn the money to pay off the poll tax; and 3. Serfs belonging to private landlords, assigned by them to factory work.

féldsher   A paramedic, officially a doctor's helper, but often the sole medical practitioner in remote country areas.

fiskál   A supervisor, appointed by Peter the Great in 1711 to root out corruption.

flagellants   *See khlystý.*

funt   (Pound) unit of weight: 410 grams (14.44 ounces). 1 *funt* = 32 *lóty* = 96 *zolotnikí*. 40 *fúnty* = 1 *pud*.

Generalitét   Collective noun denoting all those holding the top four military *chiny* in the Table of Ranks. Often more loosely used to denote holders of these *chiny* in the civil and court spheres as well.

gimnáziia (pl. gimnázii)   State academic secondary school, a 'grammar school'.

Glávnyi magistrát   The Central College (i.e. Ministry) for the urban estate until 1782.

gorodníchi   A governor of a town.

gorodskáia golová   (*lit.* 'town head') Elected by merchants (*kuptsý*), townspeople (*meshcháne*) and any other taxable town-dwellers. First introduced in the *ukáz* of 16 December 1766 for the elections to the Legislative Commission.

gradonachálnik   A city governor, or the senior state official in the town, appointed by the Tsar.

gubérniia (pl. gubérnii)   'Government' or administrative unit of pre-Revolutionary Russia, administered by a governor.

hétman   Leader of the Zaporózhian Cossack Host and ruler of Ukraine.

household serfs   Serfs taken from the land to become 'domestic servants', a term that covered everything from parlour maids, seamstresses and butlers to opera singers, actors and teachers.

Initiative Group   Menshevik body operating illegally inside Russia during the First World War.

Inter-District Group   (*Mezhraióntsy* or Inter-Raion Group) A Social-Democratic group, formed in 1913, whose political position was somewhere between the Bolsheviks and Mensheviks. Its most prominent member was Trotsky, who joined it briefly in May 1917.

Iskra   *The Spark.* A Social-Democratic paper, initially edited by Lenin and Martov, published abroad and smuggled into Russia, 1900–5.

Jewish Pale   *See* Pale of Settlement.

kabák   A state-owned pub-cum-distillery.

Kadets   Constitutional Democratic Party (after the first letters of the Russian *Konstitutsiónno-demokratícheskaia pártiia*), also known as the Party of National Freedom/*Pártiia naródnoi svobódy*.

kadétskii kórpus   Its full name was *Shliakhétskii sukhopútnyi kadétskii kórpus* (Army Cadet Corps for Noblemen). Founded in 1731 in St Petersburg, its syllabus was less military than its name implied.

Kámer-kollégiia   College of State Revenues created by Peter the Great in 1720.

khlystý 'The flagellants': a religious sect suspected of engaging in orgiastic rituals.

khútor A farm house surrounded by its own land.

knout Cat o'nine tails, weighted at the ends, used by Cossacks for crowd control.

Kollégiia ekonómii College of Economy, the body set up by Catherine I in 1726, to administer Church lands and peasants.

Kólokol The Bell, a journal published abroad by Herzen and Ogarëv.

Kommérts-kollégiia College of Trade (1720).

kopek Unit of currency, one hundredth part of a ruble.

kulák (*lit.* 'fist') Used to designate rich peasants or more generally any money lender.

kupéts (pl. kuptsý) A merchant.

kvartál A town 'quarter': subdivision of a *chast'*.

Land and Freedom *See Zemliá i vólia.*

landrát The governor of a provincial district in early eighteenth-century Russia.

liquidators A pejorative term used to describe those Social-Democrats who, in the period between the revolutions of 1905 and 1917, believed that the struggle should be conducted primarily in legal organizations (trades unions, etc.). The implication in the term was that they wished to 'liquidate' the party.

Liubomúdrye 'Lovers of Wisdom', Odóevskii's philosophical circle (1823–25).

lubók Folk pictures similar to the English chap-books or the French *image d'Épinal.*

magistrát A city council, established in St Petersburg in 1720 and administered by the College of the *Glávnyi Magistrát* (established 1721).

Manufaktúr-kollegiia College of Manufactures, one of the forerunners of the Ministries, initially created in 1723.

marshal of the nobility An elected leader of the nobility in each *uézd*, first introduced on 16.xii.1766 for the elections to the Legislative Commission.

Menshevík A 'member of the minority', originally a faction of the Russian Social-Democratic Workers' Party, who opposed Lenin at the party's Second Congress in 1903. They rejected Lenin's view of a narrow centralized party of professional revolutionaries, insisting instead on a broader-based workers' party. Also, because most of them believed that Tsarism should be replaced by a bourgeois state, they opposed the October Revolution.

meshchanín (pl. meshcháne) A town-dweller of rank lower than that of a merchant (*kupéts*), liable for the poll tax and for the military levy.

Meshchánstvo   The judicial estate to which the *meshchóne* belonged. Used figuratively to denote philistinism.

méstnichestvo   The pre-Petrine Order of Precedence of the nobility, based on birth and service.

military colonies   (or military settlements) An attempt by Alexander I to solve the rising cost of the army by allocating land to regiments, whose soldiers would sustain themselves through agriculture in peacetime. They quickly became infamous for the brutal regime inflicted on the colonists by Arakchéev, and saw many disorders as the colonists rebelled against the double burden of peasant and soldier. They were abolished by Nicholas I.

mir   A village commune.

Mir iskússtva   *World of Art*, a journal and artistic movement closely associated with Diághilev.

Molokáne   'Milk drinkers'. A religious sect that emerged in the mid-eighteenth century, so called because they continued to drink milk during Lent.

Morskói sbórnik   *Naval Miscellany*, the theoretical and historical journal of the Navy, published since 1848, which played an important part in nineteenth-century intellectual life.

Moskóvskie védomosti   *Moscow Gazette*, daily newspaper, 1754–1917.

Moskóvskii nabliudátel   *Moscow Observer*, journal published from 1835 to 1837, initially with the participation of Pushkin and Gogol, and edited by Belinskii.

Moskovskii telegraf   *Moscow Telegraph*, journal edited by N. A. Polevoi (1825–34).

Moskvitiánin   *The Muscovite*, journal edited by Pogódin 1841–56.

nakáz   An instruction.

naméstnichestvo   An administrative unit formed of two *gubérnii*, as introduced by the reform of 1775.

naméstnik   The senior of the two governors of the two *gubérnii* composing a *naméstnichestvo*.

Naródnaia vólia   'The People's Will' a populist party formed in 1879, after the break-up of Land and Freedom (q.v.). It practised social terror as a means of bringing about the social revolution. Its members assassinated Alexander II in 1881.

naródnik   A 'populist'. A member or supporter of any of the populist parties, especially the People's Will or Land and Freedom.

Nóvoe vrémia   *New Times*, St Petersburg daily newspaper, 1868–1917. Under Suvorin's editorship (1876–1912) it became the most widely read conservative newspaper.

ober-fiskál   The chief *fiskál* (q.v.).

óblast   A region not designated as a *gubérniia*, but under 'special administration.'

obrók   Money dues paid by serfs to their masters.

óbshchina   A village commune.

Octobrists   The Union of 17th October. Conservative-constitutional party formed in 1905 by P. A. Heiden, A. I. Guchkóv, M. V. Rodziánko, D. N. Shípov and N. A. Khomiakóv. Its name refers to the date on which the Tsar granted a constitution including the State Duma.

odnodvórtsy   (*lit.* 'one-homestead-men') Settlers, often of noble birth, who had been allotted smallholdings in frontier regions, especially in the Tambóv and Vorónezh areas. They had the right to own serfs, though few were wealthy enough to do so.

Okhrána   The Secret Police. Its full title was *Otdelénie po okhranéniiu obshchéstvennoi bezopásnosti* (The Department for the Preservation of Public Safety). Although always referred to as the *Okhrána* in English, the Russians actually called it *Okhránka*.

Okólnichi   The Second rank of nobility (behind boyar) from the thirteenth to the eighteenth centuries.

Old Believers   Those orthodox Christians who did not accept Patriarch Nikon's reforms of the 1650s and 1660s. They were much persecuted.

Otéchestvennye zapíski   *Notes of the Fatherland*, monthly journal founded by P. P. Svínin and edited by A. A. Kraévskii (1818–20.iv.1884).

otrúb   A farm where the house is in a village separated from its land.

Pale of Settlement   The 15 provinces of Belorussia, Lithuania, Ukraine and Bessarabia where most Russian Jews were obliged to live by law.

panslavism   A political movement of the second half of the nineteenth century that aimed at the 'liberation' of all Slavs and at the creation of a large South Slav state in the Balkans. It was seen in Western Europe as a cover for Russian expansionism.

The People's Will   *See Naródnaia vólia.*

Peredvízhniki   *The Wanderers*, an art group formed in 1870, with its centre at Abrámtsevo.

pogróm   The massacre of a particular group of people, usually used in relation to the massacre of Jews.

Poleznoe uveselenie   *Useful Entertainment*, journal edited by M. M. Kheráskov (1760–62).

Poliarnaia zvezda   *Pole Star*, 1. journal edited by Ryléev and Bestúzhev (1823–25); 2. journal published by Herzen (1855–56); 3. journal edited by P. B. Struve (1905–6).

Poméshchik   A nobleman in possession of a *poméstie*.

Poméstie   Land inhabited by serfs, granted to a nobleman by the Tsar. Originally granted for life, they became the private property of the nobility after 1714.

Porte   In full: The Sublime Porte. The Ottoman Court at Constantinople and, by extension, the government of the Ottoman Empire.

Právda   *Truth*, the Bolshevik newspaper published legally in Russia (1912–14).

prikáz   A command.

Prikáz   Department of State before 1720.

Progressists   The Progressive Party. A party in the Duma whose leading members were industrialists and *zémstvo* activists who were more progressive than their counterparts in the Octobrist Party.

Proprietal serfs   Those serfs owned by members of the nobility, as opposed to apanage serfs (q.v.) and state peasants (q.v.).

províntsiia   'Province' or subdivision of a *gubérniia*, administered by a *voevóda*. Abolished in 1775.

pud   Unit of weight: 1638 grams or 36.11 lbs. 1 *pud* = 40 *funty*.

Rátusha   A Russian attempt to say *Rathaus*, i.e. Town Hall.

raznochíntsy   People not liable for the poll tax, but not of noble birth or members of a guild or *tsekh*, i.e. not easily categorized in any of the established estates. The term was normally applied to the nineteenth-century intelligentsia.

Realschule   (German; in Russian: *Reálnoe uchílishche*) A state secondary school teaching practical rather than academic subjects.

Rech   *Speech*, the newspaper of the Kadet Party (1906–18).

Revizión-kollégiia   Audit College (1720–88).

ruble   Unit of currency = 100 kopeks.

Russkii invalid   *Russian Ex-Serviceman*, a journal.

Russkii vestnik   *The Russian Herald*, the first journal of this name was founded by S. Glinka in 1807. The second by M. N. Katkóv in 1855.

sázhen   A measure of length (2.13 metres or seven feet). Three *arshíny* = one *sázhen*.

Sech   The fortified island in the river Dniépr that was the headquarters of the Zaporózhian Cossacks. Its location, downstream of major cataracts, gave the Cossack Host its name: *Zaporózh'e*, i.e. beyond the cataracts.

Sejm **(or** *Seim***)**   Usually translated as Diet. The Assembly or parliamentary body in Poland and Finland.

serf   A peasant in bondage to a private owner.

Sévernaia pchëla   *The Northern Bee*, a conservative journal edited by F. V. Bulgárin and N. I. Grech (1825–64).

Shtats-kontór-kollégiia   College of State Expenditure (1720–83).

Skoptsý   'Castrates', a religious sect practising self-castration.

Slavophiles   A conservative political/philosophical movement of the early nineteenth century, asserting what they saw as particularly 'Slavic' values, ('togetherness'/*sobórnost*, the commune, the unity of Tsar and people, Orthodoxy), in opposition to Western values (individualism, democracy etc.).

slobodá   Settlements that had developed outside the boundaries of legally recognized towns, whose inhabitants thereby escaped taxation and state service.

sobórnost 'Togetherness', a central concept of Slavophilism.

Social-Democrat A member of the Russian Social-Democratic Workers' Party, whose policies stemmed from the belief that the socialist transformation of Russia would come about as a result of the action of the industrial working class (proletariat).

Socialist Revolutionary A member of the Party of Socialist Revolutionaries (often erroneously called 'Social Revolutionaries') whose policies stemmed from the belief that the socialist transformation of Russia would come about as a result of the action of the entire working people (peasantry and proletariat).

Sophia Not as is commonly believed a female saint, but a female manifestation of Christ as the Divine Wisdom, an important concept of Orthodox Christianity and an important image in Symbolist poetry.

sótskii An 'hundredsman' elected by the peasantry for village law enforcement.

Sovreménnik *The Contemporary*, a journal edited by Pushkin, then by Nekrasov.

stárets An 'elder', a monk whom others see as directly inspired by the Holy Ghost and consequently adopt as a spiritual guide.

stárosta The elected or appointed head of any group.

starshiná A committee of elders, especially used for the ruling group of a Cossack Host.

state peasant Peasants who belonged to the Tsar in his official capacity. This classification, created by Peter the Great, incorporated black peasants, soldier-farmers, *odnodvórtsy* and, from the reign of Catherine II, former Church peasants.

Stávka The general headquarters of the Russian Army. The place where the Commander-in-chief and his staff were to be found. In the First World War, this was initially at Baranovichi, then at Mogilëv.

steppe The grassy, treeless plain stretching from Hungary to Mongolia.

Stolýpin necktie The hangman's noose.

Stolýpin wagon A railway wagon specially designed for carrying prisoners.

Stréltsy A military body made up of non-servile town-dwellers, crushed in 1698 and replaced with Western-style military regiments.

Stundism An evangelical sect that emerged in Ukraine *c.* 1858.

Subbótniki 'Sabbatarians'. An early nineteenth-century religious sect believing in reuniting Christians and Jews. They practised circumcision, rejected the Trinity and observed the Sabbath on Saturdays.

Sunday schools Not religious instruction as in Britain but a movement started in 1859 by P. Pávlov for the (secular) education of the poor.

Syn otéchestva *Son of the Fatherland*, a conservative journal of the 1830s edited by N. I. Grech.

taigá Coniferous forest stretching across the north of Russia between the tundra and the steppe.

Teleskop *The Telescope*, a journal published in Moscow (1831–36), edited by N. I. Nadézhdin and to which Belínskii contributed.

Trudovík   Labour Party. The name adopted by populist deputies to the State Duma.

tsekh   A craft guild.

uézd   Before 1715 and after 1727, the smallest unit of local government, a subdivision of a province.

ukáz   A written Imperial decree.

ulozhénie   The code of laws.

Uniate or Uniat Churches   Churches in Eastern Christendom which retain the rite and language of the Orthodox Church yet are in communion with Rome.

upráva   A board, office or authority (from the verb *upravliát'* meaning to manage or administer).

verst   A measure of distance: 1,067 metres or 3,500 feet.

Véstnik Evrópy   *Messenger of Europe,* a journal published by N. M. Karamzín (1802–3).

Voénnyi zhurnál   *Military Journal,* Russia's first theoretical army journal, edited by P. A. Rakhmánov (1810–11), refounded 1816.

voevóda   (*lit.* 'military leader') The administrator of a province (*províntsiia*).

vólost   A unit of local administration, established by the Emancipation decree of 19 Feb. 1861, consisting of between 300 and 2,000 people living in a number of villages, with its own law courts and administered by an assembly of representatives from the various village communes.

vótchina   Hereditary, immovable inhabited property, a landed estate. In 1714, *vótchina* and *poméstie* land was merged.

Vótchina College   Department of State concerned with the records of landed estates, and of settled land in general (abolished in 1786).

The Výborg Manifesto   On 22–23 July 1906, 200 deputies from the dissolved First State Duma met in Výborg and signed a manifesto drawn up by P. N. Miliukóv urging the population not to pay taxes until a Second Duma had been convened. In December 1907 all 200 were condemned to three months' imprisonment, thereby disqualifying them from standing as candidates for the Duma. Ironically, Miliukóv, the author of the appeal, was not disqualified. As he was not a deputy to the First Duma, he had not been allowed to sign the Manifesto.

Young Turks   A group of military reformers, centred around Gúrko (q.v.), who advocated cooperation with the State Duma. The name derived from the revolutionary party in Turkey, many of whose leaders were army officers.

Zemliá i vólia   Land and Freedom. The name of two populist parties, the first in the 1860s, the second in the 1870s, which agitated among the peasantry to bring about social revolution.

zemliáchestvo   A mutual-aid society of students or workers, etc. from the same village or district, usually to organize the renting of rooms and common catering.

zémskaia ízba   The lowest level of court house.

zémskii isprávnik   The president of the lower land courts (1775–1917) who exercised judicial, administrative and police functions.

zémskii komissár   The administrator of a district (*distríkt*).

zémskii nachálnik   'Land Captain'. An official, normally from the local nobility, appointed by the law of 12 July 1889 to oversee the *vólost* assemblies.

zémskii sobór   (*lit.* 'Assembly of the Land') A parliament of boyars and 'representatives' of other classes sporadically called by Tsars before Peter the Great. N. P. Ignátev's attempt to revive this in 1882 led to his dismissal.

zémstvo   A body of local administration made up of representatives of all classes, established by the reform of 1 Jan. 1864.

Zhúpel   *The Bugbear*, a satirical magazine (1905–7).

SECTION SIX

Biographies

Adadúrov, Vasílii Evdokímovich (15.iii.1709–80): Scholar. 1733, First Russian Associate Member of the Academy of Sciences. 1744, Russian teacher to the future Catherine II. 1759, exiled to Orenburg. On her accession, Catherine recalled him from exile and made him Curator of Moscow University. His best-known work is *Rules of Russian Authography* (1768).

Akhmátova, Anna (**Gorénko**, Anna Andréevna) (11.vi.1889–5.iii.1966): Poet. Educated in Tsárskoe seló where she met her husband, the poet Nikolái Gumilёv (q.v.), whom she married in 1910 and divorced in 1918. In 1907 she graduated in law from the Kiev College for Women. 1912 saw the publication of her first book of poetry, *Evening*. Considered by many to be the best Russian poet of the twentieth century, her poems include *Requiem* and *Poem without a Hero*.

Aksákov, Ivan Sergéevich (26.ix.1823–27.i.1886): Slavophile and pan-Slav publicist, poet and anti-Semite. 1858, edited *Rússkaia beséda*. 1861–86, exerted great influence as president of the Moscow Slavic Committee. 1867–68, edited *Moskvá*, which was suppressed because of its campaign against supposed government favouritism towards the Baltic Germans. 1861–65, edited *Den'*. 1877–78, campaigned for the liberation of the South Slavs. 1880, editor of *Rus*, campaigned against 'the world-wide Jewish conspiracy'.

Aksákov, Konstantín Sergéevich (1817–60): Slavophile thinker. The main author of the idea that *sobórnost*/togetherness is the main element diffentiating the Slavs from Western individualists.

Aksákov, Sergéi Timoféevich (20.ix.1791–30.iv.1859): Writer. 1827–32, censor in Moscow. From 1843, lived in Abrámtsevo, which became a centre of Slavophilism. His works are concerned with country life and Russian-ness: *Notes on Fishing* (1847), *Notes of a Shooting Man from Orenburg Gubérniia* (1852), *Tales and Memories of Various Hunts* (1855), *A Family Chronicle* (1856), *A Russian Schoolboy* (1858).

Alekséev, Evgénii Ivánovich (11.v.1843–1918): Admiral. One of the main protagonists of an aggressive policy in the Far East. 1899, commander of Russian forces in Kwantung and of the Russian Pacific Fleet. 1903, viceroy in the Far East. February 1904, Commander-in-chief in the Far East. October 1904, replaced by Kuropátkin. June 1905, dismissed as viceroy.

Alekséev, Mikhaíl Vasílevich (3.xi.1857–25.ix.1918): General, *de facto* commander of the Russian army, 1915–17. 1898–1904, lecturer in military history, General Staff Academy. August 1915, appointed Nicholas II's Chief of Staff when the latter assumed command of the army. September 1917, Commander-in-chief of the army after the Kornílov revolt. November 1917, founded the Volunteer Army.

Antrópov, Alexéi Petróvich (14.iii.1716–12.vi.1795): Painter. 1732, in the team of painters under Matvéev (q.v.) and then Vishniakóv (q.v.), embellishing palaces and the Opera. 1752–55, interior of St Andrew's Cathedral Kiev. 1762, *Portrait of Peter III*. Never a member of the Academy of Fine Arts, he worked for the Holy Synod as Inspector of Icon Painting. 1789, he donated his house in St Petersburg to be converted into a school.

Apráksin, Fëdor Matvéevich (1661–10.xi.1728): Admiral. 1682, helped Peter the Great train his 'toy soldiers' at Preobrazhénskoe. 1700, head of the Admiralty *Prikáz* and Governor of Azóv. 1708, commander in Ingermanland and Finland. 1712–23, Governor of Estliand, Ingermanland and Karelia. 1714, defeats the Swedes at Gangut. 1718, President of the Admiralty College. 1722–23, Commander of the Caspian Flotilla against Persia. 1723–26, Commander of the Baltic Fleet.

Apráksin, Pëtr Matvéevich (1659–29.v.1728): Statesman and companion of Peter the Great. 1702–4, campaigned against the Swedes on the Izhóra. Governor of Ástrakhan in 1705, and of Kazán in 1708–13 (incorporation of the Kalmyks into Russia, 1708). 1709, the last man elevated to the rank of boyar. 1718, charged with complicity with the Tsarévich Alexéi, acquitted and served on the bench that sentenced Alexéi. 1722, president of the Justice College.

Apráksin, Stepán Fëdorovich (30.vii.1702–26.viii.1760): Field Marshal. 1737, siege of Ochákov. 1742, Ambassador to Persia and then vice-president of the War College. 1756, on Elizabeth's council; Field Marshal commanding the army in Prussia. 1757, recalled, charged with treason and exiled to his estate, where he died.

Araja, Francesco (1700–67 or 1770): Musician. Originally from Naples, he took his troupe to Russia in 1735–55. His opera, *La Forza dell'amore e dell'odio*, was the first ever performed in Russia (1736). He wrote a number of court operas: *Seleuco* (1744), *Scipione* (1745), *Mitridate* (1747), *Bellerofonte* (1750), *Eudossa incoronata* (1751). Two were particularly influential: *Asilio della pace* (1748), set in a Russian village, and *Céphale et Procris* (1755) which had a score by Sumarókov. 1762, left Russia after Peter III's murder.

Arakchéev, Alexéi Andréevich (23.ix.1769–21.iv.1834): General and statesman. 1792, joined Paul Petróvich's garrison at Gátchina, where he attracted attention as an exacting drillmaster. 1796, given the estate of Gruzinó and made Governor of St Petersburg. Dismissed briefly in 1798, he was then made inspector general of artillery, only to be dismissed again in 1799. 1803, re-engaged by Alexander I as inspector-general of artillery. 1805, did not distinguish himself at Austerlitz, and was even rumoured to have fled the field. 1808–10, Minister of War. From 1815 he was the most powerful man in Russia after the Tsar. He is most infamous for his founding and running of the Military Colonies. His health deteriorated after his mistress was killed by his serfs in September 1825. He lost all influence after the death of Alexander I.

Argunóv, Iván Petróvich (1729–1802): Painter. A serf of the Sheremétevs, he studied under Georg Christoph Grooth, with whom he was commissioned to paint icons for the church in the Great Palace at Tsárskoe seló. 1753, icons in the New Jerusalem Monastery, Istra. He was then sent by the Sheremétevs to look after their house in Moscow and, towards the end of the 1760s, he became their major-domo in St Petersburg. Most of his portraits were of his masters, but a late *genre* portrait of a fellow serf, *Portrait of an unknown peasant woman in Russian costume* (1784), is particularly fine.

Arsényi, (Alexander Matseévich) (1697–28.ii.1772): Archbishop of Rostóv, 1742–63. 1733, toured the monasteries of the North, debating with Old Believer captives. He rejected Peter's church reform, opposed lay members of the Holy Synod, and demanded the restoration of the Patriarchate. 1763, dismissed from his archbishopric and exiled to Karelia for opposing Catherine's secularization of Church lands. 1767, irritated by his continued opposition from exile and especially the doubt he cast on the legitimacy of her claim to the throne, Catherine dubbed him 'the liar' and incarcerated him for life in Réval prison, with non-Russian-speaking guards who did not know his name.

Ázev, Evno Fishelevich (Evgénii Filíppovich) (1869–1918): Police spy and Socialist Revolutionary assassin. Jewish by extraction and an electrical engineer by profession, he was recruited by the Tsarist police while he was a student in Karlsruhe. He became chairman of the Northern Union of the PSR and leader of its Battle Organization (assassination of Plehve, 1904). 1908, denounced as a police spy by Vladímir Búrtsev (q.v.), he fled to Germany where he was arrested in 1915 as a dangerous revolutionary. He died shortly after his release from prison.

Bagratión, Pëtr Ivánovich (1765–12.ix.1812): General. From a Georgian princely family. 1782, entered Russian service. 1787–91, Russo-Turkish War. 1793–94, Poland. 1799, vanguard commander of Suvórov's army in Italy and Switzerland. 1805–7, vanguard commander, distinguishing himself at Schöngraben, Eylau and Friedland. 1808–9, Finnish War. 1809–10, Turkish War. March 1812, commanded the 2nd Western Army which joined Barclay's main army outside Smolénsk. His disagreement with Barclay's strategy of withdrawal was a factor in the latter's replacement by Kutúzov. Mortally wounded at Borodinó.

Bakst, Leon (**Rozenberg**, Lev Samoílovich) (27.iv.1866–27.xii.1924): Painter and stage designer. 1889, worked as a caricaturist. 1890, joined the Society for Self-Improvement and became active in the production of *Mir iskússtva*. He then became prominent as a designer for Diághilev's *Ballets russes: Cleopatra* and *Le Festin* (1909), *Carnaval, Sheherazade, Firebird,* and *Orientales* (1910), *Spectre de la Rose, Péri* and *Narcisse* (1911), *Thamar, Dieu bleu, L'Après-midi d'un faune, Daphnis and Chloe* (1912), *Jeux* (1913), *Butterflies, Légende de Joseph* (1914). Abroad at the time of the Revolution, he returned to Russia in 1922 but soon returned to Paris, where he died.

Bakúnin, Mikhaíl Alexándrovich (18.v.1814–19.vi.1876): Anarchist. The son of a wealthy landowner, Bakúnin was, with Karl Marx, one of the founders of the First International. He subsequently broke with Marx and was expelled from the International in 1872. After developing a Left Hegelian ideology in Russia in the 1830s, he went abroad in 1840. 1848, the revolution in France and the Slavonic Congress in Prague. 1849, the uprising in Dresden. 1850–51, condemned to death in Saxony and Austria, he was handed over to the Russians and sent to Siberia.

Balákirev, Mílii Alexéevich (21.xii.1836–16.v.1910): Composer, one of the 'Five' or 'Mighty Handful'. 1853–55, studied mathematics at Kazán University. 1856, performed as a pianist. 1862, he and Lomákin organized the Free Music School in St Petersburg. 1867–69, conductor for the Russian Music Society. Works include *Overture on Three Russian Themes* (1858), *Rus: A Symphonic Poem* (1887), *In Czechia* (1906). Publication: *40 Russian Folksongs for Voice and Piano* (1866).

Balmashëv, Stepan Valeriánovich (3.iv.1881–3.v.1902): SR terrorist. Student at Kazán and Kiev universities. 1901, one of 183 Kiev University students arrested for striking. 1902, assassinated the Minister of the Interior, D. S. Sipiágin. Hanged at Shlüsselburg.

Balugiánskii, Mikhaíl Andréevich (26.ix.1769–3.iv.1847): Economist and Jurist. From TransCarpathian Ukraine, educated in Hungary and Vienna University. 1817, as chair of the commission on liquidating state debt, he established the basic principles for state credit institutions. His report on Emancipation influenced Kiselëv (q.v.). 1819–21, first rector of St Petersburg University. 1826, codified the laws with Speránskii.

Baratýnskii (**Boratýnskii**), Evgénii Abrámovich (19.ii.1800–29.vi.1844): Poet, considered second only to Pushkin (q.v.) in his time. His early life was unfortunate. Dismissed from the *corps des pages* for a prank that upset Alexander I and banned from the service, he enrolled as a common soldier and served for four years in Finland before becoming an officer in 1825. This is reflected in his poetry much of which deals with loss and hopelessness: *Elegy* (1821), *Two Fates* (1823), *Truth* (1823), *Death* (1828). A more positive note is his idealization of friendship: *The Friends* (1821), *Star* (1824).

Barclay de Tolly (**Barklái de Tólli**, **Barclay of Towie**), Mikhaíl Bogdánovich (1761–14.v.1818): General. From a Baltic family of Scottish descent. 1787–91, Turkish and Swedish Wars. 1806–7, distinguished himself at Eylau. 1808–9, Finnish War. 1809–10, Governor-General of Finland. 1810–12, Minister of War. June 1812, as commander of the main army, his strategy of withdrawal, bitterly opposed by Bagratión, led to Kutúzov's appointment as Commander-in-chief just before Borodinó. 1813, after Wittgenstein's defeats, appointed Commander-in-chief.

Bariátinskii, Alexander Ivánovich (2.v.1815–25.ii.1879): General and viceroy of the Caucasus. 1835, posted to the Caucasus. 1836, in the suite of Alexander Nikoláevich (Alexander II). 1847, on his way abroad to recuperate from a wound sustained in the Caucasus, he was ordered by Paskévich (q.v.) to quell the uprising in Cracow. 1856–62, viceroy in the Caucasus, choosing Dmitri Miliútin (q.v.) as his Chief of Staff. 1859, defeated Shamíl (q.v.), who had successfully opposed the Russians for over 30 years. 1861, after Miliútin's appointment as War Minister, Bariátinskii became one of his most outspoken opponents.

Bátiushkov, Konstantín Nikolaevich (18.v.1787–7.vii.1855): Poet, soldier and diplomat. He greatly admired Western culture, and never recovered from a depression induced by the invasion of 1812. He served in the army against the French, including the occupation of Paris in 1814. 1815, returned to Russia and suffered a nervous breakdown. 1816–21, diplomat in Italy. 1822, his depression deepened into insanity, ending his career. He was a member of Arzamás. His poetry is influenced by French, Italian and Greek classicism. Not surprisingly, his poems are unhappy and full of suffering.

Bauman, Nikolái Ernéstovich (17.v.1873–18.x.1905): Bolshevik. 1896–97, Union of Struggle for the Emancipation of the Working Class. 1897–99, 22 months' solitary confinement, then exile. 1899, fled to Switzerland and joined the League of Social-Democrats Abroad. 1901, *Iskra* agent, Moscow. 1903, Second Congress RSDRP. Killed in street fighting in Moscow.

Bazhénov, Vasilii Ivanovich (1.iii.1737 or 1738–2.viii.1799): Architect. 1760, Rastrelli's (q.v.) assistant, then in Paris, only failing to win the *Prix de Rome* because he was a foreigner. In Italy, he became a member of the Roman and Florentine Academies, returning to St Petersburg in 1765. 1769, the new Arsenal (now demolished). Although he was admired by his contemporaries, who were much influenced by his ideas, his career proved unsuccessful, as most of his projects were not adopted (e.g. rebuilding of the Moscow Kremlin, 1767). His only remaining monuments are Tsarítsyno Palace (1776–85) and the Pashkóv House, Moscow (1784–86).

Beilis, Menachem Mendel (?–vii.1934): Defendant in an anti-Semitic trial. 1911, dispatcher at a brickworks in Kiev accused of murdering a young Christian boy to use his blood to make passover bread. The case attracted world-wide attention. 1913, acquitted despite pressure for a guilty verdict from the Minister of Justice, Shcheglovítov. Emigrated to the USA.

Beliáev, Mikhaíl Alexeevich (23.ii.1863–1918): Last War Minister of Imperial Russia. 1904–5, staff officer in the Russo-Japanese War. October 1914, Chief of General Staff in St Petersburg. June 1915, Assistant War Minister. September 1916, attaché at Romanian HQ. January–February 1917, War Minister. Shot by the Bolsheviks. Beliáev was unpopular among his fellow officers, who saw him as the archetype bureaucrat and nicknamed him 'Dead Head'.

Beliáev, Mitrofán Petróvich (10.ii.1836–22.xii.1903): Patron of music. A wealthy timber merchant, he gathered around himself in the 1880s and 1890s the Russian composers of the New Russian School (also known as the Beliáev Circle). 1884, started and funded the Glínka Prize. 1885, organized the Open Russian Symphony Concerts, and founded a musical publishing house in Leipzig, exclusively for Russian composers. 1891, organized the Russian Quartet Evenings. 1892, started and funded the prizes for yearly chamber music competitions.

Belínskii, Vissarión Grigórevich (30.v.1811–26.v.1848): The foremost literary critic of the 1830s and 1840s. 1831, began publishing poems and literary reviews. 1832, expelled from Moscow University. He became the spokesman of the view that literature must serve society (see his letter to Gogol of 2 July 1847). 1838–39, editor of *Moskóvskii nabliudátel'*. 1839–46, reviewed for *Otéchestvennye zapíski*. 1847–48, directed the review section of *Sovreménnik*.

Bélyi, Andréi (**Bugáev**, Borís Nikoláevich) (14.x.1880–8.i.1934): Writer. He was a member of the younger generation of symbolists and was influenced by the ideas of Rudolph Steiner. His major work is his novel *Peterbúrg* (1913–14, revised 1922). After the October Revolution, he published the symbolist journal *Dreamers' Notes* and an historical novel *Moskvá*. His three volumes of memoirs were published in the early 1930s.

Benkendórff, Alexander Khristofórovich (23.vi.1781 or 1783–23.ix.1844): Soldier and secret policeman. 1805–7, French War, 1806–12 Turkish War, 1812–14, French War. 1821, presented Alexander with a paper on the *Union of Welfare*, naming most of the future Decembrist leaders, which the Tsar ignored. 14 December 1825, he led the cavalry unit suppressing the Decembrists. 1826, he presented Nicholas I with a plan for a secret political police force, which was the basis for the Third

Department of His Majesty's Own Chancery of which Benkendórff was the first Director.

Bénnigsen, Leóntii Leóntevich (10.ii.1745–3.x.1826): General. A Hanoverian officer, he entered Russian service in 1773 as a cavalry general. He took part in the *coup d'état* of 11 March 1801 and was rewarded by being made baron. 1806–7, Commander-in-chief of the Russian Army, defeated at Friedland (1807). 1812, Chief of the Main Staff, but dismissed in November for disagreeing with Kutúzov. 1813–14, commanded an army and continued to hold high army commands until 1818 when he was dismissed for incompetence.

Benois (Benuá), Alexander Nikoláevich (25.iv.1870–9.ii.1960): Painter and set designer. 1899, co-drafted the programme for *Mir Iskússtva*, of which he became the editor and regular contributor. 1901–2, his *History of 19th Century Russian Painting* attacked the Academic School and the Wanderers. Benois's set designs, especially for Diághilev's (q.v.) productions (*Le Pavilion d'Armide, Le Festin, Les Sylphides* (1909), *Giselle* (1910), *Petrushka* (1911), *Le Rossignol* (1914)), contributed towards the major changes that were taking place in this field. 1918–26, keeper of French and British paintings at the Hermitage. 1926, emigrated to Paris. His best-know paintings are water-colour or gouache romantic scenes set in Versailles or the Russian palaces.

Bering, Titus Jonassen (1681–8.xii.1741): Navigator. Danish by birth he entered the Russian Navy in 1703, serving in the Baltic and Azóv fleets until 1724. 1714, on the Cruys court martial. 1725–30, ordered by Peter I to discover if Siberia was joined to North America; he established that the continents were divided by the Strait that now bears his name. 1733, second expedition to explore the coast of North America, he died in the Bering Strait on the voyage home.

Bestúzhev (Marlínskii), Alexander Alexándrovich (23.x.1797–7.vi.1837): Decembrist, one of the most popular authors of the 1830s. 1816, stationed at Marlí near Peterhof (hence his pseudonym). 1823–25, edited *Poliárnaia zvezdá* with Ryléev (q.v.). 1824, member of the Northern Society, active participant in the events of December 1825 on Senate Square. Sentenced to 20 years' hard labour. 1829, sent to the Caucasian army as an ordinary soldier, where he was killed in a skirmish with mountaineers. Works: *Journey to Réval* (1821), *Roman and Olga* (1823), *Wenden Castle* (1823), *Neuhausen Castle* (1824), *The Réval Tournament* (1825), *Eisen Castle* (1826), *Lieutenant Belozór* (1831), *The Frigate Hope* (1832), *Ammalat Bek* (1832), *Nikitin the Sailor* (1834).

Bestúzhev-Riúmin, Aléxei Petróvich (22.v.1693–10.iv.1766): Statesman and diplomat. 1713, entered the service of the Elector of Hanover. 1714, when the latter became George I of Britain, he became ambassador to Russia. 1717, entered Russian service. 1720, resident in Denmark. 1730, member of Anna's cabinet. 1734–40 ambassador to Denmark. 1740, on the fall of Birón (q.v.), condemned to death, but commuted to exile. 1741, Vice-Chancellor and member of Elizabeth's supreme council. 1744–58, in charge of Russian foreign policy. 1758, disgraced and condemned to death, again commuted to exile. 1762, restored to his titles and rights by Catherine, but retired from political life.

Bestúzhev-Riúmin, Mikhaíl Pávlovich (25.v.1801–13.vii.1826): Decembrist. 1820, in the Semënovskii Guards at the time of the mutiny. One of the leaders of the Southern Society, which he joined in 1823, and a member of the United Slavs. He and Muravëv-Apóstol led the mutiny of the Chernígov Regiment. Hanged in the Peter-Paul Fortress.

Bestúzhev-Riúmin, Mikháil Petróvich (7.ix.1688–26.ii.1760): Diplomat. 1720, resident in London, expelled in November when Britain concluded an anti-Russian alliance with Sweden. 1721–25, resident in Stockholm. 1726, envoy extraordinary to Poland. 1732–41, minister in Stockholm, leaving hurriedly when suspected of complicity in the murder of a Swedish messenger from Constantinople. 1743, married Anna Gavrílovna Iaguzhínskaia, who later that year was publicly flogged, had her tongue cut out and was exiled to Siberia for her part in a plot, after which he went abroad. 1744, however, he was made ambassador to Berlin, then to Poland and finally to Vienna. 1756, member of Elizabeth's conference and ambassador to Paris, where he died.

Bétskoi (**Bétskii**), Iván Ivánovich (1704–95): Catherine II's adviser on education. 1764, Catherine ordered him to implement his *General Plan for the Education of Young People of both Sexes*, inspired by Fénelon, Rousseau, Locke and Comenius. He argued that education was about building character rather than imparting knowledge, should be moral and persuasive, not accompanied by physical punishment, and that the creation of 'new people' could only be achieved by isolating them from their illiterate and brutal environment. He opened a school for boys of all classes except serfs, a Commercial School and the first Russian girls' school, the Smólnyi Institute. 1764–94, as president of the Academy of Fine Arts, organised the first exhibitions of the works of Russian artists.

Bezboródko, Alexander Andréevich (1747–6.iv.1799): Statesman. Of Ukrainian Cossack origin, he began his service in the office of the Governor-General of Ukraine, P. A. Rumiántsev (q.v.). 1775–92, Catherine II's secretary. 1780, entered the College of Foreign Affairs. 1784–96, in charge of Russian foreign policy (annexation of the Crimea, Peace of Jassy, 1791; Third Partition of Poland, 1795). He retained his position in the College of Foreign Affairs after Catherine's death.

Bezobrázov, Alexander Mikhaílovich (1852–1931): One of the chief proponents of an active Russian presence in the Far East. 1896, persuaded the government to finance timber-felling concessions on the Yalu river. 1901, manager of the state-funded Russian Forest Products Company. 1903, member of the Special Committee for Far Eastern Affairs.

Bíbikov, Alexander Ilích (30.v.1729–9.iv.1774): General. 1767, marshal at the Legislative Commission. One of the translators of *Bélisaire*. 1763–64, punitive expedition against striking factory serfs in the Urals. 1770, host to Prince Henry of Prussia during his Russian visit. 1771, punitive expedition in Russia's Polish provinces. 1773–74, given unlimited powers to put down the Pugachëv Revolt, during which he died.

Bíbikov, Dmítrii Gavrílovich (1792–1870): General and statesman. Fought in the Turkish War and the war of 1812–15. 1825–35, director of the Department of Trade where he made a name for rooting out corruption. 1837, Governor of Kiev-Volynia and Podólsk, where he introduced the 'inventory system'. 1852–55, as Minister of the Interior he waged war on non-Russians.

Bilíbin, Iván Iákovlevich (4.viii.1876–7.ii.1942): Painter. Most famous for his set designs and book illustrations in the old-Russian style (*Boris Godunov* and *Le Festin* for Diághilev's (q.v.) productions (1908 and 1909), and *Le Coq d'Or* for Zimín's Opera Company). 1905–6, contributed to the satirical *Hell's Postbox* and *The Bugbear*. 1920, settled in Egypt, then France (1925). 1936, returned to the USSR, where he headed the Graphic Art Studio at the Leningrad Institute of Painting. Died in Leningrad during the siege.

Birón, see **Bühren**.

Blok, Alexander Alexándrovich (16.xi.1880–7.viii.1921): Symbolist poet. Greatly influenced by Solovëv's (q.v.) ideas on the Divine Wisdom, a vision that pervades his poetry but especially his *Verses about a Beautiful Lady* (1904) and *The Stranger* (1906). His poems are of quite extraordinary beauty. As well as a large number of poems, his work includes the lyrical dramas *The Puppet Show* (1906), *The Stranger* (1906), *The King on the Square* (1906), *The Song of Fate* (1908), *The Rose and the Cross* (1912).

Blúdov, Dmítrii Nikoláevich (5.iv.1785–19.ii.1864): Statesman. One of the founders of the Arzamás Circle, his career took off when he was made a member of the Commission of Investigation into the Decembrists in 1826. 1826–28, Assistant Minister of Education. 1830–31 and 1838–39, Minister of Justice. 1832–38, Minister of the Interior. 1839–62, director of the Second Department, in which capacity he oversaw the publication of *Code of Criminal and Corrective Punishments* and two editions of the *Code of Laws* (1842 and 1855). 1855, president of the Academy of Sciences, chairman of the State Council and from 1861 until his death, of the Committee of Ministers.

Bogdánov, Borís Ósipovich (1889–1956): Menshevik. 1905, joined the Mensheviks in Odessa. 1906–17, active in the St Petersburg legal trade union movement. 1915–17, secretary of the Workers' Group of the War Industries Committee. February 1917, a founder of the Petrograd Soviet. Opposed the October revolution after which he spent many years in prison and exile.

Bogdánov-Bélskii, Nikolái Petróvich (8.xii.1869–1945): Painter. A member of the *Wanderers*. Ironically, his paintings of rural poverty (*Mental Arithmetic* (1895), *At the School Door* (1897), *New Owners* (1914)) were very successful and made him rich. He is now, unjustly, condemned for sentimentality.

Bogdanóvich, Ippolít Fëdorovich (23.xii.1743–6.i.1803): Poet and translator. The work that brought him fame was *Dushenka* (1783), a free adaptation of Lafontaine's *Les amours de Psyché et Cupidon* (itself taken from Apuleius). His other works include *Lyre* (1773), *Russian Proverbs* (1785), and translations of Voltaire, Rousseau, Diderot. He also edited *Nevínnoe uprazhnéniia* (1763) and *Sankt Peterbúrgskie védomosti* (1775–82).

Bogolépov, Nikolái Pávlovich (27.xi.1846–14.ii.1901): Academic and statesman. 1883, as Professor of Roman Law at Moscow University, he was the last rector to be chosen by his colleagues according to the statute of 1863. He then served as education curator for the Moscow District. 1897, Minister of Education where he proved to be a champion of secular mass education and of a break with the repressive policies of the Holy Synod. On the other hand, he was a firm believer in authority, ordering the army in to quell the student disturbances in 1899. February 1901, assassinated by P. V. Karpóvich (q.v.), a former student of Moscow University.

Bólotov, Andréi Timoféevich (7.x.1738–4.x.1833): Writer and agronomist. Fought in the Seven Years' War. An advocate of enclosure and the selective breeding of plants. Corresponding member of the Free Economic Society, he published works on agronomy in its journal. Published (with N. I. Novikov) *Sélskii zhítel* (1778–79), *Ekonomícheskii magazín* (1780–89). His memoirs *The Life and Adventures of A. Bólotov* (1870–73) are particularly valuable.

Borodín, Alexander Porfírevich (31.x.1833–15.ii.1887): Composer and scientist. He graduated from medical school in 1856. In the 1860s he devoted himself to scientific work, becoming a member of the Academy of Sciences in 1877. He began writing musical romances in the 1850s and in 1862, as a result of his meeting Balákirev (q.v.), he joined the

Mighty Handful. His musical output was relatively small, his magnum opus, the opera *Prince Igor*, taking him 18 years to compose and remaining unfinished at his death. He was also the author of some 40 books on chemistry.

Borovikóvskii, Vladímir Lukích (24.vii.1757–6.iv.1825): Painter. From a family of Cossack icon-painters. 1780, painted the iconostasis in the church built in Mogilëv to mark the meeting of Catherine II with Joseph II. 1787, Potëmkin (q.v.) commissioned him to decorate a temporary palace at Kremenchúg for Catherine on her journey to the Crimea. This so pleased Catherine that she sent him to St Petersburg, where he continued to paint icons (Kazán Cathedral). He also became known as a portraitist, his most famous being that of Catherine II walking her dog in the park at Tsárskoe seló. Late 1790s, he joined the Freemasons, became increasingly mystical, finally joining the flagellants.

Bortniánskii, Dmítri Stepánovich (1751–28.ix.1825): Composer. Admitted to the imperial chapel choir at the age of seven, he was taught by Galuppi (q.v.) and, when the latter returned to Venice in 1768, he went with him. His first three operas, *Creonte, Alcide,* and *Quinto Fabio*, were performed in Venice (1776–78). 1779, court harpsichordist and teacher at the Smólnyi Institute. 1784, *kapellmeister* to the Tsarévich's court, where he wrote three operas: *La fête du seigneur, Le faucon* and *Le fils-rival* (1786–87). He also composed numerous instrumental works and songs. 1796, director of the imperial chapel choir, a post he retained until his death.

Briullóv, Karl Pávlovich (12.xii.1799–11.vi.1852): Painter. The son of a woodcarver. His *Last Days of Pompeii* (1828) inspired Bulwer-Lytton's novel and won him honours all over Europe. His other historical paintings include *The Death of Iñez de Castro* (1834), *The Destruction of Rome by the Vandals* (1836) and *Beersheba* (1832). He also painted some memorable portraits, including *Néstor Vasílevich Kúkolnik* (1836) and *Grand Duchess Eléna Pávlovna* (c. 1840), the best being that of the love of his life, *Countess Samóilova and her Adopted Daughter* (1834).

Brius, Iákov Vilimovich (**Bruce**, James) (1670–19.iv.1735): Field Marshal. Of Scottish ancestry, his family had lived in Russia since 1647. He fought in the Crimean campaigns of 1687 and 1689 and the Azóv campaigns of 1695–96. 1697–98, accompanied Peter on his 'Great Embassy' to the West. 1700–21, active role in reforming the Russian armed forces. 1711, with Peter on the Pruth. 1717, head of Mining and Manufactures. Bruce was extremely well educated and interested in mathematics, physics and astronomy, and was the author of a number of maps (including one of the area from Moscow to Asia Minor, subsequently published in Amsterdam, which he drew during the siege of Azóv in 1696), terrestrial and celestial globes.

Brunnóv, Filípp Ivánovich (31.viii.1797–12.iv.1875): Diplomat. From Kurland, he entered Russian diplomatic service in 1818. Took part in the congresses of the Holy Alliance and the negotiations with Turkey at Akkerman (1826) and Adrianople (1829). 1839–40, the 'Brunnóv Mission' to Britain played a major role in settling differences between the two countries during the Mohammed Ali Crisis, and he pursued this policy of *rapprochement* as ambassador to London (1840–54, 1858–74). He also attended the London Conference of 1843 and the Paris Peace Conference of 1856.

Brusílov, Alexei Alexéevich (19.viii.1853–17.iii.1926): General. 1877–78, Turkish War in the Caucasus. 1912–13, commanded the Warsaw Military District. August 1914, commanded 8th Army, and from March 1916, the South-Western Front, where he achieved fame with the 'Brusílov offensives'. 22 May–19 July 1917, Commander-in-chief of the Russian Army, replaced by Kornílov after the failure of the June offensive. For three years after the October Revolution he held no post, but in May 1920 he appealed to former Tsarist officers to join the Red Army. He then worked in the Central Apparatus of the Red Army, becoming inspector of cavalry in 1923.

Bühren (Birón), Ernst Johann (23.xi.1690–17.xii.1772): Although he was only head gentleman-in-waiting at court, he was believed to be the power behind the throne during Anna's reign, in what is normally called the *Birónovshchina*. 1737, elected Duke of Kurland and, after Anna's death in October 1740, made regent. 9 November 1740, arrested and condemned to death, commuted to exile in Siberia. Recalled by Peter III and restored to his throne in Kurland.

Bulgárin, Faddéi Venedíktovich (24.vi.1789–1.ix.1859): Journalist and proponent of Official Nationality. Born to a Polish gentry family in Western Russia (his father had joined Kosciuszko and was sent to Siberia for killing a Russian general). 1807, French War. 1808, Swedish War. 1811, cashiered 'for bad behaviour', he joined Napoleon's Polish Legion, fighting in Italy, Spain and, in 1812, against Russia. 1814, captured by Prussian partisans, he was amnestied together with other Poles by Alexander I and began a literary career in St Petersburg, becoming a proponent of Russian nationalism. 1825, founded *Northern Bee* which, after 1831, he co-edited with Grech (q.v.) (until 1864). He also wrote novels and short stories.

Búrtsev, Iván Grigórevich (4.xii.1795–23.vii.1829): Decembrist. 1813–14, French War. 1818, adjutant to Kiselëv (q.v.) in Tulchin. Member of the Holy Artél, of the Union of Salvation, of the directing nucleus of the Union of Welfare (Moscow Congress, 1821). 1825, arrested and sent to the Caucasus army. 1828–29, Turkish War, mortally wounded at Baiburt.

Búrtsev, Vladímir Lvóvich (1862–1942): Revolutionary. 1885, exiled to Siberia. 1888, fled abroad and edited *Free Russia* and *The Populist*. 1900, edited *Bylóe* (*The Past*). 1905–7, returned to Russia, publishing *Bylóe* in St Petersburg. He became the most relentless hunter of police spies in the revolutionary movement, unmasking Ázev (q.v.) and Malinóvskii. 1915, returned to Russia. 1921, emigrated to France.

Buturlín, Alexander Borísovich (18.vi.1694–31.viii.1767): Field Marshal. 1720, Peter the Great's orderly, used for confidential missions. 1722–23, Persian War. 1725–39, Turkish War. His career took off during the reign of Elizabeth, whose favourite he became. 1756, Field Marshal and member of Elizabeth's Conference. 1760–61, he proved an indecisive Commander-in-chief of the Russian Army in the Seven Years' War, was recalled and appointed Governor-General of Moscow.

Cameron, Charles (*c.* 1740–1812): Architect. He studied architecture in France and Italy, where he lived in Prince Charles James Stuart's house in Rome. 1767 and 1772, exhibited his drawings in London. 1779, began work in St Petersburg for Catherine II, who described him as 'Scottish by nationality, Jacobite by profession, a great draftsman nourished by the ancient world'. 1780–84, remodelled Catherine's apartments in Tsárskoe seló. 1782–86, Palace of Pávlovsk.

Capodistria, John (11.ii.1776–9.x.1831): Statesman. 1803–6, state secretary to the Republic of the Seven United (Ionian) Islands. 1809, invited to Russia by Alexander I. 1816–22, Secretary of State for Foreign Affairs jointly with Nesselrode (q.v.). In the summer of 1822 he resigned over Alexander's reluctance to help the Greeks. 1827, first president of Greece. He became increasingly unpopular, and was murdered in 1831 after calling in the Russian Mediterranean Squadron to suppress a revolt.

Caravaque, Louis (?–1754): Painter. 1716, brought to Russia by François Lefort (q.v.). He painted icons, portraits of Peter and his family, and decorated buildings in the capital and its environs (Winter Palace ceilings). He also devised settings for court ceremonies and theatrical performances. He had a major influence on the development of portrait painting in Russia.

Cecchetti, Enrico (1850–1928): Ballet-master. Made his first stage appearance in Genoa at the age of five. 1887, arrived in St Petersburg and was an immediate success. 1890, second ballet-master to the Imperial Theatres and instructor at the Imperial Ballet School. He was a brilliant teacher, whose pupils included Pávlova, Karsávina and Nijinski. 1902, ballet-master at the Imperial School in Warsaw. 1905, returned to Italy, but was soon back in Russia, working with Pávlova and, from 1909, as the official teacher to the Diághilev (q.v.) ballet. 1918, he and his wife opened a school in London.

Chaadáev, Pëtr Iákovlevich (27.v.1794–14.iv.1856): Writer. 1812–15, fought the French as an officer in the Semënovskii Regiment. He was close to many of the Decembrists and, in December 1821, they decided to admit him to their society. However, he had already resigned his commission and gone to Western Europe, where he remained until 1826. In the late 1820s he began writing his *Lettres philosophiques*, the first of which was published in Nadézhdin's *Teleskóp* in September 1836. Its criticism of Russia created a sensation. Chaadáev was declared mad, the censor who had passed it was dismissed and Nadézhdin exiled to Siberia. A few months later Chaadáev wrote his *Apologie d'un fou*, a partial recantation. The *Lettres philosophiques* were only published in their entirety in the original French in 1966.

Chaliápin (**Shaliápin**), Fëdor Ivánovich (1.ii.1873–12.iv.1938): Opera singer. His introduction to music was as a choirboy. He ran away from home to work on the Volga ferries and gradually drifted to the theatre, first as an actor, then as a singer. 1894–96, he joined the Imperial Opera, but was offered no roles, so joined Mámontov's (q.v.) Private Opera. 1900, left Mámontov's company for the Bolshoi, Moscow. 1901, his international career began at La Scala, Milan. After Diághilev (q.v.) invited him to sing as a soloist in his first Paris season in 1907, Chaliapin worked with him until the First World War, a partnership that brought him world fame. His most famous role was Boris in Músorgskii's *Borís Godunóv*. In 1921 he left Russia.

Chappe d'Auteroche, l'abbé Jean (1722–69): Astronomer. On the instructions of the French Academy of Sciences he travelled to Tobólsk to observe the passage of Venus across the sun (6.vi.1761). On his return to France, he published a very unflattering account of Russia, *Voyage en Sibérie* (1768), which provoked Catherine II into a reply, *L'Antidote* (1770).

Chavchavádze, Iliá Grigórevich (27.x.1837–30.viii.1907): Georgian writer and patriot. 1897–1902, editor of the newspaper *Iveriia*. 1906, elected to the Russian State Council, where he defended Georgian independence. Assassinated by Okhrána agents. His prose and verse works have a strong social and national content.

Chekhov, Anton Pávlovich (17.i.1860–2.vii.1904): Russia's greatest playwright and short story writer. The son of a petty merchant from Taganróg, his first stories were written to ease the poverty that followed his father's bankruptcy and then to finance himself through university. 1884, he qualified as a doctor and practised his profession for his entire life. His own health was poor and suffered greatly from his journey to Sakhalín in 1890, and he was forced to leave Moscow to live in the Crimea. The production of his *Seagull* in 1896 was the beginning of his association with Stanislávskii (q.v.) and Nemiróvich-Dánchenko's (q.v.) Moscow Arts

Theatre, where all his major plays (*Cherry Orchard, Uncle Vania, Three Sisters*) were premièred.

Cherepnín, Nikolái Nikoláevich (3.v.1873–27.vi.1945): Composer. 1906–9, conducted the RMS concerts in the Maríinskii Theatre and, 1908–14, in the Peterbúrgskii naródnyi dom. 1909–14, took part in Diághilev's (q.v.) Russian seasons in Paris. 1918–21, Director of the Tbilísi Conservatoire. 1921, emigrated to France. He was the composer of the *Pavillon d'Armide* (1903 and 1907), and *Narcissus and Echo* (1911).

Cherkásskii, Alexéi Mikhaílovich (28.ix.1680–4.xi.1742): Statesman. 1730, although an extremely wealthy serf-owner, he was the leader of the 'lesser nobles' opposing the 'aristocrats' who wished to limit Anna's powers, in reward for which he was made a member of her cabinet of three and, in 1740, Chancellor (trade agreement with Britain, 1734; Prussian Treaty, 1740; British Treaty, 1741). 1741, member of Elizabeth's supreme council. His daughter, Varvara Alekséevna's dowry of 7,000 serfs on her marriage to Pëtr Borísovich Sheremétev was the origin of that family's great fortune.

Cherkásskii, Vladímir Alexándrovich (2.ii.1824–19.ii.1878): Slavophile politician. 1859–61, member of Túla *Gubérniia* committee and of the Editorial Commission. Contributed to *Rússkaia beséda*. 1863–66, director of the commission on Polish internal and religious affairs (with D. A. Miliútin (q.v.) and Samárin). 1870s, mayor of Moscow, delivered liberal address to Alexander II. 1877–78, Red Cross representative with the army, civilian Governor of Bulgaria.

Cherniáev, Mikhaíl Grigórevich (22.x.1828–4.viii.1898): Pan-Slav general. 1854–55, Crimea. 1858, led a detachment supporting rebels against the Khan of Khiva. 1864, in charge of creating a defensive line between the Siberian and Orenburg steppes, in the course of which he siezed Aulie-Ata, Chimkent and Tashkent from the Khan of Kokand. 1865–66, military Governor of Turkestan, dismissed for exceeding his authority. 1875–78, co-edited with Fadéev (q.v.) the pan-Slav *Russian World*. 1876, commanded the Serbian army against the Turks after which he was refused permission to rejoin the Russian army during the Russo-Turkish War. 1882–84, promoted Lieutenant-General and appointed Governor-General of Turkestan. 1884, member of the War Council.

Chernóv, Victor Mikhaílovich (19.xi.1873–15.iv.1952): SR leader. 1892, joined a student group of the People's Will. 1894, exiled for his political activities to Tambóv *Gubérniia*, where he agitated among the peasantry. 1899, abroad, he was one of the main forces in unifying the different populist groups into the PSR, whose paper, *Revoliutsiónnaia Rossíia*, he edited, 1902–5. 1915, Zimmerwald Conference. 1916, Kiethal Conference. May–August 1917, Minister of Agriculture. 5.i.1918, president of the Constituent Assembly. 1920, emigrated. 1939–45, in the French Resistance. He was the PSR's chief theoretician, the originator of the policy of 'socialization of the land'.

Chernyshëv, Alexander Ivánovich (30.xii.1785–8.vi.1857): General and statesman. 1805–7, Austerlitz and Friedland. 1808–9, attached to Napoleon's suite. 1811–12, diplomatic mission to Sweden. 1812–15, partisan warfare. 1815, Alexander's suite. 1826, on the committee of enquiry into the Decembrists. 1827, acting War Minister. 1832–52, War Minister whose failure to reform contributed to Russia's defeat in the Crimea.

Chernyshëv, Grigórii Petróvich (21.i.1672–30.vii.1745): General. 1695, Azóv campaign. 1700–21, Swedish War, distinguishing himself at Poltáva (1709). 1710, took Výborg. 1713–14, commanded the invasion of Finland. 1718, senator and member of the Admiralty College. 1730, supported Anna Ivánovna. 1741, member of Elizabeth's supreme council.

Chernyshëv, Pável Feoktístovich (x.1854–26.iii.1876): Revolutionary student at the Military-Medical Academy. 1874, imprisoned for his part in the movement to the people. 1876, released because he had tuberculosis, he died in hospital. His funeral gave rise to major demonstrations.

Chernyshëv, Zakhár Grigórevich (1722–84): General. 1744, aide to Pëtr Fëdorovich (Peter III). 1761, commanded the troops sent to help Frederick the Great. 1763, vice-president of the War College, (as there was no president, this made him *de facto* War Minister). 1768, on Catherine's Council. After the First Partition of Poland, of which he was a strong advocate, he was made President of the War College. In 1774, however, Potëmkin (q.v.) was made vice-president and eased Chernyshëv into resignation.

Chernyshévskii, Nikolái Gavrílovich (12.vii.1828–17.x.1889): The son of a priest, he was educated at Sarátov Seminary (1842–45), but rejected the priesthood to study history and philology at St Petersburg University, where he was influenced by the ideas of Belínskii (q.v.) and by the 1848 revolution. He began his career as a teacher in Sarátov, but his radical ideas forced a move to St Petersburg. 1853–55, on the editorial staff of *Sovreménnik*. 1858, editor of *Military Miscellany*. He initially tried to reconcile socialist ideas with his religious faith, but disappointment with the Emancipation drove him to the left. He was arrested in 1862, remaining in prison and Siberia for 21 years. His best-known work, *What is to be Done?*, was written while he was a prisoner in the Peter-Paul Fortress.

Chevalier, Pierre Bressol (dates unknown): Ballet-master and Jacobin, who had taken part in the Terror at Lyon before coming to Russia in April 1798, accompanied by his wife. Paul I had Chevalier's background investigated, but still made him 'composer of ballets from this day on for always'. Madame Chevalier may have been the actress who played the part of the Goddess of Reason, in Notre Dame, Paris, on 12 November 1794. In Russia she became the mistress of Paul I's close confidant, I. P. Kutáisov, and possibly of Paul I himself. Certainly, she sang to Paul and his guests at the last dinner of his life but one, on 10 March 1801. She left Russia after Paul's murder (her husband having left three days before).

Chichagóv, Pável Vasílevich (27.vi.1767–20.viii.1849): Admiral. Joined the Navy at the age of 14, accompanying his father to the Mediterranean and to the war against Sweden. 1792–93, in England to learn navigation. 1797, dismissed from the service and imprisoned in the Peter-Paul Fortress for refusing to serve under Kushelëv, his father's former midshipman appointed by Paul I to command the Navy. 1799, released to command the fleet sailing to England to take part in the invasion of the Netherlands. 1802–11, Naval Minister. 1812 commander of the 3rd Army, which was supposed to destroy the French at the crossing of the Berezína. 1813, retired abroad, where he wrote his memoirs, refusing to return home when summoned by Nicholas I (1834), and taking British citizenship (1847).

Chichagóv, Vasilii Iakovlevich (1726–1809): Admiral. Educated in England, he entered the Navy in 1742. 1764, commander of the port of Archangel, from which he conducted two unsuccessful expeditions (1765 and 1766) to find a sea route through the Northern Ocean to Kamchátka. After the death of Admiral Greig (q.v.), he commanded the Navy in the war against Sweden (1789–90).

Chichérin, Borís Nikoláevich (25.v.1828–3.ii.1904): Liberal legal philosopher. 1861, professor of Russian Law, Moscow University. 1868, resigned in protest at breaches in the University Statute and went to live in Karaúl, where he continued to write. 1882–83, mayor of Moscow, forced to resign by Alexander III because of a speech he made at the latter's coronation. He was a founder of the 'state school of historiography' and one of the main opponents of the Slavophile worship of the Peasant Commune.

Chkheídze, Nikolái Semënovich (1864–1926): Georgian Menshevik. His early revolutionary experience was in Batumi. 1907–17, deputy and, from 1912, chair of the Social-Democratic faction in Third and Fourth Dumas, where he won a reputation as a formidable orator. 1917, co-founder and president of the Petrograd Soviet. 1919–21, president of the Georgian Constituent Assembly.

Chulkóv, Mikhaíl Dmítrievich (1743 or 1744–24.x.1792): Writer. A 'soldier's child', he was successively an actor, a lackey, rising to be a senator. Works include *Prigózhaia povaríkha* (1770), *Peresméshnik* (1766–89) and a collection of popular and Cossack songs (1770–74). He was the first Russian writer to make use of Slavic mythology.

Cruys (Kriuis), Cornelius (4.vi.1657–3.vi.1727): Norwegian by birth. 1700, Vice-Admiral in the Russian Navy, active in the creation of the Admiralty in Vorónezh, and in harbour-building in Taganróg and Azóv. 1705, drove off a Swedish attack on Kronstadt. 1714, sentenced to death for cowardice in the face of the enemy. He was, however, pardoned by Peter and made vice-president of the Naval Academy.

Cui, César Antonovich (1835–1918): Composer, one of the 'Five' or 'Mighty Handful'. The son of a French officer who had remained behind in 1812, he also entered the army, becoming professor of fortification at the St Petersburg Military Academy. He is chiefly remembered now as a composer of songs. Publications include *Music in Russia*, and *A Short Manual of Field Fortification*.

Czartoryski, Adam Jerzy (2.i.1770–3.vii.1861): Russian statesman and Polish patriot. 1795, sent to St Petersburg to enter Russian service, as a condition of the return of the family estates. 1796, a close friend of Alexander Pávlovich. 1798, Russian minister to Sardinia. 1801, member of the Unofficial Committee. 1802, assistant Foreign Minister. 1804–6, Foreign Minister. 1815, Polish Senator. 1830–31, Head of the Polish National Government. After the failure of the Revolution, he emigrated to Paris, where his residence, the Hôtel Lambert, became a centre of émigré resistance to Russian rule.

Dahl (Dal'), Vladímir Ivnánovich (10.xi.1801–22.ix.1872): Ethnographer and lexicographer, of Danish descent. 1819, in the Black Sea Fleet. 1824, resigned for health reasons and studied medicine at Dorpat University. 1829, Russian army doctor in Turkey. 1833, abandoned medicine for the Ministry of Internal Affairs. 1838, corresponding member of the Academy of Sciences. 1859, retired to Moscow to devote himself entirely to his dictionary, *Tolkóvyi slovár' zhívogo velikorússkogo iazyká* (1863–66).

Dargomýzhskii, Alexander Sergéevich (2.ii.1813–5.i.1869): Composer. 1859, elected to the committee of the Russian Musical Society. Operas include *Esmeralda* (1837–41) and *Rusálka* (1856). He also wrote songs that have become well-known: 'I loved you', 'The Wedding', 'Night Breeze'. In the 1860s he turned to orchestral music with a strong nationalist content, writing *Baba-Iaga* (1862) and *Malorossúiskii kazachók* (1864). At his death he was working on another opera, *The Stone Guest*.

Dáshkov, Dmítrii Vasílevich (25.xii.1788–26.xi.1839): Statesman. 1815, a member of the Arzamás circle. 1826–35, on the committee on the peasant question. 1829–39, Minister of Justice (introduction of the *Code of Laws of the Russian Empire*). He was also an important writer, translator and critic, who did much to discredit the 'Ancients' around Admiral Shishkóv (q.v.).

Dáshkova, Ekaterína Románovna (17.iii.1743 or 1744–4.i.1810): Writer, art connoisseur, teacher, philologist, editor, naturalist, musician. 1762, actively supported Catherine II's seizure of the throne. 1769–83, abroad, met Voltaire, Adam Smith, Diderot, etc. 1783–94, head of the Russian Academy and of the Academy of Sciences. Founder of the journals *Sobesédnik liubítelei rossíiskogo slóva* (1783–84) and *Nóvye ezhemésiachnye sochinéniia* (1786–96). 1796, dismissed from all her positions by Paul I. Her *Memoirs of Princess Dashkov* have been translated into English.

Davýdov, Denís Vasílevich (16.vii.1784–22.iv.1839): General and poet. 1806–12, Bagratión's (q.v.) adjutant in the French, Swedish and Turkish Wars. 1812–15, achieved heroic status as the main protagonist of partisan warfare. A man of liberal ideas, he was one of the first members of the Arzamás literary circle and close to the Decembrists. He published a treatise on guerrilla warfare (1821) and a collection of verse (1832).

Deliánov, Iván Davýdovich (30.xi.1818–29.xii.1897): Statesman. 1861–82, director of the Imperial Public Library, St Petersburg. 1866–74, assistant Education Minister. 1882–97, Minister of Education (University Statute depriving the universities of autonomy, 1884; closure of the Higher Women's Courses, 1886; funds cut to universities and pre-*gymnazii* courses, 1887; 'Cooks' Circular' directing education authorities not to admit those for whom education was 'unwarranted', 1887).

Délvig, Antón. (6.viii.1798–14.i.1831): Poet and school friend of Pushkin (q.v.). He worked in the Department of Mines and Salt, in the Ministry of Finance, Ministry of the Interior and in the St Petersburg Public Library. His house in St Petersburg became a literary centre. 1819, a member of the Free Society of Lovers of Russian Literature and the early Decembrist organizations, the Holy Artél and the Green Lamp. Editor of *Northern Flowers* (1825–31) and of the *Literary Gazette* (1830–31). His poetry is sensual and nostalgic, and deals with the cult of friendship and love. He was also a master of the epigram.

Derzhávin, Gavríil Románovich (3.vii.1733–8.vii.1816): Poet and statesman. He was a soldier in the Preobrazhénskii Regiment when Catherine II siezed power. 1773, first poems published. 1778, suppression of the Pugachëv Revolt. His *Odes to Felicia*, dedicated to Catherine II, won him royal favour. Governor of Olónets 1784, and of Tambóv 1785–88. 1791–93, Catherine's secretary. 1794, president of the College of Commerce. 1802–3, Minister of Justice. Considered by many to be the greatest poet of eighteenth-century Russia, his poems are Horatian odes. His *God* (1784) was the first Russian poem translated into English.

Diághilev, Sergéi Pávlovich (19.iii.1872–19.viii.1929): Promoter of the arts. 1898, first art exhibition: German and British water-colourists. 1899, founded *Mir iskússtva*. 1900, appointed to the staff of the Imperial Theatres. 1905, exhibition of Russian portraiture, Tauride Palace. 1906, exhibition of Russian painting, Grand Palais, Paris. 1907, *Concerts historiques russes*, Paris. 1908, Músorgskii's *Borís Godunóv* at the Paris Opera. 1909, first Paris season of his *Ballets russes*, thereon to be an annual event, which placed Russia at the centre of the cultural map of Europe. Abroad at the time of the Revolution, he did not return to Russia.

Díbich (-**Zabalkánskii**), Iván Ivánovich (**Diebitsch**, Johann Karl Friedrich Anton) (2.v.1785–29.v.1831): Field Marshal. The son of a Prussian officer who had entered Russian service in 1798. 1805–7, French War. 1812–13, quartermaster-general to the Russian and Prussian troops. 1821, Laibach Congress. December 1825, informed Nicholas of Sherwood's denunciation of the Decembrists in the Second Army, whose arrest he then supervised. 1828–29, officially Wittgenstein's second-in-command in the Balkans during the Russo-Turkish War, he in fact made all the decisions. 1830–31, commander of the Russian troops suppressing the Polish Revolution. Died from cholera.

Didelot, Charles Louis (1767–1837): Ballet dancer and choreographer. Studied dance in Paris and for a long time was ballet-master in London. 1801–29, ballet-master of the St Petersburg Ballet. 1801–9 and 1815–31: ballet-master at the St Petersburg Theatre School.

Dmítriev, Ivan Ivanovich (10.ix.1760–3.x.1837): Poet and Minister of Justice. 1796–1814, Ober-prokurator of the Senate. 1811–14, Minister of Justice. 1777, begins publishing sentimental poems on love, the passing of youth and nature, as well as satirical stories. Works include *A Fashionable Wife* (1792), *The Odd Woman* (1794), and *Ermák* (1794), the first romantic treatment of a national theme in Russian. His memoirs, *A View of My Life*, were published only in 1866.

Dobroliúbov, Nikolai Nikolaevich (24.i.1836–17.xi.1861): Radical writer. The son of a priest and educated in a seminary, he became literary editor of *Sovreménnik* where he argued that literature must serve a social purpose or be sterile. His writings did much to formulate radical criticism of the Tsarist order.

Dobuzhínskii, Mstisláv Valeriánovich (2.viii.1875–20.xi.1957): Painter. His first work for *Mir iskússtva* was as a book illustrator, but he is also famous for his pictures on the alienation of city life (*The Man with Glasses, In the City, The Kiss*) and for his savage satires (*October Idyll 1905, Army Recruits in the Time of Nicholas I*). During the First World War he became a war artist at the Front. After the Revolution, he took part in the Second

Congress of the Communist International, but emigrated in 1924, settling in the USA, where he worked as a stage designer.

(**Dolgorúkii** and **Dolgorúkov** are interchangeable as surnames in the seventeenth and early eighteenth centuries.)

Dolgorúkii, Alexéi Grigórevich (?–1734): Statesman. 1723, president of the *Glávnyi magisgtrát*. 1726, tutor to Peter Alexéevich. He reached the height of his power when the latter came to the throne as Peter II. Having achieved the fall of Ménshikov (q.v.), Dolgorúkii brought about the betrothal of the Tsar to his daughter Catherine. Unfortunately for him, Peter died on the morning of his wedding day. 1730, he was the only member of the Supreme Privy Council to oppose Anna's election. When she came to the throne, he and all his family were exiled to Berëzov in Siberia, the same place to which he had sent Ménshikov.

Dolgorúkii, Iákov Fëdorovich (1639–24.vi.1720): A companion of Peter the Great from the time of the struggle for power with Sofia. 1695–96, Azóv campaigns. 1696, in charge of the defence of Russia's southern border with Turkey. 1700, head of the administrative and legal departments of the War Department. 1700, taken prisoner by the Swedes outside Narva, and kept in Sweden for ten years. 1711, head of the Army Commissariat. 1717, head of the *Reviziónnaia kollégiia*.

Dolgorúkii, Vasílii Lukích (x.1670–8.xi.1739): Diplomat. Ambassador to Poland (1706), to Denmark (1707–20), to Paris (1721–22), to Poland (1724) and to Sweden (1725). 1727–30, member of the Supreme Privy Council and one of the chief instigators of the election of Anna Ivánovna and the conditions imposed on her. 1730, exiled to the Solovétskii monastery. 1739, beheaded.

Dolgorúkii, Vasílii Vladímirovich (i.1667–11.ii.1746): Statesman and soldier. 1700–21, Great Northern War. 1708, suppression of the Bulávin revolt. 1715, chairman of the commission which found Ménshikov (q.v.) guilty of corruption. 1716–17, accompanied Peter the Great abroad. 1718, disgraced as a result of the Tsarévich Alexéi affair. 1724, pardoned. 1725, commander in the Caucasus. 1730, member of the Supreme Privy Council but did not support the conditions imposed on Anna. 1731, imprisoned and exiled. 1741, pardoned and made president of the War College.

Dolgorúkov, Vasílii Andréevich (24.ii.1804–5.i.1868): Statesman. 1830–31, in Poland. 1838–41, in the suite of Alexander Nikoláevich (Alexander II). 1848, deputy War Minister. 1849, Commission of Investigation into the Petrashévskii Circle. 1853–56, War Minister. 1856, head of the Third Department. April 1866, dismissed after Dmítrii Karakózov's (q.v.) attempt on the Tsar's life.

Dolgorúkov (**-Krymskii**), Vasílii Mikáilovich (1722–82): General. Because of the disgrace his family was in under Anna Ivánovna, he began his service at the age of 13 as a common soldier in the Crimea under Münnich (q.v.). 1736, distinguished himself in the taking of Perekóp. 1756–60, served with distinction in the Seven Years' War. 1762, at her coronation, Catherine II promoted him *général-en-chef*. June 1771, defeated Selim Girey and invaded the Crimea. 29 July, arrived in Kaffa, after which he was awarded the surname Krýmskii.

Dolgúshin, Alexander Vasílevich (1848–30.vi.1885): Revolutionary. The son of a high state official. 1869, organized the Siberian Circle in St Petersburg. 1871, acquitted of participation in the Necháev (q.v.) affair. 1872–73, ran his own revolutionary circle. 1873, arrested and condemned to ten years' forced labour. Died in the Peter-Paul Fortress.

Dostoevskii, Fëdor Mikhaílovich (30.i.1821–28.i.1881): Writer. Graduate of St Petersburg Military-Engineering Institute (1843). 1847, member of the Petrashévskii Circle. 1849, condemned to death and subjected to a mock execution, then sentenced to four years' hard labour followed by service as a soldier (see his *Notes from the House of the Dead*, 1861–62). An inveterate gambler, he often wrote to pay his debts. 1873–74, edited *Grazhdanín*, where his *Diary of a Writer* first appeared, subsequently coming out as individual publications until his death. Works include *Poor Folk* (1846), *Crime and Punishment* (1866), *The Idiot* (1868), *The Devils* (1871–72), *Brothers Karamázov* (1879–80).

Dragomírov, Mikhaíl Ivánovich (8.xi.1830–15.x.1905): General. 1859, attached to the Sardinian Army during the Franco-Austrian War. 1860–69, lecturer, then professor at the General Staff Academy where he was a strong advocate of the bayonet rather than firepower. 1869–73, Chief of Staff, Kiev Military District. 1873–78, commanded 14 Division (1877–78, Russo-Turkish War). 1878, Head of the General Staff Academy. 1889–1905, commander of Kiev Military District. 1898, Governor-General of Kiev, Podólsk and Volýnia.

Dubróvin, Alexander Ivánovich (1855–1918): Politician of the extreme right. He was a doctor, editor of *Russian Banner* and chairman of the Union of Russian People (*The Black Hundreds*). 1905–7, organizer of Jewish *pogróms*. 1918, shot by the Soviet authorities.

Durnovó, Iván Nikoláevich (1.iii.1834–29.v.1903): Statesman. 1863–70, Governor of Chernígov. 1870–72, Governor of Ekaterinosláv. 1882, assistant Minister of the Interior. 1889–95, Minister of the Interior (introduction of Land Captains, 1889; reform of *zémstvos*, 1890; charter to the towns, 1891). 1895–1903, chairman of the Council of Ministers.

Durnovó, Pëtr Nikoláevich (1845–11.ix.1915): Statesman. 1884–93, director of the Police Department. 1900, deputy Minister of the Interior. 1905–6, Minister of the Interior. His presence in Witte's cabinet was the reason given by liberals for refusing to enter it. 1906, condemned to death by the SRs, who were unable to carry this out. February 1914, author of a memorandum to Nicholas II, warning him that war with Germany would be fatal to Russia.

Dúrova, Nadézhda Andréevna (1783–1866): Soldier and writer. She married in 1801, gave birth to a son in 1803, but in 1806 joined the army disguised as a man. 1807, fought at the battle of Friedland when it emerged that she was a woman. Alexander I interviewed her, gave her the surname Alexandrov and a commission in the Mariúpol Hussars. 1816, she retired from the army with the rank of staff-captain. 1836, Pushkin encouraged her to write her memoirs, *The Cavalry Maiden*, and published an extract from them in *Sovreménnik*.

Elágin, Iván Perfílevich (1725–94): Writer and impressario. 1750s, his scabrous poems circulated from hand to hand. 1758, suspected of involvement in a plot to place Catherine on the throne and exiled. Recalled on Catherine's seizure of power and showered with honours. 1766–79, director of court spectacles and music. Mid-1770s, Grandmaster of the Masonic Order (introduction of Swedish masonry of 'Strict Observance', 1777). Catherine's growing disenchantment with masonry led to his downfall. He was a linguist, one of the translators of Marmontel's *Bélisaire* and wrote in a Russian that was very close to Church Slavonic.

Eléna Pávlovna (**Románova**), (Frederika-Charlotte-Maria von Würrtemberg) (1806–73): Grand Duchess. 1823, came to Russia, where she immediately impressed people with her learning (she had already read Karamzín's (q.v.) *History*). 1824, married Mikhaíl Pávlovich, the younger brother of Alexander I. 1854, founded a nursing order to care for the war wounded. After the Crimean War her 'circle' was the centre of pro-Emancipation views. 1858, the first classes of what was to be the Conservatoire opened in her palace, under Anton Rubinstein (q.v.).

Elphinston, John (1722–28.iv.1785): Admiral. Captain in the British Royal Navy (St Malo and St Cas, 1758; Quebec, 1759; Havana, 1762). 1769, Rear-Admiral in the Russian service. 1770, one of the commanders at the battles of Nauplia and Chesme. 1771, returned to the Royal Navy.

Ermólov, Alexéi Petróvich (24.v.1777–11.iv.1861): General. 1791, entered the army as a captain. 1794, in Poland. 1796, in Persia. 1798, exiled 'eternally' to Kostromá for membership of the Smolénsk Officers Political Circle. 1801, recalled from exile. 1805–7, 1812–15 demonstrated great courage and ability in the French Wars. 1816–27, commander in the Caucasus where he showed great cruelty towards the native population.

Evdokímov, Nikolái Ivánovich (1804–73): General. The son of a simple soldier, born in the Caucasus. 1857–58, carried out the systematic deforestation of the Caucasus in an attempt to overcome the Chechens. 1862, responsible for the mass transportation of Circassians into the Russian steppe.

Fadéev, Rostisláv Andréevich (1824–83): Officer and pan-Slav ideologist. 1844, volunteer in the Caucasus Army, soon discharged for 'impermissible gossip'. 1850, rejoined the Caucasus Army, taking part in all its major operations. 1859, ordered by Bariátinskii (q.v.) to write the official history of the Caucasus war. 1866, resigned his commission because he disapproved of Miliútin's army reforms, and took up writing. 1869, his *Opinion on the Eastern Question* became the expression of pan-Slav opinion. 1870s, agitated against universal conscription. 1874, collaborated with Cherniáev (q.v.) on *Rússkii mir* (*Russian World*). 1876, offered his services to the Serbs, but was recalled by the Russian government.

Falconet, Étienne-Maurice (1.xii.1716–24.i.1791): French sculptor. The son of a cabinet maker, his first work was as a woodcarver. Recommended to Catherine by Diderot, he spent 12 years (1766–78) in St Petersburg working on his statue of Peter the Great, 'The Bronze Horseman'.

Felbiger, Johann-Ignatius (1724–88): Augustinian abbot and educationalist. 1788, director of all teachers' training schools in the Austrian Empire. Dismissed on Joseph II's accession. His ideas were influential in late eighteenth-century Russia.

Felten, see **Vélten**.

Fermór, Víllim Víllimovich (1702–8.ii.1771): General. Born an Englishman, his family had come to Russia in 1720. 1730s, adjutant to Münnich (q.v.). 1735–39, Russo-Turkish War. 1741–43 Russo-Swedish War. Commanded a corps at the outset of the Seven Years' War (Memel, Tilsit, Gross-Jägersdorff). 1757, Commander-in-chief. 1759, dismissed for indecisiveness and inactivity. 1760, reappointed acting Commander-in-chief. 1763, Governor-General of Smolénsk.

Fet, Afanásii Afanásevich (23.xi.1820–21.xi.1892): Poet. The son of A. N. Shenshín and Karolina Foeth, he took his mother's name, russified as Fet, when he was declared illegitimate at the age of 14. He served for eight years in the army, in an attempt to regain noble status. 1853, moved to the literary world of St Petersburg. 1859, Nekrásov (q.v.) excluded him from *Sovreménnik* because of an essay he wrote in defence of art for art's sake. 1863, his poems were attacked by radical critics and he lost confidence, not writing for some 20 years until his *Evening Fires* (1883). As well as a poet, he was an accomplished translator of Horace, Ovid and Goethe.

Field, John (28.vii.1772–11.i.1837): Irish composer and pianist. Studied under Clementi, who took him to Russia in 1802. Here he quickly made a reputation as a pianist and, as the teacher of Glínka (q.v.), Arkadii Rachmaninov (grandfather of the composer), and Dubuque. He played a major part in the early development of Russian pianism.

Filosófov, Dmítrii Vladímirovich (26.iii.1872–4.viii.1940): Publicist and critic, one of the founders of *Mir Iskússktvo*. He introduced Diághilev (q.v.) to his friends Benois (q.v.) and Nouvel and together they organized the first 1897 exhibition. 1900–17 lived in a *ménage-à-trois* with D. S. Merezhkóvskii and Zinaída Híppius, his association with whom led to his breach with Diághilev.

Fokine, Michel (**Fókin**, Mikhaíl Mikhaílovich) (1880–1942): Balletmaster. 1898, graduated from the Imperial Ballet School, immediately appointed soloist at the Mariinskii Theatre. 1902, teacher at the Imperial School. 1907, choreographs Saint Saens's *Swan* for Anna Pávlova. 1907–8, trained Ida Rubinstein (q.v.) for her controversial roles in the *Ballets russes*, with which company he worked until 1913. During the First World War, he worked with the Mariinskii Theatre. He left Russia in 1918, settling in New York in the early 1920s.

Fomín, Evstignéi Ipátevich (5.viii.1761–iv.1800): Composer. 1782–85, student at the Philharmonic Academy of Bologna, of which he was made a member in 1785. On his return to Russia, he was commissioned to write the music for Catherine II's libretto, *Gallant Boeslav of Novgorod*. He wrote numerous comic operas, notably *The Coachmen at the Stage* (1787) and *The Americans* (1800, libretto by I. A. Krylóv, q.v.), and a melodrama *Orpheus and Eurydice* (1792, text by I. B. Kniazhnín, q.v.). 1797, chorusmaster at the Imperial Opera.

Fonvízin, Denís Ivánovich (3.iv.1744 or 1745–1.xii.1792): Writer. His first great play, *Brigadír* (1769), satirizing Russian Gallomania, drew him to the attention of Nikíta Pánin (q.v.), whose secretary he became in 1769. He then turned to political works: *On the Recovery of Grand Duke Pável Petróvich* (1771) and *In praise of Marcus Aurelius*. His greatest play, *The Callow Youth* (1781–82), a satire on the nobility, was only performed after Potëmkin had intervened with the censors. 1783, after crossing swords with Catherine in the journal, *A Companion for Lovers of the Russian Language*, he produced the satirical *Universal Court Grammar*. His *Honest Person's Friend, or the Traditionalist* was banned by the censors. 1785, a stroke left him partially paralysed. Towards the end of his life he turned to religious mysticism.

Fonvízin, Mikhaíl Alexándrovich (20.viii.1787–30.iv.1854): Decembrist. 1801, in the Izmáilovskii Guards. 1805, Austerlitz. 1809, established a circle to study military history. 1809–10, Finnish War. 1812–14, much decorated during the French Wars. 1815–18, army of occupation, Paris. 1819, brigade commander in Tulchin. 1822, retired. Member of the Union of Salvation and of the Union of Welfare (Moscow Conspiracy, 1817; Moscow Congress, 1821), he participated in the preparation for the uprising. Condemned to eight years' hard labour in Siberia followed by exile. 1853, allowed to return home.

Galuppi, Baldassare (1706–85): Composer. Son of a barber and theatre violinist, he studied under Lotti. Composed operas for theatres in London and St Petersburg. 1763, *kapellmeister* to the Imperial Russian court. 1768, returned to Venice and placed in charge of music at St Mark's.

Gassner or **Gossner, Johann** (1773–1858): Catholic priest from Bavaria. 1819, preached reformed Catholicism in St Petersburg. 1824, his *L'Évangile selon Saint Mathieu* was burnt, and he was exiled from Russia.

Ge, Nikolái Nikoláevich (15.ii.1831–1.vi.1894): Painter. 1857–69, studied in Italy. 1870, member of the Wanderers. His work deals with major religious and moral themes: *Peter I interrogates the Tsarévich Alexéi* (1871), *What is Truth?* (1890), *Crucifiction* (1892), *Golgotha* (1893). He also completed portraits of Herzen (q.v.) (1867) and Tolstoy (q.v.) (1884).

Gertsen, see **Herzen**.

Giers, Nikolái Kárlovich (9.v.1820–95): Diplomat and Foreign Minister (1882–95). 1863, Ambassador to Iran; 1872, to Sweden. 1875, head of Asiatic department and assistant Foreign Minister. Because of Gorchakóv's (q.v.) disabilities, he was effectively in charge of foreign affairs from 1878. Although he favoured a *rapprochement* with the Central Powers, it was during his ministry that the Franco-Russian Alliance was concluded.

Glazunóv, Alexander (29.vii.1865–21.iii.1936): Composer, one of the 'Mighty Handful'. Studied under Rímskii-Kórsakov (q.v.), and wrote his first symphony at the age of 16. 1905, resigned from the Conservatoire in protest against its 'reactionary policies', returning at the end of the year as its director. After the revolution he was rector of the Conservatoire, but emigrated in 1928. Works include eight symphonies, symphonic poem *Sténka Rázin* (1895), Ballet *Raymonda* (1898), Suite *From the Middle Ages* (1902), Violin concerto (1904) and a number of chamber works.

Glazunóv: Nineteenth-century bookselling and publishing dynasty, founded when Matvéi Petrovich Glazunóv (1757–1830) opened a bookshop in Moscow around 1782. It lasted until 1917, publishing over 900 books.

Glínka, Fëdor Nikoláevich (8.vi.1786–11.ii.1880): Decembrist. 1805, Austerlitz. September 1806, retired to take up a command in the noble militia. October 1812, rejoined the army after Borodinó, fighting from Tarútino to Paris. 1817–19, editor of *Military Journal*, member of the Society of Military Men, of the Lancastrian School Movement, of the Green Lamp, and chairman of the Free Society of Lovers of Russian Literature. 1818, member of the Union of Salvation and of the directing nucleus of the Union of Welfare (St Petersburg Conference, 1820; Moscow Congress, 1821), organizer of the Glínka–Péretts Society. After 14 December 1825, exiled to Petrozavódsk and transferred to civilian work. Works include *Letters from a Russian Officer*, 7 vols (1806–16).

Glínka, Mikhaíl Ivánovich (20.v.1804–3.ii.1857): Composer, 'the father of Russian music'. Taught the piano by John Field (q.v.), he first made his name as a pianist and singer. His fame rests mainly on his two operas *Iván Susánin, A Life for the Tsar* (1836) and *Ruslán and Liudmíla* (1842). He has also written a number of songs and chamber works as well as music for the piano. Although Glínka spent much of his life abroad, his music is intensely nationalistic. He was the first Russian composer to break from the tradition of imitating Western music and to make much use of Russian themes.

Glück, Ernst (1652 or 1655–1705): Educationalist. Born in Saxony, he studied oriental languages. 1673, preached the Gospel in the Baltic region, translated the Bible into Latvian, the Slavonic Bible into modern Russian and campaigned for Russian schools. His servant, Martha, was the future empress Catherine I. 1702, taken prisoner at Marienburg and transported to Moscow. 1703, director of a school in Pokróvka.

Gnédich, Nikolái Ivánovich (2.ii.1784–3.ii.1833): Poet. Member of *Beséda*, of the Free Society of Lovers of Literature, Science and the Arts and of the group around Bátiushkov (q.v.), Krylóv (q.v.) and Olénin (q.v.). Works include *Fishermen* (1822), and translations of *Folksongs of the Modern Greeks* (1825). He also translated the *Iliad*.

Gógol, Nikolái Vasílevich (20.iii.1809–4.iii.1852): Writer. His first works, *Evenings on a Farm near Dikanka, Arabesques* and *Mírgorod*, were stories about his native Ukraine. 1829, after a short spell in the Ministry of Crown Properties, St Petersburg, he became a private tutor. 1831, part of the literary world around Pushkin (q.v.) and Belínskii (q.v.). Real success came in 1836 with *The Inspector General* and in 1842 with the first volume of *Dead Souls*. 1847, he became embroiled in an acrimonious exchange of letters with Belínskii, who saw his *Selected Passages from Correspondence with Friends* as a betrayal of his early work. For the last ten years of his life he worked on the second volume of *Dead Souls*, but in a fit of depression, he burnt the completed manuscript nine days before his death.

Golítsyn, Alexander Mikhaílovich (18.xi.1718–8.x.1783): Soldier and diplomat. Served under Prince Eugene in Austria, then in the Russian embassy in Constantinople, then ambassador to Saxony. 1756–63, in Seven Years' War, he commanded the left wing of the army at Frankfurt-on-Oder (1757). 1768, on Catherine's Council. 1768–70, Russo-Turkish War. Recalled in 1769 for failing to take Khotín, he managed to take it and Jassy before handing over his command to Rumiántsev (q.v.).

Golítsyn, Alexander Nikoláevich (8.xii.1773–22.xi.1844): Statesman and mystic. 1803, Procurator of the Holy Synod. 1810, member of the State Council. 1813, head of the Russian Bible Society. 1816, Minister of Education. 1817–24, Minister of Spiritual Affairs and Education. A close friend of Alexander I, his early life was devoted to dissipation and pleasure. He became interested in religion after being made Procurator of the Holy Synod, combining a curious mixture of Protestantism and Orthodoxy, and is probably partly responsible for Alexander's mystical beliefs in later life.

Golítsyn, Dmítrii Mikhaílovich (1665–14.iv.1737): Statesman and diplomat. 1697, sent to Italy to study, he acquired a taste for learning and culture. 1701, negotiated the agreement with Turkey for Russian ships to sail the Black Sea. 1718–22, president of the *Kámer-Kollégiia*. 1726–30, member of the Supreme Privy Council, one of the authors of the conditions imposed on Anna Ivánovna. 1736, condemned to death, commuted to imprisonment in the Peter-Paul Fortress, where he died. On his death, his library of 6,000 books in his estate at Arkhángelskoe was dispersed.

Golítsyn, Mikhaíl Mikhaílovich (1.xi.1675–10.xii.1730): Soldier and statesman. 1694, crushing of the *Stréltsy*. 1695–96, Azóv campaigns. 1700–21, Great Northern War, (stormed Noteborg, 1702; defeated the Swedes at Dóbryi, 1708; commanded the Guards at Poltáva, 1709). 1714–21, commander in Finland (naval battle of Gangut, 1714). 1728, president of the War College and a member of the Supreme Privy Council that imposed conditions on Anna Ivánovna (1730).

Golítsyn, Mikhaíl Mikhaílovich (1681–25.v.1764). Sailor and statesman. Began his service in the Dutch Fleet. 1717–21, Great Northern War, commanding a squadron of galleys raiding the Swedish coast. 1732, president of the Justice College, then Quartermaster-General. 1745–48, ambassador in Iran. 1748, commander of the Navy. 1756, in Elizabeth's conference.

Golítsyn, Nikolái Dmítrievich (31.iii.1850–1925): The last prime minister of Imperial Russia. 1885–1903, successively Governor of Archangel, Kalúga and Tver *Gubérnii*. A senator and member of the Board of Management of the Red Cross as well as chairman of the Committee to Help

Russian Prisoners of War, he was made Chairman of the Council of Ministers in December 1916, from which post he was removed by the February Revolution.

Golítsyn, Sergéi Pávlovich (1815–87): Peasant reformer. Alexander II proposed him as a member of the Editorial Commission for Emancipation, to represent the large landowners. He rapidly became one of the chief protagonists of reform and, as Governor of Chernígov, played a major part in its implementation.

Golovín, Alexander Iákovlevich (17.ii.1863–1930): Set and costume designer. 1899–1900, worked at Abrámtsevo, and made sets for Mámontov's (q.v.) private opera. 1901, stage designer for the Imperial Theatres. 1908 onwards, designed sets and costumes for Diághilev's (q.v.) productions (*Borís Godunóv*, 1908; *Iván the Terrible*, 1909; *Firebird*, 1910). He remained in Russia after the Revolution and was the first stage designer to be awarded the title of People's Artist of the Russian Federation (1928).

Golóvkin, Gavríil Ivánovich (1660–1734): Statesman. A close associate of Peter the Great, he accompanied the Tsar on his journeys. 1706, head of the Embassy Office. 1709, Chancellor. 1718, president of the College of Foreign Affairs. 1726–30, member of the Supreme Privy Council, where he opposed placing conditions on Anna Ivánovna. 1730, in Anna's cabinet.

Golovnín, Alexander Vasílevich (25.iii.1821–3.xi.1866): Statesman. 1848–59, on Naval General Staff, he edited *Morskói sbórnik* in the 1850s. 1862–66, Minister of Education (University Statute, 1863; *gymnaziia* statute, 1864; censorship law, 1865). Dismissed ten days after Karakózov's (q.v.) attempt on the Tsar, for which his failure to purge the educational system of 'materialistically inclined' textbooks and teachers was blamed.

Goncharóv, Iván Alexándrovich (6.vi.1812–15.ix.1891): Writer. Although he is chiefly known for *Oblómov* (1859), this in fact is part of a trilogy with *A Common Story* (1847) and *The Precipice* (1869) in which Russian life was to be reflected 'as in a drop of water'. His *Frigate Pallás* (1858) is a meticulous account of his trip to Japan in 1852–53 as secretary to Admiral Putiátin (q.v.).

Goncharóva, Natália (1881–1962): Painter. She met Lariónov (q.v.), with whom she lived and worked for the rest of her life, when they were students at the Moscow School of Painting, Sculpture and Architecture. Her early style was a kind of neo-primitivism, fusing post-impressionist ideas with those of the Russian *lubók* and icon. 1912, she began to explore cubism and futurism, leading to her development of rayonism jointly with Lariónov. She exhibited at the *Mir iskússtva* exhibition in Moscow and at the Salon d'Automne, Paris (1906), with *The Wreath*

(1907), the *Golden Fleece* (1908), *Jack of Diamonds* (1910–11), *Union of Youth* (1910) and participated in *Donkey's Tail* (1912) and *Target* (1913). 1914, designed the sets for Diághilev's (q.v.) production of *Le Coq d'Or*. 1915, left Moscow for Western Europe, settling permanently in Paris in 1919.

Gorchakóv, Alexander Mikhaílovich (4.vi.1798–27.ii.1883): Diplomat and Foreign Minister. 1820–22, accompanied Nesselrode (q.v.) to the Troppau, Laibach and Verona Congresses. 1854, Vienna conference of ambassadors. 1856–82, Foreign Minister. 1856–63, tried to reverse the Paris Peace Settlement (1856) through a *rapprochement* with France and when this failed, turned to *rapprochement* with Prussia (1863). 1873, League of the Three Emperors. His extreme age worked against Russia at the Berlin Congress (1878), after which, although nominally Foreign Minister, he played no real part in policy making.

Gordon, Patrick (31.iii.1635–29.xi.1699): General. The son of a minor Aberdeenshire pro-Stuart laird, he served in the Swedish, Polish and German armies. 1661, entered the Russian service. 1666, distinguished himself in the Turkish War. 1676, became friendly with Lefort (q.v.). 1687, distinguished himself in the Crimea and promoted general, at which the Patriarch prophesied disaster for Russia's armies as long as they were commanded by an 'heretic'. 1689, rewarded with great estates for his part in Peter's seizure of the throne. 1695–96, took part in both Azóv campaigns, and was entrusted with the town's fortification after its capture. 1698, suppressed the revolt of the *Stréltsy* while Peter was abroad. His diary is an important historical source.

Gorky, Maxím (**Péshkov**, Alexéi Maksímovich) (16.iii.1868–18.vi.1936): Novelist and playwright, chronicler of Russian lower-class life. Apprenticed to a shoemaker at the age of nine, he spent his youth wandering around central Russia. 1899, joined the Social-Democrats. 1905, shielded father Gapón while he was being hunted by the police. 1906–13, abroad. His relationship with Lenin and the Bolsheviks was close but troubled. His early works (*Former People, Twenty-six Men and a Girl*) reflect his early life as a vagrant. His later ones (*Lower Depths, Mother*) are powerful accounts of poverty.

Granóvskii, Timoféi Nikoláevich (9.iii.1813–4.x.1855): Historian and Westernizer. 1839–55, professor of History, Moscow University. His lectures on Russian history were a polemic with the Slavophiles and were immensely popular in progressive circles.

Grech, Nikolái Ivánovich (3.viii.1787–12.i.1867): Journalist, publisher, educator, grammarian and proponent of Official Nationality. 1812–39, editor and publisher of *Syn otéchestva*. In 1831 he joined Bulgárin's (q.v.) *Northern Bee*, which they jointly made the leading newspaper in Russia.

Satirized in the marquis de Custine's *Russia in 1839*, where his service as a police spy was mentioned, he wrote a reply, making some play of Custine's homosexuality, winning official approval. His unfinished autobiography, *Notes on My Life* (1856), is a major source for literary history.

Greig, Alexéi Samuílovich (6.ix.1775–18.i.1845): Admiral. 1785–96, served in the Royal Navy, then transferred to Russian service. 1798–1800, Russo-French War. 1806–12, Russo-Turkish War, took part in Seniávin's attack on the Aeonian islands and on the Dardanelles (1807). 1812, in Chichagóv's (q.v.) Moldavian Army. 1813, commanded the blockade of Danzig. 1816–33, commander of the Black Sea Fleet. 1834–39, in charge of building of Púlkovo Observatory.

Greig, Samuíl Kárlovich (1736–15.x.1789): Admiral. Scots by birth, he entered Russian service in 1764 as a captain. 1770, *de facto* commander at Chesme. 1770, commander of Kronstadt. 1788–89, commander of Baltic Fleet against Sweden (Hogland, 1789).

Griboédov, Alexander Sergéevich (1795–30.i.1829): Writer. A precocious genius, he entered Moscow University when he was aged 11. At the age of 16 he had completed the literary, law, natural science and mathematical faculties, learnt French, German, Italian and English and was preparing to take his doctorate. These studies were interrupted by the French invasion, when he served in the army (1812–16). He took an early interest in the theatre and translated and adapted several foreign plays. His main work is the satirical play *Woe from Wit* (1816–23). 1818, forced to leave St Petersburg after a duel, he accepted a post in the embassy in Persia. 1828, ambassador in Persia. 1829, killed when a crowd invaded the embassy and slaughtered all the Russian representatives in Teheran.

Guchkóv, Alexander Ivánovich (14.x.1862–1936): Leader of the Octobrist Party. From a family of Moscow businessmen. Fought against the British in the Boer War. November 1905, one of the founders of the Octobrist Party. December 1906, publishes *Gólos Moskvý* (daily). November 1907, elected to the Third Duma of which he became the president (Mar. 1910–Mar. 1911). 1908, chairman of the Duma Defence Committee. During the First World War he was chairman of the Central War Industries Committee and member of the Special Council on Defence. March–May 1917, Minister of War. 1918, emigrated.

Gumilëv, Nikolái Stepánovich (3.iv.1886–24.viii.1921): Poet. Husband of Anna Akhmátova (q.v.). At first influenced by the Symbolists, in 1913 he became a leader of the Acmeists. He was also a prolific translator (Voltaire, Gautier, Coleridge, Southey, Wilde as well as of the *Epic of Gilgamesh*). He fought in the Russian Volunteer Force in France during the First World War. After his return to Russia, he was shot on Lenin's orders, allegedly for counter-revolutionary activities. Works include *Path of the Conquistadors* (1905), *Romantic Flowers* (1908), *Pearls* (1910), *An Alien Sky* (1912), *The Quiver* (1916), *Camp Fire* (1918), *The Tent* (1921).

Gúrko, Iósif Vladímirovich (**Roméiko-Gúrko**) (16.vii.1828–15.i.1901): Field Marshal. 1862–66, in the Tsar's suite. 1877–78, distinguished himself in the Russo-Turkish War by a dash across the Balkan Range. 1883–94, Governor-General of Warsaw where he pursued a policy of Russification.

Gúrko, Vasílii Iósifovich (**Roméiko-Gúrko**) (8.v.1864–11.xi.1937): General. 1899–1902, military agent to the Boers. 1904–5, Russo-Japanese War. October 1906, chaired the commission writing the history of the war. 1908–10, 'Young Turk'. November 1916–February 1917, Nicholas II's Chief of Staff during M. V. Alexéev's (q.v.) illness. Emigrated, died in Rome.

Gvozdëv, Kuzmá Antónovich (1883–19?): Menshevik. 1903–7, SR sympathizer. 1902 and 1906, arrested for revolutionary activities. 1908, joins the Social-Democrats. 1910, in the Putílov factory. 1910–11, chairman of the Union of Metalworkers. January 1911, a founder of the Menshevik Central Initiative Group. 1911–14, exiled. 1914, in the Erikson factory. 1915–17, chairman of the War Industries Committee Workers' Group. February 1917, a founder of the Petrograd Soviet. After October 1917, worked in Soviet economic oganizations. Probably killed in the purges.

Hartmann, Victor Alexándrovich (23.iv.1834–23.vii.1873): Architect, watercolourist and protagonist of the 'Russian Style'. Designer of the People's Theatre for the Polytechnic Exhibition and the Studio at Abrámtsevo (both 1872). An exhibition of his watercolours, mounted by Vladímir Stásov (q.v.) in his memory, inspired Músorgskii (q.v.) to compose *Pictures at an Exhibition*.

Herzen, Alexander Ivánovich (25.iii.1812–9.i.1870): Writer and revolutionary socialist. Exiled to Viátka for five years (1834–39) for membership of Stankevich's (q.v.) circle, and to Nóvgorod for three years (1840–42), he left Russia in 1847, never to return, as a relatively minor, if oppositional, author. It was in exile in Western Europe that he achieved great fame with the publications of his 'Free Russia Press' (*From the Other Shore, The Bell*) which, although illegal, became obligatory reading inside Russia and were regarded as the nation's conscience. Ironically, it was in the West, whose values he learned to mistrust, that he developed the theory of a Russian road to socialism based on the peasant commune.

Iaguzhínskii, Pável Ivánovich (1683–6.iv.1736): Statesman and diplomat. The son of Lutheran pastor from Lithuania. 1701, in the Guards. 1719, at the Åland Congress. 1720–21, ambassador in Vienna. 1722, first

Procurator General. 1726, demoted to court appointment as a result of Ménshikov's (q.v.) *coup* against the Senate. 1730, restored as Procurator General by Anna. 1731, ambassador in Berlin. 1734, enters the cabinet on the death of Golóvkin (q.v.).

Iakúshkin, Iván Dmítrievich (28.xii.1793–11.viii.1857): Decembrist. 1811, joined the Semёnovskii Guards. 1812–15, fought from Borodinó to Paris, much decorated. 1818, retired to his estates. One of the founders of the Union of Salvation and of the directing nucleus of the Union of Welfare (Moscow conspiracy, 1817; St Petersburg conference, 1820; Moscow conference, 1821), he took part in the preparation of the uprising of 14 December. Sentenced to 20 years' hard labour, reduced to ten. 1835, active in the Lancastrian Schools movement in Siberia. 1856, amnestied and returned to Moscow.

Iaroshénko, Nikolái Alexándrovich (1846–98): Painter. Inspired to join the Wanderers after reading Dostoevskii's (q.v.) *Notes from the House of the Dead*, he became their leader after the death of Kramskói (q.v.). His works (*The Stoker*, 1878; *The Girl Student*, 1883) reflect the harshness of Russian life. *Life is Everywhere* (1888) shows convicts in a railway wagon on their way to exile. See also *Portrait of the Actress Strépetova* (1884).

Iavórskii, Stefán (Simeón Ivánovich) (1658–27.xi.1722): Priest. 1684–87, after graduating from the Kiev Academy, he studied in Poland. 1689, became a monk. 1701, president of Slavo-Graeco-Latin Academy. 1721, president of the Holy Synod. He opposed Peter's reforms and the subordination of the Church to laymen.

Iazěkov, Nikolái Mikhaílovich (4.iii.1803–26.xii.1846): Poet. One of the group around Pushkin (q.v.). A liberal when young, he moved towards Slavophile views, debating fiercly with Herzen (q.v.) and Chaadáev (q.v.), becoming xenophobic in later life. His poems are full of energy, his later ones making use of Aesopian language.

Ignátev, Nilolái Pávlovich (17.i.1832–20.vi.1906): Statesman and diplomat. 1859, envoy to China (Peking Treaty, 1860). 1861–64, director, Asiatic Department of the Foreign Ministry. 1864–77, ambassador in Constantinople. February–March 1877, tours Western European capitals to keep the Powers neutral in Russo-Turkish War. Strongly influenced the Treaty of San Stefano (1878). 1881–82, Minister of the Interior.

Ióllos, Grigórii Borísovich (1859–14.iii.1907): Journalist. Educated and lived most of his life in Germany, as Berlin correspondent of *Rússkie védomosti*. 1904, he published *Letters from Berlin*. 1905, moved to Moscow to join the editorial staff of *Rússkie védomosti*. 1907, elected as a Kadet to the Second State Duma, he was murdered by Black Hundreds, three weeks after its opening.

Iuláev, Salavát, see **Salavát Iuláev**.

Iusúpov (**Sumarókov-Élston**), Felix Felíxovich (the elder) (1856–11.vi.1926): Aristocrat and soldier. He was allowed to assume the name Prince Iusúpov on his marriage to the last of that house, Zinaída Nikoláevna Iusúpova. He introduced Rasputin to his son to 'cure' his homosexuality. 1915, dismissed as military Governor of Moscow, after his behaviour during the riots, when he appeared to be encouraging the crowd's anti-German *pogróm*.

Iusúpov, Felix Felíxovich (the younger) (11.iii.1887–27.ix.1967): Son of the above, one of the assassins of Rasputin.

Ivánov, Sergéi Vasílevich (4.vi.1864–3.viii.1910): Painter. Works include *On the Road: Death of a Migrant Peasant* (1889), *Foreigners arriving in Seventeenth-Century Moscow* (1901), *Soldiers Firing on Demonstrators* (1905).

Izvólskii, Alexander Petróvich (6.iii.1856–16.viii.1919): Statesman and diplomat. 1894–97, Minister to the Vatican. Ambassador in Belgrade (1897), Munich (1897–99), Tokyo (1899–1903) and Copenhagen (1903–6). 1906–10, Foreign Minister. 1910–17, ambassador in Paris.

Jankovich de Mirjevo, Theodore (dates unknown): Educationalist. An orthodox Serb, he came to St Petersburg in 1782 and was made a member of the school commission under Zavadóvskii (q.v.). He was chiefly responsible for the drafting of the Statute of People's Schools, 1786.

Jomini, Henri de (6.iii.1779–24.iii.1869): General and military theorist. Began his military career in the Swiss Guards at Versailles, rising to become Ney's Chief of Staff. 1804, his *Traité des grandes opérations militaires* attracted Napoleon's attention. He distinguished himself at Jena and in the Spanish campaigns of 1808. Fought in Russia in 1812 and at Lützen and Bautzen (in the French Army). Offended by Napoleon, he entered the Russian service in 1814. 1829, Russo-Turkish War (capture of Varna). Works include *Histoire critique et militaire des campagnes de la Révolution*, 5 vols (1806), *Vie politique et militaire de Napoléon*, 4 vols (1827), *Précis de l'art de guerre* (1830).

Kakhóvskii, Pëtr Grigórevich (1799–13.vii.1826): Decembrist. 1816, joined the Jäger Guards. Within nine months reduced to the ranks for disorderly conduct and transferred to an ordinary Jäger regiment in the Caucasus, where he soon regained his commission and transferred to a cavalry regiment (1818). 1821, retired for health reasons. 1823–24, in Western Europe for his health, he joined the Northern Society on his return to St Petersburg. An active participant in the events of 14 December 1825. Hanged in the Peter-Paul Fortress.

Kaliáev, Iván Platónovich (24.vi.1877–10.v.1905): SR terrorist. 1897–99, student, Moscow and St Petersburg universities. 1898, League of Struggle for the Emancipation of the Working Class. 1903, Battle Organization, PSR, Geneva. 4.ii.1905, assassinates Grand Duke Sergéi Alexándrovich for which he was executed.

Kalnyshévskii, Pëtr Ivánovich (1693–1803): Last *hetman* of the Zaporózhian Host (1762, 1765–75). 6 June 1775, surrendered to the regular army and was exiled to the Solovétskii Monastery. Freed in 1801, he remained in the monastery where he died in 1803, aged 110.

Kámenskii, Mikhaíl Fëdorovich (1738–1809): Field Marshal. 1758–59, served in the French Army. 1760–61, Seven Years' War. 1769–74, Turkish War. 1783, Governor-General of Riazán and Tambóv. 1788, defeats the Turks at Gangur. Dismissed for refusing to take orders from Kakhóvskii (q.v.), to whom Potëmkin (q.v.) handed over command. 1897, Paul I made him a count and dismissed him from the service. 1806, Commander-in-chief, but after six days fighting the French (13 Dec.) he handed over to Buxhoeveden and retired to his estates, where he was killed by one of his serfs.

Kandínskii (Kandinsky), Vasílii Vasílevich (4.xii.1866–13.xii.1944): Painter. Pioneer of abstract art. 1896–1914, abroad, a member of *Phalanx, Berlin Sezession* and *Blaue Reiter*. 1914–21 returned to Russia but left because he disagreed with the subordination of art to industrial design. 1921–33, taught at the Bauhaus. 1933, left Germany for France.

Kantemír, Antiókh Dmítrievich (10.ix.1708–31.iii.1744): Diplomat, writer and translator. Son of the reigning prince of Moldavia. 1730, active supporter of Anna Ivánovna against the Supreme Privy Council. Ambassador in London (1732) and in Paris (1739–44). He was a prolific translator from Latin and French (Montesquieu and Fontenelle, whose attack on Ptolemaic astronomy caused problems with the Church). 1725–26, his Russian–French Dictionary was published. His *Satires*, published 18 years after his death, attacked all who disparage science and perpetuate ignorance.

Kapníst, Vasílii Vasílevich (12.ii.1758–28.x.1823): Poet. 1770–75, in the Guards where he joined Derzhávin's (q.v.) literary circle. He made his reputation with the poem *Satira 1* (1780). Much of his poetry is about nature and Ukraine, with strong element of social protest (e.g. 'Ode to slavery', 1783). His most important work is a play in verse *Calumny* (1793–98).

Karakózov, Dmítrii Vladímirovich (23.x.1840–3.ix.1866): Failed regicide. Expelled from Kazán University for participating in the disturbances of 1861 and from Moscow University for non-payment of fees. 4.iv.1866, he fired on Alexander II as the latter was walking near the Summer Gardens. He was hanged and the members of his 'circle' were exiled to Siberia.

Karamzín, Nikolái Mikhaílovich (1.xii.1766–22.v.1826): Writer and historian. Briefly in the Horse Guards. Initially a writer of sentimental novels (e.g. *Poor Lisa*, 1792) and a Freemason. 1789, the shock he experienced from the French Revolution during his tour of Germany, Switzerland, France and England, led to a major change in his political ideas (see his *Letters of a Russian Traveller*, 1791–97). In 1803 he was made official historiographer and spent the rest of his life writing his *History of the Russian State*, probably the most consistent defence of autocracy as a Russian institution.

Karázin, Vasílii Nazárovich (30.i.1773–4.xi.1842): Educationalist, founder of Khárkov University (1805). 1801, his letter to Alexander I advocated the introduction of fundamental laws, public trials and military colonies. He was persecuted for his ideas, imprisoned in Shlüsselburg (1820), placed under police supervision and forbidden to live in St Petersburg.

Karpóvich, Pëtr Vladímirovich (3.x.1874–31.iii.1917): SR terrorist. Expelled from Moscow and Iurev universities for his political activities. 1899, Berlin University, but the Russian student disturbances brought him back to Russia where he assassinated the Minister of Education, Bogolépov (q.v.) (1901), for which he was sentenced to 20 years' hard labour. 1907, fled abroad and joined Ázev's (q.v.) Battle Organization. 1908, took part in an unsuccessful attempt on the life of Nicholas II. He left the Battle Organization when Ázev was exposed as a police spy. Killed on his way back to Russia after the February Revolution, when his ship was sunk by a German submarine.

Katkóv, Mikhaíl Nikíforovich (1818–87): Ultra-nationalist journalist, editor of *Moskóvskie védomosti*. Began life as an admirer of English constitutional government, but changed his ideas as a result of the rise of nihilism and the Polish revolution of 1863. 1886, conducted a successful press campaign against the Russian alliance with Austria and Germany. He is the first example in Russia of a public opinion former, who undertook many crusades against 'enemies' high and low.

Kaulbars, Alexander Vasílevich (1844–1929): General. Spent most of his career exploring Turkestan (source of the river Syr-Dari, etc.), his publications on which won him the gold medal of the Imperial Geographical Society. 1870–72, explored the Chinese frontier. 1873, combined the Khiva campaign with further geographical explorations. 1877–78, Turkish War, then on the boundary commission for Serbia, Bulgaria and Albania. 1882–83, ordered by Alexander III to become Minister of War in Bulgaria, he was dismissed after Bulgarian protests at Russian domination. 1905–9, as Governor of Odessa, he won the reputation of being an anti-Semite.

Kavélin, Konstantín Dmítrievich (4.xi.1818–3.v.1885): Historian and jurist. 1840s, a leading Westernizer. 1855, his 'Notes' (published abroad by Herzen, q.v.) advocated emancipation with land, for which he was dismissed as tutor to the Tsarévich. 1857–61, professor of civil law, St Petersburg University. He is, with Chichérin (q.v.), the founder of the 'state school of historiography'. His works, which include *A Survey of Juridical Relations in Ancient Russia* (1847), *A Brief Survey of Russian History* (1887), *Thoughts and Notes on Russian History* (1866), argue that community relations based on kinship and custom have been replaced by a system based on political and juridical legislation.

Kazakóv, Matvéi Fëdorovich (1738–26.x.1812): Architect. Exponent of classicism. 1768–74, worked with Bazhénov (q.v.) on the Moscow Kremlin Palace. 1786–93, Moscow University, 1789–96, Palace of Ostánkino.

Keith, James (11.vi.1696–14.x.1758): Field Marshal. 1715, fled Scotland after participating in the uprising. Studied in Paris, and made a member of the Académie des Sciences. 1719, spent nine years in the Spanish army. 1728, entered Russian service. 1735–37, War of Polish Succession. 1736–37, Turkish War; wounded at Ochákov. 1740, Governor of Ukraine. 1741–43, Swedish War. Grand Master of the Russian Masonic Order. 1747, having fallen from favour, left for Prussia where Frederick the Great made him Field Marshal.

Kérenskii, Alexander Fëdorovich (22.iv.1881–11.vi.1970): Statesman and lawyer. Became famous as an advocate defending the oppressed (Lena gold miners, 1912; Bolshevik Duma deputies, 1915). 1912–17, Deputy to Fourth Duma (Trudovík). March 1917, Minister of Justice and member of the Executive Committee of the Petrograd Soviet. July–October 1917, Prime Minister. 1918, emigrated.

Khabálov, Sergéi Semënovich (21.iv.1858–1924): General. 1903–14, directed a number of military academies. 1914–16, Governor of the Urals and *atamán* of Urals Cossacks. June 1916, military commander of Petrograd until removed by the February Revolution. Emigrated after October 1917.

Kheráskov, Mikhaíl Matvéevich (25.x.1733–27.ix.1807): Writer. 1755, director of Moscow University Press, where he created a literary circle. 1758, translated Molière and Pope. 1761, Rector of Moscow University. He edited a number of journals, the most influential of which was *Useful Entertainment* (1760–62), which ceased publication after the assassination of Peter III, whom it had supported. Among his many writings are *Rossiada*, an epic on the conquest of Kazán and *Friend of the Unfortunate*, a sentimental drama. He played a formative part in the life of many writers, most notably Denis Fonvízin (q.v.).

Khomiakóv, Alexéi Stepánovich (1.v.1804–23.ix.1860): Poet, religious philosopher and slavophile. 1823, member of the *Liubomúdrye*. Wrote for *Evropéets, Moskvitiánin, Rússkaia beséda*. Central to his views was the idea of *sobórnost*/togetherness.

Kiréevskii, Iván Vasílevich (22.iii.1806–11.vi.1856): Slavophile thinker. 1823, member of the *Liubomúdrye*. Chaadáev's (q.v.) first *Lettre philosophique* (1836) provoked him into writing a defence of Slavdom and Orthodoxy, the main virtue of which was that it had not been tainted by the secular humanism of the classical world. 1845, editor of *Moskvitiánin*.

Kiselëv, Pável Dmítrievich (8.i.1788–1872): Soldier, statesman and diplomat. 1807, Friedland. 1812, withdrawal to Moscow. 1814–15, Congress of Vienna in the Imperial Suite, then Chief of Staff to the Southern Army in Tulchin. Came briefly under suspicion after the Decembrist Revolt but returned to favour as a result of his courage in the Turkish War of 1828–29. 1829–34, plenipotentiary in the Principalities, which he endowed with a constitution, improving the conditions of the peasantry. 1836–56, Minister of State Domains, where his reforms of the state peasantry became the model for the emancipation of 1861. 1842, took Wallachian nationality in order to be made *hospodar* of Wallachia, but this was vetoed by the British. 1856–62, ambassador in Paris. He was the uncle of the Miliútin brothers (q.v.) whose education he supervised and whose careers he launched.

Kizevétter, Alexander Alexándrovich (10.v.1866–1933): Kadet leader. 1898–1909, lecturer then professor of history, Moscow University. 1904, Union of Liberation. 1906, Central Committee of the Kadet Party. Represented Moscow in the Second Duma. 1922, deported from the USSR, he became professor of history at Prague University.

Kliuchévskii, Vasílii Ósipovich (16.i.1841–12.v.1911): Historian. The son of a poor village priest, he became lecturer then professor of history at Moscow University. His first work, *The Boyar Duma in Old Russia*, became a classic and his lectures (published as *A Course on Russian History*) were famous. He has a beautiful style – simple, direct and uncluttered.

Klodt, Mikhaíl Konstantínovich (30.xii.1832–11.i.1902): Painter. 1870, member of the *Wanderers*. Mostly known for his landscapes: *High Road in Autumn* (1863), *Ploughing* (1872).

Kniazhnín, Iákov Borísovich (1742–91): Writer. 1757, translator to the Chancery. 1778, secretary to I. I. Bétskoi (q.v.). 1783, member of the Russian Academy. He wrote for journals and translated Corneille and Voltaire. His plays include *Dido, Rosláv, Vadím of Novgorod, The Chatterbox, Mourning or the Widow Consoled*. His best-known musical comedy is *Misfortune from a Carriage*.

Kochubéi, Víktor Pávlovich (11.xi.1768–3.vi.1834): Statesman and lomat. 1798, Vice-Chancellor. 1801–3, member of the 'Unofficial C mittee.' 1802–7 and 1819–23, Minister of the Interior. 1825, chaired t secret committee for state reform. 1827, president of the State Counc and of the Committee of Ministers.

Kokóvtsov, Vladímir Nikoláevich (6.iv.1853–1943): Statesman. 1873–79, Minister of Justice. 1879–90, prison administration. 1896–1902, assistant Finance Minister. 1904–5 and 1906–14, Finance Minister. 1911–14, chairman of the Council of Ministers.

Konválov, Alexander Ivánovich (1875–1948): Liberal politician and textile manufacturer. Educated in England. Financed *Útro Rossíi*. 1912–17, deputy to the Fourth Duma (deputy president, leader of the Progressive Block). 1915–17, vice-chairman, Central War Industries Committee. 2 March 1917, Minister of Trade and Industry. Emigrated to France.

Kościusko, Tadeusz (1746–1817): Polish patriot. Fought against Britain in America (1777), and against Russia in Poland (1792). 1794, dictator and Commander-in-chief of Poland, eventually defeated and imprisoned. 1796, released by Paul I and retired to Western Europe.

Koshelëv, Alexander Ivánovich (9.v.1806–12.xi.1883): Slavophile reformer. 1823 member of the *Liubomúdrye*. Editor of *Rússkaia beséda* (1856–60), *Sélskoe blagoustróistvo* (1858–59). Active in preparing the Emancipation, he argued for the superiority of free over bonded labour.

Koshelëv, Rodión Alexándrovich (1749–1827): A close friend of Alexander I, he was briefly Paul I's ambassador to Denmark. He travelled extensively abroad, establishing contact with the leaders of Western European mysticism (Louis de Saint-Martin, Lavater, Eckartshausen, and the disciples of Swedenborg), and was active in the promotion of Russian Freemasonry. 1810, member of the State Council and Master of the Imperial Court. 1812, resigned all his offices, but continued to occupy an apartment at the Winter Palace, devoting himself to preaching mysticism in the salons of St Petersburg.

Kostomárov, Nikolái Ivánovich (4.v.1817–7.iv.1885): Historian and Ukrainian nationalist. 1846, professor of history, Kiev University. One of the founders of the Brotherhood of Cyril and Methodius. 1847, imprisoned when the Brotherhood was closed down. 1859–62, professor of history, St Petersburg University. 1861–62, one of the organizers of the journal *Osnóva*. 1862, forced to resign from the university after his failure to protest at the exile of P. V. Pávlov (q.v.).

Kotzebue, August von (3.v.1761–23.iii.1819): Dramatist and Russian agent. Originally from Weimar, he held various posts in Russia and was briefly to Siberia in 1800. His plays (which include *Armuth und Edelsinn*, ⁊; *Menschenhass und Reue*, 1790; *Die Kreuzfahrer*, 1803 and *Der arme ≀te*, 1811) are satirical attacks on the Romantic movement. 1817–19, ⁊nile in Germany for the Russian government, he ridiculed liberal ideas ⁊and, in particular, the student movement. His assassination by Karl Sand, a student at Jena University, led to a period of reaction in Russia.

Kovalévskii, Evgráf Petróvich (1790–1886): Educational administrator. 1856, educational curator, Moscow. 1858–61, Minister of Education. He attempted to bring in a code for student life which would have allowed organized student protest under faculty supervision, but was dismissed and replaced by the reactionary Admiral Putiátin (q.v.).

Kramskói, Iván Nikoláevich (27.v.1837–24.iii.1887): Painter. 1863, led the revolt in the Academy that led to the creation of the *Wanderers*. He saw his mission as the portrayal of a Russian Christ, taking on the suffering of the world (*Christ in the Wilderness*, 1872). See also his portraits of Nekrásov and Tolstoy and his *Inconsolable Sorrow* (1884).

Kravchínskii, Sergéi Mikhaílovich (**Stepniák**, S.) (1.vii.1851–11.xii.1895): Writer and terrorist. A member of the Chaikóvskii circle, he took part in the Movement to the People. Arrested, he fled abroad and took part in uprisings in Herzegovina and Italy. 1878, back in Russia illegally, he joined Land and Freedom. 4 August 1878, assassinated gendarme chief, N. V. Mezentsóv. 1890s, renounced terror, established the Free Russian Press in London and edited *Free Russia* (1890–92). Works include *Underground Russia* (London, 1881), *Russia under the Tzars*, 2 vols (London, 1885), *The Russian Peasantry* (London, 1888).

Kriuis, see **Cruys**.

Krivoshéin, Alexander Vasílevich (19.vii.1857–28.x.1921): Statesman. 1896–1906, deputy, then head of the bureau resettling peasants in Siberia. 1908–15, Minister of Agriculture. After the death of Stolýpin (q.v.), with whom he was closely associated, Krivoshéin was probably the strongest man in the Council of Ministers, but preferred to work behind the scenes, rather than take high office himself. He was behind the dismissal of Sukhomlínov (q.v.) in 1915. His attempt to create a 'government of confidence' led to his dismissal in October 1915.

Kropótkin, Pëtr Alexéevich (27.xi.1842–8.ii.1922): Anarchist. 1864–67, on an expedition exploring Far East, he witnessed the Baikal uprising. 1871, in Paris during the Commune. 1872, member of the Chaikóvskii circle. 1874–76, imprisoned in the Peter-Paul Fortress. 1876, escaped and fled abroad. 1879, published *Le révolté* in Geneva. 1881, expelled from Switzerland. 1883, sentenced to five years in prison, Lyon. 1886, released and moved to England where he concentrated on writing.

1900–9, formed the Organization of Russian Anarchists Abroad. 1917, returned to Russia.

Krüdener, Baroness Barbara-Julia, (1764–1825). Mystic. A wealthy sentimental novelist (works include *Valérie*), she turned to mysticism, with which she managed to influence Alexander I (1815). After the French Wars she took up with Anna Golítsyna and other fashionable mystics, and opened a salon in St Petersburg. Alexander eventually cooled towards her and sent her back to her Baltic estates.

Krylóv, Iván Andréevich (2.ii.1769–9.xi.1844): Writer. The son of an impoverished army officer, he began working as an office boy at the age of 10, had no formal education, but taught himself several languages. 1782, arrived in St Petersburg, where he wrote a number of plays. A quarrel with a theatre director led him into journalism. 1794, left St Petersburg, returning only after the accession of Alexander, when he resumed writing for the theatre. 1806, began writing the fables on which his main reputation is based.

Kulísh, Pantaléimon Alexándrovich (27.7.1819–2.2.1897): Ukrainian writer and one of the founders of the Brotherhood of Cyril and Methodius for which he was sentenced to four years' administrative exile (1847). Pardoned in 1850, he entered government service. He established a Ukrainian publishing house in St Petersburg. Works include *Ukraine, a Poem* (1843), *Mikhailo Chernyshenko* (1843), *The Black Rada, a Chronicle of 1633* (1845–57).

Kurákin, Alexander Borísovich (18.i.1752–24.vi.1818): Statesman and diplomat. Brought up with Paul Petróvich, he was made Vice-Chancellor when the latter became Paul I and was in charge of the College of Foreign Affairs until 1802. He took part in the preliminary negotiations for the Peace of Tilsit (1807). 1809–12, ambassador in Vienna and then Paris.

Kurákin, Alexéi Borísovich (1759–1829): Statesman. Procurator-General under Paul I, he was given charge of the Secret Expedition in December 1796. 1801, Member of the Commission for Review of Former Criminal Cases. 1807–11 Minister of the Interior.

Kurákin, Borís Ivánovich (20.vii.1676–17.x.1727): Diplomat. In Peter's entourage since 1683, he took part in all his major ventures (Azóv, Poltáva, etc.) 1710, negotiated the Russo-Hannoverian treaty. 1711–13, at the Utrecht Congress, managing to keep Britain from open hostility to Russia. 1717, accompanied Peter to Paris and participated in the Treaty of Amsterdam with France and Prussia. Although from 1711 he was ambassador in Holland, he was *de facto* shaper of Russian foreign policy. 1724–27, ambassador in Paris.

Kuropátkin, Alexéi Nikoláevich (17.iii.1848–16.i.1926): General. 1860s–80s, in Turkestan. 1877–78, Turkish War. 1890–98, commander in the Caspian. 1898–1904, War Minister. 7.ii.1904, commander of the Manchurian Army. 13.x.1904–3.iii.1905, Commander-in-chief of the Russian Army, relieved at his own request after the Battle of Mukden. February–July 1916, commander of Northern Front. July 1916–February 1917, Governor-General of Turkestan. From May 1917 until his death he lived on his estate in Russia and taught in a local secondary school.

Kustódiev, Borís Mikhaílovich (23.ii.1878–26.v.1927): Painter. He first exhibited in 1896, then travelled extensively in Western Europe. 1905–6, contributed to the satirical journals *Ádskaia póchta* and *Zhúpel*, where he first met the *Mir iskússtva* people, whom he joined in 1910. In 1909, he developed an illness which left the lower part of his body paralysed from 1916 onwards, although he continued to paint. The theme of his pre-Revolutionary paintings is mainly Russian merchant life.

Kutépov, Alexander Pávlovich (16.ix.1882–1930?): General. Son of a forest warden. 1904–5, in the Japanese War (decorated and transferred to Preobrazhénskii Regiment). 1914–17, twice wounded and decorated. February 1917, on leave from the Front, he was given command of a detachment to crush the uprising in Petrograd (unsuccessful). 1918–21, in the White army. Active in the White movement in emigration. 26 January 1930, he disappeared in Paris, believed kidnapped by the OGPU (Soviet Secret Police).

Kútler, Nikolái Nikoláevich (1859–1924): Statesman. 1899–1904, departmental director, Finance Ministry. 1904–5, deputy Minister of Finance and deputy Minister of the Interior. 1905–6, Minister of Agriculture. 1907–12, elected to the Second and Third Dumas (Kadet). After October 1917, he worked for Narkomfin (People's Commissariat for Finance) and Gosbank (Soviet State Bank).

Kutúzov (**Goleníshchev-Kutúzov**), Mikhaíl Illariónovich (5.ix.1745–16.iv.1813): Field Marshal. 1759, mathematics lecturer, Artillery School. 1764–65, in Poland. 1768–74 and 1787–91, in the Turkish Wars. 1792–94, mission to Constantinople. 1794, director, *kadétskii kórpus*. 1795–99, in Finland. 1799–1801, Governor of Lithuania. 1801–2, Governor of St Petersburg. 1802–5, retired. 1805, at the Battle of Austerlitz, he was forced to defer to Alexander I, who lost it. 1806–7, Governor of Kiev. 1808, in Moldavia. 1809–11, Governor of Lithuania. 1811–12, in Moldavia, negotiates Peace of Bucharest (29.vi.1812). 8.viii.1812, appointed Commander-in-chief, he drives Napoleon out of Russia. Highly rated by Suvórov (q.v.), one of Kutúzov's great strengths was his ability to get his enemies to underestimate him.

Lacy, Peter (29.ix.1678–30.iv.1751): Field Marshal. Served James II in the defence of Limerick at the age of 13. 1692, entered French service. 1697, in Polish service, invited to Russia by Peter the Great. 1708, commander of the left wing at Poltava. 1709–21, fought against the Danes, Swedes and Turks. 1720–21, commanded Russian landings on Swedish coast. 1727, expelled Maurice de Saxe from Kurland. 1733, War of Polish Succession. 1736, siege of Azóv. 1737, invasion of Crimea. 1741, Finland. 1742, suppressed a mutiny against foreign officers. 1743, retired to his estates in Livonia, of which he was made Governor. His son Maurice became a famous general in Austrian service.

La Harpe, Frédéric César de (6.iv.1754–30.iii.1838): Swiss *philosophe*. 1780, invited to Russia by Catherine to be the tutor of Alexander Pávlovich. 1795, dismissed for his liberal/revolutionary views. 1798–1800, a member of the Directory of the Helvetian Republic.

Lanceray, Evgénii (23.viii.1875–13.ix.1946): Painter. Worked together with his cousin Benois (q.v.) on *Mir iskússtva*, exhibiting in the 1903 *Contemporary Art* exhibition. 1905–6, contributed to *Ádskaia póchta* and *Zhúpel*. He has done some fine cityscapes of St Petersburg, but his main work is in book illustration and stage design. After the Revolution, he lived in the Caucasus and in Paris, but returned to Moscow in 1934.

Lariónov, Mikhaíl Fëdorovich (22.v.1881–10.v.1964): Painter. Influenced by the fauvists and by Russian naïve painting (the *lubók*). Member of the *Jack of Diamonds, Donkey's Tail, Mishen*. Works include *Rain* (1904), *Soldier Resting* (1911), *Spring* (1912). From 1915, stage designer for Diághilev (q.v.) (*Midnight Sun*, 1915; *Histoires naturelles*, 1916).

Lavróv, Pëtr (2.vi.1823–25.i.1900): Revolutionary. A colonel and professor of mathematics in the St Petersburg Artillery Academy. 1862, joined Land and Freedom. 1866, court-martialled for spreading revolutionary doctrine. His *Historical Letters* (1868–69) argued that the educated must create a society based on truth and justice to repay the people whose labour makes civilization possible and that the social order can only be remodelled by a small group, the moving force of history. 1870, escaped abroad and joined the First International.

Le Blond, Jean-Baptiste-Alexandre (1679–27.ii.1719): French architect and writer, recruited in 1716 by Lefort (q.v.). He was commissioned to draw up an overall plan for St Petersburg (1717), but this was not adopted. He designed two Imperial residences on the Gulf of Finland: Strélna and Peterhof.

Lefort, François (23.xii.1655–2.iii.1699): Swiss soldier and companion of Peter the Great. Arrived in Moscow in 1676, aged 20, after serving in the French and Dutch armies. At first he made no headway, but this changed after his marriage to a relation of Patrick Gordon's (q.v.) wife. 1676–81, two Crimean campaigns and the Russo-Turkish War. 1690, became very influential over Peter. 1691, lieutenant-general. 1695–96, joint commander of the Fleet during the Azóv campaigns.

Lelewel, Joachim (22.iii.1786–29.v.1861): Polish patriot and historian. 1815–18, 1821–24, professor of history, Wilno University, dismissed for membership of the *Filomaty* and *Filarety*. 1828, elected to the Diet. 1830, president of the Patriotic Society and member of the National Government.

Le Prince, Jean-Baptiste (1734–81): Painter. A pupil of Boucher, he arrived in Russia in 1758, visiting St Petersburg, Moscow, Finland and Siberia, this last in the company of Chappe d'Auteroche (q.v.). 1763, he returned to France with a great number of sketches, which served as the basis for the Russian scenes that brought him fame.

Lérmontov, Mikhaíl Iúrevich (2.x.1814–14.vii.1841): Poet. Of Scottish descent (Learmont). 1832, expelled from Moscow University. He then attended the Junker School, emerging as a cornet in the Life Guard Hussars. His literary career began with a poem *Death of a Poet*, protesting against the death of Pushkin (q.v.), which earned him a court martial and a posting to the Caucasus. His main works are the poem, *Demon*, and the novel, *A Hero of our Time*. He was killed in a duel.

Leskóv, Nikolái Semënovich (4.ii.1831–21.ii.1895): Satirist. Works include *Lady Macbeth of Mtsensk* (1865), *Cathedral Folk* (1872), *The Sealed Angel* (1873), *On the Edge of the World* (1875), *Trivialities of Clerical Life* (1878), *Night Birds* (1891). His work is mainly concerned with the ethical and spiritual basis of Russia life. In his early period, he advocated Orthodoxy but after a visit to Western Europe in 1875, he believed that the Church should be protestantized and removed from state control. In his later years, he became a Tolstoyan.

Levitán, Isaák Ilích (18.viii.1860–22.vii.1900): Landscape painter. Exhibited with the *Wanderers* from 1884, joining the movement in 1891. 1899–1906, associate member of *Mir iskússtva*. Works include *Evening Bells* (1892), *Haystacks* (1899), *River Bank after the Rain* (1899), *Eternal Peace* (1893). He was a close friend of Chekhov (q.v.).

Levítskii, Dmítrii Grigórevich (1735–4.iv.1822): Painter, the greatest portraitist of the eighteenth century. His works include portraits of Catherine the Great (in travelling clothes, 1770; in the temple of the Goddess of Justice, 1780; as Empress, 1785), Diderot, A. M. Golítsyn, Kokórinov and, at Catherine's request, the portraits of the pupils at the Smólny Institute. His last work is *Portrait of my Brother*, P. Levítskii, 1812.

Liádov, Anatól Konstantínovich (29.iv.1855–15.viii.1914): Composer. Studied under Rímskii-Kórsakov (q.v.). 1878, lecturer at the Conservatoire. 1880s, part of the Beliáev (q.v.) circle. A champion of 'Russianism' in music associated with Rachmaninov (q.v.) and Glière, he published a collection of Russian folk music. His own work includes piano compositions, tone poems, church music and orchestrations for the Diághilev (q.v.) ballet.

Liubímov, Nikolái Alexéevich (1830–96): Professor of physics, Moscow University. 1873, wrote an article for *Rússkii véstnik* attacking university autonomy and advocating government participation in the appointment of lecturers. Government support for him in the ensuing student troubles (1876) led to the resignation of S. M. Solovëv (q.v.) as rector of the university. In March 1882, A. P. Nikolái, the Minister of Education, made a further attempt to sack Liubímov, but intervention 'at the highest level' by Katkov (q.v.) and Pobedonóstsev (q.v.) ensured that it was Nikolái who was dismissed.

Lobachévskii, Nikolái Ivánovich (20.xi.1792–12.ii.1856): Mathematician. Spent almost his whole life at Kazán University. Unrecognized in his own lifetime, he is now seen as a great geometer, a pioneer of non-Euclidian theory. Works include *Principles of Geometry* (1829–30) and *Imaginary Geometry* (1835).

Lomonósov, Mikhaíl Vasílevich (1711–65): Philologist, poet, scientist and historian. The son of a fisherman, he became the first Russian Academician (1742). 1736–41, at the University of Marburg. 1741, assistant lecturer, Academy of Sciences. 1745, Professor of Chemistry, Academy of Sciences. 1757, he published *Reflections on the Usefulness of Ecclesiastical Books in the Russian Language* and *Russian Grammar*. His *History of Russia* began to appear in 1759, but its publication was only completed posthumously in 1766.

Lósenko, Ánton Pávlovich (1737–73): Painter. 1744, engaged as a chorister in the Imperial chapel but was dismissed when his voice broke (1753). 1758, worked under Le Lorrain at the Academy of Fine Arts, then in Paris and Italy. 1769, returned to Russia where his *Cain and Abel* was accepted by the Academy. 1770, *Vladímir and Rogneda* won him election to the Academy, of which he became director in 1772. Died in extreme poverty, despite Falconet's (q.v.) pleading on his behalf to Catherine.

Lukómskii, Alexander Sergéevich (10.vii.1868–25.i.1939): General. 1908, Young Turk. 1915–16, assistant War Minister. 1916–17, quartermaster-general at Stávka. March 1917, drafted the abdication manifesto signed by Nicholas II. August 1917, active in the Kornílov Revolt. 1918–20, in the White army.

Lvov, Geórgii Evgénevich (21.x.1861–7.iii.1925): *Zémstvo* activist, the first Prime Minister of Revolutionary Russia. 1904–5, organized *zémstvo* work for the wounded. 1906, First Duma (Kadet). 1914–17, a leader of the Union of *zémstvos* and towns. March–July 1917, Prime Minister.

Lvov, Nikolái Alexándrovich (4.iii.1751–22.xii.1803): Poet, illustrator and architect. Proponent of classicism in architecture (Névskii Gates, Peter-Paul Fortress, 1784–87; Post Office, 1782–89; Cathedral of Boris and Gleb, Torzhók, 1785–96). He illustrated Ovid's *Metamorphoses* and compiled a two-volume collection of Russian folk songs. Writer of sentimentalist poetry, fables, and opera librettos (*Coachmen at the Stage*, 1787).

Magnítskii, Mikhaíl Leóntevich (1778–21.x.1844): Statesman. In his early life a supporter of Speránskii (q.v.), he radically changed his views after the latter's fall and became a tireless persecutor of liberals in education.

Maiakóvskii, Vladímir Vladímirovich (7.vii.1893–14.iv.1930): Poet. 1908, joined the Moscow Bolshevik Party. 1909, after solitary confinement in Butýrki prison, he began writing poetry. 1912, joins futurists. Works include *Vladímir Maiakóvskii* (1913), *A Cloud in Trousers* (1915), *The Spinal Flute* (1916). He committed suicide.

Maklakóv, Vasílii Alexéevich (10.v.1869–15.vii.1957): Lawyer and statesman. Defence lawyer for Tagíev, Beilis (q.v.) and the signatories of the Výborg manifesto. 1906–17, represented Moscow in the State Duma (Kadet). 1917, ambassador to France.

Mámontov, Sávva Ivánovich (3.x.1841–6.iv.1918). Railway magnate and patron of the arts. 1870–90, he supported many artists in his house, Abrámtsevo. 1885–1904, founder and sponsor of his Private Russian Opera Company, which fostered Russian music. 1899, arrested on a charge of embezzlement and, although he was released only after an ambiguous verdict at his trial in 1900, which destroyed his marriage and almost ruined him financially, he recovered to become again a major patron of the arts, this time in Moscow.

Mártov, Julius (**Tsederbaum**, Iúlii Ósipovich) (24.xi.1873–4.iv.1923): Menshevik leader. He was the first to formulate the concept of 'agitation' among the workers ('On Agitation', 1896). 1903, broke with Lenin over the nature of the party, believing that Lenin's centralized, secret party must become corrupt ('Saviours or Destroyers?', 1911) and that revolutionaries must educate workers within the legal labour movement. He accepted the October Revolution as 'historically necessary', seeing the Mensheviks as the Soviet opposition rather than the opposition to the Soviet regime.

Mattarnovy, Johann (d. 1719): German architect. He designed Peter's Kunstkamera, or Cabinet of Curiosities (1718–25), the first building in Russia devoted to science and which housed Lomonósov's (q.v.)

observatory. It later became the Library of the Academy of Sciences. He also designed the first St Isaac's Cathedral (1717) and the second Winter Palace (1716).

Matvéev, Andréi Matvéevich (1701–39): Painter. Studied in the Netherlands (1716–27). On his return to Russia he was placed in charge of the team of painters employed by the Chancery of Urban affairs. He painted icons, decorative compositions and mythological subjects (the interiors of the churches of St Peter and St Paul, St Semën and St Anne).

Mazépa, Iván Stepánovich (1645–8.ix.1709): Cossack leader. 1687–1708, *hétman* of Left-Bank Ukraine. Fought on the side of Charles XII in the Great Northern War. His exploits have been celebrated in verse and music by Voltaire, Byron, Victor Hugo, Liszt and Tchaikovsky.

Méchnikov, Iliá Ilích (3.v.1845–2.vii.1916): Biologist. 1842, forced to resign his chair in Odessa, he set up his own laboratory. 1890, joined the Institut Pasteur, Paris, becoming its director in 1905.

Mendeléev, Dmítrii Ivánovich (27.i.1834–20.i.1907): Chemist. He did important work on the liquefaction of gases and was the first scientist to organize the elements into what became known as the Periodic Table (1869). Works include *The Principles of Chemistry* (1868–70) and *Essays in Historical Chemistry* (1911).

Ménshikov, Alexander Danílovich (6.xi.1673–12.xi.1729): Of humble birth, served in one of Peter's 'toy regiments', then became his adjutant. 1697–98, on the 'Great Embassy'. 1702, Governor of Schlüsselburg, then Governor-General of Ingria, Karelia and Estonia. 1707, made Prince of Izhóra. 1708, Governor of St Petersburg. 1708, destroyed Mazepa's capital, Baturin. 1714–15, accused of corruption. 1720, Head of the War College. 1723–24, accused of concealing over 30,000 runaway serfs on his estates. 1725, supported Catherine and dominated the Supreme Privy Council during her reign. May 1727, his daughter Anna affianced to Peter II. September 1727, disgraced and exiled to Siberia.

Ménshikov, Alexander Sergéevich (15.viii.1787–19.iv.1869): Admiral. His service was confined to staff appointments (1815, accompanied Alexander I abroad). 1827–55, adviser to Nicholas I on naval affairs, he was largely responsible for the poor showing of the Navy in the Crimean War. 1831–55, Governor-General of Finland, in addition to his naval responsibilities. 1852–53, led an unsuccessful mission to Constantinople.

Meshchérskii, Vladímir Petróvich (11.i.1839–10.vii.1914): Reactionary publicist. Editor of *Grazhdanín* (1872–1914).

Messerschmidt, Daniel Gotlieb (16.ix.1685–25.iii.1735): Ethnographer. 1716, invited to Russia by Peter I. 1720–27, journeyed to Siberia to study the native peoples, publishing a 10-volume study.

Meyerhold, Vsevólod Emílievich (28.i.1874–2.ii.1940): Actor and producer. 1898, actor in the Moscow Arts Theatre. 1902–5, producer in his own New Drama Company. 1905, in Stanislávskii's studio, Moscow. 1906–7, chief producer at Komissarzhévskaia's Theatre, St Petersburg and then at the Alexandrinskii Theatre. 1922–38, a leading producer of Soviet revolutionary theatre.

Miasoédov, Grigórii Grigórevich (7.iv.1834–18.xii.1911): Painter. 1870, member of the *Wanderers*. His works deal mainly with peasant themes with a strong element of social criticism, *The Zémstvo at Lunch* (1872), *Reading the Manifesto of 19 February 1861* (1873).

Miasoédov, Sergéi Nikoláevich (31.iii.1866–18.iii.1915): Gendarme colonel, unjustly hanged on a trumped-up charge of espionage as part of a manoeuvre by Guchkóv (q.v.) and Grand Duke Nikolái Nikoláevich to get rid of War Minister Sukhomlínov (q.v.).

Mickiewicz, Adam (24.xii.1798–26.xi.1855): Polish patriot and poet. His early poems (1815–23) were only published in full in 1948. 1817, a member of the *Filomaty* and *Filarety*. 1823, arrested and exiled to St Petersburg. After the 1830 uprising, he lived abroad.

Mikhailóvskii, Nikolái Konstantínovich (15.xi.1842–28.i.1904): Populist writer, journalist and sociologist. Put forward the idea of the intelligentsia's 'debt to the people' in the journal *Otéchestvennye zapíski/Notes of the Fatherland* for which he wrote, 1868–84. 1879, associated with The People's Will. 1892, editor of the liberal-populist paper, *Rússkoe bogátsvo/ Russian Wealth*.

Miliukóv, Pável Nikoláevich (15.i.1859–31.iii.1943): Historian and leader of the Kadet Party. 1886–94, lectured in history at Moscow University, dismissed for his sympathies for the student movement. He then lectured in Russian history at the universities of Sofia and Chicago. 1905, returned to Russia, joined the Union of Liberation and organized the Kadet Party, whose president he became in 1907. Elected to the Third and Fourth Dumas. March–April 1917, Foreign Minister, resigning over the 'Miliukov Note' pledging Russia to remain faithful to its wartime alliances.

Miliútin, Dmítri Alexéevich (28.vi.1816–25.i.1912): Reforming War Minister under Alexander II. Owed his education and early career to his uncle, P. D. Kiselëv (q.v.). 1839–45, in the Caucasus. 1845–56, professor of military geography, General Staff Academy. 1856–59, Chief of Staff, Caucasus Army. 1860, assistant War Minister. 1861, War Minister, in which capacity he brought in the 'Miliútin Reforms', modernizing the Russian army. 1881, dismissed by Alexander III.

Miliútin, Nicholas Alexéevich (6.vi.1818–26.i.1872): Statesman, peasant reformer. 1846, author of new statutes for St Petersburg. 1859, assistant Minister of the Interior, and the main motive force behind the Emancipation of the serfs. 1859–61 chairman of the commission for *zémstvo* reform. Dismissed in the spring of 1861 for liberalism. 1863, drafted reforms for Russifying Poland. 1864, State-Secretary for Polish Affairs. 1867, retired for health reasons.

Montferrand, Auguste Richard de (24.i.1786–28.vi.1858): Architect. Works include St Isaac's Cathedral (1815–58), Alexander column (1834) and restructuring the round rooms in the Winter Palace.

Mordvínov, Nikolái Semënovich (17.iv.1754–30.iii.1845): Admiral. 1774–77, served in the Royal Navy in North America. 1783, on Chichagóv's expedition to the Mediterranean. 1792, begins ship-building in Khérson and thus starting the Black Sea Fleet (rewarded by Paul I with a grant of land and 1,000 serfs). 1801, Naval Minister. Worked with Speránskii improving Russian finances. 1823–40, president of the Free Economic Society. Because of his liberal views, he was one of the Decembrists' candidates for government. 1826, he alone of the judges sentencing the Decembrists refused to recommend the death penalty, pointing out that it was illegal.

Morózov, Sávva Timoféevich (1861–1905): Wealthy Moscow textile magnate. 1900–4, subsidized Moscow Arts Theatre. 1901–5 subsidized Lenin's *Iskra*. 1904, financed two Union of Liberation newspapers. Committeed suicide when the Okhrána threatened to reveal his illegal political contacts.

Münnich, Burchard Christoph von (1683–1767): Field Marshal. Son of a Danish army officer. Served with French, Hessian and Polish armies. 1721, entered Russian service, entrusted with building of Ládoga Canal. 1730, Commander-in-chief. 1732, Field Marshal, president of the War College and Governor of St Petersburg. 1741, arrested on Elizabeth's seizure of power, sentenced to death, commuted to exile in Siberia. 1762, recalled by Peter III whom he survived to serve under Catherine.

Muravëv, Alexander Nikoláevich (10.x.1792–18.xii.1863): Decembrist. 1812–15 fought from Borodinó to La Fère-Champenoise (Russian, Prussian and Austrian decorations). 1816, founder of the Union of Salvation. Member of the Elizabeth and Virtue (1810), French (1814) and Three Virtues (1816–18) Masonic lodges. Member of the Union of Welfare. 1826, exiled to Siberia. 1848, returned to the army. 1855, Crimean War, invalided out in July to become Governor of Nízhnii Nóvgorod.

Muravëv, Mikhaíl Nikoláevich (24.ix.1796–29.viii.1866). Repentant Decembrist. 1812, wounded at Borodinó. 1813, fought at Dresden. 1815, transferred to Caucasus. 1820, retired on health grounds. Member of Holy Artel, Union of Salvation, and the directing nucleus of the Union of Welfare (Moscow Congress, 1821). After the uprising, released after interview with Nicholas I. 1827, deputy Governor of Vítebsk, then Governor of Mogilëv. 1830, repressed the Lithuanian uprising, earning the sobriquet of 'hangman'. 1835, Governor of Kursk. 1839, director of tax collection. 1856, Minister of State Domains. 1863, Governor-General of Vilno, Kovno, Grodno, and Minsk, during the Polish uprising.

Muravëv, Nikíta Mikhaílovich (9.ix.1795–28.iv.1843): Decembrist. 1813–15, fought from Dresden to Paris (much decorated). 1817, member of the Three Virtues Masonic Lodge. One of the founders of the Union of Salvation, a member of the directing nucleus of the Union of Welfare, leader of the Northern Society and author of its constitution for Russia. Sentenced to 20 years' hard labour, later reduced to ten.

Muravëv (-**Kárskii**), Nikolái Nikoláevich (14.vii.1793–18.x.1866): General. Fought in the French Wars. Member of the Holy Artel. 1820, on mission to Khiva. 1828, siege of Kars. 1832, envoy to the Porte and to Egypt at the height of the first Mohammed Ali Crisis, then commander of Russian troops in the Bosphorus. 1854–56, Viceroy in the Caucasus. 18 November 1855, takes Kars from the Turks. He was dismissed when his plan to deport the Chechens into Russia gave rise to renewed resistance on their part.

Muravëv-Apóstol, Matvéi Ivánovich (18.iv.1793–21.ii.1886): Decembrist. 1811, joined the Semënovskii Guards. 1812–15, fought from Vitebsk to Paris (much decorated). 1823, resigned his commission and retired to his estates. 1816, member of United Friends and Three Virtues masonic lodges. One of the founders of the Union of Salvation (Moscow conspiracy, 1817), member of the directing nucleus of the Union of Welfare (St Petersburg conference, 1820), and of the Southern Society. Participated in the uprising of the Chernígov Regiment. Condemned to 20 years' hard labour, reduced to exile in Siberia.

Muravëv-Apóstol, Sergéi Ivánovich (23.x.1795–13.vii.1826): Decembrist. 1812–15, fought from Vítebsk to Paris (much decorated). 1815, transferred to the Semënovskii Guards. 1817, member and master of ceremonies of the Three Virtues Masonic Lodge (until December 1818). One of the founders of the Union of Salvation (Moscow Conspiracy, 1817), and of the directing nucleus of the Union of Welfare (St Petersburg Conference, 1820). Leader of the uprising of the Chernígov Regiment. Hanged in Peter-Paul Fortress.

Músin-Púshkin, Alexéi Ivánovich (16.iii.1744–1.ii.1817): Historian. 1794, published his *Historical Research on the site of the Old Russian Principality of*

Tmutarakán. 1795, purchased from the Spaso-Iaroslávskii Monastery the manuscript of *Slóvo o polkú Ígoreve*, the authenticity of which has remained in dispute ever since.

Músorgskii, Modést Petróvich (19.iii.1839–16.iii.1881): Composer. Originally a guards officer, then a civil servant. His music makes great use of Russian popular themes, which made it unacceptable to nineteenth-century audiences, who only heard versions prettified by other composers. It is only in the late twentieth century that the originals have been fully appreciated. Works include *Night on a Bare Mountain* (1867), *Borís Godunóv* (1868–74), *Khovánshchina* (1872–80), *Pictures at an Exhibition* (1874) and many songs (including the *Songs and Dances of Death*, 1875–77).

Nattier, Jean-Marc (1685–1766): Painter. Persuaded by Lefort (q.v.) to come to Amsterdam in early 1717 to paint *The Battle of Poltáva*, he then painted portraits of Catherine and of Peter the Great. 1740s, portrait painter to the French royal family.

Necháev, Sergéi Gennádievich (20.ix.1847–21.xi.1883): Revolutionary. The son of a serf, largely self-educated, he joined revolutionary circles in St Petersburg in 1868. 1869, produced the *Revolutionary Catechism* with Bakúnin (q.v.) in Switzerland. On his return to Russia he became notorious by ordering his followers to murder one of their number whose loyalty he suspected. His behaviour at his trial shocked many and he was disavowed by Marx and Bakúnin. However, he became a hero to revolutionary terrorists, with whom he continued to correspond from prison. He is the model for the anti-hero of Dostoévskii's (q.v.) *Devils*.

Nekrásov, Nikolái Alekséevich (28.xi.1821–27.xii.1877): Poet. 1842, critic for *Otéchestvennye zapíski*. 1846, part owner of *Sovreménnik*. 1868–77, editor of *Otéchestvennye zapíski*. His poems are passionate denunciations of greed, serfdom and exploitation (e.g.: *The Peddlars*, 1861; *Frost, the Red-Nosed*, 1863; *Who then is Happy in Russia?*, 1863–76).

Nekrásov, Nikolái Vissariónovich (20.x.1879–7.v.1940): Politician. 1908–17, Duma deputy (Kadet). 1914–18, vice-president of the Union of *Zémstvos* and Towns. 1916, vice-president of the Duma. March 1917, Minister of Transport. Remained in Russia after October 1917.

Nemiróvich-Dánchenko, Vladímir Ivánovich (11.xii.1858–25.iv.1943): Stanislávskii's partner at the Moscow Arts Theatre.

Nesselrode, Karl Vasílevich (2.xii.1780–11.iii.1862): Statesman. Educated in Berlin, he joined the Russian Navy as a midshipman and then served briefly in the Horse Guards before entering the Diplomatic Service (1801). He soon became the close confidant of Alexander I, and then of Nicholas I, and was effectively in charge of foreign affairs from 1814 until 1856. He attended the Congresses of Vienna (1814–15), Troppau-Laibach (1820–21), and Verona (1822).

Nésterov, Mikhaíl Vasílevich (19.v.1862–18.x.1942): Painter. 1889, joined the *Wanderers*. Worked with Vasnetsóv (q.v.) decorating St Vladímir's, Kiev. His greatest works are expressions of Orthodox faith: *Hermit* (1889), *The Boy Bartholomew's Vision* (1889), *The Bride of Christ* (1897), *The Youth of St Sergius of Radónezh* (1897).

Nikítin, Iván Nikítich (*c.* 1680–after 1742): Painter. The son of a priest, he became the pupil of the Dutch painter Schoonebeeck. 1715, portrait of Peter the Great. 1720, official court painter. 1732, accused of plotting against Birón (q.v.) and exiled to Tobólsk. 1742, pardoned by Elizabeth.

Nóvikov, Nikolái Ivánovich (27.iv.1743–31.vii.1820): Freemason and publisher. 1767–68, report writer for the Legislative Commission. 1769, published the satirical journal *Trúten'* which attacked Catherine's *Vsiákaia vsiáchina*. 1775, Freemason. 1779, manager of Moscow University Press. 1783, head of a major publishing enterprise. 1791, his publishing enterprises were suspended by the government. 1792, arrested and sentenced to 15 years in Schlüsselburg. 1796, freed by Paul.

Novosíltsev, Nikolái Nikoláevich (1768–8.iv.1838): Statesman. Introduced to Alexander Pávlovich by Czartoryski (q.v.). Member of Alexander I's 'Unofficial Committee'. 1813, vice-president of the provisional council of the Grand Duchy of Warsaw. 1816, high commissioner in Poland.

Obréskov, Alexéi Mikhaílovich (1718–87): Diplomat. 1752, ambassador to the Porte. 1769–71, imprisoned by the Turks. 1772, one of the authors of the treaty of Kuchuk-Kainardji.

Óbruchev, Nikolái Nikoláevich (21.xi.1830–25.vi.1904): General. 1858, co-founder of *Voénnyi sbórnik* which he co-edited with Chernyshévskii (q.v.). 1762–64, member of Land and Freedom. 1863, refused to take part in suppressing the Polish uprising, for which he was exiled to France. 1881–98, Chief of the Main Staff and one of the authors of the Franco-Russian Alliance.

Odóevskii, Vladímir Fëdorovich (1.viii.1803–27.ii.1869): Writer and music critic. 1823–25, president of the *Liubomúdrye*. Works include *Beethoven's Last Quartet* (1830), *The Brigadier* (1833), *Princess Mimi* (1834), *Princess Zizi* (1839), *Sylphides* (1837), *Salamander* (1840), *Russian Nights* (1844). He also wrote about Russian folk song and religious music and a number of school textbooks.

Ogarëv, Nikolái Platónovich (24.xi.1813–31.v.1877): Revolutionary publicist. Chiefly known for his collaboration with Herzen (q.v.) in publishing *Kólokol* in London (1857–67).

Olénin, Alexander Nikaoláevich (28.xi.1763–17.iv.1843): Soldier, scholar and statesman. Fought in the Swedish (1789–90) and Polish (1792) Wars. 1786, elected to Academy of Sciences, one of the authors of the Russian–Slavic Dictionary. 1806, deciphered the Tmuturakán stone. 1811, director of the Imperial Public Library. 1817, president of the Academy of Arts.

Orlóv, Alexéi Fëdorovich (8.x.1786–9.v.1861): Soldier and gendarme. 1805–14, French Wars. 1825, involved in crushing the Decembrists on Senate Square. 1831, put down the 'cholera riot'. 1833, mission to Istanbul. 1844–56, Head of the Third Department. 1856–58, Chairman of the State Council and Committee of Ministers.

Orlóv, Grigórii Grigórevich (6.x.1734–13.iv.1783): Lover of the future Catherine II and father of her son Alexéi Bóbrinskii (1762). 1756–62, Seven Years' War. Active in bringing Catherine to the throne. 1765, first chairman of the Free Economic Society. 1771, puts down the Moscow plague riot. 1772, negotiates with the Turks at Fokshani. 1772, falls from favour.

Orlóv, Iván Grigórevich (1733–91): The eldest of the five Orlóv brothers who helped Catherine to the throne in 1762. After Catherine's seizure of power, he retired from the army and refused all promotions and decorations. 1767, took part in the Legislative Commission.

Orlóv, Mikhaíl Fëdorovich (25.iii.1788–19.iii.1842): Decembrist and brother of Alexéi Fëdorovich Orlóv (q.v.). Fought at Austerlitz (1805), Friedland (1807) and from Borodinó to Paris (1812–14) where he was one of the signatories of the French capitulation. 1814, mission to Norway and Sweden. 1817, a member of the Arzamás circle. Founder member of the Order of Russian Knights. 1818, member of the nucleus of the Union of Welfare (Moscow Congress, 1821), leader of the Kishinëv organization. 1825, his brother's influence ensured that he was punished lightly. 1826–42, lived in Moscow.

Ostermán, Andréi Ivánovich (30.v.1686–20.v.1747): Statesman. The son of a Westphalian pastor, he entered Russian service in 1711. 1718, at the Åland Conference. 1721, Treaty of Nystadt. 1720–22, Peter's chief collaborator in drafting the Table of Ranks. 1726, on the Supreme Privy Council. 1725–41, in charge of Russian foreign affairs. All-powerful during the reign of Ivan VI. On Elizabeth's seizure of power, he was arrested and sentenced to be broken on the wheel, commuted to exile in Siberia, where he died.

Ostróvskii, Alexander Nikoláevich (31.iii.1823–2.vi.1886): Playwright. 1847, his first play, *Picture of a Family*, was banned by the censor for eight years. He dominated the Russian stage in the third quarter of the nineteenth century with one or two new plays every year, e.g.: *Keep it in* *the Family* (1850); *Poverty is no Crime* and *You Can't Live as You Please* (1854); *Your Drink, My Hangover* (1856); *They Could not Get on* (1858); *The Storm* (1859), etc.

Ózerov, Vladisláv Alexándrovich (30.ix.1769–5.ix.1816): The creator of Russian sentimental tragic drama. His plays – *Oedipus in Athens* (1804), *Fingal* (1805), and *Dmítri Donskói* (1806) – were extremely popular. But his *Polyxena* (1808) flopped. Ózerov was much attacked by the *Beséda* group, and he was dismissed from his job without a pension. He went mad, burnt all his papers and died.

Ózols, Ianis P. (10.ii.1885–22.xii.1919). Latvian revolutionary. Social-Democratic Duma deputy. 1907, sentenced to four years' hard labour in Siberia for fomenting mutiny in the armed forces. 1912, fled to Britain. Shot in independent Latvia for his communist activities.

Pahlen, Peter Alexéevich (17.vii.1745–13.ii.1826): General and statesman. Governor of Riga (1792), and Kurland (1795). 1797, disgraced. 1798, Governor of St Petersburg. Chancellor of the Maltese Order. 1801, one of the main conspirators against Paul, dismissed by Alexander in June.

Pallás, Peter Simon (22.ix.1741–8.ix.1811): Geographer, botanist and traveller. 1768–82, led expeditions to central Russia and Siberia (*Travels in Various Provinces of Russia*, 3 vols, 1773–78; *The Flora of Russia*, 2 vols, 1784–88). 1782, on the Advisory Commission on Education.

Pánin, Nikíta Ivánovich (18.ix.1718–31.iii.1783): Statesman. 1747–59, ambassador to Denmark, then Sweden. 1760–73, tutor to Paul Petróvich. 1762, helps Catherine to the throne. 1763–81, head of the College of Foreign Affairs. Early 1770s, involved in the plot in favour of Paul Petróvich. 1781, dismissed.

Pánin, Nikíta Petróvich (17.iv.1770–1.iii.1837): General and statesman. 1795, Governor of Lithuania. 1796, Russian representative drawing up Russo-Prussian frontier. 1797, ambassador in Berlin. 1799–1800, Vice-Chancellor. March-November 1801, head of the College of Foreign Affairs. 1805, prohibited from entering St Petersburg or Moscow, he devoted the rest of his life to embellishing his estate at Dugino near Smolénsk.

Pánin, Pëtr Ivánovich (1721–15.iv.1789): General. 1756–62, Seven Years' War. 1762, Governor-General of East Prussia. 1768–70, Turkish War (Battle of Bender). One of the leaders of the Pánin party. 1774–75, commanded troops against Pugachëv.

Pánin, Victor Nikítich (28.iii.1801–1.iv.1874): Statesman. He had a great talent for languages, his German impressing even Goethe. 1839–62, Minister of Justice. Member of the various committees on Emancipation.

Paskévich, Iván Fëdorovich (8.v.1782–20.i.1856): Field Marshal. 1806–12, Turkish War. 1812–14, French War. 1825, member of the court sentencing the Decembrists. 1827–31, commander in the Caucasus. 1830, repressed Polish uprising. 1831–56, viceroy of Poland. 1849, repressed Hungarian uprising.

Pávlov, Iván Petróvich (14.ix.1849–27.ii.1936): Physiologist. Graduate of the Riazán Theological Academy and Riazán Seminary. 1870, studied science at St Petersburg University. 1875, Medical-Military Academy. 1884–86, Breslau and Leipzig universities. 1890–1924, professor of pharmacology, Medical-Military Academy. 1904, Nobel Prize for medicine. 1925–36, head of the Physiology Institute, Academy of Sciences. His most famous work was in the field of animal behaviour, particularly conditioned reflex in dogs.

Pávlov, Platón Vasílevich (7.x.1823–29.iv.1895): Historian. 1847–59, professor of Russian history, Kiev University. 1859, one of the organizers of the Kiev Sunday Schools. 1862, implicated in the Kiev-Khárkov secret society. March 1862, exiled to Vetlúga after a lecture in which he had argued that the intelligentsia should get closer to the people. 1866, returned to teaching. 1875–85, professor of art history and theory, Kiev University.

Pávskii, Gerasím Petróvich (1787–1863): Archpriest. 1814–35, professor of Hebrew, St Petersburg Theological Academy, president of the Bible Society. Writer of Hebrew Grammar and Russian-Hebrew Dictionary. The first Russian to argue that the *Psalms* were not all the work of David. 1820, editor of the Bible Society's Russian translations. 1844, his translations of *Book of Job* and the *Song of Songs* (secretly copied and distributed by his students) were destroyed and he was dismissed. 1861, Alexander II appointed him priest in Kazán Cathedral, decorated him and gave him a pension.

Peróv, Vasílii Grigórevich (21.xii.1834–29.v.1882): Painter. 1870, member of the *Wanderers*. Works include *Village Easter Procession* (1861), *The Last Inn by the Town Gate* (1868), and portraits of Ostróvskii (q.v.) (1871) and Dostoévskii (q.v.) (1872). 1877, broke with the *Wanderers* and painted scenes of country pursuits.

Peróvskaia, Sofía Lvóvna (1.ix.1853–3.iv.1881): Terrorist. 1871–72, member of the Chaikóvskii (q.v.) circle. 1872–74, took part in the Movement to the People. Arrested in 1874, she was one of the defendants in the 'Trial of the 193' (1877–79). 1878, joined Land and Freedom. 1.iii.1881, one of the assassins of Alexander II. The first woman in Russia to be hanged for political reasons.

Pestél, Pável Ivánovich (24.vi.1793–13.vii.1826): Decembrist. 1811, joined the Litóvskii Guards. 1812–14, fought from Borodinó to Troyes (much decorated by Russians, Prussians, Austrians, Bavarians). 1821, in charge of staff work connected with Greek uprising, then regimental commander, Tulchin. Member of the United Friends and of the Three Virtues Masonic Lodges. Member of the Union of Salvation and of the directing nucleus of the Union of Welfare. Organizer and leader of the Southern Society. Author of *Russian Law*. Arrested the day before the uprising in the North. Hanged in the Peter-Paul Fortress.

Petrashévskii (**Butashévich-Petrashévskii**), Mikhaíl Vasílevich (1.xi.1821–7.xii.1866): Revolutionary. 1844, meetings in his house discuss political ideas. After 1848 they attracted police suspicion. 1849, 39 members of his group arrested and, although all that could be proved against them was a 'conspiracy of ideas', 15 of them were condemned to death, and six to forced labour or deportation to Siberia. He co-authored a *Pocket Dictionary of Foreign Words* (1845–46).

Petrunkévich, Iván Ilích (1843–14.vi.1926): Kadet leader. Late 1870s, active in the *zémstvos*. 1904, organizer and president of the Union of Liberation. 1906, Deputy to the First Duma, disbarred and imprisoned for signing the Výborg Manifesto. 1909–15, chair of the Kadet Central Committee, editor of *Rech*.

Pirogóv, Nikolái Ivánovich (13.xi.1810–23.xi.1881): Surgeon, humanist and educator. Professor of surgery, Dorpat University. At the outbreak of the Crimean War, he organized a medical corps. His article 'Vital Questions' attacked bureaucratic corruption and proposed a programme for national revival through a liberal education system open to all. 1856–61, educational curator for Odessa and Kiev, where he presided over the beginning of the Sunday School Movement. 1861, dismissed by Admiral Putiátin (q.v.). 1862, recalled and continued to press for liberal education until his retirement, which he spent as a country doctor in Ukraine.

Písarev, Dmítri Ivánovich (2.x.1840–4.vii.1868): Radical writer. An expounder of 'nihilism', he denied any value to art that did not serve social and revolutionary ends and for this reason attacked Pushkin (q.v.). 1862, arrested for spreading revolutionary propaganda. Accidentally drowned two days after his release from prison.

Plehve, Viachesláv Konstantínovich (1846–15.vii.1904): Statesman. 1881, director of the Police Department. 1889, State Secretary for Finland. 1902, Minister of the Interior. Assassinated by Egór Sazónov.

Plekhánov, Geórgii Valentínovich (29.xi.1856–30.v.1918): 'The father of Russian Marxism.' Originally a populist, he became a Social-Democrat in the 1880s, founding the Group for the Emancipation of Labour abroad. Although a major Marxist theoretician and heavyweight in the Socialist International, he had very little contact with or influence on the Russian Labour Movement.

Pobedonóstsev, Konstantín Petróvich (21.v.1827–10.iii.1907): Statesman. Tutor to the future Alexander III and Nicholas II, he exercised great influence as an advocate of autocracy and opponent of democracy, which he saw as fraudulent. 1860–65 professor of Civil Law, Moscow University. 1880–1905 procurator of the Holy Synod.

Pogódin, Mikhaíl Petróvich (ii.xi.1800–8.xii.1875): Historian and pan-Slav. Born a serf, emancipated in 1806. 1826, lecturer then professor of History, Moscow University, resigning in 1844. A lifelong champion of conservative, nationalist, pan-Slav views which he propagated in his two journals, *Moskóvskii védomosti* (1827–30) and *Moskvitiánin* (1841–56).

Poirot, Auguste (Monsieur Auguste) (1780–1844): French dancer and choreographer, came to Russia in 1798. Initially as a teacher of ballroom dancing, he became famous as a ballet dancer and choreographer. Didelot (q.v.) wrote two ballets for him: *Raoul de Créqui* (1819), and *The Captive of the Caucasus* (1823).

Polénov, Vasílii Dmítrievich (20.v.1844–18.vii.1927): Painter. 1878, joined the *Wanderers*. 1876–78, war correspondent in the Balkans. Painted *A Moscow Courtyard* (1878). He became increasingly religious, completing a cycle on the life of Christ (1909). He also designed sets for Mámontov's (q.v.) private opera.

Popóva, Liubóv Sergéevna (24.iv.1889–25.v.1924): Painter. Her first paintings were traditional landscapes but, after a year in Paris, she underwent a radical change of style reflecting cubist and futurist ideas. 1914, exhibited with *Búbnovyi valét*, and in 1915 with *Tramway V* and *0.10*, joining Malevich's *Supremus*. She died of scarlet fever, two days after her son, whom she was nursing.

Potëmkin, Grigórii Alexándrovich (13.ix.1739–5.x.1791): General, statesman and lover of Catherine II. 1762, helped Catherine to the throne. 1763, assistant procurator of the Holy Synod. 1767, on Catherine's Commission. 1768–74, Turkish War. 1770, vice-president of the War College. 1776, Governor of New Russia. 1784, president of the War College. 1787–91, Turkish War.

Priáshnikov, Illarión Mikhaílovich (20.iii.1840–12.iii.1894): Painter. Founder-member of the *Wanderers* and an influential teacher. Works include *Peasants Driving Home* (1872), *Boys on a Fence* (1883), *Religious Procession in a Village* (1893).

Prokófiev, Sergéi Sergéevich (11.iv.1891–5.iii.1953): Composer. The pre-Revolutionary Russian public was unable to accept his music. Although his first piano concerto (1912) won him the Rubinstein Prize, his second (1913) was booed and Glázunov ostentatiously walked out of his sifonietta (1915). Diághilev (q.v.), however, recognized his genius, commissioning the Scythian Suite in 1914 and *Joker* in 1915.

Prokopóvich, Feofán (8.vi.1681–8.ix.1736): Theologian. Temporarily converted to Catholicism, to study in Rome. 1702, returned to Kiev and reconverted to Orthodoxy, becoming an outspoken critic of 'Latinism'. 1718, Peter entrusted him with the writing of the *Spiritual Regulation* and had him made Bishop of Pskov despite the opposition of many senior churchmen. 1725, Archbishop of Nóvgorod. His oration at Peter's funeral is seen as one of the great defences of his achievements.

Protopópov, Alexander Dmítrievich (18.xii.1866–19.xii.1917): Statesman. 1907–17, Octobrist deputy to the Duma. 1914, vice-president of the Duma, member of the Progressive Block. 1916–1917, his acceptance of the Ministry of the Interior made him a much hated figure. Shot by the Bolsheviks.

Przheválskii, Nikolái Mikhaílovich (31.iii.1839–20.x.1888): Explorer of Central Asia. Explored the Ussuri region (1867–69), Mongolia, China and Tibet (1870–73), Central Asia (1876–77) and Tibet (1879–80 and 1883–85). A number of flora and fauna bear his name.

Pugachëv, Emelián (1742–10.i.1775): Leader of a rebellion. A Don Cossack, he served in the Seven Years' War. September 1773, pretending to be Peter III, he raised a rebellion among the Yaík Cossacks, which became widespread, incorporating Bashkir tribesmen. Executed in Moscow.

Purishkévich, Vladímir Mitrofánovich (12.viii.1870–ii.1920): Politician of the extreme right. 1905, co-founder of the Black-Hundred Union of Russian People. 1907–17, Duma deputy. 1916, makes speeches attacking Rasputin, of whom he was one of the assassins.

Pushkin, Alexander Sergéevich (25.v.1799–29.i.1837): Russia's greatest poet. Educated at the lycée in Tsárskoe seló, where he already wrote subversive poetry for which he was exiled to South Russia. The extraordinary beauty of his Russian is apparently untranslatable, despite many distinguished efforts to do so. He was killed in a duel over his wife's honour. Major works include *Ruslán and Liudmílla* (1820), *Captive in the Caucasus* (1821), *Gypsies* (1824), *Borís Godunóv* (1825), *Eugene Onégin* (1831), *Bronze Horseman* (1833).

Putiátin, Efím Vasílevich (7.xi.1804–16.x.1883): Admiral. 1822–25, circumnavigated the globe, visiting Russian America. 1827, at Navarino. 1852–55, mission to Japan. 1855–57 and 1858–61, naval attaché, London.

1857, second mission to Japan. 1861, Minister of Education, dismissed for failing to control student riots.

Quarenghi, Giacomo (1744–1817): Architect. Came to Russia in 1780. His buildings include: the English Palace at Tsárskoe seló, 1781–89; the Hermitage Theatre, 1783–87; the Academy of Sciences, 1784–87; a country house at Lialichy near Chernígov for Zavadóvskii (q.v.), 1794–95; Alexander Palace at Tsárskoe seló, 1796.

Rachmaninov (Rakhmáninov), Sergéi Vasílevich (20.iii.1873–28.iii.1943). Composer. Early success with *Aleko* (1893) and *The Rock* (1894) was followed by disaster when his first symphony (1896) met great hostility. Rescued by Mámontov's (q.v.) invitation to conduct his private opera (1897–98), he nonetheless suffered from a crisis of confidence and had to seek psychiatric help. His second piano concerto (1901) was well received, and Diághilev (q.v.) selected it for his Russian concerts in Paris (1906). His second symphony (1908), third piano concerto (1909), *The Bells* (1913), and *Vespers* (1915) established him as a major composer.

Radíshchev, Alexander (20.viii.1749–12.ix.1802): Writer. May 1790, his *Journey from St Petersburg to Moscow* (inspired by Sterne's *Sentimental Journey*) aroused Catherine's anger and he was condemned to death, commuted to ten years in Siberia and loss of noble status. 1796, freed by Paul I and permitted to live on his estates. 1801, Alexander recalled him to St Petersburg to codify the laws with Zavadóvskii (q.v.), but within a very short time he committed suicide.

Rakhmáninov, Iván Gerasímovich (1750s–27.i.1807): Translator and educator. 1785, translates Voltaire. 1788, established his own printing house. 1788–90, publishes the journals *Útrennie chasý* and *Póchta dúkhov*. 1791, begins printing Voltaire's complete works. January 1794, printing works seized by the authorities.

Rakhmáninov, Sergéi see **Rachmaninov**.

Raspútin (Nóvykh), Grigórii Efímorich (*c.* 1864–17.xii.1916): Faith healer and favourite of the Empress Alexandra. His influence derived from his ability to alleviate the symptoms of Alexéi Nikoláevich's haemophilia. He was reputed to have the power to appoint and dismiss ministers and other high officials, as well as extraordinary sexual prowess. In fact his influence has probably been greatly exaggerated. Murdered by Iusúpov (q.v.), Purishkévich (q.v.) and Grand Duke Dmítrii Pávlovich.

Rastrelli, Bartolomeo Francesco (1700–71): Architect. He reconstructed Tressini (q.v.) and Michetti's second Winter Palace in time for the Empress's return from Moscow in 1732. It was during Elizabeth's reign however that he really came into his own, rebuilding the Summer Palace on the Fontánka, Peterhof, Tsárskoe seló and the Winter Palace, completing the Aníchkov Palace, and building the Stróganov Palace, the Cathedral for the Smólny Convent and St Andrew's Church Kiev. After Elizabeth's death his influence waned.

Razumóvskii, Kiríll Grigórevich (18.iii.1728–3.i.1803): The last *hétman* of Ukraine. 1746–65, president of the Academy of Sciences, but took no part in its proceedings, except to give support to Lomonósov (q.v.). 1750–64, *hétman* of Ukraine. 1762, active in Catherine's *coup d'état.* 1768–71, on Catherine's Council.

Répin, Ília Efímovich (24.vii.1844–29.ix.1930): Painter. Son of a military colonist he studied under Ivan Kramskói (q.v.), and then in Italy and Paris. 1871, joined the *Wanderers.* 1893, professor in the Imperial Academy of Arts. Works include *The Volga Boatmen* (1873), *Easter Procession in Kursk* (1880–83), *Arrest of a Propagandist* (1880–92), *They did not Expect Him* (1884–88), *Ivan the Terrible and his Son Ivan* (1885), *The Zaporózhian Cossacks Write to the Turkish Sultan* (1891), and portraits of Músorgskii (1881), Tretiakóv (1883), Stásov (1883).

Repnín, Nikolái Vasílevich (11.iii.1734–12.v.1801): Diplomat and Field Marshal. 1756–62, Seven Years' War. Ambassador in Prussia (1762–63) and Poland (1763–68) (Warsaw Treaty, 1768). 1768–74, Turkish War (one of the authors of the Treaty of Kuchuk-Kainardji). 1779, mediator between Austria and Prussia in the Peace of Teschen. 1787–91, Turkish War. 1798, unsuccessful mission to Austria and Prussia to form an anti-French alliance.

Rimskii-Korsakov, Nikolái Andréevich (6.iii.1844–8.vi.1908): Originally a naval officer. 1871, professor in the Conservatoire. He was the dominant figure and the chief protagonist of 'Russian' music at the turn of the century. His dismissal from the Conservatoire in 1905 for supporting the students caused a sensation, as did the banning by the censors of his *Coq d'Or* shortly before his death. Although his output was great (15 operas alone), he is now chiefly remembered for *Sheherazade.*

Rinaldi, Antonio (*c.* 1710–10.iv.1794): Architect. 1751, came to Russia. 1756–90, court architect. One of the chief exponents of Baroque in Russia: Palace of Peter III (1758–62), Chinese Palace (1762–68), Sliding Hill, Oranienbaum, (1762–74), Gátchina (1768–81).

Ródichev, Fëdor Izmáilovich (1856–?): Kadet leader. 1894, one of the authors of the Tver *zémstvo* address to the Tsar, for which he was banned from public life until 1904. 1904–5, participated in the *zémstvo* congresses. 1907–17, member of all four Dumas.

Rodziánko, Mikhaíl Vladímirovich (9.ii.1859–24.i.1924): Statesman. 1907–17, elected to the Third and Fourth Dumas (Octobrist). 1911–17, President of the Duma. 1915–18, on the Special Council for Defence. He is mainly remembered for his warnings to the Tsar in February 1917 that he would lose his throne if he failed to reform.

Roerich, Nikolái Konstantínovich (27.ix.1874–13.xii.1947): Painter. He participated in *Mir iskússtva* from 1902, and was elected its chairman in 1910. His paintings and set designs are mainly of Old Rus' and in a particular old-Russian style. He designed sets for the Diághilev (q.v.) company: *Polóvtsian Dances, the Maid of Pskov* (1909), *The Rite of Spring* (1913), for the Moscow Arts Theatre and for Zimín's Private Opera. 1919, he met Rabindranath Tagore in London, and in 1923 went to India, living there from 1936 until his death.

Rókotov, Fëdor Stepánovich (1735?–12.xii.1808): Painter. Born a serf. 1765, received into the Academy for his painting *Venus and Cupid.* A fine colourist, he became much sought after. He has left an enormous number of portraits of his contemporaries.

Romme, Gilbert (1750–95): French Revolutionary. To pay for his studies in Paris, he became tutor to the Stróganov family. 1779, he followed them to Russia and continued to teach young Paul Stróganov (q.v.). 1786, he took Paul to Europe, accompanied by Voroníkhin (q.v.) whose freedom from serfdom he had just secured. 1789, after two years in Switzerland, Romme took his Russian companions round the Jacobin clubs in France, and was himself elected to the Constituent Assembly. Condemned to death by a Revolutionary Tribunal, he committed suicide to avoid the guillotine.

Romodánovskii, Fëdor Iúrevich (*c.* 1640–17.ix.1717): Statesman and childhood companion of Peter the Great. 1686–1717, first head of the *Preobrazhénskii Prikáz.* He enjoyed the Tsar's complete confidence and had great power. 1695–96 and 1697–98, *de facto* ruler of Russia in Peter's absence.

Rossi, Carlo (18.xii.1775–6.iv.1849): Architect. The son of an Italian ballerina, his work, inspired by ancient Rome, includes: the Elágin Palace (1818–22), the General Staff Arch (1819–29), the Aklexandrinskii Theatre (1827–32), the Senate and the Holy Synod (1829–34).

Rostopchín, Fëdor Vasílevich (12.iii.1763–18.i.1826): Statesman. 1798–1801, in charge of foreign affairs. 1812–14, Governor of Moscow. He always denied being the author of the fire of Moscow (1812). His daughter was the well-known French writer Madame de Ségur.

Rostóvtsev, Iákov Ivánovich (28.xii.1803–6.ii.1860): Statesman and general. 12.xii.1825, informed the future Nicholas I of the Decembrist conspiracy, but mentioned no names. Member of the Secret, Main and Editorial committees on Emancipation on which he championed peasant rights.

Rózanova, Ólga (1886–1918): Painter. 1911, joined the Union of Youth. 1913, issued her manifesto, *The Bases of the New Creation and why it is Misunderstood.* She illustrated numerous books by Kruchënykh and Khlébnikov and, in 1914, participated in the first Futurist Exhibition in the Galleria Sprovieri, Rome. 1916, joined *Supremus.* She died of diptheria.

Rubinstein, Antón Grigórevich (16.xi.1829–8.xi.1894): Musician. A pianist of international renown and a prolific composer (nine operas, six symphonies, five piano concertos, etc.), he was also the founder of the St Petersburg Conservatoire. He opposed the nationalist school in music, which he thought should be cosmopolitan.

Rubinstein, Ida (5.x.1885–20.ix.1960): Musical actress. Immensely wealthy (as a young woman she would hire an entire train for herself alone), she chose a stage career against the opposition of her family who had her confined in an asylum, from which she only escaped by means of an arranged marriage to her cousin. Her first *succès de scandale* was a private production of Oscar Wilde's *Salome* (1908) but it was Diághilev (q.v.) who made her an international sex symbol with the title role in *Cleopatra* in Paris (1909), wearing an extremely suggestive costume by Bakst (q.v.), a status further enhanced by a nude portrait by Seróv (q.v.) (1910).

Rubinstein, Nikolái Grigórevich (2.vi.1835–11.iii.1881): Pianist. Organizer of the Moscow branch of the Russian Musical Society, director of the Moscow Conservatoire.

Rumiántsev (-**Zadunáiskii**), Pëtr Alexándrovich (4.i.1755–24.i.1838): Field Marshal. 1741–43, Swedish War. 1756–62 Seven Years' War (Gross-Jägersdorf, 1757; Kunersdorf, 1759; Kolberg, 1761). 1764–96, Governor-General of Little Russia where he worked to liquidate Ukrainian autonomy (1783, poll tax). 1768–74, Turkish war (Azóv, 1769; Danube, 1770; Kuchuk-Kainardji, 1774).

Ryléev, Kondrátii Fëdorovich (18.ix.1795–13.vii1826): Poet and Decembrist. 1814–15, fought from Dresden to Poland. 1821–24, director of the Russian-American Company. 1820, published *The Favourite*, a covert attack on Arakchéev (q.v.). 1821, member of the Free Society of Lovers of Literature. 1824–25, official censor for poetry. Member of the Fiery Star and Astrea Masonic Lodges. 1823–25, edited *Poliárnaia zvezdá* with Bestúzhev (q.v.). 1823, joined the Northern Society, of which he became the director in 1824. One of the leaders of the uprising on Senate Square. Hanged in the Peter-Paul Fortress.

St Glin, Iákov Ivánovich de (1776–1864): Head of the Secret Police. The son of a French émigré, he began his career in 1793 as an interpreter. 1804, lecturer in German literature, Moscow University. 1807, gave up his academic career to join the staff of Prince P. M. Volkónskii (q.v.).

1811, Director of the Police Ministry's Special Chancellery (Head of the Secret Police).

Salavát Iuláev, (5.vi.1752–26.ix.1800): Bashkír leader in the Pugachëv Revolt and poet. 1773, deserted the army sent to repress the revolt and joined Pugachëv, rapidly becoming one of the Revolt's leaders. 24.xi.1774, captured, whipped and sent in 'eternal exile' to Rogervik on the Baltic. He is a major poet in the Bashkír language.

Saltykóv (-Shchedrín), Mikhaíl Evgráfovich (15.i.1826–28.iv.1889): Playwright. 1848, exiled to Viátka for what Nicholas I called a 'dangerous frame of mind' in his early writings. 1855, returned to St Petersburg to work in the Ministry of the Interior, preparing the Emancipation. 1858, deputy Governor of Riazán, then of Tver. 1868, dismissed and forbidden to have any kind of state appointment whatsoever. His works are wicked satires on provincial life: *Provincial Sketches* (1856–57), *History of a Town* (1869), *The Golovëv Family* (1872–76), etc.

Sanglen, see **St Glin**.

Savrásov, Alexéi Kondrátevich (12.v.1830–26.ix.1897): Painter. 1870, joined the Wanderers. His most famous painting is *The Rooks have Returned* (1871).

Schilling, P. L. (dates unknown): Physicist, member of the Russian Academy of Sciences. He invented the electric telegraph, a decade before Morse. Nicholas I sent a message ('je suis charmé d'avoir fait ma visite à Monsieur Schilling'), at its first public demonstration in 1833. Despite this, the Russian government adopted the rival Morse system for the St Petersburg-Moscow Railway (1843).

Semévskii, Vasílii Ivánovich (25.xii.1848–21.ix.1916): Historian of the peasantry. 1886, dismissed from St Petersburg University for 'harmful acts'. 1906, joined the Popular Socialists. 1913, founder and editor of *Gólos minúvshego*. Works include *The Peasantry in the Reign of Catherine II* (1881–1901), *The Peasant Question in Siberia in the 18th and early 19th Centuries* (1886), *Workers in the Siberian Gold Fields* (1898), *The Political and Social Ideas of the Decembrists* (1909), *The Society of Sts Cyril and Methodius, 1846–47* (1918), *M. V. Butashévich-Petrashévskii and the Petrashévtsy* (1922).

Senkóvskii, Ósip Ivánovich (19.iii.1800–4.iii.1858): Publisher. 1828, professor of oriental languages, St Petersburg University. 1833–56, edited *Biblióteka dlia chténiia* somewhat eccentrically, changing the articles (including, for example, works of Balzac) at will.

Serebriakóva, Zinaída Evgénievna (10.xii.1884–19.ix.1967): Painter. She first exhibited in 1910, and was hung in the *Mir iskússtva* exhibitions from 1910 to 1913. 1916, one of a team contributing paintings to the

Kazán Station in Moscow. 1924, emigrated to Paris. Her chief pre-revolutionary paintings are *Self-portait at Toilette, Girl with a Candle, Before the Storm, The Bathhouse, Village of Neskúchnoe, Harvesting, At Breakfast.*

Seróv, Valentín Alexándrovich (7.i.1865–22.xi.1911): Probably the greatest portrait painter of pre-Revolutionary Russia. He painted virtually everybody of importance during his lifetime, from Nicholas II to Ida Rubinstein (q.v.) (in the nude), from Diághilev (q.v.) to Konstantín Pobedonóstsev (q.v.). 1905, he witnessed the massacres in the streets from the Academy of Arts, and demanded that Grande Duke Vladímir Alexándrovich be removed as president of the Academy since, as commander of the Guards, he was responsible for the atrocities. When this was refused, he resigned from the Academy.

Shamíl, (*c.* 1798– March 1871): Spiritual and military leader of the Caucasus peoples against the Russians. 1834–59, led a successful guerrilla war against the Russians. After his capture in 1859, Alexander II complimented him on his fight and gave him an estate in Russia.

Shcherbátov, Mikhaíl Mikhaílovich (22.vi.1733–12.xii.1790): Historian. 1767, elected to the Legislative Commission, where he advocated a Western-style nobility defined by birth and, although supporting serfdom, humane treatment of the serfs. His *History of Russia from Earliest Times,* 7 vols (1770–90), is the first philosophical history of Russia. *On the Corruption of Morals in Russia* (1786–87), highly critical of Catherine II, was not published in Russia in its entirety until 1908. On his death, Catherine ordered the manuscript to be seized, but it was successfully concealed by his family. Its present whereabouts are unknown.

Shchúkin, Stepán Semënovich (1758–10.x.1828): Painter. Brought up in the Moscow Foundlings Hospital. 1782, awarded the Gold Medal for his *Portrait of a teacher with her pupil.* 1786, his *Portrait of the Architect I. M. Felten* gained him admission to the Academy. 1797, *Portrait of Paul I.* 1804–12, Kazán Cathedral interior with Borovikóvskii (q.v.).

Shéin, Alexander Semënovich (1662–12.ii.1700): General and statesman. 1687–89, Crimean campaigns. 1695–96, Azóv campaign. Commander-in-chief during Peter's absence on the Great Embassy, he helped Gordon (q.v.) suppress the revolt of the *Stréltsy.*

Shekhtel, Fëdor Ósipovich (26.vii.1859–7.vii.1926): Architect, son of German immigrants on the Volga. A man of extraordinary talent, patronized by the new Moscow monied class, he excelled in various styles from Gothic revival to *art nouveau.* His buildings include: the House for A. V. Morózov, Moscow (1896), Russian Pavilion, Glasgow Exhibition (1901), house for S. P. Riabushínskii (1902), Moscow Arts Theatre (1902), Iaroslávl Railway Station, Moscow (1902).

Shelgunóv, Nikolái Vasílevich (22.xi.1824–12.iv.1891): Revolutionary publicist. Professor in the Institute of Forestry. He was the author of the revolutionary manifesto of the 1860s 'To the Young Generation'. Twice arrested for political activities, he spent 20 years in prison and exile. In the 1880s he was a foremost critic of the policy of 'small deeds'.

Sherwood (**Shérvud**), Vladímir Ósipovich (1833–9.vii.1897): Architect and sculptor. Works include: the Historical Museum, Moscow (1874–83), Statue to the 'Heroes of Plévna', Moscow (1887), statue of Pirogóv, Moscow (1897).

Sheshkóvskii, Stepán Ivánovich (21.xii.1719–12.v.1794): Secret policeman. 1757, appointed secretary to the Secret Chancellery by Elizabeth. 1762, after Catherine's formal abolition of the Chancellery, it probably continued under his direction. Prominent in the investigation of the leaders of the Pugachëv Revolt. His brutality made him widely hated.

Shevchénko, Tarás Grigórevich (25.ii.1814–26.ii.1861): Ukrainian poet, artist and nationalist. Born a serf, he was sent to St Petersburg to study drawing. He became friendly with many influential artists and writers – e.g. Zhukóvskii (q.v.), Shchépkin, Briullóv (q.v.), Venetsiánov (q.v.) – who raised a fund to purchase his freedom in 1858. 1846, member of the Brotherhood of Cyril and Methodius. 1847 arrested and exiled for ten years. His poems extol the Ukrainian peasantry.

Shevyrëv, Stepán Petróvich (1806–1864): Critic and literary historian. Professor of Russian Literature at Moscow University and friend of Pogódin (q.v.). 1841, in *Moskvitiánin*, he wrote of the West as 'rotting'. 1857, his academic career ended abruptly when he was involved in a fight at the Moscow Society of Art with Count Bóbrinkskii whose words Shevyrëv interpreted as an insult to Russia. He spent most of the rest of his life abroad.

Shingarëv, Andréi Ivánovich (1869–7.i.1918): Kadet politician. 1895–1907, practised medicine in *zémstvo* hospitals. 1905–7, edited *Vorónezhskoe slóvo*. 1907–17, Kadet deputy to the Second, Third and Fourth Dumas. March–May 1917, Minister of Agriculture. May–July 1917, Minister of Finance. November 1917, arrested. He was killed in hospital by 'anarchist sailors'.

Shirínskii-Shíkhmatov, Platón Alexándrovich (18.xi.1790–5.v.1854): Sailor and statesman. 1812–14, served in the Fleet in the French War where he attracted the attention of Admiral Shishkóv (q.v.) who gave him a post in the Education Ministry. 1850–54, Minster of Education.

Shíshkin, Iván Ivánovich (13.i.1832–8.iii.1898): Painter. 1870, Founder-member of the *Wanderers*. Works include *Rye* (1878), *An Oak Grove* (1887).

Shishkóv, Alexander Semënovich (9.iii.1754–9.iv.1841): Admiral and linguistician. The foremost 'Ancient' in the dispute between 'Ancients' and 'Moderns', he opposed new trends in the Russian language, the Enlightenment and the French Revolution, arguing that Russian should remain rooted in Old Church Slavonic. 1824–28, Education Minister. Works include *Old and New* (poem, 1784), *Essay on Old and New Styles of the Russian Language* (1803) and *Conversations on Literature* (1811). He was a founder of the *Beséda* group (1811–16).

Shliápnikov, Alexander Gavrílovich (1885–1937). Bolshevik leader in Russia in February 1917. Began work at the age of 11. 1900–4, lathe operator in Sórmovo, Névskii shipyard (St Petersburg), Semiánnikov and Obúkov factories. 1904–5, organized local soviets and trade unions. 1905–7, imprisoned. 1908–14, worked in Germany, France and England. 1914–17, head of the Russian Bureau of the Central Committee of the Bolshevik Party. 1921, leader of the Workers' Opposition. 1932, expelled from the Party. Died in the camps. He is the author of a two-volume history of the Bolsheviks during the First World War, and a four-volume history of the Revolution.

Shulgín, Vasílii Vitálevich (1.i.1878–15.ii.1976): Journalist and nationalist politician. Worked on the Russian nationalist newspaper *Kievliánin*. 1912–13, broke with the nationalists over the Beilis case, and was imprisoned for three months for an article defending Beilis (q.v.). He was a member of the Provisional Committee of the State Duma in February 1917 and was sent with Guchkóv (q.v.) to Pskov to obtain Nicholas II's abdication. In the White movement during the civil war. 1944, seized in Yugoslavia and placed in a camp in the USSR, released in 1956. He has left two valuable memoirs – *Days* (1925) and *Years* (1976).

Shuválov, Iván Ivánovich (1.xi.1727–14.xi.1797): Founder of Moscow University, of many schools, and of the Academy of Fine Arts. He spoke several languages and corresponded with Voltaire and Helvétius. He encouraged the development of the arts and sciences and was a protector of Lomonósov (q.v.). 1762, forced to leave Russia after Catherine's seizure of power, he lived abroad until 1776, when his house in St Petersburg became a meeting place for leading cultural figures.

Shuválov, Pëtr Andréevich (15.vi.1827–10.iii.1889): Secret policeman and statesman. 1854, in Sebastopol during the siege. 1857, St Petersburg Police Chief. 1861, acting director of the Third Department. 1864, Governor of Estliand, Lifliand and Kurland. 1866, head of the Third Department, where his great power earned him the nickname 'Peter the Fourth'. 1874–79, ambassador in London. 30.v.1878, he signed a secret agreement with Lord Salisbury, which formed the basis of the settlement reached at the Congress of Berlin.

Shuválov, Pëtr Ivánovich (1710–4.i.1762): Statesman. 1741, participated in Elizabeth's *coup d'état*. 1750s, in charge of Russian internal policy (abolition of internal customs duties, protectionism in foreign trade, creation of merchants' and nobles' banks). 1756, a member of Elizabeth's conference. 1757, in charge of the *Oruzhéinaia kantseliáriia*, he modernized the artillery, introducing the howitzers that would be used for the next century.

Skóbelev, Matvéi Ivánovich (1885–1939): Menshevik. 1912, elected to the Fourth Duma. 1914, a leader of the Bakú oil strike. 23 February 1917, his speech in the Duma was seen as a call for revolution. 27 February, a founder of the Petrograd Soviet. May–August, Minister of Labour. Emigrated after October, returning to the USSR in 1924. 1937, arrested. Died in prison.

Skóbelev, Mikhaíl Dmítrievich (1843–25.vi.1882): General. Took part in the conquest of Central Asia. 1876–77, military Governor of Fergana. 1877–78, his ostentatious bravery in the Russo-Turkish War led to his becoming a cult figure, 'The White General'. 1880–81, Akhal-Tekin expedition (capture of Gheok Teppe, January 1881). In 1882 his anti-German speeches in St Petersburg and Paris embarrassed the government and his sudden death in July of that year at the age of 39, during a drinking bout in a brothel, gave rise to rumours that he had been assassinated.

Skriábin, Alexander Nikoláevich (25.xii.1871–14.iv.1915): Composer. Encouraged by Beliáev (q.v.), his early compositions were inspired by Chopin. Influenced by Vladímir Solovëv (q.v.), he became increasingly immersed in mysticism, believing that his shared birthday with Christ gave him divine powers, and this is reflected in his music: *Divine Poem* (1903), *Poème de l'Extase* (1908), *Prometheus* (1908–10).

Solovëv, Sergéi Mikhaílovich (5.v.1820–4.x.1879): Historian. 1842–44, lived abroad as the tutor to the Stróganov children. 1845–76, Moscow University. 1865–66 taught history to the future Alexander III. 1876, resigned from Moscow University over government support for Liubímov (q.v.). His main work is *History of Russia from Ancient Times*, 29 vols (1851–79).

Solovëv, Vladímir Sergéevich (16.i.1853–31.vii.1900): Religious philosopher. His ideas of 'Sophia', (eternal womanhood) and of Godmanhood influenced Dostoevskii (q.v.), Blok (q.v.), Bélyi (q.v.) and Viacheslav Ivánov among others. Initially drawn to the Slavophiles, he moved on to the idea of the unification of all Christian denominations and a rejection of all nationalism. Works include *The Russian Idea* (1881), *History and the Future of Theocracy* (1887), *Russia and the Universal Church* (1889).

Sómov, Konstantín Andréevich (18.xi.1869–6.v.1939): Painter. He first exhibited in 1894, and participated in *Mir iskússtva* from 1899 on. His paintings, although different in style, share Benois's (q.v.) interest in courtly scenes, pierrots and harlequins, etc. He was also a very skilled portraitist (portrait of Blok, 1907). 1923, he left for America, moving to France in 1925.

Speránskii, Mikhaíl Mikhaílovich (1.i.1772–11.ii.1839): Statesman. Son of a village priest, educated in a theological seminary, he taught for a while in an ecclesiastical institution before entering the civil service. 1808, accompanied the Tsar to Erfurt and made assistant Minister of Justice. 1809, presented his plan for constitutional reform. 1810, Minister of State. Disgraced in March 1812. He was subsequently pardoned and made Governor of Pénza (1816), and of Siberia (1819). 1821, returned to St Petersburg, appointed to the State Council and to the commission on the codification of the laws, a task he completed in 1833.

Stanislávskii (**Alekséev**), Konstantín Sergéevich (5.i.1863–7.viii.1938): Actor and director. 1888, founded the Society of Art and Literature. 1898, co-founder with Nemiróvich-Dánchenko (q.v.) of the Moscow Arts Theatre. His 'method' introduced a new approach to acting and producing. Works include *My Life in Art* (1924).

Stankévich, Nikolái Vladimírovich (27.ix.1813–25.vi.1840): Philosopher and poet. 1830s, his circle became the chief centre of Hegelianism.

Staróv, Iván Egórovich (12.ii.1745–5.iv.1808): Architect, exponent of classicism. 1771, commissioned to build a country house for A. G. Bóbrinskii at Bogoróditsa. Works include: the church at Nikólskoe (1773), the cathedral at the Alexander Nevskii Lavra in St Petersburg (1778), the Tauride Palace (1783).

Stásov, Vasílii Petróvich (24.viii.1769–24.viii.1848): Architect. Renovated the Imperial palaces at Oranienbaum, Peterhof, Tsárskoe seló. Bell Tower at Gruzinó (1822), Pávlovskii Barracks (1816–19), Moscow Gate, St Petersburg (1834–38), Cathedral of the Transfiguration for the Preobrazhénskii Regiment (1827–29).

Stásov, Vladímir Vasílevich. (2.i.1824–10.x.1906): Music and art critic. His critiques start appearing in 1847. He was a champion of Glínka (q.v.), Músorgskii (q.v.), Borodín (q.v.), and of the artists Briullóv (q.v.), Vereshchágin (q.v.), Peróv (q.v.), Répin (q.v.), Kramskói (q.v.), and supported Glázunov (q.v.), Liádov (q.v.), Chaliápin (q.v.).

Steklóv (**Nakhamkes**), Iúrii Mikhaílovich (15.vii.1873–15.ix.1941): Revolutionary. For most of his revolutionary life, he was a Bolshevik (lecturing at Lenin's School for Party Workers in Longjumeau, on the editorial staff of *Zvezdá* and *Právda*, and secretary of the Duma Faction). 1917, member of the Executive Committee of the Petrograd Soviet.

Stepniák, see **Kravchínskii**.

Stolýpin, Pëtr Arkádevich (1862–6.ix.1911): Statesman. 1887–1902, marshal of the Kovno nobility. 1903, Governor of Grodno. 1904, Governor of Sarátov. 1906, Minister of the Interior and chairman of the Council of Ministers. His term of office is associated mainly with his ruthless war on the revolutionary movement, his use of 'article 87' to force his (often progressive) legislation through the Duma, and his agrarian reforms – 'the wager on the strong' in which he attempted to replace communal by private property of the land. 1.ix.1911, shot during a performance of the Kiev Opera, by Dmítrii Bogróv, simultaneously a member of the PSR and the secret police.

Stravínskii, Ígor Fëdorovich (5.vi.1882–6.iv.1971): Composer. 1909, discovered by Diághilev (q.v.) his first great successes were ballets: *Firebird* (1910), *Petrúshka* (1911), *Rossignol* (1911), *Rite of Spring* (1914). He did not return to Russia after the Revolution, but achieved world-wide fame as one of the great composers of the twentieth century.

Stróganov, Paul Alexándrovich (Popo) (7.vi.1772–10.vi.1817): Statesman and general. Educated by Gilbert Romme (q.v.). Member of Alexander I's 'Unofficial Committee' and deputy Minister of the Interior. He left politics when Alexander abandoned liberalism. Fought in the wars against France and Sweden, 1807–14, distinguishing himself at Borodinó and Krásnoe.

Stürmer, Borís Vladímirovich (1848–20.viii.1917): Statesman. March–July 1916, Minister of the Interior, July–November, Foreign Minister. His appointment gave rise to protests from the Allies, particularly Britain, which saw him as 'pro-German'. He was arrested in March 1917, and died in the Peter-Paul Fortress.

Sukhánov (**Himmer**), Nikolái Nikoláevich (10.xii.1882–29.vi.1940): Revolutionary. 1903, joined the SRs, but turned to Social-Democracy after 1905. 1914–17, wrote articles for Gorkii's *Létopis*. February 1917, on the Executive Committee of the Petrograd Soviet and a contributor to Gorkii's *Nóvaia zhizn*. His seven-volume memoir on the Revolution is most valuable.

Sukhomlínov, Vladímir Alexándrovich (4.viii.1848–2.ii.1926). General. 1877–78, Turkish War. 1905, Governor-General of Kiev, Volýnia and Podólsk. 1908, Chief of General Staff. 1909–15, Minister of War. Seen as an enemy of liberalism, his dismissal was contrived by means of the execution of Miasoédov (q.v.). Supposedly personifying all the corruption of the old regime, he was subjected to a long trial in 1917, but was released by the Bolsheviks.

Sumarókov, Alexander Petróvich (1718–77): Playwright and translator. His *Céphale et Procris* (1755) was the first Russian opera libretto. 1756–61, director of St Petersburg's first Russian theatre. 1748, translated *Hamlet* (freely). His main dramatic works are *Khórev* (1747), *Le cocu imaginaire, la Chipie, les Monstres*. In the 1760s, he wrote a series of satires and epigrams castigating serfdom and bureaucracy.

Súrikov, Vasílii Ivánovich (12.i.1848–6.iii.1916): Painter. Works include *The Morning of the Stréltsy Execution* (1881), *Ménshikov in Berëzovo* (1883), *Boiárina Morózova* (1887), *Ermák's Conquest of Siberia* (1892), *Suvórov Crossing the Alps* (1899), *Townswoman* (1902), *Stepán Rázin* (1905–10).

Suvórin, Alexéi Sergéevich (11.ix.1834–11.viii.1912): Newspaper publisher. The son of a common soldier, he began his career in the army, leaving in 1853 to become a teacher. His writings won him a job in Moscow, where Tolstoy commissioned him to write for his journal. 1862–72, proof-reader, then writer for *Sanktpeterbúrgskie védomosti*. 1872, he compiled *Rússkii kalendár*, an annual almanac of useful information. 1876, he acquired the ailing newspaper *Nóvoe vrémia*, which he turned into Russian's greatest conservative daily. 1880s, published Russian and foreign authors for mass consumption in *Deshëvaia biblióteka*.

Suvórov, Alexander Vasílevich (13.xi.1729–6.v.1800): Field Marshal. Hero-worshipped by Russian soldiers, he is curiously undervalued elsewhere. Despite being a man of considerable learning he had the knack of getting close to his men and inspiring them. Disdaining most contemporary military theory, he relied on speed, morale and courage for his astonishing series of victories. In the early nineteenth century the cult of Suvórov had oppositional connotations.

Tatíshchev, Vasílii Nikítich (19.iv.1686–15.vii.1750): Historian. Served under Peter I in the campaigns of Narva, Poltáva and the Pruth. 1720–22 and 1734–37, director of state factories in the Urals. 1730, foremost opponent of the Supreme Privy Council. 1741–45, Governor of Ástrakhan. Writer of the *Russian History* (5 vols, published 1768–1848) and of the first Russian encyclopedia, *Leksikón Rossíiskoi*.

Tátlin, Vladímir Evgráfovich (16.xii.1885–31.v.1953): Painter and founder of Constructivism. Ran away to sea when he was aged 18, he remained a part-time painter until 1914, when he met Picasso, who inspired him. Works include *Female Model* (1910–14), *Sailor* (1911), *Board No. 1* (1916). His most famous post-Revolutionary work was his *Monument to the Third International* (1919–20).

Tchaikovsky, Pëtr Ilích (25.iv.1840–25.x.1893): Russia's most famous composer. Author of numerous operas (*Eugene Onégin, Queen of Spades*), ballets (*Sleeping Beauty, Nutcracker, Swan Lake*), six symphonies, numerous chamber works, piano music, songs, etc. Probably forced to commit suicide over a homosexual affair.

Teffi (**Lokhvitskaia**), Nadézhda Alexándrovna (9.v.1872–6.x.1952): One of the most popular writers of pre-Revolutionary Russia, she took her pseudonymn from Kipling's *Just So Story* 'How the First Letter was Written'. Her stories appeared in the daily and periodical press, but were republished in book form from 1910. 1917, joined Leoníd Andréev and Gumilëv (q.v.) on the Provisional Council for the Preservation of Cultural Treasures. After October, worked for *Novyi Satirikon* until its suppression in 1918, when she emigrated. She continued to publish in the émigré Russian press, and her flat in Montparnasse became a centre for Russian émigré culture.

Ténisheva, Maríia Klávdievna (20.v.1867–14.iv.1928): Patron of the arts. Financed her own school of painting in St Petersburg (1894–1904), and Smolénsk (1896–99). Founded the museum of Russian antiquities in Smolénsk.

Teréshchenko, Mikaíl Ivánovich (18.iii.1886–1.iv.1956): Industrialist and statesman. Owner of a large sugar enterprise. 1912–17, Duma deputy (Progressist). 1914–17, worked for the Red Cross. 1915–17, chairman of the Kiev War Industries Committee. 2 March 1917, Minister of Finance. May 1917, Foreign Minister.

Tiútchev, Fëdor Ivánovich (23.xi.1803–15.vii.1873): Poet and diplomat. Joined the *Liubomúdrye* while a student at Moscow University. 1822, in the consulates in Munich and Turin for 22 years. 1841, dismissed for 'spending too long on leave'. 1854, first anthology of verse published by Turgénev (q.v.). 1858, appointed censor of foreign publications. Although ranked by many next to Pushkin (q.v.), he did not rate himself as a poet and did not bother to keep many of his manuscripts.

Tkachëv, Pëtr (1844–86): Revolutionary populist. Made his name in the 1860s as a radical journalist. Arrested in 1869, but escaped to Geneva in 1873, where he published *Nabát/Tocsin*. He argued that revolution could only succeed if led by a tightly-knit leadership and, as such, is regarded as a precursor of Lenin.

Tocqué, Louis (1696–1772): Painter. One of the most sought-after portraitists in Paris. August 1756, came to St Petersburg at the invitation of M. S. Vorontsóv (q.v.), where he painted numerous portraits of the aristocracy, including a now famous one of the Empress Elizabeth. He left Russia in February 1758.

Tolstoy, Dmítrii Andréevich (1882–89): Procurator of the Holy Synod, Minister of Education and of the Interior. He is associated with the offensive against progressive ideas in the late nineteenth century.

Tolstoy, Lev Nikoláevich (28.viii.1828–7.xi.1910): Writer. 1849, started a school for peasant children on the family estate at Iásnaia Poliána. 1851, joined the artillery during a visit to the Caucasus, and took part in action against Shamíl. 1852, *Childhood* won him literary acclaim. 1854–55, served in Sebastopol during the Crimean War. 1856, left the army to devote himself to literature and education. 1858, nearly killed by a bear. The theme of his *Kreutzer Sonata* (1890), that sexual relations led to spiritual impurity, was extraordinarily influential among educated Russian youth. Amid the extraordinary intellectual arrogance of the Russian intelligentsia, *War and Peace* stands out in crediting the peasant, as opposed to the powerful, with political insight. Excommunicated by the Orthodox Church, he was denied burial in consecrated ground after his death in the waiting room on Astápovo railway station. Works include *Anna Karénina, War and Peace*, etc.

Tolstoy, Pëtr Andréevich (1645–1729): Statesman. Originally a supporter of Sophia and the Miloslávskiis, he changed to Peter's side in 1689. At first given only minor appointments (*voevóda* of Ustiug, 1694), he distinguished himself in the second Azóv campaign and then, although over 50 years old, went to Italy to learn Italian and navigation. 1701–14, first Russian ambassador in Constantinople. He was given the task of luring Alexéi back to Russia and was made head of the Secret Chancellery. 1720, Head of College of Trade. 1726, on the Supreme Privy Council. Exiled to Solovétskii Monastery, where he died.

Trediakóvskii, Vasílii Kiríllovich (1703–69): Translator, author and professor of eloquence in the Academy of Sciences. 1727–30 studied at the Sorbonne. Works include *Reflections on the Origins of Poetry and Verse* (1732), *Conversations on Orthography* (1748), *Russian Poetry, Ancient, Mediaeval and Modern* (1755).

Tressini (**Trezzini**), Domenico (Andréi Petróvich Trezini) (c. 1670–1734): Swiss architect. 1706, recruited to work in St Petersburg, he first built small practical buildings of wood and brick, painted to look like stone, of which only one, Peter's original residence, remains. He designed the Peter-Paul Fortress (1706–40), the Cathedral of St Peter and St Paul (1712–33), and the Twelve Colleges on Vasílii Óstrov (1722–33) (originally to house Peter's ministries, in 1819 they became St Petersburg University). 1720s, he altered Winter Palace, more than tripling its size.

Tretiakóv, Pável Mikhaílovich (15.xii.1832–4.xii.1898): Moscow merchant, founder of the Tretiakóv Gallery, the basis of which was his collection of Russian paintings. He was a patron of the *Wanderers*.

Tretiakóv, Sergéi Mikhaílovich (19.ii.1834–25.vii.1892): Moscow merchant and art collector. 1877–81, mayor of Moscow. 1892, left his collection of Western European paintings to the city of Moscow, to hang in his brother's Tretiakóv Gallery. They are now in the Hermitage, St Petersburg.

Trubetskói, Nikíta Iúrevich (26.v.1699–16.x.1767): Field Marshal. 1730, one of the main opponents of the Supreme Privy Council. 1740–60, Procurator-General (investigations into A. I. Osterman (q.v.), 1741; A. P. Bestúzhev-Riúmin (q.v.), 1758). 1741, member of Elizabeth's supreme council. 1756, member of the Conference at the Imperial Court. 1760–63, president of the War College.

Trubetskói, Sergéi Petróvich (28.viii.1790–22.xi.1860): Decembrist. 1808, joined the Semënovskii Guards. 1812–15, fought from Vilna to Leipzig (wounded, Russian and Prussian decorations). 1816, member of the Three Virtues Masonic Lodge (1818, deputy master). Member of the Union of Salvation, president and guardian of the directing nucleus of the Union of Welfare. One of the leaders of the Northern Society, one of the writers of the 'Manifesto to the Russian People', he was to be dictator after the uprising, but failed to appear on Senate Square. Arrested the next day in the house of the Austrian ambassador. Sentenced to eternal exile in Siberia (reduced to 20 years). 1856, amnestied.

Tsitiánov, Pável Dmítrievich (8.ix.1754–8.ii.1806): General, of Georgian descent. 1787–91, Turkish War. 1794, in Poland. 1796, Persian expedition with Zúbov. 1802–6, commander in the Caucasus. 1806, assassinated during negotiations outside Bakú.

Turgénev, Alexander Ivánovich (27.iii.1784–3.xii.1845): Statesman. 1810–24, Director of Spiritual Affairs in the Ministry of Spiritual Affairs and Education. 1812, a founder of the Bible Society and, in 1815, of the Arzamás circle. 1825, emigrated to Western Europe.

Turgénev, Iván Sergéevich (8.x.1818–3.xii.1883): Writer. He made his reputation with *A Huntsman's Sketches* (1847–48) whose precise descriptions of nature and the peasantry were an oblique indictment of serfdom. His novels and plays, while accurately chronicling contemporary society, are a plea for Westernism, social responsibility and tolerance together with an appreciation of Russia, its people and language. Works include *A Month in the Country* (1850), *A Nest of Gentlefolk* (1859), *On the Eve* (1859), *Fathers and Children* (1862), *Virgin Soil* (1877).

Turgénev, Nikolái Ivánovich (12.x.1789–29.x.1871): Decembrist. Educated at Göttingen University. 1812–14, worked with Baron vom Stein, then in various administrative posts. A member of the Order of Russian Knights, of the Union of Welfare (St Petersburg meeting, 1820; Moscow Congress, 1821), and of the Northern Society. 1825, on leave abroad, refused to return after the uprising and condemned to death in absentia. His memoir, *La Russie et les Russes*, 3 vols (Paris, 1847), chiefly an examination of serfdom, was banned in Russia and gave rise to much interest all over Europe.

Ukráintsev, Emelián Ignátevich (1641–12.ix.1708): Diplomat. 1688–99, head of the *Posólskii Prikáz*. 1699–1700, ambassador to Constantinople (Treaty of Constantinople, 1700). 1702–6, head of *Proviántskii Prikáz*. 1707, Ambassador to Poland. He died on an embassy to Rákószi in Hungary.

Uliánov, Alexander Ilích (31.iii.1866–8.v.1887): Lenin's brother. 1886, in the terrorist faction of The People's Will. Hanged for his part in an attempted assassination of Alexander III.

Únkovskii, Alexéi Mikhaílovich (24.xii.1828–20.xii.1893): Politician. 1857–59, marshal of the Tver nobility. August 1859, one of the authors of the address demanding political reform, for which he was deported to Viátka in 1860. 1861, defence lawyer in cases involving peasants. 1862, forbidden to practise. 1866, again practised law in St Petersburg.

Ustriálov, Nikolái Gerasímovich (4.v.1805–8.vi.1870): Historian. 1834–70, professor at St Petersburg University. 1830s, while associated with Uvárov (q.v.), he wrote a number of school history textbooks propagating official nationality. His main work remains a 10-volume history of Peter the Great (1842–63).

Uvárov, Sergéi Semënovich (25.viii.1786–4.ix.1855): Statesman. He showed great brilliance as a young man, attracting the attention of Goethe, Napoleon and de Maistre. 1815, member of the Arzamás literary circle. 1818, president of the Imperial Academy of Sciences at the age of 32 and Curator of the St Petersburg Educational District until 1821. 1832, he put forward the formula for official nationality of 'Autocracy, Orthodoxy and Nationality' (despite being a liberal, atheist and cosmopolitan, personally). 1833–49, Minister of Education.

Valúev, Pëtr Alexándrovich (22.ix.1815–27.i.1890): Statesman. 1855, extremely critical of the system leading to the Crimean defeat. 1858–61, director of the Department of State Domains. 1861–68, Minister of the Interior (*zémstvo* reform, 1864). 1872–79, Minister of State Domains (Valúev Committee on Agriculture). 1879–81, chairman of the Committee of Ministers. He is also the author of several novels.

Vasnetsóv, Victor Mikhaílovich (3.v.1848–23.vii.1926): Painter. His first paintings (e.g. *News from the Front*, 1878) were realist village scenes, but he latterly turned to the mythical, epic past: *After Prince Igor's Battle with the Polóvtsy* (1880), *Alënushka* (1881), *Knight at the Crossroads* (1882), *Three Princesses of the Underground Kingdom* (1884), *Bogatýrs* (1898).

Vélten (Felten), Iúrii Matvéevich (1730 or 1732–1801): Architect. 1754, assisted Rastrelli (q.v.) at the Winter Palace. 1760, an independent architect. He designed the granite quays and wrought-iron grilles of St Petersburg as well as the Chesme Palace, built to commemorate the naval victory of 1770.

Venetsiánov, Alexéi Gavrílovich (7.ii.1780–4.xii.1847): Painter. Portraits of A. I. Bíbikov (1805–8), M. A. Fonvízin (1812). 1807, four watercolours for his *Journal of Caricatures*, Russia's first illustrated satirical journal. 1820 onwards, he painted a number of genre works of country life.

Venevítinov, Dmítrii Vladimírovich (14.ix.1805–15.iii.1827): Poet. 1823, member of the *Liubomúdrye*. His poems are romantic, influenced by Schelling, a love of nature and the cult of friendship. He translated Goethe and E. T. A. Hoffmann.

Vereshchágin, Vasílii Vasílevich (14.x.1842–31.iii.1904): Painter. His works portray the suffering as well as the vainglory of war: *The Apotheosis of War* (1872), *Mortally Wounded* (1873), *General Skóbelev at Shipka* (1879). Killed when the Japanese sunk the battleship *Petropávlovsk*, on which he was painting the portrait of Admiral Makárov.

Viázemskii, Alexander Alexéevich (3.viii.1727–8.i.1793): Statesman. 1763, tours Urals to find reasons for disorders. 1764–93, procurator-general. 1767, chairman of the commission on the new *Ulozhénie*. 1768, on Catherine's Council.

Viázemskii, Pëtr Andréevich (12.ii.1792–10.xi.1878): Poet, literary critic and literary historian. His poems were a cry for the liberation of the serfs: *Indignation* (1820), *Sankt-Peterbúrg* (1824), *The Russian God* (1828). He was an active polemicist against the *Beséda* group, about whom he wrote malicious epigrams and parodies. He wrote biographies of Fonvízin (q.v.), Ózerov (q.v.), Dmítriev (q.v.) and Sumarókov (q.v.).

Viazmitínov, Sergéi Kuzmích (7.x.1744–15.x.1819): General. 1787–91, Turkish War. 1790s, Governor of Mogilëv, Simbírsk and Ufá, and Orenbúrg. 1802–8, first War Minister, then military Governor-general of St Petersburg. 1812, acting Minister of Police until his death.

Vigée-Lebrun, Elisabeth-Louise (16.iv.1755–30.iii.1842): Well-known portraitist of *Ancien régime* France, she arrived in St Petersburg in June 1795. During her six years in Russia, she painted 48 portraits, including those of the family of Paul I. Depressed by her daughter's marriage to the secretary of the director of the Imperial Russian Theatres, she left Russia in 1801.

Vishniakóv, Iván Iákovlevich (1699–8.viii.1761): An artisanal painter in Moscow. Summoned to St Petersburg by Peter the Great, he painted portraits, church interiors, palace ceilings, and theatrical sets, and became an important figure in the development of Russian painting.

Voéikov, Alexander Fëdorovich (30.viii.1779–16.vi.1839): Poet and journalist. 1814–20, professor at Dorpat University. 1815, member of the Arzamás circle. 1822–38, editor of *Rússkii invalíd*. His poems, *The Madhouse* (1814–39), and *Addressbook to Parnassus* (1818–20) are satyrical portraits of the literary scene.

Volkónskii, Mikhaíl Nikítich (1713–86): *Général-en-chef.* 1756–62, distinguished himself during Seven Years' War. 1764, his troops in Poland ensured the election of Stanisław Poniatowski as king. 1768, on Catherine's Council. 1775, member of the special council to judge Pugachëv.

Volkónskii, Pëtr Mikhaílovich (25.iv.1776–27.viii.1852): Field Marshal and statesman. 1810–12, quartermaster-general of the Russian Army. Founder of the School for Column Leaders. 1813–14, Chief of the Main Staff. 1815–23, head of the War Administration. 1814–15, at the Congress of Vienna. 1826–52, Minister of the Imperial Court.

Vólkov, Fëdor Grigórevich (9.ii.1729–4.iv.1763): Actor and director. 1747, established a professional theatre company in Iaroslavl, and built a theatre there in 1751. 1752, summoned by Elizabeth to St Petersburg and nominated 'first actor to the court' in 1756. 1762, granted noble status and 700 serfs for his part in Catherine's seizure of power.

Volýnskii, Artémi Petróvich (1689–27.vi.1740): Diplomat. 1715, permanent representative in Persia. 1719–24, as Governor of Ástrakhan he played a major role in planning the Persian War (1722–23). 1738, cabinet minister. An advocate of greater power for the nobility, he was accused of treason and sentenced to have one arm cut off and then to be decapitated.

Voroníkhin, Andréi Nikofórovich (17.x.1759–21.ii.1814): Architect. Remained a serf of the Stróganovs until 1785. 1777, he showed such artistic talent that his master sent him to Moscow to study painting and architecture. 1786–90, accompanied Paul Stróganov (q.v.) and Gilbert Romme (q.v.) to Western Europe. On his return, his first work was for the Stróganovs, remodelling a suite of apartments in their St Petersburg palace, and building a dacha for them on the Nevá. His major works are the Kazán Cathedral (1801–11), and the College of Mining (1806–11).

Vorontsóv, Alexander Románovich (4.ix.1741–2.xii.1805): Diplomat. 1761, envoy to Vienna. Ambassador to Britain (1762–64) and Holland (1764–68). 1773–94, president of the College of Trade. 1802–4, Chancellor, advocate of a pro-British anti-French policy.

Vorontsóv, Mikhaíl Illariónovich (12.vii.1714–15.ii.1767): Diplomat. 1741, active in Elizabeth's seizure of power. 1744, Vice-Chancellor, advocate of a French alliance. 1756, on Elizabeth's Conference. 1758–62, Chancellor. Forced into retirement as a supporter of Peter III.

Vorontsóv, Mikhaíl Semënovich (19.v.1782–6.xi.1856): Brought up in England, where his father was ambassador and where his sister married the Earl of Pembroke. 1801, returned to Russia, when Alexander I returned the family estates confiscated by Paul I. 1802, volunteered for active service in the Caucasus. 1815–18, commander of the army of occupation in France. 1823–44, viceroy in Bessarabia. 1844–54, viceroy in the Caucasus.

Vrúbel, Mikhaíl Alexándrovich (5.iii.1856–1.iv.1910): Painter. Rejected the social comment of the *Wanderers* as 'journalism'. His most famous paintings are illustrations of Lérmontov's (q.v.) *Demon: Demon Seated* (1890), *Tamara's Dance* (1890), *Lilac* (1900), *Swan Princess* (1900), *Demon Cast Down* (1902). Religious subjects include *Resurrection* (1887) and *Lamentation* (1887). He also painted portraits of Sávva Mámontov (q.v.) (1897) and V. Briúsov (1906).

Witte, Sergéi Iúlevich (17.vi.1849–28.ii.1915): Statesman. 1870, worked for the Odessa Railway. His book on railway tariffs (1883) made him famous. 1892–1903, Minister of Finance whose plan for industrializing Russia involved the large-scale building of railways. 1903–5, chairman of the Committee of Ministers. 1905–6, chairman of the Council of Ministers, one of only two who partially chose his own cabinet.

Wittgenstein, Pëtr Khristiánovich (6.i.1769–30.v.1843): Field Marshal. 1794–95, Polish War. 1805–7, 1812–14, French Wars. April 1813, succeeded Kutúzov (q.v.) as Commander-in-chief, replaced in May by Barclay de Tolly (q.v.) after defeats at Lützen and Bautzen. 1828–29, Commander-in-chief, Turkish War.

Ypsilantis, Alexander (1783–1828): Phanariot Greek and Russian General. 1812–14, in the Russian Army in the French Wars. 1820, president of *Philike Hetairia*. 1821, led an unsuccessful invasion of the Principalities.

Zakrévskii, Arsénii Andréevich (1783–1865): General and statesman. 1805–14, in the French Wars. 1823, Governor-General of Finland. 1828–31, Minister of the Interior dismissed for his heavy handed treatment of the cholera outbreak in St Petersburg. 1848–59, Governor-General of Moscow.

Zasúlich, Véra Ivánovna (27.vii.1849–8.v.1919): Revolutionary. 1869–71, imprisoned over her connections with Necháev (q.v.). 1878, her acquittal at her trial for shooting (but not killing) the St Petersburg Governor,

F. F. Trépov, who had illegally had a prisoner whipped, caused a sensation. 1883, member of the Group for the Emancipation of Labour. 1903, after the Second Congress of the RSDRP, a Menshevik leader.

Zavadóvskii, Pëtr Vasílevich. (1739–10.i.1812). Statesman. Secretary of P. A. Rumiántsev (q.v.). 1774, author of the Treaty of Kuchuk-Kainardji. 1782, chairman of Commission on National Schools. 1801, proposes reform of Senate. 1802–10, First Minister of Education.

Zheliábov, Andréi Ivánovich (17.viii.1851–3.iv.1881): Terrorist, assassin of Alexander II. 1871, expelled from Odessa University. 1877–79, acquitted in the 'Trial of the 193'. 1879, attended the Lípetsk and Vorónezh congresses of Land and Freedom. One of the foremost proponents of revolutionary terror. Hanged.

Zhomini, see **Jomini**.

Zhukóvskii, Vasílii Andréevich (1783–12.iv.1852): Poet. His first literary success was his translation of Gray's *Elegy* (1802). He subsequently translated La Fontaine, Schiller, Goethe, Byron, Goldsmith, Klopstock, and Walter Scott, as well as the *Odyssey* (1849). He became very popular with his poem 'A bard in the camp of the Russian Warriors' (1812). 1815, one of the founders of the Arzamás circle. 1817, tutor in Russian to the fiancée of the Grand Duke Nikolái Pávlovich. 1823, tutor to the future Alexander II.

Zilóti, Alexander Ilích (27.ix.1863–8.xii.1945): Pianist and conductor. Studied under Tchaikovsky (q.v.) and Liszt. Founded the Zilóti Chamber and Symphony Concerts (1903), Popular Concerts (1912), National Free Concerts (1915), and the Russian Music Fund to help musicians in need (1916). 1922, emigrated to USA.

Zínin, Nikolái Nikoláevich (13.viii.1812–6.ii.1880): Chemist. Professor at Kazán University, then (1848–74) at the Medical-Surgical Academy in St Petersburg. Developer of the military use of nitroglycerine.

Zubátov, Sergéi Vasílevich (1864–2.iii.1917): Police chief and trades unionist. 1880–83, police spy in the revolutionary movement. 1896–1902, head of the Moscow police, in which capacity he organized a trades union whose success in obtaining wage rises for the Moscow workers led to his dismissal and transfer to St Petersburg. He committed suicide.

SECTION SEVEN

Appendices

7.1 The Russian Alphabet, with Accepted Transliteration and Guide to Pronunciation

Russian	Latin	Hints on Pronunciation
А а	A a	*Stressed*: a deep 'a' as in 'arm'; *unstressed*: like the 'e' in 'worker'.
Б б	B b	
В в	V v	As a 'v' anywhere except at the end of the word, when it softens to become an 'f'.
Г г	G g	Ukrainians and South Russians make this very soft, like an 'h'.
Д д	D d	
Е е	E e	*Stressed*: 'ye' as in 'yes'; *unstressed*: a short 'yi' as in 'Yiddish'. Thus Eléna is Yi-lyé-na. Double 'e', ('ee') is never pronounced as in English but as 'e-ye'. Thus Alekséev is pronounced Aleksé-yef and not to rhyme with leaf.
Ё ё	Ё ё	Not strictly a separate letter, and mostly written simply E or e, this is always stressed and pronounced 'yo' as in 'yore'. I have always written it as Ё or ё in this book.
Ж ж	Zh zh or Ž ž	Like a French soft 'j' in 'je', or the 's' in 'pleasure'.
З з	Z z	Always soft, more like the hard s in 'please' (never pronounced like a ts in the hard German way).
И и	I i	Like the double 'ee' in 'seek'.

Russian	Latin	Hints on Pronunciation
Й й	I i or J j	A short sound like the 'y' in 'joy'.
К к	K k	
Л л	L l	
М м	M m	
Н н	N n	
О о	O o	*Stressed*: a long 'o' as in 'more'; *unstressed*: 1. Immediately before the stress: a short 'u' as in 'hun'; 2. Away from the stress: a short sound like the 'e' in 'worker'. Thus, Vorontsóv is pronounced Ver-un-tsóf.
П п	P p	
Р р	R r	Rolled like a Scottish 'r'.
С с	S s	Always soft as in 'soft'.
Т т	T t	
У у	U u	The nearest sound in English is the 'oo' in moon, but the French 'ou' is closer.
Ф ф	F f	
Х х	Kh kh or Ch ch	A harsh 'h' like the 'ch' in the Scottish 'loch', or the Spanish 'j' in 'jamon'.
Ц ц	Ts ts or C c	Ts as in 'tsetse fly'.
Ч ч	Ch ch or Č č	Ch as in 'church'.
Ш ш	Sh sh or Š š	Sh as in 'sheep'.
Щ щ	Shch shch or Šč šč	Two distinct sounds, as in the name Krushchëv.
Ъ ъ	"	Hard sign. Can safely be ignored by non-Russian speakers.
Ы ы	Y y	Somewhere between the French 'oeil' and the 'uy' in the Spanish 'muy'.
Ь ь	'	Soft sign. Can safely be ignored by non-Russian speakers.

Russian	Latin	Hints on Pronunciation
Э э	E e	A long, hard 'e' rather like the 'A' in 'Avon'.
Ю ю	Iu iu, Ju ju, or Yu yu	Long like the word 'you'.
Я я	Ia ia, Ja ja or Ya ya	*Stressed*: like the Kensington 'yar' meaning yes; *unstressed* 1. before the stress: a short 'i' as in 'little'; 2. After the stress, swallowed to sound like 'yer'. Thus Iavorksii is pronounced Yi-vórksii, but Rossíia (Russia) sounds like Russ-ee-yer (stress on the second syllable).

7.2 Julian and Gregorian Calendars

From 1700 until 1918, Russia used the (old style, normally abbreviated to o.s.) Julian Calendar as opposed to the (new style, n.s.) Gregorian Calendar now used in Western Europe. The difference between the two is that in the Julian Calendar all the century years (1600, 1700, 1800, 1900, 2000) are leap years whereas in the Gregorian Calendar only those century years divisible by four (1600, 2000) are leap years. The effect of this is that the Julian calendar falls behind the Gregorian calendar by one day in three centuries out of four, starting on the first of March on the appropriate century year. In the period covered in this book, it is 11 days behind in the eighteenth century, 12 in the nineteenth, and 13 in the twentieth. However, it will remain 13 days behind in the twenty-first century, as 2000 is divisible by four and hence a leap year in both calendars.

7.3 Russian Names

Russian names often give trouble to readers of Russian novels. People seem to be called one thing on one page, and another on another. Actually, the way Russians use names is quite simple, once one knows the system. Most Europeans have a minimum of two names, a given name and a family name (John Smith). But there seems no upper limit (Jean-François-Marie-Hippolyte-André-Georges de la Motte-Fouqué). All Russians, however, must have three names. No more, no fewer. A given name, a patronymic, and a family name (although this last can be double-barrelled). The only exception to this that I have ever come across is Mikhaíl-Kondrátii Ivánovich Dáshkov, but this is such rarity that he is normally erroneously listed as M. K. Dáshkov, rather than M.-K. I. Dáshkov or M. I. Dáshkov.

The given name, is just that: the name given to the baby at birth by its parents, say Alexander or Tatiána.

The patronymic is formed from the father's given name. If this is, say, Pável, then young Alexander's patronymic will be Pávlovich, whereas Tatiána's will be Pávlovna.

The most common Russian family name is Ivanóv. So if we assume that our two youngsters share this, then their full names will be Alexander Pávlovich Ivanóv and Tatiána Pávlovna Ivanóva.

Notice that both patronymic and family name change with gender. Men's patronymics are mostly formed by adding 'ovich' or 'evich' to the father's given name, whereas women's are formed by adding 'evna' or 'ovna'. Similarly, men's family names normally end in 'in', 'ov' or 'skii', and women's in 'ina', 'ova' or 'skaia'. Some names, however, like Ukrainian names ending in 'enko', are invariable.

Russians rarely address each other formally by their family name. Instead, the formal mode of address is given name and patronymic. Thus our couple will be addressed formally as 'Alexander Pávlovich' and 'Tatiána Pávlovna' by, say, their colleagues at work. At home, they will call each other by their given names only, but normally not in their full form. Although some Russians now use the full form of their given names ('Alexander', 'Tatiana') in imitation of Western European custom, most Russians will use the diminutive form when they use their given names only. In this case, the likelihood is that they will call each other 'Sasha' and 'Tania'. As it is here that most Western Europeans get lost, I am giving a (not complete but representative) list of the most common diminutives, with their full given name equivalents:

Aliósha	Alexéi	Líza	Elizavéta
Ásia	Anastasíia	Másha	Mariia
Bória	Borís	Mísha	Mikhail
Dásha	Dária	Mítia	Dmítrii
Díma	Dmítrii or Vadím	Nádia	Nadezhda
Gália	Galína	Ólia	Ólga
Gárik	Ígor	Pásha	Pável
Grísha	Grigórii	Pétia	Pëtr
Ída	Zinaída	Sásha	Alexander or Alexandra
Íra	Irína	Seriózha	Sergei
Kátia	Ekaterína	Sónia	Sofía
Kíra	Kiríll	Svéta	Svetlána
Kólia	Nikolái	Tánia	Tatiána
Kóstia	Konstantín	Tólia	Anatólii
Lára	Larísa	Vánia,	Iván
Léna	Eléna	Volódia	Vladímir
Lënia	Leoníd or Leóntii	Zhénia	Evgénii
Lída	Lídia	Zhóra	Geórgii
Lióva	Lev	Zínik	Zinóvii ... etc.

Guide to Further Reading

General

A good place to start is the three volumes of the *Longman History of Russia*: Paul Dukes, *The Making of Russian Absolutism, 1613–1801* (2nd edn, London, 1990), David Saunders, *Russia in the Age of Reaction and Reform, 1801–1881* (London, 1992), Hans Rogger, *Russia in the Age of Modernisation and Revolution, 1881–1917* (London, 1983). Dietrich Geyer, *Russian Imperialism: The Interaction of Domestic and Foreign Policy, 1814–1914* (Leamington Spa, 1987) is valuable for the later period, as is Marc Raeff, *Imperial Russia, 1682–1825: The Coming of Age of Modern Russia* (New York, 1971) for the early period. Old, but very readable and meticulous in its scholarship is Michael Florinsky, *Russia: A History and an Interpretation*, 2 vols (London, 1953).

Of enormous use is *The Modern Encyclopedia of Russian and Soviet History*, 58 vols (Gulf Breeze, FL, 1976–94).

What might be called interpretative studies include John Gooding, *Rulers and Subjects: Government and People in Russia, 1801–1991* (London, 1996), Geoffrey Hosking, *Russia: People and Empire, 1552–1917* (Cambridge, MA, 1997), Judith Pallot and Denis Shaw, *Landscape and Settlement in Romanov Russia, 1613–1917* (Oxford, 1990), Richard Pipes, *Russia under the Old Regime* (London, 1982), Marc Raeff, *Understanding Imperial Russia: State and Society in the Old Regime* (New York, 1984), Hugh Ragsdale, *The Russian Tragedy: The Burden of History* (Armonk, NY, 1996). A Eurasian view is given in N. S. Trubetzkoy, *The Legacy of Ghengis Khan and Other Essays on Russia's Identity* (Ann Arbor, MI, 1991).

On absolutism, there is Richard Pipes's translation of what may be considered the key to Russian nineteenth-century thinking, *Karamzin's Memoir on Ancient and Modern Russia* (Cambridge, MA, 1959). More modern works include Michael Cherniavsky, *Tsar and People, Studies in Russian Myths* (New Haven, CT, 1961), John P. LeDonne, *Absolutism and the Ruling Class: The Foundation of the Russian Political Order, 1700–1825* (New York, 1991), R. Wortman, *Scenarios of Power: Myth and Ceremony in Russian Monarchy* (Princeton, NJ, 1995).

The Central Government

Peter the Great has been much written about. The best introduction is M. S. Anderson, *Peter the Great* (London, 1978, 2nd edn, 1995). A recent, more challenging study is E. V. Anisimov, *The Reforms of Peter the Great: Progress through Coercion in Russia* (Armonk, NY, 1993). More specialized is C. Peterson, *Peter the Great's Administrative and Judicial Reforms: Swedish Antecedents and the Process of Reception* (Stockholm, 1979). See also the, unfortunately incomplete, account by Peter's Scottish General in

Passages from the Diary of General Patrick Gordon of Auchleuchries, 1635–1699 (Aberdeen, 1859).

The background to the succession crisis of 1730 is the subject of Brenda Meehan-Waters, *Autocracy and Aristocracy, The Russian Service Elite of 1730* (New Brunswick, NJ, 1982). One of its major figures is the subject of R. V. Daniels, *V. N. Tatishchev, Guardian of the Petrine Revolution* (Philadelphia, PA, 1973).

Peter III has at last found an historian in Carol S. Leonard, *Reform and Regicide: The Reign of Peter III of Russia* (Bloomington, IN, 1993), who gives Peter a much larger role in policy-making than does Robert E. Jones, *The Emancipation of the Russian Nobility, 1762–1785* (Princeton, NJ, 1973).

The best general book on the reign of Catherine the Great is Isabel de Madariaga, *Russia in the Age of Catherine the Great* (London, 1981), which is especially good on the complexities of Russian social and political structures as well as being a good read, but see also J. T. Alexander, *Catherine the Great: Life and Legend* (New York, 1989). High politics are examined in Paul Dukes, *Catherine the Great and the Russian Nobility* (Cambridge, 1967) and David Ransel, *The Politics of Catherinian Russia, The Panin Party* (New Haven, CT, 1975). The settlement of New Russia, and of other parts of the Empire, is comprehensively dealt with in Roger Bartlett, *Human Capital: The Settlement of Foreigners in Russia, 1762–1804* (Cambridge, 1979). The first major book on the Catherinian literary scene was Marc Raeff, *Origins of the Russian Intelligentsia: The Eighteenth-century Nobility* (New York, 1966). Although this is still interesting, it has to a certain extent been superseded by Walter J. Gleason, *Moral Idealists, Bureaucracy, and Catherine the Great* (New Brunswick, NJ, 1981), W. Gareth Jones, *Nikolay Novikov Enlightener of Russia* (Cambridge, 1984) and Gary Marker, *Publishing, Printing, and the Origins of Intellectual Life in Russia, 1700–1800* (Princeton, NJ, 1985). Catherine's local government reform is studied by R. E. Jones, *Provincial Development in Russia: Catherine II and Joseph Sievers* (New Brunswick, NJ, 1984). For a flavour of the times see M. M. Shcherbatov, *On the Corruption of Morals in Russia* (Cambridge, 1969), Catherine's own *Memoirs*, with an introduction by Herzen (New York, 1957), and the *Memoirs of Princess Dashkov* (London, 1958).

The standard work on Paul I is Roderick E. McGrew, *Paul I of Russia, 1754–1801* (Oxford, 1992), but see also Hugh Ragsdale, *Paul I: A Reassessment of His Life and Reign* (Pittsburgh, PA, 1979) and idem, *Tsar Paul and the Question of Madness: An Essay on History and Psychology* (London, 1988). For an eye-witness account, full of gossip, see C. F. P. Masson, *Mémoires secrets sur la Russie pendant les règnes de Catherine II et de Paul Ier* (Paris, 1859).

Alexander I has attracted much 'mystical' attention, which I shall ignore here. Among the serious works, Janet M. Hartley, *Alexander* (London, 1994), is down to earth and easy to read. See also the older, but still serviceable, A. McConnell, *Tsar Alexander I: Paternalistic Reformer* (Arlington, VA, 1970) and A. Palmer, *Alexander I: Tsar of War and Peace* (London, 1974). For Alexander's most enlightened statesman, see Marc Raeff, *Michael Speranskii: Statesman of Imperial Russia* (The Hague, 1957). (See below under Poland for books on Czartoryski.)

Contemporary sources include S. W. Jackman, *Romanov Relations: The Private Correspondence of Alexander I, Nicholas I and the Grand Dukes Constantine and Michael with their Sister Queen Anna Pavlovna, 1817–1855* (London, 1969), *The Private Letters of Princess Lieven to Prince Metternich, 1820–1826* (London, 1937) and *The Correspondence of Lord Aberdeen and Princess Lieven, 1832–1854*, 2 vols (London, 1938–39).

On Nicholas I, see W. Bruce Lincoln, *Nicholas I, Emperor and Autocrat of All the Russias* (London, 1978), Sidney Monas, *The Third Section: Police and Society in Russia under Nicholas I* (Cambridge, MA, 1961), A. E. Presniakov, *Emperor Nicholas I of Russia: The Apogee of Autocracy, 1825–1855* (Gulf Breeze, FL, 1974), Nicholas V. Riasanovsky, *Nicholas I and Official Nationality in Russia* (Berkeley, CA, 1961), P. S. Squire, *The Third Department: The Establishment and Practices of the Political Police in the Russia of Nicholas I* (Cambridge, 1968).

Two contemporary Western views of Nicholas I's Russia, the first much more hostile than the second, are the Marquis de Custine, *Lettres de Russie* (Paris, 1975) and August von Haxthausen, *Studies on the Interior of Russia* (Chicago, IL, 1972).

Curiously enough, Alexander II has not attracted very many biographers: N. G. O. Pereira, *Tsar-Liberator: Alexander II of Russia* (Gulf Breeze, FL, 1983), and P. A. Zaionchkovskii, *The Russian Autocracy in Crisis, 1878–1882* (Gulf Breeze, FL, 1979).

On the Emancipation, the best book is probably Daniel Field, *The End of Serfdom: Nobility and Bureaucracy in Russia, 1855–61* (Cambridge, MA, 1976). Other aspects are examined in Terence Emmons, *The Russian Landed Gentry and the Peasant Emancipation of 1861* (Cambridge, 1968), P. A. Zaionchkovskii, *The Abolition of Serfdom in Russia* (Gulf Breeze, FL, 1978). On the reforms in general see W. Bruce Lincoln, *The Great Reforms: Autocracy, Bureaucracy and the Politics of Change in Imperial Russia* (DeKalb, IL, 1990).

There are two biographies of Nicholas Miliútin: Anatole Leroy-Beaulieu, *Un homme d'état russe: (Nicolas Miliutine) d'après sa correspondance inédite* (Paris, 1884; reprinted 1969) and the more recent W. Bruce Lincoln, *Nikolai Miliutin: An Enlightened Bureaucrat of the Nineteenth Century* (Newtonville, MA, 1977).

Post-Emancipation Russia is the subject of D. Mackenzie Wallace, *Russia*, 2 vols (London, 1877) which ran through numerous editions until 1912, and contains many vivid insights into the Russia of Alexander II, Alexander III and Nicholas II.

On Alexander III see H. W. Whelan, *Alexander III and the State Council* (New Brunswick, NJ, 1982), P. A. Zaionchkovskii, *The Russian Autocracy under Alexander III* (Gulf Breeze, FL, 1976) and R. Byrnes, *Pobedonostsev. His Life and Thought* (Bloomington, IN, 1968). Konstantin Pobedonostsev's own view of the degeneracy of Western institutions can be read in his *Reflections of a Russian Statesman* (Ann Arbor, MI, 1965).

On the pre-Revolutionary state bureaucracy: D. Lieven, *Russia's Rulers under the Old Regime* (New York, 1989), W. Bruce Lincoln, *In the Vanguard of Reform: Russia's Enlightened Bureaucrats, 1825–1861* (DeKalb, IL, 1986), Daniel T. Orlovsky, *The Limits of Reform: The Ministry of Internal Affairs in Imperial Russia, 1802–1881* (Cambridge, MA, 1981) and R. Robbins, *The Tsar's Viceroys: Russian Provincial Governors in the Last Years of the Empire* (Ithaca, NY, 1987). Peter R. Weisensel, *Prelude to the Great Reforms: Avraam Sergéevich Nórov and Imperial Russia in Transition* (Minneapolis, MN, 1995) is a study of a man whom the author describes as 'the archetype of the transitional statesmen' in the Ministry of the Interior. Among Nicholas II's ministers only Plehve and Stolýpin have attracted attention: E. Judge, *Plehve* (Syracuse, NY, 1983), Mary S. Conroy, *P. A. Stolypin, Practical Politics in Late Tsarist Russia* (Boulder, CO, 1976), G. Tokmakov, *Stolypin and the Third Duma* (Washington, DC, 1981) and A. V. Zenkovsky, *Stolypin: Russia's Last Great Reformer* (Princeton, NJ, 1986).

The conflict between autocracy and decentralization is studied in S. Frederick Starr, *Decentralization and Self-Government in Russia, 1830–1870* (Princeton, NJ, 1972), T. Pearson, *Russian Officialdom in Crisis: Autocracy and Local Self-Government* (Cambridge, 1990), F. W. Wcislo, *Reforming Rural Russia: State, Local Society and National Politics, 1855–1914* (Princeton, NJ, 1990), N. Weissman, *Reform in Tsarist Russia: the State Bureaucracy and Local Government 1900–1909* (New Brunswick, NJ, 1981) and George Yaney, *The Systematization of Russian Government* (Urbana, IL, 1973).

Government attempts to control free expression are examined in D. Balmuth, *Censorship in Russia, 1865–1905* (Washington, DC, 1979), M. T. Choldin, *A Fence around the Empire: Russian Censorship of Western Ideas under the Tsars* (Durham, NC, 1985) and C. A. Ruud, *Fighting Words: Imperial Censorship and the Russian Press, 1804–1906* (Toronto, 1982). See also A. Nikitenko, *Diary of a Russian Censor* (Amherst, MA, 1975).

For the nobility, see S. Becker, *Nobility and Privilege in Late Imperial Russia* (DeKalb, IL, 1985), G. Hamburg, *Politics of the Russian Nobility, 1881–1905* (New Brunswick, NJ, 1984), R. T. Manning, *The Crisis of the Old Order in Russia: Gentry and Government* (Princeton, NJ, 1982) and Priscilla Roosevelt, *Life on the Russian Country Estate: A Social and Cultural History* (New Haven, CT, 1995).

The *Raznochintsy* are examined in E. W. Kimerling, *Structures of Society: Imperial Russia's 'Peoples of Various Ranks'* (DeKalb, IL, 1994).

The most noteworthy biographies of Nicholas II are Hélène Carrère d'Encausse, *Nicolas II: la transition interrompue* (Paris, 1996), Marc Ferro, *Nicholas II: The Last of the Tsars* (Oxford, 1993), Dominic Lieven, *Nicholas II Emperor of all the Russias* (London, 1993) and Robert K. Massie, *Nicholas and Alexandra* (London, 1968). See also the work of a Russian émigré historian, S. S. Oldenburg, *The Last Tsar*, 3 vols (Gulf Breeze, FL, 1977). Raspútin has not surprisingly attracted much attention. The least sensational are A. de Jong, *The Life and Times of Grigorii Rasputin* (New York, 1982) and J. Fuhrmann, *Rasputin: A Life* (New York, 1990). Rasputin's daughter has also left a memoir: M. Rasputin, *My Father* (London, 1934).

Nicholas II's statesmen and officials have left a number of memoirs: V. I. Gurko, *Figures and Features of the Past: Government and Opinion in the Reign of Nicholas II* (Stanford, CA, 1939), A. Iswolsky, *Memoirs* (London, 1920), V. N. Kokovtsov, *Out of My Past: The Memoirs of Count Kokovtsov* (Stanford, CA, 1935), A. A. Mossolov, *At the Court of the Last Tsar* (London, 1935) and S. I. Witte, *The Memoirs of Count Witte* (London, 1990). There is also a memoir by Stolýpin's daughter, Maria Petrovna von Bock, *Reminiscences of My Father, Peter A. Stolypin* (Metuchen, NJ, 1971). A highly coloured account by an opponent of the regime is M. V. Rodzianko, *The Reign of Rasputin* (London, 1927).

On the police, see Frederic S. Zuckerman, *The Tsarist Secret Police in Russian Society 1880–1917* (New York, 1996).

Samuel Kucherov, *Courts, Lawyers and Trials under the Last Three Tsars* (Westport, CT, 1953) is a fascinating account of the changes in the judicial system from 1860 to 1917 and includes, among other things, large extracts from Vera Zasulich's defence lawyer's plea for mitigation. O. Gruzenberg, *Yesterday: Memoirs of a Russian-Jewish Lawyer* (Berkeley, CA, 1981) is a particularly fine memoir by a distinguished lawyer. More specialized studies include William G. Wagner, *Marriage, Property and Law in Late Imperial Russia* (Oxford, 1994), Andrzej Walicki, *Legal Philosophies of Russian Liberalism* (Oxford, 1987) and Richard S. Wortman, *The Development of a Russian Legal Consciousness* (Chicago, IL, 1976).

The Armed Forces

Students of the military should probably begin with W. C. Fuller's thought-provoking *Strategy and Power in Russia, 1600–1914* (New York, 1992), and John Keep's *Soldiers of the Tsar: Army and Society in Russia, 1462–1874* (Oxford, 1985).

More specialized studies include Elise Wirtshafter Kimerling, *From Serf to Russian Soldier* (Princeton, NJ, 1990) and Robert H. McNeal, *Tsar and Cossack, 1855–1914* (London, 1987).

Peter Englund, *The Battle of Poltava: The Birth of the Russian Empire* (London, 1992), challenges received ideas on Peter the Great's army, and is excitingly written. The eighteenth-century army is studied in Christopher Duffy, *Russia's Way to the West: Origins and Nature of Russia's Military Power, 1700–1800* (London, 1981) and in Philip Longworth, *The Art of Victory: The Life and Achievements of Generalissimo Suvorov, 1729–1800*, (London, 1965).

Eyewitness accounts of the Napoleonic period include Carl von Clausewitz, *The Campaign of 1812 in Russia* (London, 1843), Jean Hanoteau (ed.), *The Memoirs of General de Caulaincourt, Duke of Vicenza*, 3 vols (London, 1938), Phillipe-Paul de Ségur, *Napoleon's Russian Campaign* (New York, 1942), Robert Wilson, *Brief Remarks on the Character and Composition of the Russian Army, and Sketches of the Campaigns in Poland in the Years 1806 and 1807* (London, 1810), idem, *Narrative of Events during the Invasion of Russia by Napoleon Bonaparte and the Retreat of the French Army, 1812* (London, 1860), idem, *A Sketch of the Military Power of Russia in the Year 1817* (London, 1817), and Herbert Randolph (ed.), *The Private Diary of Travels, Personal Services and Public Events by General Sir Robert Wilson*, 2 vols (London, 1861). There are two biographies of Wilson: Herbert Randolph, *Life of General Sir Robert Wilson*, 2 vols (London, 1862) and Michael Glower, *A Very Slippery Fellow: The Life of Sir Robert Wilson* (Oxford, 1977).

Secondary studies include Christopher Duffy, *Borodino and the War of 1812* (London, 1972), Curtis Gate, *The War of Two Emperors: The Duel between Napoleon and Alexander – Russia 1812* (New York, 1985), Claude Manceron, *Austerlitz* (London, 1966) and George Nafzinger, *Napoleon's Invasion of Russia* (Novato, CA, 1988). E. Tarle, *Napoleon's Invasion of Russia* (London, 1942) is to be treated with caution as it was the object of considerable political pressure.

The only work on Arakchéev in English is M. Jenkins, *Arakcheev: Grand Vizier of the Russian Empire* (London, 1969). Michael Josselson's posthumous *The Commander: A Life of Barclay de Tolly* (Oxford, 1980), does much to rehabilitate this very fine general; and his successor is studied in Roger Parkinson, *The Fox of the North: The Life of Kutuzov* (London, 1976).

A less glorious period is studied by J. S. Curtiss, *The Russian Army under Nicholas I, 1825–1855* (Durham, NC, 1979), Peter Gibbs, *The Battle of the Alma* (London, 1963) and Albert Seaton, *The Crimean War: A Russian Chronicle* (London, 1977).

Considering how important a figure he is, it is surprising that there is only one biography of Dmítrii Miliútin: Forrestt A. Miller, *Dmitrii Miliutin and the Reform Era in Russia* (Nashville, TN, 1968).

On the Russo-Turkish War of 1877–78, contemporary accounts include the *Daily News Correspondence of the War between Russia and Turkey*, 2 vols (London, 1877–78); Captain H. M. Hozier, *The Russo-Turkish War*, 5 vols (London, 1878) and, from the other side, Lieutenant-General Valentine Baker Pacha, *War in Bulgaria: A Narrative of Personal Experiences*,

2 vols (London, 1879), as well as William V. Herbert, *The Defence of Plevna, By One Who Took Part In It* (London, 1895). Charles and Barbara Jelavich have edited the letters of A. G. Jomini and N. K. Giers in *Russia in the East, 1876–1880, The Russo-Turkish War and the Kuldja Crisis* (Leiden, 1959). Secondary studies include Dorothy Anderson, *The Balkan Volunteers* (London, 1968) and David MacKenzie, *The Lion of Tashkent: The Career of General M. G. Cherniaev* (Athens, GA, 1974).

A. N. Kuropatkin, *The Russian Army and the Japanese War*, 2 vols (London, 1909) is an account by the army commander.

John Bushnell's *Mutiny Amid Repression: Russian Soldiers in the Revolution of 1905–1906* (Bloomington, IN, 1985) is superb.

On the army in the last years of the Empire, see W. C. Fuller, *Civil–Military Conflict in Imperial Russia, 1881–1914* (Princeton, NJ, 1985), B. W. Menning, *Bayonets before Bullets: The Imperial Army, 1861–1914* (Bloomington, IN, 1992) and D. Ponomareff, *Political Loyalty and Social Composition of a Military Elite: The Russian Officer Corps 1861–1914* (Santa Monica, CA, 1977).

The military implications of the Franco-Russian Alliance are dealt with in Pertti Luntinen's fascinating *French Information on the Russian War Plans 1880–1914* (Helsinki, 1984).

Memoirs and histories by participants of the First World War and the revolution of 1917 include Grand Duke Alexander, *Once a Grand Duke* (New York, 1931), Sophie Botcharsky and Florida Pier, *They Knew How to Die* (London, 1931), A. Brussilov, *A Soldier's Notebook, 1914–1918* (London, 1930), A. Denikin, *The Career of a Tsarist Officer* (Minneapolis, MN, 1975), Florence Farnborough, *Nurse at the Russian Front* (London, 1977), N. N. Golovine, *The Russian Army in the World War* (New Haven, CT, 1931), B. Gourko, *Memories and Impressions of War and Revolution in Russia 1914–1917* (London, 1918), A. A. Ignatyev, *A Subaltern in Old Russia* (London, 1944), Prince A. Lobanov-Rostovsky, *The Grinding Mill* (New York, 1935), General Loukomsky, *Memoirs of the Russian Revolution* (London, 1922), P. A. Polovtsov, *Glory and Downfall: Reminiscences of a Russian General Staff Officer* (London, 1935) and Stanley Washburn, *The Russian Campaign: April to August 1915* (London, nd). E. Ironside, *Tannenberg: The First Thirty Days in East Prussia* (London, 1925), is a damning assessment of Russia's initial campaign.

M. Mayzel, *Generals and Revolutionaries: The Russian General Staff during the Revolution* (Osnabruck, 1979) and Allan Wildman, *The End of the Russian Imperial Army*, vol. 1, *March–April 1917* (Princeton, NJ, 1980) are both essential reading.

Not surprisingly, there is relatively little written on the Tsarist Navy. What there is includes E. J. Phillips, *The Founding of Russia's Navy: Peter the Great and the Azov Fleet, 1688–1724* (Westport, CT, 1995). A. S. Novikov-Priboi, *Tsushima: Grave of a Floating City* (London, 1937) is a remarkable compilation of personal testimonies collected while the author was a prisoner of war in Japan. See also D. W. Mitchell, *A History of Russian and Soviet Sea Power* (London, 1974); Fred T. Jane, *The Imperial Russian Navy* (London, 1904; reprinted 1983) and John C. Daly, *Russian Seapower and the Eastern Question* (London, 1991). On the turbulent history of the 1917 revolution in the Fleet, see I. Getzler, *Kronstadt 1917–1921: The Fate of a Soviet Democracy* (Cambridge, 1983), Evan Mawdsley, *The Russian Revolution and the Baltic Fleet: War and Politics, February 1917–April 1918* (London, 1978) and N. E. Saul, *Sailors in Revolt: The Russian Baltic Fleet in 1917* (Lawrence, KS, 1978).

Social Unrest and Revolution

The Pugachëv Revolt is studied by J. T. Alexander, *Autocratic Politics in a National Crisis: The Imperial Russian Government and Pugachev's Revolt, 1773– 1775* (Bloomington, IN, 1969) and idem, *Emperor of the Cossacks: Pugachev and the Frontier Jacquerie of 1773–1775* (Lawrence, KS, 1973). Paul Avrich, *Russian Rebels, 1600–1800* (London, 1972), deals with Bulávin as well as Pugachëv.

Daniel Field, *Rebels in the Name of the Tsar* (Boston, MA, 1976) is a collection of annotated documents on the Bezdna and Chigirin affairs. On the Great Famine of 1891 there is R. Robbins, *Famine in Russia 1891– 1892* (New York, 1975). See also S. Bensidoun, *L'agitation paysanne en Russie de 1881 à 1902* (Paris, 1975).

The terrorists have a fairly large academic following, including D. Footman, *Red Prelude: A Life of Zhelyabov* (London, 1944), A. Geifman, *Thou Shalt Kill: Revolutionary Terrorism in Russia, 1894–1917* (Princeton, NJ, 1993), Deborah Hardy, *Land and Freedom: The Origins of Russian Terrorism, 1876–1879* (Seattle, WA, 1987), Norman Naimark, *Terrorists and Social-Democrats: The Russian Revolutionary Movement under Alexander III* (Cambridge, MA, 1983) and Derek Offord, *The Russian Revolutionary Movement in the 1880s* (Cambridge, 1986). One prominent populist assassin has himself contributed to the literature: Stepniak, (S. M. Kravchinskii), *Underground Russia* (London, 1883) and idem, *Nihilism as it is* (London, nd).

There has been much scholarship, most of it American, on working-class life in pre-Revolutionary Russia. Noteworthy are Victoria Bonnell, *Roots of Rebellion: Workers' Politics and Organization in St Petersburg and Moscow, 1900–1914* (Berkeley, CA, 1983), Barbara Engel, *Between Fields and the City: Women, Work and Family in Russia, 1861–1914* (Cambridge, 1994), Rose Glickman, *Russian Factory Women: Workplace and Society, 1880– 1914* (Berkeley, CA, 1988), R. E. Johnson, *Peasant and Proletarian: The Working Class of Moscow in the Late Nineteenth Century* (Leicester, 1979), Mark D. Steinberg, *Moral Communities, the Culture of Class Relations in the*

Russian Printing Industry, 1867–1907 (Berkeley, CA, 1992), Reginald Zelnik, *Labor and Society in Tsarist Russia: The Factory Workers of St Petersburg 1855–1890* (Stanford, CA, 1971) and idem, *Law and Disorder on the Narova River: The Kreenholm Strike of 1872* (Berkeley, CA, 1995). Victoria Bonnell has also edited a very valuable set of memoirs in translation: *The Russian Worker: Life and Labour under the Tsarist Regime* (Berkeley, CA, 1983) and Reginald Zelnik has translated *A Radical Worker in Tsarist Russia: The Autobiography of Semën Ivánovich Kanatchikov* (Stanford, CA, 1986).

On the deeper causes of social unrest and unhappiness is Laurie Bernstein, *Sonia's Daughters: Prostitutes and their Regulation in Imperial Russia* (Berkeley, CA, 1995), Laura Engelstein, *The Keys to Happiness: Sex and the Search for Modernity in Fin-de-Siècle Russia* (Ithaca, NY, 1992), S. P. Frank and M. Steinberg (eds), *Cultures in Flux: Lower-class Values, Practices and Resistance in Late Imperial Russia* (Princeton, NJ, 1994), J. Neuberger, *Hooliganism: Crime, Culture and Power in St Petersburg, 1900–1914* (Berkeley, CA, 1993) and D. L. Ransel, *Mothers of Misery: Child Abandonment in Russia* (Princeton, NJ, 1988).

The Revolutionary Movement

General studies include Philip Pomper, *The Russian Revolutionary Intelligentsia* (Arlington Heights, IL, 1970), Adam B. Ulam, *Russia's Failed Revolutions from the Decembrists to the Dissidents* (London, 1981), Franco Venturi, *Roots of Revolution: A History of the Populist and Socialist Movements in Nineteenth-century Russia* (New York, 1960) and Andrzej Walicki, *A History of Russian Thought from the Enlightenment to Marxism* (Stanford, CA, 1979).

Anatole G. Mazour, *The First Russian Revolution, 1825* (Stanford, CA, 1937) has still not been superceded as the standard work. On individual Decembrists, see Glynn Barratt, *The Rebel on the Bridge: A Life of the Decembrist Baron Andrey Rozen*, (London, 1975) and P. O'Meara, *K. F. Ryleev: A Political Biography of the Decembrist Poet* (Princeton, NJ, 1984). Glynn Barratt, *Voices in Exile: The Decembrist Movement* (Montreal, 1974), is a useful collection of translations of memoirs of the Decembrists themselves. Marc Raeff, *The Decembrist Movement* (Englewood Cliffs, NJ, 1966) is a collection of translations of their policy statements.

On Herzen, see Edward Acton, *Alexander Herzen and the Role of the Intellectual Revolutionary* (Cambridge, 1979), Martin Malia, *Alexander Herzen and the Birth of Russian Socialism, 1812–1855* (Cambridge, MA, 1961) and Judith Zimmerman, *Midpassage: Alexander Herzen and the European Revolution, 1847–1852* (Pittsburgh, PA, 1989). Herzen's autobiography has been translated as *My Past and Thoughts*, 4 vols (London, 1968), as has his *From the Other Shore and The Russian People and Socialism* (Oxford, 1979). C. H. Pearson, *Russia by a Recent Traveller* (London, 1859; reprinted 1970) is by one of Herzen's English correspondents.

See also L. Knapp (ed. and trans.), *Dostoevsky as Reformer: The Petrashevsky Case* (Ann Arbor, MI, 1987), and J. H. Seddon, *The Petrashevtsy and the Origins of Russian Socialism* (Manchester, 1985).

For books on the Bund, see under Jews below.

For Bakúnin, Necháev and Tkachëv, there is Aileen Kelly, *Mikhail Bakunin: A Study in the Psychology and Politics of Utopianism* (New Haven, CT, 1987), A. Masters, *Bakunin* (London, 1974), Philip Pomper, *Sergei Nechaev* (New Brunswick, NJ, 1979) and Deborah Hardy, *Petr Tkachev: The Critic as Jacobin* (Seattle, WA, 1977). Bakúnin's own account of himself can be found in M. Bakúnin, *The Confession of Michael Bakúnin, With the Marginal Comments of Tsar Nicholas I* (Ithaca, NY, 1977). His ideas are in *Bakunin on Anarchy* (London, 1971) and in M. Bakúnin, *Statism and Anarchy* (Cambridge, 1990). See also Woodford McClellan, *Revolutionary Exiles: The Russians in the First International and the Paris Commune* (London, 1979) and Martin A. Miller, *The Russian Revolutionary Emigrés, 1825–1870* (Baltimore, MD, 1986).

Studies of the Populist Movement include James Billington, *Mikhailovsky and Russian Populism* (Oxford, 1958), Abbott Gleason, *Young Russia: The Genesis of Russian Radicalism in the 1860s* (New York, 1980), Ronald Hingley, *The Nihilists: Russian Radicals and Revolutionaries in the Reign of Alexander II, 1855–81* (London, 1967), E. Lampert, *Studies in Rebellion* (London, 1957), idem, *Sons Against Fathers, Studies in Russian Radicalism and Revolution* (London, 1959), Philip Pomper, *Peter Lavrov and the Russian Revolutionary Movement* (Chicago, IL, 1972) and R. Wortman, *The Crisis of Russian Populism* (Cambridge, 1967). Ekaterina Breshko-Breshkovskaia, *The Little Grandmother of the Russian Revolution* (London, 1918) is a memoir by one of the participants in the Movement to the People of 1874.

On the Socialist Revolutionaries, the first major work was O. H. Radkey, *The Agrarian Foes of Bolshevism* (New York, 1958). More recent works include Michael Melançon, *The Socialist Revolutionaries and the Russian Anti-War Movement, 1914–17* (Columbus, OH, 1990), Maureen Perrie, *The Agrarian Policy of the Russian Socialist-Revolutionary Party from its Origins through the Revolution of 1905–7* (Cambridge, 1976) and Christopher Rice, *Russian Workers and the Socialist-Revolutionary Party through the Revolution of 1905–7* (London, 1988). See also Richard Abraham, *Alexander Kerensky, the First Love of the Revolution* (London, 1987) and R. Spence, *Boris Savinkov, Renegade on the Left* (Boulder, CO, 1991). I. Steinberg, Lenin's Left SR Commissar for Justice, has written a biography of *Spiridonova: Revolutionary Terrorist* (London, 1935).

The attempt to create legal Marxist parties is examined in Jonathan Frankel (ed.), *Vladimir Akimov on the Dilemmas of Russian Marxism, 1895–1903* (Cambridge, 1969), Richard Kindersley, *The First Russian Revisionists: A Study of Legal Marxism* (Oxford, 1962), Arthur P. Mendel, *Dilemmas of Progress in Tsarist Russia: Legal Marxism and Legal Populism* (Cambridge,

MA, 1961) and Andrzej Walicki, *The Controversy Over Capitalism: Studies in the Social Philosophy of the Russian Populists* (Oxford, 1969).

For the early illegal Marxist movement, see Leopold Haimson, *Russian Marxism and the Origins of Bolshevism in Russia* (Cambridge, 1955), John Keep, *The Rise of Social Democracy in Russia* (Oxford, 1963), David Lane, *The Roots of Russian Communism: A Social and Historical Study of Russian Social-Democracy 1898–1907* (The Hague, 1969), Richard Pipes, *Social-Democracy and the St Petersburg Labor Movement 1885–1897* (Cambridge, MA, 1970) and Allan Wildman, *The Making of a Workers' Revolution: Russian Social-Democracy 1891–1903* (Stanford, CA, 1967), among which this last book by Wildman is outstanding.

On individual Social-Democrats there is Stephen Cohen, *Bukharin and the Bolshevik Revolution* (Oxford, 1980), Barbara Clements, *Bolshevik Feminist: The Life of Alexandra Kollontai* (Bloomington, IN, 1979), R. H. McNeal, *Bride of the Revolution: Krupsksaya and Lenin* (Ann Arbor, MI, 1972), Robert Service, *Lenin: A Political Life*, 3 vols (London, 1985–95), I. Getzler, *Martov: A Political Biography of a Russian Social-Democrat* (London, 1967), W. H. Roobol, *Tsereteli: A Democrat in the Russian Revolution* (The Hague, 1976) and Jay Bergman, *Vera Zasulich: A Biography* (Stanford, CA, 1983).

Memoirs and histories written by revolutionaries include Eva Broido, *Memoirs of a Revolutionary* (Oxford, 1967), Theodore Dan, *The Origins of Bolshevism* (New York, 1964), N. K. Krupskaia (Lenin's wife), *Reminiscences of Lenin* (Moscow, 1959) and L. D. Trotsky, *My Life* (Harmondsworth, 1975). N. Valentinov (N. V. Volski, who disliked Lenin) has written perceptively of his *Encounters with Lenin* (London, 1968) and *The Early Years of Lenin* (Ann Arbor, MI, 1969). Rosa Luxemburg's critique of Bolshevism, 'Organizational Questions of Russian Social Democracy' (1904), can be found in her *The Russian Revolution and Lenin and Marxism* (Ann Arbor, MI, 1961).

On Kropótkin, there is Martin A. Miller, *Kropotkin* (Chicago, IL, 1976). Krópotkin's own *Memoirs of a Revolutionary* (London, 1906) make good reading, as does his *The Terror in Russia: An Appeal to the British Nation* (London, 1909).

The women's movement is studied in Barbara Engel, *Mothers and Daughters: Women of the Intelligentsia in Nineteenth-Century Russia* (Cambridge, 1983) and Richard Stites, *The Women's Liberation Movement in Russia: Feminism, Nihilism and Bolshevism, 1860–1930* (Princeton, NJ, 1978). Barbara Engel and Clifford Rosenthal have translated the memoirs of women militants of the 1870s in *Five Sisters: Women Against the Tsar* (New York, 1992).

The relationship between workers, employers and the state is examined in Heather Hogan, *Forging Revolution: Metalworkers, Managers and the State in St Petersburg, 1890–1914* (Bloomington, IN, 1992) and by Robert B. McKean's excellent *St Petersburg between the Revolutions: Workers and Revolutionaries June 1907–February 1917* (New Haven, CT, 1990).

The Social-Democracy in the Duma years is the subject of Ralph Carter Elwood, *Russian Social Democracy in the Underground: A Study of the RSDRP in the Ukraine, 1907–1914* (Assen, the Netherlands, 1974) and Geoffrey Swain, *Russian Social-Democracy and the Legal Labour Movement 1906–14* (London, 1983). R. C. Elwood, *Roman Malinovsky: A Life Without a Cause* (Newtonville, MA, 1977) looks at the man who was simultaneously a police spy and the leader of the Bolshevik Duma faction. The Bolshevik Duma deputy, A. E. Badaev, has written a memoir, unfortunately much influenced by censorship considerations, *The Bolsheviks in the State Duma* (Moscow, 1954). On the émigrés in this period see A. E. Senn, *The Russian Revolution in Switzerland 1914–1917* (Madison, WI, 1971).

The Democratic Movement

Because of the nature of the Russian intelligentsia and the intellectual heritage of Belinskii, it is often difficult to draw a line between politics and the arts. Richard Hare, *Pioneers of Russian Social Thought* (Cambridge, 1951), straddles this boundary, as does his *Portraits of Russian Personalities between Reform and Revolution* (London, 1959). More clearly political is Jacob Walkin, *The Rise of Democracy in Pre-Revolutionary Russia: Political and Social Institutions under the Last Three Tsars* (London, 1963). See also G. M. Hamburg, *Boris Chicherin and Early Russian Liberalism, 1828–1866* (Stanford, CA, 1993).

On the *Zémstvo* Movement and the closely associated movement for self-government in the towns, see T. Emmons and W. Vucinich (eds), *The Zemstva in Russia and Experiment in Local Self-Government* (Cambridge, MA, 1982), George Fisher, *Russian Liberalism from Gentry to Intelligentsia* (Cambridge, MA, 1958), K. Frölich, *The Emergence of Russian Constitutionalism 1900–1904* (The Hague, 1981), S. Galai, *The Liberation Movement in Russia 1900–1905* (Cambridge, MA, 1973), T. I. Polner et al., eds, *Russian Local Government during the War and the Union of Zemstvos* (New Haven, CT, 1930) and Robert W. Thurston, *Liberal City, Conservative State: Moscow and Russia's Urban Crisis, 1906–1914* (Oxford, 1987) as well as the contemporary Paul Vinogradov, *Self-Government in Russia* (London, 1915). Nancy Frieden, *Russian Physicians in an Era of Reform and Revolution, 1865–1905* (Princeton, NJ, 1981) examines an important sector of *zémstvo* activity.

On individual liberal leaders, there is Louis Menashe, *Alexander Guchkov and the Origins of the Octobrist Party* (New York, 1966), Richard Pipes, *Struve: Liberal on the Left* (Cambridge, MA, 1970), idem, *Struve: Liberal on the Right* (Cambridge, MA, 1980), Melissa K Stockdale's excellent new biography, *Paul Miliukóv and the Quest for a Liberal Russia 1880–1918* (Ithaca, NY, 1996) and Thomas Riha, *A Russian European: Paul Miliukov in Russian Politics* (Notre Dame, IN, 1969).

M. Szeftel, *The Russian Constitution of April 23, 1906* (Brussels, 1976) is an exhaustive examination of that problematic document. The political parties of the Duma period are dealt with in R. Edelman, *Gentry Politics on the Eve of the Russian Revolution: The Nationalist Party 1907–1917* (New Brunswick, NJ, 1980), T. Emmons, *The Formation of Political Parties and the First National Elections in Russia* (Cambridge, MA, 1983), L. Haimson, (ed.), *The Politics of Rural Russia 1905–1914* (Bloomington, IN, 1979), G. Hosking, *The Russian Constitutional Experiment: Government and Duma 1907–1914* (Cambridge, 1973), Raymond Pearson, *The Russian Moderates and the Crisis of Tsarism, 1914–1917* (London, 1977) and Ben-Cion Pinchuk, *The Octobrists in the Third Duma, 1907–1912* (Seattle, WA, 1974). J. D. Duff (ed.), *Russian Realities and Problems* (Cambridge, 1917) contains an excellent essay by Paul Miliukóv, which is by far the most readily comprehensible account of how the Duma was elected. Much more detailed are Alfred Levin's studies *The Second Duma: A Study of the Social-Democratic Party and the Russian Constitutional Experiment* (New Haven, CT, 1940), and *The Third Duma: Election and Profile* (Hamden, CT, 1973).

Important memoirs of Duma politicians are Paul Miliukov, *Political Memoirs, 1905–1917* (Ann Arbor, MI, 1967), idem, *The Russian Revolution*, vol. 1 (Gulf Breeze, FL, 1987) and V. V. Shulgin, *The Years: Memoirs of a Member of the Russia Duma, 1906–1917* (New York, 1984).

The Revolution of 1905–1907

A. Ascher, *The Revolution of 1905*, 2 vols (Stanford, CA, 1988 & 1992) is now the standard work.

The curious experiment in Police Trades Unionism that led up to Bloody Sunday has been studied in Dimitry Pospielovsky, *Russian Police Trade Unionism: Experiment or Provocation* (London, 1971), Walter Sablinsky, *The Road to Bloody Sunday: Father Gapon and the St Petersburg Massacre of 1905* (Princeton, NJ, 1976) and Jeremiah Schneiderman, *Sergei Zubatov and the Revolutionary Movement: The Struggle for the Working Class in Russia* (Ithaca, NY, 1976).

Partial studies include Laura Engelstein, *Moscow 1905: Working Class Organization and Political Conflict* (Stanford, CA, 1982), H. Mehlinger and J. Thompson, *Count Witte and the Tsarist Government in the 1905 Revolution* (Bloomington, IN, 1972), Don C. Rawson, *Russian Rightists and the Revolution of 1905* (Cambridge, 1995), Henry Reichman, *Railwaymen and Revolution: Russia 1905* (Berkeley, CA, 1987), Teodor Shanin, *Russia 1905–7: Revolution as Moment of Truth* (London, 1986), G. Suhr, *1905 in St Petersburg: Labor, Society and Revolution* (Stanford, CA, 1989), A. Verner, *The Crisis of Russian Autocracy: Nicholas II and the 1905 Revolution* (Princeton, NJ, 1990) and Robert Weinberg, *The Revolution of 1905 in Odessa: Blood on the Steps* (Bloomington, IN, 1993).

Solomon M. Schwarz, *The Russian Revolution of 1905: The Workers' Movement and the Formation of Bolshevism and Menshevism* (Chicago, IL, 1967) is an account by a Bolshevik who subsequently became a Menshevik. Eyewitness accounts by foreigners include the *Daily Chronicle* correspondent Henry Nevinson, *The Dawn in Russia* (London, 1906) and two by Bernard Pares, *Russia between Reform and Revolution* (London, 1905) and *Russia and Reform* (London, 1907).

The Revolution of February 1917

The only Soviet Russian history of the Revolution worth reading is E. N. Burdzhalov, *Russia's Second Revolution* (Bloomington, IN, 1988). T. Hasegawa's *The February Revolution: Petrograd 1917* (Seattle, WA, 1981) is the most thorough of the standard accounts. Three recent books try to place the revolution in a longer historical context: Orlando Figes, *A People's Tragedy: The Russian Revolution 1891–1924* (London, 1996), Richard Pipes, *The Russian Revolution, 1899–1919* (London, 1990) and James D. White, *The Russian Revolution, 1917–1921: A Short History* (London, 1994). Michael Florinskii, *The End of the Russian Empire* (New Haven, CT, 1931) is still worth reading. Very quirky, often misleading but nonetheless full of insights and, in its day, one of the most popular clandestine books in the Soviet Union is George Katkov, *Russia 1917: The February Revolution* (London, 1967). A good collection of revisionist essays is E. R. Frankel et al. (eds), *Russia in Revolution: Reassessments of 1917* (Cambridge, 1992).

Specialized studies include Lars T. Lih, *Bread and Authority in Russia 1914–1921* (Berkeley, CA, 1990), Tim McDaniel, *Autocracy, Capitalism and Revolution in Russia* (Berkeley, CA, 1988), William G. Rosenberg, *Liberals in the Russian Revolution* (Princeton, NJ, 1974) and M. D. Steinberg and V. M. Khrustalev, *The Fall of the Romanovs: Political Dreams and Personal Struggles in a Time of Revolution* (New Haven, CT, 1995).

An account of an important, if often overlooked, event is Nicholas de Basily, *The Abdication of Emperor Nicholas II of Russia* (Princeton, NJ, 1985).

Alexander Kerensky has left three sets of memoirs, all of them different and all of them unreliable: *The Catastrophe: Kerensky's Own Story of the Russian Revolution* (London, 1927), *The Crucifixion of Liberty* (London, 1934) and *The Kerensky Memoirs: Russia and History's Turning Point* (London, 1965). He has also edited a collection of documents on the Revolution: R. P. Browder and A. F. Kerensky, *The Russian Provisional Government, 1917*, 3 vols (Stanford, CA, 1961). Unfortunately, he has interpreted the word 'edited' very liberally, omitting sections of documents that do not suit him. V. V. Shulgin, *Days of the Russian Revolution* (Gulf Breeze, FL, 1990) is offensively anti-Semitic, but a beautifully written and often perceptive eyewitness account of events in the Duma and in Pskov in February 1917.

Memoirs by revolutionaries include V. Chernov, *The Great Russian Revolution* (New Haven, CT, 1936), S. Mstislavsky, *Five Days which transformed Russia* (London, 1988), A. Shliapnikov, *On the Eve of 1917: Reminiscences from the Revolutionary Underground* (London, 1982), V. Shklovsky, *Sentimental Journey* (Ithaca, NY, 1970), Pitrim Sorokin, *Leaves from a Russian Diary* (New York, 1924) and N. N. Sukhanov, *The Russian Revolution: A Personal Record* (Oxford, 1955), which is probably the most valuable of all.

Germany's contribution to the overthrow of the Tsar is examined in Z. A. B. Zeman, *Germany and the Revolution in Russia 1915–1918* (London, 1958), and Z. A. B. Zeman and Walter Scharlau, *The Merchant of Revolution* (London, 1965).

Religion and the Church

General introductions include G. Hosking (ed.), *Church, Nation and State in Russia and Ukraine* (London, 1991), George L. Kline, *Religious and Anti-Religious Thought in Russia* (Chicago, IL, 1968), Nicholas Zernov, *Eastern Christendom* (London, 1963) and idem, *The Russians and Their Church* (London, 1978).

Although Nikon's reforms come before our period, an understanding of them is crucial, and so one cannot do better than read P. Meyendorff, *Russia, Ritual and Reform: The Liturgical Reforms of Nikon in the Seventeenth Century* (Crestwood, NY, 1987).

James Cracraft, *The Church Reform of Peter the Great* (London, 1971) is the standard work on the subject. Cracraft has also edited a new publication of what he describes as 'the first scholarly work on Russia ever published in English': *For God and Peter the Great: The Works of Thomas Consett, 1723–29* (New York, 1982). Alexander V. Muller, *The Spiritual Regulation of Peter the Great* (Seattle, WA, 1972), is the first complete translation since Consett, and contains extremely useful notes and an introduction.

On the Old Believers, Pierre Pascal, *Avvakum et les débuts du raskol* (Paris, 1938) deals with events just before the period covered here, but is important to an understanding of the Old Belief. See also Robert Crummey, *The Old Believers and the World of the Anti-Christ: The Vyg Community and the Russian State 1694–1855* (Madison, Wisconsin, 1970). Alexander Gerschenkron, *Europe in the Russian Mirror* (Cambridge, 1970) examines the relationship between the Old Belief and the development of a capitalist class in Russia. Older but still worth consulting is F. C. Conybeare, *The Russian Dissenters* (Cambridge, MA, 1921). A Soviet view is A. Klibanov, *History of Religious Sectarianism* (Oxford, 1982).

On non-Orthodox Christianity, see J. Urry, *None but Saints: The Transformation of Mennonite Life in Russia, 1789–1889* (Winnipeg, 1989). The

Procurator of the Holy Synod, Dmitry Tolstoy, has left a history of *Romanism in Russia*, 2 vols (London, 1874; reprinted New York, 1971).

The Orthodox clergy in the eighteenth and nineteenth centuries is examined in two books by Gregory Freeze: *The Russian Levites: Parish Clergy in the Eighteenth Century* (Cambridge, MA, 1977) and *The Parish Clergy in Nineteenth-Century Russia: Crisis, Reform, Counter-Reform* (Princeton, NJ, 1983). Freeze has also edited and translated I. S. Belliustin, *Description of the Clergy in Rural Russia: The Memoir of a Nineteenth-Century Parish Priest* (Ithaca, NY, 1985).

Brenda Meehan, *Holy Women of Russia: The Lives of Five Orthodox Women Offer Spiritual Guidance for Today* (Crestwood, NY, 1997) argues from its examination of five monastic women in late Imperial Russia that feminine spiritualism is different to that of the male.

Early twentieth-century religion is studied in J. Curtiss, *Church and State in Russia: The Last Years of the Empire* (New York, 1940), Catherine Evtuhov, *The Cross and the Sickle: Sergei Bulgakov and the Fate of Russian Religious Philosophy 1890–1920* (Ithaca, NY, 1997), Samuel D. Cioran, *Vladimir Solovëv and the Knighthood of the Divine Sophia* (Ontario, 1977) and Nicholas Zernov, *The Russian Religious Renaissance of the Twentieth Century* (London, 1963).

Education

General studies of the Russian educational system include Patrick Alston, *Education and the State in Tsarist Russia* (Stanford, CA, 1969), Nicholas Hans, *History of Russian Educational Policy, 1701–1917* (New York, 1964), James C. McClelland, *Autocrats and Academics: Education, Culture and Society in Tsarist Russia* (Chicago, IL, 1979) and Cynthia Whittaker, *The Origins of Modern Russian Education* (DeKalb, IL, 1987).

On early educational efforts, see J. L. Black, *Citizens for the Fatherland: Education, Educators and Pedagogical Ideals in Eighteenth-Century Russia* (Boulder, CO, 1979). Alexander I's struggles with the universities are examined in James T. Flynn, *The University Reforms of Tsar Alexander I, 1802–1835* (Washington, DC, 1988), and the later turbulent history of the government's attempt to control the student movement is ably described in Daniel R. Brower, *Training the Nihilists: Education and Radicalism in Tsarist Russia* (Ithaca, NY, 1975) and Allen Sinel, *The Classroom and the Chancellery: State Education Reform in Russia under Count Dmitry Tolstoi* (Cambridge, MA, 1973). V. G. Korolenko, *The History of My Contemporary* (Oxford, 1972) gives a vivid eyewitness account.

Studies of education in the late Empire include B. Eklof, *Russian Peasant Schools: Officialdom, Village Culture and Popular Pedagogy, 1861–1914* (Berkeley, CA, 1986), Paul N. Ignatiev et al., *Russian Schools and Universities in the World War* (New Haven, CT, 1929), S. Kassow, *Students, Professors and the State in Tsarist Russia* (Berkeley, CA, 1989), Christine Ruane, *Gender, Class and the Professionalization of Russian City Teachers, 1860–1914* (Pittsburgh, PA, 1994) and S. J. Seregny, *Russian Teachers and Peasant Revolution. The Politics of Education in 1905* (Bloomington, IN, 1989).

Jeremy Brooks, *When Russia Learnt to Read: Literacy and Popular Literature, 1861–1917* (Princeton, NJ, 1985) is a joy that deserves to be widely read.

Industry and the Bourgeoisie

For general studies, see W. L. Blackwell, *The Beginnings of Russian Industrialization 1800–1860* (Princeton, NJ, 1968), idem, *Russian Economic Development from Peter the Great to Stalin* (New York, 1974), Olga Crisp, *Studies in the Russian Economy before 1914* (London, 1976), Peter Gatrell, *The Tsarist Economy 1850–1917* (London, 1986) and Thomas Owen, *Russian Corporate Capitalism from Peter the Great to Perestroika* (Oxford, 1995).

More specialized studies include Walter Pintner, *Russian Economic Policy under Nicholas I* (Ithaca, NY, 1967), Thomas C. Owen, *The Corporation Under Russian Law, 1800–1917: A Study in Tsarist Economic Policy* (Cambridge, 1991), Th. Von Laue, *Sergei Witte and the Industrialization of Russia* (New York, 1963) and Steven Marks, *Road to Power: The Trans-Siberian Railway and the Colonization of Asian Russia 1850–1917* (London, 1991).

A translation of a Russian nineteenth-century classic: M. I. Tugan-Baranovsky, *The Russian Factory in the Nineteenth Century* (Homeward, IL, 1970) is certainly worth looking at.

Foreign entrepreneurs are studied in René Girault, *Emprunts russes et investissements français en Russie, 1887–1914* (Paris, 1973) and John P. McKay, *Pioneers for Profit: Foreign Entrepreneurship and Russian Industrialization 1885–1913* (Chicago, IL, 1970).

On the Russian capitalists, see Valentine Bill, *The Forgotten Class: The Russian Bourgeoisie from the Earliest Beginnings to 1900* (New York, 1959), S. P. McCaffray, *The Politics of Industrialization in Tsarist Russia: The Association of Southern Coal and Steel Producers, 1874–1914* (DeKalb, IL, 1996), T. L. Owen, *Capitalism and Politics in Russia: A Social History of the Moscow Merchants, 1855–1905* (Cambridge, 1981), Alfred J. Rieber, *Merchants and Entrepreneurs in Imperial Russia* (Chapel Hill, NC, 1982), Jo-Ann Ruckman, *The Moscow Business Elite: A Social and Cultural Portrait of Two Generations, 1840–1905* (DeKalb, IL, 1984) and Robert W. Tolf, *The Russian Rockefellers: The Saga of the Nobel Family and the Russian Oil Industry* (Palo Alto, CA, 1976).

On the role of the capitalists as patrons of art, see E. W. Clowes, S. D. Kassow and J. L. West (eds), *Between Tsar and People: Educated Society and the Quest for Public Identity in Late Imperial Russia* (Princeton, NJ, 1991). Beverley W. Kean has expanded and updated her *All the Empty Palaces: The Great Merchant Patrons of Modern Art in Pre-Revolutionary Russia*

(London, 1984) in her *French Painters, Russian Collectors: Shchukin, Morozov and Modern French Art, 1890–1914* (London, 1994).

On the effects of urbanization there is J. H. Bater, *St Petersburg: Industrialization and Change* (London, 1976), J. Bradley, *Muzhik and Muscovite: Urbanization in Late Imperial Russia* (Berkeley, CA, 1965), D. Brower, *The Russian City between Tradition and Modernity, 1850–1900* (Berkeley, CA, 1990), Michael F. Hamm (ed.), *The City in Russian History* (Lexington, KY, 1976), idem, *The City in Late Imperial Russia* (Bloomington, IN, 1986) and Patricia Herlihy, *Odessa: A History 1794–1914* (Cambridge, MA, 1986). (See also on the pre-industrial city: J. Michael Hittle, *The Service City: State and Townsmen in Russia, 1600–1800* (Cambridge, MA, 1979).)

In his *Russian National Income 1885–1913* (Cambridge, 1982) and his *Before Command: An Economic History of Russia from Emancipation to the First Five Year Plan* (Princeton, NJ, 1994) Paul Gregory puts forward an optimistic view of the pre-revolutionary economy.

The Armaments Industry and the First World War are examined in Joseph Bradley, *Guns for the Tsar* (de Kalb, IL, 1990), Peter Gatrell, *Government, Industry and Rearmament in Russia, 1900–1914: The Last Argument of Tsarism* (Cambridge, 1994), Keith Neilson, *Strategy and Supply: The Anglo-Russian Alliance 1914–1917* (London, 1984), and Lewis H. Siegelbaum, *The Politics of Industrial Mobilization in Russia, 1914–1917* (London, 1983).

Serfdom, the Peasantry and Agriculture

The best studies of eighteenth-century agriculture are Michael Confino, *Domaines et Seigneurs en Russie vers la fin du XVIIIe siècle* (Paris, 1963), idem, *Systèmes agraires et progrès agricole: l'assolement triennal en Russie aux XVIIIe–XIXe siècles* (Paris, 1969) and Arcadius Kahan, *The Plow, the Hammer, and the Knout: An Economic History of Eighteenth-Century Russia* (Chicago, IL, 1985).

General studies of the nineteenth century include Lazar Volin, *A Century of Russian Agriculture from Alexander II to Khrushchev* (Cambridge, MA, 1971), E. Kingston-Mann and T. Mixter (eds), *Peasant Economy, Culture and Politics of European Russia, 1800–1921* (Princeton, NJ, 1991) and George Yaney, *The Urge to Mobilize: Agrarian Reform in Russia 1801–1930* (Urbana, IL, 1982).

The essential ingredients of Russian peasant life are examined in R. E. F. Smith and David Christian, *Bread and Salt: A Social and Economic History of Food and Drink in Russia* (New York, 1984) and David Christian, *Living Water: Vodka and Russian Society on the Eve of Emancipation* (Oxford, 1990).

Serfdom is looked at in Jerome Blum, *Lord and Peasant in Russia from the Ninth to the Nineteenth Century* (Princeton, NJ, 1961), Z. J. Deal, *Serf and State Peasant: Kharkov Province 1842–1861* (New York, 1981), Steven

L. Hoch, *Serfdom and Social Control in Russia: Petrovskoe Village in Tambov* (Chicago, IL, 1986), Peter Kolchin, *Unfree Labour: American Slavery and Russian Serfdom* (Cambridge, MA, 1987), David Moon, *Russian Peasants and Tsarist Legislation on the Eve of Reform, 1825–1855* (Basingstoke, 1992), and idem, *The Russian Peasantry 1600–1930: The World the Peasants Made* (London, 1999).

The Emancipation statute is studied in detail in Roger Portal (ed.), *Le statut des paysans libérés du servage: Recueil d'articles et de documents* (Paris, 1963).

Post-Emancipation peasant life is the subject of Roger Bartlett, *Land Commune and Peasant Community in Russia: Communal Forms in Imperial and Early Soviet History* (London, 1990), Ben Eklof and Stephen Frank, (eds), *The World of the Russian Peasant: Post-Emancipation Culture and Society* (London, 1990), C. Frierson, *Peasant Icons: Representations of Rural People in Late Nineteenth-Century Russia* (Oxford, 1993), Geroid T. Robinson, *Rural Russia under the Old Regime* (London, 1932), Teodor Shanin, *Russia as a Developing Society*, vol. 1 (London, 1986), Donald Treadgold, *The Great Siberian Migration: Government and Peasant Resettlement from Emancipation to the First World War* (Princeton, NJ, 1951), Wayne Vucinich (ed.), *The Peasant in Nineteenth-Century Russia* (Stanford, CA, 1968) and C. Worobec, *Peasant Russia: Family and Community in the Post-Emancipation Period* (Princeton, NJ, 1991).

Contemporary accounts include Henry Ling Roth, *A Sketch of the Agriculture and Peasantry of Eastern Russia* (London, 1878) and Stepniak (S. M. Kravchinsky), *The Russian Peasantry: Their Agrarian Condition, Social Life and Religion* (London, 1888).

For the last years see D. Atkinson, *The End of the Russian Land Commune 1905–1920* (Stanford, CA, 1983), R. Hennessy, *The Agrarian Question in Russia: The Inception of the Stolypin Reform* (Giessen, 1977) and Teodor Shanin, *The Awkward Class: The Political Sociology of Peasantry in a Developing Society: Russia 1910–1925* (Oxford, 1972).

Culture

James Billington, *The Icon and the Axe: An Interpretative History of Russian Culture* (London, 1966) is a good introduction, guaranteed to annoy, provoke and stimulate. Joseph Frank has also written more generally, *Through the Russian Prism: Essays on Literature and Culture* (Princeton, NJ, 1990). See also J. D. Kornblatt, *The Cossack Hero in Russian Literature: A Study in Cultural Mythology* (Madison, WI, 1992), Marcia A. Morris, *Saints and Revolutionaries: The Ascetic Hero in Russian Literature* (Albany, NY, 1993), Nicholas V. Riasanovsky, *A Parting of Ways: Government and the Educated Public in Russia 1801–1855* (Oxford, 1976), A. B. Wachtel, *An Obsession with History: Russian Writers Confront the Past* (Stanford, CA, 1994).

As its title suggests, Lev Loseff, *On the Beneficence of Censorship: Aesopian Language in Modern Russian Literature* (Munich, 1984) argues that censorship has had a beneficial effect on Russian writing.

Max J. Okenfuss, *The Rise and Fall of Latin Humanism in Early-Modern Russia: Pagan Authors, Ukrainians and the Resiliency of Moscow* (Leiden, 1995), which argues that Westernization failed in eighteenth-century Russia, is so wide in its scope and implications that its place seems to be here, rather than under more specialized headings (Ukraine, Education).

On Radíshchev, see D. M. Lang, *The First Russian Radical: Alexander Radishchev* (London, 1959), Allen McConnell, *A Russian Philosophe: Alexander Radishchev* (The Hague, 1964) as well as the book itself: Alexander Radishchev, *A Journey from St Petersburg to Moscow* (Cambridge, MA, 1958).

On Russian freemasonry, there is W. Gareth Jones, *Nikolai Novikov: Enlightener of Russia* (Cambridge, 1984) and Lauren G. Leighton, *The Esoteric Tradition in Russian Romantic Literature: Decembrism and Freemasonry* (University Park, PA, 1994).

On individual writers of the early nineteenth century, see Raymond T. McNally's *Chaadayev and his Friends* (Tallahassee, FL, 1971), Paul Debreczeny, *Social Functions of Literature: Alexander Pushkin and Russian Culture* (Stanford, CA, 1997), S. Fusso, *Designing Dead Souls: An Anatomy of Disorder in Gogol* (Stanford, CA, 1993), Robert A. Maguire, *Exploring Gogol* (Stanford, CA, 1995) and Herbert Bowman, *Vissarion Belinsky, 1811–1848: A Study in the Origins of Social Criticism in Russia* (Cambridge, MA, 1954). A contemporary account is P. V. Annenkov, *The Extraordinary Decade: Literary Memoirs* (Ann Arbor, MI, 1968).

On Slavophilism, see P. K. Christoff, *An Introduction to Nineteenth-Century Slavophilism*, 3 vols (The Hague, 1961–72), W. Dowler, *Dostoevskii, Grigor'ev and Native Soil Conservatism* (Toronto, 1982), Abbott Gleason, *European and Muscovite: Ivan Kireevsky and the Origins of Slavophilism* (Cambridge, MA, 1972), Stephen Lukashevich, *Ivan Aksakov, 1823–1886: A Study in Russian Thought and Politics* (Cambridge, MA, 1965); Nicholas Riasanovsky, *Russia and the West in the Teaching of the Slavophiles* (Gloucester, MA, 1965), Edward C. Thaden, *Conservative Nationalism in Nineteenth-Century Russia* (Seattle, WA, 1964) and Andrzej Walicki, *The Slavophile Controversy: History of a Conservative Utopia in Nineteenth-Century Russian Thought* (Oxford, 1975).

On late nineteenth-century writers, see Emil Draitser, *Techniques of Satire: The Case of Saltykov-Ščedrin* (Berlin, 1994), D. T. Orwin, *Tolstoy's Art and Thought, 1847–1880* (Princeton, NJ, 1993), C. J. G. Turner, *A Karenina Companion* (Waterloo, 1993), Leonard Schapiro, *Turgenev, His Life and Times* (Oxford, 1978) and E. C. Allen, *Beyond Realism: Turgenev's Poetics of Secular Salvation* (Stanford, CA, 1992). Turgenev's *Letters* have been edited and selected by A. V. Knowles (London, 1983). On Dostoévskii, there is Joseph Frank, *Dostoevskii: The Miraculous Years 1865–1871*

(Princeton, NJ, 1995), R. L. Jackson, *Dialogues with Dostoevsky: The Over-whelming Questions* (Stanford, CA, 1993), and R. F. Miller, *The Brothers Karamazov: Worlds of the Novel* (New York, 1992).

On the theatre, see Jean Benedetti (ed.), *The Moscow Arts Theatre Letters* (London, 1991), Konstantin Stanislavsky, *My Life in Art* (London, 1962), Robert Leach, *Vsvolod Meyerhold* (Cambridge, 1993), Feodor Chaliapin, *Man and Mask: Forty Years in the Life of a Singer* (London, 1932) and Victor Borovsky, *Chaliapin: A Critical Biography* (NY, 1988).

On the Russian ballet before Diághilev, see Roland John Wiley, *A Century of Russian Ballet: Documents and Eyewitness Accounts, 1810–1910* (Oxford, 1990). There has been enormous interest in Diághilev and his *Ballets russes*, a wealth of memoirs and even more critical studies. Biographies include Richard Buckle, *Diághilev* (London, 1993), Lynn Garafola, *Diághilev's Ballets Russes* (Oxford, 1989), John Percival, *The World of Diághilev* (New York, 1979), Serge Lifar, *Serge Diághilev: His Life, His Work, His Legend* (London, 1940) and Arnold L. Haskell and Walter Nouvel, *Diághileff: His Artistic and Private Life* (NY, 1935). See also Michael de Cossart, *Ida Rubinstein* (Liverpool, 1987) and for her admirer, Philippe Jullian, *Robert de Montesquiou: un prince 1900* (Paris, 1965).

Memoirs include Michel Fokine, *Memoirs of a Ballet Master* (London, 1961), Tamara Karsavina, *Theatre Street* (London, 1948), Léonide Massine, *My Life in Ballet* (London, 1968), Bronislava Nijinska, *Early Memoirs* (London, 1981), Vaslav Nijinski, *Cahiers* (Arles, 1995), Romola Nijinsky, *Nijinsky* (London, 1933) and Igor Schwezoff, *Borzoi* (London, 1935). See also, Isadora Duncan, *Isadora: My Life* (London, 1928) and Fredrika Blair, *Isadora: Portrait of the Artist as a Woman* (Wellingborough, 1986).

On the period just before the revolution, see J. Andrew, *Russian Writers and Society during the Rise of the Russian Revolution* (London, 1980), Christopher Barnes, *Boris Pasternak: A Literary Biography*, vol. 1, *1890–1928* (London, 1989), Avril Pyman, *The Life of Alexander Blok*, 2 vols (Oxford, 1980) and Ann Pasternak Slater, (ed.), *A Vanished Present: The Memoirs of Alexander Pasternak* (Oxford, 1984).

A good introduction to Russian music is *The New Grove: Russian Masters*, 2 vols (London, 1986). More detailed studies include Stuart Campbell, *Russians on Russian Music: An Anthology in Translation* (Cambridge, 1994), Alexandra Orlova (ed.), *Musorgsky Remembered* (Bloomington, IN, 1991), Malcolm Hamrick Brown (ed.), *Musorgsky: In Memoriam, 1881–1981* (Ann Arbor, MI, 1982), M. D. Calvocoressi, *Modest Mussorgsky: His Life and Works* (London, 1956), C. Emerson and R. W. Oldani, *Modest Musorgsky and Boris Godunov: Myths, Realities, Reconsiderations* (Cambridge, 1994), Richard Taruskin, *Musorgsky: Eight Essays and an Epilogue* (Princeton, NJ, 1992) and Peter Deane Roberts, *Modernism in Russian Piano Music: Scriabin, Prokofiev and their Contemporaries*, 2 vols (Bloomington, IN, 1995). Stravinsky's Russian roots are examined in Richard Taruskin, *Stravinsky and the Russian Traditions: A Biography of the Works through Mavra*, 2 vols (Berkeley, CA, 1996). On painting, see Alan Bird, *A History of Russian Painting* (Oxford, 1987), V. D. Barooshian, *V. V. Vereshchagin: Artist at War* (Gainsville, FL, 1993), John E. Bowlt, *The Silver Age: Russian Art of the Early Twentieth Century and the World of Art Group* (Newtonville, MA, 1979), David Buckman, *Leonid Pasternak: A Russian Impressionist* (London, 1974), Jeremy Howard, *The Union of Youth* (Manchester, 1992), Alexander Kaminsky, *The World of Art Movement in Early Twentieth-Century Russia* (Leningrad, 1991), Vladimir Markov, *Russian Futurism* (London, 1969), Anthony Parton, *Mikhail Larionov and the Russian Avant-Garde* (Princeton, NJ, 1993), E. Petrova (ed.), *Malevich, Artist and Theoretician* (Moscow, 1990), A. Rusakova, *Mikhail Nesterov* (Leningrad, 1990), Charles Spencer, *Leon Bakst and the Ballets Russes* (London, 1995), Peter Stupples, *Pavel Kuznetsov, His Life and Art* (Cambridge, 1989), Elizabeth Valkenier, *Russian Realist Art* (New York, 1989), Peg Weiss, *Kandinsky and Old Russia: The Artist as Ethnographer and Shaman* (New Haven, CT, 1995), M. N. Yablonskaya, *Women Artists of Russia's New Age* (London, 1990).

On graphic design, there is Mikhail Anikst and Elena Chernevich, *Russian Graphic Design, 1880–1917* (London, 1990) and Gerald Janecek, *The Look of Russian Literature* (Princeton, NJ, 1984).

For architecture, see Kathleen Berton, *Moscow: An Architectural History* (London, 1990), William C. Brumfield, *The Origins of Modernism in Russian Architecture* (Berkeley, CA, 1991), idem, *A History of Russian Architecture* (Cambridge, 1993) and George Heard Hamilton, *The Art and Architecture of Russia* (Harmondsworth, 1975).

Hubertus D. Jahn, *Patriotic Culture in Russia during World War I* (Ithaca, NY, 1995) deals with a specialized aspect.

Russian Expansion

General books on colonial expansion include a useful set of essays edited by Michael Rywkin, *Russian Colonial Expansion to 1917* (London, 1988), George V. Lantzeff and Richard A. Pierce, *Eastward to Empire: Exploration and Conquest on the Russian Open Frontier to 1750* (Montreal, 1973), Tatiana Mastyugina and Lev Perepelkin, *An Ethnic History of Russia: Pre-Revolutionary Times to the Present* (Westport, CT, 1996) and Boris Nolde's classic, but alas uncompleted, *La formation de l'empire russe*, 2 vols (Paris, 1952–53).

The Baltic

See Andrew Henriksson, *The Tsar's Loyal Germans: The Riga German Community, Social Change and the National Question, 1855–1905* (New York,

1983), E. Uustalu, *The History of the Estonian People* (London, 1952), Andrejs Plakans, *The Latvians: A Short History* (Stanford, CA, 1995), E. C. Thaden, *Russia's Western Borderlands, 1770–1870* (Princeton, NJ, 1984) and Andrew Ezergailis, *The 1917 Revolution in Latvia* (New York, 1974).

Poland

For the Partitions of Poland, J. T. Lukowski, *The Partitions of Poland, 1772, 1793, 1795* (London, 1998), is the first book in English on the subject since 1915! On Poland as a whole throughout the Russian period, see Norman Davies, *God's Playground: A History of Poland*, vol. 2 (Oxford, 1981) and P. S. Wandycz, *The Lands of Partitioned Poland, 1795–1918* (Seattle, WA, 1974).

The early period of Russian occupation is dealt with in A. T. Pienkos, *The Imperfect Autocrat: Grand Duke Constantine Pavlovich and the Polish Congress Kingdom* (Boulder, CO, 1987), F. W. Thackeray, *Antecedents of Revolution: Alexander I and the Polish Kingdom, 1815–1825* (Boulder, CO, 1980), Marian Kukiel, *Czartoryski and European Unity, 1700–1861* (Princeton, NJ, 1955) and W. H. Zawadzki, *A Man of Honour: Adam Czartoryski as a Statesman of Russia and Poland 1795–1831* (Oxford, 1993). Adam Czartoryski, *Memoirs and Correspondence with Alexander I*, 2 vols (London, 1888; reprinted, 1968) is not as good as the French original.

For the period from 1830, see R. F. Leslie, *Polish Politics and the Revolution of November 1830* (London, 1956), idem, *British Politics and the Revolution of November 1830* (London, 1956), idem, *Reform and Insurrection in Russian Poland 1856–65* (London, 1963) and idem, *The History of Poland since 1867* (London, 1980). See also Theodore R. Weeks, *Nation and State in Late Imperial Russia: Nationalism on the Western Frontier 1863–1914* (DeKalb, IL, 1996) and Robert E. Blobaum, *Rewolucja: Russian Poland, 1904–7* (Ithaca, NY, 1995).

The first two chapters of Jan Zaprudnik, *Belarus: At a Crossroads in History* (Boulder, CO, 1993) provide a useful survey of a topic not otherwise widely studied.

New Russia

On the southern annexations, see Alan W. Fisher, *The Russian Annexation of the Crimea* (Cambridge, 1970) and G. F. Jewsbury, *The Russian Annexation of Bessarabia, 1774–1828* (Boulder, CO, 1976).

The Russian administration of New Russia and Ukraine and the rise of nationalism and socialism, are studied in Theodore H. Freidgut, *Iuzovka and Revolution*, 2 vols (Princeton, NJ, 1989 & 1994), M. F. Hamm, *Kiev: A Portrait, 1800–1917* (Princeton, NJ, 1993), J.P. Hlinka, *Galician Villagers and the Ukrainian National Movement in the Nineteenth Century* (New

York, 1988), B. Krawchenko, *Social Change and National Consciousness in Twentieth-century Ukraine* (New York, 1985), I. S. Koropeckyj, *Ukrainian Economic History: Interpretive Essays* (Cambridge, MA, 1991), I. Majstrenko, *Borot'bism: A Chapter in the History of Ukrainian Communism* (Edmonton, 1992), I. L. Rudnytsky (ed.), *Rethinking Ukrainian History* (Edmonton, 1981), David Saunders, *The Ukrainian Impact on Russian Culture, 1750–1850* (Edmonton, 1985), O. Subtelny, *The Mazepists: Ukrainian Separatism in the Early Eighteenth Century* (Boulder, CO, 1981) and idem, *Ukraine: A History* (Toronto, 1988).

There are two studies of relatively neglected peoples: J. W. Long, *From Privileged to Dispossessed: The Volga Germans 1860–1917* (Lincoln, NB, 1988) and A.-A. Rorlich, *The Volga Tatars: A Profile in National Resilience* (Stanford, CA, 1986).

Finland

Our knowledge of the Russian period of Finnish history has benefited greatly from a spate of recent publications from Finland itself. These include Steven Huxley, *Constitutional Insurgency in Finland: Finnish 'Passive Resistance' against Russification* (Helsinki, 1990), P. Luntinen, *F. A. Seyn: A Political Biography of a Tsarist Imperialist as Administrator of Finland* (Helsinki, 1985), idem, *The Imperial Russian Army and Navy in Finland, 1808–1918* (Helsinki, 1997), T. Polvinen, *Imperial Borderland: Bobrikov and the Attempted Russification of Finland, 1898–1904* (London, 1995), L. A. Puntila, *The Political History of Finland* (London, 1975), J. E. O. Screen, *The Helsinki Junker School 1846–79* (Helsinki, 1986), idem, *The Finnish Army, 1881–1901* (Helsinki, 1996) and P. Tommila, *La Finlande dans la politique européenne en 1809–15* (Helsinki, 1962). To these can be added Edward C. Thaden (ed.), *Russification in the Baltic Provinces and Finland, 1855–1914* (Princeton, NJ, 1981), A. Upton, *The Finnish Revolution 1917–1918* (Minneapolis, MN, 1980) and the man himself: C. G. E. Mannerheim, *The Memoirs of Marshal Mannerheim* (New York, 1954).

The Jews

General studies include: S. W. Baron, *The Russian Jew under the Tsars and Soviets* (New York, 1964), S. Dubnow, *History of the Jews in Russia and Poland*, 3 vols (Philadelphia, PA, 1916–20), Zvi Gitelman, *A Century of Ambivalence: The Jews of Russia and the Soviet Union* (New York, 1988) and L. Greenberg, *The Jews in Russia, 1881–1917*, 2 vols (New Haven, CT, 1951).

More detailed studies include David E. Fishman, *Russia's First Modern Jews: The Jews of Shklov* (New York, 1995), John D. Klier, *Russia Gathers Her Jews: The Origins of the Jewish Question in Russia 1772–1825* (DeKalb,

IL, 1986), idem, *Imperial Russia's Jewish Question, 1855–1881* (Cambridge, 1995), M. Stanislawki, *Tsar Nicholas I and the Jews: The Transformation of Jewish Society in Russia 1825–1855* (Philadelphia, PA, 1983) and Steven J. Zipperstein, *The Jews of Odessa: A Cultural History 1794–1881* (Stanford, CA, 1985).

A rare autobiography is C. Aronson, *A Jewish Life under the Tsars: Autobiography 1825–1888* (Totowa, NJ, 1983). See also the autobiography of O. Gruzenberg under Central Government above.

For the depressing history of the pogroms, see I. M. Aronson, *Troubled Waters: The Origins of the 1881 Anti-Jewish Pogroms in Russia* (Pittsburgh, PA, 1990), Stephen M. Berk, *Year of Crisis, Year of Hope: Russian Jewry and the Pogrom of 1881–1882* (Westport, CT, 1985), E. H. Judge, *Easter in Kishinev: Anatomy of a Pogrom* (New York, 1992), J. Klier and D Lambroza (eds), *Pogroms: Anti-Jewish Violence in Modern Russian History* (Cambridge, 1992) and Hans Rogger, *Jewish Policies and Right-wing Politics in Imperial Russia* (Berkeley, CA, 1986).

Contemporary accounts include a valuable record by a non-Jewish opponent of the pogroms: Prince S. D. Urussov, *Memoirs of a Russian Governor: The Kishinev Pogrom* (New York, 1907; reprinted, 1970), as well as Cyrus Adler (ed.), *The Voice of America on Kishineff* (Philadelphia, PA, 1904), Michael Davitt, *Within the Pale: The True Story of Anti-Semitic Persecution in Russia* (New York, 1903), A. Séménoff, *The Russian Government and Massacres* (London, 1907; reprinted New York, 1972) and Isadore Singer, *Russia at the Bar of the American People: A Memorial of Kishinef* (New York, 1904). See also extracts in Michael Glenny and Norman Stone, *The Other Russia* (London, 1990) and, of course, L. D. Trotsky, *My Life,* (Harmondsworth, 1975).

On the Beilis Case, see Albert S. Lindemann, *The Jew Accused: Three Anti-Semitic Affairs, Dreyfus, Beilis, Frank, 1894–1915* (Cambridge, 1991), Maurice Samuel, *Blood Accusation: The Strange History of the Beiliss Case* (London, 1967), A. B. Tager, *The Decay of Czarism: The Beiliss Trial* (Philadelphia, PA, 1935). This case is dealt with fictionally in Bernard Malamud's novel *The Fixer,* which has also been made into a film starring Alan Bates as Beilis.

On the Jewish political activists, see J. Frankel, *Prophecy and Politics: Socialism, Nationalism and the Russian Jews 1862–1917* (Cambridge, 1981), C. Gassenschmidt, *Jewish Liberal Politics in Tsarist Russia, 1900–1914* (New York, 1995), E. E. Haberer, *Jews and Revolution in Nineteenth-century Russia* (Cambridge, 1995), E. Mendelsohn, *Class Struggle in the Pale: The Formative Years of the Jewish Workers' Movement in Tsarist Russia* (Cambridge, 1970), Yoav Peled, *Class and Ethnicity in the Pale* (London, 1989), H. J. Tobias, *The Jewish Bund in Russia from its Origins to 1905* (Stanford CA, 1972) and R. S. Wistrich, *Revolutionary Jews from Marx to Trotsky* (NY, 1976).

The Caucasus

John F. Baddeley, *The Russian Conquest of the Caucasus* (London, 1908) is a riveting read, but based exclusively on Russian sources. See also his later work, *The Rugged Flanks of the Caucasus* (London, 1940). This has been corrected by Moshe Gammer, *Muslim Resistance to the Tsar: Shamil and the Conquest of Chechnia and Daghestan* (London, 1994), whose account of the terrible cruelty of the Russian conquest makes the bitterness of the conflict in Chechnia today readily understandable. See also A. Altstadt, *The Azerbaijani Turks: Power and Identity under Russian Rule* (Stanford, CA, 1992), Muriel Atkin, *Russia and Iran 1780–1828* (Minneapolis, MN 1980), D. M. Lang, *The Last Years of the Georgian Monarchy 1658–1832* (New York, 1957), idem, *A Modern History of Georgia* (London, 1962), R. Hovannisen, *The Republic of Armenia*, 2 vols (Berkeley, CA, 1971 & 1982), R. G. Suny, *The Making of the Georgian Nation: From Prehistory to Soviet Rule* (London, 1989) and T. Swietochowski, *Russian Azerbaijan, 1905–1920: The Shaping of a National Identity in a Muslim Community* (Cambridge, 1988). A. L. H. Rhinelander, *Prince Michael Vorontsov: Viceroy to the Tsar* (Montreal, 1990) is about one of the more humane Russian viceroys of the Caucasus. See also below in the section on Russia in Asia for general books about Islam in Russia. See also M. Atkin, *Russia and Iran, 1780–1828*, (Minneapolis, MN, 1980).

Contemporary accounts include W. F. von Freygan, *Letters from the Caucasus and Georgia* (London, 1823), J. Milton Mackie, *Life of Schamyl and Narrative of the Circassian War of Independence Against Russia* (Boston, MA, 1856), W. Monteith, *Kars and Erzeroum. With the Campaigns of Prince Paskiewitch in 1828 and 1829 and an Account of the Conquests of Russia beyond the Caucasus from the Time of Peter the Great to the Treaty of Turcuman Chie and Adrianople* (London, 1856). Alfred J. Rieber (ed.), *The Politics of Autocracy* (Paris and The Hague, 1966), contains the correspondence between Alexander II and his viceroy in the Caucasus, Prince A. I. Bariátinskii.

On Caucasian culture, see Donald Rayfield, *The Literature of Georgia: A History* (Oxford, 1994). From the other side of the hill, there is Susan Layton, *Russian Literature and Empire: Conquest of the Caucasus from Pushkin to Tolstoy* (Cambridge, 1994). On Georgia's great painter, see Erast Kuznetsov and Ketevan Bagratishvili, *Niko Pirosmani, 1862–1918* (Leningrad, 1983).

Russia in Asia

On Siberia, see M. Raeff, *Siberia and the Reforms of 1822* (Seattle, WA, 1956), John Stephan, *The Russian Far East: A History* (Stanford, CA, 1994), already described as a classic, and A. Wood (ed.), *The History of Siberia: From Russian Conquest to Revolution* (London, 1991).

On Central Asia, there is E. Allworth (ed.), *Central Asia: 120 Years of Russian Rule* (Durham, NC, 1989), Elizabeth Bacon, *Central Asia under Russia Rule: A Study in Cultural Change* (Ithaca, NY, 1966), S. Becker, *Russia's Protectorates in Central Asia: Bukhara and Khiva, 1865–1924* (Cambridge, MA, 1968); H. Carrère d'Encausse, *Islam and the Russian Empire: Reform and Revolution in Central Asia* (London, 1988), David Dallin, *The Rise of Russia in Asia* (London, 1950), George Demko, *The Russian Colonization of Kazakhstan 1896–1916* (Bloomington, IN, 1969), A. S. Donnelly, *The Russian Conquest of Bashkiria, 1522–1740, A Case Study in Imperialism* (New Haven, CT, 1968), N. A. Khaflin, *Russia's Policy in Central Asia 1857–1868* (London, 1964), M. Khodarkovsky, *Where Two Worlds Met: The Russian State and Kalmyk Nomads, 1600–1771* (Ithaca, NY, 1992), Richard A. Pierce, *Russian Central Asia, 1867–1870. A Study in Colonial Rule* (Berkeley, CA, 1960), D. Rayfield, *The Dream of Llasa: The Life of Nikolay Przhevalsky, 1839–88: Explorer of Central Asia* (London, 1976), Michael Rywkin, *Russia in Central Asia* (New York, 1963), Edward Sokol, *The Revolt of 1916 in Russian Central Asia* (Baltimore, MD, 1953) and Serge Zenkovsky, *Pan-Turkism and Islam in Russia* (Cambridge, MA, 1962).

Contemporary accounts include Andrew Kalmykov, *Memoirs of a Russian Diplomat: Outposts of Empire, 1893–1917* (New Haven, CT, 1971), Nikolay Muravyov, *Journey to Khiva through the Turcoman Country* (London, 1977) and R. A. Pierce (ed.), *Mission to Turkestan: Being the Memoirs of Count K. K. Pahlen, 1908–1909* (London, 1964).

Russian America

See B. Dmytryshyn (ed. and trans.), *The Russian American Colonies: A Documentary Record, 1798–1867* (Portland, OR, 1989), J. Gibson, *Imperial Russia in Frontier America: The Changing Geography of Supply of Russian America, 1784–1867* (New York, 1976), Howard I. Kushner, *Conflict on the North-West Coast: American Russian Rivalry in the Pacific North-West 1790–1867* (New York, 1975), and in his *Distant Friends* and *Concord and Conflict*, (Lawrence, KS, 1991 & 1996) Norman Saul examines the relationship between Russia and America.

Urey Lisiansky, *A Voyage Round the World in the Years 1803, 1804, 1805, and 1806* (London, 1814; reprinted Amsterdam, 1968) includes detailed studies of the Pacific islands.

Foreign Policy

Barbara Jelavich, *A Century of Russian Foreign Policy, 1814–1914* (Philadelphia, PA, 1964) and her *St Petersburg and Moscow: Tsarist and Soviet Foreign Policy* (Bloomington, IN, 1974) are both good introductory books.

On the Seven Years' War, see H. H. Kaplan, *Russia and the Outbreak of the Seven Years' War* (Cambridge, 1968) and L. J. Oliva, *Misalliance: French Policy in Russia during the Seven Years' War* (New York, 1964). Catherine's policy towards Poland is examined in A. S. Kaminski, *Republic versus Autocracy: Poland-Lithuania and Russia, 1686–1697* (Cambridge, MA, 1993), which is very hostile to Russia. Herbert Kaplan, *Russian Overseas Commerce with Great Britain during the Reign of Catherine II* (Philadelphia, PA, 1995) covers much more than the commercial relations suggested by the title. On this, see also D. K. Reading, *The Anglo-Russian Commercial Treaty of 1734* (New Haven, CT, 1938).

We are fortunate in the analyses of Alexander I's foreign policy, which is well covered by Patricia Kennedy Grimsted, *The Foreign Ministers of Alexander I: Political Attitudes and the Conduct of Russian Diplomacy, 1801–1825* (Berkeley, CA, 1969), Norman Saul, *Russia and the Mediterranean 1797–1807* (Chicago, IL, 1970), Hugh Ragsdale, *Détente in the Napoleonic Era: Bonaparte and the Russians* (Lawrence, KS, 1980), Albert Vandal, *Napoléon et Alexandre Ier: l'Alliance russe sous le Premier Empire*, 3 vols (Paris, 1891–96), Henry Kissinger, *A World Restored: Metternich, Castlereagh and the Problems of Peace 1812–22* (Boston, MA, nd), Harold Nicolson, *The Congress of Vienna: A Study in Allied Unity 1812–22* (London, 1946), F. Ley, *Alexandre I et la Sainte Alliance* (Paris, 1975) and H. G. Schenk, *The Aftermath of the Napoleonic Wars: The Concert of Europe – An Experiment* (New York, 1967).

The best general book on the Eastern Question is M. S. Anderson, *The Eastern Question, 1774–1923: A Study in International Relations* (London, 1966). More specialized studies include John C. K. Daly, *Russian Sea Power and the Eastern Question 1827–41* (London, 1991).

The Greek Revolt is well covered by Douglas Dakin, *The Greek Struggle for Independence, 1821–1833* (London, 1973), Barbara Jelavich, *Russia and the Greek Revolution* (Munich, 1966), Theophilus C. Priousis, *Russian Society and the Greek Revolution* (DeKalb, IL, 1994) and C. M. Woodhouse, *Capodistria: Founder of Greek Independence* (Oxford, 1973).

Russia's complex relations with the Balkan Slavs have also been the subject of much scholarship. See Barbara Jelavich, *Russia's Balkan Entanglements, 1806–1914* (Cambridge, 1991), Charles and Barbara Jelavich, *The Establishment of the Balkan National States, 1804–1914* (Seattle, WA, 1977). A good corrective to Russo-centric historiography is William Miller, *The Ottoman Empire and its Successors, 1801–1927* (London, 1966). Early Russo-British conflict in Serbia is the subject of Stevan K. Pavlovitch, *Anglo-Russian Rivalry in Serbia, 1837–39, The Mission of Colonel Hodges* (Paris, 1961). Other conflicts with Britain are examined in William Habberton, *Anglo-Russian Relations Concerning Afghanistan 1837–1907* (Urbana, IL, 1937), F. Kazemzadeh, *Russia and Britain in Persia, 1864–1914* (New Haven, CT, 1967) and G. Morgan, *Anglo-Russian Rivalry in Central Asia, 1810–1895* (London, 1981).

On two of Nicholas I's foreign policy misconceptions, friendship with Britain and Austria, see Harold Ingle, *Nesselrode and the Russian Rapprochement with Britain, 1836–1844* (Berkeley, CA, 1978) and Ian W. Roberts, *Nicholas I and the Russian Intervention in Hungary* (Basingstoke, 1991). On the Crimean War, Norman Rich, *Why the Crimean War? A Cautionary Tale* (Hannover, NH, 1985) is a good introduction. David Goldfrank, *The Origins of the Crimean War* (London, 1994) is an excellent, balanced study. P. W. Schroeder, *Austria, Great Britain and the Crimean War* (Ithaca, NY, 1972) examines the question from the Austrian viewpoint, seeing Britain's policy as being quite cynical, a view strongly contested in Richard Millman's very persuasive *Britain and the Eastern Question, 1875–1878* (Oxford, 1979). For the politics of the war itself, see D. Wetzel, *The Crimean War: A Diplomatic History* (New York, 1985). Andrew D. Lambert, *The Crimean War: British Grand Strategy against Russia, 1853–56* (Manchester, 1990) adopts a very interesting approach, arguing that the term 'Crimean War' is a misnomer, and shifting the emphasis to British strategy against Russia in the Baltic. See also J. H. Gleason, *The Genesis of Russophobia in Great Britain* (Cambridge, MA, 1950) and Ann Saab, *Reluctant Icon: Gladstone, Bulgaria and the Working Classes 1856–78* (London, 1991).

B. H. Sumner, *Russia and the Balkans 1870–1880* (Oxford, 1937) is still the best book on the Russo-Turkish War of 1877–78. Richard Crampton, *Bulgaria 1878–1918: A History* (Boulder, CO, 1983) is an invaluable corrective to the Russian perspective. See also Barbara Jelavich, *Russia and the Romanian National Cause 1858–59* (Bloomington, IN, 1959), Charles and Barbara Jelavich, *Tsarist Russia and Balkan Nationalism: Russian Influence in the Internal Affairs of Bulgaria and Serbia 1879–1886* (Berkeley, CA, 1958) and David MacKenzie, *The Serbs and Russian Pan-Slavism, 1875–1878* (Ithaca, NY, 1967).

At the time, the Bosnian revolt and the Russo-Turkish War of 1877–78 attracted much attention in the rest of Europe. Sir Edwin Pears, whose reports for the *Daily News* first drew attention to the Turkish atrocities in the Balkans, has left memoirs, *Forty Years in Constantinople* (London, 1916). Januarius A. MacGahan's follow up reports to Pears's initial investigations have been reprinted as a book, *The Turkish Atrocities in Bulgaria* (Geneva, 1966). In turn, these reports gave rise to W. E. Gladstone, *The Bulgarian Horrors and the Question of the East* (London, 1876). Contemporary memoirs include H. C. Barkley, *Bulgaria before the War, during Seven Years' Experience of European Turkey and its Inhabitants* (London, 1877), Arthur J. Evans, *Through Bosnia and Herzegovina on Foot during the Insurrection* (London, 1876) and G. Muir MacKenzie and A. P. Irby, *Travels in the Slavonic Provinces of Turkey-in-Europe*, 2 vols (London, 1877), which has a foreword by Gladstone. Lord Augustus Loftus, the British Ambassador in

St Petersburg during the Russo-Turkish War has left us his rather uninspired *Diplomatic Reminiscences*, 2 vols (London, 1894).

On the decline of the League of the Three Emperors and the rise of the Franco-Russian Alliance, George F. Kennan, *The Decline of Bismarck's European Order: Franco Russian Relations 1875–1890* (Princeton, NJ, 1979), and his *The Fateful Alliance: France, Russia and the Coming of the First World War* (Manchester, 1984) are both thoughtful and a pleasure to read. Almost all books on the subject refer back to Baron Boris Nolde's meticulous *L'Alliance Franco-Russe: Les origines du système diplomatique d'avant-guerre* (Paris, 1936). See also George H. Rupp, *A Wavering Friendship: Russia and Austria 1876–1878* (Cambridge, MA, 1941). Contemporary accounts include Barbara and Charles Jelavich (eds), *The Education of a Russian Statesman: The Memoirs of Nicholas Karlovich Giers* (Berkeley, CA, 1962) and J. Y. Simpson (ed.), *The Saburov Memoirs, or Bismarck and Russia, Being Fresh Light on the League of the Three Emperors* (Cambridge, 1929).

For the Russo-Japanese War and its aftermath, see R. M. Connaughton, *The War of the Rising Sun and Tumbling Bear: A Military History of the Russo-Japanese War, 1904–1905* (London, 1988), Andrew Malozemoff, *Russian Far-Eastern Policy 1881–1904* (Stanford, CA, 1958), Ian Nish, *The Origins of the Russo-Japanese War* (London, 1985), Boris Romanov, *Russia in Manchuria 1892–1906* (Ann Arbor, MI, 1952), J. A. White, *The Diplomacy of the Russo-Japanese War* (Princeton, NJ, 1964), Ernest Price, *The Russo-Japanese Treaties of 1907–16 concerning Manchuria and Mongolia,* (Baltimore, MD, 1933) and Peter S. Tang, *Russian and Soviet Policy in Manchuria and Outer Mongolia, 1911–31,* (Durham, NC, 1959).

The Balkan crises in the run-up to the First World War are covered by K. A. Roider, *Austria's Eastern Question* (Princeton, NJ, 1982), Andrew Rossos, *Russia and the Balkans: Inter-Balkan Rivalries and Russian Foreign Policy, 1908–1914* (Toronto, 1981), Edward C. Thaden, *Russia and the Balkan Alliance of 1912* (University Park, PA, 1965), Bernadotte E. Schmitt, *The Annexation of Bosnia, 1908–1909* (Cambridge, 1937), and Wayne S. Vucinich, *Serbia Between East and West: The Events of 1903–1908* (Stanford, CA, 1954). See also Stephen Constant, *Foxy Ferdinand, 1861–1948: Tsar of Bulgaria* (London, 1979). David M. McDonald, *United Government and Foreign Policy in Russia, 1900–1914* (Cambridge, MA, 1992) argues that fear of internal disorder lay behind Russian determination not to become involved in Balkan conflicts in this period.

For the foreign policy issues of the First World War, see Dominic Lieven, *Russia and the Origins of the First World War* (London, 1987), W. Bruce Lincoln, *Passage through Armageddon: The Russians in War and Revolution* (Oxford, 1986), Keith Nielson, *Britain and the Last Tsar: British Policy and Russia, 1894–1917* (Oxford, 1995), C. Jay Smith, *The Russian Struggle for Power, 1914–1917: A Study of Russian Foreign Policy during the*

First World War (New York, 1956) and Norman Stone, *The Eastern Front 1914–1917* (London, 1975).

Diplomatic memoirs include Sir George Buchanan, *My Mission to Russia and Other Diplomatic Memories*, 2 vols (London, 1923). His daughter Muriel has written a number of memoirs aimed at exonerating her father from the charge of bringing about the Revolution. The most readily available is *Petrograd: The City of Trouble, 1914–1918* (London, 1918). Alfred Knox, *With the Russian Army, 1914–1917*, 2 vols (London, 1921) is by the British military attaché, R. H. Bruce Lockhart, *Memoirs of a British Agent* (London, 1933) is by 'our man in Moscow' and Samuel Hoare, *The Fourth Seal* (London, 1930) is by the head of the British Intelligence Mission. M. Paléologue, *An Ambassador's Memoirs*, 3 vols (London, 1923–25; reprinted 1973) should be treated with great caution because, although presented in diary form, it was written after the event and is extremely unreliable. Bernard Pares, *My Russian Memoirs* (London, 1931) and idem, *The Fall of the Russian Monarchy* (London, 1939) are written by a man who enjoyed very close contact with Duma circles.

Memoirs of Russian Foreign Ministers and diplomats during the last period of the Empire include Dmitri Abrikosov, *Reminiscences of a Russian Diplomat* (Seattle, WA, 1964), Nicholas de Basili, *Diplomat of Imperial Russia, 1903–17* (Stanford, CA, 1973), V. N. Charykov, *Glimpses of High Politics: Through War and Peace, 1855–1929* (London, 1931), A. P. Izvolsky, *The Memoirs of Alexander Izvolsky* (London, 1920), K. D. Nabokov, *Ordeal of a Diplomat* (London, 1921), S. D. Sazonov, *The Fateful Years: The Reminiscences of Serge Sazonov* (NY, 1928) and Eugene de Schelkin, *Suicide of a Monarchy: Recollections of a Diplomat* (Toronto, 1918).

SECTION NINE

Placenames

Placenames change with political change. Lwow becomes Lvov, Lviv or Lemberg, according to whose possession it is at any particular time. In this table, the left-hand column gives the placenames current in the period covered by this book, the right-hand column gives the modern name and country, sometimes with a short explanation. Some placenames are deliberately devised to have political meaning: Fort *Groznyi* (Fort Threatening), for example, was built by the Russians in Chechnia to tell the native population what Russian rule was all about. In these cases, the left-hand column gives the Russian name, the right-hand column gives a translation. Finally, in Finland, the Russians used the Swedish names still used by Swedish-speaking Finns, and here the left-hand column gives the Swedish and the right-hand column the Finnish name, both of which are still current.

Åbo	Turku (Finland)
Adrianople	Edirne (Turkey)
Akkerman	Bilhorod Dnistrov'skyy (Ukraine)
Andizhan	Andijon (Uzbekistan)
Archangel	Arkhangelsk
Austerlitz	Slavkov (Czech Republic)
Batum	Batumi (Georgia)
Bayazid	Bayezit (Eastern Anatolia, Turkey)
Belostok	Białystok (Poland)
Bessarabia	Moldova
Borgå	Porvoo (Finland)
Breslau	Wrocław (Poland)
Cattaro	Kótor (Montenegro)
Chesme	Çeşme (Turkey)
Chigirin	Chyhyryn (Ukraine)
Chimkent	Shymkent (Kazakstan)
Circassia	North-western Caucasus, now Krasnodar Krai and Karachaievo-Cherkasskaia Republic
Constantinople	Istanbul (Turkey)
Courland	See Kurland
Dalnyi	('Distant') Dalian (China)
Danzig	Gdansk (Poland)
Dorpat	Tartu (Estonia)
East Prussia	Now divided between Poland and Russia (Kaliningrad Oblast)
Eastern Rumelia	Created by the Congress of Berlin (1878) as an autonomous province of the Ottoman Empire, in 1885 it became the southern part of Bulgaria
Enos	Enez, (Eastern Thrace, Turkey)

Eriván	Ereván (Armenia)
Estliánd or *Estaliándia*	Northern part of Estonia. From 1346 to 1561 ruled by the Livonian Brothers of the Sword; from 1561 to 1710, by Sweden; from 1710 to 1991 by Russia
Eylau (East Prussia)	Bagrationovsk (Kaliningrad Oblast)
Fort Ross	(Ross = Rossíia) Former Russian settlement in California
Fridrikshamn	Hamina (Finland)
Friedland	Pravdinsk (Kaliningrad Oblast)
Gangut	Russian name for Hango or Hanko (Finland)
Gazy-Kerman	Beryslav (Ukraine)
Glatz	Kłodzko (Poland)
Grodno	Hrodna (Belarus)
Groznyi	('Threatening') Russian fort now the capital of Chechnia
Gumbinnen	Gusev (Kaliningrad Oblast)
Helsingfors	Helsinki (Finland)
Ingermanland	'No man's land,' Ingria, former Swedish Province, now Leningrad Oblast
Izmail	Izmayil (Ukraine)
Jassy	Iaşi (Romania)
Kaffa	Feodosiya (Crimea, Ukraine)
Karelia	Finnish-speaking area to the east of the present Finnish frontiers
Kay	Prussian name for the battle of Paltzig (1759)
Khárkov	Kharkiv (Ukraine)
Khodjent	Khudzhand (Tajikistan)
Kiaochow	Jiao Xian (China)
Königsberg	Former capital of East Prussia, now Kaliningrad, Russian Federation
Kovno	Kaunas (Lithuania)
Kuldja	Yining (China)
Kunersdorf	Kunowice (Poland)
Kurland	Baltic Duchy, now divided between Latvia and Lithuania
Laibach	Ljubljana (Slovenia)
Lemberg	L'viv (Ukraine)
Libau or *Libava*	Liepāja (Latvia)
Livonia or *Lifliándia*	Originally the name for the whole of Latvia and Estonia. In 1561, with the creation of Kurland, it became the name of a new state

formed out of Northern Latvia and Southern Estonia. It was acquired by Poland during the Livonian War (1558–61), by Sweden at the Peace of Altmark (1629), and by Russia in 1721 (Nystadt), when its name was changed to Lifliándia. Now divided between Estonia and Latvia

Lwow or L'vov	L'viv (Ukraine)
Manchuria	Dongbei (China)
Memel	Klaipėda (Lithuania)
Midia	Midye (Eastern Thrace, Turkey)
Mitau	Former capital of Kurland, now Jelgava (Latvia)
Mogilëv	Mahilyow (Belarus)
Mukden	Shenyang (China)
Nakhicheván	Naxçivan (Azerbaijan)
Nezhin	Nizhyn (Ukraine)
Nyslott	Olavinlinna, (Finland)
Ochakov	Ochakiv (Ukraine)
Olmütz	Olomouc (Czech Republic)
Peking	Beijing (China)
Petrograd	The name given to St Petersburg between 1914 and 1923
Plevna	Pleven (Bulgaria)
Pólotsk (Polish: *Polock*)	Polatsk (Belarus)
Pomerania	Former Prussian province, now divided between Germany (Mecklenburg-Vorpommern) and Poland (Zachodniopomorskie and Pomorskie).
Port Arthur	Lüshun (China)
Posen	Poznań (Poland)
The Principalities	Wallachia and Moldavia (Romania)
Réval or Rével	Tallinn (Estonia)
Sanjak of Novi Bazar	Province of the Ottoman Empire now part of Serbia (Novi Pazar)
Shumla	Shumen (Bulgaria)
Silesia	Śląsk (Poland)
Silistria	Silistra (Bulgaria)
Stettin	Szczecin (Poland)
Tammerfors	Tampere (Finland)
Tannenberg	Stębark (Poland)
Thorn	Toruń (Poland). From 1793 to 1918 part of Prussia, (except for a brief interlude in the Grand Duchy of Warsaw)

Tientsin	Tianjin (China)
Tiflis	Tbilísi (Georgia)
Trebizond	Trabzon (Turkey)
Tsargrad	('The Emperor's Town') Istanbul (Turkey)
Vasilkóv	Vasylkiv (Ukraine)
Vernyi	'Loyal' fortress, in 1921 renamed Alma-Atá. Now Almaty (Kazakhstan)
Vilna or *Vilno*	Vilnius (Lithuania)
Vindava	Ventspils (Latvia)
Wilmanstrand	Lappeenranta, (Finland)
Wilno	Vilnius (Lithuania)
Windau	Ventspils (Latvia)
Zips	Spiš (Slovakia)

Index

General references to Moscow and St Petersburg have been omitted as they are too numerous. Numbers in *italic* refer to short biographies.